Successful Business Planning for Entrepreneurs

JERRY W. MOORMAN

JAMES W. HALLORAN

THOMSON
SOUTH-WESTERN

Australia · Canada · Mexico · Singapore · Spain · United Kingdom · United States

Successful Business Planning for Entrepreneurs, 1st edition

by Jerry W. Moorman and James W. Halloran

VP/Editorial Director
Jack W. Calhoun

VP/Editor-in-Chief
Karen Schmohe

Executive Editor
Jane Phelan

Project Manager
Enid Nagel

Production Manager
Patricia Matthews Boies

Production Editor
Diane Bowdler

VP/Director of Marketing
Carol Volz

Marketing Manager
Valerie A. Lauer

Marketing Coordinator
Georgianna Wright

Manufacturing Coordinator
Kevin Kluck

Art Director
Michelle Kunkler

Editorial Assistant
Linda Keith

Cover and Internal Designer
Liz Harasymczuk Design

Cover Images
© Getty Images, Inc.

Production House
New England Typographic Service (NETS)

Printer
Quebecor World
Dubuque IA

Printed in the United States of America
2 3 4 5 09 08 07 06 05

Student Edition: ISBN 0-538-97182-7
Student Edition with CD:
ISBN 0-538-43921-1

For more information contact,
Thomson Higher Education
5191 Natorp Boulevard,
Mason, Ohio, 45040
USA.
Or you can visit our Internet site at:
http://www.swlearning.com

ASIA (including India)
Thomson Learning
5 Shenton Way
#01-01 UIC Building
Singapore 068808

AUSTRALIA/NEW ZEALAND
Thomson Learning Australia
102 Dodds Street
Southbank, Victoria 3006
Australia

LATIN AMERICA
Thomson Learning
Seneca, 53
Colonia Polanco
11560 Mexico
D.F. Mexico

CANADA
Thomson Nelson
1120 Birchmount Road
Toronto, Ontario
Canada M1K 5G4

UK/EUROPE/MIDDLE EAST/AFRICA
Thomson Learning
High Holborn House
50-51 Bedford Road
London WC1R 4LR
United Kingdom

SPAIN (includes Portugal)
Thomson Paraninfo
Calle Magallanes, 25
28015 Madrid, Spain

Other Career Solutions from Thomson South-Western

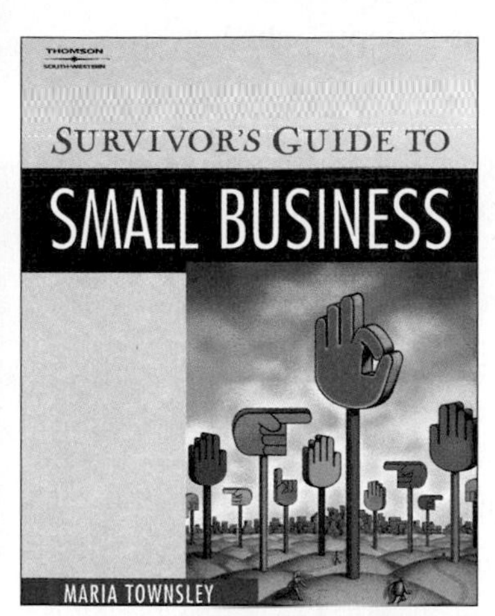

Survivor's Guide to Small Business

Townsley (0-538-72573-7)

Designed for those who need to know the basics, this text/CD package will guide users through the world of small business and the skills needed to survive. This comprehensive, easy-to-use guide for small business development and ownership reflects the most current topics and issues that entrepreneurs face in an easy to understand manner.

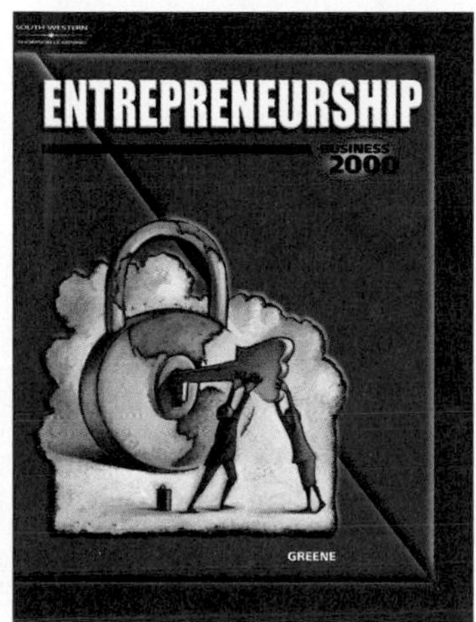

Business 2000: Entrepreneurship

Greene (0-538-69875-6)

As a part of the innovative ***Business 2000*** series, this text provides information on becoming an entrepreneur, selecting a type of ownership, developing a business plan, marketing your business, hiring and managing a staff, and financing, protecting, and insuring your business. The way this textbook can be used is unlimited! By incorporating critical thinking exercises, vocabulary building, business math, technology, and career awareness into this textbook, we've made ***Business 2000: Entrepreneurship*** inviting and informative.

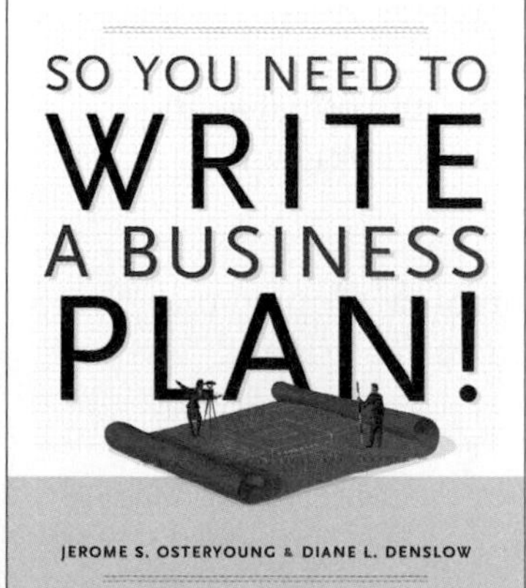

So You Need to Write a Business Plan

Osteryoung and Denslow (0-03-031533-6)

This text teaches students how to create a business plan by taking them through many real-life examples and exercises demonstrating in detail the process of writing a business plan. Throughout the text the examples will be drawn from product type companies, service companies and retailers, covering the majority of issues that are unique to each of these industries.

About This Book

What an exciting time it is for you to begin your study of entrepreneurship. At no time in recent history has the world market been in such a state of flux. China, Eastern Europe, and the states of the former Soviet Union have made drastic changes in the way they conduct business. They have begun to embrace capitalism with vigor and anticipation. At the heart of that anticipation is the belief that individuals can own and operate their own businesses with success. This interest and belief in entrepreneurship is sweeping the world.

In the course of America's history, you can trace the country's phenomenal success to the spirit of individual entrepreneurs who were not afraid to strike out on their own in pursuit of business dreams. Large companies such as Dell Computer Corporation and Wal-Mart began as dreams of individuals. From those small dreams grew large, successful corporations.

The teaching of entrepreneurship is a very important task in today's schools. Without proper instruction, the entrepreneurial spirit may not be properly nourished. If the needed nourishment is denied, the spirit could well falter.

Successful Business Planning for Entrepreneurs reflects an awareness of the tremendous importance of the first course in entrepreneurship. A learning program has been created to maximize students' understanding and appreciation of entrepreneurship.

A BOOK FOR ENTREPRENEURS

Successful Business Planning for Entrepreneurs is designed with entrepreneurs in mind. It is written in simple and understandable language. All topics were carefully chosen with an eye toward presenting practical material for use in real entrepreneurial situations.

Both authors have extensive experience as small business consultants and are full-time college faculty members. Dr. Moorman is Professor of Business at Mesa State College in Grand Junction, Colorado, and Mr. Halloran, owner of several small businesses, serves as an instructor of entrepreneurship and management at Wesleyan College in Macon, Georgia. The expertise they have developed as a result of working with and advising hundreds of clients, owning and operating businesses, as well as their years of teaching experience, are reflected throughout the book. Their experience and expertise have been combined with the latest learning theory to create a text that is both technically accurate and educationally sound.

TEXT ORGANIZATION

Successful Business Planning for Entrepreneurs is divided into four units, each containing four chapters. The topics are arranged so that readers examine the steps to successful entrepreneurship in a logical order.

Unit 1 is an introduction to and overview of entrepreneurship and you. It deals with the individual as an entrepreneur and presents an overview of the process necessary to plan a small business. Purchasing an existing business or a franchise and legal requirements are also covered.

Unit 2 is an examination of marketing research that begins with a detailed explanation of developing the marketing plan, followed by conducting the industry analysis. Conducting the competitive analysis and deciding on location and facilities follow those chapters.

Unit 3 is devoted to marketing the small business. Topics include getting to know your customers and discussions of pricing and promotional strategies. It concludes with a discussion of e-entrepreneurship and the many aspects of online businesses.

Unit 4 moves into the management and financing of the small business. Chapters in this unit cover human resource management, initial capitalization and personal finances, and financial planning and analysis of financial sources. A discussion of management control tools brings the unit to a close.

To further help new entrepreneurs, an appendix is devoted to small business assistance. It provides information about the numerous state, federal, and private sources of information available to assist in the start-up and management of small businesses. A glossary is also included.

Profile of an Entrepreneur Each unit opens with the profile of an entrepreneur. Three of the profiles are of famous entrepreneurs and the fourth is an example of a hometown entrepreneur who has achieved success.

Case Study Each unit closes with a comprehensive case study that utilizes concepts presented in one or more of the unit's chapters.

Each chapter opens with chapter objectives, followed by the chapter narrative. Chapter features include:

Ethics for Entrepreneurs a situation in which an ethical decision is needed,

The Global Entrepreneur which addresses global business concepts,

Small Business Technology which describes new technology that is useful for small businesses,

Fun Facts in which interesting tidbits of information are presented.

Ongoing Case Study: Ship in a Bottle

Each chapter concludes with an ongoing case study entitled *Ship in a Bottle,* which tracks the growth of a new business. Fred Johnson, a fictional entrepreneur, and his wife Jeanie apply the concepts presented in the specific chapter to their business. The case study will stimulate students' interest as it illustrates a type of part-time business with full-time promise that students can develop themselves. It is a multifaceted learning experience that describes an Internet retail business with wholesale and international dimensions.

End-of-Chapter Assessment

Summary

A Case in Point

Vocabulary Builder

Review the Concepts

Critical Thinking

Project: Build Your Business Plan Allows each student to apply chapter concepts in the development of a business plan around a hypothetical entrepreneurial venture of his or her own choice.

To complement the text, the authors have developed a Student CD that contains a study guide to reinforce the material presented.

Contents

©INDEX STOCK IMAGERY, INC.

©GETTY IMAGES/PHOTODISC

©GETTY IMAGES/PHOTODISC

©GETTY IMAGES/PHOTODISC

©GETTY IMAGES/PHOTODISC

©GETTY IMAGES/PHOTODISC

©GETTY IMAGES/PHOTODISC

Chapter 10
Pricing 206

Chapter 11
Promotional Activities 228

©GETTY IMAGES/PHOTODISC

©GETTY IMAGES/PHOTODISC

©GETTY IMAGES/PHOTODISC

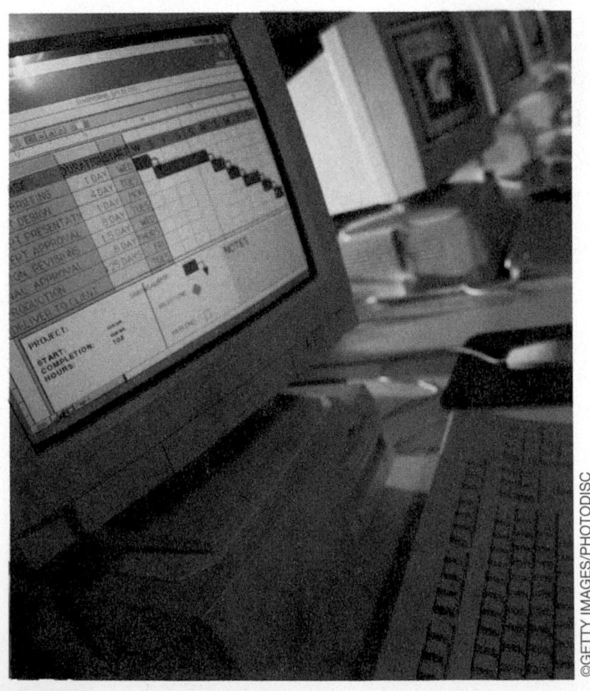

©GETTY IMAGES/PHOTODISC

Reviewers

Judith Gaffney
TCI
New York, NY

Elaine Giuliano
Director of Education
Central Coast College
Salinas, CA

Elizabeth M. Nichols
Instructor
Indiana Business College
Lafayette, IN

Jana Schrenkler
Business Program Coordinator
Rassmussen College
Eagan, Minnesota

Candace Schiffer
Instructor
Mercyhurst College
Erie, PA

Dennis Schoenwetter
Program Coordinator Business Adm/Mgmt & Professor
Hamilton College
Mason City, Iowa

Gilda L. Taylor
Director of Education
HTI Online
Phoenix, AZ

Juno Taylor
Owner
J Taylor Consulting
Phoenix, AZ

Serena Tong
Coordinator, Business and Accounting
Long Island Business Institute
Flushing, NY

ABOUT THE AUTHORS

Jerry Moorman

Jerry Moorman is Professor of Marketing at Mesa State College in Grand Junction, Colorado. Dr. Moorman is an active consultant and the author of more than fifty publications, including two novels and four textbooks. His academic interests include entrepreneurship, technical writing, and market research. Dr. Moorman has been on the staff at Mesa State College since January of 1990.

James Halloran

James Halloran serves on the faculty of Wesleyan College in Macon, Georgia, as an Instructor of Entrepreneurship and Management. He is an active entrepreneur having owned numerous retail, wholesale and Internet enterprises. Mr. Halloran is a small business consultant and has authored or co-authored three textbooks and four professional books on the subject of entrepreneurship.

Unit 1

Entrepreneurship and You

Profile of an Entrepreneur

Mary Kay Ash, 1915–2001

Mary Kay Ash was an extraordinary woman who possessed an uncanny business ability. Her influence on the cosmetics industry will long be remembered. Known for rewarding sales success with pink cars, Mary Kay founded Mary Kay Cosmetics and grew it into one of the largest and most successful beauty products corporations in the country.

Mary Kay's actual date of birth is something of a mystery. She is rumored to have said, "A woman who will tell her age will tell anything." When asked her age, she would often respond, "How much do you weigh?" Most records place her year of birth as 1915, in Hot Wells, Texas. She died in 2001.

Life was not kind to Mary Kay during her early years. Born the youngest child in the family, she soon discovered the realities of being poor when her father became sick. With her mother working long days, she assumed responsibility for housework and caring for an invalid father stricken with tuberculosis. She was seven.

"You can do it, honey," her mother constantly assured her. Mary Kay developed a high level of confidence in her own abilities. This personality trait later proved invaluable as she built her dream company.

In school Mary Kay was very bright and extremely competitive. She excelled in front of a crowd as a public speaker and debater. Being bright was not enough, however, for Mary Kay to pursue her dream of being a doctor. Financial hardships prevented her family from sending her to college. Instead, she followed a more traditional route, getting married and starting a family. To help the family budget, she took a job selling books door-to-door.

By the age of 27, however, she was enrolled at the University of Houston, studying medicine. Her medical studies were cut short when her husband came home from World War II and asked for a divorce.

With three children to support, Mary Kay went to work selling Stanley Home Products. Regarding the Stanley experience, she was later quoted in a magazine article as saying, "I worked under a branch manager who promoted at his discretion, and I began to see that my whole world was hemmed in by a man who didn't want me to succeed."

Leaving Stanley Home Products as the top sales producer, Mary Kay went to work for World Gift Company in the early fifties. Through hard work and successful selling, she was eventually appointed to the board of directors.

©GETTY IMAGES/PHOTODISC

©DOUGLAS KIRKLAND/CORBIS

Mary Kay soon experienced the "glass ceiling," the invisible barrier to promotion sometimes encountered by women and minorities. In the early sixties, she quit to pursue early retirement.

Mary Kay decided to spare other women the ordeal she had experienced by writing a sales book. It was to be a guide for women in the workplace. Once she started writing, it occurred to her that she had created the perfect plan for a successful business. With the business plan in hand, she quit writing and started doing. She was on her way.

The first step to becoming a successful businesswoman was a good product. She decided on skin care products because Avon and other companies were primarily selling cosmetics. By not competing directly with these well-established companies, Mary Kay thought her business had an excellent chance for success.

Mary Kay Ash started the company when she discovered a cream that softened the skin and made it look good. It was a concoction made by a local hide tanner, and she had been using it herself for almost ten years. Mary Kay took her life savings of $5,000 and bought the formula.

Unfortunately its smell left something to be desired. After experimentation and remixing the formula, she developed a cream that smelled good. She hired a local manufacturer with instructions to create a line of skin care products based on the original formula.

In 1963, with her son's help, Mary Kay Cosmetics was born. The small direct-sale company began operating out of an 800-square-foot storefront in Dallas, Texas. Sales for the first three months of operation totaled approximately $34,000. First-year sales were $198,000, and the amount grew to $800,000 by the end of year two.

Today Mary Kay Cosmetics is one of the highest-selling cosmetics companies in the world, with annual sales of over $1.2 billion. Representatives number approximately 850,000 in 37 countries.

Mary Kay set out to create nontraditional employment opportunities that gave women the freedom to set their own hours and to earn either primary or supplemental income. She wanted women to work as independent salespeople and develop their own clientele. She also made it possible for women to be successful Mary Kay representatives without formal education or special work experience. It was her goal to allow them unlimited potential and access to unlimited success. Today her dream has come true.

In addition to being one of the most successful entrepreneurs of her time, Mary Kay was also a successful author. Her books include *You Can Have It All;* her autobiography, *Mary Kay;* and *Mary Kay on People Management.*

Mary Kay Cosmetics has always been noted for rewarding successful representatives with recognition and cash. By awarding pink Cadillacs, diamond jewelry, bumblebee pins, and expensive vacations, the company ensures that women feel good about themselves and their careers.

Mary Kay Cosmetics is also a company that believes in worthy causes. In 1989, it was one of the first in the cosmetics industry to stop testing on live animals. Mary Kay was personally involved in the struggle to fight and find a cure for cancer.

She is also the only woman to be profiled in *Forbes* magazine's "Greatest Business Stories of All Time." She was honored by President Reagan and was one of the women entrepreneurs featured in the National Federation of Independent Business Report. Her company is the only one that has been featured three times in *Fortune* magazine's "100 Best Companies to Work for in America."

Mary Kay was a strong believer in entrepreneurship and private enterprise. Her overall philosophy can be summarized in two of her sayings: "If you think you can, you can. And if you think you can't, you're right." And "People fail forward to success."

Chapter 1

You as an Entrepreneur

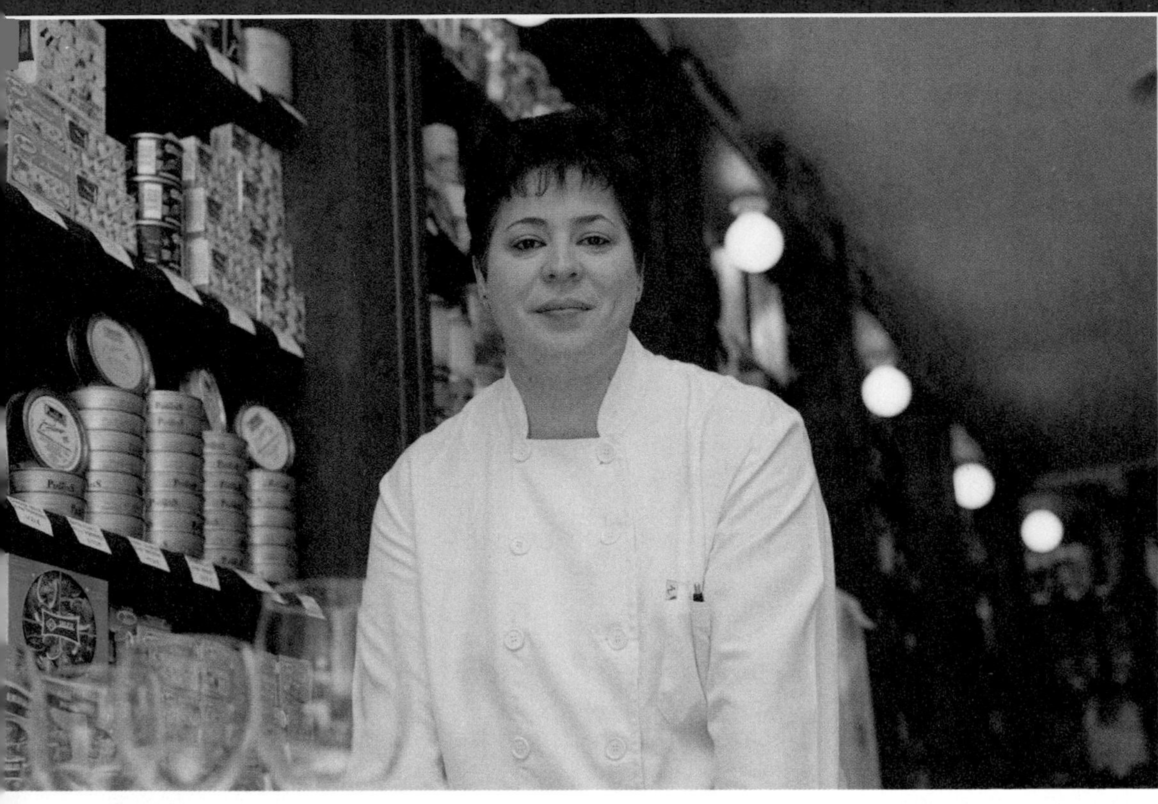

©GETTY IMAGES/PHOTODISC

Objectives

1-1 Describe the nature of entrepreneurship.

1-2 Define what it takes to be a successful entrepreneur.

1-3 Explain the importance of choosing the right environment in which to work.

1-4 Explain the process of setting personal goals according to your values, attitudes, needs, and expectations.

1-5 Identify the sources of new business ideas.

1-6 Discuss the advantages and disadvantages of part-time entrepreneurship.

WHAT IS AN ENTREPRENEUR?

The development of the United States economy can be traced directly to **entrepreneurs** who possessed the vision and ambition to reach goals that many of us can barely imagine. From Henry Ford 100 years ago to Bill Gates today, these individuals were the founders of businesses and industries that have enhanced our standard of living. They were entrepreneurs—individuals who took great risks to pursue their dreams. They created businesses that produced wealth for our society in the forms of tax revenues, employment, and new products to make life more pleasurable. This is what entrepreneurs do. They invest money and/or time in commercial enterprises with the hope of achieving profits but also with the understanding that they are risking losses. Successful entrepreneurs can sense the needs of the marketplace and work to satisfy those needs. Whether they start a new business or create a new direction for an existing corporation or nonprofit organization, they are innovators. They make things happen.

The Role of the Entrepreneur

Entrepreneurs come from all types of backgrounds and are active in all forms of enterprise. They may be independent business owners, franchise owners, corporate or organization leaders (often referred to as intrapreneurs), or professionals such as lawyers, doctors, or artists who operate their own offices or galleries.

Figure 1-1 illustrates the percentages that small businesses account for in various categories. The small business sector generates more than half the jobs in the U.S. and a majority of product innovations. Small businesses often act as suppliers or distributors for large businesses. In recent years they have gained importance in the international marketplace as well. They are essential to the economic strength of our country. It is important for us to understand the entrepreneurs who lead these small businesses and what makes them successful.

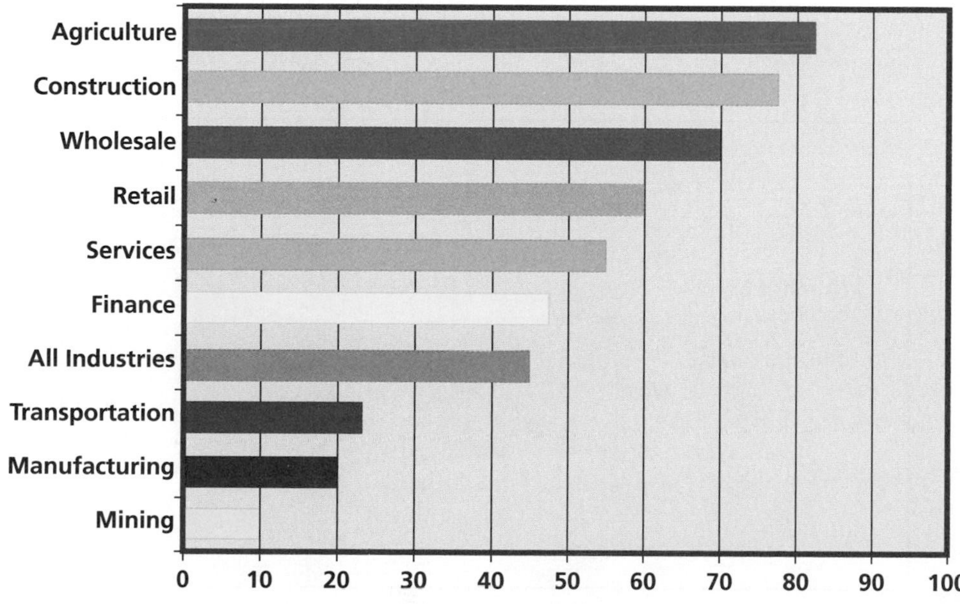

FIGURE 1-1

Small Businesses in Different Categories

Why Become an Entrepreneur?

There are three basic reasons to consider becoming an entrepreneur: to control your own destiny, to achieve independence from supervision, and to gain profits greater than a salary earned by working for others.

Controlling Your Destiny This benefit is normally the greatest motivator to the path of self-employment. As business owners, individuals can determine how they wish to run both their professional and private lives. Entrepreneurs plan their own business activities and schedule these activities around their personal commitments. They can prioritize for themselves rather than have a boss do it for them. Entrepreneurs are not told that they must attend an out-of-town meeting at the expense of important events in their personal lives such as a child's Little League game or other important family events. Entrepreneurs make these decisions based on how important they feel a business activity is and not how important someone else believes it is. An entrepreneur works for his or her own goals, not someone else's. This right is the greatest reward of entrepreneurship.

Independence from Supervision Although entrepreneurs must answer to the many people they depend on, including customers, lending institutions, suppliers, or, in the case of franchisees, the franchisor, they do not have a boss. Their business relationships are based on partnering, not supervising.

Achieving Great Profits The first two reasons are guaranteed, but achieving profits is not. Entrepreneurs are willing to take risks in order to achieve profits while at the same time recognizing that they may incur losses. Profits are the most difficult objective to achieve and often take considerable time to realize. Unfortunately, more new small businesses fail than succeed in the very competitive marketplace (Figure 1-2). It is important to note, however, that the majority of those failed businesses are poorly planned. If the entrepreneur is determined to succeed and the new business venture is properly researched and planned, the odds are greater for success than for failure. Taking entrepreneurship courses prepares an individual to take on the challenge of starting a profitable business.

FIGURE 1-2

Small Business Start-ups and Failures

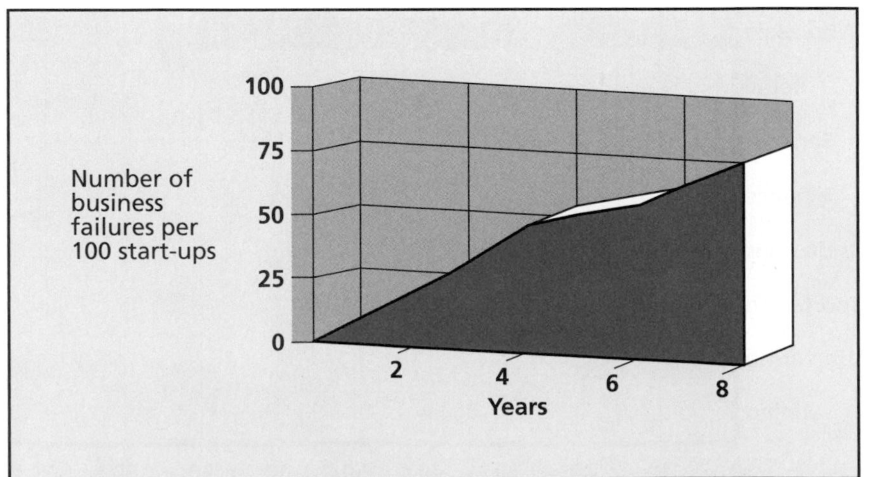

CHARACTERISTICS OF SUCCESSFUL ENTREPRENEURS

The **Small Business Administration** (SBA), a federal government agency created to assist the development of the country's small businesses, reports that 24 out of every 100 businesses starting out today will not be open in two years. An additional 27 will close within four years, and within six years, 60 will no longer be operating. Although some businesses close for reasons other than failure, it is apparent that it is very difficult to succeed as a small business owner.

So who succeeds? In short, those who carefully plan and research their ideas are way ahead of those who don't. They write a business plan. A business plan serves as a blueprint or map that leads the aspiring entrepreneur to achieving the goal of a successful business. It validates the entrepreneur's intuition about the venture. Much of this textbook will discuss writing a proper business plan. However, certain personal characteristics are also essential for entrepreneurial success.

FUN FACTS

Did you know that the number of businesses owned by women has increased by 77 percent since 1983?

Self-confidence Entrepreneurs must feel confident in their ideas and in their ability to succeed. Small business owners cannot "pass the buck." They make the key decisions that determine the success or failure of an enterprise, without the advantage of the professional research staffs or numerous committees found in large corporations. As decision makers, entrepreneurs must trust their instincts and abilities. If a decision turns out to be wrong, they need the confidence to bounce back and face the next situation that requires a decision.

Determination and Perseverance There are times when things do not go as planned for the new business. It may be tempting to give up, fold up the tent, and go home. Successful entrepreneurs hang in there until the objective is achieved.

Creativity Why do some businesses selling the same product or service in the same marketplace succeed while others fail? It's likely because the successful entrepreneurs are doing some things better than their competitors. A competitive marketplace is dominated by those who can think and move quickly to attract and retain customers. This takes creativity. From the initial idea to the finished product, creativity is demonstrated in subtle but distinctive ways. Sensing the needs of the marketplace and generating ideas to meet those needs is a highly creative process.

The Need to Achieve Successful entrepreneurs are constantly setting new goals. The challenge of attaining those goals is fun for them. They are energetic, possess a high need for self-fulfillment, and feel good about their achievements. Sam Walton, founder of Wal-Mart, often said, "It's knowing what you want to achieve and then going about doing whatever is necessary to achieve it."

Questions to Ponder

To determine if you have the characteristics of an entrepreneur, consider the following thought-provoking questions.

1. Do you give up on your favorite football team when it is two touchdowns behind with five minutes to play? (Determined entrepreneurs do not give up easily.)
2. If you see a stream, are you curious as to where it started and where it ends? (Entrepreneurs are constantly asking questions, looking for answers and information. Curiosity is part of the creative process.)
3. Do people look to you for leadership in critical times? (As a small business owner, the entrepreneur is captain, leader, and motivator. These roles require self-confidence.)
4. Are you constantly resetting your goals as you work toward a long-term objective? (Always reaching for new heights means achieving goals and striving toward new ones.)
5. Do you consult with others on most decisions? (Successful entrepreneurs must have the confidence to make decisions on their own.)
6. Do you tend to be a daydreamer? (Entrepreneurs are dreamers. Their dreams motivate them and produce creative energy. But the dreams must be based on reality.)
7. Do routine chores make you restless? (Entrepreneurs are action-oriented goal seekers who are somewhat restless. Keep in mind, however, that every venture involves routine and even boring tasks.)
8. Are you stubborn? (A certain amount of stubbornness comes with determination. Entrepreneurs are stubborn, but they're also sensible.)
9. Do you like yourself? (Confidence comes from within. Good leadership stems from self-assuredness.)
10. Is making money your only goal in starting a business? (For a true entrepreneur, the satisfaction of doing things on one's own ranks higher than making money.)

Small Business Technology

Network Solutions is a private, online, for-profit company that registers all web site names. Go online to www.networksolutions.com and investigate what domain names are available for a small business idea. Commercial businesses normally use the .com suffix, not-for-profit businesses use .org, educational institutions use .edu, and government institutions use .gov.

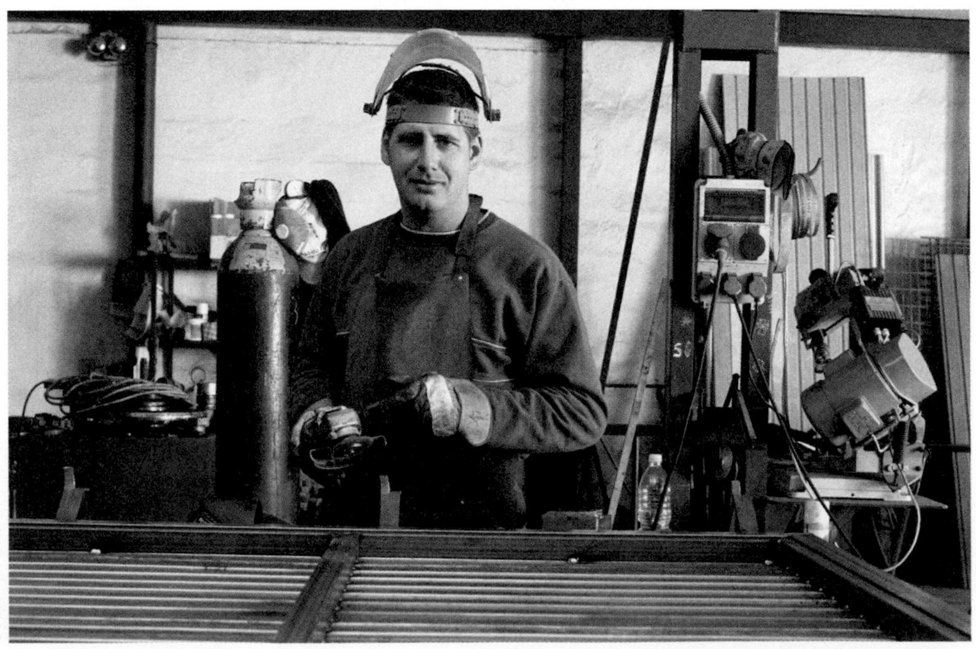

©GETTY IMAGES/PHOTODISC

Other questionnaires directed toward established, successful entrepreneurs have led to some interesting discoveries. For example, the Center for Entrepreneurial Management cites the following characteristics as common among entrepreneurs.

1. Many are the children of self-employed parents.
2. Many are descendants of parents or grandparents who immigrated to the United States.
3. Many were enterprising in their youth, operating part-time, independent enterprises such as lawn mowing, newspaper routes, house-sitting services, and so on.
4. Many are the oldest child.
5. The majority state that their prime reason for starting a business was to be on their own and not work for someone else.

WORK IN THE RIGHT ENVIRONMENT

Success as an entrepreneur requires being committed to a business and an idea. Commitment often involves long hours and an abundance of energy. If you are not in the right field, you will have difficulty making the necessary commitment over the long term. Working in an environment compatible with your interests allows you to reach your full potential. Setting goals in such an environment is stimulating and exciting.

The choice of a field or vocation should not be made without considering past experiences that were meaningful and fulfilling. An administrator who is restless while working at a desk but enjoys interacting with people needs to weigh that factor before considering opening a business that would confine his activities to an office. Analyzing past experiences gives the aspiring entrepreneur an idea of the environment that would most likely bring personal satisfaction and success in attaining goals.

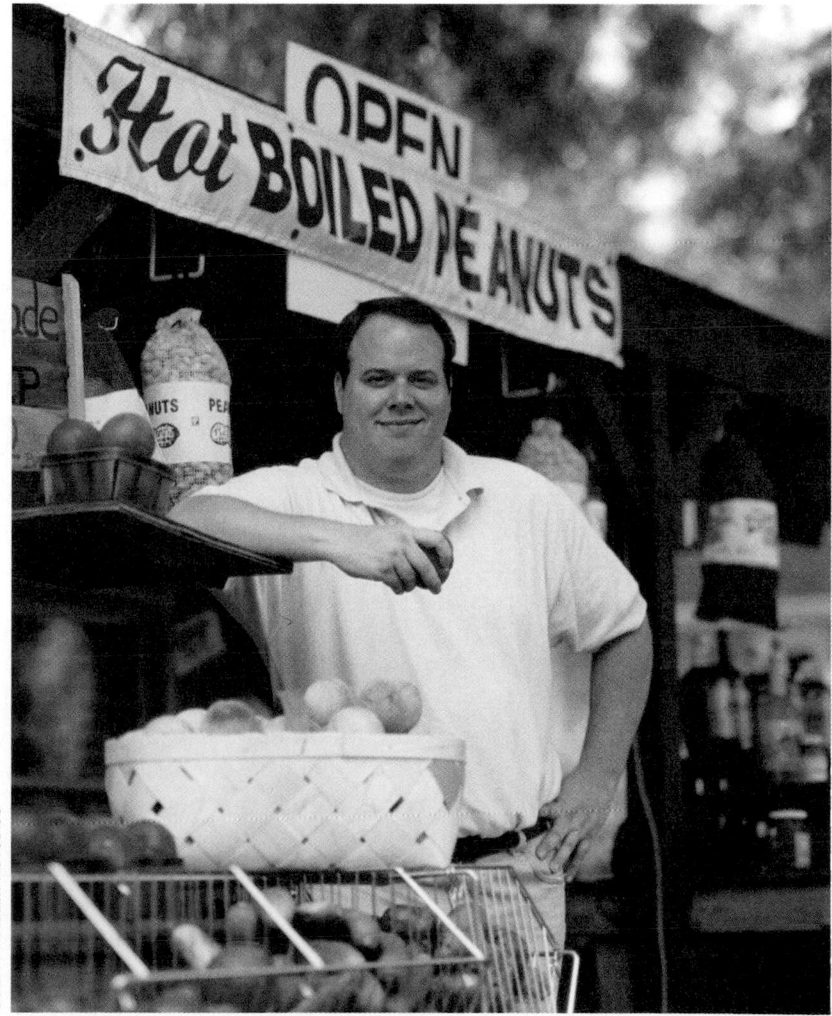

©GETTY IMAGES/PHOTODISC

Career Anchors

Dr. Edgar Schein of the Massachusetts Institute of Technology has identified five **career anchors**: technical, managerial, security, creativity, and autonomy. Within each of these anchors he identified vocational choices. Anchors in this context are important career motivators that help you make choices, determine directions, pursue ambitions, and measure success. They can help determine business choices and influence changes.

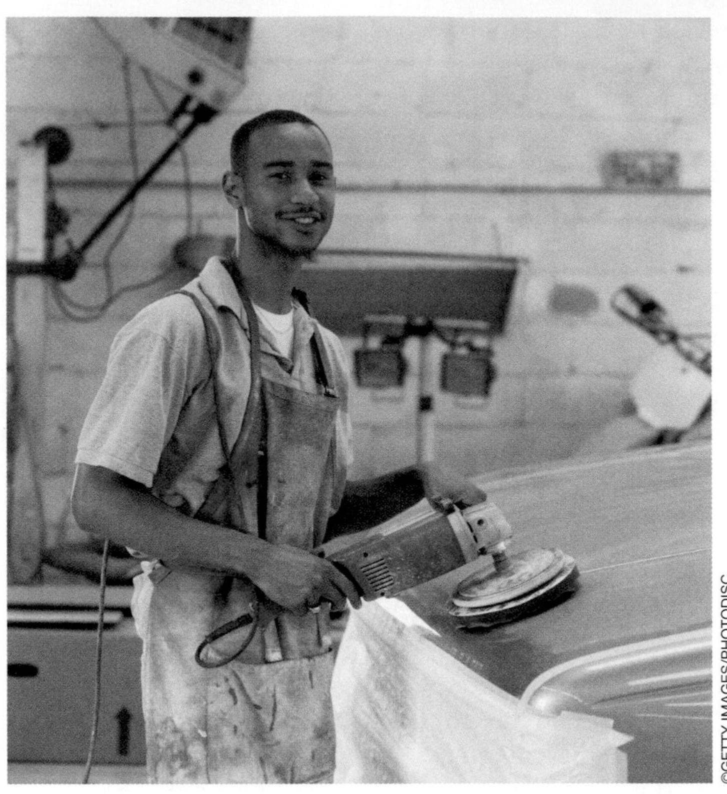
©GETTY IMAGES/PHOTODISC

An individual with a **technical anchor** gains satisfaction from being able to do a specific job correctly. People with technical anchors might be technicians, surgeons, craftsmen, or any kind of specialist. Such individuals are less concerned with titles and promotions than with being considered experts in their fields. They seek self-employment in areas that allow them to concentrate on a specific mission. Automobile mechanics, computer repair shop owners, hobby shop owners, and small technology manufacturers are examples of entrepreneurs who work at specific pursuits.

Individuals with a **managerial anchor** are generalists as opposed to specialists. They enjoy working with people. They are able to handle many duties and responsibilities. As entrepreneurs, they do well in businesses with multiple outlets, or in businesses producing and selling many products. Chain store owners and manufacturers who produce a variety of products are examples of entrepreneurs with managerial anchors.

People with a **security anchor** are generally not equipped to handle the risks of self-employment. They are content to work in large organizational environments that offer regular paychecks, company benefit programs, and the assurance of long-term employment. Someone with a security anchor who is determined to be self-employed might purchase a well-established franchise such as McDonald's or Pizza Hut, or an existing business with a proven track record. However, businesses such as these are expensive to acquire because they have proven to be successful. The initial risk was taken by someone else who is entitled to additional compensation for successfully developing the franchise or business. Starting up a new business provides little in the way of security.

FUN FACTS

Did you know that America's 25 million small businesses employ more than 58 percent of the private work force and generate more than 51 percent of the nation's gross domestic product?

Individuals with a **creativity anchor** enjoy coming up with unique ideas. They do not like routine tasks and are constantly looking for new ways of doing things. They are often successful as small business owners because they can devise better ways to sell products or services. People with creativity anchors should be wary of business opportunities that depend principally on administrative talents. Promotion-based businesses such as advertising and retail merchandising are a better fit.

People with an **autonomy anchor** are free thinkers and individualists. They are seldom concerned with security. They like to do things their own way, with little interference from others. Individuals with an autonomy anchor have a natural aptitude for starting small businesses, although they sometimes lack the patience and endurance needed to stick with it. Inventors, writers, and artists are examples of this anchor classification.

Sample Career Anchor Questions

To determine what your career anchor may be, consider the following questions. Answering them truthfully and realistically can help lead you to the work environment that is right for you.

1. What are your primary career ambitions?
2. Do you prefer changes in your work responsibilities rather than permanent, unchanging tasks?
3. What do you dislike about your work?
4. Is it important for you to receive recognition?
5. When do you feel the most fulfilled by your work?
6. What will be most important to you when you seek your first job after graduation?
7. What strategy will you use to achieve job promotions?
8. What intangible characteristics of a career are most important to you?

Discuss your answers with a colleague or mentor. See if there appears to be a trend in your answers that confirms your initial guess as to your career anchor.

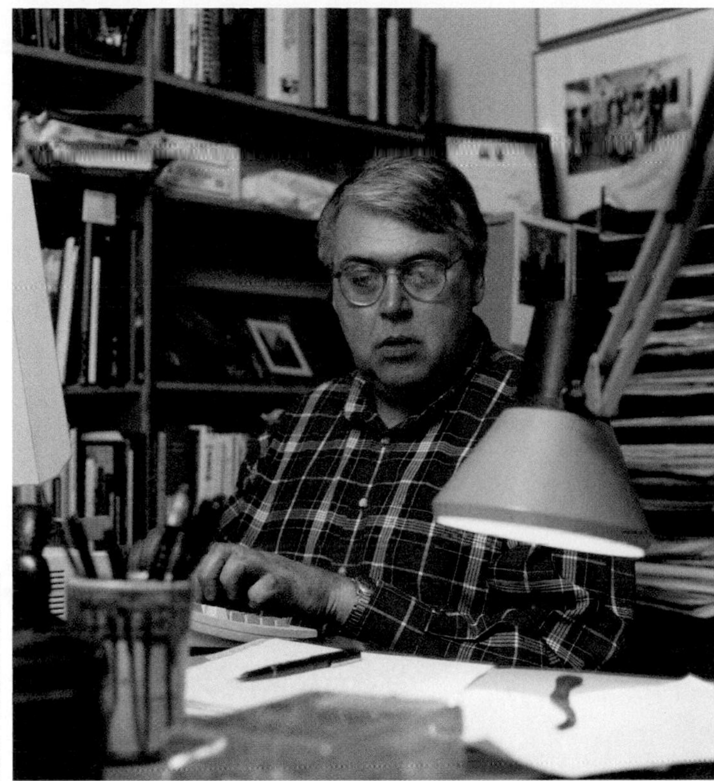
©GETTY IMAGES/PHOTODISC

VALUES, ATTITUDES, NEEDS, AND EXPECTATIONS

The ultimate goal of all entrepreneurs should be to match their values, attitudes, needs, and expectations with a business opportunity. The acronym **VANE** refers to these personal characteristics.

Values are the beliefs and inner convictions that you hold dear. When your actions do not reflect your values, you feel discomfort. Your **attitude** is how you feel about something. It transforms into habitual ways of viewing your environment. A positive attitude makes an optimist; a negative attitude makes a pessimist. There is no correlation between successful entrepreneurship and pessimism. **Needs** are the tangibles (the things you see) and intangibles (the things you feel) that you must have to maintain an acceptable lifestyle. When you identify a need, you are motivated to satisfy it. Successful entrepreneurs are good at identifying customer needs and also at working hard to satisfy their own needs. **Expectations** are the minimum goals that you attempt to achieve. Entrepreneurs are constantly raising their expectations as their business develops.

Aspiring entrepreneurs who have given thoughtful analysis to their values, attitudes, needs, and expectations will feel confident that they are personally prepared for the challenge ahead of them. If they are equipped with a proper business plan as well, they have greatly enhanced their chances for a successful business.

Ethics for ENTREPRENEURS

Mary Hamilton wanted desperately to be a stay-at-home mom, but she knew she would have to find a way to replace the income from her current job first. She was intrigued by some of the start-up business offers that came through her e-mail. "Earn $2.50 For Each Envelope You Stuff! Stuff 800 envelopes, earn $2000. Sign up now and receive a 2-night stay free at a plush resort!" Or "Invest $1900, $200,000 Annual Income Guaranteed! Receive commissions of 5% to 50%."

When she made direct inquires by telephone, she found the offers to be very misleading. One company requested a $30 information fee. Another company was vague regarding the merchandise she would be buying for resale. Other companies informed her that her future income would depend on the efforts of those to whom she sold distributorships.

Discouraged, Mary decided that these companies had misrepresented the truth in their e-mail ads.

Think Critically

1. Do you believe that e-mail advertisements like these are misrepresentations? Do the companies have an obligation to be more forthcoming when attracting potential applicants?
2. Do your own Internet research on business offers like the ones above. Compare what you find with what your classmates discover.

Setting Personal Goals

Once career values, attitudes, needs, and expectations are determined, aspiring entrepreneurs need to look specifically at what business opportunities they should consider. Since successful entrepreneurs are goal-oriented individuals, it is important that the goal setting begins with stating priorities in their personal lives. Personal goals are established with respect to income, personal satisfaction, and status.

Income When setting realistic income goals, the new business owner must be aware that initially there is a direct correlation between how much time and money is invested and how much profit is realized. Over time, the owner's experience, perseverance, and creativity determine profits. For instance, in most retail and service businesses, the owner will do well to make a profit of 15 percent of gross sales. To make a profit of $45,000, the business must generate annual sales of $300,000. Enough money must be invested in inventory, fixtures, and equipment to generate sales of $300,000. If some of the initial money is borrowed, any principal and interest that is paid back must come from the $45,000.

You have probably heard that it takes five years to get a business on its feet. Five years is the most commonly used payoff period on a new business loan. Until the initial debt is paid, there is seldom much extra income available for the owner. For example, an entrepreneur starts a business that requires an investment of $100,000. The owner has $50,000, borrows $50,000, and promises to pay back the loan over five years ($10,000 per year plus interest). The first year, the business sells $300,000 and makes a profit for the owner(s) of $45,000. The owner(s) must pay the lender out of earned profits each year until the loan is paid off. The business finances will look like this after the first year:

Total investment	$100,000
Borrowed funds	50,000
Sales	300,000
Profit	45,000
Less principal and interest	–13,000
Available to owner (before taxes)	32,000

Because the owner is forced to borrow, she or he will not be able to realize the goal of a $45,000 personal profit until the debt is paid or there is growth in sales and profits. In reality, the owner has invested $50,000 in personal capital and $50,000 in borrowed capital, and has most likely given up a salary to make a risky $32,000 per year. Before a business can be considered a success, not only should the original debt be paid but the owner should regain the initial investment as well. Although this takes time, once it has been achieved and sales increase, the profits can be generous enough to pay a good salary and show healthy retained earnings. **Retained earnings** are profits that remain in the business for either future use for business expansion or for distribution to the owner(s) as investment payback. The investment payback is termed **return on investment**.

In this case, the owner hopes to be paid back the original $50,000 investment once the debt is retired. The same business five years later might look as follows:

Sales	$400,000
Profit	60,000
Less principal and interest	–0
Available to owner as salary	45,000
Retained earnings (or return on investment)	15,000

Goal setting with respect to income needs and expectations must be realistic concerning amount invested, returned, and future potential return. Business owners should not expect a 100 percent payback on their investment within one year. They must realize they will likely have to make some financial sacrifices in their personal lives and, as a result, may have to adjust their goals and be flexible because of unexpected changes in business earnings.

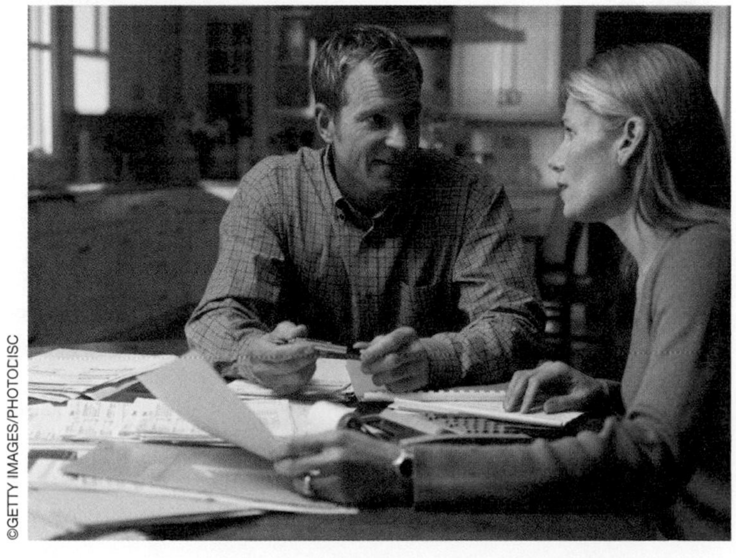
©GETTY IMAGES/PHOTODISC

Personal Satisfaction Goals for personal satisfaction are usually intangible and may include such things as what one wishes to contribute to one's family or community. People need to feel satisfied with what they do with their lives. Working in a career that is personally rewarding adds greatly to a feeling of satisfaction.

Status In the context of entrepreneurship, status refers to the respect a business owner receives based on how others feel about his business or vocation. Declaring a status goal is an important step in determining the best business arena to enter. The noted psychologist Dr. Abraham Maslow includes status, the need for respect from others, as a fundamental need that we all share. Since owning a business involves great personal investment, it is important that the entrepreneur take pride in his efforts. Assuming the risks of business ownership earns recognition and respect from others, which in turn further motivate the entrepreneur.

Type of Work

After declaring your personal goals, your next step is to match those goals with the type of work that really excites you. Your preferences might include sales, office work, working with numbers, working with your hands, working outdoors, and others. This decision dictates what your main occupation will be for the many hours required to operate a successful business.

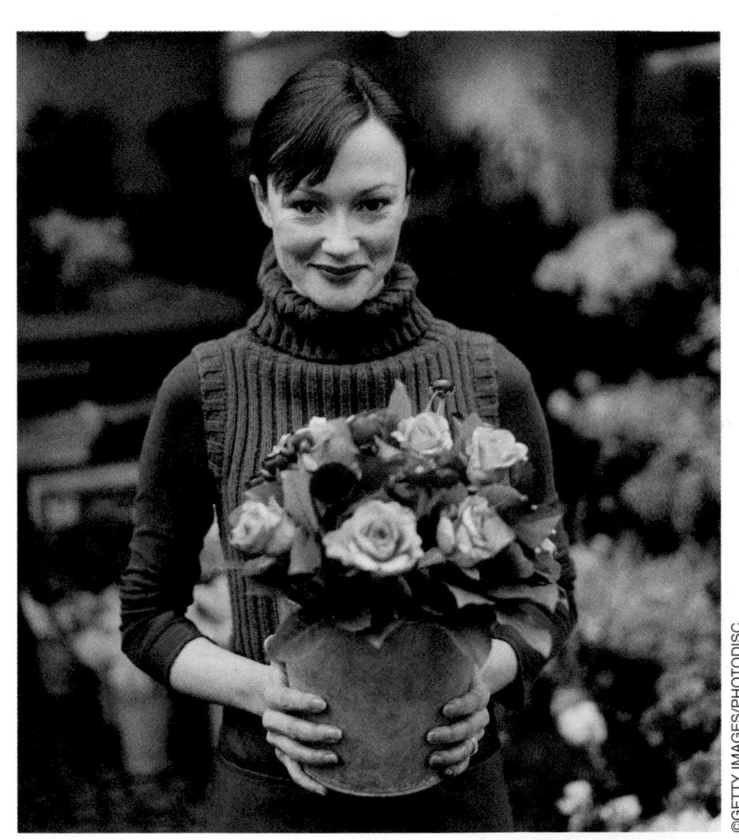

©GETTY IMAGES/PHOTODISC

Another consideration is how you feel about working with people. Would you rather work alone? How do you feel about selling? Profits are generated by the exchange or sale of goods or services. Therefore selling is an important business function. Some entrepreneurs engage in direct, face-to face-selling with customers. Others assign this responsibility to someone else or choose a business in which selling can be handled through the mail, through the Internet, or by telephone. In any selling situation there is interaction with employees, suppliers, and customers. Some businesses place more emphasis on one group than another. You must decide on the selling environment in which you feel most comfortable.

You will also have to decide the amount of time and involvement required to run the business. Is it to be a full-time endeavor, a part-time project, or possibly a business that will start small, with the goal of growing into a full-time business? Small businesses lend themselves to different arrangements, ranging from weekend or off-hours involvement to full-time management. Many businesses operate under **absentee management** in which the owner oversees the business but is not present on a regular basis. Often timing and the nature of the situation dictate the arrangement, as they did for Flora Ramirez.

During Flora's maternity leave from her job, she had more time available to work on her favorite hobby, making custom jewelry for her family and friends. Her imaginative creations were received with great enthusiasm. The husband of one of her friends was a manufacturer's representative for several clothing and accessory companies. After seeing Flora's creations, he offered to take some samples with him to the fall fashion show at the Atlanta Apparel Mart. He returned with orders totaling more than $25,000. Flora had the start of a prosperous full-time business and eventually hired her husband on a full-time basis as well.

Many successful businesses start out as part-time operations until sufficient demand for the product or service allows the owner to leave full-time employment.

Lifestyle

Small businesses come in all forms and sizes. Your preferred lifestyle should have a bearing on the type of business you open. Do you like to travel, work at night, entertain clients, or be entertained? For many, the idea of shaping and controlling their lifestyle is the greatest advantage and appeal of small business ownership. Starting your own business is a declaration of independence.

Capabilities

Your abilities and talents play an important role in the decision-making process. You need to give thought to the physical and psychological demands of your chosen venture. An inventory of skills—developed through education, career, hobbies, and interests—is also useful when assessing your capabilities.

Finally, what are your financial capabilities? This question is usually the toughest to answer and represents the biggest obstacle to effective planning. You must carefully determine how much money is available to you and how much you are willing to invest in a business. Your degree of confidence in your business idea and the amount of risk you're willing to take will help determine the optimum investment amount. You should not risk everything in a new business venture. You also need to consider personal living expenses for yourself and your family.

Tables 1-1 and 1-2 can serve as guides in determining your personal goals and financial resources. Determining available capital is further discussed in Chapter 14.

The Global ENTREPRENEUR

The international market is open for small businesses as well as large ones. It is estimated that over 25 percent of small businesses are engaged in international activities. Many are importers and exporters. The U.S. government encourages small businesses to enter the global marketplace, particularly as exporters. Products produced in the U.S. and sold overseas bring our country revenue and at the same time provide manufacturing jobs, a double bonus. Our economy prospers when we have a surplus trade balance, which is reached when we have more exports than imports. The Department of Commerce works closely with the Small Business Administration to offer assistance to small business owners interested in entering the global market.

Think Critically

1. List three small businesses that you believe would be good international businesses. Explain why you think they would do well.
2. Find the Small Business Administration office nearest to your city.

TABLE 1-1 GUIDE FOR SETTING PERSONAL GOALS

GOALS	**Income Needed** $_______ 1st year $_______ 2nd year $_______ 3rd year	**Personal Satisfactions** *(Rank from 1 to 5)* _____ recognition by others _____ helping others _____ expressing creativity _____ developing expertise _____ other	**Status Considerations** *(Rank from 1 to 4)* _____ status in community _____ personal growth potential _____ expertise _____ other
TYPE OF WORK DESIRED	**Type of Activity** *(Rank from 1 to 6)* _____ sales _____ clerical _____ working with hands _____ working outdoors _____ technology _____ other	**People Contact** *(Rank from 1 to 5)* _____ direct contact with customers _____ indirect contact with customers _____ frequent contact with suppliers _____ close contact with personnel _____ work alone	**Business Involvement** *(Rank from 1 to 5)* _____ part-time _____ 40 hours/week _____ 10–12 hours a day, 5–7 days a week _____ weekends and off-time hours only _____ absentee management
LIFESTYLE CONSIDERATIONS	**Travel** _____ Yes _____ No	**Entertainment** _____ Yes _____ No	**Community Involvement** _____ Yes _____ No
PHYSICAL AND PSYCHOLOGICAL CAPABILITIES	*Example: age, stamina, ability to cope with pressure* ________________ ________________ ________________		
LEARNED ABILITIES	*Example: specialist (languages, bookkeeping), generalist (office management)* ________________ ________________ ________________		
FINANCIAL CAPABILITIES	*Example: How much money can you invest?* ________________ ________________ ________________		
DEGREE OF RISK ACCEPTABLE *(Circle one.)*	1. High risk, high profit potential. 2. Moderate risk, moderate growth potential. 3. Lower risk, slower profit growth potential.		

TABLE 1-2 DETERMINING CAPITAL AVAILABLE

ASSETS		LIABILITIES	
Cash on hand and in bank	$________	Notes payable to bank	$________
Government securities	$________	Notes payable to others	$________
Stocks and/or bonds	$________	Accounts and bills due	$________
Accounts and notes receivable	$________		
Real estate owned			
Home	$________	Real estate mortgage	
Auto	$________	Home	$________
Other	$________	Other	$________
Cash surrender value	$________	Other debts	$________
Life insurance	$________		
TOTAL ASSETS	$________	TOTAL LIABILITIES	$________

NET WORTH CALCULATIONS	
Total assets	$________
Less total liabilities	$________
Equals capital surplus	$________
Amount of capital willing to risk	$________

SOURCES FOR NEW BUSINESS IDEAS

Ideas for new businesses can come from a variety of sources.

1. **Previous Employment** People who do well at their jobs learn a profession and a great deal about market needs and how to satisfy those needs. They build a network of potential customers, suppliers, employees, and distributors. They are confident they can sell to this market more effectively than their present employer does. It's time to give it a try.
2. **Hobbies** A strong interest in a particular pastime may lead to commercial opportunities. Perhaps the individual has built a collection of artifacts or, like Flora Ramirez, finds a way to market a hobby.
3. **Intentional Search** The individual sets out on an extensive research project to find out what is missing in a particular market, what needs are begging to be satisfied. Many information networks are readily available, such as chambers of commerce, small business development centers, or small business consultants, to assist in the search for the perfect opportunity.

4. **Accidental Invention or Discovery** Someone may invent a new tool for working on a car engine or a gardening device that works better than what is sold at the local nursery. He takes the idea one step further and does research to see if it can be patented, who the competition is, what the manufacturing process would entail, and who the target market is.

Figure 1-3 illustrates the **creativity process** as described by an early American psychologist, Graham Wallas. It starts with discovery and interest, proceeds through research, and ends with the entrepreneur as captain of his domain—a successful new business owner. Each step involves a particular mindset, some dealing with simple intuition, others with details and rational thinking.

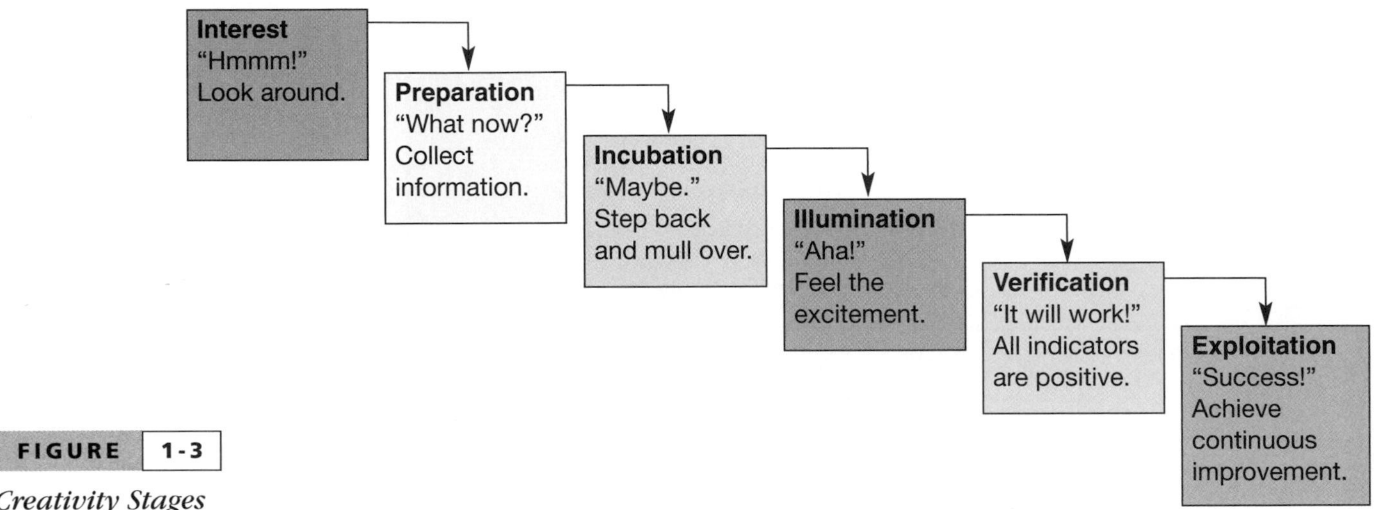

FIGURE 1-3

Creativity Stages

THE PART-TIME ENTREPRENEUR

Many enter the world of entrepreneurship on a part-time basis until the business has developed enough to support full-time occupation. It is estimated that there are over 10 million part-time businesses operating in the United States. Often these businesses are started at home after work hours and during weekends.

Advantages The goal of many part-time businesses is to build a market demand for a product or service until the owner can leave full-time employment and focus on the new business. Phasing in allows the entrepreneur to reduce much of the risk associated with new business start-ups. During this phase, the entrepreneur develops a customer base, sets up supplier relationships, and, most importantly, gains valuable experience.

Disadvantages It can be very tiring to operate a business and at the same time maintain full-time employment. One or both may suffer because of conflicting interests. The entrepreneur may feel as though she is always working. It can be difficult on family members as well. Whenever possible, it is wise to involve family members in the new enterprise.

The business plan for a part-time business should give particular attention to time management. It helps to make a list of all current responsibilities and block off the necessary time to complete them. Potential conflicts between regular employment, part-time business interests, and family obligations should be addressed from the very beginning.

Table 1-3 can be used as a guide to part-time business possibilities.

TABLE 1-3 CHECKLIST FOR SELECTING A PART-TIME BUSINESS

On a scale of 1 to 5, with 5 being the highest, rate each of the following businesses in terms of your level of interest, your personal strengths in that area, and the local market strength of the business.

	My Level of Interest	Personal Strength	Market Strength	Total Points
Personal Services				
housecleaning	______	______	______	______
babysitting	______	______	______	______
tutoring	______	______	______	______
secretarial	______	______	______	______
catering	______	______	______	______
direct mail	______	______	______	______
Handicrafts				
needlework	______	______	______	______
ceramics	______	______	______	______
jewelry design	______	______	______	______
upholstering	______	______	______	______
Artistic work				
painting	______	______	______	______
photography	______	______	______	______
prints	______	______	______	______
wire sculpture	______	______	______	______
engraving	______	______	______	______
Repair services				
small appliances	______	______	______	______
furniture	______	______	______	______
clothing	______	______	______	______
TV and radio	______	______	______	______
automotive	______	______	______	______
Instruction skills				
languages	______	______	______	______
math	______	______	______	______
gourmet cooking	______	______	______	______
music	______	______	______	______
home repairs	______	______	______	______
Mail-order ideas				
product sales	______	______	______	______
repairs	______	______	______	______
business service	______	______	______	______
Seasonal products				
foodstuffs	______	______	______	______
clothing	______	______	______	______
gift items	______	______	______	______
Party sales				
cookware	______	______	______	______
plants	______	______	______	______
plastic goods	______	______	______	______
cosmetics	______	______	______	______
Your own ideas				
For other ideas, check your local public library.				
______	______	______	______	______
______	______	______	______	______
______	______	______	______	______

Source: Small Business Administration, Publication MP15.

Ship in a BOTTLE

The Idea

"Honey, where did you buy my ship-in-a-bottle?"

"I got it at a closeout sale at that nautical gift store in Maine. It was going out of business, remember? Why do you ask?"

"Because I really like it. I'd like to start collecting them."

Little did Fred Johnson know that this simple exchange of information with his wife, Jeanie, would lead to the start of a successful Internet business. His search for a new ship-in-a-bottle model led him to retail stores, catalogs, and the Internet, without success. He even attended, as a guest, the gift trade show at the Atlanta Merchandise Mart. He couldn't find a single well-built model. Fred wondered how many other people were looking for the same thing. Had he stumbled on an unsatisfied need in the marketplace? He sensed that he had.

From his initial research, Fred learned that ship-in-a-bottle models had been around for 200 years. Sailors had created the first of these unusual artifacts during their long hours at sea. Today they are constructed much the same way. Each tiny ship is built outside the bottle with collapsible masts. Then it is inserted through the neck of the bottle with the masts down and attached to a blue putty base. The masts are hoisted with a wire, which is then cut.

Fred delved deeper into the Internet for information. He did find modelers who would sell customized models at exorbitant prices. He also found distributors of inexpensive souvenir versions. The souvenir types did not match the quality of the model that Jeanie had purchased in Maine.

Fred expanded his search to international web sites, where he finally found the exact model Jeanie had purchased three years earlier. The craftsman/manufacturer was Johann Schneider of Hamburg, Germany. Johann produced a line of over 100 models with retail prices ranging from 50 to 500 euros, depending on size and detail of work (the euro at that time was roughly equivalent to the U.S. dollar). Fred e-mailed Johann for information on how to purchase a model and also inquired as to the possibility of selling Johann's products in the U.S. Johann was as excited as Fred about the chance to explore a new market. The Schneider family had been producing ship-in-a-bottle models for over 25 years. Johann had learned the craft from his seafaring grandfather. His annual European sales were over $300,000, and he believed that he could produce more models if American demand were great enough. He immediately sent Fred sample bottles in three sizes.

Fred showed the samples to everyone who might have even the remotest interest, including the owner of an executive gift catalog company. She told Fred she would order a dozen models if he decided to import them.

An exchange of e-mails with Johann followed. They agreed on wholesale prices and some basic goals. They also decided that Johann would travel to the U.S. to discuss further possibilities.

"Wow," thought Fred. "I do believe I've stumbled on a great business idea!"

Think Critically

1. Where is Fred in regard to the creativity process?
2. At this point should Fred consider ships in bottles as a part-time or full-time business venture?

Summary

Entrepreneurs are risk takers who are able to sense the needs of the marketplace. They are often small business owners who are willing to invest their money, time, and abilities in pursuit of achieving profits at the risk of incurring losses.

Entrepreneurs come from all backgrounds and form enterprises in all sectors of the economy. They open businesses not just for the sake of making profits but also from an overpowering need to achieve independence and control their own destiny.

Entrepreneurs are also found in large organizations and businesses, where they are often the most innovative, forward-thinking employees. They possess the personal characteristics of self-confidence, determination, creativity, and the need to achieve.

In order to perform at their highest potential, entrepreneurs need to work in environments that are personally satisfying to them. Their values, attitudes, needs, and expectations must match the goals they set out to accomplish.

It is mandatory that aspiring entrepreneurs write out a good business plan that serves as a guide to achieving their objectives. The research performed while preparing the business plan will validate whether the entrepreneur's idea serves a true market need. The business plan must take into consideration personal goals with respect to income, personal satisfaction, status, work content, and lifestyle.

If the entrepreneur is not working in an environment compatible with personal interests and goals, success will be very hard to achieve due to the amount of personal sacrifice often required in starting a new business. Opportunities that allow an individual to utilize personal and learned capabilities should receive priority attention.

Entrepreneurship is available to anyone with the necessary personal characteristics to succeed in building a business. Often entrepreneurs begin with a part-time venture that grows into a full-time occupation. Ideas for new businesses come from previous employment experience, hobbies, accidental discoveries, or an intentional search for a marketplace need.

A Case in POINT

Unrealistic Expectations

"I'll tell you, Jerry, I'm paying the price for success." Bill Lankford was chatting over coffee with his friend, Jerry Gold. "I'm a senior executive, I'm financially set, but I'm too exhausted to enjoy it. Except for weekends, I've been home three nights in the past month. I'm losing touch with my family. My job has turned into a PR job—all I do is travel and make speeches. Success may be great for the ego, but what about the soul? I envy you owning your own business and being in charge of your life. I don't need the money as much as I need to slow down and smell the roses." Bill paused for a moment. "That's why I called you. I want your opinion on a business opportunity. There's a chain of six laundromats for sale here in the metro area. It sounds ideal to me. Take a look at this income statement from last year." Bill pulled a sheet of paper from a folder and handed it to Jerry, who looked it over carefully.

According to the income statement, the business was producing an $80,000 net profit before the owner's salary was deducted. The selling price was $150,000. Bill explained that he could cut his present salary to $50,000, which would allow a $30,000 payback

continued

on the $150,000, a 20 percent return on the investment. "I really want to do it, Jerry. It sounds ideal. Each unit has its own part-time manager, so if I want to take a trip with the family or play golf, I can do so. I can open more outlets to generate greater profits. I'll control my own priorities, have the independence I want, and make good profits. No more corporate world. What do you think? Should I write the seller a check?"

Jerry scratched his head. "Bill, I think you need to slow down a bit. It may not be quite what you're expecting. Believe me, I've owned a business for sixteen years, and it's harder than you think. I don't know the laundromat business, but I can guarantee you there will be unexpected surprises. You need to make sure this opportunity is what it appears to be and that it's really something you want to do fifty-two weeks a year."

"Aw, come on, Jerry, this will be a piece of cake compared to what I've been doing the past twelve years. I appreciate your concern, but unless I find problems with this proposal, I'm going to be an entrepreneur."

Bill handed in his resignation the following month. There were good-bye parties, and a genuine display of sorrow on the part of his associates. He was deeply touched.

In many ways, Jerry proved to be right. Bill had not taken the time to thoroughly analyze his projected career and lifestyle. It was not a "piece of cake." Equipment maintenance alone was a nightmare. He spent many afternoons surrounded by pieces of washing and drying machines. Store manager turnover was a problem because of the low wages. Bill had not realized that controlling an expense budget of $180,000 of his own money could be as difficult as controlling the much larger budget of his previous employer. Every added expense was a subtraction from his already decreased salary. His first attempt at opening a new laundromat was a shock when he realized that it normally takes a few years for a business to become profitable.

Bill wondered if he had chosen the wrong business. Maybe he should have taken Jerry's advice and not been in such a hurry.

Think Critically

1. List the steps Bill should have followed before deciding to buy the laundromat.
2. What should Bill do at this point?
3. Many aspiring entrepreneurs place their desires before their good sense. What can an entrepreneur do to make sure his plan supports his goals?

Vocabulary Builder

Write a brief definition of each word or phrase.

1. absentee management
2. needs
3. attitude
4. retained earnings
5. autonomy anchor
6. return on investment
7. career anchors
8. security anchor
9. creativity anchor
10. Small Business Administration
11. creativity process
12. technical anchor
13. entrepreneur
14. values
15. expectations
16. VANE
17. managerial anchor

Review the Concepts

18. Describe what makes a successful entrepreneur.
19. Why is writing a business plan necessary to achieve success?
20. How does determining an individual's career anchor(s) help in deciding on a business endeavor?
21. What are meant by values, attitudes, needs, and expectations as applied to entrepreneurship?
22. Why does it normally take five years for a business to become successful?
23. List the six steps of the creativity process.
24. What are the advantages and disadvantages of starting a part-time business?

Critical Thinking

25. Explain why entrepreneurs are so vital to the economic well-being of our country.
26. How do the four essential characteristics of successful entrepreneurs relate to the reasons individuals open small businesses?
27. Discuss the importance of working in the right environment and the risks involved in working in unfamiliar occupations.
28. Apply your personal VANE analysis to choosing a business.
29. Explain the danger of not considering return on investment when deciding on a business opportunity.
30. Describe a source of new business ideas other than the ones listed in the chapter.
31. What businesses do you believe are needed in your community? Why?

Project

Build Your Business Plan

As you proceed through the textbook, write out a business plan for a hypothetical business of your choice. Each chapter will give you suggestions for each step. The challenge for this chapter is to determine what type of business you wish to investigate. Once you have decided, write a paragraph describing why you have chosen that particular business.

Chapter 2

Plan the Small Business

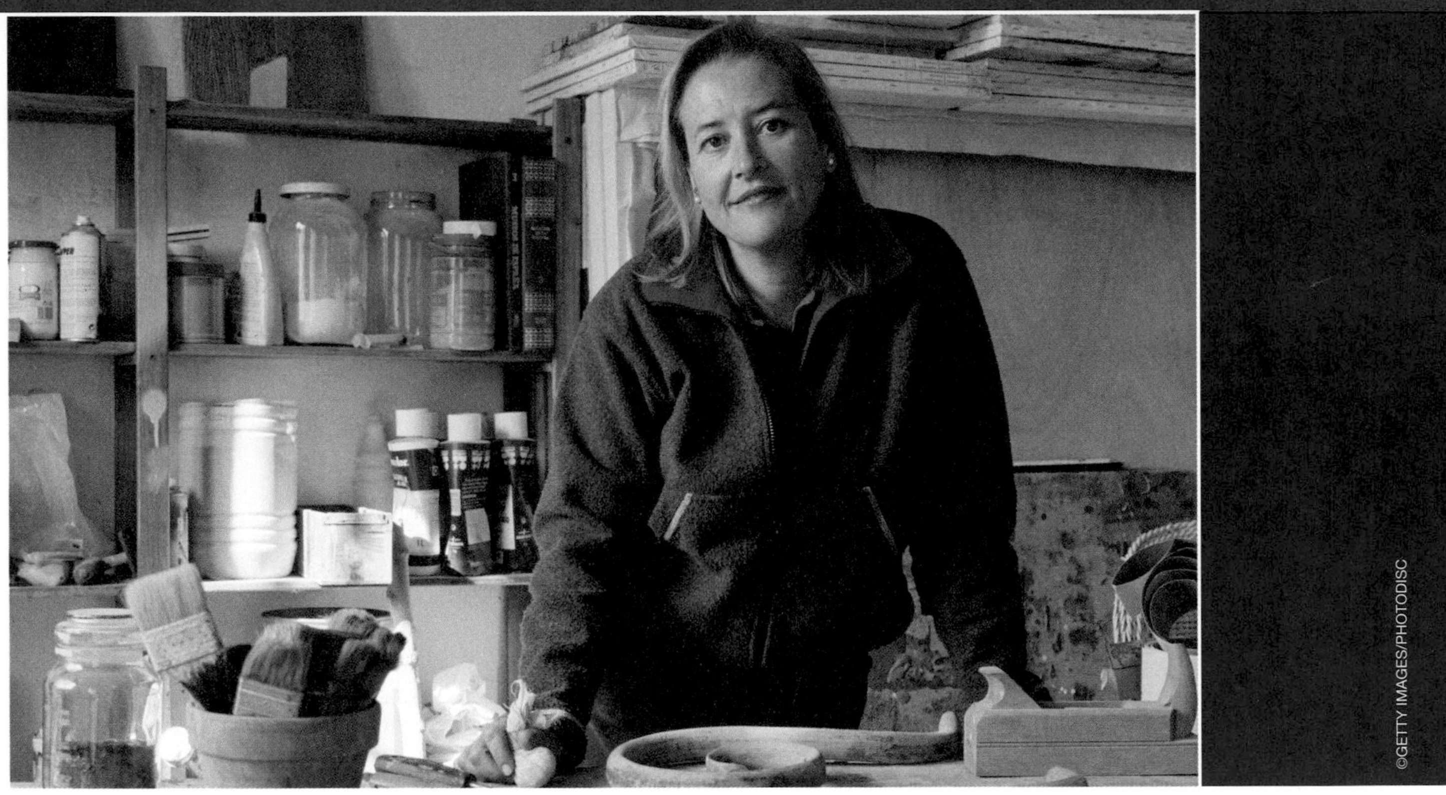
©GETTY IMAGES/PHOTODISC

Objectives

2-1 Explain the importance of planning to the small business.

2-2 Define the term *business plan.*

2-3 Describe the components of a business plan and explain the importance of each.

2-4 Identify the sources for assistance in planning a small business.

GET STARTED

This chapter discusses the business planning process and provides an overview of chapters to follow. In the Project you will be developing a business plan. You have probably heard that writing one of these things takes forever and you never really know what to put in it. Anyone who has ever gone through the complete business planning process would say there is a measure of truth to that rumor.

The value of a business plan in getting financing or serving as a guide for your new business will probably be in direct proportion to how seriously you take the process and how much time you devote to its writing. As far as what to put in it, there are as many suggestions out there as there are cars on an L.A. freeway.

Your first question is probably "Isn't your business plan suggestion just another addition to an already long list?" In a way the answer is yes, but in what is probably a more important way, the answer is no. The business plan outline provided in this text is a result of in-depth research into what commercial lending officers want in a plan. Additional research involved comparing the contents of several mainstream business plan outlines. Consequently, the business plan outline recommended here includes all the major categories and subcategories required by bankers plus those appearing in other business plan outlines. A business plan written using the recommended outline should meet the requirements of most lenders.

©GETTY IMAGES/PHOTODISC

In business planning, the secret is not to overthink or overwork the process. You should decide why you are writing the business plan. Is it to get your local banker to loan you the money to start? Is it to get your Aunt Mary to bankroll the operation? Is it a way to examine the feasibility of the proposed business? How are you going to use the final business plan? Only you know that. Based on your answer, put as much or as little effort into developing the plan as is required to meet your goal.

According to the Small Business Administration, "Starting and managing a business takes motivation and talent. It also takes research and planning. Although initial mistakes are not always fatal, it takes extra skill, discipline, and hard work to regain the advantage." Starting a new business is much like going on a long journey. Both undertakings require time, effort, know-how, and a sense of adventure. Both are more enjoyable and rewarding if you know how to go, what to take along, how long it will last, and what to expect along the way. You may still encounter some surprises, but chances are you will be prepared to deal with them.

THE BUSINESS PLAN

Once aspiring entrepreneurs have identified a business idea that seems promising, they must begin preparing for the journey that will transform the idea into a business success. The key step in preparation is planning. Planning is the systematic process of developing an outline for the accomplishment of a goal or set of goals. A well-prepared outline serves as a road map that guides the traveler to the desired destination.

Planning is one of the most important skills needed for starting a business. Whether the entrepreneur is going to start a new business, buy an established business, or purchase a franchise, good planning is the key to business success.

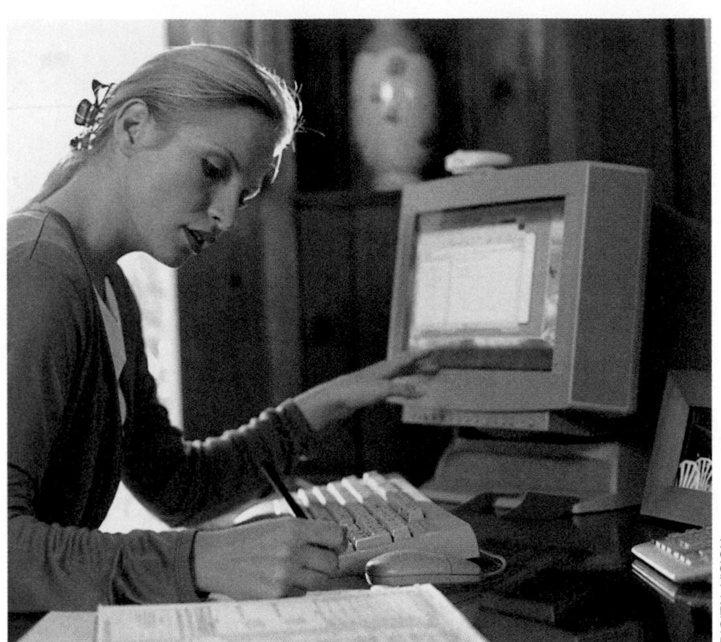

DIGITAL VISION

A **business plan** serves as a manual to help the entrepreneur during the design and start-up phases of the business. It also states the entrepreneur's expectations, which serve as criteria by which business performance can be periodically evaluated. A good business plan is an ever-evolving resource that grows and changes with the business. As such, it should be consulted regularly and updated annually.

Many entrepreneurs stumble upon an idea that seems certain to be a success. They are tempted to skip the planning phase and jump right into business. After all, a day spent planning is a day without profit. That temptation must be resisted. The steps involved in starting and maintaining even the smallest business can be overwhelming. Neglecting even a minor detail may cause unnecessary aggravation and expense. Overlooking a major detail may ultimately lead to business failure.

Writing a comprehensive business plan ensures that all the details of your proposed business are addressed. It helps you avoid many of the pitfalls that can delay or prevent business success. If you carefully explore and evaluate your proposed business, the time you invest will be a small price to pay for achieving your goals.

Many entrepreneurs have plenty of ideas but very little capital with which to start a business. Most of them have to go to a bank or other financial institution for a loan. A majority of banks require a written business plan before they will consider loaning money for a small business start-up. A comprehensive and detailed business plan shows the bank that you are serious about your new venture and have invested considerable time and effort in planning what will be a successful business. Such a proposal is more likely to win the bank's support than one that presents only vague details.

FORMULATE A BUSINESS PLAN

Below is an outline of a typical business plan. Several of the headings may not be applicable to certain types of businesses and may be omitted. The amount of information required under each heading will also vary from business to business.

Outline of Typical Business Plan

COVER SHEET
STATEMENT OF PURPOSE
TABLE OF CONTENTS
EXECUTIVE SUMMARY

1. Concept History and Background
   A. Description of Product or Service
   B. Idea History
   C. Summary of Experience
2. Goals and Objectives
3. Marketing Plan
   A. Consumers and Demand
   B. Competition
   C. Geographic Market
   D. Pricing Policy
4. Legal Requirements
5. Form of Ownership
6. Financial Plan
   A. Initial Capitalization Plan
   B. Projected Income Statement
   C. Projected Operating Statement
   D. Cash Flow Projection
7. Organization, Management, and Staffing Plan
   A. Organization Chart
   B. Employee Requirements
   C. Resumes
   D. Personal Financial Statements
   E. References
8. Special Considerations
   A. Production and Manufacturing Needs
   B. Facility Needs
   C. Education and Training Needs
   D. Land and Utility Needs
   E. Research and Development
   F. Other

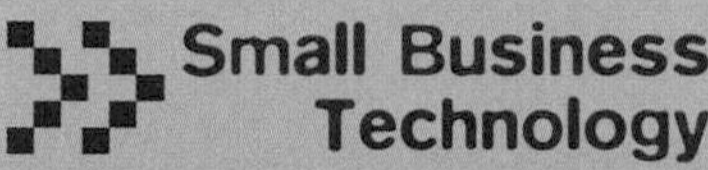

Small Business Technology

For the entrepreneur needing examples of business plan components or samples of suggested content, business planning software is an option. Two leading business planning software companies are BizPlan™ and Business Plan Pro™.

©GETTY IMAGES/PHOTODISC

The individual components of a business plan and how they are developed will be described in detail in later chapters. For the purpose of discussing the general principles of business planning, however, these components and their importance in the planning process are covered briefly here.

Plan Layout

> **FUN FACTS**
> Wrigley's Chewing Gum was the first product to have a bar code.

First, your business plan should be "pretty." Specifically, it should look professional. Use high-quality paper and make sure the print is dark and easy to read. Present the plan in an attractive folder or binder with good use of color on the front. The plan should be free of spelling errors and grammatical inconsistencies. Carefully proofread the final version or get a family member or friend to do it.

The overall appearance of a business plan can never be as important as what it says, but if the plan is sloppy and not visually appealing, it may never get read. Remember, "pretty" is important.

A business plan opens with a cover page, a table of contents, and an executive summary.

Cover Page The cover page answers these questions: Who wrote the plan and how can they be contacted? Why was the plan developed? To whom is it presented?

Since the cover page is one of the first things the reader sees, make sure it is neat and easy to read. Include your name, phone number, and address.

If the plan was developed for bank financing, say so. If you are sending it to a bank lending officer, say the plan is being presented to Gene Miller at the Bank of Clarksdale, for example. If the plan is for planning purposes only or will be viewed by many types of people, leave this section out.

Table of Contents The table of contents follows the cover page and lists the major components of the plan and corresponding page numbers. The table of contents is written when the business plan is in its final draft.

Executive Summary The **executive summary** follows the table of contents and provides a two- to three-page summary of what is in the plan. Because it is a summary, it should also be written after the business plan is in its final draft.

©GETTY IMAGES/PHOTODISC

What should you put in the summary? Put in the most interesting and most important details of the plan. Pretend you have a maximum of three pages to sell your idea to the reader. That is not far from the truth. If you are providing the plan to a banker for funding consideration, keep in mind that he or she probably has to read several similar plans each day. The usual drill is for the banker to read the executive summary and then decide if it is worth spending any more time reading the whole plan.

Write the first paragraph of the executive summary as if your business life depends on it. It probably does! Then write the remaining summary with equal care.

Concept History and Background

The first part of the business plan itself describes the business concept, how it was developed, and what qualifications the potential entrepreneur has for the intended business.

Description of Product or Service The entrepreneur should describe in very specific terms the product or service that the business is going to offer. The description should highlight how the product or service is different from or better than existing products or services. Such details aid in determining the feasibility of the proposed business.

Idea History An idea history summarizes when, how, and why the potential entrepreneur developed the idea for the business. This component is important primarily during the loan application process. At least half of all bank loan officers require applicants to include an idea history in their business plans because it provides insight into the thought processes of the potential business owner.

Summary of Experience Most banks consider a written summary of the entrepreneur's experience an essential component of the business plan. The summary should emphasize practical exposure to the intended business. Relevant volunteer work and hobbies, as well as paid employment, may have provided valuable experience that could be helpful in running the business. Such experience may greatly increase the business owner's chances of success both at the bank and in the marketplace.

Goals and Objectives

A goal can be defined as the overall end toward which one directs one's efforts. An objective is a specific result that is desired. For example, a well-defined goal should answer the question "What do I want to achieve?" An objective answers the question "What specific results do I need to accomplish that will help me reach my goal?"

Goals and objectives are important because they provide direction and focus for your activities. How will you know where you are going unless you identify where you want to go? A new business might set a goal of becoming the number-one business of its type in the metropolitan area. One of its objectives may be to grow its customer base by 10 percent per year. By setting the goal and several objectives, the business has established the direction it will take.

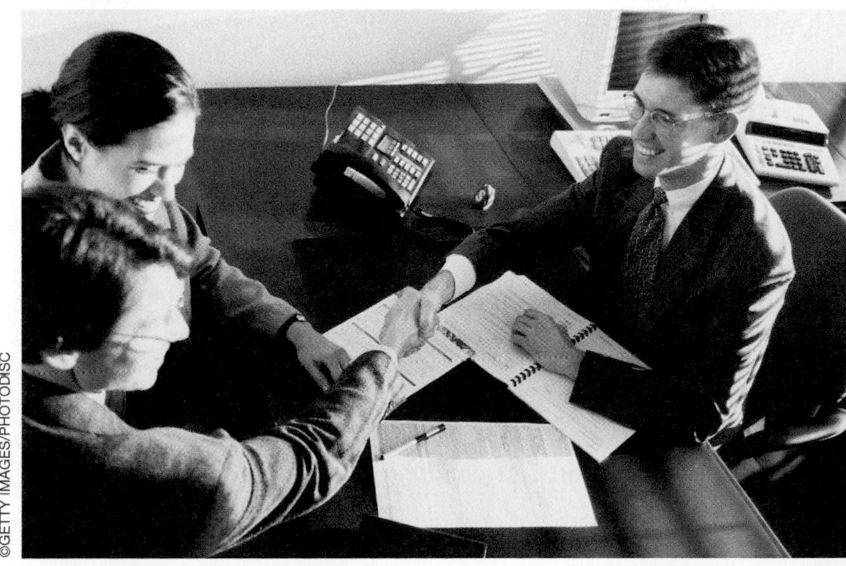

©GETTY IMAGES/PHOTODISC

Goals and objectives work in much the same way for entrepreneurs—by keeping business owners focused on what they are trying to achieve. Many entrepreneurial goals deal with profitability. Goals and objectives are also useful to banks because the lender must know the entrepreneur's intentions. More than two-thirds of banks require written goals and objectives for at least the first year. For this reason, entrepreneurs should be insightful, realistic, and concise when writing goals and objectives for the business plan.

Short-Term and Long-Term Goals A short-term goal is one that can be achieved in a short period of time, perhaps within several months or a year. A long-term goal is one that is to be achieved over a longer period of time, such as a number of years. The entrepreneur should set short- and long-term goals concerning both financial and personal interests, always focusing on the ultimate goal of the business.

©GETTY IMAGES/PHOTODISC

As an example, a short-term personal goal might sound like this: Work part-time while planning my new business, then, at the end of one year, quit my job and devote all my efforts to opening and managing the new business. A long-term financial goal might sound like this: Pay back my $20,000 start-up loan within six years.

Using Goals and Objectives to Measure Success Success can be measured by how close entrepreneurs come to reaching their goals and objectives. Certainly one of the most satisfying feelings for entrepreneurs comes from achieving the goals and objectives they established—personal as well as financial. If they accomplish this, they should consider themselves successful.

If, after some period of time, goals or objectives are not being met, they may have been unrealistic in the first place. The entrepreneur should re-evaluate the business and try to determine what went wrong. The important thing to remember is to review, reevaluate, and, if appropriate, reestablish goals and objectives at least once a year to make sure that the business venture is on the right track.

FUN FACTS

On May 5, 1978, Jerry Greenfield and Ben Cohen opened the first Ben & Jerry's ice cream shop in a converted gas station in Burlington, Vermont.

Marketing Plan

Just speculating that many people will want to buy a product or service is not enough. Entrepreneurs need to quantify information about their potential markets—that is, they need to express that information in specific, measurable terms.

The **marketing plan** defines and quantifies consumers, demand, competition, geographic market, and pricing policy for a specific small business. Most business experts consider the marketing plan a key component of the planning process. Drawing an accurate picture of the potential market for a product or service helps the entrepreneur to set realistic goals and objectives for the business. Bank loan officers devote considerable attention to the marketing plan.

Consumers and Demand The first part of the marketing plan describes the consumers and demand for the product or service. It may profile a typical customer in terms of age, sex, income, occupation, family status, or other characteristics that make that person likely to frequent the business. It may also estimate how often a typical customer will want to buy the product or service and at what price.

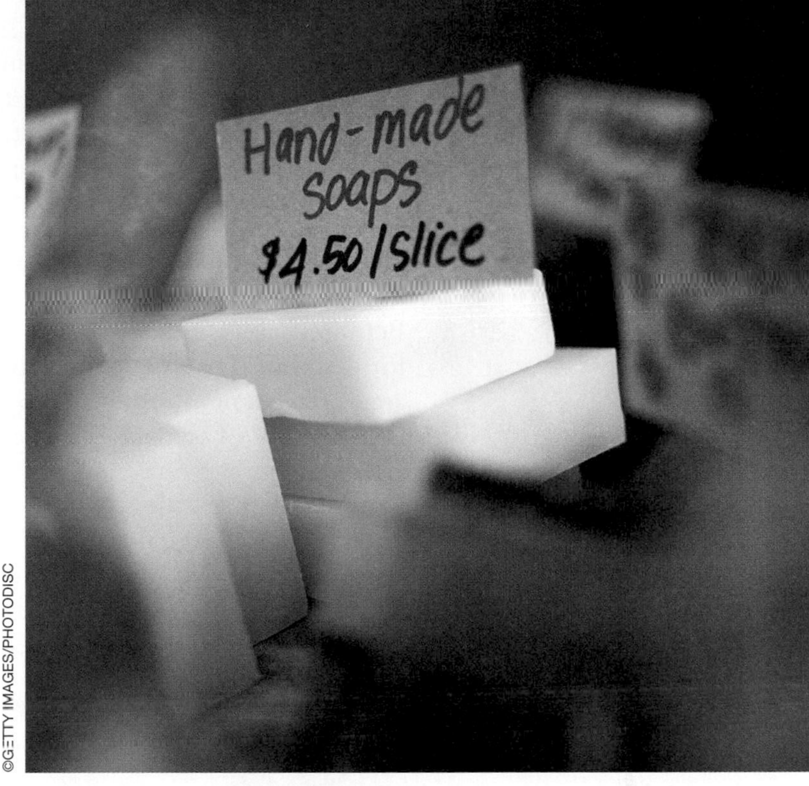

©GETTY IMAGES/PHOTODISC

Competition The second part of the marketing plan deals with competition. Suppose you decide that a shoe store is a good venture. You know that everybody in town is already wearing shoes—in other words, they are shopping at your competitors' stores. The only way for you to bring customers into your new store is to lure them away from the competition. One way you can do this is by making your store different from the others in terms of location, selection, quality, price, or service. But in order to make your store different, you need to know about the competition. In addition, you need to consider what your competitors' reaction will be to your business. What will you do to counteract their responses?

As you plan your business, then, you should learn as much as possible about the competition. In particular, you should determine how the competition is different from the business you have in mind. All of this information should be summarized in your marketing plan.

Do banks think you should be concerned with your competition? You bet they do! One of the first questions many loan officers ask is, "What can you tell us about your competition?" If your answer is "Nothing," their next statement may well be "Good-bye!"

Geographic Market This part of the marketing plan describes the geographic area from which the business will draw its customers. The entrepreneur must project how far people will be willing to travel to frequent the business, and from which areas they will come. Correctly identifying the geographic market makes setting realistic sales goals easier.

Pricing Policy The last part of the marketing plan is the **pricing policy**, which determines how you will set prices for the product or service. Your prices will have a direct impact on the number of customers you will have and the profits you accumulate. A carefully considered pricing policy can help you achieve your sales and profit goals.

Legal Requirements

As aspiring entrepreneurs consider opening their new businesses, legal problems are the last thing on their minds. But if they do not devote time and attention to the legal aspects of a new business, legal problems may soon be the only thing on their minds. Entrepreneurs must consider potential legal problems before they actually go into business.

The legal requirements for conducting almost any business today can be extensive and complicated. Certain patents, copyrights, agreements, contracts, or other legal arrangements will be needed to carry out day-to-day business. The planning phase is the proper time to consider these requirements and how they will be met. Indeed, 94 percent of the banks doing business with entrepreneurs in new small business ventures require that the legal aspects of the ventures be addressed in the planning process.

Form of Ownership

Before you seek financial assistance, you must decide on a form of ownership for your business. If you are going it alone, this part of the plan is easy. If you are starting a new business with one or more other persons, however, choosing the form of ownership becomes a critical decision. Form of ownership affects business management, division of profits, division of labor, liability, and many other issues.

The most common forms of ownership are sole proprietorship, partnership, LLC (limited liability company), and corporation. Each of these will be discussed briefly in Chapter 4. Entrepreneurs must decide during the planning phase which form of ownership best suits the needs of the business and the people involved.

Ethics for ENTREPRENEURS

In a well-written business plan, the entrepreneur presents the proposed business in a positive, upbeat manner, by personally gathering the information and stating it in an optimistic way. The question is, when do facts presented in a positive light cross the ethical line and become lies? Are they lies if you did not really develop the plan yourself?

Lies occur when the entrepreneur misrepresents the facts in such a way that the reader reaches an incorrect conclusion. For example, Lee always had a passion for gourmet coffee. Six months after being fired as a foreman at a local manufacturing plant, he decided to become an entrepreneur and open an Internet coffee shop.

Lee's first stop was at his bank, where he spoke to a commercial lending officer. The banker told Lee that in order to be considered for financing, he had to write an original business plan.

Like most entrepreneurs, Lee was in a big hurry to get the new business up and running. Writing a comprehensive business plan can take months. Perhaps, Lee thought, he could find a business plan on the Internet. Then he could simply change the name and a few facts and submit it to the bank.

Good ethics and good business go hand-in-hand.

Think Critically

Would Lee be lying to the banker by presenting an online business plan as his own? Is this an ethical approach?

Financial Plan

Along with the marketing plan, the financial section of the business plan is a key component in the overall planning process. A basic **financial plan** contains the entrepreneur's estimates for the following categories:

©GETTY IMAGES/PHOTODISC

1. cost of starting the business and maintaining it for a specified period of time (initial capitalization plan)
2. projected income
3. projected operating expenses
4. projected cash flow
5. initial balance sheet

Some small business experts say that potential entrepreneurs should start their business planning process with the financial plan. They argue that, until the entrepreneur determines what the proposed venture will cost and whether or not it is feasible, other planning is fruitless.

All experts agree that the financial plan must be developed very carefully. Poor financial planning at the start of a business venture almost inevitably leads to overall business failure. Therefore most bank loan officers carefully scrutinize all five categories in the financial plan.

Organization, Management, and Staffing Plan

Although opening day may be a long way off, the entrepreneur must determine how many employees the business will require and what their responsibilities will be. Such concerns are addressed in the organization, management, and staffing plan section of the business plan.

Organization Chart The **organization chart** deals with the actual management of the business. The chart defines who will be responsible for tasks such as purchasing, advertising, accounting, and hiring personnel. The chart also shows who reports to whom in the organizational hierarchy.

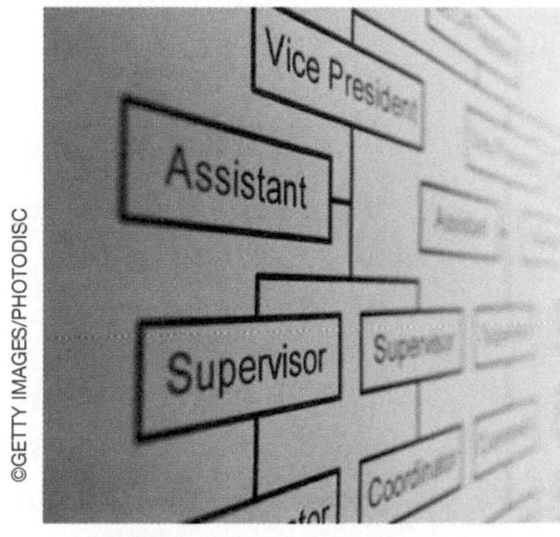

©GETTY IMAGES/PHOTODISC

The Global ENTREPRENEUR

The entrepreneur planning expansion into global markets must approach the business planning process from a slightly different perspective. An excellent place to start is the Small Business Administration's Online Guide to Exporting. The SBA offers several suggestions. First, select the most exportable products. Determine what makes your products unique for an overseas market. Ask yourself why international buyers would purchase the products from your company. How much inventory will you need to sell overseas? Identify customers within your chosen markets. Determine what companies, agents, or distributors would be prospective customers for your export products. Decide your method of exporting. How do other U.S. firms sell in the markets you have chosen? The SBA offers information to guide you through the entire planning process. Use their help. The global entrepreneur must face more complex issues and answer additional questions during the business planning process.

Think Critically

Which of the questions above do you consider the most important? Why?

Employee Requirements Planning for an appropriate number of employees is essential. If too few employees are hired, there will not be enough people to meet customers' needs. On the other hand, if too many employees are hired, the excessive labor costs will decrease profits. During the business planning phase the entrepreneur should use information such as the organization chart and projected sales figures to estimate how many employees will be needed.

Resumes, Personal Financial Statements, and References If opening a new business will require bank financing, each borrower must prepare a resume, a personal financial statement, and a list of references. The resume outlines the borrower's education and work experience. Banks use the resume to determine whether the entrepreneur has the necessary background for the proposed business. The **personal financial statement** describes the borrower's financial condition. In particular, it shows what assets the borrower could use as **collateral**—something of value pledged as security—for the loan. Banks use the personal financial statement to evaluate the borrower's ability to repay the loan. The list of references contains the names and addresses of people who can supply information concerning the borrower's character and history.

Special Considerations

The last component of the business plan deals with any special considerations that apply to the entrepreneur's chosen business. Some small businesses will have many special considerations; some will have none.

If the business will involve manufacturing a product, the list of special considerations may be quite lengthy. If the business will consist exclusively of selling a service, however, the only special consideration may be a facility. Other special considerations may include training for the entrepreneur or employees, land and utility needs, and research and development. The entrepreneur's goal is to recognize and deal with all these special considerations during the planning process.

Decide Whether to Go into Business

Once the business plan is complete, the entrepreneur can make the final decision as to whether or not to go into business. The three most useful pieces of information are the marketing plan, the financial plan, and the personal financial statement. If the entrepreneur has worked carefully, these items should reveal whether there is a market, how much money it will take to reach that market, and whether enough resources are available to pull it all together.

DIGITAL VISION

SOURCES FOR PLANNING ASSISTANCE

Many entrepreneurs bring enthusiasm and a wealth of technical knowledge to their new venture. What is usually lacking is management expertise and specific information about the nuts and bolts of starting a business. Fortunately, a variety of resources can offer assistance. Three of the most commonly available resources are community colleges, chambers of commerce, and the Small Business Administration.

Local Community Colleges Many community colleges have small business development centers designed to assist local small businesses. The first such center established in the state of Colorado almost two decades ago by one of the textbook authors is located at Pueblo Community College. It serves a three-county area in the southern part of the state and provides a wide array of services. In addition to community colleges, many four-year colleges and universities have resources available to the aspiring entrepreneur. Before embarking upon the planning process, check your local community for higher education resources.

Pueblo Community College

Small Business Development Center

Pueblo's Small Business Development Center offers "one-stop" assistance to small businesses, making a wide variety of information and guidance available in central and easily accessible locations. The Pueblo SBDC provides services for Pueblo, Fremont, and Custer counties, and has office locations in Pueblo and Canon City.

The Small Business Development Center provides free one-on-one counseling for both existing and start-up businesses. It also sponsors seminars and workshops designed to help small business owners improve their business knowledge and entrepreneurs plan their start-up business.

The center's mission: "To promote a vigorous and viable small business community by providing high-quality counseling and training to owners and prospective owners of small businesses in Pueblo, Fremont, and Custer counties, and to proactively work with lenders, government entities, and other small business service providers to enhance the probability of success of these businesses."

Chamber of Commerce In many communities, the chamber of commerce has a small business development committee that can offer guidance to entrepreneurs. One such example is discussed in the section on Internet resources later in this chapter.

Small Business Administration The SBA is an independent federal government agency with offices in most metropolitan areas. It offers a range of services, including seminars, counseling, and loans. For entrepreneurs contemplating the small business planning process, the SBA offers excellent information in the following areas:

Start-up Basics	Financing
Business Planning	Marketing
Business Plan Basics	Employees
Writing the Plan	Taxes
Using the Plan	Legal Aspects
Specific Training	Special Interests

Entrepreneurs should contact the closest SBA office or go online to retrieve information in any of the above areas.

Accountants and Attorneys

Accountants and lawyers should not be overlooked as sources for planning assistance. During the planning process, the entrepreneur should establish a working relationship with an accountant and an attorney who have experience with small businesses. The accountant should review or, in some cases, help to develop the financial plan. The attorney should be consulted to determine the legal requirements of the proposed business.

These professionals are a necessary part of the planning process regardless of whether you are starting a new business, buying an existing business, or purchasing a franchise. Their fees, which usually run $100 an hour and up, must simply be viewed as part of the expense of doing business.

Internet and Electronic Indexes

The Internet is probably the best place to start searching for planning assistance. Your local chamber of commerce likely has a web page providing local business and community information. For instance, the Grand Junction, Colorado, Area Chamber of Commerce lists community information, economic outlook, demographics, transportation, community resources, and much more valuable information for entrepreneurs. The SBA also has an excellent site.

Many private sites offer excellent links. A good example is the web page of one of the authors. It has been developed over the course of many years for use by his entrepreneurship students. Comprising over 400 links, the site is organized into sections for ease of use. Sections currently include links to information about finance and taxes, government, industry/company information, Internet search and directories, international business, legal and hiring law, marketing, news and journals, business protocol, and start-up and planning. It is available for use by any entrepreneur planning a business.

Electronic indexes are sites that usually charge a fee to access their collection of publications. A good example of a useful index for entrepreneurs is Business Source Premier. It offers full-text articles from over 2,804 business-related publications, with indexing and abstracts for nearly 3,335 journals. It is updated daily.

Another index is the Fortune 500 Annual Reports, which offers the full text of official annual reports for the current year and six previous years for Fortune 500 companies, company home pages, stock reports, and news wire articles. Mergent's (formerly Moody's) offers full-text updates on news and financial information for publicly traded companies and municipal and government entities covered in the annual Mergent Manuals.

Using your computer is a quick and easy way to locate business assistance and other valuable information.

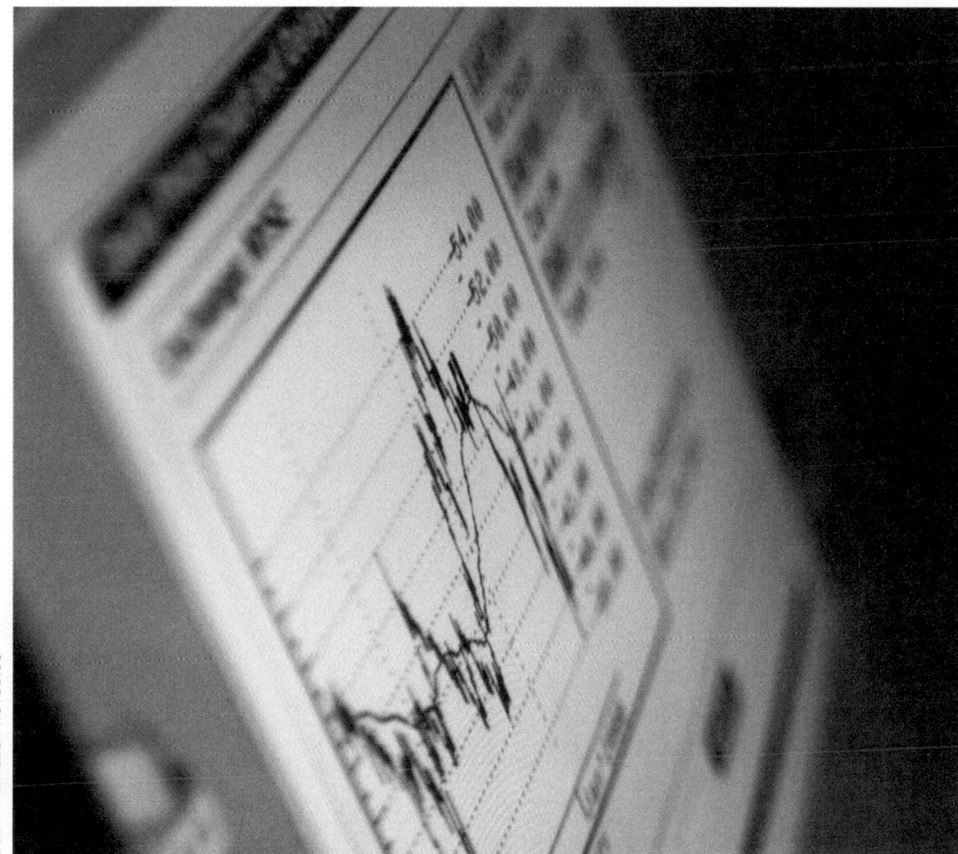

Ship in a BOTTLE

The Plan

One month after their first exchange of e-mails, Fred Johnson was at the Atlanta airport meeting Johann Schneider. He was pleased to learn that they had much in common. They were about the same age, had families, were sports fans, and wanted to develop a successful business venture.

They set about developing a business plan. The first step was to decide that for the time being they would restrict themselves to selling ships-in-bottles manufactured in Germany. Later on, they agreed, they might expand into other product lines in which Johann had experience and resources. But first they needed to develop their advantage in their special area.

They decided that Fred would distribute their products in two ways. He would serve as a wholesaler to retail gift and nautical stores and also as an Internet retailer. The business would be called Ship in a Bottle. They would create a color brochure showing 75 different models. They compiled wholesale and retail price lists, devised billing terms and credit application forms, and set up a bank account and credit card vendor arrangements. Fortunately for Fred, Johann was not only fluent in English but also experienced in computer design. Together they set up a simple web site similar to the one Johann had developed in Germany. They secured a web site domain listing and launched a five-page retail site.

The other part of the distribution plan would require taking the products to wholesale trade shows. They decided to lease exhibition booths for the two-day to week-long events that were attended by retail buyers. Since one of the largest merchandise marts in the country is in Atlanta, they made plans to exhibit at the January Atlanta gift show two months later. In the meantime Fred would travel to various coastal towns and visit potential retailers.

Their financial plan began to take shape. There would have to be enough money for the brochure, initial inventory, shipping materials, supplies, exhibit booth space, and, it seemed, a million incidentals. Ship in a Bottle would be Fred's business. Johann would be the supplier. They agreed on an initial order of samples, basic inventory, and terms and estimated they would need $10,000 to get the fledgling business off the ground.

After five days of feverish work, Fred threw Johann a going-away party featuring bratwurst, sauerkraut, and German beer. Not only had they created a business, they had also launched a friendship.

Think Critically

1. Sketch an outline of a business plan for Fred and Johann.
2. What resources can they turn to for help in writing their business plan?

Summary

Planning is critical to the ultimate success of a small business. At the heart of the process is the business plan, which contains the following components:

1. Concept History and Background: The first part of the business plan itself describes the business concept, how it was developed, and what qualifications the potential entrepreneur has for the intended business.
2. Goals and Objectives: A goal can be defined as the overall end toward which one directs one's efforts. An objective is a specific result that is desired.
3. Marketing Plan: Most business experts consider the marketing plan a key component of the planning process. Drawing an accurate picture of the potential market for a product or service helps the entrepreneur to set realistic goals and objectives for the business.
4. Legal Requirements: The legal requirements for conducting almost any business today can be extensive and complicated. Certain patents, copyrights, agreements, contracts, or other legal arrangements will be needed to carry out day-to-day business.
5. Form of Ownership: Entrepreneurs must decide during the planning phase which form of ownership best suits the needs of the business and the people involved.
6. Financial Plan: Poor financial planning at the start of a business venture almost inevitably leads to overall business failure.
7. Organization, Management, and Staffing Plan: The entrepreneur must determine how many employees the business will require and what their responsibilities will be.
8. Special Considerations: This component deals with considerations such as a manufacturing facility or special training that apply to the chosen business.

A business plan serves as a manual to help the entrepreneur during the design and start-up phases of the business. It also states the entrepreneur's expectations, which serve as criteria by which business performance can be periodically evaluated. A good business plan is an ever-evolving resource that grows and changes with the business. As such, it should be consulted regularly and updated annually.

The value of a business plan in getting financing or serving as a guide for your new business will probably be in direct proportion to how seriously you take the process and how much time you devote to its writing.

Writing a comprehensive business plan ensures that all the details of your proposed business are addressed. It helps you avoid many of the pitfalls that can delay or prevent business success. If you carefully explore and evaluate your proposed business, the time you invest will be a small price to pay for achieving your goals.

The completed business plan contains the information a potential entrepreneur needs to decide whether or not to start a business. The three most useful pieces of information are the marketing plan, the financial plan, and the personal financial statement. If the entrepreneur has planned carefully, these items should reveal whether there is a market, how much money it will take to reach that market, and whether enough resources are available to pull it all together.

Most banks also require a written plan before they will consider lending money for a new business venture. Planning assistance is available from community college business development centers, chambers of commerce, and the Small Business Administration. The services of an accountant and an attorney are invaluable in the planning process.

Chapter Review

A Case in POINT

To Loan or Not to Loan

Evan Yang lives in a small town 250 miles west of Denver. Recently he started thinking about opening his own small business. After a lot of thought and discussion with his friends, he decided to open a bicycle sales and repair business.

Knowing that he needed a loan to get his business started, Evan went to his bank. He had been doing business at Thunder Mountain National Bank since he was a teenager. Before going, he called ahead and made an appointment with Marty Swink, the commercial loan officer.

After Evan explained his idea, Marty's first question was, "How much money do you need?" Evan answered that he thought $10,000 or $15,000 should be enough.

"There's a lot of difference between $10,000 and $15,000, Evan," said Marty. "Let me see your business plan and I'll help you figure the exact amount you need."

Evan hesitated for a moment, then asked, "What's a business plan?"

Think Critically

1. Do you think Ms. Swink will loan Evan the money he needs? Would you? Why or why not?
2. Which part of the business plan will Ms. Swink probably want to see first? Why?
3. What is the first thing Evan needs to do after leaving the bank if he doesn't want his business dream to die?

Vocabulary Builder

Write a brief definition of each word or phrase.

1. business plan
2. collateral
3. executive summary
4. financial plan
5. marketing plan
6. organization chart
7. personal financial statement
8. pricing policy

Review the Concepts

9. Why is careful planning crucial to developing a small business?
10. What are the eight components of a business plan?
11. How can a business plan help an aspiring entrepreneur decide whether or not to go into business?
12. What are three sources of assistance available to entrepreneurs?
13. What services can an accountant and an attorney provide during the business planning phase?

14. What are electronic indexes?
15. Describe two examples of electronic indexes.

Critical Thinking

16. What are the two key components of a business plan and why are they so important?
17. Why must entrepreneurs consider the competition when developing a business plan?
18. What is the importance of staffing to business success?
19. What is the importance of the form of ownership to the business operations of a small business?
20. Why is the Internet a good place to start searching for planning assistance?

Project

Build Your Business Plan

In the last chapter you decided what type of business you were interested in investigating. As you will see, the decision you made then will guide the rest of the business planning process.

As the first step in the planning process, start a business plan notebook. Briefly respond to each of the following points.

1. Write a one- or two-paragraph description of the product or service that your business will sell.
2. How did you get the idea for this business?
3. What experience do you have in the intended business?
4. Develop two goals you hope to attain during the first year in business. Develop two goals you hope to attain within five years. Do not skip this section; it is very important to the planning process.

Now, using your responses, write the first component of your business plan—the concept history and background. Remember that this should include a description of your product or service, an idea history, and a summary of your experience and qualifications. It is very important that you do as thorough job as possible planning the first section.

The information developed here will form the foundation for other decisions that have to be made later in the business planning process. As you proceed through the chapters of this text, you will be adding other components of the business plan to your notebook.

Chapter 3

Purchase an Existing Business or Franchise

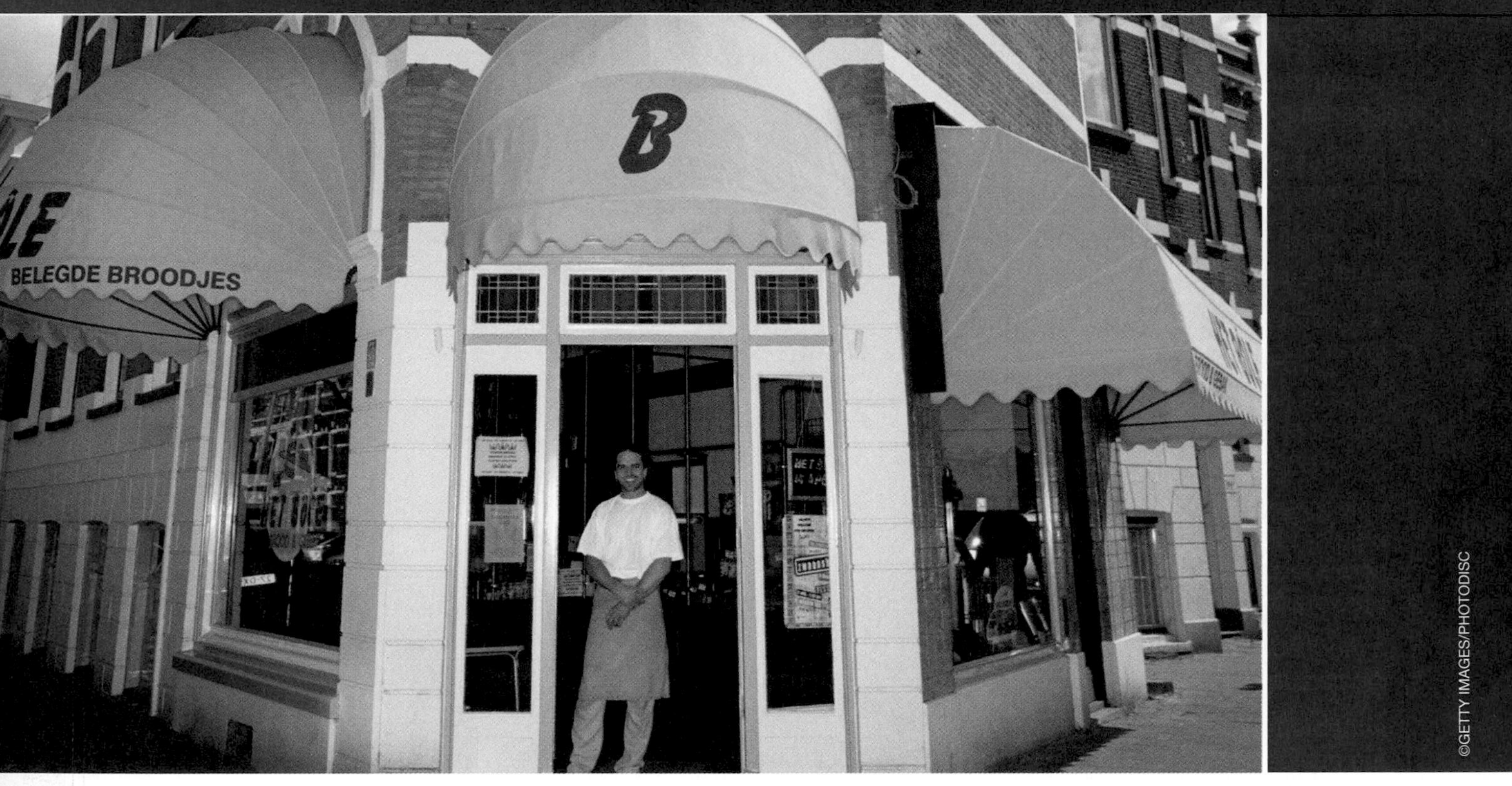

©GETTY IMAGES/PHOTODISC

Objectives

3-1 Describe the advantages and disadvantages of buying an existing business.

3-2 Explain how to evaluate a business for sale opportunity.

3-3 Understand and explain various legal aspects and requirements of franchising.

PURCHASE AN EXISTING BUSINESS

For many aspiring business owners, the best way to enter the world of entrepreneurship is through the purchase of an existing business. Before you decide to open a new business, it would be wise to investigate the business-for-sale market. Why? Talking to a current business owner is an excellent way to learn about market conditions in your community. As a potential buyer, you will be able to examine firsthand the sales revenues of an industry member and a possible future competitor. In addition, you will have a chance to determine the potential **market value** of the type of business you are interested in once it is established and any start-up problems have been worked out. Market value is the price at which buyers and sellers trade similar items in the open marketplace. Furthermore, it might lead to an opportunity to enter the market at a lower cost than you originally anticipated. For these reasons it makes sense to inquire about businesses for sale, even if buying an established business was not your original intention.

How to Find Businesses for Sale

Business owners wishing to sell their businesses commonly advertise their intentions in the classified section of newspapers, list their businesses with business brokers, or get the word out through industry and community networks.

Classified Advertising Potential buyers should first check the "Business Opportunities" pages in the classified section of local newspapers. There they are likely to find numerous advertisements for a variety of businesses for sale. The information provided in these ads is often very general. However, a telephone call or mail inquiry should provide enough basic information to determine whether the business is worth investigating. If the idea shows promise, you should arrange a time to meet with the seller to discuss the opportunity. Since buying a business requires intensive research, the first meeting is normally a general discussion of why the business is for sale and how well the seller thinks the business will do in the future. If you are still interested after this initial discussion, you and the seller should schedule further meetings so that you can observe business operations during working hours.

Restaurant for Sale

Established 3 years. Good location. Seats 50. Profitable, family oriented. Must sell. $65,000. Call 404-555-1060.

Business Brokers Business sellers often work with agents called **business brokers**, who function in the same way real estate brokers do for people selling homes. Brokers represent sellers and bring them together with potential buyers. As part of handling a business sale, brokers advise sellers to have specific information available to answer potential buyers' questions. Brokers also handle advertising. Many sellers go through brokers to keep their intention to sell confidential. Brokers advertise without giving the name of the business and provide their own business phone number and address for interested parties to contact. Only when they have screened the prospects and identified qualified buyers do they tell the prospects how to contact the seller. Business brokers may also assist in drawing up sales contracts and arranging financing. Brokers are paid for their services with a percentage of the selling price, normally 10 to 15 percent.

Industry Sources Another way business owners publicize their intent to sell is by alerting other industry members. They do this either by advertising in industry publications or by encouraging referrals from salespeople. Since potential new business owners frequently ask industry suppliers about business opportunities, both are effective ways to learn about businesses for sale. Many companies have referral systems that put people making inquiries in touch with people wishing to sell. Industry sources normally get involved with the selling process only in a referring role.

Entrepreneurs may also find businesses for sale through other sources, such as

- landlords/leasing agents
- attorneys
- bankers
- SBA
- Small Business Development Centers
- management consultants
- shopping center management offices
- venture capitalists
- chambers of commerce
- acquaintances
- bankruptcy announcements

Often the best business opportunities come from businesses that are *not* for sale. If an existing business meets all the criteria a potential buyer is looking for, the buyer can make the owner an offer. The owner may, of course, refuse. However, if the offer is attractive enough, he or she might consider the opportunity to sell.

©GETTY IMAGES/PHOTODISC

Advantages of Purchasing an Existing Business

There are many advantages to buying an existing business, particularly for entrepreneurs with little experience. It is an ideal way to "learn the ropes" because, in many cases, the previous owner will stay on for a period of time to train the new owner or be available for consultation.

It is also a less risky way to become self-employed. The existing business has a track record—procedures are in place, suppliers are lined up, and a customer base has been established. New owners will have an idea of what to expect for revenues, expenses, and profits. These figures are easier to forecast for an established business than for a start-up. If new business owners have some of the security anchor characteristics described in Chapter 1, buying a business will alleviate some of the anxiety of owning and operating a business.

Purchasing an established business may also be financially advantageous. Sellers often assist with financing arrangements. It is not uncommon for sellers to accept an initial partial payment with the agreement that the balance will be paid off in monthly installments in the form of a promissory note. This arrangement may reduce or eliminate the need for bank financing and is often negotiated at a lower interest rate. If the seller does not wish to help with financing, buyers are still (in most cases) more likely to receive financing from a bank or other financial institution for an established business than for a start-up. Why? It is less risky for the lender.

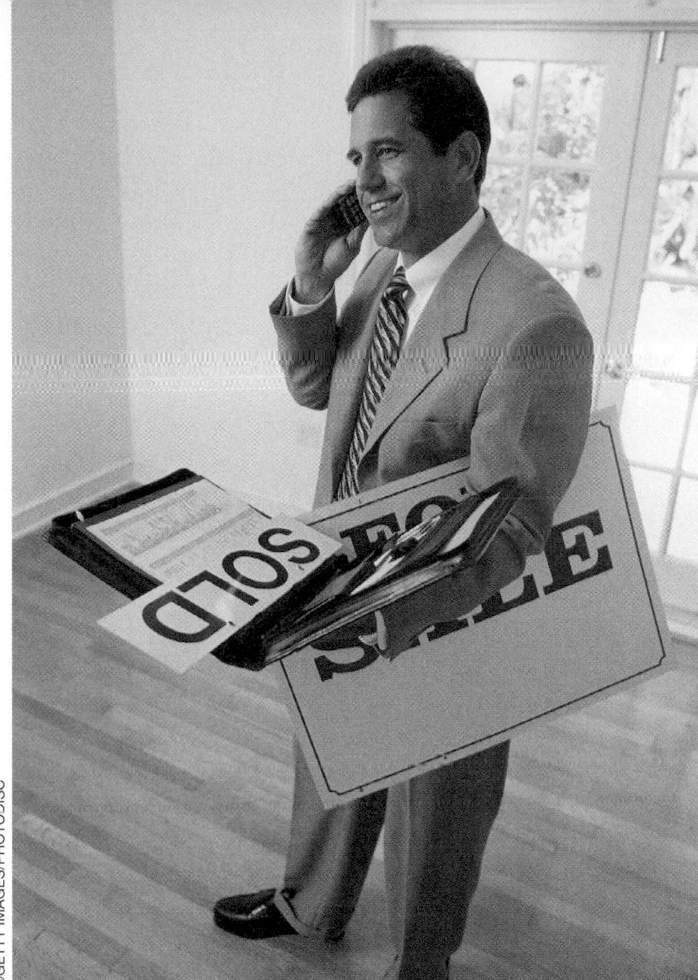

©GETTY IMAGES/PHOTODISC

Entrepreneurs sometimes purchase businesses because it is the only way to successfully enter the market. If a particular business dominates the market because of its superior location and reputation, buying that business might be the best way to ensure success.

Other advantages of buying an existing business include the following:

- No business start-up is required.
- Suppliers have already been tried and tested.
- The company has survived the start-up phase (the first year or two) and has a better chance of succeeding.
- Experienced employees will already be functioning and will probably require little, if any, training.

Disadvantages of Purchasing an Existing Business

Many businesses are for sale because of internal problems. It is not a good idea for aspiring business owners to assume someone else's problems. If a business has a poor reputation with customers, has trouble with suppliers, or is inconveniently located, it is unlikely that new ownership will automatically change customers' negative opinions. Too many business buyers have learned the hard way that it takes a long time to restore customer confidence.

Another disadvantage is that buying a profitable business will initially cost more. The seller has built a business, poured time and energy into it, and will usually expect to be rewarded with a selling price that reflects those efforts. Capital limitations on the part of the buyer, however, might prevent the purchase. It might be economically more feasible to take the risk of creating a new business with a smaller capital investment.

Some entrepreneurs might consider investing in, or purchasing part of, a business. The risk is that the parties, who have essentially been forced together for economic reasons, might not be compatible. A bad partnership arrangement hinders the growth of the camaraderie that is so essential for small business success.

Another drawback to purchasing an existing business is that current employees may have to be replaced because of poor training by the former owner or unacceptable work habits. It may also be necessary to invest money in modernizing the operation.

Reasons Businesses Are Sold

When considering the purchase of a business, the potential buyer should find out why the business is for sale. This will help the buyer determine a fair price. If owners are under pressure to sell, they may be more flexible about the selling price. Some of the many reasons businesses are sold are

- insufficient profits
- owner's retirement
- death or illness of a working partner
- business heirs not interested in inheriting the business
- partner or shareholder dispute
- management "burnout"
- growth too slow or too rapid
- forced liquidation or sale
- fear of new competition
- fear of current or predicted economic conditions
- lack of desire or capital to do necessary remodeling
- owner's desire for a change of career
- owner's desire to take advantage of another opportunity requiring liquidation of business assets

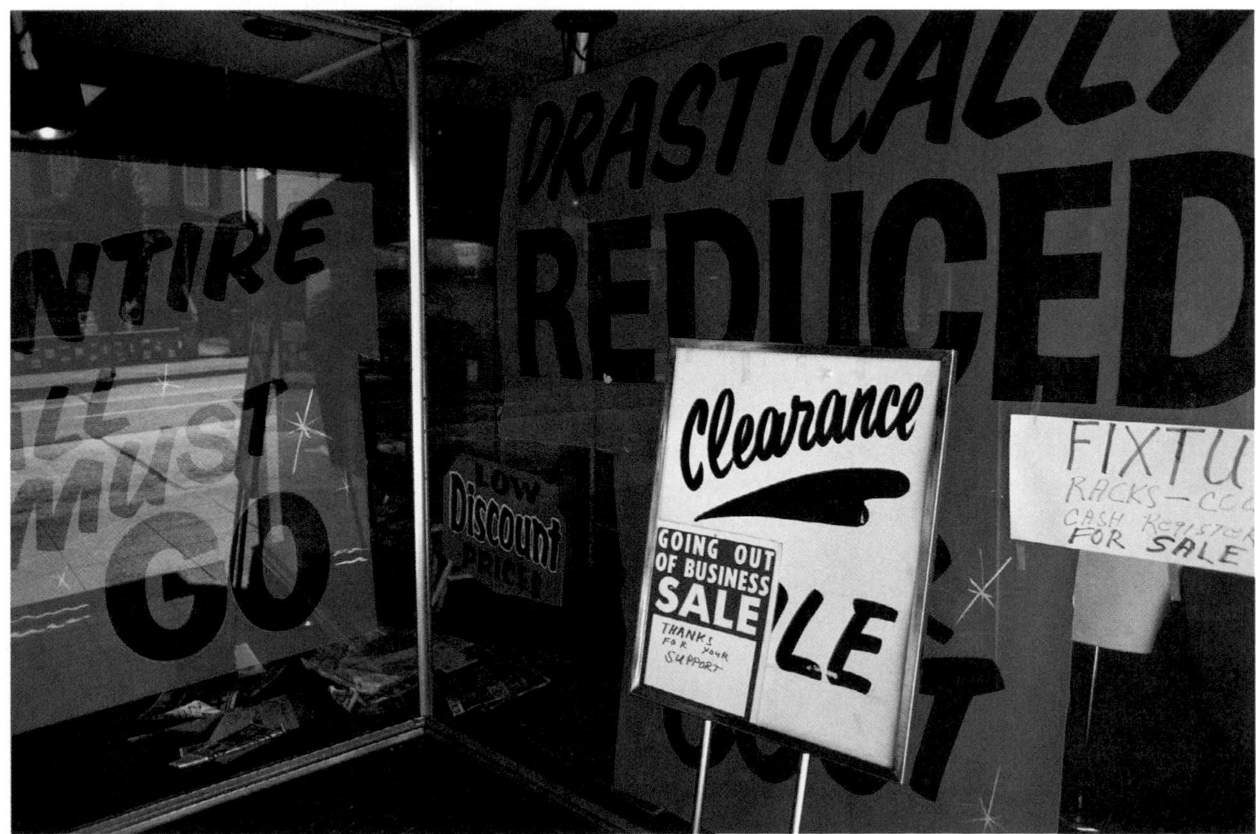

HOW TO PURCHASE A BUSINESS

Buying a business is an intricate process that requires the same thoroughness as starting a business from scratch. As a potential business buyer, you should follow these steps:

1. Write clear, specific, personal, and financial objectives about the kind of business you want to buy. Whatever the type of business for sale, it must match these statements before you consider it for purchase.
2. Identify business opportunities that offer growth and provide an attractive return on investment. Read classified ads, discuss opportunities with business brokers, and check industry sources as you compile a list of potential opportunities.
3. Meet with business sellers or brokers for an introduction to specific business opportunities. The initial information provided by the seller should include a brief financial report, the history of the business, the selling price, and the reason for the sale.
4. Request a second meeting to probe for more information if the seller's material fits the objectives you stated in step 1.
5. Inspect the facility closely to determine how well it has been maintained.
6. Prepare a checklist of information you need, including the following:
    - complete financial accounting of operations—income statements, federal income tax returns, state sales tax forms, and balance sheets—for at least the previous three years, or from the beginning of operation if the business is less than three years old
    - list of all assets to be transferred to the new owner, including an itemized list of all inventory as of the last accounting period
    - statement about any past or pending legal action against the business
    - copy of the business lease or mortgage
    - list of all suppliers
7. After you have examined the information, you should meet with several key individuals to receive their professional recommendations or approval before going any further.

    First, consult an accountant and a lawyer. They should be able to provide you with any further interpretation of the financial and legal information you received. Your accountant will review all the financial information and may uncover flaws or inaccuracies that provide a more accurate financial picture than the seller presented. Among other things, your lawyer will need to check if the lease or title may be transferred to you. You will need to conduct an on-site meeting with the landlord or mortgage holder to ensure the facility is in satisfactory condition. In the case of a lease, you should discuss the expiration date and, if possible, negotiate the terms and price to fit your needs.

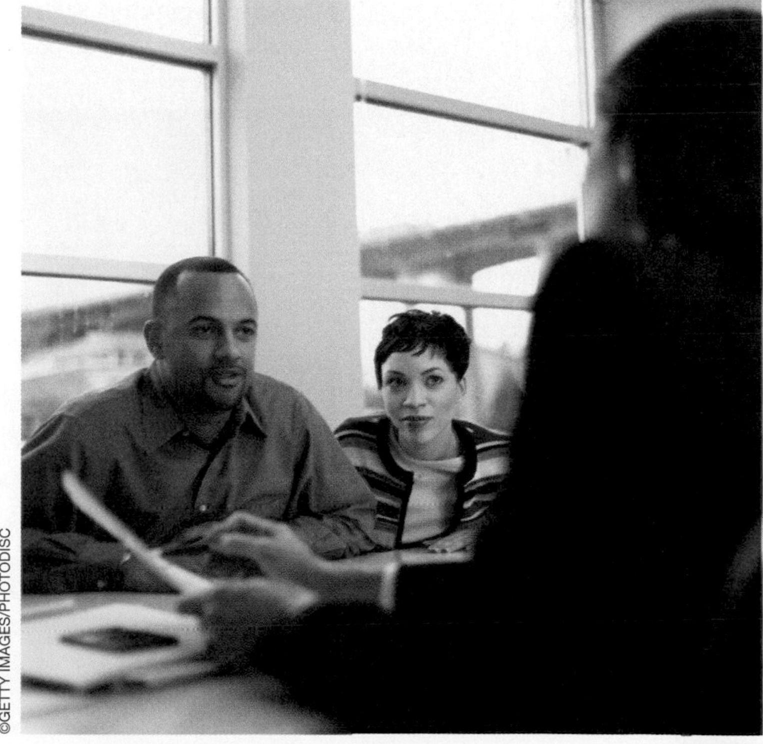
©GETTY IMAGES/PHOTODISC

Potential buyers are wise to consult the chamber of commerce and other local assistance centers to discuss the future of the market and the location. It is also a good idea to contact industry representatives presently selling to the business to validate the sales reported and to get their assessment of the business's future growth.

8. Arrange a convenient time with the seller to observe operations. Evaluate employee and customer satisfaction and/or dissatisfaction, as well as the pros and cons of the operation in general. All these considerations enter into the final sales price.
9. Determine a fair price to offer the business owner. In some cases, the owner will have already stated a price; you now must make a counteroffer based on your research. Determine what financing arrangements are available through a lending institution or with the seller. Present a letter of intent to the seller that says, in essence, "I will purchase the business at the stated price and under the stated terms provided an audit shows that the inventory, work in process, accounts payable, and accounts receivable are as presented."

   At this point there is normally some negotiation. You will have to use your best persuasion techniques to point out the fairness of your offer and the advantages to the seller of accepting it. Either party may bring his or her attorney, or another agent, to assist in negotiations.
10. If an agreement is reached, an attorney should draw up a suitable sales contract. The terms of the contract address such questions as whether the seller is permitted to open a competing business within the buyer's market area. Which party will be responsible for paying any unreported claims, liens, or unpaid taxes on the business following its sale? What should be done about customers' long-standing debts? What about union contracts for unionized employees? Are employee benefits and pensions in order? How will costs for insurance coverage, taxes, and utilities be divided? As you can see, a lawyer can be very helpful at a business closing and can protect you from costly, unforeseen complications. The contract should be contingent upon examination of all assets to validate that what is represented is true.
11. Before signing a sales contract, the buyer should be present when the seller takes final inventory of assets.

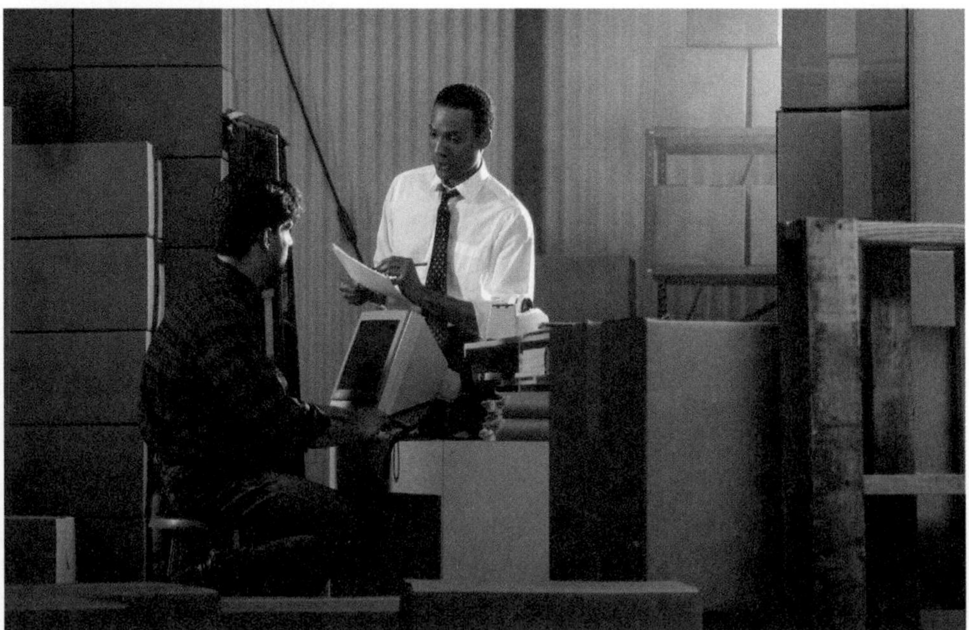

COMSTOCK IMAGES

Evaluating Business-for-Sale Opportunities

Normally an investigation of businesses for sale produces opportunities that range from bad to promising to good. Categorizing a business opportunity helps prospective buyers determine the value of the business and, therefore, the price they are willing to offer.

Types of Opportunities The first sign of a bad business opportunity is poor bookkeeping. If a business owner has been negligent in maintaining proper financial records, it is more than likely that the business has suffered because of it. Failure to present adequate verification of sales revenues and expenditures is often a sign that the seller is attempting to hide information. It would not be wise to pursue this opportunity.

Many business opportunities are not easy to classify or measure. For example, a business's record keeping may be adequate but not entirely complete; a solid but unspectacular customer base may have been established; relationships with suppliers may be satisfactory but not as efficient as they could be. Often these are the best business opportunities because their

FUN FACTS

On July 2, 1962, Sam Walton, entrepreneur, opened the first Wal-Mart in Rogers, Arkansas. Today, Wal-Mart is the biggest company in the world.

Ethics for ENTREPRENEURS

Millie Tan has worked in the hotel business for the last 14 years. Immediately upon graduation from high school, she went to work as a maid at a 200-room hotel in her hometown. She financed her college education by continuing to work in the hotel for the next four years.

As she progressed toward a business degree in marketing, she worked her way up in responsibility. During her sophomore year in college, she was hired by a large multinational hotel chain to work the front desk. With success at that position came a promotion to night auditor, then to director of marketing. After college she continued to work for the hotel chain.

Recently, Millie has been looking for a small, owner-managed motel where she can apply her years of hotel experience on a smaller scale and in a fashion she thinks best. She is tired of the corporate style of management. In short, Millie wants to become an entrepreneur.

Yesterday she met with the owner of a small beachfront motel on the Gulf Coast of Mississippi. The property met all her requirements for her new business venture. It was in a resort location, it had fewer than 100 rooms, and it was generating a profit of at least $50,000 annually. There was one problem, though.

The owner told Millie that the way he kept the profit margin up was by using a contract employment agency for his cleaning staff. He paid the agency $7 per maid per hour for the service. He knew the agency used undocumented illegal immigrants, but that was not his concern. By using the agency, he saved on wages and benefits. The owner admitted that even though he was not technically breaking the law, some might consider the practice unethical.

Think Critically

Do you consider the employment practice either illegal or unethical? What would you advise Millie to do?

greatest need is better management. Proper management might generate greater sales, better customer reception, and goodwill. **Goodwill** is an intangible but salable asset, such as the reputation or location of a business, that makes the business worth more to a buyer. Since previous management has not been able to reach all its objectives, the selling price of the business should not include goodwill. Therefore, it might be a bargain for the right buyer.

An example of a promising business opportunity is a store that has leveled off in sales at a certain point and cannot seem to increase them even though the market is good. Management is evidently not doing some things right or else does not have the capital to aggressively pursue the market. If a new owner can make some changes, such as remodeling, adding new inventory, or increasing advertising expenditures, he or she could quite possibly increase profits and receive a healthy return on investment. Potential buyers should look for this type of opportunity.

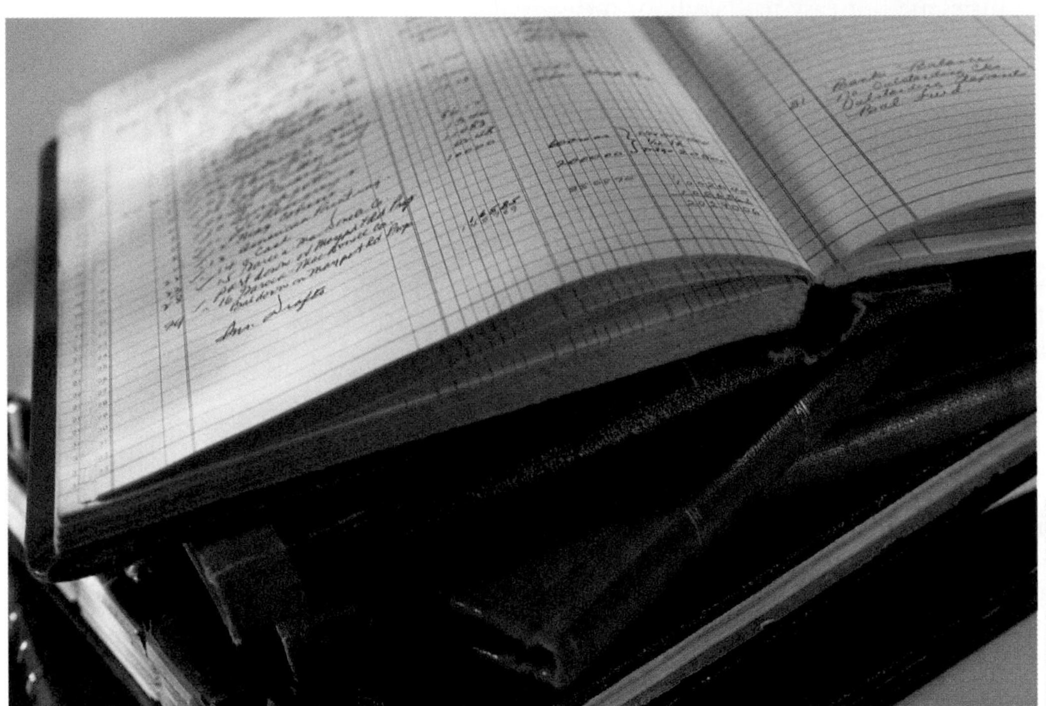
©GETTY IMAGES/PHOTODISC

Good businesses keep good records and maintain a good customer image. Buying a business that has been properly managed is an asset to the new owner. Customers will not have to be convinced that they will be given better service, quality, or prices under the new management. However, if a business has been profitable and managed well, it will cost more to purchase. It is customary for the seller of a successful business to specify a dollar value for goodwill.

Evaluation Considerations Unfortunately, there is no easy, standard formula for computing the value of a business. Many deals are based on how motivated both the seller and the buyer are to close the deal. Sometimes the terms are more important than the price. However, the following evaluation methods will help you generate a price at which you can begin negotiating.

Prospective buyers must evaluate opportunities for buying a business in terms of profit earnings and return on investment. The most important factor to look for is the business's potential to make money. Unfortunately, this is not always easy to determine because the buyer is dealing with what he or she thinks *might* happen. To help, most buyers use a method called the **earnings approach**, in which they determine whether the business will be able to pay them for their time. Potential buyers should identify their proposed changes and develop pro forma (projected) financial statements to examine the impact of those changes on the business. If this forecast looks positive, they then need to examine their return on investment.

Entrepreneurs should expect earnings to provide a return on investment over a period of time. Usually that period is five years, or 20 percent per year. Too often, businesses are bought with the assumption that as soon as the new management takes over, business will improve dramatically. It takes time to change operations procedures, employee performance, and customer buying habits. Opportunities must be evaluated by considering the long-term potential.

Buyers must also research the market value of the business for sale. This requires learning the selling prices of similar businesses and comparing them to the price of the business being considered. It is a good way to get a general idea of the market, but since no two businesses are exactly alike, it is not always accurate. Buyers would be wise to hire an appraiser to appraise the building and other assets.

Buyers must determine the **replacement value** of the assets they are considering for purchase. Since the value of assets such as equipment, furniture, fixtures, and inventory listed on a balance sheet is based on their previous purchase price, the buyer should determine their current replacement value. The replacement value is usually higher than the asset value.

A final measure should be the **liquidation value** of a business's assets. Using a worst-case scenario, the prospective buyer should determine the immediate cash value of all assets (including the present value of future income) in the event a problem arises that requires the immediate sale of the business.

It is a good idea for prospective buyers to review the current income statement of a business for sale and indicate any foreseeable adjustments to that statement due to the new owner. Table 3-1 is an example of such a list of adjustments.

TABLE 3-1 INCOME STATEMENT ADJUSTMENTS FOR YEAR ENDING DECEMBER 31, 2003

ACTUAL		NEW OWNER COMMENTS
Sales and revenues	$180,000	Should increase 10%
Less cost of goods	93,000	Add $25,000 for new inventory
Gross profit	$87,000	Minus approximately $7,000
Operating expenses		
Payroll	26,000	–$5,000 cut one employee
Rent	19,500	No change
Utilities	2,200	No change
Maintenance	1,600	+$500 for new lights
Insurance	2,400	+$200 to cover additional inventory
Accounting	2,000	–$1,000 keep own books
Advertising	2,800	+$550 announce new owners
Supplies	4,100	+$600 new bags, boxes
Miscellaneous	4,000	+$1000 other changes
Total operating expenses	$64,600	Minus approximately $3,150
Net operating profit	$22,400	Approximately $18,500

Inadequate review and investigation before buying a business can lead to problems such as those experienced by Bailey Robinson, who bought a retail clothing business believing she could increase profits as soon as she took over. The business financial statement looked like this:

Sales	$ 250,000
Cost of goods	–130,000
Gross profit	120,000
Operating expenses	–95,000
Net profit	$25,000

To buy the business, Bailey borrowed from the bank with a promise to pay back $20,000 per year. She knew that this would leave only $5,000 per year for her salary, but she was sure that she could immediately increase sales by $50,000. This would allow her a salary of $25,000. One year later she was forced to sell the business. Although she had increased sales by $10,000, it was not enough and she ran out of time.

PURCHASE A FRANCHISE

FUN FACTS

Most franchise companies have fewer than 100 units.

A person who has a burning desire to become an entrepreneur and own a small business may have no real idea what particular business to choose or how to run a business. This aspiring entrepreneur may want to consider a **franchise**, which is the contractual right to market a product or service. There are an estimated 1,500 franchised companies in the United States from which entrepreneurs can choose. Well-known franchises include Subway, McDonald's, Kentucky Fried Chicken, Curves, Midas, Wendy's, Century 21, Dunkin' Donuts, Dairy Queen, and Ramada Inn.

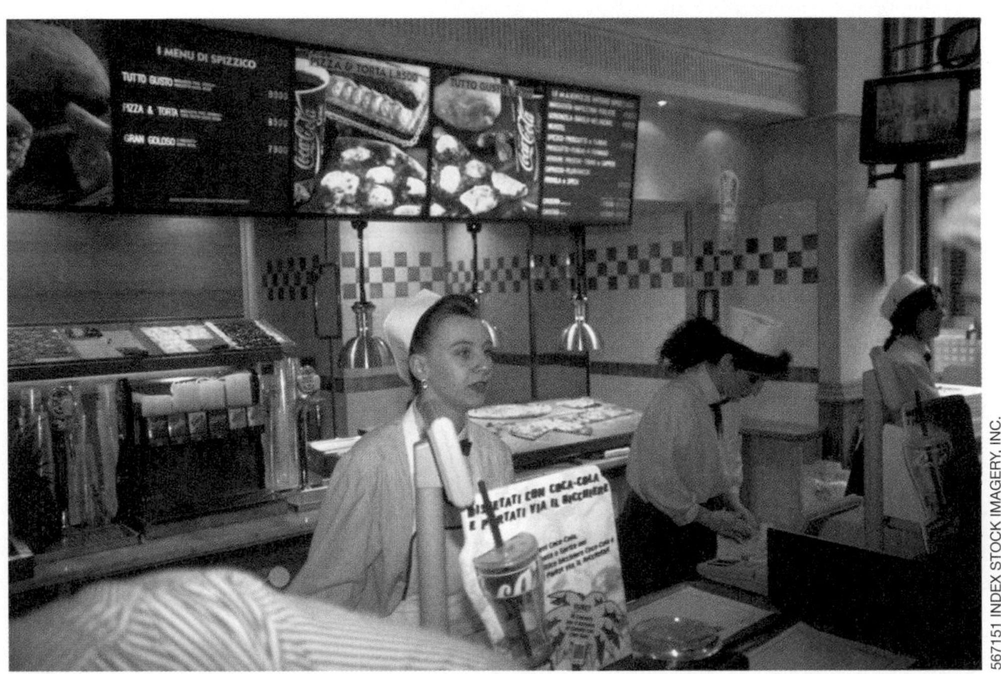

567151 INDEX STOCK IMAGERY, INC.

There are numerous benefits—as well as some drawbacks—to franchising. One of the benefits of franchising is business experience. When someone purchases a franchise, the past experiences of other entrepreneurs who have chosen that franchise are included in the purchase. In other words, practical business advice, based on the experiences of all other owners of the same franchise, comes with the franchise. This advice is a valuable asset.

Purchasing a franchise is a desirable option for some entrepreneurs. For others it is not. Read the following information carefully and decide if a franchise may be the right decision for you.

Definition

The U.S. Department of Commerce defines **franchising** as a method of doing business in which a franchisee is granted the right to engage in offering, selling, or distributing goods or services under a marketing format that is designed by the franchisor. The International Franchise Association defines franchising as a method of distributing products or services. At least two levels of people are involved in the franchise system: the franchisor and the franchisee.

1. The **franchisor** lends his trademark or trade name and a business system.
2. The **franchisee** pays a **royalty** (percentage of sales or outright fee) and often an initial fee for the right to do business under the franchisor's name and system.

Technically, the contract binding the two parties is the "franchise," but that term is often used to mean the actual business that the franchisee operates.

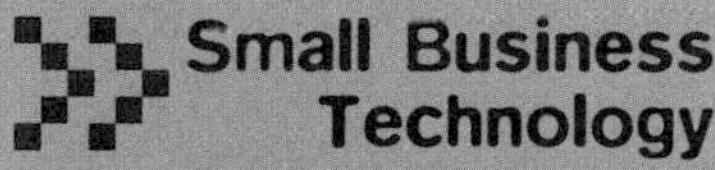

Many franchises now use an extranet to speed up communication with their network of franchisees. An extranet is a shared network that uses Internet technology to link businesses with suppliers, customers, or other businesses. It is designed to share information or operations with authorized business users. An extranet can be viewed as part of a company's intranet that is extended to users outside the company.

Classifications

Franchising opportunities are available in many types of business in all areas of the U.S. A publication available from the Department of Commerce, the *Franchise Opportunities Handbook*, lists these franchise opportunities by category. Entrepreneurs have more than three dozen categories from which to choose. The publication includes information about costs, capital required, number of franchises already operating, and so on. A current copy can be obtained from the U.S. Government Printing Office in Washington, D.C.

Some of the categories in the *Franchise Opportunities Handbook* are

- automotive products/services
- business aids/services
- campgrounds
- clothing/shoes
- cosmetics/toiletries
- dental centers
- educational products/services
- employment services
- foods
- motels/hotels
- printing
- real estate
- security systems
- vending

Other sources for information about franchise opportunities include the Small Business Administration, the Federal Trade Commission, *Franchising World Magazine*, the International Franchise Association, and *Entrepreneur* magazine.

Advantages of Purchasing a Franchise

There are many advantages to purchasing a franchise. The entrepreneur should evaluate these (as well as the disadvantages) carefully before deciding to purchase.

A franchise provides an established product or service. One of the most challenging problems any entrepreneur faces when starting a new business is that of product/service acceptance by the consumer. The process of becoming established can take years. With a franchise, the process has already been under way for some time and is usually reinforced by large-scale advertising.

Many, but not all, franchisors offer management and/or technical assistance. Management assistance usually includes providing the knowledge needed to start the new business and handle daily operations as well as crises. This assistance is available through on-site training or classes at the franchisor's base. Technical assistance can include anything from site selection and building design to equipment purchase and food recipes.

For consumers, one of the main attractions of franchised businesses is consistency. A franchise contract mandates a certain level of quality, which is determined by past business experience. Most franchisees realize that they must match or exceed the quality available in related franchises if they are to be successful. The consumer knows that a franchised business in New Jersey will offer the same basic range of products or services as the same franchised business in California. It is unlikely there will be any major surprises.

The operating capital required for a new business can be considerable. Association with a franchise may reduce some of those expenses. General supply purchases are a good example. Franchisors may be able to negotiate low prices because of the large volume they purchase. Independent entrepreneurs usually do not have that advantage. The same holds true for equipment, insurance, and other expenses.

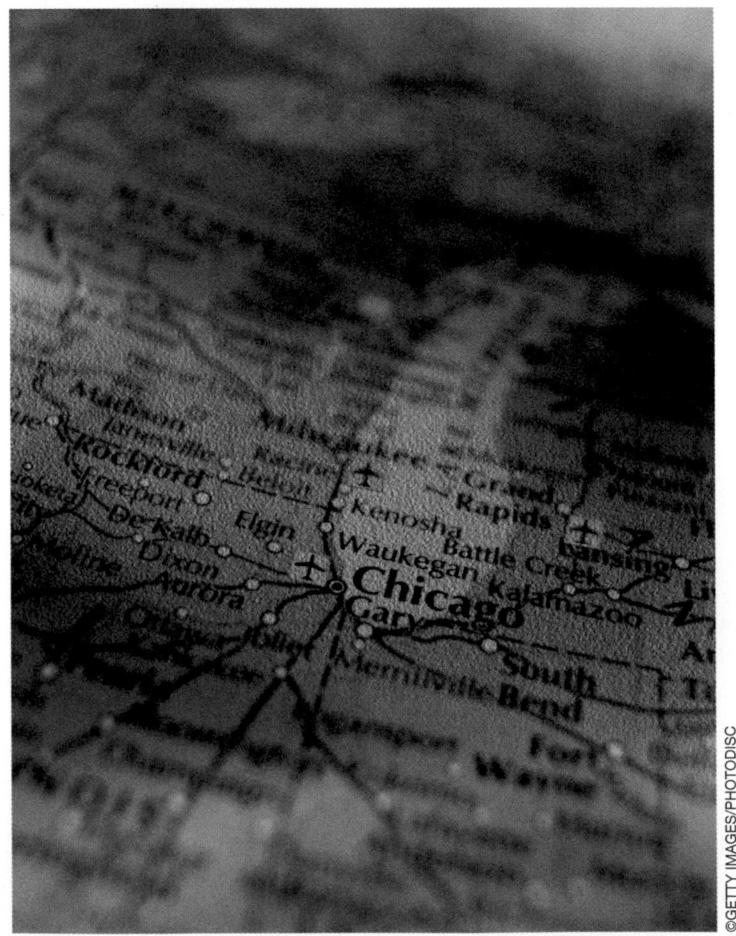

A franchise contract may provide for the franchisee's professional growth. If the contract guarantees a certain geographic territory to the franchisee, future competition within that territory cannot come from within the same franchise. Any growth in the territory is limited to the purchase or sale of additional locations by the original franchisee. For example, if you purchased a franchise for a certain submarine sandwich business and, as part of the contract, were given an exclusive geographic territory, you may be able to purchase franchises for additional locations within that territory or sell franchises to others.

Disadvantages of Purchasing a Franchise

Entrepreneurs who purchase franchises may have certain expectations as to services they are to receive from the franchisor. If these services are not clearly spelled out in the contract, they may not be provided. The franchisor's only legal responsibilities are those included in the contract.

A franchisee is required to pay the franchisor on an ongoing basis. If the value of the services the franchisee receives does not at least offset the payment, the payment becomes a financial drain on the new business.

Franchisees may depend heavily on the advice of the franchisor at first but should aim for greater self-reliance over time. Overdependence often clouds common sense and interferes with sound business practices. The level of dependence should decrease as time passes.

The Global ENTREPRENEUR

According to the International Franchise Association (IFA), "Franchised businesses continue to grow in all corners of the world." It has been estimated that one in seven American franchisors attempts to market franchises abroad.

When it comes to international franchising, business is rarely business as usual. One of the biggest concerns for franchisors such as fast food companies is the need to consider language and cultural differences.

McDonald's International Division was created in 1969. Since then it has expanded to include 119 countries all over the world. With the expansion often comes a need to adapt the food to local tastes.

In India, for instance, McDonald's had to accommodate religious beliefs. The hamburgers at McDonald's in New Delhi are made of chicken and called Maharaja Macs. Also offered is the McVeggie, which is made from a breaded fried vegetable patty (peas, carrots, green beans, red capsicum, potatoes, onions, rice, and seasoning), lettuce, and eggless mayo, served on a toasted sesame seed bun. An additional menu item is the McAloo Tikki Burger, consisting of a fried breaded potato-and-peas patty (flavored with special spice mix), fresh tomato slices, onion, and tomato mayonnaise, served on a toasted bun.

In Israel, all meat served in McDonald's restaurants is 100 percent kosher beef. McDonald's operates kosher and non-kosher restaurants.

Other international issues for McDonald's include translating "quarter pounder," an English measurement term. When selling food in countries that use the metric system, an alternate approach is necessary. Franchises in many European and Asian McDonald's have replaced the name with "McRoyal" or "Hamburger Royal."

The global franchisor faces many challenges unheard of in this country. Planning the small business becomes even more critical.

Think Critically

Can you think of other U.S. products that have to be modified to sell in another country? Name two and discuss the necessary modifications.

The franchise package usually carries restrictions involving products or services to be offered, types of customers to be served, geographic territory, and pricing. Many entrepreneurs object to this type of control because it inhibits the freedom they seek as business owners.

Franchise contracts usually control to some degree the terms of a sale or closure. This means that a franchisee may have little or no say about the terms of a termination of the franchise agreement. For franchises that are part of a chain, the performance of existing locations may influence the success of new businesses. If service and quality slip at one location, customers may associate that decline with the other locations as well.

Legal Aspects of Franchising

An entrepreneur should not sign a franchise contract without the advice of a competent attorney. Only an attorney can properly analyze the legal documents that are required for a franchise arrangement. These documents are covered in the **Federal Trade Commission Franchise Rule**.

FTC Rule The FTC states the following purpose for the Rule: "The Rule is designed to enable potential franchisees to protect themselves before investing by providing them with information essential to an assessment of the potential risks and benefits, to meaningful comparisons with other investments, and to further investigation of the franchise opportunity."

Rule Requirements The Rule imposes six requirements in connection with the "advertising, offering, licensing, contracting, sale, or other promotion" of a franchise in or affecting commerce.

1. ***Basic Disclosures*** The Rule requires franchisors to give potential investors a basic disclosure document at the earlier of the first face-to-face meetings or ten business days before any money is paid or an agreement is signed in connection with the investment (Part 436.1(a)).

2. ***Earnings Claims*** If a franchisor makes earnings claims, whether historical or forecasted, they must have a reasonable basis, and prescribed substantiating disclosures must be given to a potential investor in writing at the same time as the basic disclosures (Parts 436.1(b)-(d)).

3. ***Advertised Claims*** The Rule affects only ads that include an earnings claim. Such ads must disclose the number and percentage of existing franchisees who have achieved the claimed results, along with cautionary language. Their use triggers required compliance with the Rule's earnings claim disclosure requirements (Part 436.1(e)).

4. ***Franchise Agreements*** The franchisor must give investors a copy of its standard-form franchise and related agreements at the same time as the basic disclosures, and final copies intended to be executed at least five business days before signing (Part 436.1(g)).

5. ***Refunds*** The Rule requires franchisors to make refunds of deposits and initial payments to potential investors, subject to any conditions on refundability stated in the disclosure document (Part 436.1(h)).

6. ***Contradictory Claims*** While franchisors are free to provide investors with any promotional or other materials they wish, no written or oral claims may contradict information provided in the required disclosure document (Part 436.1(f)).

Amended Franchise Rule (12/30/93) The Rule was amended in 1993 with the intention to: "improve the clarity of disclosures by requiring the use of 'plain English' and of tables that highlight important information; add new and enhanced disclosures; and enhance uniformity among the states by minimizing state-specific requirements."

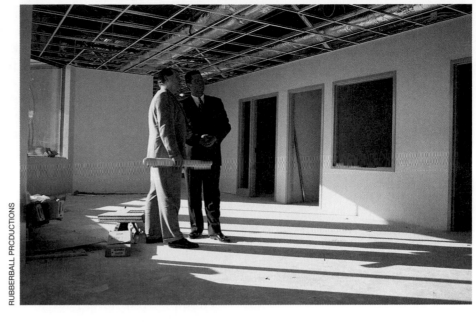

RUBBERBALL PRODUCTIONS

Registration Requirements There is no requirement by the Federal Trade Commission that franchisors register with it or any government agency. The following states, however, do require registration: California, Hawaii, Illinois, Indiana, Maryland, Michigan, Minnesota, New York, North Dakota, Oregon, Rhode Island, South Dakota, Virginia, Washington, and Wisconsin.

Buying A Subway® Franchise

Subway Restaurants, which were started in 1965 by Fred DeLuca and Dr. Peter Buck as a single sandwich shop called "Pete's Subs" in Bridgeport, CT, opened its 20,000th location in November 2003.

Offering franchise opportunities since 1974, Subway receives more than 1,000 requests for information each week. The total investment required for a Subway franchisee ranges from $86,300 for a lower-cost store to $213,500 for a higher-cost store.

Subway offers these services to new franchisees prior to opening:

- *Training* An intensive two-week program takes place at Subway HQ in Milford, CT. Programs are also conducted in Miami, Australia, Germany, and China.
- *Site Selection* Subway works with franchisees to secure a location for the business.
- *Restaurant Design* Subway provides floor plans for the specific location.
- *Equipment Ordering* Subway helps the franchisee order the necessary equipment package for timely delivery.

After the Subway is open, a high level of services continues:

- *Operations Manual* An in-depth manual covers a full range of topics important to running the business.
- *Field Support* Each franchisee is assigned a field consultant who will help them get started and provide ongoing operational evaluations.
- *Franchisee Services* Each franchisee is assigned a coordinator who serves as the main contact person at headquarters and is just a phone call or e-mail away.
- *Research and Development* Subway continually strives to make its food better.
- *Continuing Education* Franchisees receive periodic newsletters, e-mails, and voicemails. Videos and additional training classes are also available.

Subway information from the official Subway web site.

The 15 states have franchise investment laws that require franchisors to provide pre-sale disclosures, known as "offering circulars," to potential purchasers. Thirteen of these state laws treat the sale of a franchise like the sale of a security. They typically prohibit the offer or sale of a franchise within their state until a franchise offering circular has been filed on the public record with, and registered by, a designated state agency.

These state laws give franchise purchasers important legal rights, including the right to bring private lawsuits for violation of the state disclosure requirements. The FTC encourages potential franchise purchasers who reside in these states to contact their state franchise law administrators for additional information about the protection these laws provide.

Questions to Ask

Entrepreneurs should ask several pertinent questions before they purchase a franchise. The final decision to purchase should not be made until these questions have been answered satisfactorily. These questions involve the franchise, the franchisor, the franchisee (entrepreneur), and the franchisee's market.

The Franchise Prospective franchisees should ask these questions about the franchise in general.

1. Was the franchise agreement approved by a lawyer?
2. Are any of the requirements of the contract illegal in the area where business is to be conducted?
3. Will the franchisee receive an exclusive territory for the duration of the franchise term, or can the franchisor sell additional franchises in the territory?
4. Is there a connection between the franchisor and any other franchise company dealing in similar merchandise or services?
5. If there is a connection between the franchisor and another franchise company, is the franchisee protected against competition from the second franchise company?
6. What is required if the franchisee wishes to cancel the contract?
7. Will the franchisee receive any payment for goodwill (customer loyalty) if the franchise is sold?

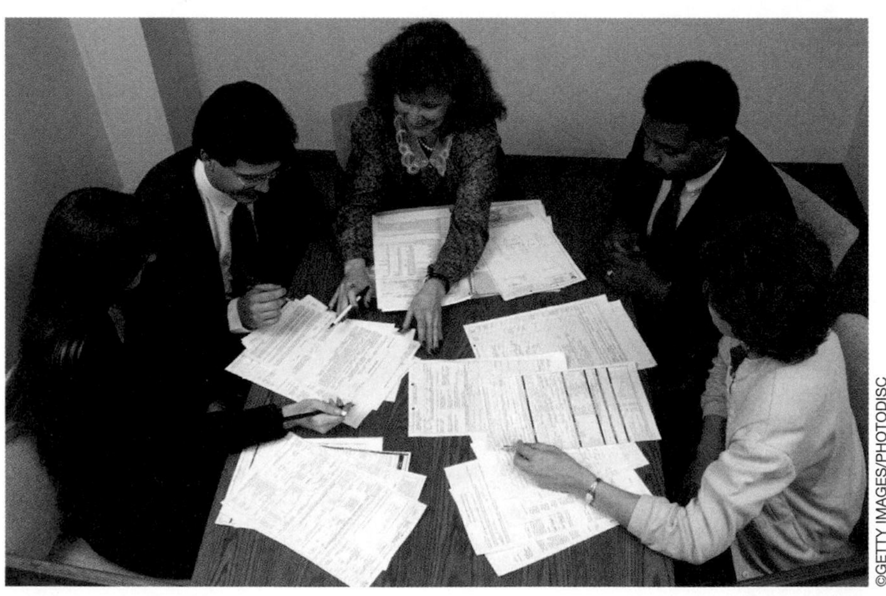

The Franchisor Prospective franchisees should ask these questions about the specific franchisor with which they are dealing.

1. How long has the company existed, and how long has the franchisor been in business?
2. Do other franchisees consider the franchisor honest and fair?

3. Has the franchisor shown the franchisee profit statements for several franchise locations? Have they been verified by the franchisee at each location?
4. Does the franchisor provide the following services?
   - credit
   - capital marketing assistance
   - management training
   - employee training
   - marketing and/or marketing assistance
   - merchandising assistance
   - site selection assistance

DIGITAL VISION

5. Is the franchisor on firm financial ground?
6. Is there an experienced management team from which the franchisee can seek advice?
7. What services or opportunities can the franchisor provide that the franchisee cannot otherwise obtain?
8. In what kind of detail has the franchisor investigated the franchisee and the franchisee's ability to run a profitable business?
9. Has the franchisor followed all state, federal, and local laws that govern the sale of franchises?

The Franchisee Each prospective franchisee must determine the answers to these questions before he or she can make a decision about investing in a franchise.

1. How much money is required to open and run the business until it becomes profitable?
2. Does the value (monetary and/or psychological) of the franchise outweigh the loss of the freedom of being an independent business owner?
3. Does the franchisee have what it takes to open the franchise and turn it into a profitable business?
4. What kind of commitment is the franchisee willing to make to the franchise? Is the franchisee willing to devote years to its success?

The Franchisee's Market And, finally, prospective franchisees should consider these questions about the market and the location of the franchise.

1. Has the franchisee conducted in-depth marketing research to determine that the franchise will be successful in the intended location?
2. What does marketing research indicate about potential future changes in the intended location?
3. What is the projected demand for the franchised product or service in the area surrounding the intended location?
4. What is the competitive environment for the franchised product or service?

Ship in a BOTTLE

New Opportunity

"The only way to see if this idea makes any sense is to take it on the road and talk to retailers," Fred told his wife, Jeanie. "We can learn more from them than from any other source. So let's plan a trip."

They decided to use their vacation time to travel up the East Coast, from Florida to Maine. They would visit gift shops, show samples, and, they hoped, take some orders.

Initially they were disappointed. Store owners liked the idea, but it was not a buying season and they questioned whether the product would sell well once the wholesale cost was doubled. The news improved the further north they traveled. When they got to the New England coast, they were amazed at the number of stores that sold nautical items. Their ships in bottles were enthusiastically received. Fred was pleased, but also cautious—he was still trying to coordinate delivery times from Germany and deciding which models to stock. He was not guaranteeing anything at this point, but he welcomed the retailers' comments and suggestions.

In a picturesque village on the Maine coast, Fred was taken aback when he walked into The Maritime Store. The proprietor, John Wilkins, talked at length about setting up a display of the models in the best section of his 1,500-square-foot store. Fred recalled Johann telling him about a similar display in a restaurant in Hamburg, Germany, that outsold all his other retail outlets. John told Fred that he planned to sell The Maritime Store after the current tourist season. He had opened the store 12 years earlier after a career as a teacher and was looking forward to retirement in Florida.

That evening Fred and Jeanie discussed their future. Since it appeared that ships in bottles would sell better in the Northeast than in the South, wouldn't it make sense to relocate? And wouldn't a nautical gift shop make a good home base from which to sell their products? They could easily imagine living in Maine. It would mean giving up their jobs and leaving friends and family, but their two children were in college, so they were "empty nesters" with more freedom than they had experienced in years. Tomorrow they would look into buying The Maritime Store.

John, of course, was more than pleased to discuss a possible sale. They reviewed the previous year's finances.

Sales	$ 354,000
Less cost of goods	– 183,000
Gross profit	171,000
Less operating expenses	– 124,000
Net profit	$47,000

John was willing to sell the store for the retail value of his inventory, $125,000, $35,000 for his display cases and equipment, and $20,000 for leasehold improvements he had made to the property—a total of $180,000. Three years remained on the lease, and he was sure it could be extended with a minimal increase. Although sales had been stagnant for the previous three years, John admitted he had not advertised during that period. He pointed out that if Fred and Jeanie could produce a $50,000 annual profit, they would achieve a return on investment of 27 percent and earn back the $180,000 investment in a little over three years. Fred and Jeanie had a lot to discuss on their way back to Georgia.

continued

Fred was excited—a new beginning, an adventure in a beautiful setting, sailing, fishing, becoming active in the community. Jeanie was more cautious. The lifestyle sounded wonderful, but the risks were great. Was the return on investment really 27 percent, since the profit would be their salary? Did they know enough about retailing to make it a career? Should one of them operate the store while the other worked a salaried position? If so, were there job opportunities in the area? Had John given them enough information to make such a big decision? Where would they get $180,000—a bank loan, selling their retirement plans, taking investors, or asking John to finance part of the purchase? There were so many questions it made Jeanie's head spin. By the time they reached their home, they agreed that buying a business now would be too much too soon.

Think Critically

1. Address Jeanie's concerns. Is this a good, promising, or bad opportunity?
2. How important is experience to such a decision?

Summary

Many entrepreneurs choose to buy an existing business rather than create a new business. To find business-for sale-opportunities, prospective buyers research the classified sections of the newspaper, make inquiries to business brokers, discuss their interest with industry representatives, and inquire throughout the community.

The advantages of buying an established business include owning a business with a history, which reduces risk because the buyer knows what to expect. The new owner inherits a customer and supplier base and often receives preferable financial arrangements through seller financing. However, many businesses that are for sale have poor customer relations or negative images that take new ownership a long time to improve.

Buying an existing business requires detailed research and planning, just as in starting a new business. Buyers must make sure that all documents presented are accurate and that the final price is fair. If the opportunity does not appear to be a good investment, it should be avoided. The buyer should realistically project what impact the change of ownership will have on the business. The buyer should not expect an immediate turnaround of profits and growth.

A person who wants to become an entrepreneur but does not know what business to choose or how to run a business may want to consider a franchise. Franchising is a method of doing business in which a franchisee is granted the right to engage in offering, selling, or distributing goods or services under a marketing format designed by the franchisor.

An entrepreneur should not sign a franchise contract without the advice of a competent attorney who can analyze the legal documents required for a franchise arrangement. These documents are covered in the Federal Trade Commission Franchise Rule.

Several pertinent questions should be asked and answered before the entrepreneur purchases a franchise. These questions involve the franchise, the franchisor, the franchisee (entrepreneur), and the franchisee's market.

Chapter Review

A Case in POINT

Career Decision

Joe Ramos is a third-generation Mexican-American who lives in a suburb of Chicago. He has worked for his uncle Paco in the restaurant business for 20 years. Uncle Paco's restaurant, Casa de Mexico, is very successful.

When Joe began working for Uncle Paco, he bussed tables. Over the years he has performed every job in the restaurant, including chef. Since Uncle Paco went into semiretirement five years ago, Joe has managed the restaurant.

Joe has always been very happy working at Casa de Mexico. He figured he would stay there until he retired. All that changed recently, however. Uncle Paco's oldest son, Luis, moved back from the West Coast and began working at the restaurant.

During the six months that Luis has been working with Joe, things have been changing. Joe is sure that it is just a matter of time before Uncle Paco makes his son manager of Casa de Mexico. Joe sees his career suffering a serious setback when that happens.

Because of what is happening, Joe has decided that going into business for himself might be a good idea. He has always invested a portion of his earnings and now has quite a nice nest egg. He plans to either purchase a franchise or open a small restaurant on his own.

Think Critically

1. Would you advise Joe to purchase a franchise or open his own restaurant? Why?
2. What should Joe consider as he decides which option is best for him? What questions should he ask?

Vocabulary Builder

Write a brief definition or explanation of each word or phrase.

1. business broker
2. earnings approach
3. franchise
4. franchisee
5. franchising
6. franchisor
7. FTC Franchise Rule
8. goodwill
9. liquidation value
10. market value
11. replacement value
12. royalty

Review the Concepts

13. Why is it a good idea to investigate business-for-sale opportunities before deciding to start a new business?
14. What are three advantages of buying an existing business?
15. What are three disadvantages of buying an existing business?
16. Why is it important to determine why a business is for sale?

17. What information should a prospective buyer collect to properly evaluate a business opportunity?

18. What does an earnings approach determine when used to evaluate a business for sale?

19. What is determined when calculating liquidation value?

20. Why is it wise to make a pro forma (projected) income statement before purchasing a business?

21. Name four advantages and four disadvantages of franchising.

Critical Thinking

22. What are some characteristics of a promising business opportunity?

23. What steps should an entrepreneur take to investigate a business for sale?

24. How does replacement value differ from the asset value listed on a balance sheet? Why should prospective buyers determine the replacement cost?

25. What are royalties? What effect do they have on business profits?

26. What are three of the questions entrepreneurs should ask about a franchisor before purchasing a franchise?

Project

Build Your Business Plan

Review the classified section of the newspaper to find a business for sale similar to the hypothetical one you are planning. Contact business brokers and inquire if they have any current listings of similar businesses. How do the newspaper or brokers' descriptions compare with what you have learned about your business project? Write a report that analyzes the existing business opportunities and compares them with your planned new business.

Choose a franchise, gather as much information as you can, and answer the questions that were presented in this chapter to decide if this franchise would be a viable option for you. Then answer the following questions.

1. What are the advantages and disadvantages of purchasing a franchise in your particular situation?
2. Is purchasing the franchise you researched a suitable option for you? Why or why not? If not, might you consider purchasing a different franchise? Why or why not?

Chapter 4

Legal Requirements

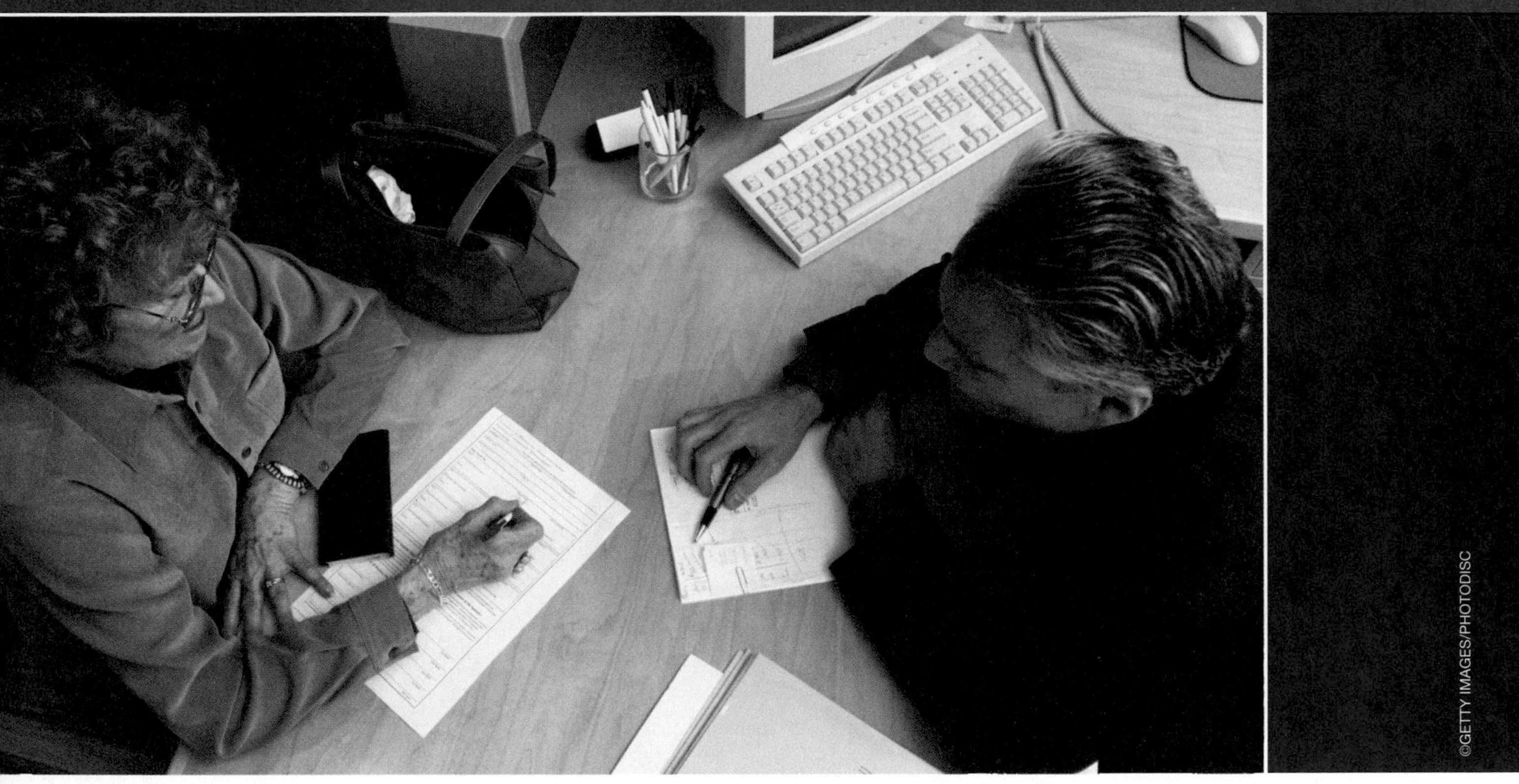

©GETTY IMAGES/PHOTODISC

Objectives

4-1 Discuss the process of legally naming a business.

4-2 Explain the nature of a sole proprietorship.

4-3 Describe the types of partnerships.

4-4 Name and define the five classifications of corporations.

4-5 Explain the benefits and disadvantages of a limited liability company.

4-6 Explain the Federal Trade Commission and its impact on advertising, pricing, product warranties, and competition.

4-7 List and explain the components of a legally enforceable contract.

4-8 List the employer's responsibilities for taxes, licenses, and employment regulations.

NAME THE BUSINESS LEGALLY

When the time comes to choose a name for the new business, certain basic principles apply. The name should be easy to spell, pronounce, and remember. It's best not to get too fancy. Fancy names can pose problems with spelling and pronunciation for customers. Sometimes the simplest name is the best choice.

When Sam Walton first started his franchise of five-and-dime stores, he called them "Ben Franklin." Most customers, however, referred to the stores as "Sam Walton's Five and Dime." Mr. Walton wanted a different name for his business. The name that would one day be associated with the biggest company in the world came about one day when Sam was flying with Bob Nogle, his first manager. During the flight, Sam proposed a number of new names.

Bob suggested they use something simpler, with fewer letters in it. He was thinking of the cost of big signs. He wrote W-A-L-M-A-R-T on a napkin and passed it to Sam, who was piloting the plane.

Mr. Walton read the suggestion but did not respond. To Bob's surprise, the next store opening featured a new Wal-Mart sign.

FUN FACTS

How do you think Hershey's Kisses got their name? No one seems to know for sure. One popular theory says the candy was named for the sound and motion of the chocolate being extruded during the manufacturing process.

Legal Requirements

Wal-Mart neglected to register the name immediately. By some accounts, it was 15 years before someone remembered to file for the registered trademark.

You may not be as lucky as Wal-Mart in protecting the name of your new business. After you decide on a name, you should find out if state law requires that you register it. Registration requirements differ from state to state, but there are many similarities. For instance, all companies doing business in Colorado with trade names must register those trade names. Sole proprietorships and general partnerships must register their trade names with the Department of Revenue. According to state law, a **trade name** is any name other than the full first and last name(s) of the owner(s) of a business entity, including a general partnership. Under this law, the following are trade names:

- John Doe's Plumbing Supply
- Jane Doe's Chiropractic Clinic
- Joe Doe & Associates
- Jane Doe's Accurate Accounting

The following are not trade names:

- John Doe, Plumber
- Jane Doe, Chiropractor
- John Doe, Attorney at Law
- Jane Doe, CPA

If you are in doubt about whether or not you have to register your business's name, either contact the Secretary of State's office or consult an attorney. Failure to register a trade name could result in the loss of your right to use it.

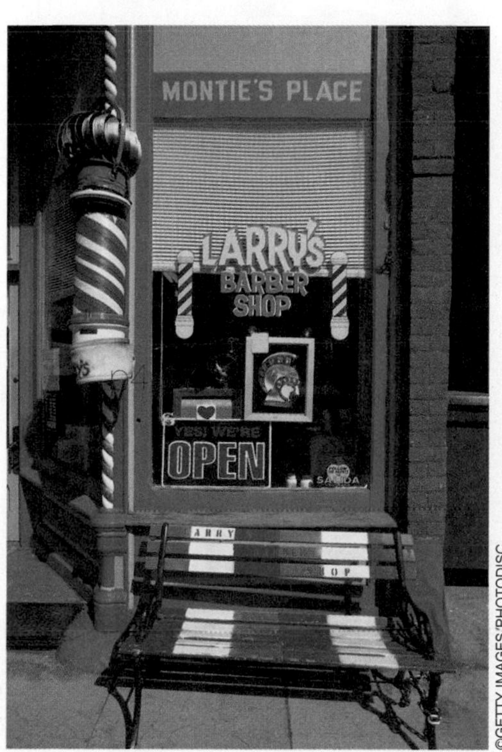

©GETTY IMAGES/PHOTODISC

FORMS OF OWNERSHIP

A key decision for any entrepreneur is one of ownership of the new business. Will you choose to make a go of it by yourself? Will you establish a business with one or more other people? Or do you want a business in which many people share ownership?

The form of ownership an entrepreneur chooses has important legal, financial, and personal implications throughout the life of the business. Each form has advantages and disadvantages. As you read through this chapter, keep in mind the type of business you would like to start someday, and try to determine which form of ownership is right for you.

The four basic forms of business ownership are sole proprietorship, partnership, corporation, and limited liability company. Which of these is best for the entrepreneur thinking of starting a new business?

SOLE PROPRIETORSHIP

Do you want to go it alone? If you are willing to be solely responsible for all aspects of a new business, a sole proprietorship may be the best form of ownership for you. A **sole proprietorship** is a business established, owned, and controlled by a single person.

©GETTY IMAGES/PHOTODISC

Sole proprietorships come in all shapes and sizes. They may be very small businesses with only one employee, the owner. A sole proprietor may hire a manager to run the business on a daily basis or may own a very large business with hundreds of employees. The owner realizes all the profits from the business and assumes responsibility for all losses. In this sense, the owner of a sole proprietorship is truly an entrepreneur.

The sole proprietorship is the most prominent of the four forms of ownership. In fact, more than 95 percent of all businesses in the United States are sole proprietorships. They are easy to form and allow almost unlimited control of the business. The same characteristics that prompt individuals to be entrepreneurs—the desire to control their own destiny, the freedom from direct supervision, and the potential to achieve profits greater than a salary from someone else—prompt them to choose the sole proprietorship form of ownership.

Formation of a Sole Proprietorship

Of the four forms of ownership, the sole proprietorship is by far the easiest to form. The government exercises very little control over the establishment of new sole proprietorships. Start-up can be immediate and simple, providing you have all the necessary resources—capital, knowledge, and merchandise or a service to sell. Keep in mind that you may need to obtain licenses or permits for your particular type of business, such as the license to operate a hair salon.

Operation of a Sole Proprietorship

Sole proprietors make all the decisions regarding the operation of the business. Although they have the luxury of being the boss, sole proprietors are not exempt from financial risk. They must obtain the necessary funds to open and run the business, and they must pay taxes.

The assets of sole proprietors are not considered legally separate from the assets of the business. This means that if the business does not succeed and any debts remain, the proprietor's assets may be taken to pay those debts. Despite this drawback, reporting taxes is fairly simple. Owners of sole proprietorships report business income and expenses on their personal income tax returns.

©GETTY IMAGES/PHOTODISC

Advantages and Disadvantages of a Sole Proprietorship

To summarize, some of the advantages of a sole proprietorship are as follows:

- Sole proprietorships are simple to start. No formal action is required.
- A sole proprietorship may be started immediately.
- The owner has total control of all aspects of the business.
- The owner receives all the profits.
- The business itself pays no income tax; the owner pays income tax as an individual.

A sole proprietorship also has some disadvantages:

- The owner has unlimited responsibility for losses, debts, and other liabilities the business might develop.
- The owner must make all the decisions.
- The owner is the only person who can arrange financing or capitalization.
- The existence of the business ends upon the owner's death.

Small Business Technology

It is important to protect the name of a new business through registration. Part of any registration process is a search to determine if the name is already in use. Both the name search and name registration can be accomplished in most states using the Internet. The best place to start is the Secretary of State's home page. A process that used to take weeks can now be completed in minutes.

Federal Tax Forms for Sole Proprietorships

The following is only a partial list of tax forms, as listed on the SBA Internet site, and some may not apply to your business.

- Form 1040: Individual Income Tax Return
- Schedule C: Profit or Loss from Business (or Schedule C-EZ)
- Schedule SE: Self-Employment Tax
- Form 1040-ES: Estimated Tax for Individuals
- Form 4562: Depreciation and Amortization
- Form 8829: Expenses for Business Use of Your Home
- Employment Tax Forms

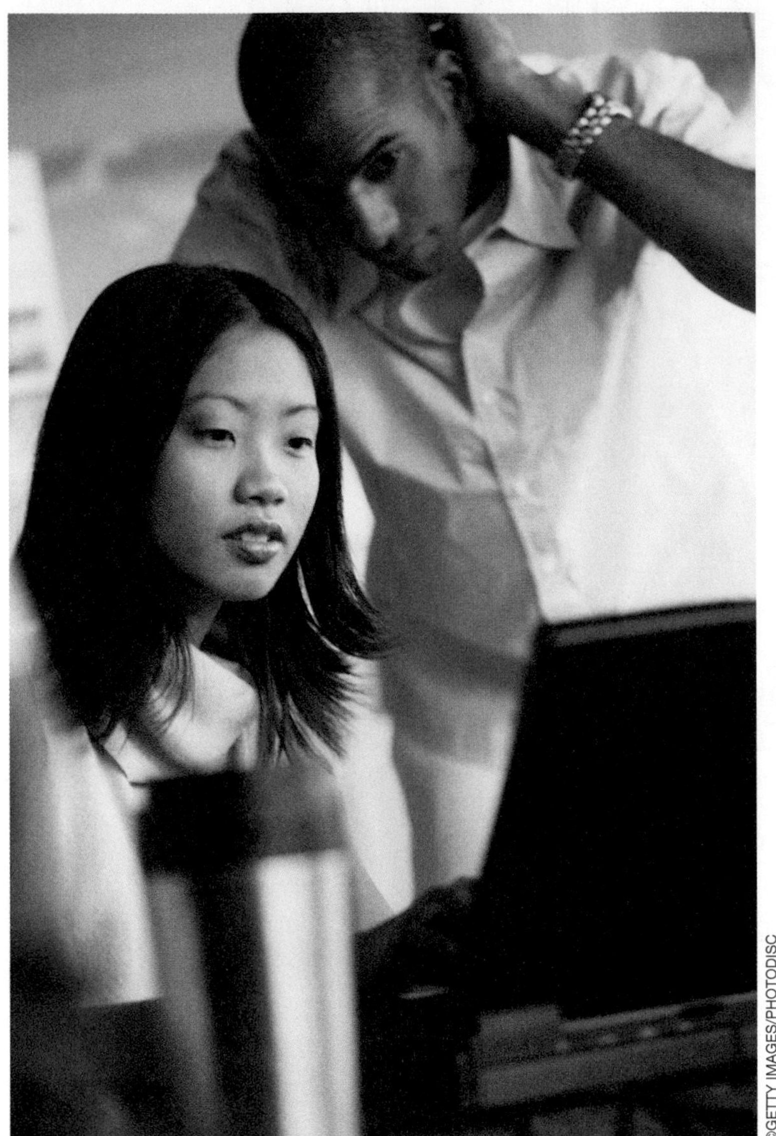
©GETTY IMAGES/PHOTODISC

PARTNERSHIP

As defined by the Uniform Partnership Act (UPA), a **partnership** is an association of two or more persons to carry on as co-owners of a business for profit. Partners with complementary skills or knowledge often team up to form a partnership. For example, a person experienced in manufacturing may form a partnership with an individual with marketing expertise. Partnerships offer the benefit of combined finances as well as combined talents.

The Uniform Partnership Act has been adopted by almost every state to provide a degree of uniformity to partnership laws. Entrepreneurs should check to see if the UPA has been adopted by the state in which their new business is to be located. If it has not, they should approach the formation of a partnership more cautiously. Without the UPA, there are no guidelines to protect individuals in partnerships.

Partnership Agreement

One of the first things that must be done when two or more entrepreneurs are considering a partnership arrangement is to write a **partnership agreement,** such as the one in Figure 4–1 on page 69. Written partnership agreements are not required by law in all partnerships; oral agreements are perfectly legal in some cases. However, a written agreement is strongly recommended. Many future conflicts can be avoided by defining in writing all important aspects of the partnership. At a minimum, partnership agreements should contain the following points:

- Name of the business or partnership
- Names of the partners
- Type of investment of each partner (such as cash, equipment, real estate) and its value
- Managerial responsibilities of each partner
- Accounting methods to be used
- Rights of partners to review and/or audit accounting documents
- Information about how profits will be divided and how losses will be shared
- Salaries/money to be withdrawn by partners
- Duration of the partnership
- Information concerning dissolution of the partnership
- Distribution of assets upon dissolution
- Procedure relating to the death of a partner

FIGURE 4-1

Partnership Agreement

PARTNERSHIP AGREEMENT

We, L. J. Doray, Jake Meyer, and Janet Feldman, do mutually agree to conduct a business as general partners under the fictitious trade name of STYLE 'N SPEED, on the following terms and conditions:

PURPOSE, LOCATION — I The purpose of the business shall be the operation of an automobile body customizing shop to be located in rented quarters at 5500 Auto Row, Atlanta, Georgia.

DURATION, DISSOLUTION — II The partnership shall continue for a period of five (5) years, with the expectation that it will be renewed thereafter for additional five-year periods by unanimous mutual consent. However, any partner may withdraw without liability with ninety (90) days' notice in writing, sent by registered mail to the other partners, with time to commence five (5) days from date of posting. In such event, either or both of the other partners may decide to terminate the business. In the alternative, either or both may elect to continue the business, buying the interest(s) of the withdrawing partner(s) at book value with no allowance for goodwill. Book value shall be determined as of the date of withdrawal, by the firm's certified public accountant. Payment shall then be made in equal monthly installments over a three (3) year period, unless otherwise agreed, with interest at ten (10) percent a year on the unpaid balance. The continuing partner(s) may accelerate the payments at will. In the event of death of any partner, the same terms shall apply.

CAPITAL — III The initial capital shall be the sum of thirty thousand dollars ($30,000) to be contributed in equal amounts by the partners within ten (10) days of this agreement. Additional contributions of no more than ten thousand dollars ($10,000) from each partner may be required by majority vote at any time within one year from this date. Any further contributions of capital shall require unanimous agreement.

DUTIES AUDIT, BANK — IV Doray and Meyer shall work in the shop; Feldman shall run the office, promote sales, make all necessary purchases and disbursements, and keep or supervise...

...fiscal year by allocating the year's total profit to all working days equally. Any sum thus deducted shall be added to the share of profits of the partner(s) who remained at work on the day(s) in question.

COMMENCEMENT, WORK DAYS — VII Business shall commence on the day this agreement is signed. The work of this partnership shall constitute the full-time, gainful occupation of each of the partners. Unless and until otherwise agreed, the business shall be open from 8:00 a.m. until 6:00 p.m. every weekday. It shall be closed on Saturdays, Sundays, and officially designated federal holidays.

IN WITNESS WHEREOF WE HAVE SET OUR HANDS THIS ________________ day of September, 20--.

L. J. Doray   Jake Meyer   Janet Feldman

L. J. Doray   Jake Meyer   Janet Feldman

Types of Partnerships

Partnerships may take many forms, but the general partnership and the limited partnership are the most common. Entrepreneurs should be familiar with the characteristics of each.

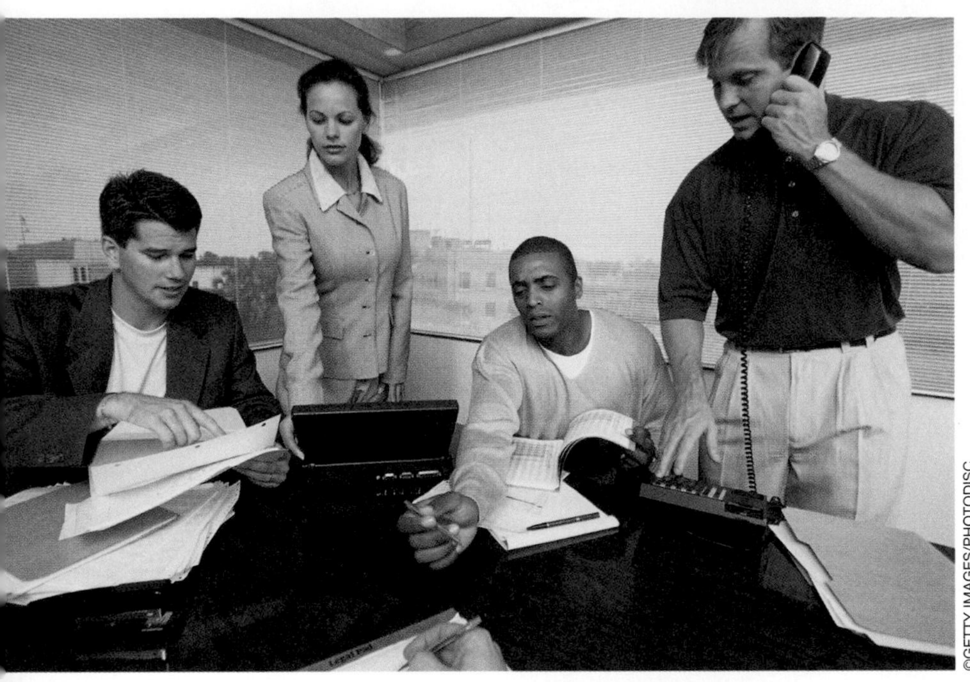
©GETTY IMAGES/PHOTODISC

General Partnership A general partnership is made up of two or more general partners. A **general partner** is a partner who actively engages in the day-to-day management of the business and is fully liable for any actions for, by, and against the business. General partners are sometimes referred to as "ordinary" or "regular" partners. Partnership agreements are not always required by law for this type of partnership. They are, however, advisable.

Limited Partnership A limited partnership is made up of one or more general partners and one or more limited partners. A **limited partner** is a partner who does not actively engage in the day-to-day management of the business and whose liability is limited to the extent of his or her investment in the business. Limited partners are investors in the business. For example, if Marty Junkin wants to be a limited partner in Dana Simpson's video store business, she is limited in two ways. First, Marty cannot participate in the day-to-day management of the video store. Second, her liability is limited to the amount she invests in the business. If she invests $3,000, then $3,000 is the maximum amount she can lose.

In a limited partnership, there must be at least one general partner. This means that at least one partner in the business is both fully liable for losses and involved in the daily management of the business.

Unlike a general partnership, which has minimal start-up requirements, there must be a partnership agreement in a limited partnership. States generally require that the limited partnership agreement be filed with the state in which it is located. Entrepreneurs forming a limited partnership should seek the assistance of a competent attorney when writing and filing the agreement.

Termination of a Partnership

A partnership may be terminated for any number of reasons. Partners may agree to terminate the partnership. A partner may leave or a partner may be added, in which case the old partnership is terminated and a new one initiated. A partnership agreement may provide for the expulsion of partners under certain circumstances, such as the unauthorized use of funds.

The law also dictates the termination of partnerships under certain circumstances. These include the death, bankruptcy, or insanity of a partner. In addition, a partnership may be terminated if the purpose of the business is determined to be illegal.

Advantages and Disadvantages of a Partnership

There are numerous advantages for the partnership as a form of ownership.

- Start-up can be simple because the law does not always require a partnership agreement.
- The partnership, as an entity, pays no income tax.
- Partners share the responsibilities of decision making, management, and capitalizing the business.
- Partners share any and all liabilities.
- Liability is limited in the limited partnership.

There are also disadvantages to partnerships:

- A high percentage of partnerships are terminated.
- General partners carry unlimited financial liability (in the general partnership).
- Each general partner carries liability for the errors of his or her partners.
- Because decision making and management are shared, partners have potentially less control.
- Partners must share profits.
- Partnership termination may disrupt business.

Federal Tax Forms for Partnerships

This is only a partial list of tax forms, taken from the SBA Internet site, and not all may apply.

- Form 1065: Partnership Return of Income
- Form 1065 K-1: Partner's Share of Income, Credit, Deductions
- Form 4562: Depreciation
- Form 1040: Individual Income Tax Return
- Schedule E: Supplemental Income and Loss
- Schedule SE: Self-Employment Tax
- Form 1040-ES: Estimated Tax for Individuals
- Employment Tax Forms

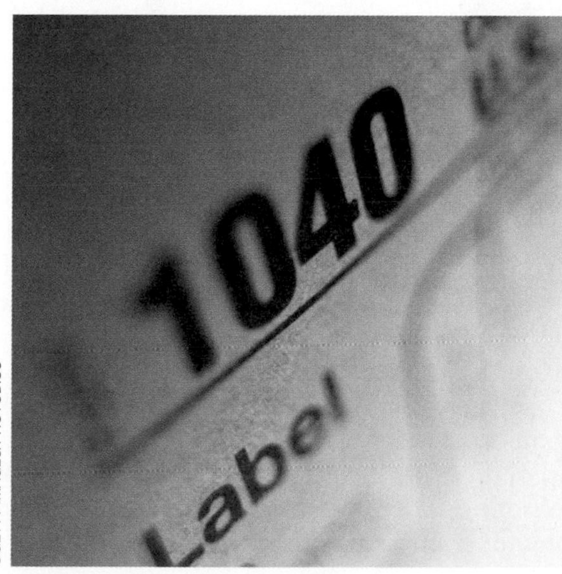

CORPORATIONS

A **corporation** is a legal entity created by law. In some ways a corporation is like an artificial person. For example, a corporation pays taxes, accrues debt, enters into contracts, can be held liable for negligence, and can make a profit.

Starting a Corporation

A corporation is created by one or more people. The individuals who start the process of incorporation—creating the corporation—are called promoters. The promoters file articles of incorporation with a state agency, usually the Secretary of State. Typically, articles of incorporation must contain the following information:

- Name of the proposed corporation
- Promoters' names and addresses
- Address of the corporate office
- Explanation of why the corporation is being formed
- Number of years desired for operation of the corporation (most states allow an indefinite number)
- Names and addresses of the people who will direct the corporation

Once the articles of incorporation are in order, the promoters pay the required state fees, which vary from state to state. When all requirements have been met, a state official—again, usually the Secretary of State—issues a charter. Entrepreneurs should have an attorney file all papers.

©GETTY IMAGES/PHOTODISC

Ownership and Management of a Corporation

Ownership of corporations is handled through the possession of stock. **Stock** represents a share of ownership in a corporation. The promoters and/or executives of a corporation divide a specified amount of stock into a certain number of shares. People who buy these shares are called **shareholders** or **stockholders**. All shareholders hold partial ownership in the corporation, according to the amount of stock they own.

The amount of ownership represented by one share of stock is determined by the amount of stock issued upon incorporation. If 1,000 shares of stock are initially issued, each share represents 1/1,000 ownership of the corporation. If the initial issue is 50,000 shares of stock, each share represents 1/50,000 ownership. The greater the number of shares issued, the lower the value of each share.

After the charter has been issued for a new corporation, a shareholders' meeting is held. Any person owning stock in a company has the right to attend and vote on issues during this and all future meetings. During the first meeting, a board of directors is elected. The board is responsible for electing the senior officers of the corporation, setting their salaries, and deciding the corporation's rules for conducting business.

Classifications of Regular "C" Corporations

Corporations are usually classified in five categories: domestic, foreign, public, private, and closely held.

Domestic or Foreign A corporation doing business within the state of incorporation is referred to as a domestic corporation. When employees of the corporation go out of the home state to do business, the corporation is considered a foreign corporation in the other states in which it does business. As an example, consider Leonard, Inc., a business that sells musical greeting cards. It is incorporated in the state of North Carolina. When it does business in North Carolina, it is a domestic corporation. When it does business in Texas, or any state other than North Carolina, it is a foreign corporation. Foreign corporations sometimes need to obtain permission to do business in other states.

Public or Private Corporations can be either public or private. Public corporations are incorporated government entities. For example, public utility companies fall into this category.

A private corporation is one owned by one or more individuals. As a rule, it is freer to operate than public corporations because it is bound by fewer regulations. Entrepreneurs who choose to incorporate form private corporations.

Closely Held Closely held corporations are similar to private corporations. Closely held corporations are private; the difference is that stock is sold to people other than the promoters, but only on a small scale. Even though the corporate structure is used and shares of stock are issued, there is nothing in corporate law that requires large-scale or public sale of the stock. The promoters may choose to retain all or most of the stock themselves. Some notable examples of closely held corporations are Mary Kay Cosmetics and the Amway Company.

Subchapter S Corporations

A popular variation, the subcharter S designation must be requested from the IRS by the stockholders. Once requested, it becomes a tax election only. This means it still has all the advantages of a corporation but is taxed differently. It eliminates double taxation by enabling shareholders to treat the earnings and profits as distributions and have them pass directly to their personal tax returns. This eliminates double taxation.

Advantages and Disadvantages of a Corporation

Because of their legal structure, corporations offer numerous advantages.

- **Limited Liability** This is probably the primary reason many entrepreneurs choose the corporate form of ownership. In many ways it is less risky than other forms. Shareholders' liability for debts, taxes, and lawsuits is limited to the amount of money they have actually invested in the purchase of stock. However, you should be aware that most lenders require a top executive of an incorporated small business, such as the chief executive officer (CEO), to sign both personally and as the business owner. In such cases, liability may not be limited for that individual.
- **Ability to Raise Capital** The ability of a corporation to raise additional capital through the sale of stock is a very important advantage of this form of ownership. Lenders are generally more willing to loan money to corporations than to sole proprietorships or partnerships.
- **Continuity of Business** Unlike the sole proprietorship and partnership, the corporation is not directly affected by events such as the death or bankruptcy of an owner. The business continues to exist and operate regardless of what happens to individual shareholders.
- **Transferable Ownership** Since shareholders (owners) do not manage the business, ownership can change through the buying and selling of stock without disrupting the day-to-day business of the corporation.

The legal structure of the corporation can also lead to disadvantages.

- **Double Taxation** There are several instances in which individuals are taxed more than once on income generated from a corporation. Functioning as a legal entity, the corporation pays income tax on profits earned. Shareholders pay additional income tax on any dividends they receive from the corporation. Employees who are shareholders must, of course, pay income tax on their salaries, so they are taxed one more time. This is a disadvantage, especially for a closely held corporation.
- **Charter Costs** The cost to incorporate a business can be high. Attorneys can be expensive, and fulfilling state requirements generally involves paying fees.
- **Regulation** A corporation is subject to a considerable amount of regulation that does not apply to the sole proprietorship or partnership. Examples include holding board meetings, keeping records of board meetings, and completing public disclosure reports. A corporation's business activities are also regulated; it may pursue only the business activities stated in the charter. If the owners wish to expand those activities or do business in other states, they must complete the necessary paperwork first.

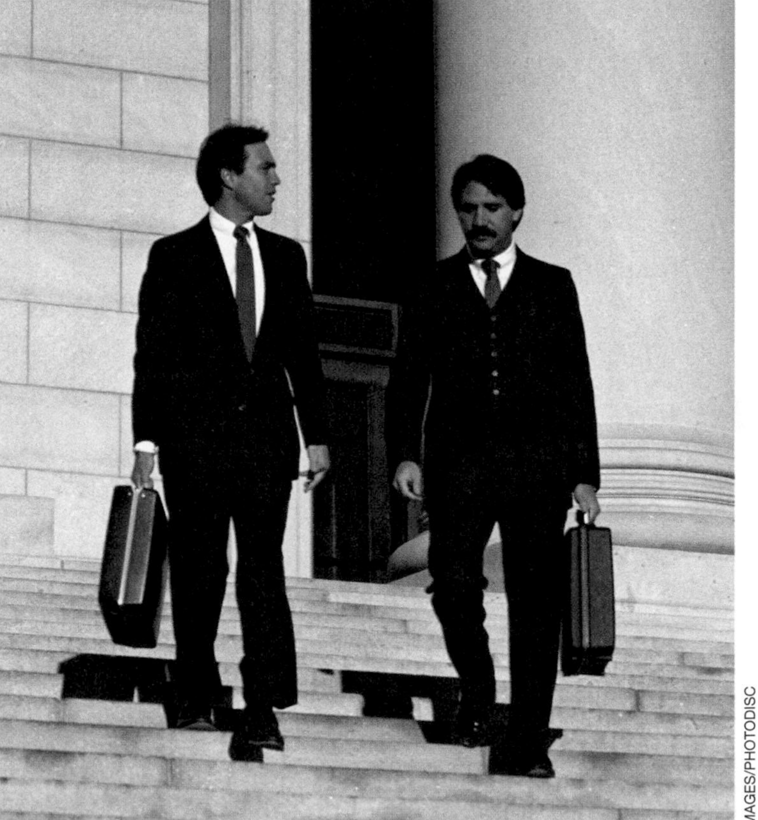

©GETTY IMAGES/PHOTODISC

- **Lack of Control** Ownership in a corporation does not guarantee any control or say in the day-to-day operation of the business. Remember, stockholders only vote for the board of directors. The president or CEO actually decides how the business is run. Even if you are a major stockholder, unless you are the president or CEO you may not have much control over the management of the company.

Federal Tax Forms for Corporations

Federal tax forms for regular "C" corporations (as listed on the SBA Internet site) include:

- Form 1120 or 1120-A: Corporation Income Tax Return
- Form 1120-W: Estimated Tax for Corporation
- Form 8109-B: Deposit Coupon
- Form 4625: Depreciation
- Employment Tax Forms
- Other forms as needed for capital gains, sale of assets, alternative minimum tax, etc.

Federal tax forms for subchapter S corporations include:

- Form 1120S: Income Tax Return for S Corporation
- 1120S K-1: Shareholder's Share of Income, Credit, Deductions
- Form 4625: Depreciation
- Employment Tax Forms
- Form 1040: Individual Income Tax Return
- Schedule E: Supplemental Income and Loss
- Schedule SE: Self-Employment Tax
- Form 1040-ES: Estimated Tax for Individuals
- Other forms as needed for capital gains, sale of assets, alternative minimum tax, etc.

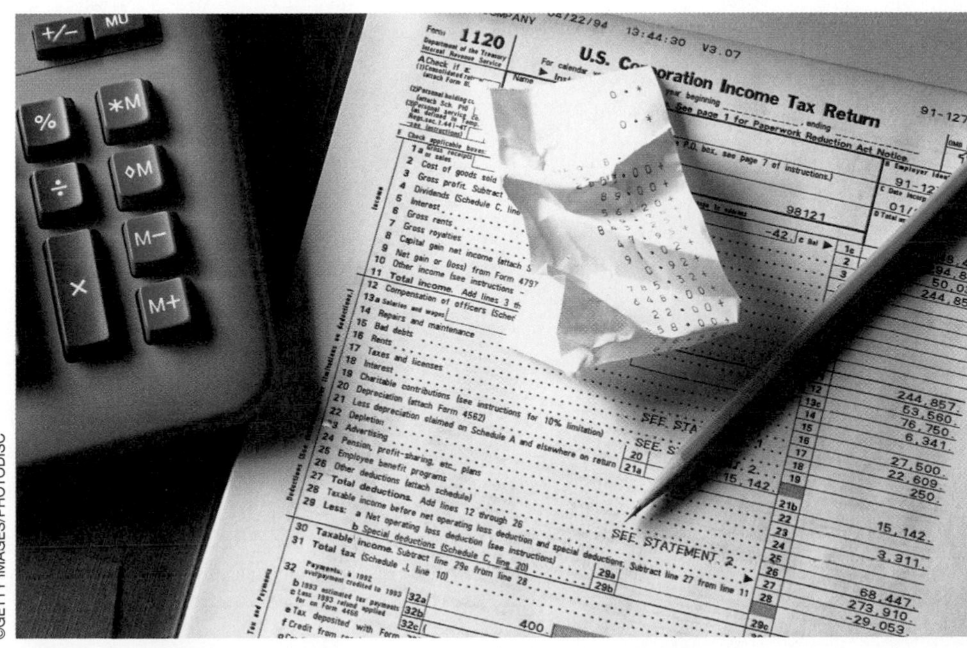

LIMITED LIABILITY COMPANY

A **limited liability company (LLC)** is an alternative form of ownership that has been around since the late 1980s. It has become a very popular form of ownership for small business owners. It offers the limited liability protection of a corporation but is taxed like a partnership.

Advantages and Disadvantages of an LLC

Forming an LLC has several benefits:

- It has limited liability.
- It is taxed like a partnership.
- It is not subject to all the rules involved in an S corporation.

LLCs have certain drawbacks as well:

- The body of case law around this form of ownership may not be fully developed.
- The type of businesses may be limited by state law.
- A single owner usually cannot establish an LLC.
- Many states limit the life of an LLC to 30 years.

As with a corporation, different versions of the LLC are available in different states. In Colorado, for instance, the entrepreneur may choose an LLC, a limited liability partnership, or a limited liability limited partnership.

Federal Tax Forms for LLC

The LLC is taxed as a partnership in most cases.

TABLE 4-1 COMPARE FORMS OF OWNERSHIP

Factors of Ownership	Sole Proprietorship	Partnership	Corporation	Subchapter S	Limited Liability Company (LLC)
Ease of start-up	A	A (except limited)	D	D	D (depends on state)
Liability	D	D (except limited)	A	A	A
Regulation	A	A (except limited)	D	D	D (depends on state)
Ownership control	A	A (except limited)	D	D	A
Initial costs	A	A	D	D	A (depends on state)
Ability to raise capital	D	A	A	A	A
Taxes	A	A	D	A	A

A Advantage of this particular form of ownership D Disadvantage of this particular form of ownership

SPECIAL REGULATIONS

There is more to successfully operating a business than hanging a sign and opening the door. You have examined the process of naming the business and the different forms of ownership. Now it is time to look at some legal considerations.

As an entrepreneur, you will enjoy considerable freedom to operate your business as you see fit. This freedom may be somewhat restricted, however, by certain laws and regulations. To prevent costly lawsuits and other unpleasant matters, you should understand certain basic laws that regulate business activities.

FUN FACTS

H. J. Heinz created the "57 varieties" tag line in 1896 as a marketing ploy. At the time, the condiments company was producing well over 57 different products. He simply liked the way "57" looked on a sign.

FEDERAL TRADE COMMISSION

The **Federal Trade Commission** (FTC) is a federal administrative agency charged with the responsibility of ensuring fair, free, and open business. In general, it is concerned with unfair business practices in interstate commerce. Its scope is very wide, affecting advertising, consumer credit, product safety, and business competition.

The FTC accomplishes its job in several ways. It interprets laws and creates regulations. It also advises businesses when it is requested to do so. If unfair business practices are suspected, the FTC will investigate. Based on its findings, it may issue "cease and desist" orders, and businesses can then voluntarily discontinue unfair, deceitful, or illegal business practices. If a business does not agree to stop such activities, the FTC may prosecute. As you read about some of the FTC's major areas of responsibility—advertising, pricing, product warranties, and competition—in the following paragraphs, think about which ones might apply to the business you would like to start.

Advertising

The FTC's role in advertising is to ensure that accurate information is being presented in advertisements to the public. Being accurate is not enough, though. The information must also be presented in a way that is not misleading. The following are some circumstances in which the FTC might take an interest in the advertising methods of a small business.

False Advertising False advertising is any advertising containing information that is not true or would cause the average consumer to reach a false conclusion about the product or service concerned. For example, if marketers of products containing oat bran claim that oat bran lowers cholesterol levels, it must be a proven fact. Otherwise, they are engaging in false advertising.

Deceptive Advertising Deceptive advertising is any advertising containing information that would mislead the average consumer about a particular product or service. Marketers presently advertise many foods as "diet" by virtue of "low fat" content. In fact, the products may actually contain a very high calorie count. Many consumers consider this to be deceptive advertising.

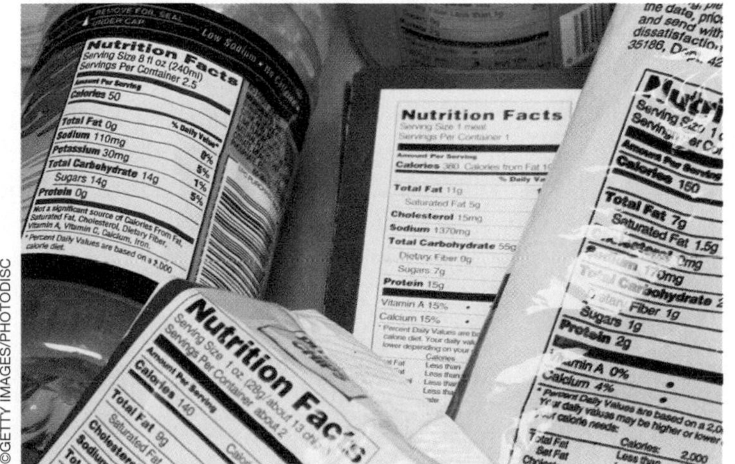

©GETTY IMAGES/PHOTODISC

Billie's Steppin' Out Shoes
Lowest Prices In Town!
BRAND NAME SNEAKERS
Hours 10 – 8 Mon thru Fri
401 Dodge Road

Prior to the establishment of the FTC in 1914, false and deceptive advertising were fairly common. Since then they have become less common, but they have not disappeared altogether.

There is a fine line between false advertising and deceptive advertising. For example, consider Billie's Steppin' Out Shoes. Billie's sales have been lower than normal for the past month. She has decided that a little advertising is what she needs to pump some life back into her business. In her newspaper ad is an illustration of a popular, national brand-name sneaker. The caption indicates that Billie offers these shoes at the lowest price in town. In reality, Billie has not checked prices outside her own shopping area. She has no idea what the sneakers cost at the mall across town. Billie has just engaged in false advertising. Her claim of offering the sneakers at the lowest price in town is just a claim. She does not know whether it is true or not. Her reason for making the claim is to entice customers into her store.

Now consider Billie's competitor, the owner of Frank's Fine Footwear. Seeing Billie's ad, Frank decides to fight back. He places an ad in the newspaper with this statement: "BRAND-NAME SNEAKERS FOR SALE. SNEAKERS PRICED AT $10." Frank thinks he is being smart. What he says is true. He does have brand-name sneakers for sale and he does have some sneakers for $10. They are not the same sneakers, however. Therefore, Frank has engaged in deceptive advertising. The average consumer would probably assume that the brand-name sneakers are priced at $10. Both Billie and Frank have broken the law and are subject to penalties prescribed by the FTC.

Bait and Switch Advertising The practice of advertising a lower-priced item to lure customers into the store for the real purpose of selling them a different, higher-priced item is called **bait and switch advertising**. With bait and switch, an actual attempt is made to convince the customer that the advertised product is inferior and should be ignored in favor of higher-priced merchandise. As an example, take Frank's advertisement for $10 shoes. His ad lures customers in. The "bait" is the inexpensive shoes. If Frank tries to "switch" the customer's preference from the lower-priced sneakers to higher-priced brand-name sneakers, he has engaged in bait and switch advertising. Again, he will have violated the law.

Sometimes salespeople claim that all the advertised models have been sold, when in fact the items were never in stock in the first place. This practice is often difficult to prove, especially if the store later has the advertised product in stock.

The Global ENTREPRENEUR

When businesses advertise to children 12 and under in the United States, the FTC pays particular attention because children may be more vulnerable to certain kinds of deception. Advertising directed to children is evaluated from a child's point of view, not an adult's.

To monitor the ads, the FTC works with the Children's Advertising Review Unit (CARU) of the Council of Better Business Bureaus. The advertising community established CARU to serve as an independent manager of the industry's self-regulatory program. CARU publishes self-regulatory guides for children's advertising.

In summary, advertising to children in the U.S. is self-regulated, with little legislation to enforce it. Entrepreneurs should realize, however, that other countries regulate advertising to children through laws.

As an example, Sweden, commonly seen as the strictest European country in this area, bans advertising aimed at children under 12 and does not allow advertisements before or after children's TV programs. Swedish public opinion considers advertising to children "not fair play." The law also prohibits displays of sweets in shops within reach of little children. Additionally, it is against the law to address direct marketing mail to children under 16.

A number of other European countries have also tightened their rules concerning marketing to children. Greece, for example, bans all toy advertising on TV between 7 A.M. and 10 P.M.

Global entrepreneurs should carefully investigate local laws before advertising in another country. Failure to do so could have serious legal consequences.

Think Critically

Pick a member country of the European Union and investigate its advertising laws. Are they significantly different from U.S. laws?

Deceptive Pricing

You have probably noticed that many stores—especially some major chains—always seem to be having sales. These repeated sales have attracted the attention of the FTC because of a concern that the advertised sale price is actually the true value of the merchandise, not a reduction from the original price.

As an example, imagine that Merchandise for America is a large general merchandise company found in malls across the country. Because it has so many stores, it can go directly to a factory and have clothing made exclusively for its stores. Recently, Merchandise for America had the factory make 20,000 swimsuits for the summer season. The swimsuits have a retail value of $20 each. The company had the factory put a price tag on each suit listing the suggested retail price at $30.

In a memo to store managers, a store executive instructed them to put the swimsuits on sale after displaying them for only one week. If the FTC investigated this, it would probably conclude that the pricing was deceptive. The only reason the price was originally set at $30 was so that it could be marked

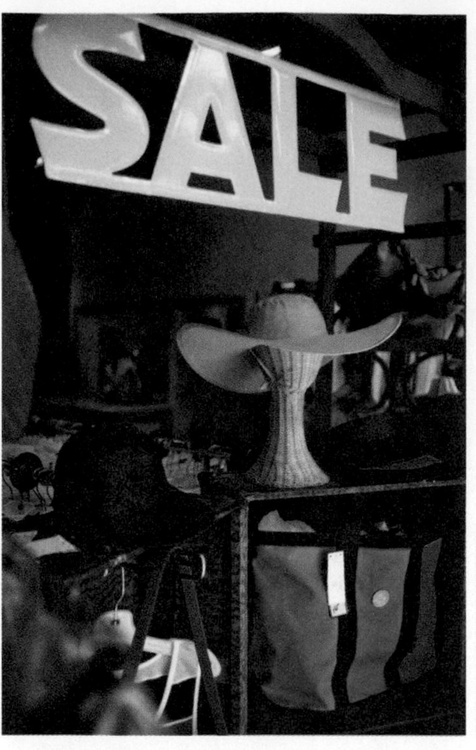

©GETTY IMAGES/PHOTODISC

at a sale price. The lower price would deceive customers into thinking they were getting a bargain when, in fact, they were not.

For entrepreneurs unsure about the legalities of pricing, the Federal Trade Commission offers an excellent publication, *FTC Guides Against Deceptive Pricing*. It is written in plain English, easy to understand, and offers excellent examples illustrating the basics of pricing regulations.

Product Warranties

Generally speaking, a warranty is a guarantee of the integrity of a product. Entrepreneurs need to be aware of two types of warranties—express and implied.

Express Warranty An **express warranty** is a clearly stated fact, either written or verbal, about the quality or performance of a product. For example, a label on a sweater saying "100 percent cashmere" is an express warranty. The warranty often serves as an important factor in a consumer's buying decision.

Entrepreneurs must exercise caution when purchasing goods from suppliers. They need to judge whether or not the products can deliver what their manufacturers or their labels state they can. Furthermore, business owners and their salespeople must watch what they say about product performance or quality when talking to customers. If they are not careful, sales talk may become an enforceable warranty.

As an example, consider Barbara Ellis. She works at Mountain Products Limited, a sporting goods store. A customer, Mary, enters the store and wants to look at sleeping bags. During her sales pitch, Barbara says, "I guarantee that this bag will keep you warm even if the temperature drops to 30 degrees below zero." Whether the bag was designed for that temperature or not does not matter: Barbara has issued an express warranty. The store can now be held liable if the product fails to protect the buyer at minus-30 degrees. This bit of sales talk can ultimately be costly to the store if it is not true. The salesperson should never warranty a product in any way that is not supported by the manufacturer.

Implied Warranty Almost all purchases are covered by implied warranties. They are created by state law, and all states have them. An **implied warranty** is an unwritten warranty ensuring that a product will perform under normal use and circumstances. In other words, the consumer is entitled to certain minimum levels of quality when purchasing products.

As an example, a customer purchases from your retail store a radio designed for use in the shower. The first time the buyer uses the radio, it stops playing as soon as it gets wet. Since the radio was designed to be used in the shower, getting it wet would be considered normal use. Therefore, based on the implied warranty, the customer can legally return the radio to your store and get a replacement.

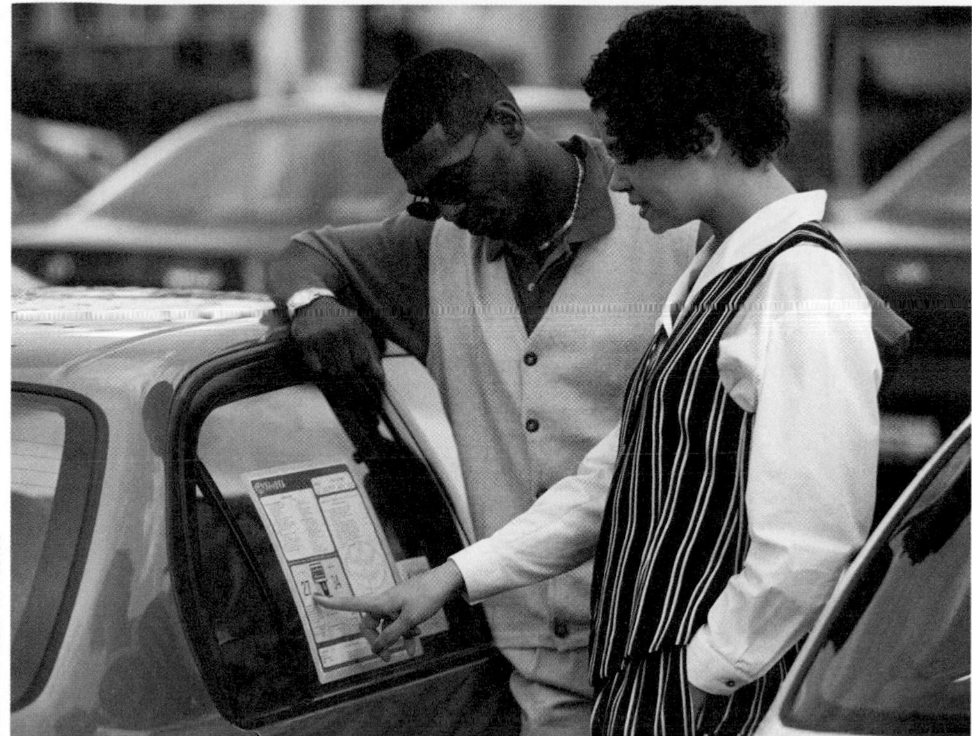

If the purchase does not come with a written warranty, it is still covered by implied warranties unless the product is marked "as is," or the seller otherwise indicates in writing that no warranty is given. Several states, including Kansas, Maine, Maryland, Massachusetts, Mississippi, Vermont, West Virginia, and the District of Columbia, do not permit "as is" sales.

FTC's Role in Warranties The FTC is charged with enforcement of the Magnuson-Moss Warranty Act, which provides standards for companies that choose to give written express warranties on consumer products. Under the FTC's Disclosure Rule, five basic components of warranty coverage must be described.

1. What does the warranty cover? What does it not cover? If there are exclusions or exceptions, you must state specifically what they are.
2. What is the period of coverage? If coverage begins at some point in time other than the purchase date, your warranty must state the time or event that begins the coverage. One example is when the warranty coverage begins upon product installation, which may be different from when the product is purchased. Also, if coverage is terminated by a particular event, that must be clearly stated. For instance, coverage might last until the first purchaser transfers the product to someone else.
3. What will you do to correct problems? You must explain what remedy you offer under the warranty. This could be repair or replacement of the product, a refund of the purchase price, or credit toward subsequent purchases.

   If necessary for clarity, you must also explain what you will *not* do—the types of expenses, if any, that you will not cover. These might include labor charges, consequential damages (the costs of repairing or replacing other property that is damaged when the warranted product fails, such as food that spoils when a refrigerator breaks down), or incidental damages (the costs a consumer incurs in order to obtain warranty service, such as time lost from work or charges for towing, telephone calls, transportation, or renting a product to temporarily replace the warranted product).

4. How can the customer get warranty service? Your warranty must tell customers whom they can go to for warranty service and how to reach those persons or companies. The warranty must include the name and address of your company and any person or office customers should contact.
5. How will state law affect your customer's rights under the warranty? Your warranty must answer this question because implied warranty rights and certain other warranty rights vary from state to state. Rather than require a detailed explanation on a state-by-state basis, the FTC adopted the following boilerplate disclosure, which must be included in every consumer product warranty: "This warranty gives you specific legal rights, and you may also have other rights which vary from state to state."

Competition

The FTC guarantees fair competition among U.S. businesses through the enforcement of the Sherman Antitrust Act, the Clayton Act, and the Robinson-Patman Act. Sometimes, however, a business may do something that does not violate one of these acts but still interferes with fair competition. The FTC can step in if a valid complaint is filed. As an example, consider a bank that wants to increase its deposits. As an incentive, it offers an interest rate that is a full percentage point higher than the rate other local banks are offering. Consumers who want to earn this higher rate, however, must agree to do all their banking business with this particular bank. The bank is not violating any antitrust laws, but it is still trying to interfere with fair competition. The FTC has the authority to step in and investigate.

CONTRACTS

Entrepreneurs deal with contracts and agreements—both formal and informal—on a daily basis. These contracts take many forms and address a wide range of situations. Because of the variety—and potential complexity—of contracts, it is important that entrepreneurs understand the basic principles by which contracts and agreements operate.

Contractual Requirements

A **contract** is a legally enforceable agreement negotiated between two or more persons. A "person" may be either a juristic person or a human being. A juristic person is an entity, such as a corporation, created by law. A legally enforceable contract fulfills requirements in five areas:

- agreement (offer and acceptance)
- legality
- consideration
- contractual capacity
- contractual form

Agreement (Offer and Acceptance)

A contract must provide for an offer by one party and an acceptance by another. This is not as simple as it sounds. Certain requirements must be met for the offer and for the acceptance.

Offer A contractual offer is an offer that is intended to be legally binding. The intent is judged to be legally binding if a reasonable person would consider it binding.

Marty, a salesperson, is taking a client to lunch and her car won't start. She says, "I'd sell this thing for two cents. It's no good." Marty is angry; she wouldn't really sell her car for two cents. This is not an offer in the legal sense.

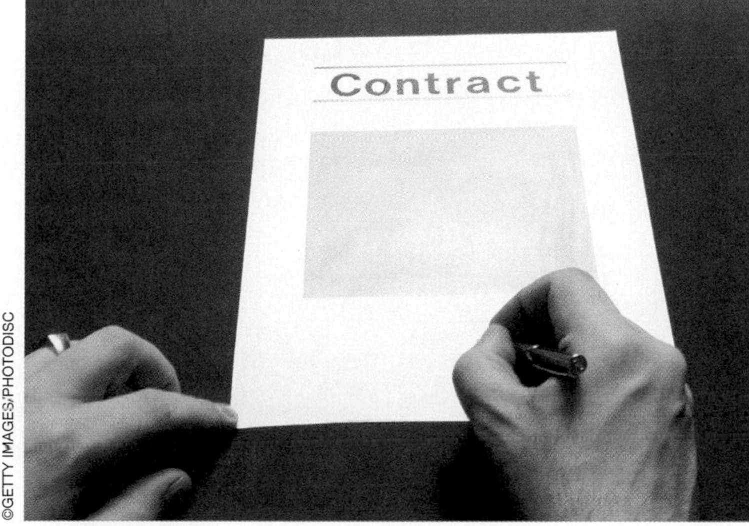

©GETTY IMAGES/PHOTODISC

Marty calls her friend Bill and says, "I'm buying a new car. Would you like to buy my old one for fifteen hundred dollars?" Marty really wants to sell her car. An offer has been made in the legal sense.

The offer must also be in definite terms and communicated in some ordinary fashion. In the second example above, Marty made a definite offer—the sale of her car. Marty also communicated the offer to Bill in an ordinary fashion—verbally.

Once communicated, the offer does not remain open forever. It may be ended in several ways:

1. The party making the offer retracts it prior to acceptance.
2. The party receiving the offer rejects it. Once the offer is rejected, the party that rejected it cannot later demand that the offer be honored.
3. The party receiving the offer makes a counteroffer. The original offer is ended and a new offer exists. In the second example above, Bill might tell Marty that he will give her $1,000 instead of $1,500. At that point, the original offer is ended and replaced by the second.
4. An offer ends after the passage of a reasonable length of time.
5. The death or mental incapacity of either party ends an offer.
6. Any change in a law that makes an offer illegal ends an offer.

Hector offers to sell a three-wheeled recreational vehicle to Tom for his customers at the hotel to use. After the offer has been made, a law is passed that makes it illegal to drive a recreational vehicle with less than four wheels. The offer is now illegal and, therefore, ended.

Acceptance An acceptance must be clear and positive. The party accepting an offer must agree unconditionally to all the terms of the offer. The acceptance may be communicated to the party making the offer in any fashion unless a specific method of acceptance is designated. If, however, the acceptance is not communicated in a manner equal to or better than that of the communication of the offer, the acceptance is not effective until thus received.

Marty writes Bill a letter offering her car for sale. Bill writes back accepting the offer. His acceptance is effective when he mails the letter. Marty cannot change her mind, even if she has not yet received the letter.

Legality

A legally enforceable contract must have a lawful objective. If the satisfaction of a contract requires breaking the law or violating a statute or policy, it does not have a lawful objective.

Jo tells Ben she will use her employee discount at a retail computer store to buy a computer for his new clothing store if he'll sell her two new outfits at cost. Since the discount is intended for Jo's personal use and is not transferable, the contract does not have a lawful objective and is not enforceable.

Consideration

Each of the parties involved in a contract must receive value. The legal term for that value is **consideration**. Think back to the first example.

If Bill accepts Marty's offer, the consideration (value) to Marty is Bill's $1,500, and the consideration to Bill is Marty's car.

©GETTY IMAGES/PHOTODISC

Contract law does not require that the considerations be equal. Marty's car may be worth $2,000. That does not matter; as long as consideration is involved, the contract is binding.

Something that has already been done or something that a person has a legal duty to do is not consideration.

If Mario comes back from his vacation and discovers that two of his employees were responsible for the apprehension of a would-be thief, he may be so happy that he promises to give them each $100. This is not a legal contract. Consideration is current or future value. Past actions are not part of a legally enforceable contract.

Gloria agrees to purchase a certain percentage of the remote-controlled airplanes she sells from her competitor, the only other company that sells the planes, in exchange for the competitor's promise not to sell planes to consumers at prices below a certain level. This is not consideration on the competitor's part. The agreement would interfere with fair competition. (*Note:* There are exceptions to the consideration requirement.)

Contractual Capacity

All parties to a legally enforceable contract must meet the legal requirements for capacity. Among those who do not meet these requirements are minors (persons under age 21), persons who are under the influence of alcohol or drugs when the agreement is made, and persons who are mentally deficient.

Minors can choose to fulfill the terms of a contract, but since they do not meet the requirements for legal capacity, they are not required to do so. A party who enters into a contract with a minor, however, is obligated to fulfill the terms of the contract. Business owners take great risks if they enter into contracts with minors. A minor may void or enforce the contract. The business owner has no choice—the wishes of the minor must be honored.

If a minor chooses not to honor a contract, the other parties involved may try to recover any goods given to the minor as a part of the contractual agreement, but they cannot legally enforce any other aspects of the contract.

Laura Marcus, a 16-year-old high school junior, is an avid reader. She reads an average of three novels a week. With the price of books increasing steadily, Laura's reading is getting very expensive.

Last month a book club offer came to Laura's house in the mail. Laura could get 10 novels for 99 cents by joining the club. She would then have to purchase 10 novels at their regular prices within 12 months. The offer stated that regular prices would be at least 25 percent less than bookstore prices and that future selections could be made from a list of hundreds of books.

Laura decided it was a great offer. After all, the required 10 novels represented less than one month's purchases. What could go wrong if the purchase requirement was only 10 in one year? Laura signed the form and returned it with the 99 cents. The 10 novels would soon be on their way.

A few days later, Laura's mother noticed the book club brochure and asked Laura about it. Laura explained why accepting the club's offer had been a good decision. Her mother sat down and carefully read the brochure.

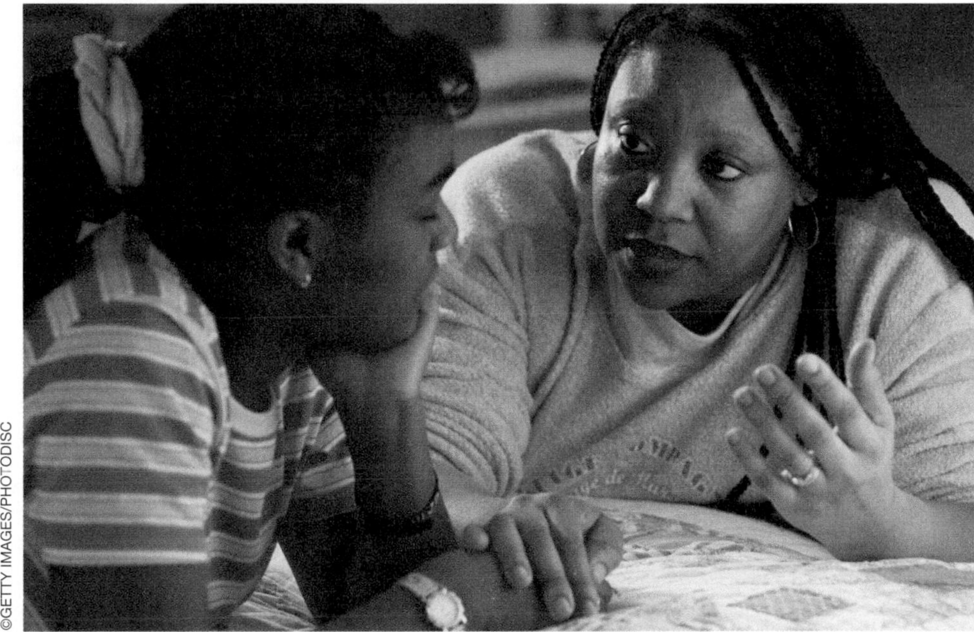
©GETTY IMAGES/PHOTODISC

After a few minutes she said, "Buying 10 hardcover novels may be very expensive, Laura." Laura had not read the statement that all novels except the first 10 would be in hardcover! Laura intended to pay for the books with earnings from a part-time job. Instead of spending about $40 as she had calculated, she was obligated to spend much more. Even with a 25 percent discount, the total would be more than $300.

Sending the signed form to the publisher meant that Laura had entered into a contract. Is there any help for Laura? Is there a way out of this mess?

Laura may either honor the contract and purchase at least 10 more novels, or she may return the 10 paperbacks as soon as she receives them and void the contract.

In another example, a person who is under the influence of alcohol when a contract is negotiated may void the contract, but only if the other party can be restored to pre-contract condition.

Lu-Yin was intoxicated at the time she told Carla she would buy 50 books of the coupons that Carla was selling in her store. Lu-Yin took the coupons and promised to pay Carla $150 the following week. Later that day, the coupons were stolen from Lu-Yin's car. She sought to void the contract on the grounds that she was intoxicated at the time the contract was made, but since she cannot restore Carla to her pre-contract condition (return the coupons), she must honor the contract and pay the $150.

A person who claims mental deficiency as a reason for voiding a contract must prove that the mental deficiency existed at the time the contract was made. The condition does not, however, have to be permanent. Lack of knowledge is not considered mental deficiency.

Jamie is a business owner who can sign his name and read a little, but that's about all. Jamie signed a contract to purchase some expensive equipment from Walt. Afterwards, he explained the deal to his attorney and showed him the contract. After reading it, the attorney told Jamie that, according to the contract, Jamie's cost for the equipment would be about 10 percent higher than the price Walt had quoted verbally.

Jamie sought to void the contract on the grounds that he could not read it and thus did not fully understand what was involved. Jamie must honor

Ethics for ENTREPRENEURS

Jim Tanzi owns an unusual auto body shop in Pueblo, Colorado. He specializes in rebuilding antique automobiles. When Jim started his business 10 years ago, he had very few customers. However, the last five years have been very busy and very profitable.

Five years ago Jim rebuilt a classic Model A Ford for a customer from Detroit. Shortly after Jim delivered the car, a story featuring the car's owner was printed in a national magazine. The story included a description of the car and mentioned Jim Tanzi. As a result, Jim has been getting business from all over the country. Sometimes he has more than he can handle.

Jim recently agreed to rebuild a 1965 Corvair for a man from Florida. Although he was busy, he thought he could complete the car by the time the man wanted it. They signed an agreement specifying the charges and the delivery date, and Jim scheduled his time so that he could start the Corvair job on June 3.

Jim encountered an unusual problem while working on another project and had to spend a lot of time taking care of it. He knew he was taking more time than he had planned, and there was no way he could get to the Corvair on time. That meant he would not finish it on schedule.

Jim called his cousin Blaine, who was also in the auto body business, and asked him to do the work on the Corvair. Blaine agreed and started immediately. When he finished, Jim checked the work. He was a bit disappointed. Blaine had done a good job, but not as good as Jim might have done. But it would have to do.

When the man from Florida came for his car, Jim told him what he had done and gave him the bill. The man was very angry and refused to pay. He claimed that Jim had breached the contract.

Think Critically

1. Whether or not Jim breached the letter of the contract is something that can only be decided in a court of law. In your opinion, did Jim breach the intent of the contract, which was that he would personally do the work?
2. What would you advise Jim to do?

the terms of the contract, however, because lack of understanding is not the same as lack of legal capacity.

Contractual Form

Contracts can be verbal or written; both are legally enforceable. Some contracts are regulated by the Statute of Frauds and must be written and signed. The **Statute of Frauds** is a collective term describing assorted statutory provisions that render certain types of contracts unenforceable unless they are executed in writing.

Several major examples of contracts that are covered within the Statute of Frauds are the sale of land, the sale of goods exceeding $500, contracts for services that cannot be performed in one year, and promises to assume the debt or legal responsibility of another. It is always a wise business practice to insist on a written contract anytime a contractual relationship is established.

Do not be fooled into thinking a contract is only a document with "CONTRACT" written at the top of the page. A written contract may be simply a letter addressed to you, as long as it contains all five requirements.

TAXES, LICENSES, AND EMPLOYMENT LAW

Be aware of the personal and business tax implications of starting your own business. Self-employment tax will double, as you must pay both the employer's and employee's share of social security and Medicare taxes. Property tax is collected on all personal property owned by a business. Special licenses may be required. City and county government may have special business regulations, sales taxes, personal property taxes, and zoning restrictions that will affect your business.

Make sure you understand your responsibilities as an employer in the following areas: employees vs. independent contractors, leased employees, seasonal employees, personnel policies, finding and hiring employees, employer/payroll registration forms, payroll taxes (filing requirements and forms), workers' compensation, the Occupational Health and Safety Administration, and the Americans with Disabilities Act.

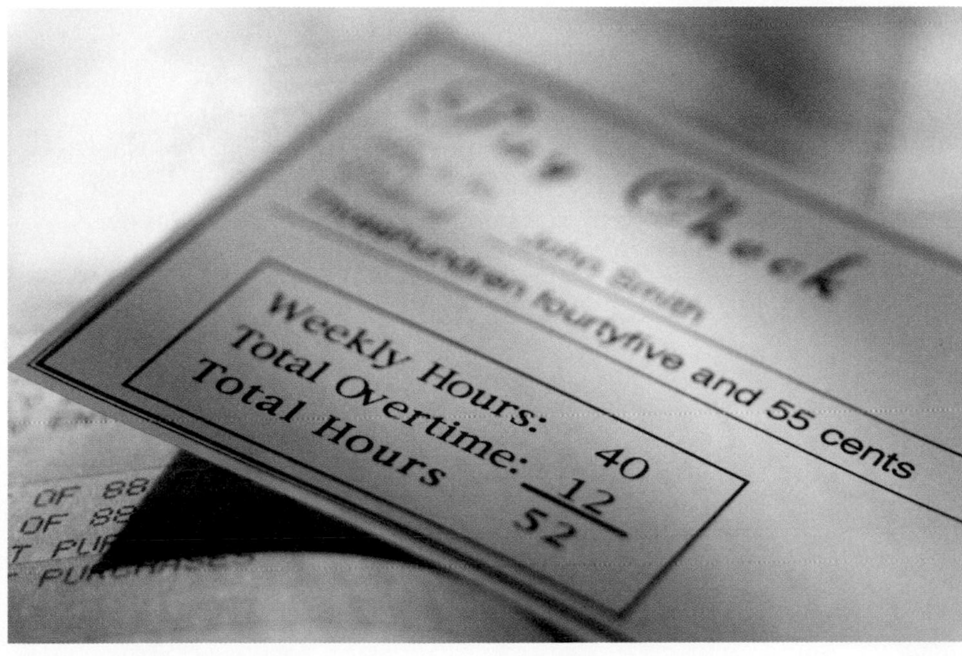

Ship in a BOTTLE

Clearing Customs

Fred was feeling excited as he drove his van to the Atlanta airport to pick up his first inventory shipment of ships in bottles. The $3,200 shipment had arrived at the Lufthansa Air Cargo Center. When he got there, he was surprised to learn he could not take possession of the goods until they had cleared customs. The woman at the counter sent him to the U.S. Customs Office to arrange clearance.

The process was not as simple as Fred had hoped. The customs agent explained that he could not pick up an overseas shipment worth more than $2,000 without being bonded. The agent showed Fred an official document stating that importers are required to post a bond "to protect the revenue of the United States or to assure compliance with any pertinent law, regulation or service." In other words, said the agent, an importer must post a bond to guarantee to U.S. Customs that all import duties, taxes, and charges will be paid and all import laws and regulations be complied with. To post a bond, Fred would have to fill out several forms. Once approved, he could pick up his shipment and all future shipments as well. The agent told Fred it might take a few days to process the paperwork. He suggested that Fred use a customs broker.

A customs broker is a bonded company or agent that handles all paperwork for imported shipments. The broker is notified of incoming shipments and prepares the necessary paperwork to receive clearance. This includes paying all tariffs, taxes, transportation costs, and bond fees. The broker informs the client when a shipment is ready for pickup, and the importer can then go directly to the air cargo center of the delivering airline. The customs broker bills the importer for all charges incurred, plus a fee for its services.

Fred selected JRM International Forwarding Company from a list of customs brokers at the U.S. Customs Office and drove to their nearby office. It quickly became apparent to Fred that using a customs broker was the answer to his dilemma. Since he would initially be bringing in only four to six shipments a year, the cost of the service would be reasonable and would certainly save time. Rose Marie, the manager, was very helpful in explaining the laws covering the intricacies of importing goods. She also made some phone calls and arranged the release of Fred's shipment later that day.

As it turned out, Fred would not have to pay tariffs on his ships in bottles. Tariffs are taxes imposed on imported goods to protect domestic manufacturers from being severely undermined by low prices in the marketplace. Since there was no ships-in-bottles industry in the U.S., there was no need to impose tariffs.

Fred drove home from the airport with his van full of ships in bottles. It had taken a few extra hours but he had certainly learned a lot about international business.

Think Critically

1. How would you find out the tariff rates imposed on particular products? Select a product line and research the tariffs imposed on importing it.
2. Call or visit the nearest customs broker office and inquire about career opportunities.

Summary

The name of a business should be easy to spell, pronounce, and remember. Do not try to get too fancy. Fancy names can pose problems with spelling and pronunciation for customers. Sometimes the simplest name is the best choice.

Name registration requirements differ from state to state, but there are many similarities. For instance, all companies doing business in Colorado with trade names must register those trade names. Sole proprietorships and general partnerships must register their trade names with the Department of Revenue. According to state law, a trade name is any name other than the full first and last name(s) of the owner(s) of a business entity, including a general partnership.

There are four basic forms of business ownership: sole proprietorship, partnership, corporation, and limited liability company. A sole proprietorship is a business established, owned, controlled, and operated by a single person. The sole proprietorship is the most prominent of the four forms of ownership. In fact, more than 95 percent of all businesses in the United States are sole proprietorships. They are easy to form and allow almost unlimited control of the business.

A partnership is an association of two or more persons to carry on as co-owners of a business for profit. The two major types of partnerships are general and limited. One of the first things that must be done when two or more entrepreneurs are considering a partnership arrangement is to write a partnership agreement. Law in all partnerships does not require written partnership agreements; oral agreements are perfectly legal in some cases. However, a written agreement is strongly recommended. Many future conflicts can be avoided by defining in writing all important aspects of the partnership.

A corporation is a legal entity created by law. One or more people create a corporation. The individuals who start the process of incorporation—creating the corporation—are called promoters. The promoters file articles of incorporation with a state agency, usually the Secretary of State.

Corporations may be domestic or foreign, public or private, or closely held. A popular variation, subchapter S designation must be requested from the IRS by the stockholders. Once requested, it becomes a tax election only. This means it still has all the advantages of a corporation but is taxed differently.

A limited liability company (LLC) is an alternative form of ownership that has been around since the late 1980s. It has become a very popular form of ownership for small business owners. It offers the limited liability protection of a corporation but is taxed like a partnership.

The Federal Trade Commission is a federal administrative agency responsible for ensuring fair, free, and open business. It interprets laws and creates regulations, advises businesses when requested, and investigates when unfair practices are suspected. In the area of advertising, entrepreneurs should be sensitive to false and deceptive advertising, bait and switch advertising, and deceptive pricing. Generally speaking, a warranty is a guarantee of the integrity of a product. Entrepreneurs need to be aware of two types of warranties—express and implied. They are regulated by the FTC through enforcement of the Magnuson-Moss Warranty Act.

Entrepreneurs deal with contracts and agreements—both formal and informal—on a daily basis. Because of the variety and potential complexity of contracts, it is important that entrepreneurs understand the basic principles by which contracts and agreements operate. A contract is a legally enforceable agreement that is negotiated between two or more persons. A contract must fulfill requirements in five areas: agreement, consideration, contractual form, legal capacity, and legality.

A Case in POINT

Career Decision

Stan Beasley has been working for the past two months on a business plan involving a health club. For most of his life, Stan has been a very successful athlete. In high school he excelled in football and went on to earn a scholarship to a major university. After college he joined a professional team and, for 10 years, was the best defensive safety in the National Football League.

Thanks to his tremendous success in the NFL, Stan is quite wealthy. He doesn't really have to work again, but he thinks he needs to stay busy at something to be happy. Opening a health club seems to be the perfect business, since he has been involved in athletic training for most of his adult life. He feels he possesses the technical know-how to start such a business and keep it running.

Stan has looked at either buying an existing gym or investing in one of several franchise options available. After careful analysis of the pros and cons of each, he has decided to buy an existing gym.

What to call the gym is the next issue. Because he is a football celebrity, he decides that naming the gym after himself would be a wise business move. He finally settles on "The Stan Beasley Health Club." He runs a name check on the Internet to make sure that the name is not already being used and then to register it.

Now Stan is at the point in his business planning where he needs to decide which form of ownership is most appropriate for the new business. He has listed the following points as factors to consider:

1. Capitalization (money) is no problem.
2. He possesses technical expertise.
3. He possesses no business management experience.
4. The current gym owner has agreed to stay and work for Stan for one year.
5. The gym has an established clientele.
6. Health clubs have experienced great financial difficulty in recent years.
7. Lawsuits against health clubs have been increasing.
8. Several friends (ex-football players) have expressed an interest in participating in some way in the venture.

Think Critically

Stan has a difficult decision to make. Give him some help by answering these questions.

1. Should Stan seriously consider a sole proprietorship? Explain your answer.
2. There are at least two ways that Stan could involve his friends as owners of the new business. What are they?
3. If you were Stan, what would be your primary area of concern regarding form of ownership?
4. What form of ownership would you recommend to Stan? Why?

Vocabulary Builder

Write a brief definition of each word or phrase.

1. bait and switch advertising
2. consideration
3. contract
4. corporation
5. deceptive advertising
6. express warranty
7. false advertising
8. Federal Trade Commission
9. general partner
10. implied warranty
11. limited liability company
12. limited partner
13. partnership
14. partnership agreement
15. shareholder/stockholder
16. sole proprietorship
17. Statute of Frauds
18. stock
19. subchapter S corporation
20. trade name

Review the Concepts

21. What is the legal requirement for naming a business?
22. What are the four basic forms of business ownership?
23. What are the two major types of partnerships? How do they differ?
24. What are the advantages of forming a corporation?
25. What is a limited liability company?
26. What five requirements must a legally enforceable contract fulfill?

Critical Thinking

27. Describe a sole proprietorship, including its advantages and disadvantages.
28. What is false advertising? Deceptive advertising? Give examples of each.
29. Explain the function of the Federal Trade Commission.
30. What are the employer's responsibilities in terms of taxes, licenses, and employment laws?

Project

Build Your Business Plan

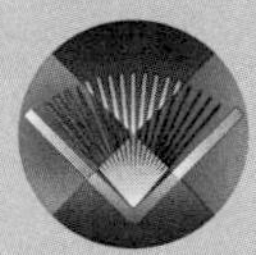

1. Choose a name for your business. Justify your choice.
2. Choose two forms of ownership that are possibilities for your business. List the advantages and disadvantages of each form, being specific about your hypothetical business.
3. Choose your form of ownership and list the two most important reasons why you chose it.

Writing a Business Plan

Nancy Hickam was feeling nervous as she waited for her appointment with Ms. Ferlaino, a vice president with First National Bank and a family friend. Nancy's husband, Tim, had suggested she go to the bank for advice on how to get her business idea off the ground.

Ms. Ferlaino greeted her cordially. "Hi, Nancy, it's good to see you. Have a seat. How are Tim and that future president you two are raising?"

"We're fine, Ms. Ferlaino. Little Henry is definitely keeping us busy. And so are our jobs. Tim and I feel like we're always on the run. That's why I'm here to see you. I have an idea for a new business, and I need some guidance. I want to open my own antiques shop. I have sales and buying experience from my present job, and I've been buying and learning about antiques for myself as long as I can remember."

"My goodness, Nancy, that's quite a step. Have you considered all the risks involved in owning a business? What information have you collected to support your idea?" Ms. Fairlano asked.

"Actually, I only have a few notes. I've been reading about antiques stores in the antiques magazines I get, and it sounds perfect for me. I estimate it will cost around $25,000, but I think I can make a good profit. What information do I need?"

"It's a big job, Nancy. You'll need some assistance. You might want to visit with a business consultant. Try the Small Business Development Center at the college, or go downtown to the Small Business Administration and talk to one of their counselors. They'll help you write a business plan. Then come back here, and we'll see if the bank can help you get started financially."

Nancy went home and looked in the yellow pages of the telephone book. She jotted down the phone numbers and addresses of the SBA office and the Small Business Development Center. She also noted a few private business consulting firms. Out of curiosity she called B&B Consulting Services. They invited her to come in and told her that, for a fee, they could write a business plan in a couple of days. It sounded great to Nancy.

Nancy took her notes and her dreams to the consulting firm. They asked her how much money she had available for the new business and how much she hoped to make. True to their promise, they produced a professional-looking, 15-page report a day later that explained how she could open an antiques store with a $25,000 investment that would produce a $50,000 profit by the end of the second year of operations. The report provided a general description of the local market and the potential of antique shops. It included some information on setting up a retail store, such as location considerations and expected costs. The fee for the report was $800. Nancy rushed it to Ms. Ferlaino for her opinion.

The banker's reaction shocked her. "Nancy, the bank needs a business plan that specifically addresses your concept and capabilities. This is just a list of statistics about antiques stores. It has very little to do with you or the local market. You need to personalize a business plan to your specific situation. I'm afraid you spent money on information that you could easily have found on the Internet or at the library. I suggest you take your information to one of the agencies I mentioned before. They'll show you at no charge how to write a business plan for your antiques shop."

The next day Nancy visited Tom Porter at the Small Business Development Center. Tom explained the ingredients of a business plan and directed her to the proper resources for information, including seminars held at the college. "Simplify your approach as much as possible," he said. "Start by writing out a two-paragraph description of your objectives. The first paragraph should address your personal objectives, meaning the personal satisfaction you hope to achieve from this endeavor. The second paragraph should address your financial objectives. State these in terms of the minimum amount of money you must make from the business during the first year to meet your personal obligations. Write down what you anticipate the profits will be after three years and five years. Then list all the things you need to research to complete the business plan. Don't worry too much about the final structure of the plan. I can help you with that later. The main thing is to start writing it out. Putting your idea on paper begins to make it real and helps clarify your thoughts. When you put your objectives in writing and then write a plan to reach those objectives, you've started down the path to owning a successful small business."

That evening, with Tim's help, Nancy wrote the following.

Personal Objective *For the purpose of achieving self-employment, I wish to open a retail antiques shop in Spring County that will primarily sell 19th- and early 20th-century American furniture and household items. As a business owner I will be able to control my own destiny and be responsible for all decisions I make concerning the business operation. I will use my previous experience in the management and merchandising of antiques. I will own a business that I will be proud of and receive recognition from my community for my efforts. It will be an enterprise that I can share with family members.*

Financial Objective *I am willing to invest $25,000 of my own resources in this venture if I feel confident that the business will produce a profit of $20,000 in its first year of operation. I anticipate that the profits will grow to $40,000 by the end of year three and that I will recapture my initial investment within a five-year period. I am hopeful that the store will open within the next twelve months.*

"Hey, Tim, I'm excited," Nancy exclaimed. "We still have a lot of information to collect and we need to go to some business seminars, but we've taken the first step. Ms. Ferlaino was right. This won't be easy, but anything worthwhile is worth the extra effort."

Case Questions

1. Why isn't it possible for a consulting firm to do a complete business plan?
2. List the elements of a business plan that Nancy will need to address.
3. How does a personal business plan differ from one that is offered to a bank or group of investors to review?

Unit 2

Small Business Research

Profile of an Entrepreneur

Bruce Hill, 1959–

Bruce Hill is the owner of a very successful business, Superior Alarm, in Grand Junction, Colorado. His entrepreneurial journey has been an interesting one.

As a high school student, Bruce was the manager of the Grand Junction office of H & R Block, the seasonal tax company. When clients were led into his office, their initial question was invariably, "Do you know what you're doing?" The reason for the question: Bruce was only 17 years old. That's right—he was certified as an H & R Block tax consultant at the tender age of 16 and a year later was promoted to manager.

When questioned about his ability, Bruce's response was always, "If you feel uncomfortable with me, you can get back in line and wait for another consultant." He never had a taker! At this point you might think that Bruce Hill was a child prodigy, a natural-born whiz with numbers.

Bruce Hill, future entrepreneur, was born and raised in Grand Junction. When he got his driver's license, Bruce became the "runner" for his father's accounting business and began his lifelong association with the Grand Junction business community.

In high school Bruce was an average student. He was class president and a talented athlete in track and football. By his own admission he "coasted through," but he was bored with school.

After graduating and marrying, he started college. But college, too, proved to be boring and not much of a challenge.

One night, while at a social function with his wife, Bruce was introduced to the owner of a local security firm. After a brief conversation he was offered a job. His response was, "Is it inside?" Since leaving college he had been working as a laborer in the snow and cold and wanted more comfortable employment. Bruce learned that the business owner was thinking of getting out of the business in a couple of years and that if Bruce went to work for him, he would have the opportunity to purchase the business.

Bruce didn't know anything about the security business, but he did know that he wanted to be his own boss. Several dead-end jobs and constant exposure to the elements had convinced him he wanted to give orders, not take them. Although the offer sounded too good to be true, Bruce accepted it.

He jumped right into his new job, making significant contributions almost immediately. His boss was amazed to see such a young man tackle tasks no one else had accomplished, such

COMSTOCK IMAGES

COURTESY OF BRUCE HILL

COURTESY OF BRUCE HILL

as computerizing the administrative work. True to the owner's promise, less than two years later Bruce and another employee were given the opportunity to buy the business. The owner told them they had six months to decide.

Over the next few months Bruce used his accounting expertise to evaluate the business. He concluded the company was solid and potentially very profitable. There was one catch: where would he get his share of the down payment? Although the owner was willing to carry the note himself, he required a substantial payment up front. By mortgaging their home, Bruce's parents came through with the necessary capital. Bruce Hill, 22-year-old entrepreneur, was born. Already the astute businessman, he held a 51 percent position in the new venture.

Superior Alarm, Inc., is a company that installs, services, and monitors alarm systems. Although profit is made from the sale and installation of alarm systems, the company's real bread and butter is its monitoring function. After a system is installed, the customer pays a monthly fee to have it monitored. The volume of people paying regular monitoring fees yields a healthy profit.

As happens with many entrepreneurs, the demands of business eventually took their toll. A rift developed between the two partners. As if that were not trouble enough, husband and wife also drifted apart. Ultimately both partnership and marriage were dissolved.

For the next 10 years Bruce built a strong business while raising two kids by himself. One philosophy that came to permeate everything Bruce did was that family must come first. This is evident in his management style, which treats long-term employees more like family than employees.

The best description of Bruce's management style is "interconnected flat." All employees are cross-trained so that if an employee is absent, the job still gets done. Bruce uses the analogy of a circle in which all employees are holding hands. One employee is just as important as another. If one person steps out of the circle, the circle becomes smaller, but all necessary jobs are still taken care of. Employees are self-directed and may call something to the attention of any other employee, including Bruce.

Another aspect of Bruce's management style is that he treats people the way he wants to be treated. In any contract negotiation he asks himself, "If I were the other guy, would I feel the contract is fair?"

Superior Alarm has a written marketing plan in which the main strategy is word-of-mouth promotion. Any advertising is designed for name recognition only. Unlike others in the security business, Superior Alarm refuses to stoop to scare tactics in its promotion.

Bruce's community involvement also generates company publicity. Activities include serving as city councilman, Kiwanis Club member, and vice president for the Junior College Baseball World Series held in Grand Junction every spring. Bruce attributes about 30 percent of his business to contacts made through this involvement. He is quick to add, however, that service to his hometown, not profit, is the reason he participates.

Bruce's overall business strategy is one of wise and efficient money management. He stresses that a business is smarter if it saves for what it wants instead of paying interest rates. "I despise debt," he says. He feels that part of what is wrong with government and business today is the tendency to borrow and go into debt instead of paying as they go.

Bruce has this advice for young entrepreneurs: "All work must be checked and double-checked every time, quality has to be the first and foremost concern, enter business with a long-term perspective, be timely in all aspects of business, and above all else, stand behind your word."

When asked to rate his success on a scale of 1 to 10, with 10 being high, Bruce rates himself a 6. "If I say I'm a 10, I'm done, I'm history, I'm out of here, I'm on my way down. I have to try harder every day, keep refining it. My worst competition is myself. As soon as I say I'm an expert or I'm great, somebody will roll over me."

If Bruce Hill's worst competition is himself, his best employee and best ally are also himself. He has made Superior Alarm immensely successful. Its future rests squarely in his very capable hands.

Chapter 5

Develop the Marketing Plan

Objectives

5-1 Explain the marketing concept.

5-2 Discuss target marketing and market segmentation.

5-3 Explain the role of product, place, price, and promotion in a marketing plan.

5-4 Analyze the process involved in the development of marketing strategies.

THE MARKETING CONCEPT

To be successful, entrepreneurs must develop effective marketing plans. But first they must have a full understanding of the marketing concept.

The **marketing concept** is the belief that consumer wants and needs are the driving force behind any product development or marketing effort. There was a time when producers, such as automobile manufacturers, designed and produced their products with little regard to consumer wants and needs. Decisions were made primarily on investment reasoning. With little competition in the marketplace, it worked. Consumers were forced to purchase what was available, not necessarily what they desired. That has changed greatly in the past 50 years. Consumers are more educated, and competition has increased, particularly in regards to globalization. Consumers now expect to have their needs satisfied and can choose from a much broader array of goods than ever before.

The United States has evolved from a product-driven market to a consumer-driven market. A business owner who believes he or she can survive simply by introducing a product or service to the market quickly learns that the product is only part of the concept. The marketing concept works to the advantage of small business owners, who know their customers better than large businesses do. They can communicate on a more personal level and can be more flexible and more responsive in satisfying customer needs.

Market Research

Developing a marketing plan starts with a market research process designed to learn as much about the potential customer as possible. The American Marketing Association defines **marketing research** as "the systematic gathering, recording, and analyzing of data about problems relating to the marketing of goods and services." Marketing research requires completing six steps.

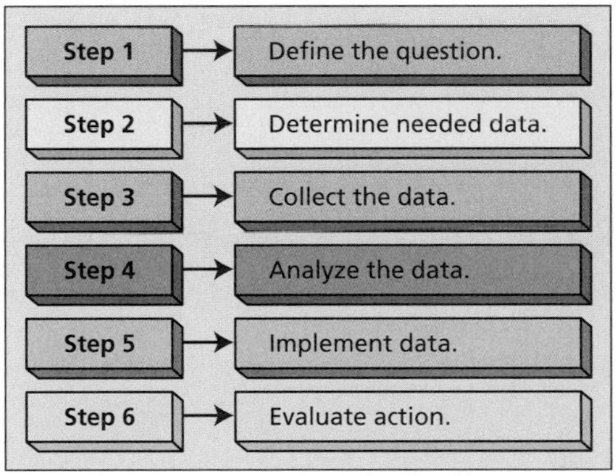

FIGURE 5-1 *Marketing Research Steps*

Step 1	Define the question.
Step 2	Determine needed data.
Step 3	Collect the data.
Step 4	Analyze the data.
Step 5	Implement data.
Step 6	Evaluate action.

Step 1 Define the Question Entrepreneurs often have concerns or are not sure about certain aspects of their business. By putting their concerns into words, they define the question that will be the focus of the research. A typical question entrepreneurs ask themselves is, "Which people are likely to buy from my business?"

Step 2 Determine What Data Is Needed After the question has been determined, data must be collected to provide the answer. Entrepreneurs must determine what kind of data will be the most helpful. Not all data will provide the needed information. For example, data about the number of customers who visit a certain mall each year does not indicate what those customers purchase.

Step 3 Collect the Data Entrepreneurs determine if there is a market for a product or service by collecting and studying information about consumers in the desired market. In a demographic study, data is collected about the age, employment status, education, per capita income, ethnic ratio, gender ratio, and economic stability of the target population. The **psychographics** of the market should also be researched. Are the people socially active, or do they tend to stay at home? Do they have a lot of leisure time? The answers to these questions will be important in determining if the intended product or service can be sold successfully to this market.

If the product or service is industry oriented, such as surgical equipment for hospitals, the entrepreneur should conduct a study of the targeted industry. Such a study would include the number of potential customers in the industry, their locations, and their sizes in terms of sales revenues and number of employees. It is also helpful to learn the particulars of the industry, such as economic trends and which companies are the leaders.

The collected information will include primary and secondary data. **Primary data** is original research data often collected through surveys and questionnaires. **Secondary data** is available at the local chamber of commerce, library, or community college in the form of published information about the number of people living in a community, average education level, per capita income, and gender ratios. Secondary data is also readily available through the Internet. An entrepreneur who wants to learn more about potential new markets for a chain of shoe stores, for example, could collect and analyze the information shown in Tables 5-1 through 5-6.

Table 5-1 is an example of how secondary data collected from a chamber of commerce can be useful. It is a population chart for the five communities that make up Spring County. It shows the population of each community in 1990 and 2000 and the projected population for 2010.

In addition to focusing on specific communities, entrepreneurs should collect data about geographic areas larger than the intended market so they can understand the total picture. In this case, data can be collected about Spring County, the surrounding counties, and other cities in the state.

TABLE 5-1 COMMUNITY POPULATION ESTIMATES

Community	1990	2000	2010
Spruce City	52,000	75,000	99,000
Wallington	25,000	28,000	31,000
Henry	17,600	17,800	17,500
Riceville	24,300	26,300	28,500
Newton	33,600	39,500	47,400
TOTALS	152,500	186,600	223,400

Step 4 Analyze the Data After compiling primary and secondary data, entrepreneurs must analyze the information in a systematic manner. The analysis should include both the results and an interpretation of those results. All useful data should be included. A thorough analysis and interpretation can provide answers to many kinds of questions.

Table 5-1 not only provides basic population figures but also shows a growth pattern. You can see what areas of the county are growing the fastest and which are likely to continue growing. If a business is to grow, the entrepreneur must consider what may happen five or ten years down the road.

The information in Tables 5-1 and 5-2 tells you that Spruce City's population is young, densely populated, centrally located, and growing faster than

TABLE 5-2 AGE AND ETHNIC STRUCTURE						
Community	**Median Age**	**White non-Hispanic (%)**	**African American (%)**	**Asian (%)**	**Hispanic (%)**	**Native American (%)**
Spruce City	32.1	87.5	6.9	1.6	2.3	1.7
Wallington	34.5	91.6	4.4	0.0	1.8	2.2
Henry	37.0	83.2	10.5	3.3	0.7	2.3
Riceville	42.5	76.4	14.6	4.8	0.0	4.2
Newton	38.4	92.0	3.2	1.2	2.6	1.0

the population of any other community in the county. The information in Tables 5-3, 5-4, and 5-5 tells you that the county head-of-household income and per capita income are higher than average and are expected to continue to grow. These facts are positive indicators for opening a new business in Spruce City in Spring County.

A county map is useful in determining the best location for a new business. By pinpointing the county's population centers, the entrepreneur can estimate the traveling time between populated areas and determine the accessibility of the business to potential customers.

TABLE 5-3 AVERAGE HEAD-OF-HOUSEHOLD INCOME BY COUNTY	
County	**Average Income**
Jackson	$20,427
Spring	19,978
Concord	19,865
Wilson	18,696
Newton	18,480
Walton	18,205
Cory	17,680
Denton	17,435

TABLE 5-4 INCOME GROWTH. TOP 8 CITIES IN STATE	
City	**Income Growth (%)**
Springfield	38.8
Smithville	37.8
Winston	37.0
Spruce City	35.4
Canton	34.7
Jonesborough	31.8
Green City	31.5
Howard	29.6

TABLE 5-5 PER CAPITA INCOME, TOP 5 COUNTIES IN STATE			
County	**1990**	**2000**	**2010**
Atlas	$12,940	$15,540	$19,500
Spring	12,861	15,120	19,380
Desmond	12,140	14,800	18,700
Concord	11,985	13,980	17,310
Pacific	11,620	13,870	16,940

Another information ingredient of value to entrepreneurs is a breakdown of sales in the county by industry classification. By comparing the information in Table 5-6 with the same information from other counties, an entrepreneur can tell which categories of products sell better in Spring County. Industry sources can often provide information on the average per capita sales of a product or service in the national or regional market. The same sources may also be able to help an entrepreneur determine how many customers it will take to support the new business under consideration. This information will tell the entrepreneur if sales of the product in the intended market are higher or lower than the national, regional, and local marketplaces.

TABLE 5-6 COUNTY ANNUAL SALES, BY INDUSTRY CLASSIFICATION

Store Type	Total Sales	Per Capita Sales
Restaurants	$7,340,000	$389.71
Apparel	3,419,000	182.61
Furniture	1,760,000	89.89
Shoes	792,000	40.18
Records, music	388,000	20.16
Gifts/novelties	313,000	16.85

Step 5 Implement the Data The next step in the market research process is to use the research data to make a decision and develop a plan of action.

For example, a shoe store is a good possibility in Spring County. The research shows a growing population with a higher-than-normal per capita income, indicating a healthy economy. Further research would show the average spent per capita on shoes in Spring County, $40.18, is below the national average, $42, and slightly below that of the neighboring county, suggesting a shortage of shoe outlets. It is possible to carry the research quite a bit further. It can be used to forecast potential sales and to determine if the shoe store should be large and located in a centrally located community, or small, more specialized, and in a smaller community.

Step 6 Evaluate Action The last step in the market research process is evaluation. Entrepreneurs should not be satisfied with just developing a plan of action. The actions taken as a result of the plan should be evaluated regularly after implementation.

To be sure the market research will accomplish its purpose, the entrepreneur should consider the following:

1. Demographic information is only valuable if compared to the same information for other markets.
2. The process of market research should be ongoing, because the marketplace is constantly changing. It is important to stay informed about current events and changes in the marketplace and continually try to project what may happen next.
3. To keep up with and take advantage of market changes requires knowledge. Knowledge is the result of research.
4. Determination and creativity are necessary for success.

TARGET MARKETING

Identifying the customer begins with **market segmentation**. Since small businesses do not serve mass markets, the entrepreneur must determine which portion of the market is most likely to buy the product or service offered. An example of market segmentation would be to separate country western music fans from those who listen to hard rock and classifying the listeners as different market segments. Markets can be segmented on the basis of who benefits from the product or service, age, geographic location, or other demographic or psychographic factor.

After completing a general marketing segmentation process, entrepreneurs go a step further by targeting their particular market or **niche**. It is imperative that the small business target its marketing efforts to a small and manageable segment of the market that can be effectively reached and influenced. Entrepreneurs need to make sure, however, that the targeted market is stable, permanent, and large enough to support the business.

Properly identifying a new business's ideal customer is a very important step in writing an accurate business plan. Creating a **customer profile** tells the entrepreneur to whom the marketing plan should be directed. This group is the **target market** and should be quite narrowly defined. Think of the customer profile as the center of a target. The marketing arrow is aimed at the bull's eye, with some ripple effect, or overflow, onto the outer rings. The outer rings represent customers who have some of the characteristics of the ideal customer and who might buy the product. Since small businesses do not have the capital to attract the mass market through mass media advertising, they must concentrate their efforts on the group of customers most likely to buy their goods and services. This is target marketing. Once the target market is determined, the business can start to develop a marketing plan to attract this segment of the market.

The identification of the target market allows the business owner to select a specific product style or type—for instance, designer clothes versus everyday wear—determine an acceptable price, find a proper location, and select the appropriate promotional tools to communicate with the customer. If the target market is incorrectly identified, the entire business plan will be incorrectly projected.

FIGURE 5-2 *Customer Profile*

Male, 25-30 years old

High school graduate
Annual salary range, $20,000–25,000
Married, with two young children
Owns home, two cars
Hobbies: automobile maintenance
fishing
hunting
spectator sports
movies
camping
Enjoys: working with hands/outdoors
time with family, travel
Appeal to safety, self-esteem, and self-actualization needs.

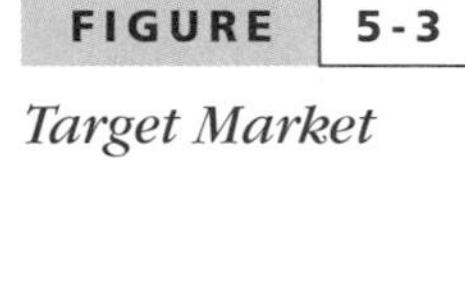

FIGURE 5-3 *Target Market*

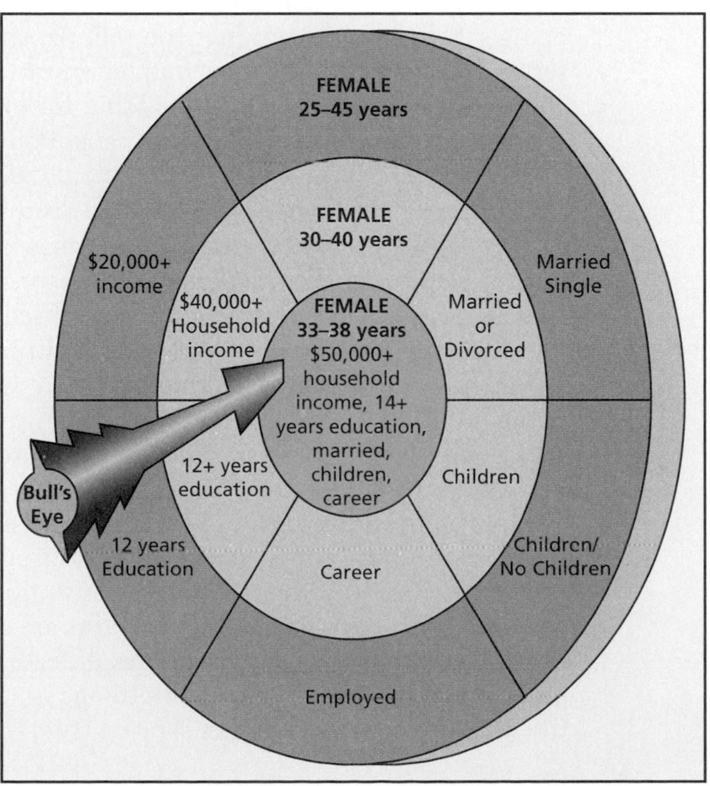

THE FOUR P'S OF THE MARKETING MIX

The four P's of the **marketing mix**—product, place, price, and promotion—are the heart of a marketing plan for any business, large or small. Small businesses take a different and more personal approach to the four P's than large businesses do (Figure 5-4).

FIGURE 5-4

The Marketing Mix

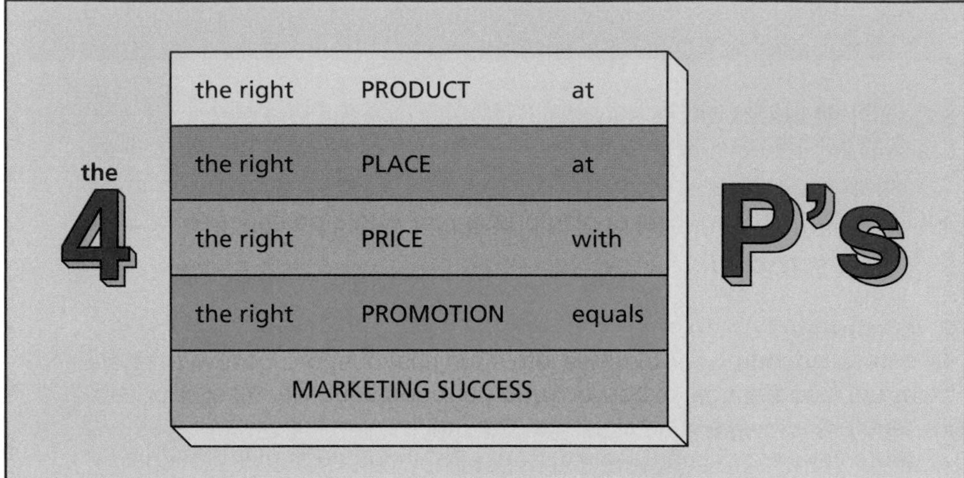

the 4 P's
the right PRODUCT at
the right PLACE at
the right PRICE with
the right PROMOTION equals
MARKETING SUCCESS

Product

Product is a marketing tool if you are able to convince consumers that your product best satisfies their needs. Every product has both tangible features (things you can see and touch) and intangible features (things you feel). A product is much more than the item you take off the shelf. The total product also includes the packaging, the warranty, and all other elements intended to satisfy consumer needs. It is essential to understand the needs being satisfied by the product you sell. An expensive, designer-label gown serves a different need than a simpler, more practical dress. One is purchased for a special occasion, the other for everyday wear. Before you can develop a marketing plan, you must know the need your product will satisfy.

Your next step is to narrow your focus to the specific products you will offer. A bookstore owner must decide what books to stock. If she makes the wrong decision for her marketplace, the consumers will find other outlets. Not all products in her **product mix** will sell equally well. Best-sellers will outsell American history books, but she must carry some history books if she is truly consumer driven, because there will always be some consumers with a need for history books. The challenge is to determine how large a selection of history books will be sufficient to satisfy the needs of her marketplace.

In a consumer-driven business, entrepreneurs recognize that they must include products in their product mix that may not be profitable from a sales standpoint but that create the perception that their store "has it all." It is often said that 80 percent of profits are derived from 20 percent of the products. Although the exact figures differ from industry to industry, the basic premise that a minority percentage of the product selection makes up the majority of sales revenues is often true.

Place

Place—the exchange point of a product—is an effective marketing tool if the business can create the perception that the product is easy to acquire. The entrepreneur has to make sure that the right product is in the right place at the right time. In retailing, the product must be on the shelves ready to be sold when the consumer walks into the store. If it isn't, then all the marketing planning in the world will not make the business a success.

A manufacturer must decide the best way to get the product into the hands of the consumer. The available distribution networks are called **channels of distribution** (Figure 5-5).

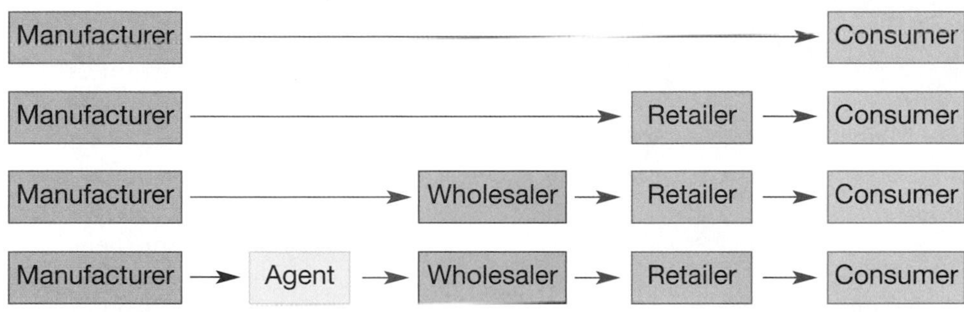

FIGURE 5-5

Channels of Distribution

FUN FACTS

The number of U.S. companies exporting goods has increased more than 200 percent in the past 10 years. (U.S. Department of Commerce)

One option is for the manufacturer to sell directly to the consumer. The product can be sold through the Internet, television infomercials, direct mailing pieces such as catalogs, or media advertising. It would certainly appear to be the most cost-effective option, as there are no middlemen. However, it may not reach the sales objective.

Another possibility is to create a sales force to sell to retail stores, which then pass the product on to the final consumer. Although this channel is more expensive than selling directly to the consumer, it offers potentially far more sales opportunities.

If a large market is anticipated, the manufacturer might sell the product to a wholesaler, who then sells to a retailer, who sells to the final consumer. This method is particularly appealing when large bulk amounts are involved, as the wholesaler buys in large quantities and breaks those down into more manageable quantities for the retailer. It adds another middleman at greater expense, but it may also add substantially to sales and allow the manufacturer to produce more, thereby lowering the cost of unit production. Manufacturing in greater quantities to lower unit cost is called **economies of scale**. Often economies of scale offset the cost of adding middlemen to the channel of distribution and can even add to profits.

A final option for distribution is for the manufacturer not to get involved at all with the marketing or distributing efforts but to turn those responsibilities over to an agent. This is often done in overseas marketing. The domestic company may not understand the peculiarities of the foreign marketplace and uses a host country agent to represent the company.

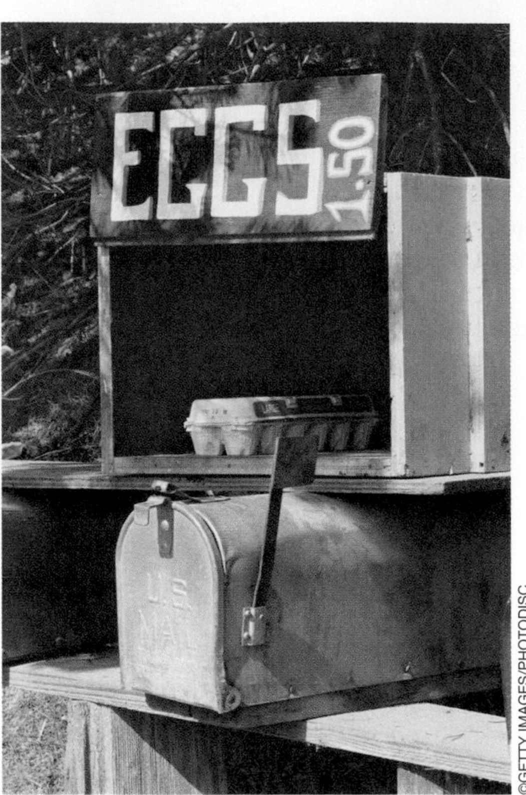

©GETTY IMAGES/PHOTODISC

Price

Price is the marketing tool that sells value to the consumer. The price charged must be low enough that the consumer will want to buy, but high enough for the entrepreneur to make a reasonable profit. Often entrepreneurs are not careful to protect their profit margins and end up setting their prices too low. An adequate profit margin must be built into the marketing plan.

Successful small business owners know their product and customers better than large businesses do. Because of this they generally do better work, are more flexible, and offer more services. Consequently they should be able to receive a fair price for their product or service, not a discounted one. When they do not receive full value for their efforts, they cannot make the necessary profits to sustain their business for the long term.

Setting a price demands that the business owner

1. Cover the cost of the products or services sold, including the cost of acquiring and receiving them
2. Cover the cost of all business operating expenses
3. Make sure that profits are sufficient to pay the owner a fair salary for efforts and risk invested
4. Retain a certain portion of the revenue for future expansion and improvement of the business
5. Entice customers to return because of the high value they perceive for the prices charged

When price is an effective marketing tool, there is no reason to hide it. Good pricing tells your customers that you are proud of what you sell and that they will be pleased with the exchange.

Promotion

Promotion is the way a business communicates with its market. Good communication tools are very important to marketing success and should be built into the marketing plan. It is through promotion that the entrepreneur informs the potential customer about the product or service. Promotion includes advertising, sales promotion, personal selling, visual merchandising, and public relations. These activities are termed the **promotional mix**.

Advertising Although considered by many to be an expensive part of starting and operating a business, advertising is a sales tool that cannot be ignored by entrepreneurs offering products or services directly to consumers. **Advertising** is defined as a paid-for, nonpersonal presentation of a sales-enticing message. Small business owners should look at it as a personal presentation, however, since they are closer to their customers and know them better than large businesses do.

There are several reasons advertising is so important.

- Advertising lets customers know that the new business exists and where it is located.
- Advertising informs customers about the products or services that the business offers.
- Advertising provides ongoing communication with the customer.
- Advertising keeps the business's name in front of the buying public.

As an entrepreneur, you must select the form of advertising that best suits your business. The most common forms of advertising are newspaper, radio, and television. All three media reach a large audience but can be quite expensive, so a decision to use any of them for advertising must be made carefully. Other types of advertising you might consider are yellow pages ads, direct mail, billboards, Internet pop-ups, and specialty advertising. Examples of specialty advertising are calendars or key chains with the business name imprinted on them. (Advertising is discussed in greater detail in Chapter 11.)

Sales Promotion To ensure effective **sales promotion**, entrepreneurs must understand the communication channel. The communication channel, illustrated in Figure 5-6, consists of five steps or points in the sending of a message: message sender, encoding, message vehicle, decoding, and message receiver. The message sender decides what message is to be relayed, creates the message (encoding), and determines the best method for relaying the message (written, verbal, or by means of a second person). Once sent, the message is interpreted (decoded) and absorbed by the message receiver. The sender waits for the feedback, or response, from the receiver. The feedback might be a returned message or an action taken as a result of the message.

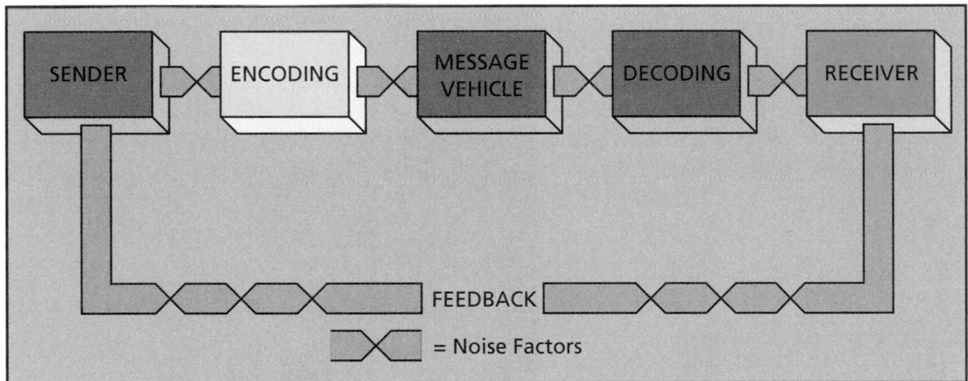

FIGURE 5-6

The Communication Channel

In sales promotion, the entrepreneur is a message sender hoping for a positive response from the message receiver, such as confirmation of a sale. To maintain an effective communication channel, the entrepreneur must recognize that distortions and interruptions will disrupt the messages. The distortions, called "noise factors," impose severe limitations on how intended messages are received and interpreted. A simple analogy is the game of sending a message around a group—each person whispers the message to the next person, who then passes it along to the next, and so on. The message received by the last person usually bears little resemblance to the original message. In sales promotion, noise factors are any interruption of or distraction from a sales message.

In sales promotion, the best way to get a message across is through repetition. The more times a message is sent, the better the chances that it will be received in its intended form. This is why advertisements are repeated many times. The advertiser believes that with continual and repetitive exposure, the intended message will eventually get through the noise factors and be received in its intended format, resulting in more sales.

One of the most common tools for sales promotion currently used by businesses is coupons. Businesses give away coupons to their target customers through newspapers, magazines, direct mail materials, free samples, and free gifts. The smart entrepreneur chooses sales promotion tools carefully. Because they can be very expensive, sales promotions should be focused, well planned, and well implemented.

Personal Selling The importance of personal selling to the success of a business cannot be overstated. Customers are more likely to purchase a product or service from knowledgeable people they like and trust. New business owners may hire salespeople or have family members help out, but they often do most of the personal selling themselves because they generally have few employees and they usually know the product better than anyone else. With their confidence, determination, and need to achieve, entrepreneurs are often natural salespeople.

The selling process involves six steps.

1. ***Approach*** This is the technique used to introduce the product and make the transition into the sales presentation.
2. ***Presentation*** A carefully orchestrated declaration of the features, advantages, and benefits of the product follows the initial approach.
3. ***Handling objections*** Objections or possible resistance should be anticipated by the salesperson. Answers and solutions should be practiced in advance of the presentation.
4. ***Trial close*** A good salesperson learns how to test the waters to determine if the customer is prepared to buy. If the time does not appear to be right, the salesperson goes back to the presentation or makes sure all objections have been overcome.
5. ***Close*** A sale is not complete until the purchaser declares his or her intent to buy. It takes a certain skill to ask for the order in the proper way and close the sale.

6. ***Follow-up*** In many sales situations the buyer may feel **cognitive dissonance**—that is, uncertainty as to whether the purchase was the correct one to make. Good salespeople know how to follow up a purchase with a personal compliment, a thank you note, or even a telephone call. This may also be a good time to set the stage for the next appointment.

There are many sales programs, courses, and books available on effective selling techniques. Selling takes knowledge not only of the product but of the proper technique. The entrepreneur is the number-one salesperson in the small business and must make sure that all personnel are taught how to sell and feel confident in their approach.

FUN FACTS

Online retail marketing is experiencing about 200 percent annual growth. Internet sales accounted for approximately 6 percent of all sales during the 2003 Christmas selling season.

Visual Merchandising Window displays are a common form of **visual merchandising**. Interior uses of merchandise to attract customers attention are another form—for example, shadow boxes, display cases, and mannequins. Retail stores are not the only businesses that use visual merchandising. Wholesalers and manufacturers use product displays at trade shows to attract retailers. Displays are called "silent salespeople" and, if properly designed, can be a very valuable and affordable addition to the company's sales force.

Public Relations A complete marketing plan should include a strategy for public relations. **Public relations** (PR) consists of planned events that demonstrate the goodwill of a business. Often these are in the form of sponsorships or charitable volunteer work. Although these activities do not give an immediate feedback, they do give a long-run return in the form of customer and community attitude toward the business.

Good entrepreneurs often use PR to promote their businesses more directly. They learn what parts of their business might be of interest to the public and then keep the news media informed of any interesting developments. For example, a bridal shop receives a new line of bridal gowns and notifies the local newspaper, which runs a feature story about the latest bridal look available at that store.

The Global ENTREPRENEUR

The vast majority of U.S. entrepreneurs engaged in international trade start by developing a business relationship in Canada, Mexico, or the United Kingdom. The reasons are simple—language, geography, and cultural similarity. The most difficult aspect of international trade is developing a marketing plan that will work in a foreign country. Marketing efforts must be designed for markets often quite different from the domestic market. Entrepreneurs prefer to start out in countries with fewer language and cultural barriers before they move on to more complex situations. A business that starts with a simple export or import arrangement with a seller or supplier in Canada often matures into a multinational business with host-country sales representatives or distributors all over the world.

Think Critically

1. Describe a channel of distribution that would be effective for selling flags in Spain.
2. Call the consulate of a foreign country and request any materials they may have for potential international trade partners.

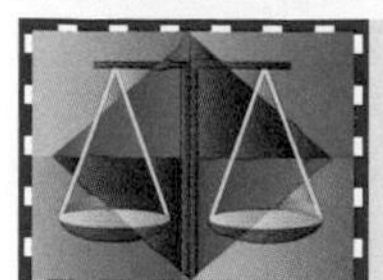

Ethics for ENTREPRENEURS

Ned and Barbara were working on a layout for their new housing development, called The Orchard. The centerpiece would be a restored farmhouse and barn, and the homes would have a rural, early-20th-century look. There would be a meadow, walking trails, and a covered bridge over a meandering stream. The development would include 50 home sites on small lots, rather closely clustered together.

Barbara gave Ned a final plan for his approval. He noticed that two spaces originally listed as lots for sale were labeled as parks.

"Barbara, what's the deal on these two lots? I thought we were going to sell them. You have them labeled as parks."

"I know, Ned. I thought we could show them as parks in the brochure in the beginning and sell them later, after we've sold most of the other lots. It will help our marketing if we show more green space."

"Isn't it illegal to misrepresent lots for sale as park space?"

"Not really. We aren't changing how they're legally listed at the county property tax office. I don't think any buyers will check the courthouse records about those two lots."

"I don't know, Barbara. Just because it's legal, is it ethical? We need to rethink these plans."

Think Critically

1. How would you feel if you bought a house lot beside what was advertised as a park, but was later sold as a lot for a home?
2. Cite examples of other legal actions in selling real estate that may not be ethical.

MARKETING STRATEGIES

Strategies are developed to accomplish goals. The goal of all new business start-ups is growth. Once the four P's are thoroughly analyzed, the entrepreneur can put together a strategy to gain growth by achieving a marketing superiority over the competition. Decisions must be made regarding where to buy the products or materials and how they will be shipped to the business. An appropriate inventory system must be designed to assure the right product is there at the right time. Final pricing decisions need to be made. Finally, a promotion plan to attract and keep customers must be created.

Implement Marketing Strategies

There are six steps to developing a complete marketing and promotional strategy.

Step 1 Establish an Advertising Budget A certain amount of advertising must be done to launch a new business. Entrepreneurs need to decide what kind of advertising will best serve their type of business. For assistance, the entrepreneur should contact the newspaper, radio station, or other media that will be used. Media specialists will be available to discuss schedules, costs, and other necessary information. A little extra time should be devoted to comparing the costs for different types of advertising as well as costs between competing media, such as two radio stations or two newspapers. The information from this investigation should be used to develop an advertising budget. Although the expense of advertising may seem excessive, it is a necessary expense.

If the entrepreneur feels there is no money available for advertising, it may be an indication that there isn't enough money to start the business. A delay in the start-up schedule should probably be considered.

Whatever the type of business, some form of "grand opening" advertising is usually recommended. The budget for this advertising is a one-time expense and should be separate from the operating advertising budget. If newspaper, radio, or television rates are too high, the entrepreneur may devote the advertising budget to direct mail pieces such as brochures, circulars, catalogs, or sales letters to potential customers.

New businesses would do well to consult with trade associations to determine the percentage of annual revenues normally spent on advertising. Suppliers can also be helpful, as they work with many businesses similar to the one the entrepreneur is planning.

Step 2 Plan and Schedule Advertising Once the advertising budget has been calculated, a plan should be developed. Working with the media specialists mentioned above, you should plan and schedule actual advertising. One key to successful advertising is consistency. It is recommended that you follow an advertising calendar laid out 6 to 12 months in advance that assures your business of regular, consistent exposure. The advertising expenditures for a retail store will ordinarily be higher for the holiday selling season, but advertising should also be scheduled for smaller events, such as a Labor Day sale, back-to-school events, white sales, Valentine's Day specials, and so on, that occur throughout the year (Figure 5-7).

Step 3 Make Decisions about Sales Promotions Entrepreneurs should make decisions about sales promotions well in advance of the planned opening of the business. For example, if you decide to use coupons as

Small Business Technology

Marketing web sites were originally listed on search engines according to how their content related to the subject being searched. But small e-commerce companies can no longer count on this exposure and have had to turn to "pay per hit" network support services. The service arranges for search engine listings and charges the company a fee (10¢ to $2 or more per hit) each time a potential customer clicks on its web site. The goal of most companies is to be listed among the top three, on the first page of a search listing.

FIGURE 5-7

Advertising Calendar

Dates To Remember

Month	Date	Event	Month	Date	Event
JANUARY	13–16	White Sale	**JULY**	14–15	Sidewalk Sale
	20–21	Sidewalk Sale			
FEBRUARY	14–	Valentine	**AUGUST**	15–30	Back to School Promotion
	20–	President's Day Sale			
MARCH	17–	St. Pat Promotion	**SEPTEMBER**	10–	Moonlight Madness Sale
	15–24	Easter Promotion			
APRIL	8–	Moonlight Madness Sale	**OCTOBER**	9–	Columbus Day Sale
	19–	Anniversary Sale		31–	Halloween
MAY	20–	Mother's Day	**NOVEMBER**	20–	Launch Xmas Program
				23–	Thanksgiving
	24–	Launch Wedding Promotion		30–	Pre-Xmas Sale
JUNE	10–	Bridal Fashion Show	**DECEMBER**	7–	Xmas Open House
	19–	Father's Day		26–	After Xmas Sale

promotional tools, you must design the coupons (or have them designed), contact printers to obtain quotes for the work, select a printer, order the coupons, and distribute them in time for the opening. This process can take weeks, even months, so planning is imperative for any promotional event your business sponsors during the opening or after it is well established. A grand opening is considered a major promotional event that must be planned months in advance.

Step 4 **Decide How Personal Selling Will Be Handled** Many decisions have to be made concerning personal selling, such as whether to hire salespeople, how many to hire, when to hire them, how to compensate them, and how to train them. These decisions and others should be made and implemented long before the business is open and ready for customers.

Step 5 **Create Visual Merchandising** If the new business is retail, visual merchandising will set the tone for the enterprise. The store owner cannot wait until the merchandise arrives. Decisions have to be made much earlier so that supplies and props can be purchased or constructed. If the entrepreneur is a manufacturer or wholesaler and plans to display his products at a trade show, it may be necessary to have a display backdrop customized, which takes considerable time.

Step 6 **Develop a Strategies Calendar** In addition to an advertising calendar, a more inclusive strategies calendar should be developed. A strategies calendar, such as the one in Figure 5-8, displays all marketing activities and their implementation strategies. It is a valuable tool that should be continuously updated as plans are developed and changed.

FIGURE 5-8

Strategies Calendar

Strategy	Begin Planning	Complete Planning	Implement Plan	Strategy Complete
1. Christmas open house	Sept. 1	Dec. 1	Dec. 10–12	3-day event—food, entertainment, men's evening Dec. 11
2. Valentine's Day contest	Jan. 2	Jan. 19	Jan. 20	Announce winner, award prize
3.				
4.				
5.				
6.				
7.				
8.				
9.				
10.				

Small Business Marketing Guidelines

The entrepreneur faces many challenges in defining the marketing plan, the primary one being less capital than is available to larger businesses. It takes creativity to compete and a certain amount of aggressiveness to get noticed. The best strategy is to use the advantage of knowing your customer better. In his book *Guerilla Marketing,* Arthur Levinson suggests that small business marketers

- Invest time, energy, and imagination, not just money
- Measure their success by making profits, not sales
- Use good sense to make up for experience
- Focus on excellence, not diversification
- Place emphasis on making larger transactions with existing customers and referrals, not just on adding new customers
- Use a combination of marketing strategies instead of just sticking to one that appears to work
- Look for free ways to promote the business
- Keep track of the number of relationships they establish, not just the number of sales
- Find ways to add drama to their promotional activities and products in order to get the customer's attention
- Invite their customers to get involved
- Communicate in a believable and clear manner

The marketing challenge is an exciting part of being an entrepreneur. Unit III will describe specific tools for taking on the competition. It is enough for now to understand the importance of creating a well-defined plan that will guide the business and provide the momentum for future growth. No business can survive without an exciting marketing concept in today's competitive marketplace.

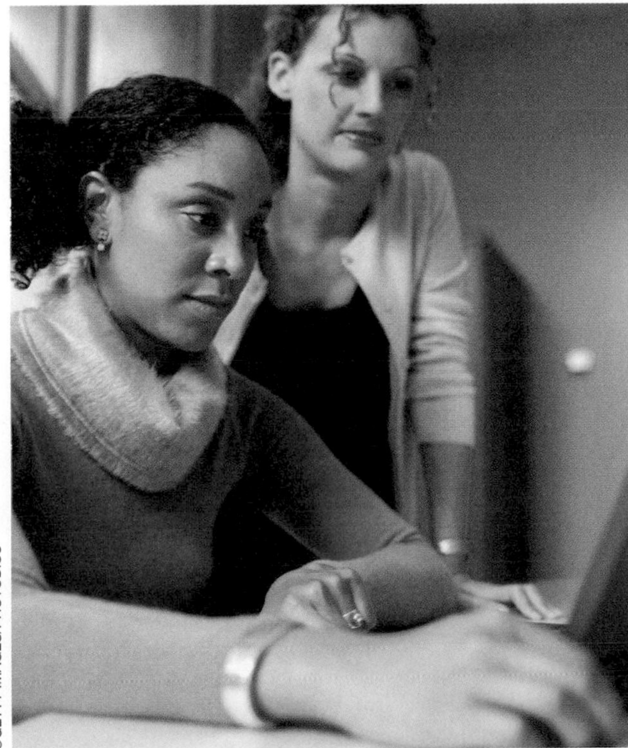

Ship in a BOTTLE

Looking for the Target Market

Fred realized that his initial visits to stores, the trial web site, and the numerous direct mail letters he had sent out were the elements of a market research study. He had taken careful notes as he proceeded. The results thus far:

35 stores visited, 8 sales: 5 to nautical gift shops, 2 to a museum gift store, and 1 to a general gift store.

50 letters with product photos mailed: 20 to nautical-theme gift stores, 10 to nautical museum gift stores, 10 to general gift and souvenir stores, and 10 to seafood restaurants. 12 responses for more information were returned: 8 from nautical-theme gift stores, 2 from museum stores, 2 from gift stores, and none from the restaurants.

Although he realized that these limited results were far from conclusive, a trend was starting to show. Certainly nautical gift shops were very interested, particularly in coastal towns. Museum gift stores showed promise and needed to be researched further. Gift shops were potential buyers, but he would have to determine what type of gift store would have the greatest interest. Using ships-in-bottles as decorations or retail items had apparently not appealed to the seafood restaurants. Fred also had some other ideas he wanted to investigate.

The Internet results at this point were not consistent, nor did they show much of a pattern. The first 50 purchases were about equally divided between people buying gifts and people buying for themselves. The average purchase price was approximately $75, which pleased Fred. Buyers were happy to answer his questions about how they found the site, whom they were purchasing for, and what other items they were seeking. All were delighted to find his unique product, as they had been searching for it without success for some time.

At this point Fred was quite optimistic. If he could find a way to contact the right type of gift shops, design and produce a professional-looking brochure for direct mail, and get noticed on the Internet, he was sure the business would be successful. He needed to draw up a marketing plan that would help him accomplish these goals. He hoped the upcoming gift trade show would teach him more about the wholesale gift market and give him a sense of the best target for his marketing emphasis.

Fred felt he had learned enough to design an effective product brochure. He met with a graphics design expert, Kiki Pollard, and discussed ideas for product layout and photos. Two weeks later Kiki presented a 3.5 x 8.5-inch triple-fold brochure that showed over 50 models in various sizes. It was attractive and would fit in a standard-size mailing envelope, which was important for controlling mailing costs. Kiki would design two price-list inserts (one wholesale, one retail) so that the one brochure could be used for both intended markets. It was agreed that an initial run of 1,000 would be produced at a cost of $2,500, plus a $500 fee for Kiki's work. The brochure would be completed in time to distribute at the gift show the following month.

The goal of getting properly launched and listed on the Internet was an area in which Fred did not feel completely comfortable. Although he was not computer illiterate, he did not feel he could design a web site that would attract potential customers and stand up to the competition. He arranged an appointment with Dick Crooks, a professional webmaster. Dick reviewed the temporary website that Johann and Fred had initially put together and went to work redesigning it into a more customer-friendly site. He reshot many of the photos, added automatic enlarge and

continued

order clicks, listed easy-to-use contact information, and developed a great-looking home page. The total design and launch fee was $3,000. Included was the task of making sure that the various web services would show "Ship in a Bottle" in their information source list. The marketing plan was starting to take shape. Fred believed it would take six months and at least two gift-show exhibits before he could develop a complete and consistent plan.

Think Critically

1. Develop a preliminary customer profile of Fred's target market.
2. What other primary and secondary sources of data can Fred pursue?
3. What other market possibilities should Fred investigate?

Summary

Before entrepreneurs can begin developing a marketing plan, they must understand the marketing concept. They should follow the six-step approach to market research: defining the question, determining what data is needed, collecting the data, analyzing the data, implementing the data, and evaluating actions. With the data they have collected, they can then segment the market into manageable groups of potential consumers with similar characteristics and needs. Additional information allows entrepreneurs to target a very specialized group of customers. The final step is creating a customer profile that describes the ideal customer for the planned business.

For effective planning, decisions must be made regarding the marketing mix, or the four P's: product, price, place, and promotion. Successful entrepreneurs know the product, understand the role of the price, select an effective channel of distribution to make sure the product is in the right place at the right time, and implement an effective promotion plan. The promotion part of the mix includes advertising, sales promotion, personal selling, and public relations.

Once the marketing plan is developed, the entrepreneur has a number of marketing strategies to implement: establishing an advertising budget, planning and scheduling advertising, creating a sales promotion program, deciding how to handle personal selling, creating visual merchandising, and developing a strategies calendar.

The ultimate goal of the business is to offer a product or service to potential customers at a convenient location and at an affordable price, so the business will make a profit. If all this happens, both the consumer and the business owner will be satisfied.

As each strategy is completed, the dream of being a successful business owner is one step closer to becoming a reality.

A Case in POINT

Selecting a Personal Shopper

Ingrid Harrison plans to open a business in three months. Her business will offer what she considers a needed service in her community: customized shopping for senior citizens who wish to avoid the inconvenience of going to the grocery store or are simply unable to go themselves.

After researching her community, Ingrid has collected the following data:

Twenty percent of the city's population are senior citizens. The current city population is 115,000.

The average annual income of each senior citizen household is $25,000.

Most senior citizens (80 percent) live in the same section of town, the south side, because of the concentration of retirement housing there.

Although Ingrid knows that she wants to sell her services as a personal shopper, she hasn't decided what specific services senior citizens would be willing to buy.

Think Critically

1. Do you think Ingrid's idea will work? Why or why not?
2. What would you suggest Ingrid do to determine the specific services she should offer?
3. What other demographic and psychographic information might be useful to Ingrid in developing her marketing plan?

Vocabulary Builder

Write a brief definition of each word or phrase.

1. advertising
2. channels of distribution
3. cognitive dissonance
4. customer profile
5. economies of scale
6. marketing concept
7. marketing mix
8. marketing research
9. market segmentation
10. niche
11. primary data
12. product mix
13. promotion
14. promotional mix
15. psychographics
16. public relations
17. sales promotion
18. secondary data
19. target market
20. visual merchandising

Review the Concepts

21. Describe the marketing concept.
22. What are the six steps of marketing research?
23. What is the difference between primary and secondary data?
24. Describe the four P's of the marketing mix.
25. What is meant by communication channel "noise" factors?
26. What are the steps of the selling process?

Critical Thinking

27. Explain why correctly identifying a business's target market is essential to writing an accurate business plan.
28. Discuss the various elements of a demographic study and how they can be applied to determining if a market is suitable for a new business.
29. How is it possible to add middlemen to the distribution channel and at the same time increase the profit margin?
30. What should be included in a customer profile?
31. Create a 12-month strategies calendar for a new bridal shop.

Project

Build Your Business Plan

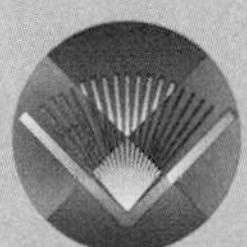

At this point in your business plan it is time to start building a marketing plan. It should start with a list of information that you will need to collect in order to do market research. You should also design a preliminary market strategies calendar, taking into consideration all parts of the marketing mix.

1. Describe a demographic study of the market you are researching.
2. Explain how each of the four P's relates to your intended business.
3. Create a strategic marketing and advertising calendar for the first 12 months of the business.
4. Develop an approximate budget for your grand opening event and your annual advertising expenditures.

Many of these steps will be defined in more detail later on in the course. However, it is important at this point to lay out a preliminary plan of action.

Chapter 6

Conduct the Industry Analysis

Objectives

6-1 Define industry analysis.

6-2 Discuss the influence of market size on business planning.

6-3 Analyze demographic issues and how they affect the business planning process.

6-4 Discuss the role of economic issues in an industry analysis.

6-5 Explain how industry trends are important to business planning.

6-6 Explain how laws and legal issues impact an industry.

6-7 Discuss the impact of ecological issues on an industry.

6-8 Discuss how technological issues impact an industry.

6-9 Describe barriers to entry into an industry and the factors that make an industry attractive.

6-10 Explain the importance of a thorough industry analysis.

INDUSTRY ANALYSIS

Industry analysis is a form of exploratory business research that examines the overall condition of a particular industry. Your industry is made up of the companies providing products and services similar to yours.

It is essential that you, as an entrepreneur, complete an industry analysis as part of the business planning process. You should become an expert in your chosen industry. Understanding and anticipating the various conditions of your industry will form the foundation for success in the future.

Sources of Information

An industry analysis is no better than the resources used to gather the information. Where does the entrepreneur start such a daunting process?

One of the authors maintains a comprehensive Internet site for use by entrepreneurs preparing a business plan. The site is accessible from the textbook web site and contains industry and company information under the Resource Links section.

Other sources of industry analysis include libraries and library web sites, investment firms, business and trade periodicals, trade associations, government agencies, and numerous others. Talk to people in the same business or industry. Read industry-specific publications. Attend trade fairs and seminars. Gather as much information as possible.

The following are a few major sources of industry information. Use an Internet search engine to locate current electronic addresses.

Current Industrial Reports from the U.S. Census Bureau The Census Bureau's Internet site contains a wealth of information. Since 1904, the Current Industrial Reports (CIR) program has provided monthly, quarterly, and annual measures of industrial activity. The primary objective of the CIR program is to produce timely, accurate data on the production and shipments of selected products. CIR surveys measure manufacturing activity in important commodity areas such as textiles and apparel, chemicals, primary metals, computer and electronic components, industrial equipment, aerospace equipment, and consumer goods. These data are used to help formulate economic policy and for market analysis, forecasting, and decision-making in the private sector.

Table 6-1 is an example of the type of information available about the apparel industry, including business ventures at both the manufacturing and retail levels. The apparel industry was selected here because of its popularity with many entrepreneurs.

TABLE 6-1 SUMMARY OF PRODUCTION AND VALUE OF SHIPMENTS FOR APPAREL

Product Description	Year-to-date 2003	
	Quantity (in thousands of units)	Value (in millions of dollars)
Total	1,787,649	11,977.4
Men's and boys' apparel		
Suits	2,045	229.9
Coats	10,404	439.1
Tops	478,824	1,566.8
Bottoms	186,563	2,297.8
Underwear and nightwear	135,316	272.5
Other garments	30,267	382.5
Women's and girls' apparel		
Dresses	56,382	1,188.1
Coats	5,920	154.5
Tops	229,954	1,571.9
Bottoms	181,472	1,817.4
Underwear and nightwear	362,327	1,187.9
Other garments	54,897	670.1
Infants' apparel		
Dresses	1,287	14.3
Sets	1,607	10.1
Pants and shorts	8,179	30.4
Play clothing	6,763	28.7

Business.com This resource for entrepreneurial planning covers over 28 industries and provides a directory of industry web sites. Developed by a team of industry experts and library scientists, the directory contains more than 400,000 listings within 25,000 industry, product, and service subcategories. Its stated mission is "to help you, the business professional, find exactly what you're looking for."

Hoover's Online According to the company web site, Hoover's, Inc. delivers comprehensive company, industry, and market intelligence that drives business growth. Its database lists 12 million companies, with in-depth coverage of 40,000 of the world's top business enterprises. Many college libraries provide Hoover's free to students.

Reuters Investor The "Industry Overview" section of Reuters Investor describes key, up-to-date developments in the industry. Information includes industry statistics, price performance, company rankings, news, market capitalization, research reports, and risk alerts.

Statistical Abstract of the United States The Statistical Abstract is an excellent resource for the entrepreneur seeking basic statistics on an industry. The Census Bureau has compiled it every year since 1878. The latest edition contains over 1,400 tables, charts, and graphics. Highlights include a "New Congressional Districts Profiles" section, which contains selected data for each congressional district, such as population, educational attainment, housing, and the newly defined boundaries of the 108th Congress.

Also new in this edition, Appendix II lists the names of new metropolitan and micropolitan areas, current-year population estimates, and trade and employment figures. **Micropolitan** is a term used to designate areas with at least one urban cluster of 10,000 to 50,000 people, plus adjacent territory that has a high degree of social and economic integration with the core, as measured by commuting ties.

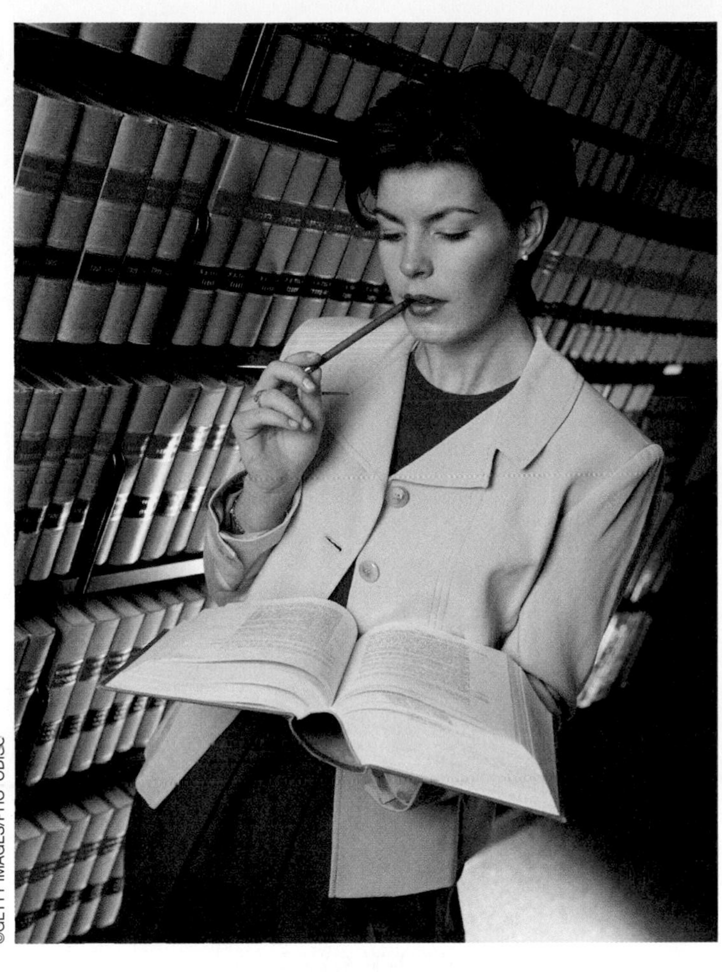

©GETTY IMAGES/PHOTODISC

Thomas Register of American Manufacturers

The Thomas Register has long been recognized as one of the most comprehensive online resources for finding companies and products manufactured in North America. Readers of *Design News* magazine rated the Thomas Register Internet site the number-one site for detailed product, pricing, and supplier information.

More than 173,000 companies, both American and Canadian, are found in Thomas Register in Print and on CD-ROM or DVD. Over 152,000 brand names are also listed in the Thomas Register database. There is no charge for accessing any of the Register information.

Census Bureau States Initiative The Census Bureau has an ongoing effort to make economic data and statistics more widely available at the state and local levels.

A good example is the Business and Industry Data Center (BIDC) program for the state of Texas. This program is a cooperative effort between the Census Bureau, the Office of the Governor's Economic Development and Tourism (ED&T), and the State Data Center at Texas A&M University. State participation in the program requires no direct outlay of state funds. The Census Bureau and the Bureau of Economic Analysis provide data to participants at no cost. Under state law, ED&T is required to share and exchange data and statistics with other agencies and organizations in order to facilitate access by the general public. All the organizations affiliated with the BIDC program maintain a depository of economic data (in print and electronic formats) from the Census Bureau and the Bureau of Economic Analysis.

Check with your state government to determine if it is cooperating with the Census Bureau to provide economic data and statistics for entrepreneurial use. If it is, the site could prove a valuable resource when completing an industry analysis.

Components of an Industry Analysis

A comprehensive industry analysis consists of ten components.

1. market size
2. competitive analysis
3. demographic issues
4. economic issues
5. industry trends
6. laws or legal issues
7. ecological issues
8. technology issues
9. barriers to entry in the industry
10. factors that make the industry attractive

FUN FACTS

The weight of all the plastic bags used by dry cleaners and disposed of annually in New York City is almost 3 million pounds. Great market if you're selling disposable plastic garment bags!

If the list above seems intimidating, do not let that bother you. Starting a business *should* be intimidating. Consider your potential investment of time and money. But time invested now in an industry analysis will save you time and money in the future. Most small business experts point out that the better you know your industry, the better your company's chance of success.

The competitive analysis is that component of the industry analysis in which you quantify and qualify the competition. The competitive analysis occupies such an important place in planning a new business that the next chapter is devoted entirely to that activity.

MARKET SIZE

What is the size of your industry in terms of revenue and number of firms? You should gather information about the local market, state market, and national market. If the market is small, it is less likely that you will attract big new competitors. A large market, on the other hand, often draws the attention of major national competitors.

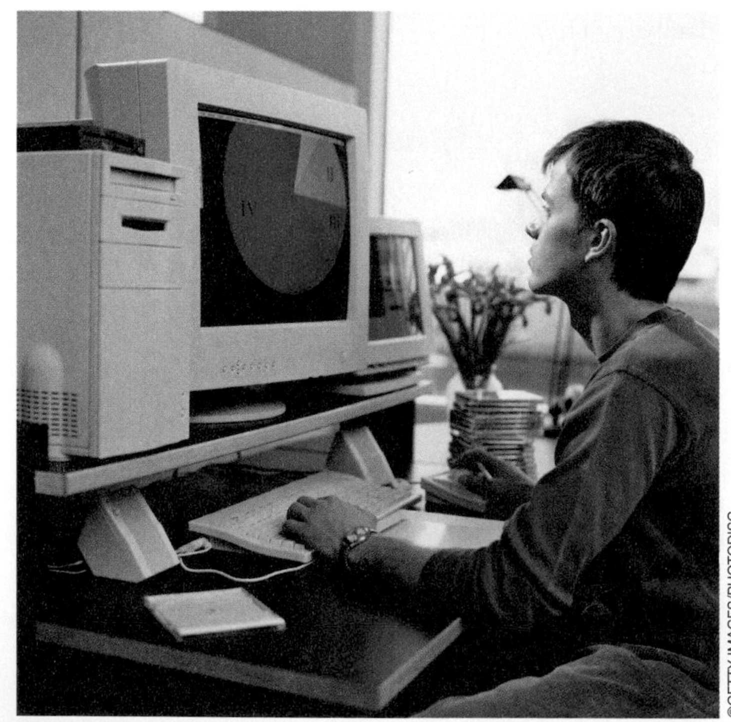
©GETTY IMAGES/PHOTODISC

Market growth rate at the local, state, and national levels is also of interest to entrepreneurs. A rapid growth rate encourages new business entrants. If the growth rate is slow, competition will be much stronger and weak companies will fall by the wayside.

Where does the entrepreneur start the search for information? Start with the wine industry as an example. Go to a major Internet search engine and type in "wine statistics." It will likely bring up over 20 pages of potential information links. If you enter the name of any one of hundreds of industries, the results will no doubt be similar.

Continuing with the wine industry example, click on a site that seems interesting. The site should also appear to have official or other legitimate status. Beware of sites created and maintained by individuals with no association to the industry other than personal interest.

It quickly becomes evident that the state of California is the largest producer of wine in the U.S. Perhaps, then, a California Internet site would be a good place to start. Further research yields the "Wine Institute" site, which bills itself as "The Voice of California Wine" and yields some interesting market size data.

Table 6-2 lists the total wine consumption per U.S. resident from 1982 to 2002. It also shows the total gallons of wine consumed during the same time period and its retail sales value.

What does the table tell you about market size? First, if you know the amount of wine consumed nationally per person, you can use that information to compute the wine consumption in your state and community. When you factor in the data showing wine sales, you can determine the revenue value of consumption and the market revenue growth rate. For example, in 1999 wine consumption per person in the U.S. was 2.02 gallons. The market growth rate between 1999 ($18.1 billion) and 2002 ($21.1 billion) was 16.57 percent. That represents an average yearly growth rate of over 5 percent in sales. The industry is obviously growing.

As you work your way through your industry analysis, make sure to record all the information you discover. It is also a good idea to make a note of or "bookmark" Internet sites of interest. You may need to revisit them later to answer questions about your chosen industry.

TABLE 6-2 WINE CONSUMPTION & SALES IN THE U.S. 1982–2002

Year	Wine Consumption per Person	Total Gallons Consumed	Retail Sales
2002	—	595 million	$21.1 billion
2001	—	561 million	$19.8 billion
2000	—	558 million	$19.0 billion
1999	2.02 gals.	551 million	$18.1 billion
1998	1.95 gals.	526 million	$17.0 billion
1997	1.94 gals.	520 million	$16.1 billion
1996	1.89 gals.	500 million	$14.3 billion
1995	1.77 gals.	464 million	$12.2 billion
1994	1.77 gals.	459 million	$11.5 billion
1993	1.74 gals.	449 million	$11.0 billion
1992	1.87 gals.	476 million	$11.4 billion
1991	1.85 gals.	466 million	$10.9 billion
1990	2.05 gals.	509 million	$11.7 billion
1989	2.11 gals.	524 million	$11.3 billion
1988	2.24 gals.	551 million	$11.0 billion
1987	2.39 gals.	581 million	$11.2 billion
1986	2.43 gals.	587 million	$11.4 billion
1985	2.43 gals.	580 million	$10.8 billion
1984	2.34 gals.	555 million	$9.7 billion
1983	2.25 gals.	528 million	$9.1 billion
1982	2.22 gals.	514 million	$7.3 billion

DEMOGRAPHIC ISSUES

The entrepreneur should pay careful attention to the targeted population and demographic issues affecting it. **Demographics** are defined as characteristics of a population as classified by age, sex, income, and other factors for market and other forms of research.

Changes and/or trends in demographics can have dramatic effects on business. For planning purposes, the entrepreneur should research (at a minimum) changes in age, gender, income, educational levels, race, marital status, and other trends. If other demographics are relevant to a particular industry, they should also be investigated.

Age

Age is an important demographic issue. For instance, consider the largest age group in the U.S. today. Baby boomers (the 77 million Americans born between 1946 and 1964) are radically changing the age mix. In the late 1990s, the baby-boom group defined the United States' age configuration. Each year the population gets older, primarily because of the aging of this huge group.

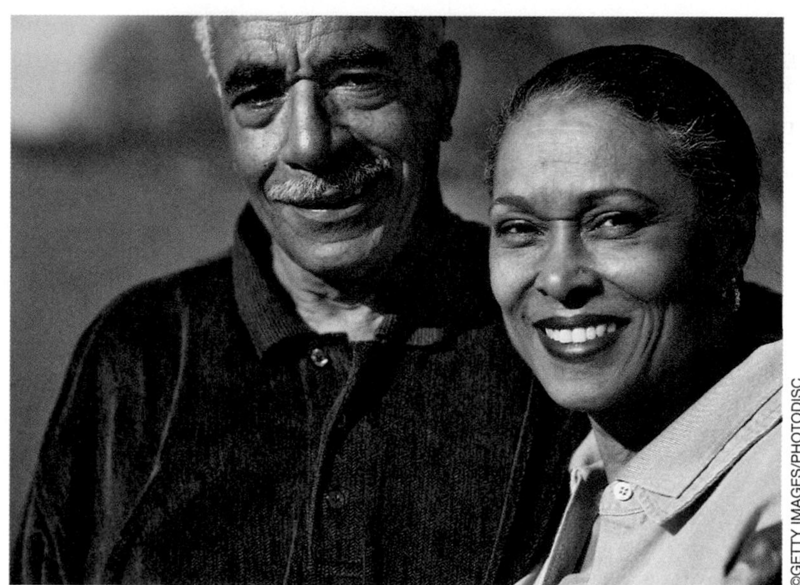
©GETTY IMAGES/PHOTODISC

Over the next three decades, most baby boomers will reach retirement age, causing rapid growth of the population over age 65. According to the Census Bureau, by 2025 the age structure of the population will change noticeably. As a result of declining birth rates and increasing longevity, the percentage of those 65 years or older in the U.S. rose from approximately 8.2 percent in 1950 to approximately 12.6 percent today. By 2025, according to "Government Spending in an Older America" (Population Reference Bureau), some 20 percent of Americans will be over the age of 65.

According to the United Nations, one out of every 10 persons in the world is now 60 years or older. By 2050, one out of five will be 60 years or older, and by 2150, one out of three. In 2000 there were an estimated three women for every two men age 65 or older, according to "Elderly Americans," a new publication of the Population Reference Bureau. The gender ratio is even more skewed among the oldest-old. At ages 85 and older, the ratio is 41 men to 100 women. The preponderance of women among the elderly reflects the higher death rates for men than women at every age.

The aging of the U.S. population should be closely monitored by entrepreneurs with an eye to its potential impact on business. Few businesses will escape this impact. Some will cease to exist because they ignore the trend. Others will prosper because they are paying attention.

Gender

Women's spending power and pressure on the marketplace have grown considerably. As a result, women have become more influential, better-educated consumers. They have different buying habits than men, and they view and process advertisements differently. In many important ways, women are different consumers than men and must be treated so.

Regardless of what you are selling, keep women in mind. You need to understand and take advantage of this significant market sector. Here are some useful facts about women consumers.

- More than 80 percent of women aged 25 to 44 work at full- or part-time jobs.
- Roughly 22 percent of working wives earn higher incomes than their husbands, and women make up nearly half of all adults with a net worth of $50,000 or more.
- Approximately 50 percent of business travelers are now female. This has made a significant difference to the travel industry as it adapts to the change.
- Women buy 80 percent of household goods and are increasingly responsible for buying bigger items such as houses and cars.
- Women purchase or influence the purchase of 80 percent of all consumer goods, including stocks and computers.
- Women instigate the decision to buy cable in 74 percent of households and sign up for pay channels in 78 percent.
- Women aged 45 to 64 spend more than $21 billion annually on clothes and more than $5 billion on beauty products.
- By 2010, women are expected to control $1 trillion, or 60 percent of the country's wealth, according to research conducted by *Business Week* and Gallup.
- Almost three-fourths of women in the labor force are concerned about the conflicts between work and home. Implications for marketers of consumer products are enormous.

Business from both an ownership and consumer perspective is no longer the exclusive domain of men. Take Dallas, Texas, for example. According to the Center for Women's Business Research, there are almost 90,000 majority-owned, privately held firms owned by women in Dallas. These firms represent approximately 28 percent of all privately held firms in the metropolitan area. They employ over 144,000 people and account for over $19.9 billion in sales.

When it comes to women entrepreneurs, not all states are created equal. The top states for women are all in the western U.S.

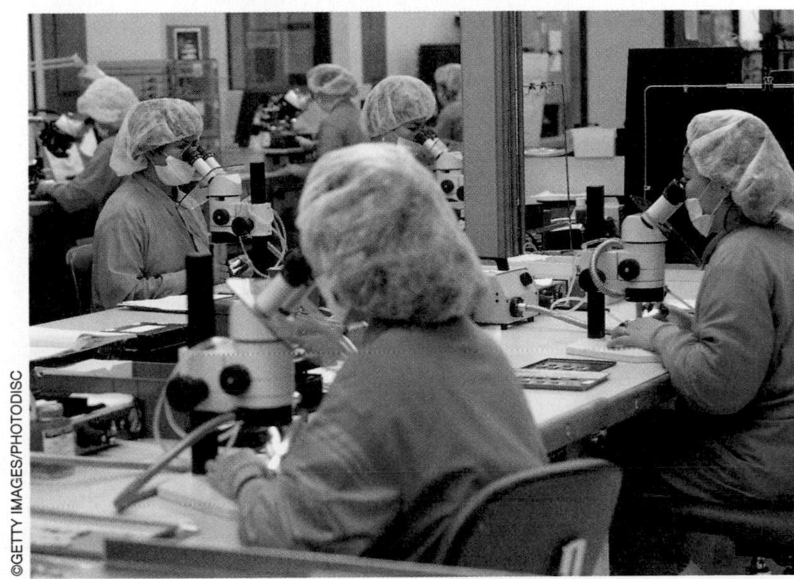
©GETTY IMAGES/PHOTODISC

According to a new study by the Center for Women's Business Research, the top five states in the nation for growth and expansion of women-owned businesses are Idaho and Wyoming (tied for first place), Utah, Nevada, and Arizona. Between 1997 and 2002, on average, the number of women-owned businesses in these five states grew at more than twice the rate of the rest of the country, an average of 28.8 percent, compared to 14.0 percent for all other states.

The Small Business Administration has developed a special online site for women, the *SBA Online Women's Business Center.* According to the site, "America's 9.1 million women-owned businesses employ 27.5 million people and contribute $3.6 trillion to the economy—yet women continue to face unique obstacles in the world of business. The U.S. Small Business Administration is doing more than ever to help level the playing field for women entrepreneurs, and the SBA's Office of Women's Business Ownership is leading the way."

Income

Research on the income level of your target market—per capita income, average family income, and so on—is critical to the planning of your new business.

As an example, take an entrepreneur who would like to start a franchised car repair service in Grand County, Utah. The area is full of beautiful terrain visited by hikers and tourists from all over the world. In addition to the other

The Global ENTREPRENEUR

According to the U.S. Department of Commerce's International Trade Administration, U.S. exports of goods and services rose $2.2 billion to $88 billion in October 2003 and imports increased $2.7 billion to $129.7 billion. Business in the world marketplace is growing.

Global entrepreneurs wanting a piece of the world's business pie should be extremely careful. They are not exempt from the industry analysis process. If anything, they should pay even more attention to their research.

Just as there are sources of information about U.S. industries, there is also information about internationally based industries.

The *Encyclopedia of Global Industries* presents the history, development, and current conditions of "125 business sectors of global significance." It profiles industry leaders and lists the major countries involved in an industry.

The *Handbook of North American Industry: NAFTA and the Economy of Its Member Nations* presents data provided by the Canadian, Mexican, and American governments. Part II provides detailed, 10- to 15-page descriptions of 31 industries, including statistical data.

Think Critically

What country is the top trading partner of the U.S.? Can you name at least one difference between the two countries in the way they do business?

components of the industry analysis, income is very important. What is the median household income in the area? What are the retail sales per capita? Sample information for Grand County, Utah, is presented in Table 6-3. By examining income demographics, the entrepreneur gathers information that will affect such factors as merchandising and pricing for the new business.

Educational Level

Should the entrepreneur be concerned with the educational level of targeted consumers? The wise entrepreneur is.

Educational levels have changed considerably in the past 30 years. According to the Census Bureau, the percentage of the population aged 25 and over with less than a high school diploma declined from 44 percent in 1970 to 17 percent in 1998. Within the same period, the percentage of adults who completed at least some college has more than doubled, from 22 percent to 58 percent. The number of Americans 25-plus with a bachelor's degree or higher is now estimated at slightly less than 25 percent. Although the trend has slowed somewhat in recent years, the change in America's literacy level has been exciting to follow.

By examining the educational demographics in Table 6-3, the entrepreneur can gain information useful for such things as promotional activities and customer service.

TABLE 6-3 SELECTED DEMOGRAPHICS FROM THE U.S. CENSUS BUREAU FOR GRAND COUNTY, UTAH

Population	8,633
Percent persons 65 years and older	12.5%
Percent female persons	50.9%
Percent white persons	92.6%
Percent American Indian persons	3.9%
Percent Hispanic or Latino origin persons	5.6%
Percent high school graduates 25+	82.5%
Percent bachelor's degree or higher 25+	22.9%
Housing units	4,062
Home ownership rate	71%
Median value of owner-occupied housing units	$112,700
Persons per household	2.44
Median household money income	$32,387
Per capita money income	$17,356
Persons below poverty level	14.8%
Retail sales per capita	$9,506
Persons per square mile	2.3

Race

Many believe that racially based marketing is a fad. But most experts agree that, as the racial makeup of the country changes, so should marketing strategy. Entrepreneurs should determine for themselves if race is a demographic with potential business implications.

Other facts may further reveal the way Americans view race. For the first time, the 2000 census made it possible for people to identify with more than one race. The Census Bureau provided this option because of the rising rates of interracial marriage and the growing number of people who view themselves as members of multiple races. Children and people from minority groups are more inclined to do so.

Of the 281.4 million people included in the 2000 census, approximately 6.8 million identified with multiple races. About 4 percent of children were identified as multiracial, compared with 2 percent of adults.

©GETTY IMAGES/PHOTODISC

Some specific racial changes reported by the Census Bureau are worthy of note. For instance, the Hispanic population in the U.S. gained about 13 million people between 1990 and 2000. That 58 percent increase makes the Hispanic population more or less equal in size to the black population.

More recent research reveals that 193,000 Hispanic households have an annual income over $100,000. Between 2000 and 2003, Hispanic Americans increased spending by 15.5 percent. The annual buying power of Hispanics is $270 billion, a 150 percent growth since 1996.

Are racial demographics important to entrepreneurs? You bet they are. To ignore the business implications of the changing statistics is to ignore very important consumer purchasing trends.

Marital Status

For many entrepreneurs marital status is an important demographic. Consider some of the facts revealed by cursory research.

Americans are less inclined to marry today. Between 1975 and 2002, the percentage of Americans who had never married increased from about 24 percent to approximately 29 percent. There are an estimated 86 million single adults in the U.S. today, and unmarried adults head nearly half the nation's households.

According to the National Marriage Project at Rutgers University, whites and Asians are most likely to be married. Black men and women are least likely to be married. The Northeast has the lowest percentage of married people (52.7 percent) and the highest percentage of those never married (29.3 percent).

Views of what most consider the traditional family are changing, despite television commercials and magazine ads to the contrary. By 2002, only 7 percent of all U.S. households consisted of married couples with children and with the husband working and the wife staying home. Two-income families with children were more the norm.

Many consumer products are marketed to married couples. Many are marketed to singles. It is important to understand marriage demographics.

Demographic Trends

The entrepreneur researching demographics will no doubt uncover numerous trends. For instance, the size of American homes has been changing. Between 1970 and 2000 the average size of a new single-family home increased from 1,500 square feet to over 2,200 square feet. During the same period, the average household size declined from 3.1 to 2.6 people per household.

Cocooning is the tendency of people to create a home retreat and then stay there. The home is designed as a stress-free zone, a safe haven from the outside world. Consumer purchases associated with cocooning include elaborate homes, big-screen televisions, saunas, gourmet kitchens, and extensive landscaping.

Hiving involves people without children who seek an in-city environment. This urban trend puts people in the center of activities with city amenities just out the front door. In a recent market research survey, about two-thirds of the respondents identified themselves as "hivers" and one-third as "cocooners."

In another trend, Census Bureau statistics show that Houston, Seattle, Chicago, Denver, Portland (OR), Atlanta, Memphis, and San Diego all experienced greater increases in their downtown populations than in their entire urban areas over the past decade. Other major cities are also reporting growth in their downtown areas.

ECONOMIC ISSUES

Entrepreneurs should research the local economy in which their new business will be located. What is the unemployment rate? Unemployment is important for several reasons. A low level of unemployment, such as 5 percent, may have a positive impact on the new business. It could mean a healthy economy and potentially high sales of the entrepreneur's product.

A low level of unemployment could also have a negative impact if the entrepreneur must hire employees for the new business. An unemployment rate such as 5 percent could mean a higher pay scale and difficulty finding qualified employees.

Other local issues of economic interest to the entrepreneur include the cost of living index, income levels, and overall economic health of the area. Table 6-4 is an example of economic information available online for a major city in South Carolina.

TABLE 6-4 ECONOMIC FACTS ABOUT GREENVILLE, SC

Gross sales	$78,617,121,000
Cost of living index rate	98.3
Business failure rate	52 per 10,000 concerns
Percent union members in manufacturing	2.9
Right-to-work law	Yes
Leading agricultural products	forestry, poultry, tobacco, cotton, soybeans
Average hourly earnings, manufacturing	$10.55
Average hourly earnings, all jobs	$12.53
Median household income	$26,256 (35th in state ranking)
Number of residents per physician	513
Largest foreign investor country	Germany
Median value of owner-occupied homes	$61,000
Percent homes owner-occupied	69.8
Average monthly contract rent	$276

INDUSTRY TRENDS

A major part of becoming an expert in a given industry is recognizing and even predicting trends. Industry trends can encompass product design, new target markets, new ways of promoting, offshore competition, and numerous other things.

As an example, the following are some recent trends in the wine industry.

©GETTY IMAGES/PHOTODISC

- One of the newest trends is "organic wines," which are produced using organically grown grapes. No pesticides, herbicides, fungicides, chemical fertilizers, or synthetic chemicals of any kind are allowed on the vines or in the soil. Strict rules govern the winemaking process and storage conditions of all imported and domestic wines that acquire certification. Moreover, organic winemakers often avoid many of the chemical substances used to stabilize conventional wines.
- Another wine trend has to do with corks. Many in the industry think alternative closures should be found for wine bottles, such as screw-top caps and synthetic corks.
- Inexpensive table wine is a popular new trend. One wine creating a new urban legend is Charles Shaw's $1.99 table wine, known in local California circles as "Two-Buck Chuck."
- Because of an overabundance of grapes flooding the wine market from places like Chile, Australia, and New Zealand, the price of grape juice is very low. This allows wineries like Charles Shaw to produce inexpensive wine—an estimated 5 million cases so far. It's easily outselling more famous brands in California.
- Mead wine is another growing trend in the industry. Mead is honey wine and was the first alcoholic drink that humans learned to brew, earlier than wine or beer. It is once again growing in popularity.

LAWS AND LEGAL ISSUES

What laws and legal issues may affect your entrepreneurial venture? Do you have a working knowledge of the major laws influencing your industry? Are there any laws on the horizon that might impact your business, either positively or negatively?

Table 6-5 lists and explains many federal laws common to all types of businesses. Not all laws are included here. If in doubt about your specific legal obligations, consult your lawyer.

TABLE 6-5 COMMON BUSINESS LAWS	
Fair Labor Standards Act (FLSA)	Addresses minimum wage and overtime.
Social Security	Establishes a number of social programs that provide for the material needs of individuals and families.
Federal Insurance Contributions Act (FICA)	Includes two separate taxes: social security and Medicare. Taxes are paid by both employer and employee (withheld from wages).
Equal Pay Act (EPA)	Prohibits discrimination in pay on the basis of sex where jobs are performed under similar conditions and require equal skill, effort, and responsibility.
Immigration Reform and Control Act (IRCA)	Requires employers to verify that applicants for employment are authorized to work in the U.S.
Federal Unemployment Tax Act (FUTA)	Provides workers payments for a given period of time or until they find a new job, if job was terminated through no fault of their own.
Occupational Safety & Health Administration Act (OSHA)	Requires all employers to provide a workplace free from recognized hazards that cause, or are likely to cause, death or serious physical harm to employees.
Title VII Civil Rights Act	Prohibits discrimination in hiring, firing, promoting, compensation, or terms, conditions, or privileges of employment on the basis of race, color, sex, religion, or national origin.
Americans with Disabilities Act (ADA)	Prohibits discrimination in employment on the basis of physical or mental impairments that limit one or more major life activities.
Pregnancy Discrimination Act	Prohibits discrimination in employment based on pregnancy, childbirth, or related medical condition.
Age Discrimination in Employment Act (ADEA)	Prohibits discrimination against individuals over 40 with respect to hiring, compensation, terms, conditions and privileges of employment on the basis of age.
Older Worker Benefit Protection Act (OWBPA)	Amendment to the Age Discrimination in Employment Act that prohibits discrimination with respect to employee benefits on the basis of age.
Regulatory Flexibility Act (RFA)	Requires federal agencies to review regulations for their impact on small businesses and consider less burdensome alternatives.
Small Business Regulatory Enforcement Fairness Act (SBREFA) of 1996	Provides new avenues for small businesses to participate in andhave access to the federal regulatory arena.
Paperwork Reduction Act of 1980	Requires that all proposed regulations be analyzed for the paperwork they require and that paperwork be reduced to a minimum.
Small Business Paperwork Relief Act of 2002	Institutes a process to make paperwork reduction a serious, on-going effort and make it easier for small businesses to comply with the law.
Consumer Protection Laws	Ensure safety, fair labeling, privacy, and other matters.

What about laws that are not common? Even though the entrepreneur must be aware of the common body of business law, there are laws specific to all industries that are not common knowledge. How do you determine those?

A comprehensive industry analysis is never complete until you have researched the idiosyncratic laws of your own industry. Take the wine industry example. Table 6-6 lists some laws peculiar to that industry. There are many others.

TABLE 6-6 EXAMPLES OF LAWS AFFECTING THE WINE INDUSTRY

The body of law concerning interstate shipment of wine varies widely from state to state. For example, it is a felony for wineries to direct-ship wine to the following states:

- Florida
- Georgia (except in compliance with limited direct provision)
- Kentucky
- Maryland (except in compliance with special order provision)
- Tennessee
- Utah

In these states direct shipments via common carrier is prohibited:

Alabama	New Jersey
Arkansas	New York
Delaware	Ohio
Kansas	Oklahoma
Maine	South Dakota
Massachusetts	Vermont
Michigan	

State laws vary in regard to labeling requirements. (Laws are subject to change and may not be current as of your reading.)

Ignorance of the law is no defense for breaking it. Research all the legal aspects of your proposed industry.

FUN FACTS

Did you coffee drinkers know it takes approximately 4,000 hand-picked Arabica coffee beans to make one pound of roasted coffee? A mature coffee tree produces one pound of coffee per growing season.

ECOLOGICAL ISSUES

During the planning stage, entrepreneurs must determine if there are ecological issues facing the business. Take, for example, an entrepreneur considering opening a retail mountain bike store. The attitude of the general public and/or government entities toward the off-road impact of mountain bikes in wilderness areas could have a significant impact on business. The entrepreneur should keep a close eye on prevailing attitudes. A turn in the wrong direction could spell disaster for the new business.

Ecological issues may be more direct. For an entrepreneur planning to open a restaurant, they might include concerns such as the disposal of used cooking oil.

If ecological issues are overlooked during the planning stage, serious problems may occur. Areas of concern should be identified through research during the industry analysis, not later by a local health official or other government employee.

TECHNOLOGY ISSUES

Entrepreneurs also need to carefully research any technological issues facing the industry. Is there a product innovation on the horizon that will make your product obsolete? Is a new manufacturing technology being developed that will make your way of doing things less cost-effective?

Take the example of the mountain bike industry. What are some of the technological issues impacting it? A cursory examination of industry information reveals new technology in suspension frame design. Other advances involve cantilever brakes, use of titanium in frames, carbon fiber "shock-absorbing" seat posts, more gears (some bikes have as many as 27), advances in sprocket technology that make changing gears easier, shift levers that automatically go up or down one gear at a time, and new brakes, including hydraulic disc brakes. If you were starting a mountain bike retail store, would you be interested in these advances? How about the latest developments in folding bike technology?

©GETTY IMAGES/PHOTODISC

As you can see, if the mountain bike entrepreneur does not keep up with technology changes, the store might end up with an inventory of antiquated, old-tech bikes.

Investigate technological changes in your industry. You will never be perceived as an expert without this very important piece of product knowledge.

INDUSTRY BARRIERS AND ATTRACTIONS

When considering a new business venture, entrepreneurs should examine any factors that may make it difficult to enter an industry as well as factors that make the industry particularly attractive.

Barriers to Entry into the Industry

Are there barriers that may stand in your way, and are those barriers insurmountable? For example, what is the level of competition? Who are your competitors, and how are they likely to respond to another entrant? If they are well established, well funded, and have high visibility, their reaction to your entry into the industry could be a very aggressive opposition. Careful planning will be required to offset it.

Is the industry too crowded already? For instance, if you are planning to start a health food store in a small city of 40,000 people, you need to know how many health food stores already exist. Your research should include the approximate number of people it takes to keep a health food store in business. You should then compare the size of the city to the number of stores already in business, including your planned one.

What start-up costs are required to open a new business and compete in the industry? Some businesses are a lot more expensive to start than others. If you intend to start a small consulting business, you may do it from the extra

Small Business Technology

When doing any business research, try the indexes and databases available online through most libraries. One good example is *Business Source® Premier.* Designed specifically for business schools and libraries, it contains full-text articles from over 3,500 scholarly journals and business periodicals. Topics include management, economics, finance, accounting, international business, and many others.

bedroom in your home for very little up-front capital. If, however, you plan to start a small company to manufacture snowshoes, the initial capital requirements can be considerable.

Is the required equipment available? For a consulting business, basic office equipment is available from any number of sources and obtainable on short notice. A snowshoe manufacturer, though, may require a complex plastic injection-molding machine that has to be specially built and cannot be delivered for months. The wait and the expense could present a formidable barrier to entry.

Are the necessary product vendors available, and will they do business with a new company? This is one area of planning often overlooked by entrepreneurs, especially those opening retail stores. For instance, just because you plan to sell snow skis and accessories does not mean snow ski manufacturers will be willing to do business with you. Your business skills are probably limited and you have no proven track record in sales. How can they be sure you will pay your bills? Many are not willing to risk new retail customers. Checking out and contacting potential product vendors during the industry analysis is a good idea.

Many factors can make entry into a specific industry difficult or undesirable. Those described above are only a few of the barriers. Spend some time brainstorming those specific to your chosen industry.

Ethics for ENTREPRENEURS

Madison Reeder is planning to buy a vineyard and open a winery. She has done extensive research and has chosen to locate her business in the Grand Valley area of western Colorado.

Colorado is a nationally recognized wine region. Currently, it has an estimated 400 acres of vineyards and 40-plus licensed commercial wineries with more than $5 million in sales. The quality of the grapes that can be grown in Colorado meets Madison's requirements for producing a high-quality product. She has a dilemma, though.

Madison wants to label her wine "organic." Only one other Colorado winery is producing organic wine, so she feels she can use the designation to create a competitive advantage. Organic wine is made with grapes grown without chemical fertilizers, weed killers, insecticides, or other synthetic chemicals. Wine labeled 100 percent organic cannot have added sulfites, typically used as a preservative.

Madison is aware of the controversy about what "organic" means. The Department of Agriculture has several categories for the term: "100 percent organic," "organic," and "made with organic ingredients." If she decides to go with the third designation, her wine can consist of up to 30 percent non-organically-produced ingredients. An advisor from the California wine industry tells her that the average wine consumer does not know the difference between the three categories.

Think Critically

1. What marketing advice would you give Madison?
2. Do you think she should rely on the consultant's advice? If she does, do you think the approach is ethical?

Factors that Make the Industry Attractive

While researching the industry, you should discover several compelling reasons for going ahead with the planned start-up of your new business. If you do not, you may need to revisit your decision.

Starting a business from scratch can be both expensive and time consuming. Typical small-scale entrepreneurs invest their life savings in businesses that require 60 to 80 hours a week of their time. Their reasons for doing so must be obvious and compelling. They may not seem so important before the doors of the new business are opened, but after about six months of 80-hour weeks, they become an absolute necessity.

Also, putting in writing the factors that make the industry attractive can be a powerful motivator to complete the planning process and get the business under way. These factors perform the same function as the carrot does for the donkey. They keep you putting one foot in front of the other until the job is done.

IMPORTANCE OF THE INDUSTRY ANALYSIS

As an entrepreneur, you can demonstrate expertise in your chosen industry with the amount of detail you provide in each component of your industry analysis. Take your time and do the required research. The more you know about the intended industry, the stronger your business plan will be.

If you use your business plan to secure traditional bank financing or to convince people to invest, keep in mind that it will be read by any number of outsiders. As they read this section of the business plan, they will make judgments regarding your expertise. Make sure they have adequate information on which to base those judgments.

Ideally, all ten components should be addressed in the industry analysis. In reality, however, time may be at a premium and that may not be possible. In that case, try your best to include the first five. These components are absolutely critical to all entrepreneurial ventures. Then, as time allows, choose components from the second five that are most important to the new business venture.

Whatever happens, do not skip over this section of the business plan. The industry analysis is your best chance at proving you are a knowledgeable entrepreneur who has done the required research to ensure future business success.

Ship in a BOTTLE

The Industry

Fred knew the best place to research an industry was at trade shows. In addition to setting up an exhibit in Atlanta to test his product, he did some research. The general gift industry was huge. The Atlanta Gift Mart had 650 permanent and almost 500 temporary exhibitors, representing about 3,000 manufacturers. Most exhibitors also exhibited in other regional shows. Nationally over 1 million visitors shopped these shows each year. To Fred these were mind-boggling statistics. He knew he had to narrow his research to a more manageable target.

He defined his industry as two segments of the general gift industry: nautical gifts and collectible gifts. At the Atlanta show 114 exhibitors offered nautical gifts, and over 150 showed collectible gifts. Fred visited each exhibitor and learned that many sold inexpensive souvenirs, many represented the same manufacturers, and a few extended the term "nautical" to include anything with a fish or seashell design. The collectible gifts ranged from hand-painted porcelain to imported dolls.

Fred's final tally was 55 true nautical gift sellers who offered quality products to nautical gift stores, including ship models, lighthouses, brass items, plaques, stationery, and other decorative items for the home. Thirteen collectible exhibitors sold one-of-a-kind nautical pieces, primarily to museum stores. The only sellers of ships in bottles were a few souvenir companies offering very inexpensive models.

This was a good start, but further research lay ahead. Fred exhibited in a smaller, more regional show in Miami. Many, but not all, of the Atlanta true nautical exhibitors were present. There was also a large contingent of Far East importers who had missed the Atlanta show. Several were showing in the U.S. for the first time and exhibited good ship models and brass pieces. Fred was still the only exhibitor of ships in bottles. The Miami show was not as successful for Fred as the Atlanta show because of its smaller size and the low-priced imports.

Fred attended an East Coast museum-store trade show next. Over 60 museum stores were in attendance, 12 of which had a nautical theme. Fred opened six accounts at that show.

Fred's research was giving him a good conceptual view. Nautical gift stores bought from about 50 distributors. Museum gift stores were more particular and bought from collectible sellers and higher-end nautical gift distributors. Importers would play a larger competitive role in the industry as trade barriers were eliminated. The industry had few entry barriers, many sellers, and only a handful of large manufacturers.

Think Critically

1. What other sources of information can Fred research to learn more about the industry? What demographics should he study?
2. Is there anything the gift industry should be doing to protect itself against the rising number of low-price imports?

Summary

Industry analysis is a form of exploratory business research that examines the overall condition of a particular industry. Your industry is made up of the companies providing products and services similar to yours.

A typical analysis includes the following components.

1. Market size: revenue and number of firms; information on local, state, and national markets
2. Competitive analysis: quantifying and qualifying the competition
3. Demographic issues: targeted population and demographic issues that affect it, such as age, gender, income, educational levels, race, marital status, and others
4. Economic Issues: local economy (unemployment rate, cost of living index, income levels, overall economic health)
5. Industry trends: product design, promotion, target markets, offshore competition, and others
6. Laws or legal issues: current and potential laws that may affect the business positively or negatively
7. Ecological issues: aspects of the business that may have an environmental impact
8. Technology issues: product innovations, new manufacturing technologies
9. Barriers to entry in the industry: level of competition, start-up costs, equipment availability, lining up product vendors
10. Factors that make the industry attractive: compelling reasons for starting up the new business

There are many sources of industry analysis, including library sites, investment firms, business and trade periodicals, trade associations, government agencies, and numerous others. Talk to people in the same business or industry. Research industry-specific publications. Attend trade fairs and seminars. Gather as much information as possible to enhance your image as an expert.

What is the market size? What is the size of your industry in terms of revenue and number of firms? The competitive analysis is that part of the industry analysis in which you quantify and qualify the competition.

Pay careful attention to the targeted population and any demographic issues affecting it. Demographic issues ultimately have an impact on most businesses.

Researching the local economy is another crucial task. What is the unemployment rate? Other local issues you need to explore are the cost of living index, income levels, and the overall economic health of the area.

A major part of becoming an expert in a given industry is learning to recognize and even predict trends. Industry trends can include product design, new target markets, new ways of promoting, offshore competition, and many other things.

What laws and legal issues may affect your business venture? Do you have a working knowledge of the major laws that impact your industry, both currently and in the future?

Are there any ecological and technological issues facing the industry? Do any other barriers stand in the way of the success of your business? As you do your research, you should discover several compelling reasons to go ahead with your plans and start your new business.

A Case in POINT

Charles and Melissa Taft, both in their mid-fifties, have enjoyed long and successful careers as restaurant entrepreneurs. They have just sold their nationwide chain of restaurants and for the first time in their lives don't have to worry about money.

Over the years, whenever they felt stressed with the day-to-day pressures of running the business, the Tafts would spend a long weekend at some small bed-and-breakfast inn. After years of staying at different B&Bs, the couple feels they have a good knowledge of the business.

Now that money is no object, they have decided to start a B&B of their own, in a small scenic community on the coast. They want the business to be a size they can manage themselves. It will be more of a hobby than a business. They do, however, want it to be profitable and competitive.

After exhaustive research, they have located a B&B for sale near Pawley's Island, South Carolina, and one on the Georgia coast near Savannah. Now they must do more targeted research on the two locations. Having purchased options on both properties, they have 30 days to make a final decision.

Think Critically

1. How would you advise the Tafts to start their analysis of the bed-and-breakfast industry?
2. Should the Tafts be concerned with the number of other B&Bs in the two areas? Which of the two locations has the most B&B competition?
3. Should the Tafts be concerned with trends in the B&B industry? Can you identify at least one trend?

Vocabulary Builder

Write a brief definition of each word or phrase.

1. Business.com
2. Census Bureau States Initiative
3. cocooning
4. Current Industrial Reports
5. demographics
6. hiving
7. Hoover's Online
8. industry analysis
9. micropolitan
10. Reuters Investor
11. Statistical Abstract of the United States
12. Thomas Register of American Manufacturers

Review the Concepts

13. Why is industry analysis important to the planning process?
14. What is the primary objective of the Census Bureau's Current Industrial Reports?
15. How can an entrepreneur research market size and growth?
16. Which major demographics should be researched during the industry analysis process?
17. How has the education level in the U.S. changed over the past 30 years?
18. How did the reporting of race change during the 2000 census?
19. What is the importance of unemployment trends to entrepreneurs?
20. Describe at least five laws that may affect an industry.
21. Why are ecological issues important to entrepreneurs?
22. Why are technological issues important to entrepreneurs?
23. What are some of the barriers to entry in industries?
24. Summarize the importance of an industry analysis in business planning.

Critical Thinking

25. In your opinion, why should global entrepreneurs pay even more attention to their industry analysis than domestic entrepreneurs do?
26. In Table 6-2, what basic fact is evident concerning the wine industry?
27. How do age demographics affect entrepreneurial decisions?
28. Compare the demographic trends of cocooning and hiving.
29. What are the likely consequences of skipping the industry analysis when planning a business?

Project

Build Your Business Plan

As an aspiring entrepreneur, you should give thought to the need to be perceived as an expert in your chosen industry. Remember, a well-done industry analysis is the first step in becoming an expert.

1. Choose at least 7 of the 10 industry analysis components and start the research process. As you uncover information relevant to your particular business, record the highlights for use in completing your business plan.
2. File the information according to the major headings of the business plan laid out in Chapter 2.

Chapter 7

The Competitive Analysis

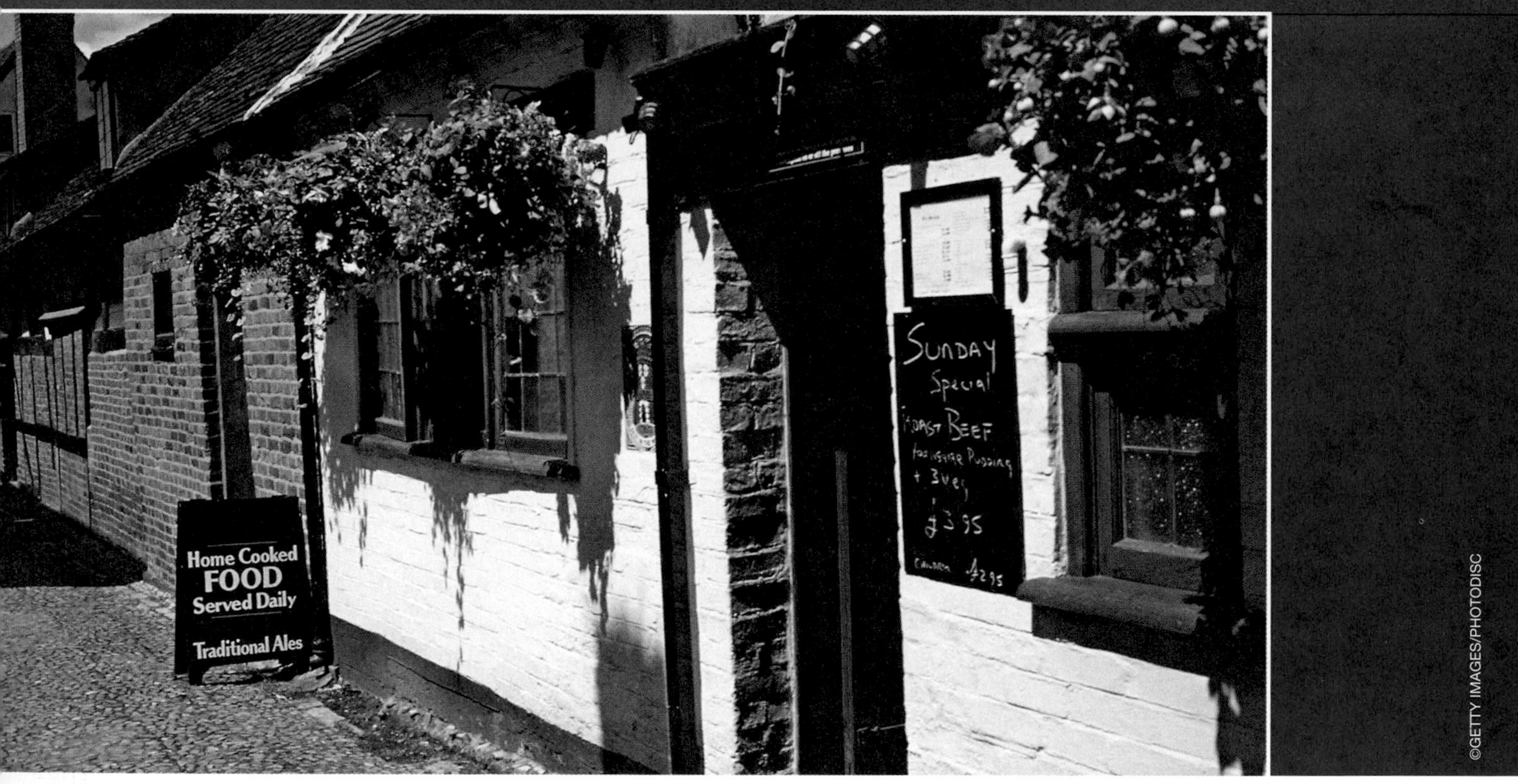

Objectives

7-1 Explain competitive impact.

7-2 Discuss the role of competition in private enterprise.

7-3 Explain Porter's Five-Forces Model of Competition.

7-4 Explain direct and indirect competition.

7-5 Determine the geographic distribution of potential customers.

7-6 Conduct a competitive analysis.

7-7 Discuss the importance of competitive intelligence to entrepreneurial success.

THE IMPACT OF COMPETITION

New businesses need new customers. Opening a store or service is only one step toward future success. Real success occurs only if you attract customers—many customers.

Where are these customers currently shopping? Entrepreneurs must be able to answer that question, as well as many others. After all, they start out with no customers at all. Everyone who wants to buy products similar to theirs is buying from other, already established businesses. The only way to get customers, then, is to convince them to stop purchasing from those other businesses. To do that, entrepreneurs must have as much information about the competition as possible.

Competition, when used in a business sense, means a rivalry between companies that sell similar products or services. If you are to survive in the business world, you will have to get to know your competition. You must have **competitive impact**, which means the ability to effectively compete with other businesses.

Competition grows out of the fact that, in a country such as ours, consumers have freedom of choice. They can spend their money anywhere they please. They make the decision to spend their money in your store or down the street at another store that is in competition with yours.

Because there is freedom of choice in spending, you as a businessperson must be as competitive as possible. Your store must be of the highest quality and your merchandise of the type consumers demand. These positive attributes must then be combined with prices that are lower than or at least equal to those of your competitor.

Every day that the doors of your business are open to the public, you must strive to develop better products and better ways to serve your customers. If you do not, your competition will. At the same time, you have to keep an eye on your competitors and what they are doing. You cannot allow them to get a competitive edge on you. Once they do, your customers will become their customers.

COMPETITION AND PRIVATE ENTERPRISE

Competition is a very necessary part of private enterprise. If a private enterprise system is to serve the people efficiently, there must be competition among those who produce the products and among those who sell them. That competition is created by the following factors.

Similar Products and Services

©GETTY IMAGES/PHOTODISC

Competitors offer similar products or services for sale. Take sporting goods as an example. The owner of any one sporting goods store must consider all other sporting goods stores as competition for customers.

Multiple Buyers and Sellers

If there is to be competition within an economic system, there must be many buyers and many sellers. When these conditions exist in a market, no individual or business can exert undue pressure. For example, if there were only one sporting goods store in town, that store's owner could charge whatever price he or she wanted for the products. Local customers would have no choice but to pay the price or travel out of town to shop. Likewise, if there were only one buyer, the buyer could exert undue pressure on the seller to give price concessions. Multiple buyers and multiple sellers ensure competition by offering choices. Choices, in turn, help keep prices at fair levels.

Freedom to Enter or Exit Business

Competition in private enterprise means that a new business can start at any time. It also means that a company or an individual can stop doing business at any time. This freedom is what gives private enterprise its strength. Because new people are entering the marketplace on a regular basis and others are leaving, competition is assured.

The Guarantee of Fair Competition

Competition is a critical component of private enterprise, but private enterprise can be effective only if fair competition is guaranteed. The United States government, along with many state governments, has taken steps to ensure fairness in competition. Through the enactment of certain laws and the creation of the Federal Trade Commission (FTC), the U.S. Congress has undertaken to create an environment in which entrepreneurs can receive fair treatment from competitors, no matter how small or large their companies are.

Three laws that protect competition are the Sherman Antitrust Act, the Clayton Act, and the Robinson-Patman Act. Collectively, these laws help prevent monopolies. A **monopoly** is a business environment in which a single company, by controlling a specific supply of products or services, sets prices, prevents other businesses from entering the market, and controls the available supply of the product or service. Because these practices are anti-competitive, the government does not approve of them. The only monopolies the government allows are those in industries in which the product or service offered necessitates one supplier. This is often the case with local utilities.

The laws and the regulatory agency described below help protect fair competition in the United States.

FUN FACTS

According to a leading online source for small business statistics, there are over 24 million business entities in the U.S. filing income tax returns, but nearly 60 percent reported annual receipts of less than $25,000.

Sherman Antitrust Act This act, passed in 1890, makes any business deal illegal that unreasonably restricts trade or commerce among states. It outlaws **price fixing**, the agreement between competitors to establish and maintain prices for their goods and services, a practice that leaves customers with few price choices. The act also makes owners or directors of a violating business guilty of a crime. Even though this law is over a hundred years old, it is one of the laws most often invoked today. At any given time, there are major cases in the U.S. courts based on the Sherman Antitrust Act.

Clayton Act This 1914 legislation is a follow-up to the Sherman Antitrust Act and provides additional powers for dealing with companies involved in illegal deals. Specifically, it prohibits businesses from acquiring companies that would create a monopoly environment and reduce competition. It also makes **tying agreements** illegal. In a tying agreement, a customer must buy one type of product before he or she can buy another type from the same seller. As an example, an automotive wholesaler agrees to sell an auto parts retailer hard-to-find vintage car parts, in return for which the retailer buys all his tires from the wholesaler as well.

Robinson-Patman Act This act extended the Clayton Act in 1936 by outlawing **price discrimination**, the practice of charging different prices to different customers for the same goods. It also outlaws mergers in which large companies acquire all the stock of competing companies.

Federal Trade Commission The FTC is a regulatory agency that was established to enforce and monitor these laws. It ensures fair competition among businesses, encourages free trade, carefully reviews business mergers and acquisitions to prevent monopolies from forming, and regulates advertising so that it is not deceptive. (See Chapter 4.)

©GETTY IMAGES/PHOTODISC

FIVE-FORCES MODEL OF COMPETITION

When it comes to the analysis of competition, Harvard Business School Professor Michael Porter's body of work is the acknowledged standard. In his research, Porter identifies five forces that drive competitive activity:

1. Intensity of rivalry among existing competitors
2. Threat of entry by new competitors
3. Pressure from substitute products
4. Bargaining power of suppliers
5. Bargaining power of buyers

Any entrepreneur contemplating entering a new industry should examine these forces. Current entrepreneurs can benefit from a similar analysis as they struggle to stay competitive in markets where they already operate.

Another essential point entrepreneurs should keep in mind is the direct relationship between competition and profit. With increased competition often comes deep discounting of prices, increased advertising expenses, and other activities that negatively impact profit margins.

The level of competition is often the deciding factor in whether or not to enter a particular industry. Just as important, competition often drives an entrepreneur to leave an industry.

Rivalry Among Existing Competitors

Professor Porter typically identifies rivalry among competitors as the strongest of the competitive forces. He identifies nine specific areas of rivalry.

1. *Rivalry intensifies as the number of competitors increases and as competitors become more equal in size and capability.* In an industry with few competitors, competition is minimized. As the number of competitors increases, so does the level of competition. What does this mean for an entrepreneur thinking of starting a new business? It means you should investigate the industry carefully and determine how many potential competitors exist in the geographic market of your proposed business. Based on the number, estimate the level of competition.
2. *Rivalry is usually stronger when demand for the product is growing slowly.* In a mature industry, competitive rivalry is stronger because the market size is fairly well established. In a growing industry, competitive rivalry is less intense because new customers are easier to find. Aspiring entrepreneurs should seek out growth industries in which competition is not likely to be as aggressive toward new entrants.

3. *Rivalry is more intense when industry conditions tempt competitors to use price cuts or other competitive weapons to boost unit volume.* When business conditions put pressure on companies to sell more product units to protect cash flow, they are more inclined to use price as a competitive weapon. If you enter a business driven by the need for large unit sales, evaluate your company's economic health and the nature of your product to determine the best time to enter the market.
4. *Rivalry is stronger when the cost to customers of switching brands is low.* If a customer is using a $50,000 piece of equipment, the cost to switch brands would be very high. If, on the other hand, the customer is using a $10 item, the cost to switch would be very low. The price of the products you sell will be a very important variable in the potential competitive environment.
5. *Rivalry is stronger when one or more competitors is dissatisfied with its market position and launches moves to bolster its standing at the expense of rivals.* A large competitor may seek to enhance its position in the market by using aggressive competitive tactics. If you are considering entry into such a market, take into account the already heightened level of competitiveness.

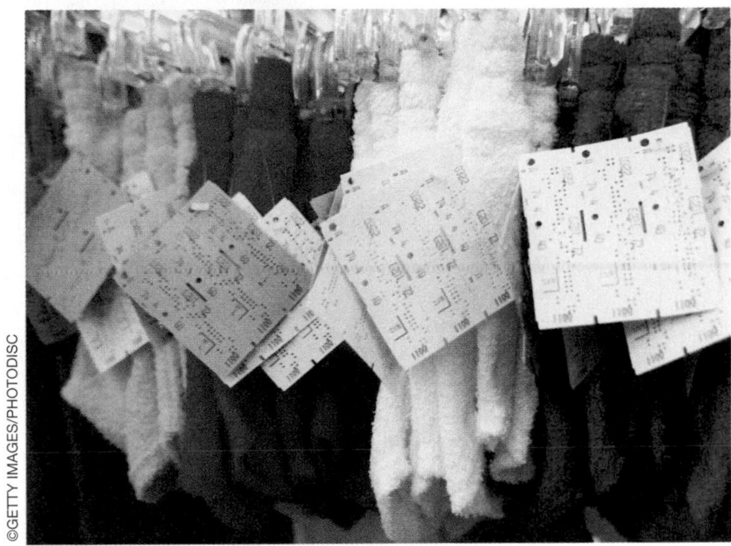
©GETTY IMAGES/PHOTODISC

6. *Rivalry increases in proportion to the size of the payoff from a successful strategic move.* If a strategic move such as a new product introduction results in a rapid increase in market share, the competition to make that move is very high. Obviously, in an industry where the payoff for a new product is very high, the risks of entry are also very high.
7. *Rivalry tends to be more vigorous when it costs more to get out of a business than to stay in and compete.* If an entrepreneur has several million dollars invested in a business, the cost of closing that business would be extremely high. Consequently, such a businessperson is inclined to stay in the business even though the profit margin is low. It is better than losing millions of dollars. You should carefully examine the costs of starting the proposed business. The higher the initial costs, the harder it is to exit the business later.
8. *Rivalry becomes more volatile and unpredictable when competitors are more diverse in terms of their strategies, personalities, corporate priorities, resources, and countries of origin.* The more diverse the group, the harder it is to predict competitive response. Gather as much competitive intelligence as possible on all your major competitors. You can never know enough about those with whom you compete.
9. *Rivalry increases when strong companies outside the industry acquire weak firms in the industry and launch aggressive, well-funded moves to transform their newly acquired businesses into major market contenders.* Competition grows more intense when larger companies enter the industry by purchasing small, already existing companies and transforming them into major competitors. You should understand that if the industry is attractive to you, it might also be attractive to a large company wishing to expand its offerings.

Threat of Entry by New Competitors

Whether you are already doing business in an industry or merely contemplating such a move, you should give careful consideration to a couple of factors. First, what are the barriers to entering the new market? Second, what will be the reaction to your new company by businesses already actively operating there?

Barriers to Entry The first barrier to entry is often the question "How big do I have to be to enter the business and be successful?" For example, take an entrepreneur who is thinking about opening a sporting goods store in a small metropolitan area. She wants to offer hunting, fishing, camping, and other lines to make her store a comprehensive, broadly based option for local customers. She will need enough money to successfully compete with two large, well-established national sporting goods chains already in business in the area. The barriers she faces are the size of building required to house the store and the large amount of start-up cash she will need to stock it. The size of the store alone may be a big enough barrier to keep her from entering the business.

©GETTY IMAGES/PHOTODISC

Another barrier to entrepreneurs may be the technology or specialized skills necessary to enter a particular business. Are any special technologies or training necessary for success in the business? Are they available and affordable? Do patents control any critical part of the business? If so, are the necessary patents available? Trade skills necessary for success may be carefully guarded secrets.

If you have no experience in the planned business, how long will it take you to get up to speed? The wrong answer can be a significant barrier to business success.

Brand loyalty—the consumer's preference for familiar, well-established brands—is an important entrance barrier facing many new entrepreneurs. The difficulty of penetrating and diffusing brand loyalty is one of the tenets of marketing theory. Barriers to switching brands include not only psychological issues but also real costs. What will be the cost in real dollars for potential customers to switch to your brand? Is it a reasonable expectation that they will do so? If it is, does your start-up budget allow for the promotional expenses necessary to overcome brand loyalty?

Then there are the start-up expenses associated with buildings, equipment, and supplies necessary for successful entry into the industry. Do you have to construct a building from the ground up and then equip it with costly machinery? If you do, how long will it take before the new business starts to generate revenue? Does your start-up budget allow for these initial expenditures?

Access to product and/or equipment vendors is another factor to assess. Will the vendors do business with you? Often, fear of losing a major client who happens to be your competitor may cause hesitation on a vendor's part. Difficult access to the necessary equipment, parts, and inventory may prove a formidable barrier to entering the industry.

Competitive Reaction How will firms already doing business in the industry react to a new start-up? Take the previous example of the entrepreneur planning to open a sporting goods store in a market in which two well-established national chains are already operating. Will they ignore the new entrant as an insignificant competitor, or will they wage all-out war? Their reaction will probably be driven by the overall health of the industry and its potential for growth.

If there is little potential for growth in the sporting goods market and the retail pie will simply be divided among more players, some sort of retail war is inevitable. If the market is still growing and entrance of another competitor is not as critical, minor price competition may be the only reaction.

Will the competitors put pressure on their vendors not to sell to the new business? Will they create promotional campaigns aimed at solidifying brand loyalty? Will they send secret shoppers into the new business? The answer to all these questions is probably yes. Will the competitors go so far as to break the law? No, but they will no doubt go as far as the law allows.

Beware of the competition's reaction to your new business. Your competitors will learn about the start-up when you make your business plan available to bankers, vendors, and potential customers. Some of these individuals will likely mention your plan to the competition. It is very important to try to predict competitive reaction; it is even more important to plan for it.

©GETTY IMAGES/PHOTODISC

Small Business Technology

The starting point for entrepreneurs doing a competitive analysis should be the Internet. If, for instance, you are starting a small winery in Grand Junction, Colorado, and want to check out the competition, you would simply type "Grand Junction Colorado wineries" into an Internet search engine. One of the first search options offered would take you to a page that links you to a list of the 14 wineries in the area. Further links take you to the wineries' web sites, which provide a great deal of useful competitive information.

Pressure from Substitute Products

Are substitute products readily available in a sufficient quantity and at a price that might cause your potential customers to switch? In 2004, the price of natural gas for home heating was very high. The cost of electricity was considerably lower. Entrepreneurs selling natural gas heaters soon realized the competitive pressure created by an abundant supply of electric heaters. Their only real salvation was the high cost of switching. To switch from natural gas to electric heat, customers had to invest in electric heaters or even convert their furnaces. Obviously, this would be very expensive.

If substitute products are available for the products you are planning to sell, how do you plan to deal with them? The danger from substitute products should be addressed during the business planning process.

What about the danger from substitute distribution channels? Again, consider the entrepreneur planning to open a retail sporting goods store. Her intent is to open a bricks-and-mortar store—in other words, a traditional retail store in a local shopping center or other convenient location. She is planning her business around the competition from other similar businesses. What if her potential customers are planning to use a substitute approach to purchasing sporting goods? What if they intend to shop at one of the large online sporting goods retailers? Again, this kind of potential substitution should be included in the planning process. Issues such as cost of switching, quality of substitutes, and availability should be researched as well.

Bargaining Power of Suppliers

The power of suppliers to the desired industry is another factor to evaluate. Are the suppliers in a position to withhold supplies of needed products? Can they extort a higher price because supply is either limited or closely controlled?

Take diamonds, for instance. For many years one European company closely controlled the supply of diamonds. Dealers wanting a supply of high-quality stones dealt with the company or one of a few designated wholesalers. The suppliers wielded considerable power over the industry. Even though the supply of diamonds has opened up over the past few years, suppliers are still a major competitive consideration.

You should question and investigate the availability of raw materials, inventory, and supplies for your planned business. What can interrupt the flow of these items? If the flow is interrupted, what are the alternatives?

If the bargaining power of suppliers is a major consideration for the new business, you must plan accordingly. Lack of sales is not the only thing that kills businesses; lack of necessary supplies or raw materials can be just as deadly.

The Global ENTREPRENEUR

So you're starting a new business with an international component. Maybe the company is totally internationally based. How can you conduct a competitive analysis?

There are numerous resources for the international entrepreneur. The secret is knowing where to look. As with a domestic venture, the Internet is a good place to start. You'll need to make a few adjustments in your strategy, however.

First, you'll need to use a search engine that can provide country-specific Internet sites related to your new business. One such site is Search Engines Worldwide®, a list of global and local search engines sorted by country. If you are interested in doing business in Australia, for instance, you'll find 60 Australian search engines at this site.

Another great place to start is the U.S. Department of State. It offers a series of publications called *Background Notes* that contain information on all countries with which the U.S. has relations. They include facts on each country's land, people, history, government, political conditions, economy, and relations with other countries and the U.S. The *Notes* are updated regularly and are available free on the Internet to entrepreneurs needing timely information on an international market.

Another interesting site is the Central Intelligence Agency (CIA) site called *The World Factbook.* It offers a staggering array of information about countries of interest to entrepreneurs. Under the heading "Economy — Overview" for each country, it describes the type of economy, the degree of market orientation, the level of economic development, the most important natural resources, and the unique areas of specialization. It also characterizes major economic events and policy changes in the most recent 12 months and often includes a statement about one or two future macroeconomic trends. The site is a good resource for an overall perspective of a country's business climate.

A competitive analysis is probably more critical to the future success of an internationally based business than to that of a domestic company. If you grew up in America, you are familiar with the culture, laws, and other idiosyncratic aspects of doing business here. How could you possibly know about doing business in another country without extensive research? Do your homework! Competitive surprises in another country may not be much fun.

Think Critically

Pick a country of personal interest to you. Using the Internet, log on to the CIA site. Prepare a brief overview of the country that would be useful to an entrepreneur considering doing business there.

Bargaining Power of Buyers

Just as you should carefully research the power of suppliers to the desired industry, you should also investigate the power of buyers. If, for example, you are starting a business to manufacture computer chips, are there a few large buyers that control the industry? If so, are they in a position to exert undue price and/or quality pressure on the new company?

What should the entrepreneur look for in relation to buyers? The first thing is probably the number of buyers. If there are so many they cannot all be identified, they may not be a major concern. If there are a lot of buyers but only two or three major ones, that may be a concern if those major buyers control a majority percentage of the market.

Quantifying buyers/customers is always an important planning activity. How do you plan for an industry in which buyers have a great deal of bargaining power? Look at the availability of substitute products and the cost of switching. Analyze potential buyers carefully. The problem is not always their reluctance to buy your product. Rather, it may be the pressure they can bring to bear on the way you do business.

TYPES OF COMPETITION

Every business that sells sporting goods of any kind is a potential competitor for a new retail sporting goods store. Not all the businesses are the same, though. Some compete more directly than others. As entrepreneurs analyze their competition, they must first consider into which classification the competing firms fall—direct or indirect competition.

Direct Competition

Direct competition refers to businesses that derive the majority of their profits from the sale of products or services that are the same as or similar to those sold by another business. A good way to start an analysis of direct competition is by looking in the Yellow Pages of the telephone book for other stores that deal in the same product you are planning to sell.

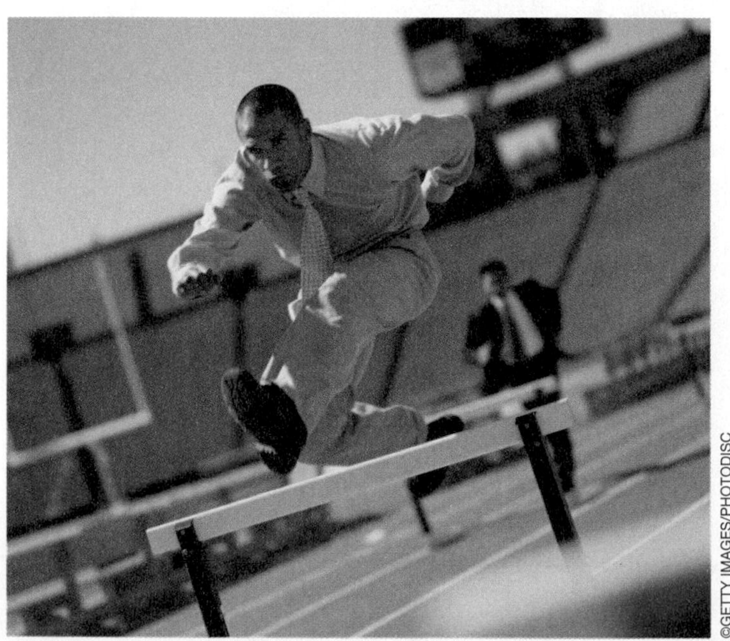
©GETTY IMAGES/PHOTODISC

Another method of identifying direct competition is to contact the local chamber of commerce. A quick review of its membership list should identify organizations that will be direct competition. Many communities have planning departments that compile annual data books in which the communities are divided into shopping zones and the number and types of retailers in each zone are listed.

Yet another valuable way to scope out the competition is by conducting a physical check of the geographic market. A good way to do this is to drive through all retail centers within the competitive area to see if there are other competitors you have not already identified. The check should also include walking through any enclosed malls.

The number of direct competitors you identify and their behavior in the marketplace will ultimately have a profound effect on the new business. It is important to evaluate your findings and try to determine the reputation of your competitors. For example, you should address these questions: "What are they doing that appeals to customers? What could I do better? What have I seen that I want to avoid?"

Indirect Competition

Indirect competition is competition from businesses that derive only a small percentage of their profits from the sale of products or services that are the same as or similar to those sold by another business. If a small entrepreneurial business sells sweatshirts, for example, its indirect competitors might be Wal-Mart, Kmart, Target, and other large general-merchandise retailers.

If you have lived in the area for some time, identifying indirect competition should not be too difficult. You should take time, however, to include all businesses that fall into this category.

Indirect competition can often prove to be the most dangerous kind. For a business like a sweatshirt store, indirect competition will almost always come from a large national chain, which usually has more capital than a small business and is capable of purchasing in much greater quantities. Because the large chain does not have to rely simply on the one product line, it can choose to deal only in those items that produce the greatest profit. It can carry as few or as many of an item as it desires.

Small business owners do not have that option. Not only can they not be as selective, they cannot buy in as large a quantity, either. To attract and keep customers, the sweatshirt store owner must try to satisfy all customer needs for athletic apparel and merchandise. In addition to high-profit items, the store owner must also carry items that are in demand even though they produce much lower profits.

Just as the number and behavior of direct competitors have a profound effect on the new business, so do the number and behavior of indirect competitors. Assess your findings about indirect competitors and try to determine their reputations and roles in the marketplace.

GEOGRAPHIC CUSTOMER DISTRIBUTION

As entrepreneurs begin the process of formally getting to know the competition for the planned business, they need to be concerned with geography—not geography in the sense of the world but in the sense of customers. Getting to know customers is a critical ingredient in the success formula for your new company. Where do your potential customers live? How far will they travel to do business with you?

To determine the geographic distribution of potential customers, get a map of the area in which your business will be located. Mark the probable location of the business. You have likely not chosen the exact location yet, but you probably have a good idea of the general neighborhood.

Next, mark the areas on the map in all directions that represent the farthest distance customers will likely be willing to travel to do business with you. Then draw a circle that includes all the communities in which your potential customers live.

If the business is a small retail store, the circle may be relatively small and cover only a portion of the city. If, on the other hand, the intended business is a production facility with widely based appeal, the circle might include one or more states. It could even cover entire regions of the country.

The circle on the map represents the geographic distribution of your potential customers. It also, to some extent, represents the geographic distribution of your future competition. Have you ever noticed that fast-food restaurants tend to come in clusters? That's because they have all determined where their potential customers live and work and how far they are likely to drive for a hamburger and a soft drink. This is just one illustration of the fact that once you have located the customers, you have probably located the competition as well.

COMPETITIVE ANALYSIS

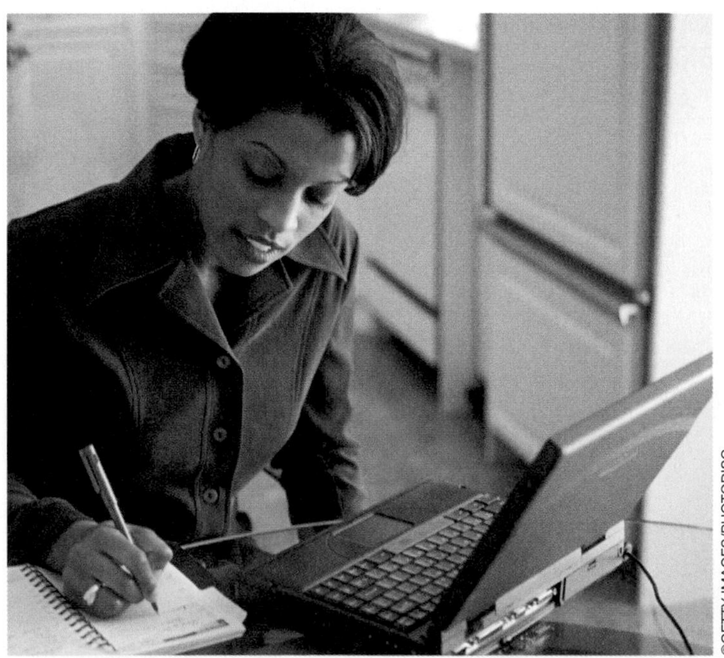

Now that you understand types of competition and geographic distribution, it is time to do a more detailed competitive analysis. A **competitive analysis** is defined as the identification and examination of the characteristics of a specific competing firm. A business-specific competitive analysis provides you with the information you need to pinpoint strengths and weaknesses, both yours and the competition's. This knowledge is essential for marketing success.

How do you know the names of your competitors? Every business providing the same product you plan to offer within the geographic distribution of potential customers is your competitor. As suggested earlier, check the Yellow Pages, look for advertisements, drive the geographic area if you can, talk to people, ask questions, and put together a list. You will need it to analyze your competition.

Analysis of Competitors Who Have Failed

Not only should all the identified direct and indirect competitors be analyzed, so should any that have recently gone out of business. Most of these would probably have fallen into the category of direct competitors. It is important to include them in your analysis so that you can benefit from their mistakes. But first you need to determine the reasons for these mistakes. A good analysis provides that information.

Table 7-1 is a form designed for analyzing competitors who have failed. List as many competitors that have gone out of business as possible, consulting chamber of commerce records, community data books, personal knowledge, Yellow Pages from previous years, and any other source of local business data.

After identifying failed competitors, try to determine why they failed. Casual conversations with existing competitors will often yield useful information. Most will probably have an opinion on why the business in question failed.

Some of the possible reasons for failure are listed in the table. They include poor management, undercapitalization, lack of knowledge about the business, and the competition's influence. If you can identify any trends among the failures, note those as well.

TABLE 7-1 REASONS FOR FAILURE

Names	Poor Management	Under-capitalization	Lack of Knowledge	Competition	Other
1.					
2.					
3.					
4.					
5.					
6.					
7.					
Trends					
1.					
2.					
3.					
4.					
5.					

Analysis of Direct and Indirect Competition

The next step is to look at both direct and indirect competition from an analytical perspective. Table 7-2 is a convenient way to record data from that analysis. Five factors should be analyzed: price, location, facility, competition type, and rank.

- **Price** In this sense, price refers to the price range into which each competitor's prices fall for products or services that are the same as or very similar to what your new business will offer. Based on your competitive analysis, indicate if the competition is in the high (H), middle (M), or low (L) range.
- **Location** The location of competitive businesses must be examined in comparison to the new business's anticipated location. Is the competition located in a better (B), worse (W), or about the same (S) quality location?
- **Facility** Facility refers to the actual buildings occupied by competitors. Compared to the new business's anticipated facility, is the competitor's facility better (B), worse (W), or about the same (S)?
- **Type of competition** Based on the previous information presented, determine if other businesses are direct (D) or indirect (I) competition.
- **Rank** The competitors should be ranked in terms of their degree of competitiveness. If there are 10 competitors, number 1 should be the strongest, number 10 the weakest.

TABLE 7-2 ANALYSIS OF THE COMPETITION

Names of Competitors	Price (H/M/L)	Location (B/W/S)	Facility (B/W/S)	Direct (D) or Indirect (I)	Rank (1 to 10)
1.					
2.					
3.					
4.					
5.					
6.					
7.					
8.					
9.					
10.					

Table 7-3 is a form that takes the competitive analysis one step further. With this form you can use the information recorded in Table 7-2 to identify your strengths and weaknesses as compared to the competition's. First list two strengths, then two weaknesses. As you identify each weakness, try to determine how it might be overcome.

By this point you should have the information you need to understand your competition. If you do a good job, competitors should not be able to surprise you in the future.

TABLE 7-3 STRENGTHS AND WEAKNESSES OF MY PLANNED BUSINESS
Strengths 1. 2. 3. 4.
Weaknesses 1. *How will I overcome this?* 2. *How will I overcome this?* 3. *How will I overcome this?*

What if you are having trouble finding information about your major competitors? Are there other things you can do? Of course there are. The secret is to try to continually discover new sources of information. The following list offers several possibilities.

- **Yellow Pages** After you have identified a competitor, check the Yellow Pages in the local telephone book for an ad. Does the ad provide useful competitive information? If so, make a record of it.
- **Promotional Brochures** Do any of your competitors print and distribute brochures? If so, these usually contain a wealth of information about the business.
- **Promotional Advertisements** Paid promotional advertisements in print media, on the radio, and on TV are usually built around one or two major selling points your competitor feels are important. Pay careful attention and try to identify them.
- **Competitors' Customers** Have you run across potential customers for your business who are currently shopping at the competition? If so, ask them questions such as what they like and dislike about the competition and what it would take for you to win their business.
- **Competitors' Vendors** As you check out vendors for equipment, supplies, and inventory for the new business, ask them questions about the competition. Ask which business is the biggest, most profitable, best managed, and so on. Ask who they think your biggest competitors will be.
- **Trade Associations** If there are trade or business associations dealing with your specific business, join them if possible. That way you can get membership lists and other valuable information about the industry and who the major players are.

©GETTY IMAGES/PHOTODISC

- **Competitors' Web Sites** Companies often put things on their web pages that they never should. Check them out for things such as number of employees, major clients, employee resumes, future plans, and anything else that might be listed. You will find that good competitive sense is often sacrificed for ego, and poor decisions concerning what to put on the Web are the result.
- **Competitors' Employees** Depending on the size of your community, you may meet or already know one or more employees of some of the competitive businesses. If you do, ask them about their company. Why do they like working there? Is it a strong company? Who are some of the company's biggest clients? A word of caution: Do not try to deceive the people with whom you are talking. Tell them you are interested in getting into the business.
- **News Stories About Competitors** Keep a careful eye on the news media for stories about the competition. Again, sensitive competitive information sometimes slips out when a news story is being developed. Also, newspeople have a tendency to do in-depth background work on interviewees and include it in the story.
- **Shop the Competition** If the competitive business is the kind that encourages customers to walk in and wander around, take advantage of the opportunity to see them in action. Check out the physical facility, prices, customer service, and anything else you can think of.

COMPETITIVE INTELLIGENCE

Competitive analysis has achieved such a prominent place in business success that it has spawned a whole new industry. Today entrepreneurial ventures all over the world sell the service of gathering competitive intelligence. The industry is large enough to have its own professional association. SCIP, the Society of Competitive Intelligence Professionals, describes itself as an organization that is "serving professionals who are leveraging knowledge for competitive advantage."

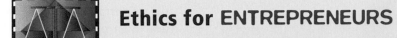

Ethics for ENTREPRENEURS

Candice graduated from Colorado State University 10 years ago with a business degree in human resource management. For the first five years after college, she worked in the personnel department of a large computer manufacturing facility in Fort Collins, Colorado. The work was challenging and the pay was good, but with 60-hour workweeks, Candice had little time or energy to devote to other aspects of her life.

Candice progressed well in the company. She gained solid experience in all aspects of human resource management, especially hiring and benefits. Life was good, if somewhat boring and predictable.

Toward the end of her fifth year, the company decided to outsource the human resource management function. As Candice contemplated unemployment for the first time in her adult life, the phone rang. It was the manager of the company that had been awarded the outsourcing contract. He wanted to know if Candice was interested in working for them.

Fast-forward four years to the present. Candice has advanced to the level of manager of the outsource company. Realizing she is doing the lion's share of the work but receiving little of the profit, she is planning to strike out on her own. The title "entrepreneur" has a nice sound to it.

She has been working on a business plan that will lay the groundwork for her new company. It is now time to start on the competitive analysis. Candice faces an ethical dilemma. One of the major competitors for her venture will be the company she currently manages. How much company information can she ethically use?

Two years ago Candice's boss responded aggressively to the challenge of a new competitor. He cut prices to a bare minimum, pressured clients, and called in favors all over town. She knows she can expect the same treatment. Her advantage, in addition to being able to predict the competitive response, is that she is the one who has been working with clients. She is the face of the company around town. Plus, the owner has seemingly lost interest in the business.

Candice decides she would probably have the competitive advantage in any struggle that might arise when she opens her own company. She continues to work on her business plan.

Think Critically

1. Do you think it is ethical for Candice to use her personal knowledge of the company to compete against it?
2. Is there another way for Candice to work more for herself, yet not have to compete against her current employer?

Many entrepreneurs do not understand the concept of competitive intelligence and its importance to modern businesses. **Competitive intelligence (CI)** is a systematic and ethical program for gathering, analyzing, and managing external information that can affect a company's plans, decisions, and operations.

Regardless of whether you are selling competitive intelligence as a service or conducting it for your own entrepreneurial use, CI is important. Consider the pace of business change. What was true yesterday may not be true tomorrow. Managing "by the seat of your pants" is no longer a viable option.

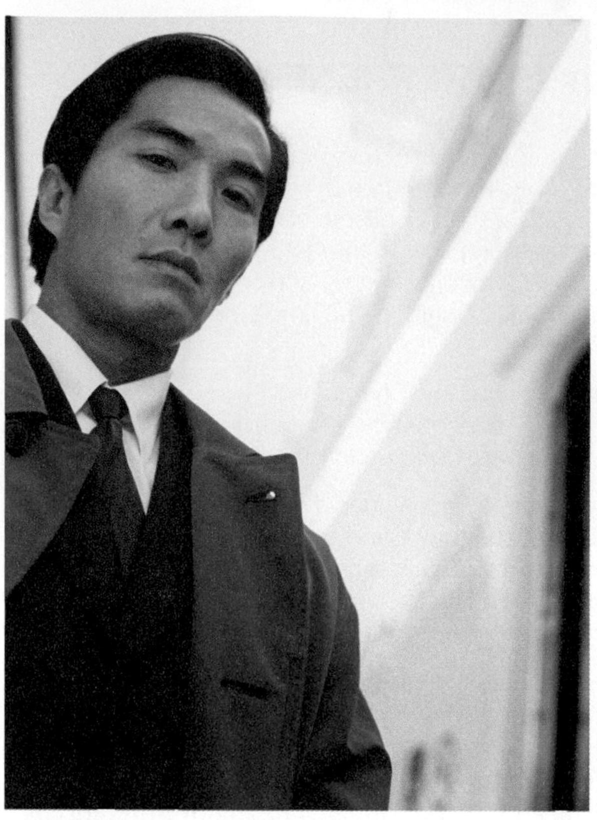
©GETTY IMAGES/PHOTODISC

Instinct and intuition are still important assets, but they must be applied to data gathered through intense competitive intelligence activities.

The price of bad business decisions is often business failure. This is especially true for the small business still in its infancy. Limited financial resources and restricted cash flow make every decision a critical juncture for the business owner.

The price is equally heavy for big business. Sam Walton, the founder of Wal-Mart, noted in his autobiography, *Made in America: My Story,* "One reason Sears fell so far off the pace is that they wouldn't admit for the longest time that Wal-Mart and Kmart were their real competition. They ignored both of us, and we blew right by them."

Ethics and Competitive Intelligence

Is competitive intelligence legal? Yes. With the information published on company web sites and the preponderance of written material available today, there is little competitive information that cannot be uncovered using legal, ethical means.

To help guide those gathering competitive intelligence, SCIP has published "Society's Code of Ethics," which "forbids breaching an employer's guidelines, breaking the law, or misrepresenting oneself." SCIP's guidelines for intelligence-gathering professionals are the following:

- To continually strive to increase respect and recognition for the profession at local, state, national, and international levels
- To pursue their duties with zeal and diligence while maintaining the highest degree of professionalism and avoiding all unethical practices
- To faithfully adhere to and abide by their own company's practices, objectives, and guidelines
- To comply with all applicable laws
- To accurately disclose all relevant information, including their identity and that of their organization, prior to all interviews
- To fully respect all requests for confidentiality of information
- To promote and encourage full compliance with these ethical standards within their company, with third-party contractors, and within the entire profession

FUN FACTS

Mattel's Barbie® and Ken® were a couple for 43 years. In 2004, the company's vice president of marketing said they were "breaking up." It seems nothing lasts forever. Competitors are probably trying to determine why. Do you think there is a competitive implication here?

Many firms dealing in CI have incorporated SCIP's code of ethics and made additions to it as well. Some examples follow.

1. Employees never lie when representing themselves.
2. They do not provide false or misleading information.
3. They do not try to confuse or deceive during interviews.
4. They never use threats or intimidation.
5. They do not deal in corporate espionage by stealing trade secrets.
6. They conduct all Internet research in a legal manner.
7. They do not offer money or special favors for information.
8. They do not install listening devices in competitors' businesses.
9. They do not record conversations without permission.

The Competitive Intelligence Industry

According to the Society of Competitive Intelligence, the market for business intelligence is worth about $2 billion a year worldwide. Services range from detailed investigations to clipping news articles. According to research in the late 1990s, 60 percent of all surveyed U.S. companies had a structured intelligence system.

Competitive intelligence is not just for big business, though. Entrepreneurs starting small businesses need it just as much. The major difference is that while big business may hire a CI firm to gather information, small businesses must educate themselves in CI procedures and perform the work themselves.

Regardless of your size, big company or small, to a large degree your success lies in knowing what your competition is doing. Business decision-making should be more of a science than an art. A big part of making it a science is having accurate data upon which to base decisions.

Analyze your competition carefully. You can be sure they are watching and analyzing you.

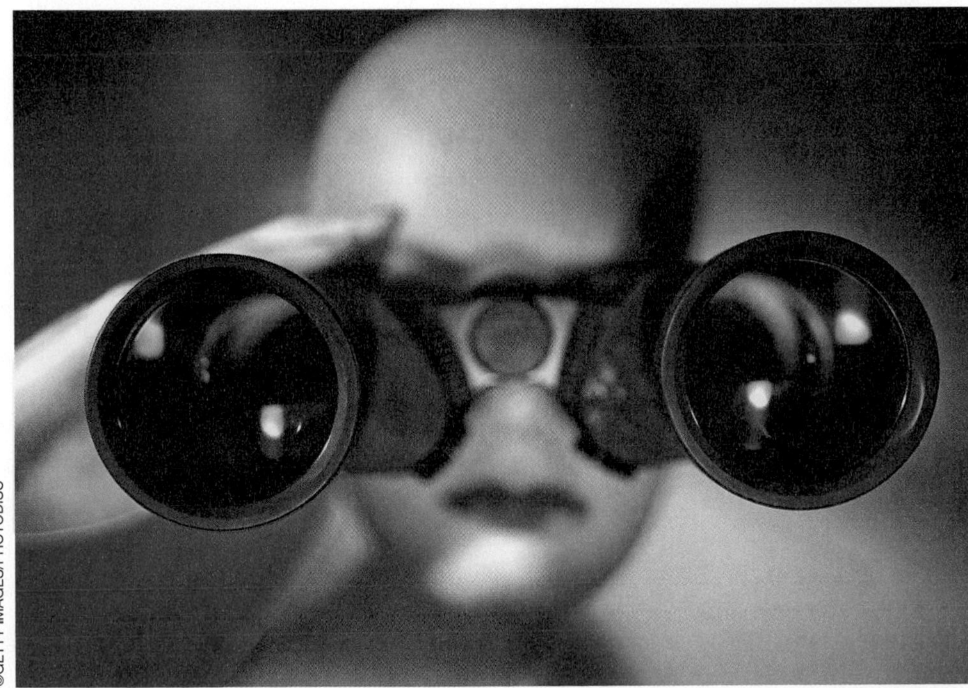

Ship in a BOTTLE

Survey the Competition

One of the attractions of the ships-in-bottles business to Fred was the lack of competition. At first glance he believed he had the market pretty much to himself, but when he did some research he learned he was far from alone when he considered the tremendous amount of indirect competition and substitute products.

In the wholesale business, indirect competition came from the 50 plus wholesalers and manufacturers who were active in the quality specialty nautical product business. Although their products did not duplicate his, they were after the same target market that Fred was. Their presentations and sales of items such as ship models, kits, and nautical artifacts could quickly absorb the retail buyer's open to buy budget. During the trade show Fred often heard "Well, I'd be interested, but I've already gone over my purchase budget in ship models."

Fred started a list of the companies he'd heard the most about in order to design a competitive strategy. He would have to create arguments why a buyer should stock ships in bottles in addition to ship models and other related items. He would point out the advantages of ships in bottles in terms of uniqueness, space requirements, and sometimes price compared to large ship models. He would not pretend that the competition did not exist and would offer his product as one that complemented the other. The argument that a complete nautical gift display should offer ships in bottles as well as ship models, nautical instruments, kits, and other artifacts held considerable merit.

Fred also learned he should not dismiss the inexpensive souvenir competition. He worked on designing presentations that demonstrated that his product was distinctly different and served a different market.

The retail Internet market was filled with nautical gift sellers. Again, although they did not offer the same product, they were selling to the same market. Their web sites often advertised a complete selection of all nautical gifts, including one or two models of ships in bottles purchased from a souvenir wholesaler. Fred's new web site would address this potential competition by announcing boldly that he had the largest selection available in the U.S.

One area he felt confident about was that it was a very difficult market for new entrants. Building ships in bottles was a rare skill. It was practiced by some modeling experts, but few would turn it into a commercial business because of the lack of trained labor and the difficulty of acquiring parts. Some of Johann's relatives were trained in the craft, and he had a source for bottles and materials in the Philippines that was not known to many. In the past there had been competition, in particular another German manufacturer. However, he had left the market because of material supply problems and a lack of qualified help and returned to making customized models.

Fred did not consider the modeling experts competition, as they served an entirely different market.

A buyer looking to purchase an individual customized model for $1,500 and willing to wait six months for its completion was not part of Fred's target market. He was only too glad to pass along the names of professional modelers to inquirers.

continued

Think Critically

1. What other sources of information should Fred investigate to determine the strength and number of his competition?
2. Fred is very vulnerable to the bargaining power of his supplier. Johann could change distributors or decide to manage the U.S. market himself. What should Fred be doing to protect himself from this threat?

Summary

Knowledge of the competition is vital to all entrepreneurs if they are to survive in the business world. Competition and private enterprise are dependent on each other. Competition in the United States is created by the following factors: similar products and services, multiple buyers and sellers, freedom to enter or exit business, and the guarantee of fair competition. Fair competition is ensured by three acts of Congress: the Sherman Antitrust Act, the Clayton Act, and the Robinson-Patman Act. In addition, the Federal Trade Commission regulates business activities to prevent unfair competition.

When it comes to business competition, Harvard Business School Professor Michael Porter's body of work is the analytical standard. Porter identifies five forces that drive competitive activity:

1. Intensity of rivalry among existing competitors
2. Threat of entry by new competitors
3. Pressure from substitute products
4. Bargaining power of suppliers
5. Bargaining power of buyers

Any entrepreneur contemplating entry into a new industry should examine all these forces. Current entrepreneurs should also study these forces as they struggle to stay competitive in markets where they already operate.

There are two types of competition, direct and indirect. All competitors, whether direct or indirect, must be identified and analyzed. The geographic distribution of both customers and competitors is one of the first factors an aspiring entrepreneur should consider.

In the next step, specific competitors must be identified and a more detailed analysis begun. Businesses that have failed in the recent past must also be analyzed to determine why they failed and to look for any trends that may be useful for planning purposes.

The next step is to look at both direct and indirect competition from an analytical perspective. Current competitors must be analyzed in five areas: price, location, facility, type of competition, and rank. After competitors are analyzed, the information should be used to identify strengths and weaknesses of the new business.

Competitive analysis has become so essential that it has spawned a whole new industry. Today, entrepreneurial ventures all over the world sell the service of gathering competitive intelligence, or CI. Competitive intelligence is a systematic and ethical program for gathering, analyzing, and managing external information that can affect a company's plans, decisions, and operations. SCIP, the Society of Competitive Intelligence Professionals, has created guidelines for the conduct of CI professionals.

Chapter Review

A Case in POINT

"A GOOD JOB" FOR THE COMPETITION

Two weeks ago Benjamin Dinges opened his new business, a store called Sporting Life. It offers a full range of athletic equipment designed for weekend athletes.

Business has been very slow for Ben, and he is getting discouraged. The new business has not lived up to his expectations at all. In the beginning he thought that once he got enough money together to open the store, customers would automatically start coming in. He had put up the equity on his home as security, done the necessary work to get the rented facility ready, and chosen the right kind of merchandise.

A few customers had come in, but most left without buying anything. He had been so frustrated he'd asked several of them why they didn't buy. They told him they could get the same merchandise at a lower price from the competition. When he pressed them for names, they mentioned several. He had heard of only one of the competing stores.

Back in the planning stage, he had known there would be competition, but he didn't worry about it. "Just do a good job," he had told himself. "That's all it takes. Let the competition worry about me. I'm going to be the problem, not them."

Think Critically

1. If you were a friend of Ben's and he asked you for advice, what would you say to him at this point?
2. Do you think there is any chance of salvaging Ben's business? What is the biggest mistake he has made so far?
3. Do you think Ben gave himself good advice when he said, "Just do a good job"? Why or why not?

Vocabulary Builder

1. Clayton Act
2. competition
3. competitive analysis
4. competitive impact
5. competitive intelligence
6. direct competition
7. indirect competition
8. monopoly
9. price discrimination
10. price fixing
11. Robinson-Patman Act
12. Sherman Antitrust Act
13. tying agreements

Review the Concepts

14. What is competitive impact?
15. How does competition relate to private enterprise?
16. What is the difference between direct and indirect competition?

17. What is meant by geographic distribution of customers?
18. What is Porter's Five-Forces Model of Competition?
19. What does Porter mean when he says, "Rivalry is usually stronger when demand for the product is growing slowly"?
20. What does Porter mean by the bargaining power of suppliers?
21. Why is it important to analyze competitive strengths and weaknesses?
22. Define competitive intelligence.
23. Is competitive intelligence legal? Is it ethical?

Critical Thinking

24. Name the four factors that create competition in the U.S. Briefly explain each factor.
25. How does a monopoly eliminate competition?
26. What role do customers play in determining the geographic distribution of competition?
27. Why is it important to analyze competitors that have failed?
28. What are the five factors to consider when analyzing current competitors?

Project

Build Your Business Plan

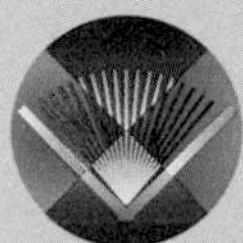

As you continue the planning process for your new business, it is now time to take the information presented in this chapter and use it to get to know your competition. Complete the following steps in your business plan notebook.

1. Take a map of your area and put a star on the general site of your new business. With a marker, draw a circle around your anticipated geographic market area.
2. Using the Yellow Pages and other available resources, make a list of businesses that are potential competitors within the geographic market area.
3. Try to find out if businesses similar to yours have failed in the past year. List those businesses on a separate sheet of paper.
4. Now make your own copies of Tables 7-1, 7-2, and 7-3. Complete the tables as fully as you can.

Chapter 8

Location and Facilities

Objectives

8-1 Explain the role of convenience in choosing a location for a business.

8-2 Differentiate the three categories of consumer goods.

8-3 Describe the location options available for retail businesses, industrial businesses, professional offices, and home-based businesses.

8-4 Discuss various aspects of commercial leases.

8-5 List the advantages of buying a commercial space.

8-6 Explain the importance of properly evaluating potential facilities and their surrounding environment.

THE IMPORTANCE OF CONVENIENCE

You may have heard that the three most important ingredients in starting a successful business are location, location, location. Although this statement is somewhat exaggerated, for some businesses it holds much truth. Choosing the proper location is one of the most important decisions an entrepreneur makes.

Our society demands convenience. Driving along a busy commercial strip with its fast-food restaurants or visiting a super-sized shopping mall gives you an idea of the extremes businesses go to in order to be accessible to their customers. The question is no longer whether to eat pizza but rather from which pizza restaurant to order and whether to go to the restaurant to eat it, pick it up, or have it delivered. The entrepreneur who understands the importance of being in the right place at the right time is the one most likely to succeed.

Entrepreneurs must understand the relationship, or correlation, between time and place. Whether the prospective purchases are consumer goods or services or industrial products, customers' decisions are affected by what they perceive to be convenient. Making a business convenient intensifies the consumer's desires. If it is convenient to buy pizza, people will buy more. If they have to drive 5 miles to buy pizza instead of 1 mile, they will buy fewer pizzas.

Convenience saves time, and time is finite. Time cannot be created or extended. There are only 24 hours in a day. In increasingly busy lives, saving time has become very important. By offering convenience, the entrepreneur saves time for the consumer, thus persuading the consumer to buy more.

Americans have grown accustomed to obtaining goods with little effort. If you are pressed for time and cannot easily find what you want, you often buy substitute goods or services. Many businesses profit from consumers' time limitations. Fast food restaurants are a good example. The tremendous growth of the fast food industry occurred when women started to enter the workforce in greater numbers. Because of the hectic lifestyle of the dual-career family, it became more convenient to go through a drive-through window on the way home from work or order a home-delivered pizza.

©GETTY IMAGES/PHOTODISC

Saving time is often worth money to customers. Time becomes a commodity for which they are willing to pay. Certainly it is less expensive to buy basic grocery items at a supermarket than at a convenience store. But in a convenience store, customers are paying for the convenience, which provides the merchant with a higher markup. Figure 8-1 illustrates what happens when a business is perceived as more convenient than its competition.

FIGURE 8-1 *Convenience Theory*

Convenience

Retail Image → Ease of Acquisition → Increased Sales → Increased Profits

Convenience

↑ Repeat Sales

Time and convenience are responsible for the growth of many other industries, such as catalog sales and vending machines. Internet sales have surged because Internet shopping is convenient and saves time and travel. Time is also why small manufacturers can compete successfully with large manufacturers, as they are often able to deliver goods faster. It is very important to have the right assortment of goods and the right image, but if the goods are not easy to acquire, the business will not succeed.

TYPES OF CONSUMER GOODS

To determine the best location for selling consumer goods and services, entrepreneurs must first classify their products as one of three types of goods—convenience goods, shopping goods, or specialty goods.

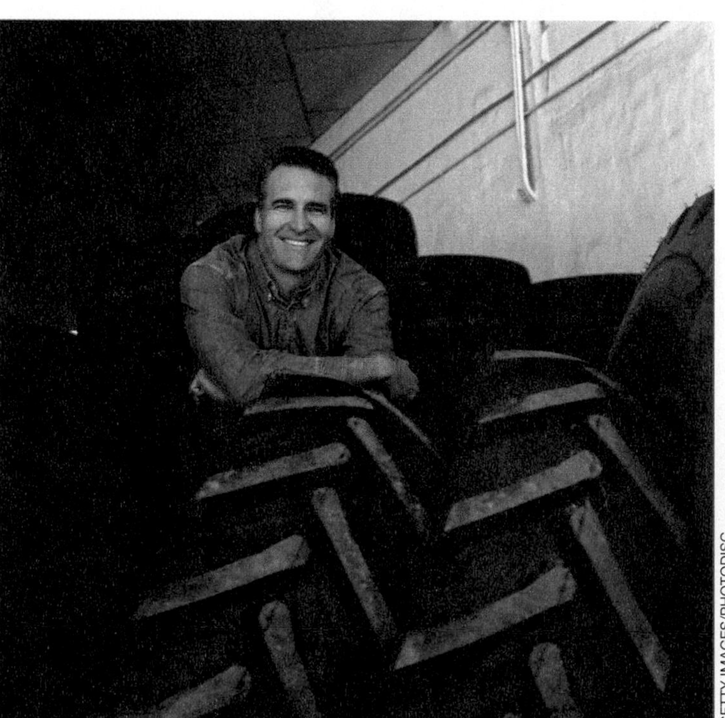
© GETTY IMAGES/PHOTODISC

Convenience goods are products that people expect to find in many places. They are readily available in a variety of stores, including convenience stores, drugstores, and grocery stores. It is imperative that a business that sells convenience goods be accessible to large markets.

Shopping goods are products that are also easily found, although they are not as widely distributed as convenience goods. They are normally available in all communities in sufficient quantities to meet average consumer needs. Tires, jewelry, popular fashions, and compact discs are examples of shopping goods. Purchase of these products often requires going to a particular type of store and usually involves more planning and decision making than does the purchase of convenience goods. Consumers often comparison-shop for these products, looking for the best value. To sell shopping goods successfully, businesses must be convenient to intended markets.

Specialty goods are products that people are willing to go out of their way to buy. The purchases are usually planned in advance. Wedding dresses, cars, and computers are examples of specialty goods. Since these are usually major purchases, the consumer does not mind taking extra time to get the best product. Success in specialty goods sales requires that the business be accessible, that potential customers know its location, and that it is located in an area that is compatible with the image of the product or service.

Small Business Technology

Telecommunications technology has been a great advantage to small business owners. With affordable long distance telephone rates, e-mail, and faxes, small businesses can communicate with their customers as easily as large businesses do. Potential customers cannot tell if the communication comes from the skyscraper office of a large company in New York City or John Smith's home office on Cherry Street. Transactions also occur more quickly than ever before. Inquiries can be made and answers received in a matter of minutes.

CHOOSE A BUSINESS LOCATION

The first decision you need to make is which community will be the best one for your business. Completing a demographic study will help to determine this (see Chapter 5).

If the demographics of your local community support your business idea, you would be wise to locate there for several reasons.

1. You will be working in a familiar area.
2. There will already be a small nucleus of customers in place, made up of friends and acquaintances.
3. You may know bankers, attorneys, or accountants who would be part of an important support system for your new business.

The grass might look greener in another community, but your hometown is often the best bet. Once you have chosen the community, you can consider specific location possibilities.

Retail Businesses

A wide variety of shopping areas offer different advantages and drawbacks, depending on the type of retail business you are starting.

Downtown Shopping Districts In the past, the downtown area of a town or city was where the commercial activity was centered. Almost everyone worked and shopped downtown. After World War II, however, a population shift toward suburban areas began. More and more people chose to reside outside of cities, so retail establishments started to move to these areas as well.

Suburban shopping areas began as small shopping centers and grew into major shopping complexes. Downtown stores branched out to the suburbs and left the downtown areas in many communities almost deserted. In recent years, many cities have recognized the deterioration in their downtowns and have made efforts to reverse it. It is often difficult to rebuild these areas because of parking problems and limited shopping hours, but many towns have managed to create attractive downtown shopping districts.

Locating in a downtown shopping district offers certain advantages to business owners, the chief one being the lower cost of doing business. Since the buildings are often older, rental costs may be considerably lower. Also, the hours of operation are often shorter than in suburban malls, which reduces operating expenses. However, when considering a downtown location, the entrepreneur must identify any disadvantages, such as parking limitations, as well as the overall suitability of the facility. Although many of today's shoppers prefer evening shopping, if the downtown area is active during the day and the surrounding businesses are well maintained, it is certainly a location worth considering. College towns, tourist areas, and active commercial districts make attractive downtown locations.

FUN FACTS

The Country Club Plaza in Kansas City, Missouri, is considered the country's first shopping center. The Plaza opened in 1924 as the first shopping area specifically designed to accommodate automobiles.

Shopping Centers Shopping centers have come a long way since they first appeared, primarily after World War II. There are four classifications of shopping centers, and each is indicative of the market it serves.

Neighborhood shopping centers often have a supermarket and small service and convenience goods stores. The customers are nearby residents who shop in these centers for convenience. The population density of the surrounding residential areas determines the amount of activity. Rental expense is usually reasonable. Businesses that sell mainly convenience goods or services can be profitable in these shopping centers.

Community shopping centers are designed to serve residents of many neighborhoods. Although rents are higher than in neighborhood shopping centers, locating in community shopping centers can mean more profit for businesses that sell shopping goods, convenience goods, or both. Normally, these centers have at least one, and often two, major tenants called **anchor stores**, and 20 or more smaller stores. Anchor stores, which are often department stores, large discount stores, supermarkets, or drugstores, advertise

actively and attract customers from an entire community. The smaller stores attempt to attract those customers as well, often as they walk by, comparison-shopping between the anchor stores.

Regional shopping centers are designed to attract customers from a region, or more than one community. These larger shopping areas usually have three or more anchor stores and more than 50 other stores and are often enclosed malls. A regional shopping center or mall offers convenience, shopping, and specialty goods, but because renting the space is expensive, the products offered often have a higher **profit margin** than most convenience-goods stores can support. The profit margin, or markup, is the difference between the cost of a good or service and its selling price.

©GETTY IMAGES/PHOTODISC

The entrepreneur who sells shopping goods or specialty goods and needs substantial pedestrian traffic to be successful might want to do business in a regional shopping center, but the high cost of operation adds to the risk of starting a business.

Super regional shopping centers are found in major metropolitan areas and may contain more than a hundred of the most contemporary stores. For example, the West Edmonton Mall in Edmonton, Canada, and the Mall of America in Bloomington, Minnesota, each has approximately 800 stores. These giant complexes also feature entertainment facilities, such as skating rinks, miniature golf courses, hotels, and amusement parks. The Toronto Blue Jays' baseball stadium is attached to a shopping mall. Stores in these centers are extremely expensive to operate and are not usually recommended for new business owners. Most tenants are chain operations that can make large investments in their operations.

Big box store centers are being developed in medium and larger communities. These centers comprise very large shopping goods stores that sell in great quantities, usually at discounted prices. Stores such as Best Buy, Circuit City, Barnes & Noble, and Toys "R" Us, which offer a complete selection of their industry's products, have found a profitable platform of operations in such locations. They are not the best choice for smaller stores, but strip shopping centers are often located near box stores and take advantage of the traffic they create.

Discount outlet centers have also become more widespread, but these stores are usually owned by the manufacturer of the products they sell, and are therefore not an option for start-up entrepreneurs.

If the new business is to be located in a shopping center, the entrepreneur must research the advantages and disadvantages of each type. For example, the high cost of a large center is offset by its appeal to customers, and, theoretically, more people shopping means more chances to sell. Also, if paying more rent gives the business greater exposure, the business will not have to spend as much money on advertising. Malls and shopping centers charge rent based on traffic flow. A store in a high-traffic mall will cost more than one in

FIGURE 8-2 *Shopping Center*

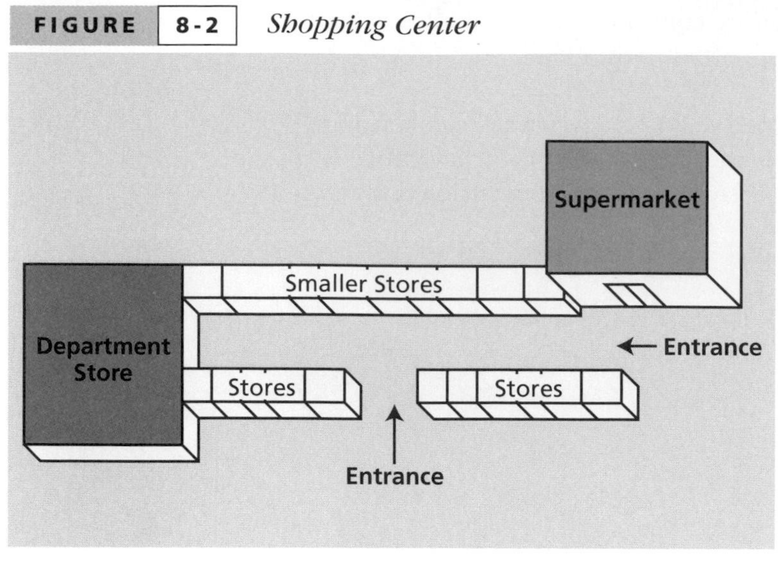

FIGURE 8-3 *Competing Shopping Center*

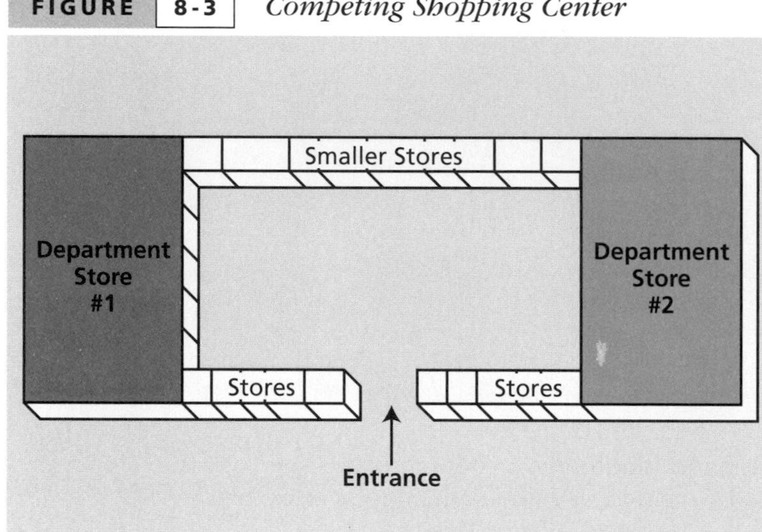

a low-traffic mall. Entrepreneurs must determine whether the extra traffic will generate enough additional sales to offset the higher rent. Stores that depend on a large number of fairly low-cost transactions must locate where there is a high volume of pedestrian traffic. Also, larger shopping centers usually have larger advertising budgets.

"You get what you pay for" is often true when it comes to choosing a retail location. Two shopping centers that appear to be very similar in makeup might be quite different in traffic flow, as illustrated in Figures 8-2 and 8-3. Suppose two community malls were located within a mile of each other on the same side of the same busy highway. One is anchored by two major department stores, the other by a major department store and a major supermarket chain store. Both shopping centers have approximately 55 stores and the same tenant mix of smaller stores. The shopping center with the two department stores rents for $25 per square foot base rent, and the other center rents for $20 per square foot. If you were considering a 1,500-square-foot store, the difference in base rent would be $7,500 per year ($30,000 versus $37,500). That $7,500 could be used to buy additional inventory, which could produce more sales. But look closely at the traffic flow. The two department stores create a constant cross flow of traffic past the other tenants as shoppers go from one to the other, comparing prices and selection. This does not happen with a grocery store anchor, as shoppers leave for home immediately after collecting their groceries. The shoppers at the department store at the other end of the mall have no compelling reason to walk past the other stores. If your business is dependent on enticing customers walking by your storefront, it might be a critical mistake to save $7,500 and lose unknown potential customers. It is worth the effort to take careful traffic counts during different times of the day to determine which location has the most walk-by customers. An entrepreneur who gives up $50,000 in sales to save $7,500 in rent will be kicking herself 365 days a year.

Super regional, regional, and most community shopping centers have **merchant associations**. The dues collected from tenants by these associations are used to advertise and to pay for entertainment events designed to attract customers. Special attractions such as Christmas decorations, antique automobile shows, or circus clowns are usually arranged by merchant associations.

Stand-Alone Stores Stores that depend on drive-by traffic are often **stand-alone stores**. They must have ample parking, good signing, and effective lighting if they are to be successful. Stand-alone stores may be located adjacent to large malls, or on the streets leading to the malls, to take advantage of the traffic flow. Since they are located away from shopping areas, the business owners pay less rent or might even own the buildings. Restaurants and automobile dealerships are examples of businesses that do well in stand-alone store space.

Industrial Businesses

Manufacturers and wholesalers also recognize the importance of location, but for different reasons. It is important that these businesses efficiently address logistical, transportation, and communication needs. A sizable part of the operating expense of an industrial company is shipping costs, both for material received and for products shipped. A manufacturer or wholesaler must deliver products in a timely manner and will therefore want to locate close to transportation facilities and, if possible, to customers. In addition, this kind of business often hires a sales force. Traveling to make sales calls is both time-consuming and expensive, so a geographically centralized location is more efficient.

Industrial Parks Good space at a reasonable rent and access to transportation couriers are two advantages offered by industrial parks. The cost is often partially subsidized by city, county, or state agencies in order to attract industrial businesses that create jobs and expand the community's tax base. Industrial parks offer large spaces that are ideal for manufacturers and bulk wholesalers.

Incubators In recent years there have been a growing number of subsidized business rental spaces called **incubators**. Incubators make it possible for new small businesses to share space and certain operating expenses, such

The Global ENTREPRENEUR

Some entrepreneurs are truly globally located. Greg Myers, an Atlanta entrepreneur, spends 80 percent of his time traveling the world and considers his office as wherever he happens to be at any time. Greg often rents temporary office space at airports around the world. Many large airports rent office space on an hourly or daily basis to international business travelers. Entrepreneurs can meet with clients and hold conferences at a convenient location, which saves considerable time traveling to and from airports. Greg believes this is a great idea: "I can meet with a client in Japan in the morning and another client in Australia in the afternoon."

Think Critically

1. Discuss with your classmates the advantages and disadvantages of a lifestyle like Greg's. Does it appeal to you?
2. Why is it important to meet face to face with customers rather than conduct business via conference calls or video transmissions?

as rent, utilities, property taxes, office equipment, and salaries for some supporting staff, such as a receptionist. The businesses may be located on different floors of a large building or in adjacent smaller buildings. Ideally, similar business start-ups are grouped together, such as technology businesses or small manufacturers, in order to share ideas as well as equipment and space.

An incubator manager assists the small businesses with certain kinds of tasks—helping to find trade shows for tenants to exhibit their products, for example, or putting them in touch with outside experts. The manager's salary is paid by the supporting agency.

Incubators are usually subsidized by state and local business development agencies and sometimes have access to federal programs. Often they are located near state universities and receive their support from educational institutions. The arrangements are not long term. Many have a time limit of three years, after which the new business must leave the incubator and find a permanent space. It is the hope of the supporting agency that by the end of the allotted time the business has fully developed into a successful enterprise with a sizable employee base, thus contributing back to the community.

The entrepreneur who needs only a small amount of space for technological development or light manufacturing should find out whether there are incubators in the community with available space.

Professional Office Space

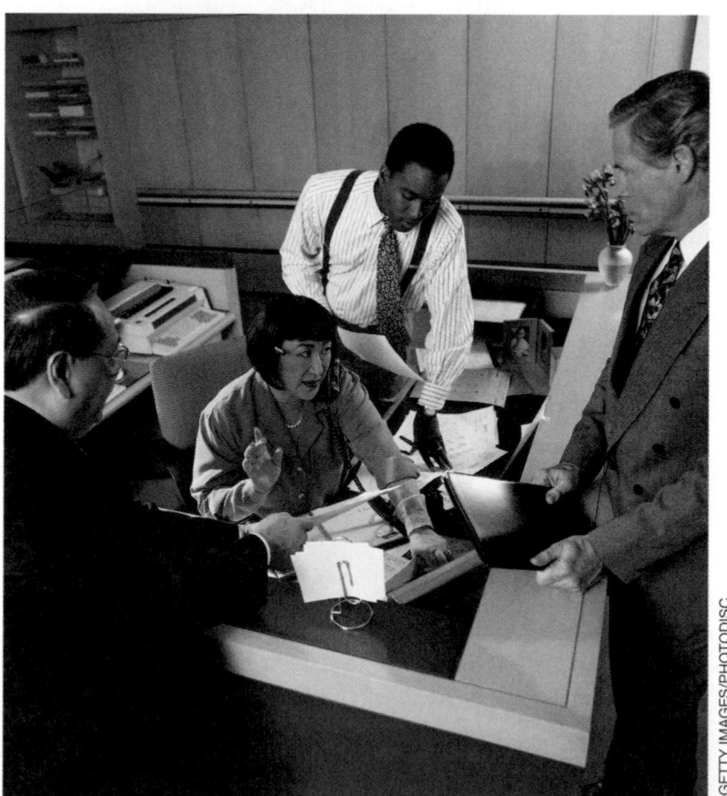

©GETTY IMAGES/PHOTODISC

Many entrepreneurs—real estate agents, accountants, business consultants, and architects, among others—need a professional office to meet with and sell to their clients. It is important that their offices present a professional image and be conveniently located. Many types of offices are available, from small suites in standalone buildings to penthouses at the tops of skyscrapers. The spaces are leased, and expenses vary depending on location, size, and what services the landlord offers. Rental costs are based on cost per square foot, as for retail space.

Various arrangements are available—some landlords offer furniture and equipment, and others lease just the empty space. Office suites that include a waiting room and a receptionist area are often needed to serve clients professionally. Some office complexes also rent out space, which allows tenants to share common expenses such as copying machines, a receptionist, and rest rooms. This arrangement is similar to that of an incubator, but is not normally subsidized by development agencies.

Home-Based Businesses

There has been a tremendous growth in home-based businesses over the past decade, and for some very good reasons.

- Doing business from the home is an excellent way to run a business on a limited budget. Rent, utility costs, and maintenance fees are avoided, so there is more money to purchase income-producing inventory and to advertise.
- Home-based business owners are not subject to the restrictions and obligations imposed by lease agreements.
- The owner can be at the business site around the clock.

A home-based business is excellent for the part-time entrepreneur. Many businesses start out in the owner's home, on a part-time basis, until demand is established. Then the entrepreneur can afford to move to a larger site.

You may recall the story of Flora Ramirez in Chapter 1. Flora successfully turned a part-time jewelry business into a full-time career. She started a home-based business selling handmade jewelry to retailers. She worked in her basement to fill the orders, then took the finished products to a shipping office. Once a steady demand for her merchandise had been established, she hired four people (including her husband) and moved to a nearby industrial park, where she had more working space and better access to transportation couriers.

Anyone with the desire and a good idea can operate a home-based business. Many services, such as babysitting, house and office cleaning, and lawn maintenance, can be coordinated and managed from a home office. All that is needed is a telephone to contact customers, a personal computer, and a fax line. It is also possible to sell goods via the Internet or direct mail. These goods can be offered through magazine advertisements, catalogs, or a web site. When an order is received, the product can be packaged and taken to the post office or picked up by a courier service.

There are some disadvantages to operating a home-based business. Space limitations are often a drawback. It may also be difficult to keep the business separate from family activities. The result can be constant interruptions. Also, many entrepreneurs find themselves feeling isolated from the business community. They miss the social interaction and information exchange with business colleagues. Many owners learn to treat their home business as if it were located downtown, by dressing in suitable attire, arranging lunch appointments, and getting out of the office regularly to visit customers, attend meetings, and spend time with colleagues.

FUN FACTS

There are over 18 million home-based businesses of all types and sizes operating in the U.S. The Census Bureau estimates that home-based businesses are increasing at the rate of 2.7 percent per year.

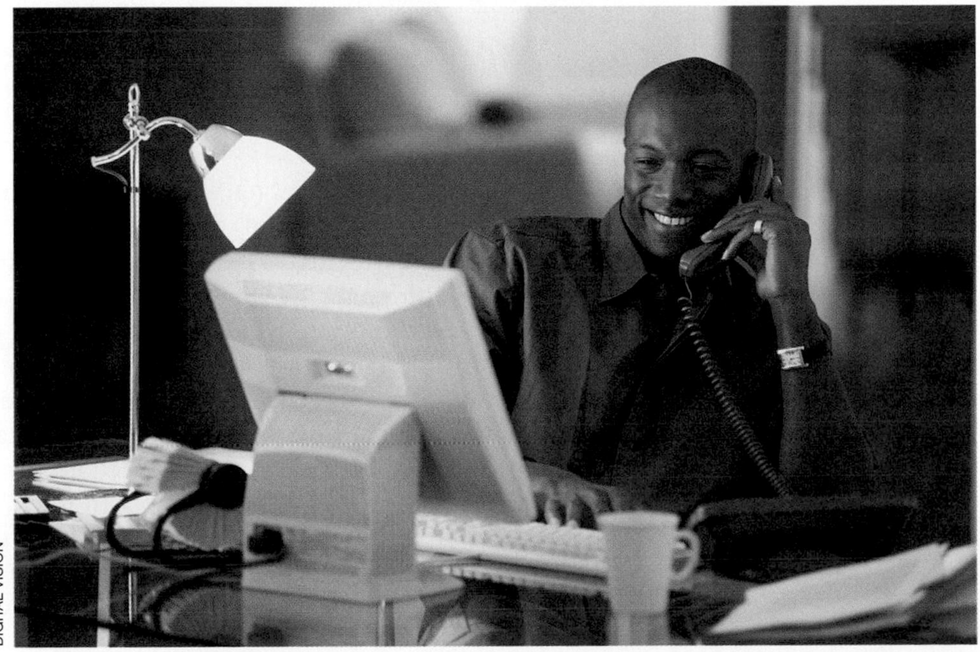
DIGITAL VISION

LEASE ARRANGEMENTS

Unless they work from home, business owners either enter into commercial lease agreements or buy commercial property. Lease agreements for commercial property are usually long and complex contracts that should not be viewed lightly. If inexperienced, the **lessee** (the tenant) should hire an attorney to carefully review the fine print. A shopping center lease may be 30 pages long and tie the lessee to a very tight contractual agreement. It is a contract that is in effect for the stated duration of the agreement whether the space is being occupied by the tenant or not. Rent payments do not stop just because the tenant wishes to stop doing business. Too often businesses close with time still left on the rental contract, and the owner must continue to pay rent for a nonexistent business. Lease contracts are like bank notes—they are for a stated amount of a guaranteed total divided by the number of months. The typical lease is written to protect the **lessor**, or landlord, from tenants vacating the property before the end of the lease.

Commercial leases are written in terms of a stated base rent per square foot of leased space. The rent cost is declared on an annual basis by multiplying the number of square feet by the stated per-square-foot charge. For instance, 2,000 square feet at $15 per square foot equals an annual rent of $30,000. The annual rent is divided by 12 to arrive at a monthly rental fee, in this case $2,500 per month. These are only the basic terms. The full terms of the lease may include anything from the amount of property and liability insurance the tenant has to carry to what type of business the tenant can operate and during what hours.

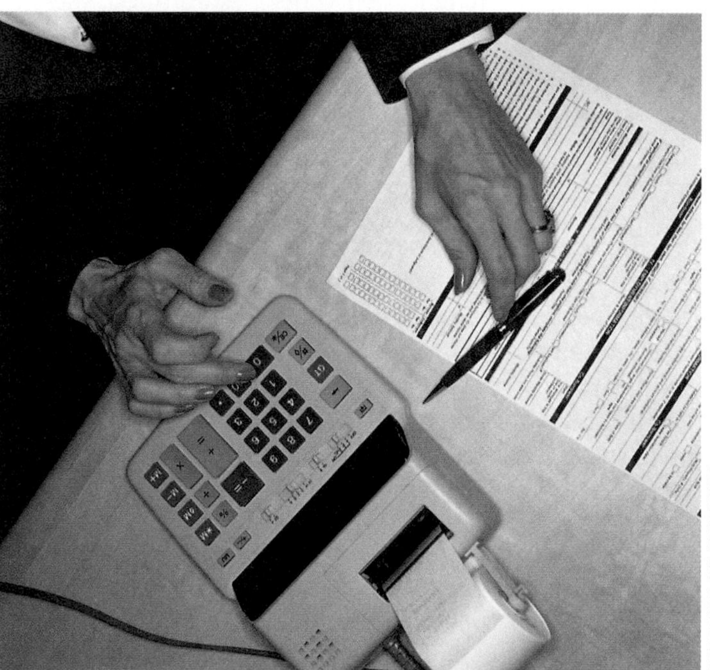
©GETTY IMAGES/PHOTODISC

Retail leases often include a **percentage rent clause**, which requires that the tenant pay additional rent if and when revenues exceed a certain dollar amount. The landlord is in effect receiving a reward for offering the tenant a convenient location. Figure 8-4 illustrates a cover sheet for a retail lease that includes a percentage rent clause. The business owner has agreed to pay 6 percent of gross sales if that figure is higher than the guaranteed base rent of $1,200 per month or $14,400 per year. The percentage rent kicks in when annual sales exceed $240,000 ($20,000 per month). If the merchant does a great job, the shopping center brings in a lot of traffic, and sales reach $300,000, the annual rent will be $14,400 plus 6 percent of the $60,000 overage, or $3,600, for a total rent of $18,000 per year.

FIGURE 8-4 *Cover Sheet, Retail Lease Agreement*

This lease, entered into the ______ day of ______________, 20___, between the Landlord and the Tenant hereafter named.

ARTICLE 1. Definitions and Certain Basic Principles

a. "Landlord" Smith Development Co. .

b. Landlord's address 120 Main Street .
Springfield, IL 22573 .

c. "Tenant" Mr. John Doe DBA Card Town .

d. Tenant's mailing address 32 Washington Ave. .
Springfield, IL 22513 .

e. Tenant's trade name Card Town .

f. Tenant's address in Shopping Center A-8 .

g. Demised Premises approximately 1500 square feet in Building A (computed from measurements to the exterior of outside walls of the building and to the center of interior walls) having approximate dimensions of 30 feet x 50 feet, such premises being shown and outlined on the plan attached hereto as Exhibit A and being part of the Shopping Center situated upon the property described in Exhibit B attached hereto. "Shopping Center" shall refer to the property described in Exhibit B, together with such additions and other changes as Landlord may from time to time designate as included within the Shopping Center.

h. Lease term: Commencing on the "Commencement Date" as hereinafter defined and ending thirty-six (36) months thereafter except in the event the Commencement Date is a date other than the first day of a calendar month, said term shall extend for said number of days in addition to the remainder of the calendar month following the Commencement Date.

i. "Estimated Completion Date" day of October 15, 20XX .

j. Minimum Guaranteed Rental $ 1,200.00 per month, payable in advance.

k. Percentage Rental 6 % of gross sales in excess of $ 20,000.00 per month during the calendar year, payable on or before the 10th day of each following month subject to Article IV, Section 3 below.

l. Initial Common Area Maintenance charge per month $ 92.08 .

m. Initial Insurance Escrow Payment per month $ 40.42 .

n. Initial Tax Escrow Payment per month $ 82.50 .

o. Security Deposit $ 2,998.00 refundable upon expiration of term less any damages for unusual wear and tear or charges necessary to restore the Damaged Premises to satisfactory condition.

p. Permitted use Card and gift store – retail sale of cards and gifts .

The sum of

Minimum Guaranteed Rental as set for in Article 1, Section 1.1j and 1,200.00

Initial Common Area Maintenance charge, as set forth in Article 1, Section 1.1l and 92.08

Initial Insurance Escrow Payment as set forth in Article 1, Section 1.1m 40.42

Initial Tax Escrow Payment as set forth in Article 1, Section 1.1n 82.50

Initial Base Sales Tax Payment as set forth in Article 1, Section 1.3 . . . . 84.00

MONTHLY PAYMENT TOTAL 1,499.00

1.3 In addition to its obligation to pay the Monthly Payment total, adjusted from time to time as provided herein, Tenant shall pay simultaneously herewith any sales tax, tax on rentals, and any other charges, taxes, and/or impositions now in existence or hereafter imposed by any governmental authority based upon the privilege of renting the Demised Premises or upon the amount of rent collected thereof. All payments provided for herein shall be in lawful (legal tender for public or private debt) money for the United States of America.

Ethics for ENTREPRENEURS

Inexperienced entrepreneurs often enter leasing agreements without a complete understanding of all the clauses in the lease contract. The excitement and enthusiasm of opening their first business keeps them from asking pertinent questions and doing careful research.

Leasing agents can find themselves at a lease signing asking, "Have you carefully read the lease, and do you have any questions?" The excited entrepreneur might answer, "It looks like a bunch of legal mumbo jumbo to me, but I'm sure it's what we discussed and the rent is what we agreed on. I'm ready to sign."

Think Critically

1. Does the leasing agent have an obligation to suggest postponing the signing until the entrepreneur has a chance to consult with an attorney or an experienced entrepreneur?
2. What articles in a lease might be the most difficult to understand and require further clarification?

A lease agreement may include other charges besides rent.

- **Common Area Maintenance (CAM)** Often included in retail and industrial leases. Maintenance might include anything from the cost of lighting the parking lot to having the parking spaces striped. The charge reimburses the landlord for keeping up the property and is determined by the percentage of total leased space the tenant occupies.
- **HVAC Charges** These charges, for heating and air conditioning the common property of the mall or office complex, are also determined by the percentage of total leasable space in the complex occupied by the tenant.
- **Tax Escrow Payment** The tenant agrees to pay the proportional amount of real estate property tax assessed on the complex.
- **Insurance Escrow** The tenant agrees to pay a portion of the liability insurance to protect against injuries that might occur to anyone on the common property.
- **Merchant Association Fee** Retail tenants often pay a monthly fee that might be combined with the monthly rent.

As you can see, the extra charges on a lease can add up to a substantial percentage of the total lease payment. Each situation is different. Entrepreneurs must make sure the agreements they are entering are exactly what they perceive them to be.

Leasing is a bargaining confrontation between the lessor and the lessee. Terms are normally negotiable depending on supply and demand and the desired tenant mix. If the landlord is seeking the type of business the entrepreneur represents, there may be considerable room to negotiate the lease on more favorable terms. This might include requesting that the landlord be responsible for all interior finishing work, or leasehold improvements, to the property. In all cases it never hurts to try to negotiate.

The following interview, with a former retailer who now acts as a leasing agent for community shopping centers, will give you some insight into commercial real estate.

What are the main determinants used in site selection of a shopping center?

The main considerations are competition and land costs, which include the cost to develop the land. The objective is to locate as close to the population area as possible. You do not want a location where a competing shopping center could be built between yours and the population area, thereby cutting you off from your market. The cost of the land is important, but we are not interested if there are problems such as no utilities or other complications that will drive up the building cost. We use market research to gather demographic information and try to find out if any anchor store tenants would like to locate in the area. We share the demographic information with all potential tenants.

How are rent charges determined?

Rent charges are determined by the total cost of the site, the con-struction costs, and the cost of financing. The developer needs to show the bank a projected income statement showing that he can pay loans back based on projected rental fees. The final rent is determined in consideration of recovering costs, rent surveys of area shopping centers, and a desired rate of return on the investment. In the end, of course, it's decided by supply and demand. The anchor tenants are major determinants of rents, since they will contribute greatly to the demand for the space. Excess competition will drive the price down. Keep in mind, however, the shopping cen-ter developer has made a financing contract with the lender that he will receive X dollars per square foot of space, and anything too far removed from this figure will raise the lender's eyebrows. Regardless of market supply and demand, there is a point in negotiations at which the developer is better off carrying a vacancy than renting at reduced rates for an extended period of time.

©GETTY IMAGES/PHOTODISC

How do you find tenants, and what do you look for?

We want tenants that complement the shopping center. We do not want to put an auto supply store in an exclusive specialty store center. The great majority of my time is spent canvassing existing merchants in the general area to alert them to our project. We prefer established businesses to new business owners. An established owner can show us a track record and we know what to expect. We really like established businesses that advertise a lot,

©GETTY IMAGES/PHOTODISC

because they contribute to a more vibrant shopping center. We screen new business owners closely. We request financial information and detailed plans for the proposed operation. We like to see a source of outside income in the event initial plans do not work. If the tenant has absolutely no experience, we might attempt to direct him to a franchise. If there is limited capital and little experience, we will back away from leasing to that individual. New businesses usually call us in response to a sign on the property or an announcement of our project in the newspaper.

The landlord is sometimes considered an adversary of the tenant, rather than an ally. Having been on both sides, would you comment?

The landlord is a businessperson just as the tenant is, with the same objective—to make a profit. I have found the industry to be very ethical. The developer is concerned with the tenant's success, as it ultimately determines the landlord's future success. Landlords are not villains in black hats. They are legitimate businesspeople with fair objectives. Although commercial real estate is not as strictly regulated as residential real estate, it is for the most part a very professionally run industry. However, in commercial real estate I would recommend "Caveat emptor"—let the buyer beware—as a guideline for the inexperienced entrepreneur.

BUY A BUSINESS LOCATION

The alternative to leasing is buying commercial property. Rarely is this a good choice for a new business start-up. However, once the business is established and proven, it can be a very profitable step. Successful stand-alone operations in particular should consider owning the property from which they operate. Needless to say, lease concerns become a thing of the past. There will be no landlord to raise the rent or make demands. Owning can also be a very good investment. Commercial property can escalate in value just as residential property does. The entrepreneur can achieve on two fronts: a business that makes a profit residing in a facility that appreciates in value.

The down payment on commercial property may be higher than that for a home. Lenders do not normally offer mortgages of the same duration as residential mortgages. Lenders seek shorter paybacks for commercial ventures, which are considered riskier. Like rent payments, mortgage interest is tax deductible.

EVALUATE THE FACILITIES

Choosing the facility for a new business is an important decision for business owners. Once the best location has been found, the owner must determine whether the facility is suitable for the intended business operation. It must be large enough, and it must be structurally sound. Many leases assign responsibility for all property maintenance to the lessee; if there is a leak in the roof or the plumbing or air conditioning fails, the tenant has to pay all repair costs. It is imperative that the prospective tenant carefully examine the property for structural soundness before signing the lease.

The chosen site must fit the image of the intended business. Selling fine, expensive jewelry requires a different image than selling tires does. People shopping for a $5,000 diamond ring will not shop in a run-down section of town. On the other hand, for most people, the price of a tire is more important than where the tire store is located. If you are selling to a specific market, the facility and its surroundings must appeal to that market.

Different businesses have different environmental requirements. For example, the aspiring restaurateur should consider the following:

1. Restaurants should not be in areas that are noisy, have unpleasant odors, or are frequented by vagrants.
2. The type of neighborhood will influence whether customers come in family groups, as couples, or singly.
3. Restaurants located in industrial areas will be dependent on surrounding businesses and their employees' lunch arrangements.
4. Restaurants should not be located near funeral homes or cemeteries.
5. Restaurants in residential areas rely mostly on evening trade.
6. Schools or churches are not particularly desirable as neighbors to a restaurant. They may cause congestion, and they can affect a restaurant's right to sell alcoholic beverages.
7. There must be good lighting and ample parking for customers.

The prospective business owner must fully research the location and facility requirements of the intended product or service.

Ship in a BOTTLE

Setting Up Operations

After Fred and Jeanie decided against a retail store, the location decision for Ship in a Bottle came down to two options: either lease exhibit and office space at the Merchandise Mart in downtown Atlanta, or set up operations in the Johnsons' home.

Fred spent a day visiting with the Merchandise Mart leasing agent, Henry Richmond. Henry showed Fred a number of available spaces in various sections—the general gift floors, the home decor floors, and the patio and garden area. A 400-square-foot space in the gift area drew Fred's interest. The leasing cost of $2,500 per month was something of a shock, but Fred knew it would be expensive based on his experience as a temporary exhibitor, which cost that much for just five days. Leasing a permanent showroom would replace the cost of four temporary rentals per year, or $10,000. Deducting the $10,000 from the one-year total lease of $30,000 meant the added cost of permanent space would be $20,000 per year.

Fred knew that selling from a permanent showroom during the shows would greatly increase his exposure and sales. In addition, it would provide office space for Fred and a showroom in which to meet with customers when there were no shows. The idea of a deluxe showplace, a nice office, and some extra prestige was certainly appealing.

However, the benefits of working from home were equally attractive—low overhead, no lease obligation, a flexible schedule, and the casual atmosphere of home. Certain decisions and expenses were involved, however. An up-to-date computer system, including a scanner and a printer, was a must. One room, probably the spare bedroom, would have to be changed to an office. He would need to arrange for voice mail service, a toll-free 800 number for customers, and office furniture, including file cabinets and a credenza. In addition, where would he store his inventory? The garage would not work, as the ships in bottles were somewhat heat sensitive. So it would have to be the basement, which he would have to finish—another expense. All told, Fred calculated the total cost of setting up in his house would be approximately $10,000.

Fred weighed this $10,000 against a lease that would cost an added $20,000 per year. Even recognizing that sales would initially be greater from the leased space, it was not a hard decision. The fact that the business was new and still a part-time operation was the determining factor. Tax savings were another consideration—Fred could deduct 15 percent of his mortgage interest and utilities costs as legitimate business expenses as long as the business was in a separate room and the basement was used primarily for inventory storage.

The day might come when Ship in a Bottle had a fancy full-time showroom, but for now Fred would work from his home and enjoy the benefits of free rent *and* a tax deduction.

Think Critically

1. If you were in Fred's situation, would you prefer to work from your home office, or from a nicely decorated showroom downtown? Defend your choice.
2. Sketch an office layout for Fred. Indicate the various pieces of equipment he would need to carry on his business.

Summary

Successful entrepreneurs know the importance of choosing the right location. Being in the right place at the right time is an important ingredient of success. Our society has become accustomed to accessibility and convenience, and businesses should be located with that in mind.

Entrepreneurs must classify their products or services in terms of degree of convenience to the consumer. They can then determine what type of location should be chosen to successfully sell the products. This choice will depend on the product, the community, and the amount of money available to operate the business.

Entrepreneurs who sell or manufacture industrial goods might locate in an industrial park. Some small industrial and technological businesses might choose to locate in partially subsidized spaces called incubators.

Many entrepreneurs operate small businesses from their homes, and some then move to a larger space after demand has been established. A home-based business is an excellent starting place for the part-time entrepreneur.

It is important that inexperienced entrepreneurs learn the intricacies of commercial leases. Many clauses in leases address the obligations of the tenant and can affect the amount paid to the landlord. It is generally advisable to seek the assistance of an attorney before signing a lease.

A Case in POINT

Stacy Roper had wanted to open a ladies' fashion boutique on posh Park Avenue since moving to the neighborhood five years ago. The tree-lined shopping area comprised four blocks of unusual boutiques, jewelry shops, craft stores, and European-style restaurants. The shopping area was so busy and successful that openings for new stores were rare. When a vacancy did occur, the lessor would simply contact the next person on a long tenant waiting list.

When Stacy learned that the old movie theater on the busiest block was to be converted into a three-story complex of small stores, she contacted the developer. The developer's plan provided for 18 store spaces of approximately 800 square feet each. The developer was hoping for a balanced tenant mix of specialty retail stores and food services. The idea was to have a restaurant, a gift shop, an apparel store, and three other stores on each level. This would ensure a good traffic flow throughout the complex. Stacy leased the ground-floor apparel space, just inside the entrance. She had carefully scrutinized the shops across the street, and they all seemed to be very successful. Stacy was confident she had made a good decision.

During the nine months that it took to remodel the theater, Stacy planned an exciting presentation. She bought her inventory from the leading apparel designers and consulted with top professionals on store layout. The finished store was truly eye-catching. It had the latest in display pieces and mannequins, elegant color-coordinated decor, and a sophisticated sales checkout system.

The Colony Theater Shopping Galleria opened with great fanfare. Of the 18 spaces, 15 opened on time, and the initial reaction was enthusiastic. Stacy was very pleased with the first month's receipts, but during the second month the pace was inconsistent, traffic seemed to thin, and sales leveled off. Some days were so busy it was hard to keep up, and others were so slow there might as well have been a barrier in front of the building. Business across the street continued at its usual hectic pace.

continued

Chapter Review

A year later Stacy contemplated closing. Six of the original merchants had already moved out. Four had been replaced, but the new tenants were not of the same stature as the original stores. Meanwhile, businesses on the other side of Park Avenue continued to prosper.

Think Critically

1. Examine Figure 8-5. Can you identify some of the reasons why the Colony Theater Shopping Galleria had difficulty attracting shoppers?
2. Based on your knowledge of the importance of convenience, what could be done to help the stores in the Galleria?
3. Do you think Stacy should close her store?

FIGURE 8-5

Colony Theater Shopping Galleria

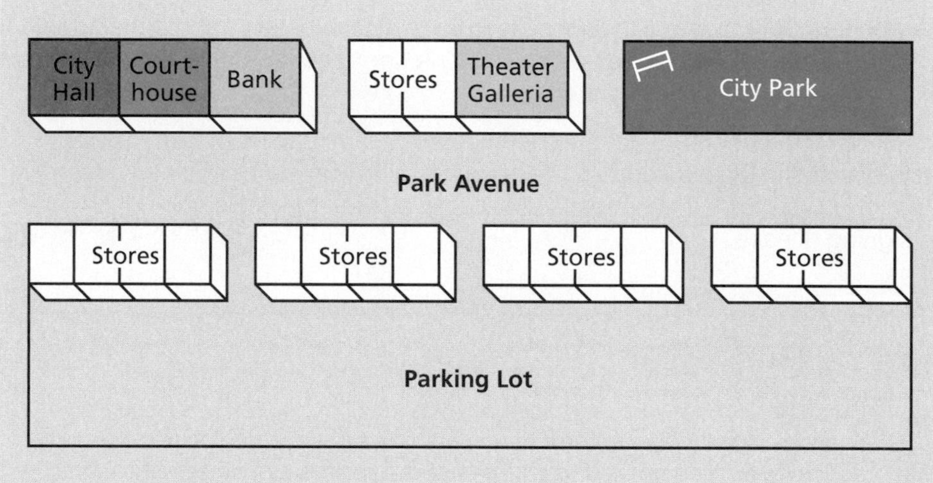

Vocabulary Builder

Write a brief definition of each word or phrase.

1. anchor store
2. big box store center
3. community shopping center
4. convenience goods
5. discount outlet center
6. incubator
7. lessee
8. lessor
9. merchant association
10. neighborhood shopping center
11. percentage rent clause
12. profit margin
13. regional shopping center
14. shopping goods
15. specialty goods
16. stand-alone store
17. super regional shopping center

Review the Concepts

18. What role does convenience play in choosing a business location?
19. What are the differences between convenience goods, shopping goods, and specialty goods?
20. How do neighborhood, community, regional, and super regional shopping centers differ?
21. What is the purpose of a merchant association?
22. List the advantages of a home-based business.
23. What is a percentage rent clause?
24. When is buying a business location a good idea?
25. What considerations must be taken into account when evaluating a facility?

Critical Thinking

26. Explain what is meant by the convenience theory.
27. List location considerations in starting a retail business.
28. List location considerations in starting an industrial business.
29. How can the choice of location be a competitive advantage?
30. Are there any drawbacks to operating a home-based business?
31. Why is a commercial lease considered a contract?
32. Describe three clauses often found in commercial leases that add to the overall cost of the rental agreement.

Project

Build Your Business Plan

Choose a location for your business, applying what you have learned.

If your business sells retail, classify your product or service as convenience, shopping, or specialty goods. Visit shopping areas in your community where you would expect to find similar products. Note how successful these areas seem to be, based on the number of shoppers and how well the individual businesses appear to be doing. Call leasing agents and inquire about costs and other leasing considerations. Request to see a sample lease.

If you are starting an industrial, wholesale, technological, or professional business, ask leasing agents for information about industrial parks, incubators, and professional office space, including terms and considerations.

If you want to start a home-based business, decide how you would use your home as a place of business.

Now make your location decision. Remember to consider the surrounding environment and the facility itself. Defend your reasons for choosing the location.

Which Business?

The time was right for Jarrid Barton to explore new career opportunities. He was completing his bachelor's degree in business administration, and his job with a large West Coast computer contractor was probably going to be eliminated due to industry-wide downsizing. With a degree, experience as a purchasing agent, and the knowledge that he wanted to be his own boss, Jarrid was ready to identify the employment options available to him.

Jarrid decided to start by creating a list of jobs he felt would interest him. He first evaluated his past work experiences to determine which responsibilities and tasks he enjoyed most. Working with people, accepting greater responsibility, and initiating new projects headed the list. Personal choice criteria included a desire to serve the community, maintain professional satisfaction, and earn the respect of clients and peers. Skills that Jarrid identified included his management style, computer expertise, and ability to negotiate contractual agreements. From this information he compiled a list of industries that he found appealing:

food services
recycling
manufacturing parts, wholesale
delivery services
restaurant supply
sporting goods, retail

Jarrid's next step was to do some analysis of each industry. First he gathered relevant information from various local agencies. The Los Angeles Chamber of Commerce provided statistics concerning the economic health and growth projections of surrounding communities. The Small Business Development Center offered leads to sources of specific industry information. The LA Economic Development Agency gave him a list of industries they considered to be underrepresented in southern California. Jarrid ended up with a small library of information from over a dozen agencies. After more than a month of research, telephone calls, and personal visits, Jarrid narrowed his findings to three primary markets.

1. ***Restaurant supply*** The Los Angeles area appeared to have a need for a restaurant supply business specializing in gourmet produce. In his initial research, Jarrid found a directory of produce suppliers in the greater LA area. Much to his surprise, there were only 13 major suppliers. He also discovered that many restaurateurs were dissatisfied with the service they received from these suppliers. The deliveries arrived late in the day and the produce frequently did not look fresh.

   The restaurant supply business had possibilities. With so few potential competitors, it would be fairly easy to establish name recognition. The competitive analysis would also be greatly simplified because of the small number of competitors. The business met his personal choice criteria of providing professional satisfaction and the ability to earn respect from clients and peers.

2. ***Recycling*** Initial research revealed that small communities on the fringe areas of Los Angeles did not have adequate recycling services. There were not enough

municipal or private recycling companies to fill this growing need. Jarrid recognized several opportunities in the industry, including trash/recycling collection services and beverage container recycling. Through further research, Jarrid discovered that the California Refund Value (CRV) was 2.5 cents for containers smaller than 24 ounces and 5 cents for containers 24 ounces or larger.

The recycling business also had possibilities. Jarrid estimated he could make a living with a well-run beverage recycling center. According to the California Beverage Container Recycling and Litter Reduction Act, many containers other than aluminum were subject to CRV, including glass, plastic, and bimetal containers.

Working in the recycling business would make use of his past experience dealing with people and initiating new projects. Additionally, it met his personal choice requirement of serving the community.

3. ***Exporting manufacturing parts*** Requests and orders for manufacturing parts from Pacific Rim companies were not being filled. At the same time, there appeared to be a surplus of inventory among many smaller local parts manufacturers. When Jarrid conducted his initial research, he was amazed at the huge number of companies in California producing manufacturing parts.

   Further research did turn up a few major competitors in the LA market. They were well established, with many international clients. Jarrid knew the international manufacturing parts business would require more business sophistication than his other two choices would. It would definitely be more of a challenge. His computer expertise and ability to negotiate contractual agreements would certainly come in handy. Exporting manufacturing parts, like the other two options, had real possibility.

Jarrid was now ready for the next step. All three opportunities interested him. How would he decide which one had the most potential? As you answer the case questions, keep in mind Jarrid's work experience, personal choice criteria for a business, and job skills.

Case Questions

1. Jarrid must research potential target markets for each business. How do you suggest he proceed?
2. Jarrid has barely begun to examine the competitive environment for each business. Where should he start?
3. For each business, suggest to Jarrid the two most important "P's" he should consider and why each is important to a particular business.
4. Given what you know about Jarrid, which business would appear to offer him the greatest potential satisfaction? Explain your choice.

Unit 3

Market the Small Business

Profile of an Entrepreneur

Oprah Winfrey, 1954–

According to EinfoNEWS, "Oprah Winfrey has to be one of the most admired Black entrepreneurs of all time." TopBlacks.com says, "Oprah Winfrey is considered one of the most powerful women of our time." Many who have met and worked with this extraordinary woman would remove any qualifiers and simply say, "Oprah Winfrey is one of the most admired and successful entrepreneurs living today."

The television talk-show host, actress, and producer was born in 1954 in Kosciusko, Mississippi. The family home in rural hill country lacked the most basic facilities, such as running water and electricity. It is hard to imagine any entrepreneur emerging from such humble beginnings.

Following a troubled adolescence, Oprah moved with her businessman father to Nashville, Tennessee. According to the official Oprah web site, she began her broadcasting career at WVOL radio in Nashville while still in high school. At 19 she was the youngest person and first African-American woman to anchor the news at Nashville's WTVF-TV. In 1971 she won the Miss Black Tennessee Pageant and entered Tennessee State University. She continued her radio and TV broadcasting career in college.

In 1977 Oprah moved to Baltimore, where she had been given the co-anchor slot for the WJZ-TV six o'clock news. She also co-hosted WJZ-TV's popular local talk show, *People Are Talking*, for eight years.

On the coattails of her Baltimore success, a Chicago TV station recruited Oprah to host her own morning show, called *A.M. Chicago*. As luck would have it, her chief competitor in the time slot was Phil Donahue. History was to prove the match-up inconsequential. Within a few months, Oprah's warm, personal style proved too much for the competition. Her show attracted 100,000 more viewers than Donahue's and moved from last place to first in the ratings.

In 1986 *The Oprah Winfrey Show* was aired in national syndication. It was soon available on 120 channels, had an estimated audience of 10 million people, and grossed $125 million its first year. Oprah's cut was reportedly in the neighborhood of $30 million—not a bad neighborhood, most would agree.

Realizing the benefits of owning the show herself, Oprah made the necessary personal and business moves to

REUTERS/LANDOV

DAVID YOUNG-WOLFF/PHOTO EDIT

do so. She created her own production company, Harpo Productions ("Oprah" spelled backwards), to manage the show. *The Oprah Winfrey Show* was soon in syndication and making even more money.

When it comes to formal business training, Oprah Winfrey has had little. Often joking she cannot even read a balance sheet, she does not seem to care for the term *businessperson*. (One wonders what she thinks of the term *entrepreneur*.) But it is clear she developed considerable business skills somewhere along her life's journey. Any marketing expert would qualify her as a major business success. Her brand equity (the value of associating her name with something) is in a league of its own. Just the mention of a book title in relation to her book club propels the book onto the *New York Times* Best Sellers list. Where would Dr. Phil be today were it not for his association with Harpo Productions?

Oprah's brand equity carries through all her major endeavors. Acting was an early extension of her brand. She first appeared in 1985 as Sofia in Steven Spielberg's *The Color Purple* and received Academy Award and Golden Globe nominations for her performance. Thirteen years later she starred as Sethe in the widely acclaimed *Beloved.*

Oprah did not limit her acting to the big screen. She has also appeared in the made-for-television movies *The Women of Brewster Place* (1989), *There Are No Children Here* (1993), and *Before Women Had Wings* (1997).

According to the official Oprah web site, "Oprah has been honored with the most prestigious awards in broadcasting, including the George Foster Peabody Individual Achievement Award (1996) and the IRTS Gold Medal Award (1996). In 1997 Oprah was named the most important person in books and media by *Newsweek,* and *TV Guide* crowned her the Television Performer of the Year."

In 1998 *Time* magazine included her among the 100 most influential people of the 20th century. The publishing industry recognized her contribution to reading and books by awarding her the National Book Foundation's 50th Anniversary Gold Medal (1999) and the Association of American Publishers AAP Honors Award (2003). In 2002 Oprah was given the first-ever Bob Hope Humanitarian Award at the 54th Annual Primetime Emmy Awards.

Oprah and *The Oprah Winfrey Show* have received 39 Daytime Emmy Awards. In 1998 she received the National Academy of Television Arts & Sciences' Lifetime Achievement Award.

Oprah has added magazine founder and editorial director to her long list of entrepreneurial job titles. In 2000 Oprah and Hearst Magazines introduced *O, The Oprah Magazine. O* is published monthly and today is considered a leading contemporary lifestyle publication for women. Given the intense competition in the women's magazine field, *O* is something of a phenomenon. It is the most successful magazine start-up of the last decade, with an audience of over 2 million readers each month.

Another hat Oprah wears is that of educator. In 1999 she joined Stedman Graham as an adjunct professor at the J. L. Kellogg Graduate School of Management at Northwestern University to co-teach "Dynamics of Leadership." The goal of the course was to help students cultivate their own leadership skills and develop an approach to management, leadership, and organization suited to their individual circumstances.

Philanthropy is another of Oprah's many passions. The mission of the Oprah Winfrey Foundation is to support women, children, and families around the world. Because of her work in this area, some refer to her as "the socially conscious entrepreneur."

In 2003 Oprah became the first African-American woman to make the annual *Forbes* magazine list of the world's wealthiest people, with a fortune of about $1 billion. Not bad for a poor country girl from Mississippi.

So, is Oprah an entrepreneur or an entertainer? You know what they say: "If she walks like an entrepreneur and talks like an entrepreneur, then she must be an entrepreneur."

Chapter 9

Get To Know Your Customers

©GETTY IMAGES/PHOTODISC

Objectives

9-1 Describe the characteristics of customers.

9-2 Explain the components of a consumer psychological profile.

9-3 Compare the four consumer personality styles.

9-4 Describe the consumer decision-making process.

9-5 Discuss what makes a satisfied customer.

WHAT ARE CUSTOMERS?

Customers are individuals or organizations with unsatisfied needs who possess the resources needed to fulfill those needs. The single greatest competitive advantage that small businesses have over large businesses is that they know and understand their customers better. Therefore they can better serve their unsatisfied needs. Customers are the most important part of a business. Without customers, there can be no business.

©GETTY IMAGES/PHOTODISC

To be sure of having customers, entrepreneurs must determine the needs of the marketplace and identify groups of consumers who are likely to have an unsatisfied need for the product or service to be offered. These consumers must also have the means to satisfy their needs, as this determines the size of a business's market. If an entrepreneur markets a high-priced luxury item that appeals to many, such as a 48-inch television, those who cannot afford such a purchase must be eliminated from the marketing strategy since they do not qualify as potential customers. This requires effective target marketing, which is achieved by addressing the following questions.

1. Where do my customers live and work?
2. What is the lifestyle of the people who are most likely to need my product or service?
3. What level of income is needed to purchase my product or service?
4. Which of my potential customers will receive the greatest benefit from my product or service?
5. Which group will buy the most of my product or service?

The answers to these questions can help the entrepreneur create an accurate demographic profile (see figures in Chapter 5).

CONSUMER PSYCHOLOGICAL PROFILES

After establishing a demographic profile, you should take a close look at your target customer's psychological profile. A consumer profile includes needs, perceptions, motivations, and attitudes. A basic understanding of these concepts as they apply to customer behavior allows you to efficiently satisfy the demands for your product or service.

Needs

There are many opinions as to what needs are as compared to wants. For the purpose of understanding consumer decision making, wants are defined as anticipated desires. Needs, on the other hand, are of greater priority. Needs are those things, tangible and intangible, that you require to maintain your standard of living or expected lifestyle. Using this definition, it becomes clear that people may have different needs depending on their standard of living and lifestyle expectations. To many people, designer clothing is a frivolous want, but to those who live in an environment in which they perceive that wearing designer clothes is essential to maintaining their lifestyle standards, designer clothes can be a need. Parents of teenage children learn this as they observe fashion peer pressure changing a want to a need very quickly. Human needs are rarely fully satisfied and, when unsatisfied, motivate behavior.

The noted psychologist Dr. Abraham Maslow developed his **need satisfaction theory** while studying human motivation. His premise was that as you fulfill your lower-level, physiological and safety needs, you begin to crave the upper-level needs for love and belonging, self-esteem, and self-actualization (Figure 9-1). More simply, you have a need to maintain and improve your standard of living. To be successful, entrepreneurs must identify how their products or services will allow their customers to fulfill their needs, which will then lead to a craving for a higher standard of living. Once the proper need is identified, you must learn to sell to that need.

FIGURE 9-1

Maslow's Hierarchy of Human Needs

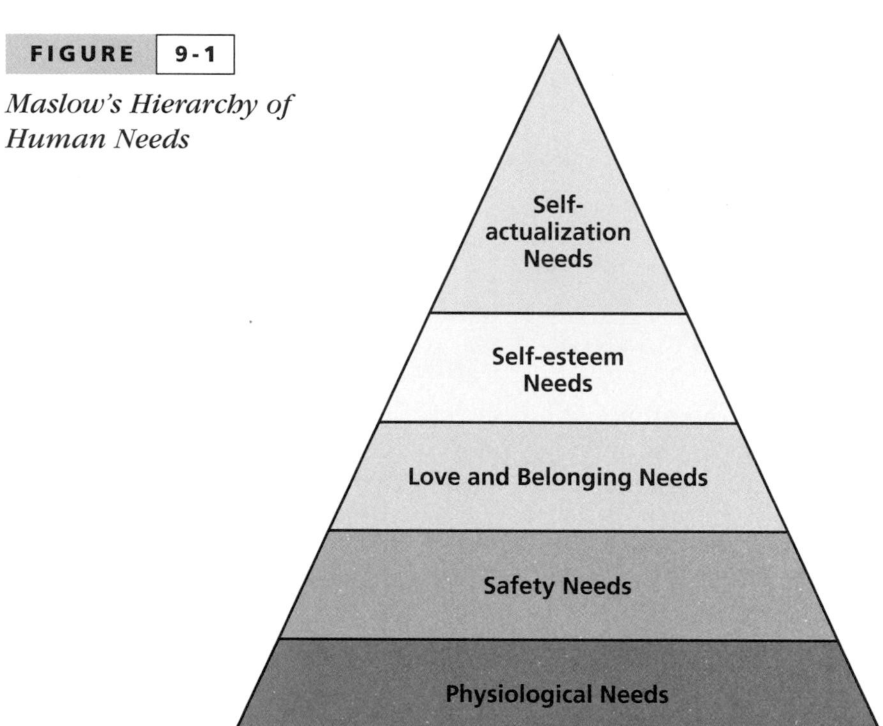

For instance, an apparel store might sell to a multitude of needs, depending on the customer. Customers looking for a basic outfit suitable for work are satisfying a belonging need. They need the right look to fit in with the rest of the workforce. However, others in the same store who are shopping for high-fashion outfits for social events are seeking to fulfill a self-esteem and/or self-actualization need—to appear attractive in the eyes of others—or they believe they deserve such an outfit for achieving a certain level of social prestige. Another example is someone purchasing a basic car to drive to work or to visit family and friends. This belonging need is certainly different from the need that motivates the purchase of a luxury car, a need to be recognized or to be rewarded for financial success. Each need level requires a different marketing strategy on the part of the entrepreneur. Through experience, questioning, and testing, you will learn what needs your products appeal to.

Often consumers are not fully aware of their needs until stimuli are applied to expose them. If a buyer is fully aware of her needs, only supplemental information may be needed to reinforce these **conscious needs**. For example, a person shopping for a particular car model for the specific purpose of transportation may require only information and assistance to direct the purchase.

A more challenging situation arises when a consumer's needs are not fully developed or conscious. The consumer may be aware of a general need for a product but may not be fully aware of what specific needs the product must fulfill. For instance, the general need may be for a car, but the specific needs may be for a car that is both fun to drive and economical. This **preconscious need** level requires additional stimuli to develop greater need awareness before a buying decision can be made.

Sometimes people do not know why they buy a particular product or service. An **unconscious need** might be an unsatisfied need exposed years before and suppressed until the purchase opportunity is presented. A need for fine china might be an unconscious need developed from admiring a grandmother's china years earlier as a child. Until the purchase opportunity arises at a time when the necessary funds are available, it remains a suppressed, unconscious need.

Perceptions

The ways you view and understand things, as determined by your background and mental framework, are your **perceptions**. They are largely formed by the amount of information and knowledge you possess about particular subjects or about a business's products or services.

Perceptions are difficult to interpret and understand. What some people perceive as needs, other people perceive as unnecessary luxuries. Perceptions may depend on how and in what environment a person was raised. People raised in great wealth certainly have a different perception of luxury goods and services than those who have not had access to them. Successful sellers learn through providing sufficient information and education how to alter perceptions to make an otherwise unappealing product appealing. Entrepreneurs must determine how their potential customers perceive their products or services and what can be done to improve that perception. Desire can be awakened by making a consumer perceive a difference between what is and what should be.

Perceptions help explain why a person makes a decision to purchase. To a certain extent you may fall victim to hearing what you want to hear and seeing what you want to see, based on your past experiences. This **selective distortion** often drives buyers to transpose information that is not in agreement with their perceptions into information that does agree. If a salesperson is

©GETTY IMAGES/PHOTODISC

providing information that tells you a certain television is a quality model, and you believe otherwise based on a prior experience with a similar model, you may subconsciously decide not to listen. Likewise, **selective retention** can influence perception. In this case the buyer remembers and retains only information that aligns with personal beliefs and values and discards or ignores information that does not.

Motivations

Customers are persuaded into action when they are given a reason, or **motivation**. Unsatisfied needs create internal tensions that motivate them to act to fulfill those needs. An individual walking by a greeting card store is reminded that it is Aunt Mary's birthday and feels an anxiety or tension to take action. This exposure may direct the individual into the store to relieve the tension (satisfy the need), or the individual may decide on another method to relieve the anxiety, such as a telephone call or flowers.

©GETTY IMAGES/PHOTODISC

Consumers are directed toward what they feel will be pleasant and away from what is unpleasant. They seek pleasure, which can be relief from the pain or anxiety of an unsatisfied need. They are motivated to relieve that pain. If you understand what motivates your target customers, you can create reasons for them to act. Knowing your target market well allows you to create ads, displays, and sales presentations that will expose unsatisfied needs, thus creating tensions that may be relieved by buying your product or service. Successful entrepreneurs are very good at exposing unsatisfied needs and suggesting ways to relieve the tensions created.

A total marketing strategy takes into account the strong motivators that direct the consumer's behavior.

- **Selfishness** Everyone has the right to satisfy their own personal needs. "You deserve a break today."
- **Greed** The product or service is a bargain. "Two for one, limited time only."
- **Hedonism** Pleasure or relief are readily available. "Tired of that tired feeling?"
- **Indolence** Perceived convenience allows ease of acquisition. "Just a phone call away."
- **Fear** Missing out can cause pain. "Buy now, limited quantities available."

Attitudes

A person's attitude can be defined as the way he or she feels about something. You want your customers to feel positive about your product. Large businesses do this through brand identification. Entrepreneurs do it through personal interaction with the customer that builds confidence. Knowing the attitudes of your target market allows you to create a strategy that appeals to positive influences. The more confidence you instill in the customer about your business, the more sales you will achieve.

Combining good service with quality products pays off. The previous Aunt Mary birthday problem will be resolved at the greeting card store if the buyer's confidence in the type of cards sold at the store is combined with positive shopping experiences there. A store that sells Hallmark cards ("When you care enough to send the very best") and also has a solid reputation for customer service is combining a well-known brand image and good customer relations to create a positive consumer attitude.

In the initial stages of developing a business plan, aspiring business owners should learn as much about how their target market thinks and behaves as possible. Primary research tactics such as surveys will help you determine your target customers' likes and dislikes, what excites them, and their expectations of the kind of product or service you are planning.

CONSUMER PERSONALITY STYLES

The importance of customers to a successful business cannot be overstated. Without customers there can be no sales, and sales are the lifeline of any business. Sales success comes from your knowledge of your customers, demographically and psychographically. It is essential that you seek as much information about your customers as possible, whether demographic descriptions of age, gender, and education or an analysis of what they need to maintain or improve their life-style. The success of the enterprise depends on how well you apply this information.

One important application is designing a marketing strategy that stimulates your target customer. This involves understanding the personality types your business will be selling to. Personality is made up of an individual's distinguishing character traits, attitudes, and habits. Carl Jung, the noted psychologist, categorized human awareness into four functions: thinking, intuiting, feeling, and sensing. Personality styles can be described in terms of these functions.

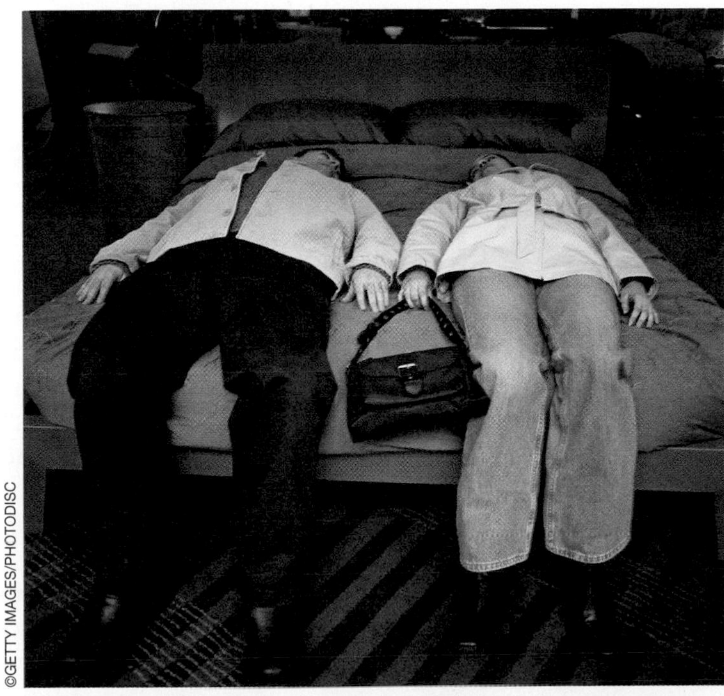

Personality Styles

FUN FACTS

In 30 years the number of Americans over age 50 will double. They will be 25 percent of the population.

Thinker Style Thinker-style personalities place great emphasis on logic and the systematic gathering of information. They take their time making a decision. They are very deliberate people who are objective and ask questions. Selling to a thinker requires presenting information in a logical and analytical manner. If your target market is made up largely of thinking-style people, your marketing information and approach must be geared toward information presentation.

Intuitor Style Intuitive people are future oriented. They are creative, broad minded, idealistic, and charismatic. They are long-range conceptual thinkers. Selling to this personality type requires demonstrating the overall concept of the product or service and its long-range benefits.

Feeler Style Feeler-style personalities are people oriented and sensitive to others' needs. They are not afraid to show their emotional side. They are spontaneous, impulsive, and rooted in the past more than the future. You should use a personal marketing approach and appeal to their people-oriented nature to gain their trust and confidence.

Sensor Style Sensor-style individuals are action oriented. They are decisive and do not like getting bogged down in detail. They are down to earth, impatient, and seek perfection, but live in a chaotic environment. Marketing efforts that attract them are to the point and often start with the results. These are present-oriented people who want immediate satisfaction.

Self-Concepts

It is not easy to judge a personality, particularly since not everyone is a psychologist. However, you can get a sense of the dominant styles of a target market through observation. Keep in mind that an individual's self-concept can change, depending on circumstances. People see themselves in four different images:

- **Real Self** How they really are.
- **Self-image** How they think other people see them.
- **Ideal Self** What they would like to be.
- **Looking-glass Self** How they want others to regard them.

The entrepreneur needs to understand the buyer's self-concept in order to design the best sales and marketing approach. Selling the latest women's fashions or diet fad is selling to the ideal self and requires a different approach than does selling life insurance, which appeals to the looking-glass self as a good provider. Successful selling requires insight and study into the target market.

Behavior Patterns of Consumer Groups

Marketers classify consumers according to their buying behavior. You can use information to determine where to position your product or service as you continue to refine your target market.

You are probably familiar with the term "baby boomer." Baby boomers are the generation born between 1946 and 1964. They are a large percentage of the buying public. Because of the size and buying power of this group, marketers have been following this generation through its various life stages. In many cases they have changed their product image to accommodate the desires of this group. Now these consumers are moving into their early retirement years, so you can expect to see more advertising directed to senior citizens than ever before.

Marketers have also identified other categories of consumers.

- **Generation Y** The youngest category of shoppers drives the market for high-tech products. Born after 1982, this generation loves to shop.
- **Generation X** This is considered by many the first generation of dual-career households and single parents. Born between 1968 and 1982, they grew up with influences such as Madonna's "Material Girl" lyrics.
- **Older Consumers** The current population of seniors is much healthier, wealthier, and better educated than previous generations.
- **Ethnic Markets** The U.S. marketplace has been greatly influenced by the growth of three large racial and ethnic minorities: African-Americans, Asian-Americans, and Hispanics.

Marketers recognize that the most basic unit of buying behavior is the household. Table 9-1 illustrates the life cycle of the household and what each group purchases at each stage of maturity.

FUN FACTS

Generation X contains over 50 million Americans, or more than 17 percent of the U.S. population.

TABLE 9-1 CONSUMER LIFE CYCLE

Stage in Life Cycle	Buying Behavior Pattern
Bachelor stage	Few financial burdens. Fashion leaders, recreation oriented.
Newly married, no children	Highest purchase rate. Cars, refrigerators, furniture.
Full nest I: youngest child under 6	Home purchasing at peak. Baby needs, washers, dryers, etc.
Full nest II: youngest child over 6	Financial position better. Many wives working. Buy large packages.
Full nest III: older couples with dependent children	Financial position still better. Hard to influence with advertising.
Empty nest I: older couples, no children at home	Home ownership at peak. Not interested in new products.
Empty nest II: older couples	Drop in income. Stay home, buy medical care products.
Solitary survivor, in labor force	Income good, but likely to stay home.
Solitary survivor, retired	Drop in income, medical needs.

Consumer Classifications

How do consumers make purchasing decisions? In addition to gathering information through information media, they rely on personal contacts, or **reference groups**, who are buyers with similar needs. This is particularly true with new or different purchases. If you are selling fashion apparel, such as ladies' sweaters, you would be wise to consider the five consumer classifications—**innovators, early adopters, early majority, late majority,** and **laggards**—as described in the following example.

Katrina arrives at a gathering of her friends wearing a new sweater. She is considered an innovator, and if the sweater receives favorable attention she will start a cycle. At the next get-together two or three other women may be wearing sweaters in the same style; they are the early adopters. By the third get-together more members of the group may be wearing the style; they are the early majority. By the fourth gathering most of the women are wearing the new look. They are the late majority. At the fifth meeting Katrina shows up wearing a new, completely different style. Some of the women are still wearing what is now the old look; they are the laggards.

It is important for the entrepreneur to sell to the innovators. They are the pacesetters and opinion leaders. They might be the popular student, the mayor, the banker, or any of the people considered to be the "movers and shakers."

Jeffrey Neff owned an air-conditioning/heating sales and service business in a large city. His business was confined to middle-class homeowners in the south part of the city. Most of his sales for new units ranged from $3,000 to $5,000. Business was decent but could have been better. Being a baseball fan, Jeff bought season tickets to the hometown team's games. His seat was beside Bill Uhler's, and they quickly became close friends. When Bill mentioned his need for a new air-conditioning/heating system, Jeff volunteered to visit his home and give him a fair quote. What Jeff did not know was that Bill was the CEO of a large company and lived in an area of the city known for its elegant mansions. Jeff received the contract to install a new unit in Bill's 8,000-square-foot home. The total price came to over $20,000. Within a month, Jeff received inquiries from one of Bill's chief executives as well as Bill's next-door neighbor. Within a year, Jeff was sending work crews on a regular basis to some of the largest homes in the city. His business had quadrupled because he had attracted an opinion leader.

CONSUMER DECISION MAKING

Customers strive for **utility satisfaction**. They choose from various products those that will give them the greatest satisfaction in exchange for their money or barter (utility). The decision-making process is not always simple; it requires effort and often causes great anxiety. Simple, almost reflex decisions such as what brand of toothpaste to buy do not require scrutiny and research and are considered **routine decisions**. **Nonroutine decisions** involve a more complex process as they are infrequent, or are sometimes first purchase decisions that may require a greater utility exchange. Purchasing tires, new furniture, or a dress for a holiday party are all nonroutine decisions. The most difficult purchase decisions are **extensive decisions**. They are characterized by the belief that the decision is extremely important and has a long-term impact on personal budgets or lifestyles. Purchasing insurance, a car, or a house are examples of extensive decisions that require much time and research.

A young man with $20 in his pocket has to determine what will give him the greatest utility satisfaction for his money. It may be a situation of deciding between a new CD or asking a young lady he recently met for a movie-and-pizza date. The CD represents an item he has purchased many times and can use over and over. Except for the choice of artist it is a fairly routine purchase. The date, however, is not routine since it is a first date. He must think about his feelings regarding the young lady, the anxiety of asking her out, his chances of success, and perhaps even the possibility of a good-night kiss. All of these factors may enter into his decision. Will the utility satisfaction of the date be worth the effort and anxiety of the nonroutine decision process? A third choice might be to decide against both these alternatives and instead set the money aside for the future purchase of a car, which would be an extensive decision.

A purchase decision requires several steps (Figure 9-2).

1. Recognize a need.
2. Analyze the cause of the need.
3. Review alternatives to relieve the need.
4. Select from the desired alternatives.
5. Make the exchange transaction.
6. Evaluate the purchase.

FIGURE 9-2 *Consumer Decision-Making Process*

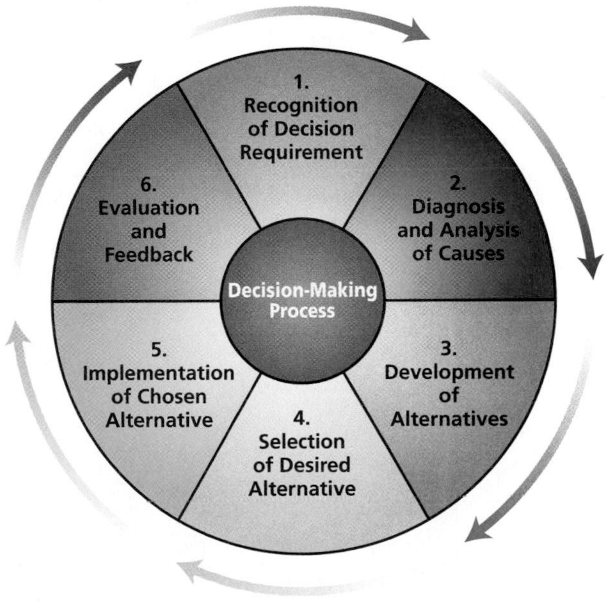

Through marketing efforts the entrepreneur can play an important role in each step of the process. Stimuli in the form of displays, advertisements, telephone calls, or other media can expose the need, cite the cause ("Is your present car no longer reliable?"), compare the particular product to its competitors, demonstrate the ease of acquisition, and illustrate the pleasure of the purchase.

Successful entrepreneurs take an active role in leading potential customers through the decision-making process. They understand the anxieties and tensions and the need to review alternatives. They provide information that gives confidence to the purchaser. Very importantly, they recognize that consumers often feel cognitive dissonance, or the feeling of anxiety and uncertainty as to whether the purchase decision was right or wrong. A good entrepreneur follows the sale with a compliment, a phone call, or a letter to foster a positive evaluation of the purchase decision in the customer's mind.

The Black Box Approach

Obviously you cannot know the complete psychological makeup of each customer. Even if you did, it could change according to the situation. The question of why people buy is an intriguing one that has provoked much thought and study for many generations.

FIGURE 9-3 *Black Box Stimulus Model*

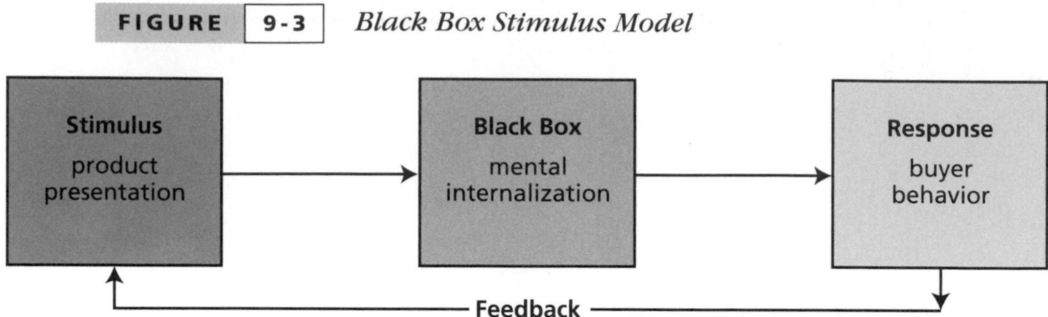

The **black box approach**, illustrated in Figure 9-3, has been used to describe the mystery of what goes on in the buyer's mind. Entrepreneurs can apply a stimulus (an advertisement or a sales presentation) and observe the reaction but cannot be positive of the customer's actual decision-making process. The black box approach describes a stimulus response model. A stimulus is applied, which results in a reaction. The approach assumes that

The Global ENTREPRENEUR

The international entrepreneur must learn the needs, perceptions, motivations, and attitudes of the many markets in which he or she competes. The customs in many countries are very different from those in the United States. Entrepreneurs often do not take the time to research foreign markets and end up offending potential customers with their poor choice of marketing techniques. Entrepreneurs who insist on doing business as they do in their own society are considered *ethnocentric*. Those who conduct business according to the attitudes and values of the host country are considered *polycentric* and are more successful because of it.

Think Critically

1. In the U.S., business lunches and dinners are standard practice. In some other cultures, it is impolite to discuss business during a meal. If someone from such a culture is visiting an American company, should his or her American host refrain from talking business during meals?
2. What are the dangers of an ethnocentric attitude?

the reaction should occur in a predictable manner, such as to buy or not to buy, but it does not tell you the reason for the reaction. That information is hidden in the black box that is the buyer's hidden mental process. If you could determine what goes on inside that mental process, you would become a marketing genius. In the meantime you have to be content with gathering as much information as possible in order to choose the best marketing strategy to reach the greatest number of potential customers.

The Informed Consumer

The difference between routine, nonroutine, and extensive decisions is the degree of uncertainty surrounding the decision. The greater the uncertainty, the more effort is required of the decision maker. More information equates to less risk equates to easier decision making.

Consumers have never been smarter or had as much power as they do in the 21st century. The tremendous exposure and access to technology has created a more educated consumer than ever before. Consumers can research questions and reduce uncertainty with a click to a web site or a change of TV channel. They are exposed to much more information about many more products. In addition, consumers have never had more disposable income.

©GETTY IMAGES/PHOTODISC

The combination of more education and bigger incomes has given the consumer more tools to use in decision making. No longer do consumers buy strictly on the basis of brand loyalty, which in the past served as a confidence builder but is being replaced by product education. The growing availability of generic-name products in the market can be attributed to better-informed customers.

This increased product knowledge works to the advantage of the entrepreneur. It is now possible to compete directly with more established brand names because consumers have the tools and ability to research and compare product quality, advantages, and value. Comparison shopping and customer service are becoming more important to consumers today.

When selling business to business, successful entrepreneurs use educational tools to illustrate to potential clients how buying their product can improve the client's business. The entrepreneur performs a service for the client by providing information. Whether or not that results in a sale, it creates trust that will lead to future sales.

THE SATISFIED CUSTOMER

©GETTY IMAGES/PHOTODISC

Walking to his car after writing a check for repairs, Ron was feeling a bit down in the wallet. Although he felt sure the repairs were well done and the price was fair, it is never fun to pay for car repairs. As he approached his three-year-old car his spirits were lifted. The car, which he had dropped off with a coat of dust on it, now shone like a new car. Getting behind the wheel, he noted the vacuumed carpet, the clean dashboard, and the smell of a clean car. To his surprise, the car had been washed and cleaned inside and outside as well as repaired. Suddenly the sting of the check was not as hard to bear.

Washing cars that were in for service and repairs was standard practice at Bob Fischer's Pontiac. Satisfied customers more than made up for the cost of hiring a high school student to wash cars for two hours after school. Bob understood customer service.

Satisfied customers return. It is much less expensive and more profitable to sell to current customers than to attract new customers. Once a business is established, the single most important ingredient to future success is the return of satisfied customers. A good business makes every effort to ensure its customers' return. This is the **total customer concept**. If a customer leaves with a feeling of cognitive dissonance and there is no effort to follow the sale with a gesture of confidence, the business will most likely lose that customer. Even with small purchases, customers should be sent away with a friendly salute and an offer to assure satisfaction, such as "Enjoy your pizza, and let us know if we can be of any further service."

In the total customer concept, customers are viewed in terms of their total lifetime value to the business. If the average customer spends $100 per year on your product and you expect to be in business for 20 years, that customer is worth $2,000 in present dollar value. Do not lose $2,000 over a $20 refund dispute. Winning the argument for $20 will gain you the gross profit on the $20 purchase and lose the gross profit on $2,000. You must establish clearly defined and carefully thought-out policies concerning customer satisfaction.

Policy setting in a large business can be very bureaucratic. Often many rules guide employees on how to act in order to protect the company. The small business holds a strong advantage in that it has greater flexibility and less red tape when it comes to setting policies. There is no need for time-consuming meetings to make decisions; the business owner can make a decision on the spot and change a policy if necessary to satisfy a customer. The ability to offer personalized service and approach each situation individually is a key reason small businesses can prosper. For customers it is often worth an added cost to do business with a company that can react quickly to address their needs. It is essential that customers have a high regard and positive image of the business and the business owner they are patronizing. The entrepreneur's objective is to do as much as possible for customers to ensure their satisfaction without sacrificing long-term profits.

Small Business Technology

Telecommunications technology is a great asset to small businesses. Small manufacturers and wholesalers can respond immediately to product information requests by sending photographs and specs from their web sites. They can also be listed on the Internet as information providers at no charge and receive questions forwarded to them from potential customers. Consumers now have more choices than ever because they can access small businesses as easily as larger ones.

Customer Relations

The best policy is one that treats all customers equally. Small businesses that ignore small customers to please their larger or perceived "better" customers may regret their actions. The best-dressed shopper is not always the best customer or the one with the biggest bank account.

Small manufacturers must not become dependent on one or a few customers. For example, a small paint manufacturer is ecstatic to receive an order from a large retail chain for 25,000 gallons of paint at $15 per gallon. To get the order, the owner has lowered his price 15 percent, but he is sure he will make this up through economies of scale. Upon receiving the purchase order, he buys the necessary capital equipment to handle the increase in volume. To make sure he completes the order on time, he turns down orders from smaller established accounts. He produces the paint for the retail chain for two years and then loses the contract to a lower bid. The result is that he has lost his nucleus of regular customers and has an abundance of underutilized capital equipment. He must basically start over and rebuild his business. Similar situations can happen to any small business—retail, wholesale, or manufacturing—that gives preferential treatment.

Services can be offered without necessarily driving up costs. Employees can do more while on the payroll. Gift-wrapping, writing thank you notes, or making follow-up telephone calls do not cost money but can add profits. They are on-the-job tasks that require little or no investment in product. Good customer relations mean repeat sales.

Often tact and diplomacy are necessary to satisfy a customer. For example, Diane, who owns an apparel store, is confronted by an irritated Sharon, one of her best customers. "Diane, I think you owe me a $40 refund. You've reduced the price on the $200 dresses, like the one I bought, by $40 and I haven't even had a chance to wear mine yet." Diane recognized the dress as one that had been on the rack well past the three months during which her clothes were sold at full price before being reduced.

©GETTY IMAGES/PHOTODISC

Diane always tried to avoid putting any clothes sold to a regular customer on sale until she was sure there would be no problems. "I'm sorry, Sharon. Let me see what I can do."

When she checked the receipt, Diane found the problem. Sharon had originally put the dress on layaway for over two months, long past the 30-day layaway policy. When she finally paid in full, she had requested additional alterations, which took another five days before pickup. Although she had tied up the dress for over 60 days, she now believed she had paid $200 for a dress she could have bought for $160. Diane recognized that she had a serious problem, as she could not give Sharon $40 without setting a precedent for other customers to request refunds for items purchased before they went on sale. "Sharon, I understand why you're upset. Please understand that sales are a necessary part of the business. I can't give you a direct refund, because you had the dress on layaway. However, since you're one of our best customers, I'd like to offer you a 20 percent discount on your next purchase to make up for it."

Sharon was agreeable with this, and a problem was resolved without the loss of a customer. Diane had used her flexibility as a small business owner to satisfy a customer. At the same time she recognized Sharon as a valuable part of her business and set up a future sale.

The customer comes to a business with a need to be fulfilled. It is the responsibility of the business to do its very best to fill that need.

Relationship Marketing

The entrepreneur faces many challenges in creating the marketing plan, the primary one being access to less capital than is available to larger businesses. It takes creativity to compete and a certain amount of aggressiveness to get noticed. Knowing your customers is a strategic advantage—it builds relationships, a vital ingredient to the success of a small business.

Relationship marketing allows the small business to

- receive more volume on fewer transactions
- spend less money on attracting new customers, which is more costly than selling to established customers
- concentrate on continuous improvement
- get more involved with its customers by providing education and building future sales
- be seen as credible, sincere, and trustworthy
- receive strong referrals from a satisfied customer base

Ethics for ENTREPRENEURS

A lot has been written recently about marketers and the media exposing youth to excessive sexual content in advertisements and productions. Lingerie modeling, Super Bowl halftime shows, and risqué apparel catalogs are commonly cited examples. Entrepreneurs and advertisers base their livelihood on creating buying motivations.

Think Critically

1. Is it proper to use sexual innuendo to sell products to young people? Is it necessary for a store selling youth apparel to emphasize the sexual appeal of its fashions?
2. Where do you think the line should be drawn between suitability and censorship? Should there be more laws covering public decency, or would they be a threat to freedom of expression?
3. How do your classmates view these marketing programs?

Keep in mind that the small business owner has limited capital for marketing expenditures and cannot afford to spend money frivolously. Satisfying established customers builds sales and at the same time attracts new customers through word-of-mouth referrals. It is not as expedient as mass media advertising but is more effective in the long term.

The total customer concept keeps a customer for the lifetime of the business. Remembering clients' birthdays, anniversaries, and other special occasions are examples of ways to stay in touch and build a loyal customer base. This strategy easily outperforms the inconsistency of a constantly changing client base. Success comes to patient and determined entrepreneurs who devise the best plan for building customer relationships.

Social Responsibility

Good customer relations equate with strong goodwill. A successful business is recognized by the community as one that has earned trust and confidence. In addition to satisfying customers, it is the entrepreneur's responsibility to give something back to the community from which the business derives its success.

Businesses receive numerous requests to support not-for-profit organizations. It is not possible to support all requests, but there is a moral and practical responsibility to do one's share. Whether it is the Chamber of Commerce, the YMCA, the hospital auxiliary, or the local theater group, entrepreneurs gain goodwill and recognition with their active support. A portion of the business's advertising budget should be set aside to help publicize community groups and activities. The dollars spent and the time and effort donated to support these causes does not show up immediately on the profit and loss statement, but over time the business gains customers and respect. A community relations program shows that you care and in the long run will produce a handsome return on your investment.

Ship in a BOTTLE

Finding an Unsatisfied Need

Fred had learned a great deal about his customers during the start-up stage of the business. Although he personally sold to two categories of buyers—retailers and consumers—he recognized that in both instances the goal was to satisfy the needs of the final user. How could he stimulate the motivations of potential customers?

The logical question when creating product differentiation versus a low-cost marketing strategy is "What makes it different?" Certainly a ship in a bottle is different from other ship models, but is that the whole story? From his experience of trying to find more ships in bottles to add to his wife's initial purchase, Fred recognized another marketing stimulus—discovery. Making a discovery—the "Aha!" experience of stumbling into the unexpected—can be a stimulus to buy. "Look at this! I didn't know they made these!" or "Can you believe someone can do this?" are reactions that may lead to a buying decision. Fred remembered his own reaction when he found the German ships-in-bottles web site.

So Fred built a marketing strategy around the discovery theme. His brochure and web site headline was "Now Available in the USA: European Crafted Ships in Bottles." He felt that if he could convince buyers that his product was not only unusual but difficult to find, he would expose a need and they would buy out of fear of not finding the product anywhere else. By explaining how his ships in bottles were built in a German seaport city by Johann Schmidt, whose history was tied into his grandfather's seafaring life of 100 years earlier, Fred would create a positive image of the product. This could alter the perception that the price was too high for a relatively small model. The phrase "European crafted" would also convey the idea of quality and tradition. With the right wording, photographs, and layout, Fred believed he could motivate buyers to act on satisfying a need.

Indeed, the strategy worked. Almost 90 percent of the inquiries from retailers and web site buyers began, "I'm so glad to find these. I didn't know anyone still made them."

Think Critically

1. In what other ways can Fred influence the needs, perceptions, motivations, and attitudes of potential customers?
2. Sketch a brochure cover to introduce ships in bottles to customers. What information would you include in the text of the brochure?
3. What type of decision making would be evident in the purchase of a $75 ship in a bottle?
4. How would you identify an "opinion leader" among customers for ships in a bottle?

Summary

Successful entrepreneurs are successful because they know their customers better than the competition does. It is important that they take the time to analyze and understand what motivates a consumer to make a decision to buy or not to buy. Effective target marketing requires an understanding of consumers' needs, perceptions, motivations, and attitudes. The entrepreneur applies certain stimuli to direct the consumer's motivations and assists in the buying decision.

Entrepreneurs must plan their marketing strategies around the various groups to whom their product or service appeals. There are four general personality styles: thinker, intuitor, feeler, and sensor. The entrepreneur should also take into account the overall self-concept of the target market as well as its demographics.

Understanding the consumer decision-making process is essential to entrepreneurial success. Marketing is successful when it is directed at the right group of influential buyers or innovators, who then influence the desires and purchasing decisions of others in the group. Marketing efforts or stimuli should be developed with the awareness that today's consumers have access to more information, and therefore more chances to compare products and services, than ever before.

Knowing the customer does not stop with the sale. It is important to ensure post-purchase satisfaction as well. A satisfied customer becomes a repeat customer and will bring others to the business. The total customer concept requires that attention be paid to all customer requests and that vigorous efforts be made to ensure that the buyer remains a customer for the life of the business. These efforts include supporting community activities and being perceived as a valuable member of the community.

A Case in POINT

The China Shop

"Why not?" thought Katie Barron. "A fine china department would add a great look to the store, and we could get out of the summer doldrums by selling to newlyweds." There were no china shops in her town of 30,000 people. The only retailers who sold china at all were a flower shop and a jeweler. Katie felt sure that a complete china department in her 4,500-square-foot gift shop would be welcomed by her customers.

She discussed the idea with a representative from a prestigious china company, and he agreed with her assessment. A friend who worked in the china department of a large department store 200 miles away was also positive about the idea and offered to explain the bridal registry system to Katie and her staff when the department opened.

Katie designed an attractive space for the china, with chandeliers, plush white carpeting, and exquisite wallpaper. The department opened to an enthusiastic response. The compliments seemed unending: "Absolutely beautiful," "Just what our town needs," and "We'll be back."

The china department was a failure. Sales were only 25 percent of projections. The bridal registry business was almost nonexistent. Katie wondered what she had done wrong.

continued

Chapter Review

Think Critically

1. What did Katie fail to recognize with regard to perceptions of her store? What demographic and competitive research might have given Katie more insight into her business's future as a bridal registry store?
2. What would you recommend to Katie as a strategy for selling to influential groups of consumers?

Vocabulary Builder

Write a brief definition of each word or phrase.

1. black box approach
2. conscious needs
3. customers
4. early adopters
5. early majority
6. extensive decisions
7. ideal self
8. innovators
9. laggards
10. late majority
11. looking-glass self
12. motivations
13. need satisfaction theory
14. nonroutine decisions
15. perceptions
16. preconscious needs
17. real self
18. reference groups
19. routine decisions
20. selective distortion
21. selective retention
22. self-image
23. total customer concept
24. unconscious needs
25. utility satisfaction

Review the Concepts

26. Why is knowing the customer a competitive advantage for small businesses?
27. What is the importance to the entrepreneur of understanding basic psychological concepts as they apply to consumers?
28. How can understanding personality styles influence marketing decisions?
29. What are ways that a business can assist in the consumer's decision-making process?
30. What are the differences among routine, nonroutine, and extensive decisions?
31. Explain how following a total customer concept pays huge financial dividends to a business in the long run.
32. How does cognitive dissonance inhibit future sales of the same product?
33. What "self" are you when you purchase a textbook?
34. Do you know anyone who is considered an opinion leader? If you do, how would you describe that person?

Critical Thinking

35. Explain how needs differ from individual to individual.
36. Describe yourself in terms of personality style. How does your personality style affect your purchase decisions?
37. Describe how your self-image has changed in various buying situations.
38. What was the last extensive purchase decision you encountered? How did you respond to it?
39. Describe a feeling of cognitive dissonance that you have recently experienced. What did you or the business do to relieve the anxiety it caused?
40. Describe a scenario that would enable you to sell a wedding dress to an opinion leader.
41. Defend the concept of spending money for socially responsible reasons when that money could be used to expand your business and create more jobs.
42. Imagine you are confronted by a customer who is requesting a refund for a gift bought for her at your store. Apply the total customer concept to this situation.

Project

Build Your Business Plan

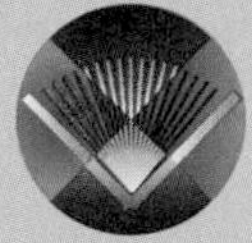

Write a psychological profile of your intended target market. Include any marketing ideas you would use to influence the needs, perceptions, attitudes, and motivations of your customers. Also describe the personality type your product or service would appeal to and how you would tailor your marketing campaign to accommodate that personality.

Be sure to address the following questions.

1. How would you group your target market with regard to household life cycle?
2. What reference groups might you address to gain product acceptance?
3. What information can you provide to help your target customers make decisions?
4. What policies will you instill to adhere to the total customer concept and ensure customer satisfaction?

Chapter 10

Pricing

©GETTY IMAGES/PHOTODISC

Objectives

10-1 Explain the functions of price.

10-2 Explain how to determine the breakeven point for pricing.

10-3 Define and calculate markups and markdowns.

10-4 Describe different pricing strategies and how they are applied.

10-5 Describe the various external and internal factors that can affect prices.

THE ROLE OF PRICE

Price is included among the 4 P's of the marketing mix because setting prices directly affects the perceived needs, attitudes, perceptions, and motivations of the consumer. If a product or service is properly priced, price becomes a customer relations tool. If the price is not perceived as a fair exchange, it becomes a buying inhibitor.

Proper pricing of a product or service serves as a positive marketing incentive and ensures enough profit to the seller to allow the business to continue serving the market.

The price of a product or service must accomplish the following objectives. By satisfying these requirements, the entrepreneur is operating under the **total pricing concept**.

1. The total cost of the item to be sold must be covered. This includes the direct expenses of manufacturing or buying the product and the operating and overhead expenses incurred in operating the business.
2. Pricing must contribute to the long-term stability of the business. There must be enough profit to generate retained earnings, which can be put back into the business for future growth and development.
3. The entrepreneur must be rewarded for the effort expended and the risk assumed in owning and running the business.
4. Customers must perceive the price as giving a fair value.

Supply and Demand

It is important for entrepreneurs to understand the relationship between **supply and demand**. Proper allocation of goods and services to the market at an affordable cost helps maintain a healthy economy. Consumers can buy only what they can afford, so the higher the price of the product or service, the smaller the market. If the market perceives the price of a product as too high, then the demand for the product will be low. This will cause a surplus

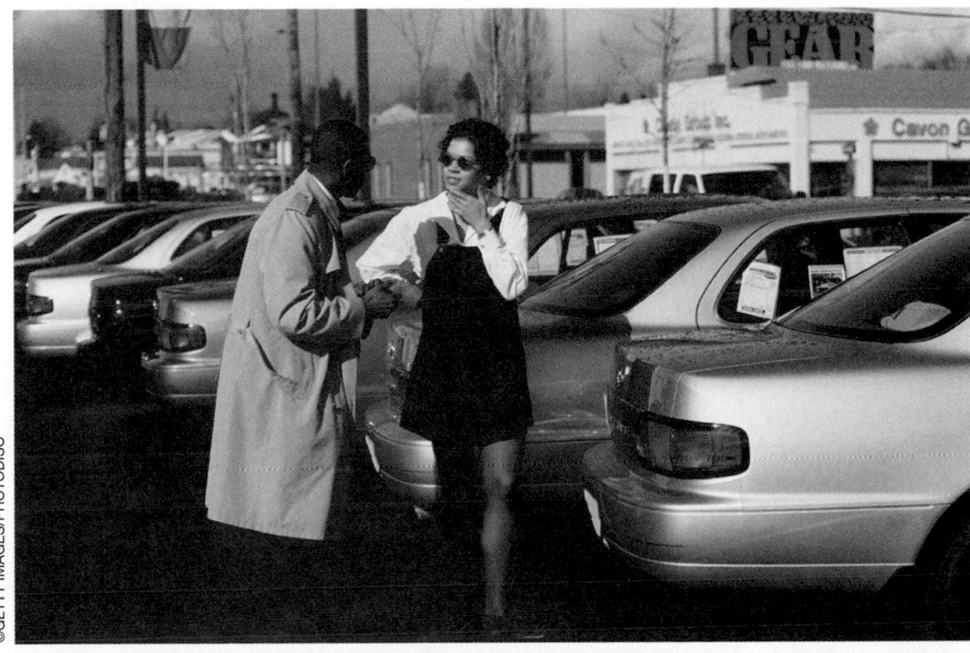

of the product in the marketplace, and production will have to be slowed or stopped. Conversely, if a product is priced below the perceived value, the demand will be great. This will cause a shortage in the marketplace, and production will need to be increased to bring supply in line with demand.

FUN FACTS

The consumer price index (CPI) is a measure of the average change over time in the prices paid by urban consumers for a market basket of consumer goods and services. It is one of the factors affecting such economic indicators as the rate of inflation. In 2003 the CPI rose 1.9 percent.

The entrepreneur's goal is to find the price point that allows a balance between supply and demand. When a price is set high enough to ensure a profit for the seller, certain portions of the market will switch their demand to other products. This guarantees that the supply of the higher-priced product will be adequate for demand. On a supply and demand graph, such as that in Figure 10-1, the equilibrium or balance point is reached when the demand line intersects with the supply line. To read the graph, use the vertical (price) scale in conjunction with the supply line. Use the horizontal (quantity) scale in conjunction with demand line. For example, if an item costs $2, read across the graph until you reach the point where the demand line intersects the horizontal "2" line. The demand for a $2 item would be eight units.

FIGURE 10-1

Supply and Demand

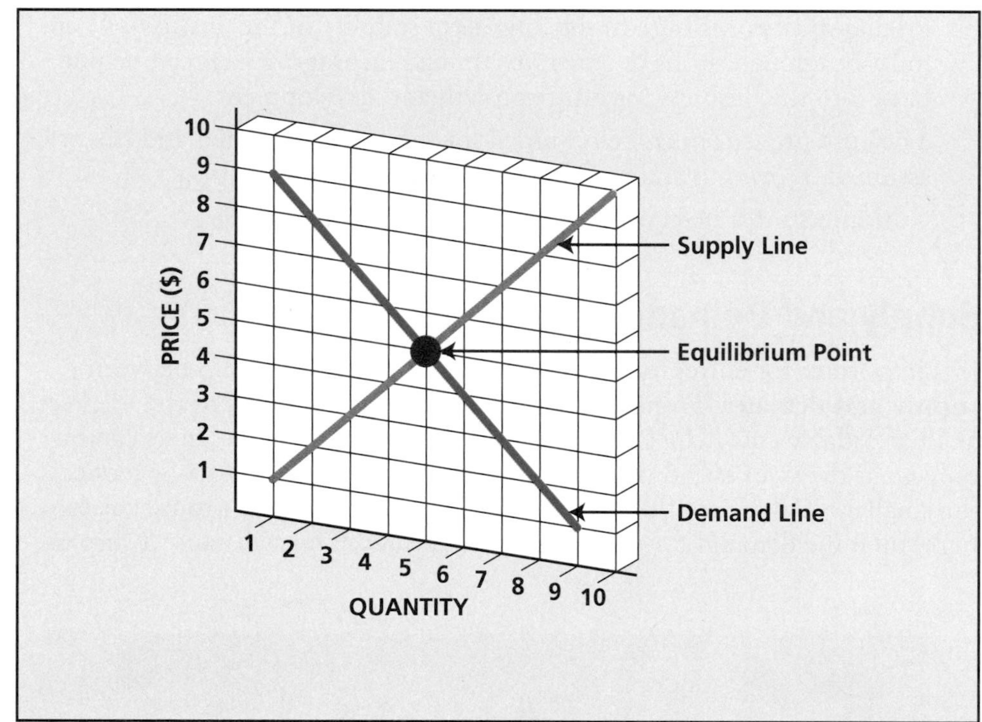

It is not difficult to sell a product at below-market prices. The challenge is to sell products and services at a high enough price to ensure profit and still pass on customer value. Too often small businesses get caught up in playing the sales game and not paying enough attention to profit, the bottom line. Anyone can sell ice cream at a low price, but to sell ice cream at a profitable price requires entrepreneurial skills.

The prices that entrepreneurs set need to be low enough to encourage a high demand for their products or services but high enough to ensure a profit. Low prices will certainly increase demand, but they may yield little or no profit. High prices could mean more profit, but only if demand does not drop. Therefore, it is important to find a price point that is acceptable to the buyer and yields a satisfactory profit to the seller. In a relatively free marketplace, the determination of the acceptable price point ultimately comes from the buyers. They will not buy what they cannot afford. Using the various strategies employed in the marketing plan, the entrepreneur attempts to determine what that price is.

BREAKEVEN POINT

Price setting begins with determining the breakeven point. The **breakeven point** is reached when the cost of producing and/or selling a product or service is covered. You can determine that point by first analyzing your **fixed costs**, which are the costs that do not vary even when there are changes in production and/or sales volume. Examples of fixed costs are rent, utilities, and insurance. You will also need to analyze your **variable costs**, which are costs that fluctuate with changes in production and/or sales volume. Examples of variable costs are the cost of goods or materials, payroll, and advertising. Fixed and variable costs should then be broken down to determine the cost of each unit sold.

Once the breakeven point is reached, additional sales produce profit for the entrepreneur. The more units are sold, the greater the profit per unit. Total profits can be projected by multiplying the amount of money that will be made per unit by the number of units that will be sold, then subtracting the total cost (fixed plus variable) of selling the units.

Figure 10-2 is a graphic illustration of the breakeven point for a small manufacturer of a product—call it a Gizmo. The price of $10 will cover all fixed and variable costs of making Gizmos when 1,000 units have been sold. If fewer than 1,000 units are sold at this price, there will be a loss. Each sale in excess of 1,000 will mean a profit.

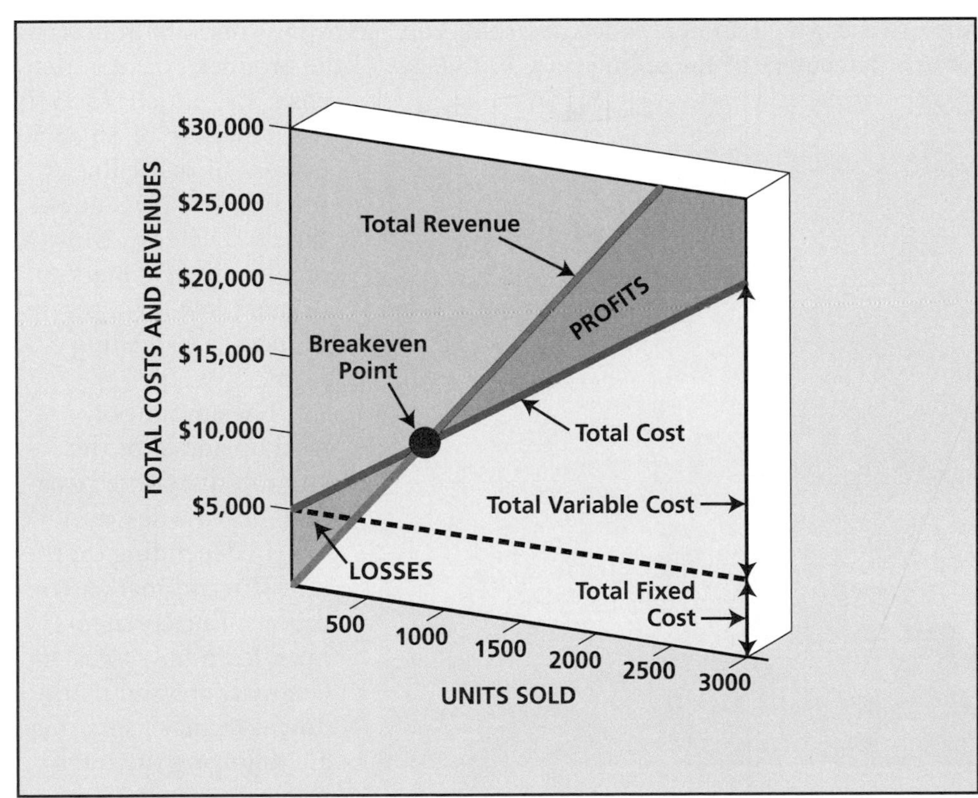

FIGURE 10-2

Breakeven Point

Businesses become exciting and profitable as they go further past the breakeven point. The first Gizmo sold after the breakeven point, unit 1,001, will return just a small fraction of its price as profit. However, as you can see from Figure 10-2, the margin grows as more units are sold. At unit 2,000 the revenue is approximately $20,000, the total cost is $15,000, and therefore the profit is $5,000, which is $2.50 for each $10 unit sold above the breakeven point. That profit on each unit sold will continue to increase as more units are sold.

The **contributing margin** is the gross profit derived from the sale of the product, that is, the selling price less the cost of the goods or materials. The contributing margin for the Gizmo is $4.

Selling price	–	Cost of goods	=	Contributing margin
$10	–	$6	=	$4

Breakeven Formula To find the breakeven point when you know the total fixed cost and the contributing margin of the units sold, divide the fixed costs by the contributing margin. If the fixed cost is $100,000 per year and the average contributing margin is $4, the breakeven point is reached when you sell 25,000 units.

Fixed costs	÷	Contributing margin	=	Breakeven point
$100,000	÷	$4	=	25,000 units

At the breakeven point, the revenue and the total cost are equal.

25,000 units × $10 = $250,000 revenue
$100,000 fixed cost + $150,000 variable cost = $250,000 total cost

MARKUPS AND MARKDOWNS

A **markup** is the amount added to the cost of an item to arrive at a selling price. A **markdown** is the difference between the original selling price and the price at which an item is actually sold. You can express markup in dollars or as a percentage of the selling price or the cost of the product. An item that costs $5 and sells for $10 has a markup of $5 or 50 percent of the selling price or 100 percent of the product cost. Most retailers express markup or markdown as a percentage of the selling price.

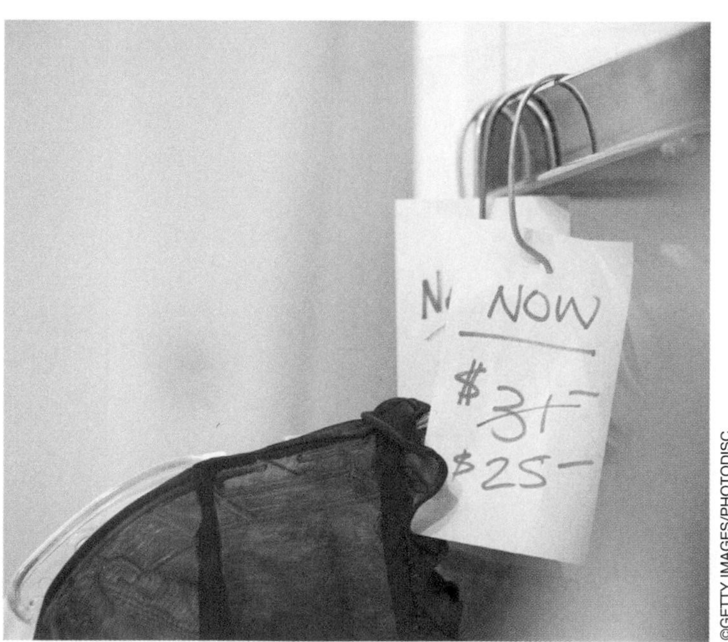

©GETTY IMAGES/PHOTODISC

The amount of markup added or the amount discounted as a markdown will vary widely depending on the industry and market conditions. Entrepreneurs must learn how to calculate markups and markdowns to make sure they are following the total pricing concept.

Find the Selling Price To calculate the selling price at a percent markup when the cost is known, simply divide the cost by 100 percent minus the desired markup percent.

Cost	÷ (100% –	Markup percent)	=	Selling price	
$5	÷ (100% –	50%)	=	$10	Cost: $5; Markup: 50%
$6	÷ (100% –	40%)	=	$10	Cost: $6; Markup: 60%

Find the Cost To calculate the cost when the selling price and the markup percent are known, multiply the selling price by the markup percent and subtract the answer from the selling price.

$10 selling price × 40% = $4 markup
$10 selling price – $4 markup = $6 cost

Find the Markup Percent To determine the markup percent when the cost and the selling price are known, subtract the cost from the selling price. Divide the difference by the selling price.

$10 selling price – $6 cost = $4 markup
$4 ÷ $10 = 0.4 or 40% markup

Manufacturers and wholesalers use the same formulas to determine the markup on their selling price to retailers. However, they are often operating in a more volatile environment because materials, transportation, and labor costs are more variable and time sensitive than in retail purchasing. Once a desired markup percentage is achieved, the cost of materials, goods, and transportation must be closely monitored to prevent an unexpected decrease in the contributing margin of the company's product sales.

Protecting Your Profit Margin

Many small businesses do not adequately protect their profit margins—their markup is too low. For example, a retail store sells its products at a 50 percent markup: for every $1 of product sold, the average cost is 50 cents. The profit and expense for each dollar sold is calculated as follows:

Sale price	$1.00
Cost of product	– 0.50
Freight cost	– 0.02
Gross profit	0.48
Operating expenses	– 0.34
Net operating profit before taxes	0.14

Averaging a 50 percent markup allows the owner to receive a profit of 14 cents for each dollar of product sold. The 14 cents must cover the owner's salary, taxes, and loan principal payments and contribute to retained earnings. If the selling price of the $1 example was cut to 90 cents (a 44 percent markup rather than 50 percent) and if all operating and freight expenses remained the same, the profit would be only 4 cents on each dollar sold. The owner would have to sell considerably more products to make the same amount of money. Too often entrepreneurs engage in price wars with larger competitors, which results in severely decreased profits.

©GETTY IMAGES/PHOTODISC

Taking Markdowns

Markdowns are taken when a product does not sell at the desired price. When a product is "on sale," its original selling price has been reduced. To calculate a markdown, decide on the percent of markdown. Multiply the original selling price by the percent of markdown, and then subtract the result from the original selling price to get the sale price.

$10 selling price × 40% markdown = $4 markdown
$10 original price – $4 markdown = $6 sale price

There are a number of reasons for taking markdowns.

- **Damaged Merchandise** A defective item usually cannot be sold at its original selling price.
- **Old Merchandise** Some products remain on the shelves too long and go out of style or become obsolete. The entrepreneur needs to divest old products in order to raise capital to buy new products.
- **Broken Assortments** Items that were intended to be sold in sets or groups lose their salability when part of the grouping is missing or damaged.
- **Special Promotions** Low prices are offered to increase demand and, therefore, customer traffic.
- **Limited Space** Markdowns are needed to clear shelves in order to make room for new inventory.

When setting markups for new items, be sure you consider future markdowns. The initial markup must be high enough to accommodate periodic markdowns.

PRICING STRATEGIES

In the initial stage of selling a product or service, the entrepreneur must set prices to determine what is acceptable to customers. Ultimately the customers determine what is an acceptable price, as they will not buy if the value is not perceived as fair.

©GETTY IMAGES/PHOTODISC

To arrive at a pricing strategy, the seller must take into consideration the total pricing concept and the marketing objective of the business. The strategy will depend on the maturity of the business, the particular cycle of the economy, the newness of the product, and the reaction of the competition. Common pricing strategies include skimming, market penetration, loss leader pricing, price lining, price bundling, status quo pricing, and price points.

Skimming

Skimming is a short-term profit strategy often used for products that are not expected to remain on the market for an extended period of time. These products are fads that take advantage of current—but temporary—demands in the marketplace. The products are sometimes tied into a current market happening, such as a popular movie or a music or fashion trend. Manufacturers produce these items with the expectation of selling a lot quickly, then getting out of the market. These products carry a high risk, since sales are dependent on whether or not the fad catches on and how long it lasts. Prices are set very high in the anticipation that the short selling period will encourage customers to pay a high price for the "in" product. The higher markup also gives manufacturers and retailers a cushion in the event they are caught with a high inventory and must take large markdowns when the fad subsides.

A good example of this is the Pet Rock, a novelty product that became popular during the Christmas holiday season a number of years ago. It was an ordinary garden rock, 2 to 3 inches in size, packaged in a small carton that looked like a doghouse. The Pet Rock came with instructions on how to train it to do tricks such as "sit," "stay," or "roll over." It caught the country's attention on late-night television programs and became the rage as a novelty Christmas present. At a price of $6.95, it sold millions within a six-week selling period and just as quickly disappeared from store shelves immediately after the holidays. A price of $6.95 for a common rock was truly a price set as part of a skimming or short-term profit strategy. More recently Pokemon, Power Rangers, and ET dolls were products with intended short-term life cycles, priced to get in and get out of the marketplace quickly. Some did well, while others (ET dolls) failed miserably.

Market Penetration Pricing

Sometimes entrepreneurs use the opposite of the short-term profit strategy—selling at the lowest possible price for a short-term period. This strategy, known as **market penetration pricing**, is often used to introduce a new product or business with an expected long-term life cycle. The idea is to gain market share. By setting a low price to entice people to try a new product, the business is hoping to gain customers at their competitors' expense. Taking customers from the competition dilutes the competition's portion of the market while increasing the market penetrator's portion. By gaining market share, the entrepreneur increases demand for the product or service. Once a desired share of the market is attained, prices gradually rise to the level of the competition.

Grocery stores and new restaurants often rely on the market penetration strategy. Small businesses need to be careful not to permanently violate the tenets of the total pricing concept by not protecting their proper profit margin. Market penetration pricing can be effective as an introductory tool to acquaint the marketplace with a new business or product but should not be used on a continuous basis.

©GETTY IMAGES/PHOTODISC

Loss Leader Pricing

A **loss leader pricing** strategy consists of purposely pricing some products at a level that eliminates profit and incurs losses on those particular products. This is done to increase customer traffic and thereby the likelihood that other, related products will be purchased at a normal or higher markup. By enticing customers to come in and buy certain products at bargain prices, business owners hope that those customers will also buy other products at full price to offset the losses incurred on the bargain prices. The bargain prices are advertised on television and radio and in newspapers, and there is usually a time limitation on the price. Department stores, variety stores, toy stores, grocery stores, and drugstores utilize this marketing/pricing strategy on a regular basis. Manufacturers and wholesalers also offer loss leader bargains to their customers to entice them to buy more related products in large volumes. But small business owners are advised not to use it, as it requires additional expenditures on advertising and can be detrimental to achieving the overall desired markup percentage of the business.

Price Lining

When businesses group products at certain price points—such as all items for $9.99—they are **price lining**. By grouping items, they make shopping easy for the consumer and average out their desired markup. Some items are priced under the desired markup and others over it, but the average reaches the desired results as long as the products sell evenly. It can be risky, but rewarding, if customers respond to a simple one-price-for-all strategy.

Price Bundling

Selling a product in multiple units—such as "Two for the price of one" or "Buy three and receive one free"—is a type of pricing strategy called **price bundling**. Many retail outlets use it. Price bundling is similar to penetration pricing in that it can in-crease market share. It can also be used to reduce surplus inventory. The latter use can be effective for small businesses, but price bundling is not recommended as a permanent tool because it does not normally sustain a proper profit margin.

Status Quo Pricing

Most businesses settle into a **status quo pricing** strategy in which price levels are firmly established and remain relatively fixed until something happens in the marketplace that requires a change or adjustment. Such events include new competition, changes in the established competition's pricing strategies, changes in demand due to market shortages or overflows, or changes in the economy. New competition causes disruption in the market. Established business owners must react by increasing advertising, matching prices, or holding their position until the disruption settles down. When an established competitor makes a dramatic shift in prices, other business owners must react either with similar action or by adding value to their offerings. If a product is undersupplied (such as Cabbage Patch Dolls or Pokemon) or oversupplied (gasoline availability), supply and demand will affect prices. Prices will also change if the economy enters a prolonged period of inflation or recession, as either condition will change consumer buying behavior. It is wise to keep a close eye on these conditions in order to react quickly.

©GETTY IMAGES/PHOTODISC

You can reach your profit goals only if you use the right pricing strategy for your particular type of business. Strategies appropriate for certain target markets may not work for others. You must be realistic in your expectations and knowledgeable about the supply and demand conditions of the market you wish to serve in order to determine the best pricing strategy. This requires constant evaluation of market conditions and your pricing policies.

Price Points

It is very important to understand the psychology of violating **price points**, which are the price levels with which consumers feel psychologically comfortable. Normally they fall at even dollar levels in increments of fives, tens, or hundreds. Price points vary from industry to industry, but the general guidelines are consistent. In the minds of many consumers there is a big difference between $9.95 and $10.50. $10 is a recognized price point in many consumer goods categories. Going above $10 is a violation of that particular price point. A car selling for $19,900—below the $20,000 price point—appeals to a larger market than one that sells for $20,750.

Sellers need to be sensitive to making decisions that may violate consumers' psychological perception of value exchange. Staying below a price point is possible when the entire price point ranges are considered. For instance, there is not much difference between perceptions of $18.95 and $19.95—they are both below the price-sensitive point of $20. Taking this into account, you can increase an $18.95 price tag to $19.95, which allows you at the same time to lower the suggested markup of a $20.95 item and price it at $19.95. The goal is to receive the desired markup on the entire product line as an average.

Small Business Technology

The complications of determining values in foreign currencies are behind you. Small businesses can now convert a foreign currency to a U.S. dollar value with a click of the computer mouse. A search of "currency exchange" brings up a number of conversion web sites. Say you wish to explore the wholesale purchase of weather instruments from South Africa and the seller quotes a price of 300 rand per piece. A quick visit to a conversion site will tell you that 300 rand equals $47.39. Also, banks can send bank drafts overseas in a matter of minutes and automatically convert the receipt into the seller's account. The huge growth of international trade has prompted new technology to solve a problem that once deterred many businesses from considering foreign commerce.

Discounts

Small business owners must be careful not to fall prey to larger businesses by competing strictly on price. This is not the entrepreneur's strong point. Big businesses compete for a cost leadership position and are able to offer larger discounts because they have greater capital resources. You make your profits through differentiation, with a unique product or personalized customer service.

The drawbacks of discounting can be illustrated by the following example. A small business sells 5,000 units at $100 each, an average 45 percent markup, resulting in revenues of $500,000.

Revenues	$500,000	5,000 units @ $100
Cost of goods	– 275,000	5,000 units @ $55
Gross profit	225,000	
Operating expenses	– 200,000	
Net operating profit	$25,000	

The entrepreneur decides to reduce prices 20 percent, or $20 per unit, to compete with a large discount operation. He first assumes a minimum sales increase of 20 percent more units, or 6,000 units, at $80, the new selling price.

Revenues	$480,000	6,000 units @ $80
Cost of goods	– 330,000	6,000 units @ $55
Gross profit	150,000	
Operating expenses	– 200,000	
Net operating loss	<$50,000>	

He changes his calculation to show a 100 percent increase in the number of units sold, 10,000, at the $80 selling price.

Revenues	$800,000	10,000 units @ $80
Cost of goods	– 550,000	10,000 units @ $55
Gross profit	250,000	
Operating expenses*	– 225,000	
Net operating profit	$25,000	

**includes additional advertising, payroll, and supplies to sell extra units*

It isn't until he increases projected unit sales to 300 percent, 15,000, that it makes any sense to lower prices 20 percent.

Revenues	$1,200,000	15,000 units @ $80
Cost of goods	– 825,000	15,000 units @ $55
Gross profit	375,000	
Operating expenses	– 300,000	
Net operating profit	$75,000	

Taking the risk of discounting requires ample capital, space, and advertising. Certainly a 300 percent increase in unit sales would require additional payroll, an aggressive advertising campaign, more supplies, and moving to a larger space in order to house and display or assemble inventory.

Strategic planning requires that you identify your objective in terms of sales and profits and how they can be obtained. The choice is normally to achieve goals by cost and price leadership or by differentiation and service leadership. Small businesses should build their strategies around the latter course. Although it may take longer to reach and surpass the breakeven point, it will result in a more stable business.

©GETTY IMAGES/PHOTODISC

FACTORS THAT AFFECT PRICES

There are a number of factors that can affect the price of a product, both externally and internally. Legal considerations and the customer's perception of fair value also affect prices.

External Factors

Elements surrounding a business that indirectly affect its operations are called **external factors**. They may be economic cycles, societal changes, technological developments, the market entry of substitute products, new competition, or other disruptions in the marketplace.

Economic Cycles Changes in the economic environment can encourage or discourage consumer buying. You may read many economic stories from Washington and sometimes think they will not affect you. However, just the mention of inflation, recession, stagnant economy, rising interest rates, or increasing and decreasing taxes has a psychological impact on consumers.

Inflation says prices will be going up, and consumers may wish to purchase before they do. Recession says the economy is faltering, jobs are being lost, and production is down, in which case consumers become conservative and watch prices more closely. If interest rates are rising, consumers put off making major purchases. When interest rates drop, consumers charge and buy more freely. If there are tax rebates and decreases, consumers feel free to spend extra money and are not as cautious. If taxes go up, consumers have less spending money. Entrepreneurs must keep an eye on the economic environment and be prepared to change prices as necessary to accommodate the impact of any changes.

FUN FACTS

The market basket of consumer goods used to measure CPI consists of a selection of goods from eight major categories: food and beverages, medical care, housing, recreation, apparel, education and communication, transportation, and other goods and services, from haircuts to funeral expenses.

Societal Changes Whether they are short-term fads or long-term lifestyle changes, societal attitudes affect the marketplace and price acceptability. Certainly this is evident in the fashion industry. What opinion leaders decide to wear often determines demand, which of course determines prices. Examples of longer-term changes are the growing ethnic populations, dual-career families, and the sexual revolution. In a changing social environment, some entrepreneurs can increase their prices while others have to decrease them as demand changes. Successful entrepreneurs stay abreast of the changes that surround them.

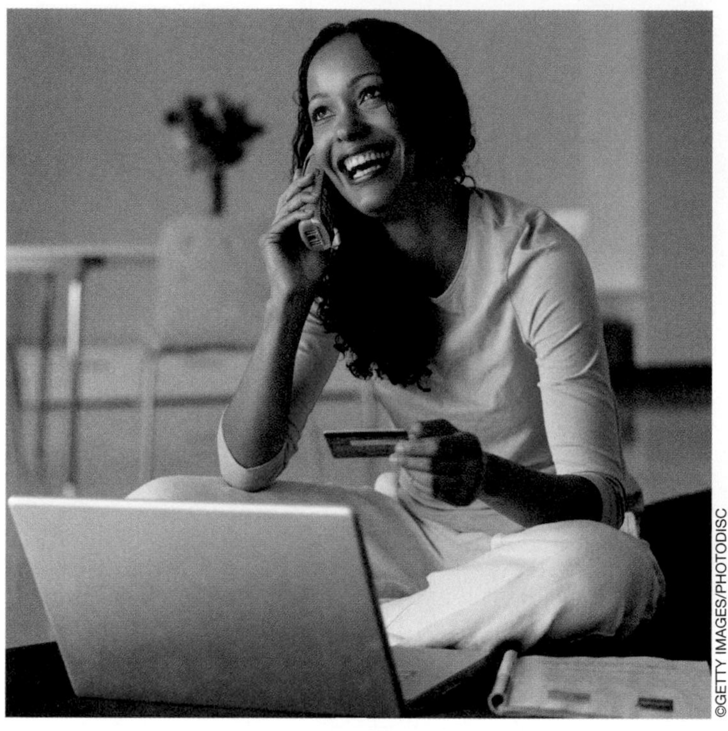
©GETTY IMAGES/PHOTODISC

Technological Developments When new technology is introduced, older technology suffers. A business may be stuck with obsolete products and little demand unless it stays up to date with new technology. New technology also offers great opportunity for entrepreneurs. Being among the first to sell or manufacture a new technology is often a road to riches as demand outweighs supply and allows the seller to receive maximum prices. It was not long ago that a simple handheld electronic calculator sold for over $100. Now they are giveaways for businesses like banks and insurance companies.

Substitute Products One characteristic of the free market system is that if a product is selling at a greater profit than expected, other entrepreneurs will at some point introduce similar or substitute products to gain a share of the market and its profits. Established business owners need to be on the lookout for new products that serve the same target market and change their prices accordingly to counter the threat of these new product entries.

Ethics for ENTREPRENEURS

During emergencies some businesses raise the prices of essential products, such as candles and batteries during power outages. Even during the 9/11 disaster some gas station owners raised gasoline prices as rumors of pending oil shortages spread. Those who engage in this type of price gouging refer to the principles of the free market and assert that under high-demand conditions it is acceptable to raise prices to what the market will bear.

Think Critically

1. Do you believe these businesses are following acceptable business practices?
2. Who is hurt by price gouging? Should it be illegal?
3. Give examples of other price gouging situations that you are familiar with.

New Competition New entrants into the market have an immediate impact and should always be taken into account when determining prices. If a new sandwich shop opens and sells 20 sandwiches a day, that means 20 sandwiches have been taken from other businesses. Those businesses will respond, often by lowering prices. The new business will set prices according to how it believes the market will respond but at the same time must be prepared for a reaction from the competition.

Internal Factors

Internal factors are elements within a business that directly affect prices. They may be an increase in fixed costs, supplier shortages, increases or decreases in the cost of materials or goods, or more efficient technology that allows increased production.

Increase in Fixed and Variable Costs If a business is faced with an increase in fixed costs, it has to adjust in some manner, often by raising prices. An increase in rent, freight charges, or other fixed costs changes the bottom-line profit figure. If a business is holding on to a slim profit margin of 7 percent and its fixed costs rise 2 to 3 percent, an adjustment must be made or the business will cease to exist. One alternative is to increase prices. During inflationary times the competition will have to respond, and the winner may be the one who can hold out the longest. This scenario also occurs when the cost of materials or goods to the final seller is increased, and prices rise accordingly.

©GETTY IMAGES/PHOTODISC

Supplier Shortage If a supplier shortage slows the supply of a product in great demand, the entrepreneur with excess inventory or better access to the product may decide to increase prices. Because of the supplier shortage there will be little competition. If it is a short-term shortage, the entrepreneur may choose not to raise prices in order to avoid appearing to be a "price gouger."

New Technology Businesses that can improve efficiency with better technology and thereby benefit from economies of scale may be able to increase production and decrease their costs. This, in turn, may allow them to lower their prices and gain a larger market share. Economies of scale work to the advantage of consumer and entrepreneur alike.

©GETTY IMAGES/PHOTODISC

Legal Considerations

There are many types of legal considerations that affect prices, including price discrimination and tie-in sales.

Price Discrimination As you have learned, the practice of charging different prices to different customers for the same goods is called price discrimination. It is in violation of the Robinson-Patman Act of 1936 if it interferes with competition and injures the discriminated buyer. The Robinson-Patman Act *does* allow sellers to allow quantity discounts to larger buyers, citing that this can save in manufacturing costs. In other words, an entrepreneur can sell a product at a different price to Wal-Mart than to Smith Brothers Hardware, but only if it is truly a quantity discount.

Tie-in Sales A related legal consideration is **tie-in sales**. For promotional purposes it is legal to offer an additional item for the same price as for the original item alone. However, you cannot tie in the purchase of one product line to the purchase of another without violating the Clayton Act. In other words, it is legal to sell two for the price of one, as long as the offer is made to all customers, but it is not legal if the customer must also buy another product that is not related directly to the original offer.

Types of Prices Often it can be very confusing for the consumer to determine the final price, particularly in such instances as buying an automobile. Some common types of prices are the following.

- **List Price** The **list price** is the standard price charged to customers.
- **Net Price** After all discounts are subtracted, the balance is the **net price**.
- **Zone Price** The price set for a particular geographic area is the **zone price**.
- **FOB** With free on board or **FOB** pricing, the buyer must pay transportation charges to deliver the products, and the title or ownership of the products is passed to the customer when the items are loaded on the shipping vehicle.

Entrepreneurs who manufacture products must make sure that all their salespeople are knowledgeable about discounts and price components and that their products are sold legally and ethically.

Fair Value

In Chapter 9 utility satisfaction is defined as the search for value—that is, the consumer's search for those products or services that give the greatest satisfaction in exchange for his or her money. It is imperative for a business that its customers believe they have received fair value. In the mind of the seller it is the price charged, but in the mind of the customer it is the cost incurred for a purchase. To a buyer, true cost consists of what has been received in comparison to what has been given up. It can be expressed as a ratio.

true cost to customer = price:value

The seller has determined the price, but the value will differ depending on the customer's needs. Value is the total package of benefits, which may not always be immediately identifiable but is anticipated. Life insurance or an IRA are examples of products that you buy with the anticipation that in the long term they have a greater value than in the immediate transaction.

Customers' View of Quality Customers have undergone quite a transformation in the way they view price in regard to quality. Shifting from the product concept of marketing to the customer concept has changed marketing strategies to emphasize value and quality more than in the past. When there were only three major automobile manufacturers or three television networks, customers were limited in what they could purchase or view and often settled for second-rate products of questionable value. Since the invasion of Japanese goods in the 1960s—initially cars and electronics, then a steady stream of other quality products—American manufacturers have awakened to the idea that to compete effectively they must offer value through quality products.

Japanese automobiles coming into America offered superior quality at lower prices than American automobile manufacturers were offering. The impact was so great that the U.S. government placed high tariffs and quotas on imported automobiles to protect domestic manufacturers and the huge number of jobs related to the automobile industry. The tariffs and quotas were not intended to last forever but were installed to give American companies time to retool and rethink their manufacturing processes. The result was a better-quality American automobile and at the same time a message to all manufacturers that quality *does* count and that contemporary consumers have many more choices about how to spend their money. Prices and perceived values were affected in many industries.

THINKSTOCK

The Global ENTREPRENEUR

Hurray for the euro! Since 2002, 12 European nations have used a standard currency, the euro, for international business purposes. The value of the euro at the time was determined by the value of the U.S. dollar. In its initial implementation, the dollar and euro were equal in value. Since then the euro has risen in value past the value of the dollar, and over time its value will continue to fluctuate. The transition went more smoothly than many experts had predicted and has made monetary exchange between countries and businesses much easier. This development has been a boon for further globalization.

Think Critically

1. If one euro is of greater value than one dollar, what effect does that have on American and European imports and exports?
2. There were, and still are, some European countries reluctant to accept the euro as their currency. Why do you believe they hesitate?

Managing Quality A new management style, **total quality management** or TQM, became a buzzword in many organizations. TQM theory was essentially taken from the Japanese method of manufacturing. Its basic premise is one of continuous improvement in quality and customer service. The idea of setting up various methods of ensuring quality and improving customer service has caught on with many American companies. It has also carried over into the international business community and is the cornerstone of ISO9000 regulations. These regulations are international standards of quality control management that set uniform guidelines for manufacturing processes to ensure that products conform to customer expectations. In order for a company to receive endorsements for its products in many foreign markets, it must follow ISO9000 recommendations for product manufacture and guarantees.

The result of all this is a market that offers more choices to more informed customers who have a much clearer understanding of value. Entrepreneurs who attempt to price-gouge with inferior products will not be successful in the long term.

Price Objections

Price is considered the hidden objection when it comes to selling. Many times interested buyers are persuaded not to buy because of the price of a product, but they are reluctant to admit it. They might say, "No, I don't like the color," when what they really don't like is the price. Professional salespeople learn how to handle price objections by being knowledgeable about the value of the product and about ways to assist the buyer in overcoming the objection. They become experts at finding this hidden objection, bringing it out, and handling it with carefully chosen questions and constructive suggestions. A price objection to an expensive item might be countered with, "If we can spread the payments out over a period of time, would that help you make the purchase?" Price objections should always be handled from a positive standpoint, using positive words.

©GETTY IMAGES/PHOTODISC

You must be able to defend your pricing strategy and counter the consumer's quite normal reaction. For customers the difficult part of the purchase decision is giving up what they have for something they do not have, no matter how good the product or the sales presentation.

Pricing Criteria

Before determining your final prices you should do the following.

1. Compute what will be required to cover the four points of the total pricing concept.
2. Determine the breakeven point.
3. Gather information on competitors' prices and how long they have maintained those prices.
4. Ask selected representatives of the target market or a focus group for input.
5. Ask members of the industry what has worked for them.
6. If necessary, experiment with introductory pricing strategies, keeping in mind that it will be easier to lower prices at a later date than to raise them.
7. Examine closely the image of the product and the price consumers would be willing to pay for that image.
8. Scan the business environment for external and internal factors that might influence customer buying attitudes.
9. Give careful consideration to the chosen strategy and its long-term goal.
10. Determine the best way to defend your prices when questions and objections are raised.

Ship in a BOTTLE

Setting Prices

Determining the prices was a two-part process: wholesale and retail. Fred had a starting price based on his cost and on Johann's prices at his Hamburg store and web site. By calculating the cost to an American of ordering a model from Johann, including the cost of shipping from Germany, Fred could calculate a fair value to the customer. His research and conversations with Johann had convinced him that Johann's retail prices were perceived as a fair value. Therefore he could calculate his initial retail prices by adding the cost of an individual shipment to a U.S. address from Germany to the advertised prices on Johann's web site. He also believed he could justify adding a small premium for the convenience of buying in the U.S., which saved customers considerable time and allowed personal communication with the seller.

Arriving at a wholesale price would not be difficult once the retail price was set. Fred knew that independent retail operations expected a 50 percent markup. His objective was to determine a retail selling price on the web site that could be discounted 40 to 50 percent to his retail store clients so their prices would be in line with his. The difficulty was making sure these prices would cover the four requirements of the total pricing concept: cost of product, cost of operations, a reasonable profit, and a return of earnings for business expansion and/or debt reduction. Fred tried a few approaches.

1. First he calculated his fixed costs. Four trade shows per year, including travel and accommodations, would cost $10,000. Road travel to visit retail stores would cost $6,000 for 20,000 miles per year and 16 nights on the road, plus $4,000 for lease payments on a van. Total fixed costs would be at least $20,000 per year.
2. Variable costs were more difficult to estimate. Fred had not yet decided how much to order or how much to spend on advertising, wages for office and trade show assistants, and office supplies.

Fred knew there would be some guesswork involved and that it was possible prices would have to be revised after final financial projections and plans were in place. His best course of action was to be aggressive initially and, if the prices were too high, back off later.

Using a ship-in-a-bottle model that Johann offered for $100 on his web site, Fred added $22 as the savings in shipping and a $3 premium for ease of acquisition to arrive at a retail price of $125. Could he sell it wholesale for $65 to $70 to retailers, who could then sell it for $130 to $150? Johann was willing to sell to Fred at 40 percent of his retail prices, assuming at least $3,000 per order. The $100 model would cost Fred $40 plus shipping costs and customs fee. The shipping cost would average $4 per unit. So the cost of goods was $44 on Johann's $100 model. His final calculation showed:

Web site retail price:	$125 – $44 = $81	64.8% contributing margin
Wholesale price:	$70 – $44 = $26	37% contributing margin

Assuming a 50 percent ratio of retail to wholesale sales, Fred added the $81 margin to the $26 margin and divided by 2 to estimate an average contributing margin of $53.50 on each unit. This gave an average markup of 50.9 percent, since (64.8% + 37%) ÷ 2 = 50.9%.

Would these margins hold up after factoring in the cost of operations? Fred thought they would. Using the breakeven formula, he estimated that with fixed costs of $20,000 per year and an average contributing margin of $53.50, he would be all right

continued

as long as he sold at least 374 units per year, well under his expectations. Fred decided the 50.9 percent average unit markup would be his initial objective.

Think Critically

1. How would you classify Fred's initial pricing strategy? As a new entrepreneur, what other pricing strategies should he consider?
2. Is it possible that Fred is setting his wholesale margin (37 percent) too low, considering that it represents 50 percent of his total projected sales volume?

Summary

If products or services are not properly priced, customers will not buy. The entrepreneur's goal is to set prices low enough to ensure a demand for the product and high enough to ensure a sufficient profit to successfully operate the business. Consumers will buy what they perceive will bring them the greatest need satisfaction for their money.

Successful entrepreneurs follow the total pricing concept by pricing their products to ensure good customer relations and long-term profits. To accomplish these objectives, they must find the breakeven point for a product, service, or business operation. They then apply markup formula calculations and determine the best pricing strategies for the business.

Numerous external and internal environmental factors must be taken into account when determining prices. Shifts in economic cycles, lifestyles, and marketplace competition are a few considerations analyzed by successful entrepreneurs. Pricing should be considered a marketing tool with many legal and financial considerations.

A Case in POINT

A Shortsighted Pricing Decision

Charlie's Tobacco Patch Store used a discount pricing strategy on cigarette cartons to entice customers into the store. Charlie felt that once they were inside, they would buy enough related smoking items to offset the lost profit margin on the cigarettes. The strategy was working to his advantage until a national chain drugstore in the same mall undercut Charlie's prices by 10 percent. Charlie countered with a similar discount. A few weeks later the drugstore cut prices again, and Charlie followed suit. At this point Charlie was selling his cigarette cartons for less than he actually paid for them—a true loss leader. However, his customer count continued to rise, and his sales revenue was growing as well.

But now Charlie has received a rent bill that includes a percentage rent charge, and he realizes the mistake he has made by competing with a discounter on price. His loss leader cigarette sales have risen to 60 percent of his total revenue. Therefore 60 percent of sales are not even covering the cost of goods. To make matters worse, he is now paying additional rent as a result of his increasing sales volume. For every dollar of revenue he receives from the sale of cigarette cartons, Charlie is paying 6 cents in rent plus the cost of the product itself.

Charlie had better do something fast, or he could be out of business.

Think Critically

1. Can you help Charlie with some suggestions on how to raise prices on his cigarettes?
2. Should Charlie visit the landlord and request that the percentage rent clause be eliminated because he has to compete with a tenant in the same mall?

Chapter Review

Vocabulary Builder

1. breakeven point
2. contributing margin
3. external factors
4. fixed costs
5. FOB
6. internal factors
7. list price
8. loss leader pricing
9. markdown
10. market penetration pricing
11. markup
12. net price
13. price bundling
14. price lining
15. price points
16. skimming
17. status quo pricing
18. supply and demand
19. tie-in sales
20. total pricing concept
21. total quality management
22. variable costs
23. zone price

Review the Concepts

24. Describe the role of price in the marketing mix.
25. What objectives are addressed by the total pricing concept?
26. Explain the relationship between supply and demand.
27. What is the difference between fixed and variable costs?
28. How is the breakeven point calculated?
29. Distinguish markups from markdowns.
30. If the cost of an item is $50 and it is sold for $100, what is the markup percent? If an item retails for $50 and has a 40 percent markup, what was its cost to the seller?
31. List and describe the six pricing strategies.
32. Name three external factors and three internal factors that can affect the pricing decisions of a business owner.

Critical Thinking

33. In a free market economy, how do supply and demand correct prices and protect against monopolies?
34. If the fixed costs of a business operation are $50,000 and the average contributing margin of its products is $11, how many units must be produced to reach the breakeven point?
35. What are the factors that must be considered in arriving at the variable cost of a product?
36. What pricing strategy would you suggest for a new technology product? A brand-name set of tires? A new addition to a restaurant's menu? A grand opening for a new wholesale business?
37. What products have you purchased recently that were loss leaders?
38. What dangers and risks does discounting present to the small business?
39. Why is it necessary for an entrepreneur to scan the environment for external factors if they do not have a direct, immediate impact on the business?

Project

Build Your Business Plan

At this point in the business planning process, it is time to set the initial prices of the products or services you will be selling. Apply the breakeven analysis and total pricing concept to this process.

1. Defend your reasons for the prices you have set.
2. Describe or show your products to classmates and friends and ask their opinions as to their perceived value.
3. Choose a pricing strategy. Do you plan to change this strategy once it has been established?
4. Which of your competitors do you consider price leaders?

Chapter 11

Promotional Activities

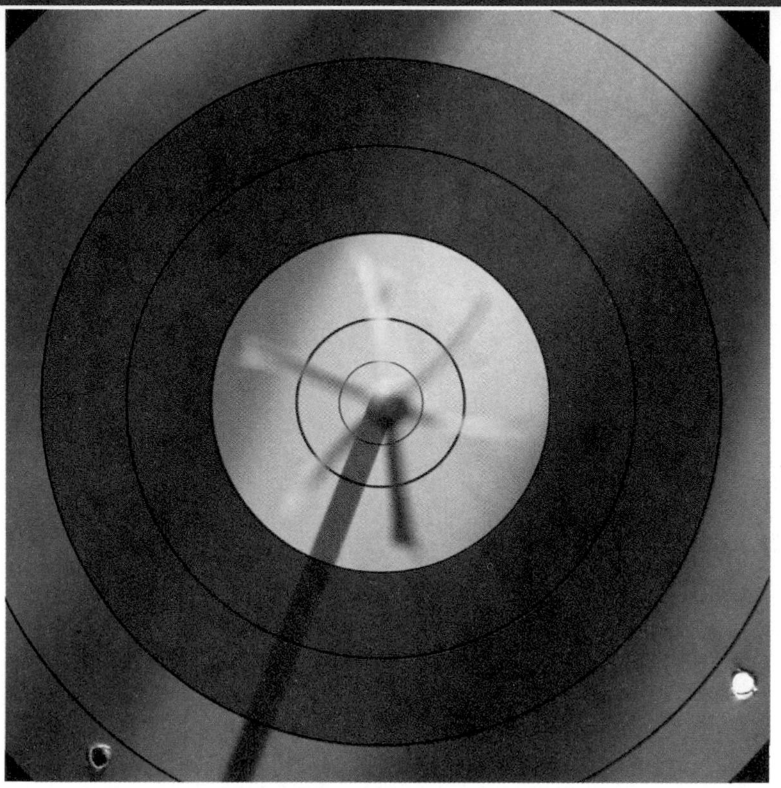

©GETTY IMAGES/PHOTODISC

Objectives

11-1 Describe the promotional strategies available to entrepreneurs.

11-2 Explain the three advertising stages of a business and how they affect advertising choices.

11-3 Discuss the guidelines and considerations for selecting the most effective advertising vehicles.

11-4 Explain the considerations involved in staging a successful promotional event.

11-5 Define the different selling methods and explain how each is used.

11-6 Discuss the importance of good public relations to a small business.

IMPLEMENT THE PROMOTIONAL MIX

In Chapter 5 the promotional mix was defined as consisting of four parts: advertising, promotion, personal selling, and public relations/publicity. These communication strategies are designed to promote customer acceptance of the product or service. Once the entrepreneur has determined the complete product, selected a location, and set a price that ensures a comfortable profit margin, she can turn her attention to the final P of the four P's, designing sales-enticing promotional strategies.

In the free enterprise system, businesses have a myriad of ways to communicate with their intended target market. However, many of these methods are not within the budget constraints of the small enterprise. It is important that you learn how to outthink your competitors because, in many instances, you will not be able to outspend them. There will be hard choices to make in regard to how you spend money—on advertising, promotional activities, or personal sales programs. To develop an effective promotional strategy, it is imperative that you have a thorough understanding of your customers' needs as well as the best methods to satisfy those needs.

Strategic Considerations

Determining which overall promotional strategy is best suited to the business and its products is your first step. Always keep in mind that the strength of a small business lies in its ability to be more personal and flexible than a large business. The promotional strategy begins with reviewing the competitive advantage of your business. Is it a cost leader? Does it offer the greatest convenience? Does it offer a unique product or service? What you are promoting determines which tool would be the most effective.

Some products or services demand a very aggressive strategy of enticing customers to try them. For other products or services it is better to use a strategy of creating a demand and then delivering the product. The former, known as a **push strategy**, depends on the seller making the product immediately available. The latter, a **pull strategy**, is intended to create so much interest in the product beforehand that customers are literally demanding that it be made available. Push strategies place the products on retail shelves for customers to choose, while pull strategies enlighten customers to the products' existence before the retailer has offered them for sale.

Strategies

A **viral promotional strategy** is a commonly used type of pull strategy. The business sets in motion a plan to capture the attention of a particular segment of the market with the expectation that the opinion leaders of that segment will spread the word—just as a virus spreads from one person to another.

A good example of viral marketing was the opening of the movie *The Passion of the Christ* in 2004. It was released on a very limited and controlled basis to certain churches and religious organizations, with the hope that the leaders of these groups would tell others about the movie and lay the groundwork for an enthusiastic reception when the movie was released to the general public. The $30 million production grossed well over $200 million within a few weeks of its debut.

Small businesses can use viral marketing with their target markets as well. A well-designed promotional strategy and mix can spread the word about the features, advantages, and benefits of buying from a certain business. Once it is set in motion, word-of-mouth promotion becomes the strongest type of promotion a business can rely on. There is nothing more effective than praise and personal recommendations passed from one person to another.

Network promoting is another example of using personal references to spread the word and sell products. Networking strategies have grown tremendously over the past decade. The use of networking started years ago with Tupperware parties and has expanded to include activities such as demonstrating the uses of Mary Kay cosmetics and selling Amway cleaning products to friends and relatives. The success of these businesses comes from the personal contact.

As a small businesses owner, you can learn from this success and use your own network of customers and friends to promote your product or service. Be on the lookout for any opportunity to discuss your business in front of groups of interested individuals. This activity may take many forms, such as seminars at your local community college on subjects such as home decorating (if you own a furniture store) or speeches on retirement planning at local civic organizations (if you own a financial planning service). By placing yourself in the public eye this way, you are building a network of people who will spread the word about your business.

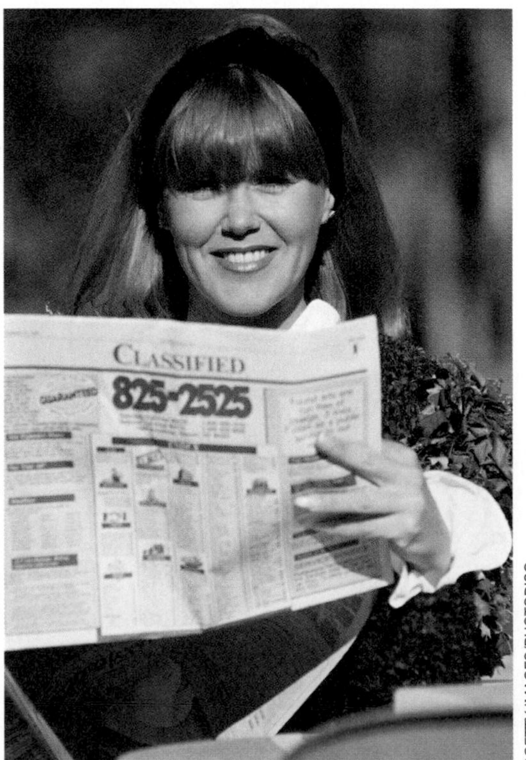

ADVERTISING

The function of advertising is to draw attention to the features, benefits, and advantages of a product, service, or business. As noted in Chapter 5, for small businesses this should be done on as personal a basis as possible. Rarely can a small business afford the cost of mass media vehicles that larger businesses use—large metropolitan newspapers, national magazines, and major television and radio networks. The success of a small business is far more dependent on the personal, customer-oriented approach, and that includes the business owner's approach to advertising. It is not necessary to spend lavishly to achieve the desired results from an advertising campaign. It *is* necessary to focus on advertising activities that yield the greatest return for the dollar.

Advertising Guidelines

It is impossible to evaluate the results of an advertisement in strictly quantitative terms. Therefore there are no definite rules to follow. However, experience has generated some general guidelines for effective advertising for small businesses.

1. A business that engages in advertising must design a consistent approach. Too many businesses jump in and out of the marketplace based on impulse and cash flow fluctuations.
2. You must be careful not to overreach your intended market. Too often small businesses assume they are more powerful in attracting customers than they really are. They tend to overreach their target audience by paying for advertising circulation that extends beyond their market. For instance, a single retail unit should not spend advertising dollars in a metropolitan newspaper that is distributed to areas that are not part of the business's marketplace. If it does, it is paying as much to reach readers 20 miles away as it is to reach those in the immediate marketplace.
3. Small businesses should keep their advertising message and approach personal. They should employ advertising vehicles that allow, as closely as possible, a direct or one-on-one presentation, as in direct mail.
4. Business owners must understand the stage of development their business is in to choose the most effective advertising copy.

Advertising Stages

Businesses must look at their stage of development to determine what type of advertising will be most effective. The goal is to always look fresh and exciting to customers. The spiral in Figure 11-1 represents a business's continuous effort to stimulate and restimulate the market's interest in a product or service.

New businesses are in the **pioneering stage** of development and therefore should concentrate their strategies on introducing themselves to the marketplace. Key words such as "introducing," "welcome," "brand new," and "announcing" are often used at this stage.

Once the business has settled into the marketplace, it enters the **competitive stage** of advertising. In this stage distinctive or exceptional features of the product that are not shared by the competition are emphasized. Themes such as "compare," "better than," and "less expensive than" are used in an effort to increase market share. Often this stage begins when competitors react to the new business by increasing their advertising.

FIGURE 11-1

Advertising Spiral

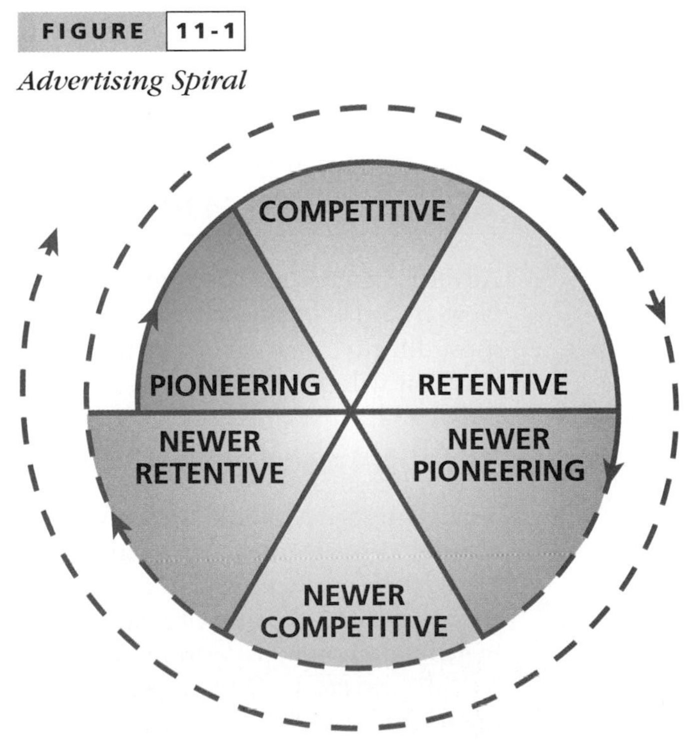

Once firmly established, the business enters the **retentive stage**, in which the intention is to maintain market share. Themes such as "established since," "reliable," and "serving your needs since" remind customers of the business's staying power, loyalty, and dependability. This is considered the least effective form of advertising and is used only for businesses and products that are already well known in the marketplace.

Advertising in the first two stages is normally **product advertising**, since it focuses on the benefits and advantages of buying the particular products or services of a business. **Institutional advertising** is used in the retentive stage. It is designed to broadcast a good image of the business itself by emphasizing the benefits and advantages of doing business with it.

Businesses in the retentive stage should look for ways to reenter the pioneering stage. At this point it is important to add a new dimension to existing products or services or the business may fall behind and become obsolete. Often a new look can be achieved by expanding the selection, redesigning the product, or showing new uses for it. Arm & Hammer is an excellent example of a company that has used this strategy successfully. It has cast the usefulness of baking soda in a variety of ways, from refrigerator deodorizer to tooth cleanser to antacid. Johnson's also used this strategy when it ran ads showing a well-known football player using its baby shampoo, and in that way entered the adult shampoo market. It is common for companies to return to the pioneering stage of advertising by announcing a "new and improved" or "bigger and better" product. Small businesses can do the same thing in a smaller capacity. Inviting customers to "come see our new look," or announcing that "we now carry the new" can accomplish the same result.

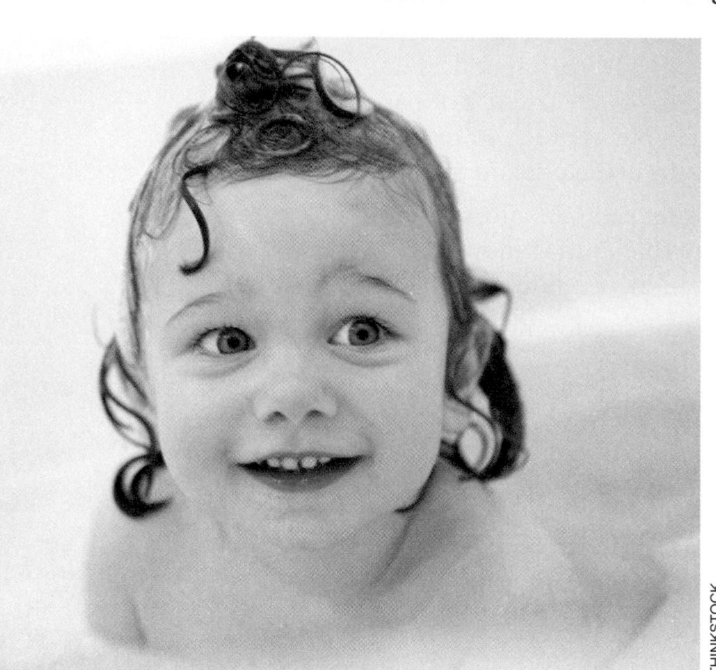
THINKSTOCK

ADVERTISING FOR SMALL BUSINESSES

Advertising rates are based on exposure, whether it is to readers, listeners, or viewers. Small business owners are constantly on the watch for the media that most directly reach their specific market, without needless exposure to markets that will not react to their message.

Local Newspapers

Small enterprises should use only those newspapers that are circulated to their specific target market, from which they expect to derive the greatest percentage of their business, and not to areas outside of their domain. These newspapers are usually community dailies or weeklies. In some larger markets the metropolitan newspaper runs **zoned editions**, which are distributed only in specific areas to serve the needs of marketers in that area. By limiting advertising to the immediate market, the entrepreneur saves money that would otherwise have been spent on unnecessary exposure.

Rates for newspaper advertising are based on cost per **column inch**. Newspapers are laid out in a 6- or 8-column format. The total number of column inches per ad is calculated by multiplying the width of the ad, measured in columns, by the depth, measured in inches or lines (there are 14 lines to a column inch). A 4-by-4-column-inch ad is 4 columns wide by 4 inches (56 lines) deep. If the rate is $24 per column inch, the cost of the ad would be 4 x 4 x $24, or $384. The charge per column inch is derived from the stated circulation number of the newspaper. A metropolitan newspaper with a circulation of 200,000 might charge $40 per column inch, whereas a zoned edition of a local community newspaper with a circulation of 50,000 might charge $20 per column inch. Newspapers generally allow discounts on their published rates if the advertiser signs a contract guaranteeing purchase of a stipulated number of column inches over a specific period of time.

It is very difficult for a small business to compete with larger businesses in terms of ad size and competitiveness. Size is the single most important factor in getting an ad noticed, as illustrated in the survey results from Starch Marketing Reporting Service in Table 11-1.

FUN FACTS

The great increase in information sources (television, Internet) has taken its toll on newspaper readers. Newspaper readership has declined almost 40 percent in the past 40 years. Today fewer than 55 percent of adults read a daily newspaper, compared to over 80 percent in 1964.

TABLE 11-1 SUMMARY OF 32 NEWSPAPERS AND 6,400 PERSONAL INTERVIEWS

Size of Ad	Women Noted	Women Read Most	Men Noted	Men Read Most
1 page or more	48%	19%	34%	11%
¾ to 1 page	43%	13%	30%	8%
½ to ¾	36%	10%	31%	9%
¼ to ½	29%	10%	22%	7%
⅛ to ¼	28%	10%	20%	7%
Under ⅛	15%	5%	13%	5%
All ads	31%	11%	24%	7%

It is clear that if you cannot afford to run an ad large enough to make an impact in a high-circulation newspaper, you should concentrate on less costly but more target-specific print media. For example, a 6-by-8-column-inch ad (approximately half a page) in the 200,000-circulation newspaper described above would cost $1,920 (48 x $40), compared to $960 (48 x $20) in the more tightly distributed 50,000-circulation newspaper or zoned edition. Not only is the latter cheaper, it is also more efficiently targeted for your needs.

Magazines

Magazine advertising has the benefit of a longer exposure time. While newspapers generally have a one-day exposure, magazines have an extended reading window. They may be left on coffee tables, in waiting rooms, or on library shelves for many weeks, even months. As with newspapers, rates are based on subscriber and circulation statistics. The advantage to small businesses is that magazines are targeted by subject material. The disadvantage is that unless they are very tightly distributed geographically, they usually overreach the target market.

Many small businesses use the classified section of major magazines to reach targeted markets. Classified ads are affordable and can serve either to sell directly or to gain prospects. They often direct readers to call or send for more information. Classified ads are also an effective means for advertising web site addresses.

Classified advertisements, whether in newspapers or magazines, are sold on a per-word basis. There is a flat rate for a set number of words, with an additional charge for every word over the initial number—for example, $150 for the first 20 words and $12 for each additional word. A 25-word classified ad would then cost $150 plus $60, or $210. For an additional fee, many publications print simple artwork as the headline. There may also be additional charges for bold print. If you sell specialized products to a niche market, such as fishing lures to fishermen, classified magazine advertising can be very profitable and should be considered.

Radio

FUN FACTS

The average listener over 12 years old in the U.S. spends over 1,100 hours a year listening to the radio.

Many small businesses use radio advertising effectively, citing its affordability. Radio advertising is charged a fee per spot. Rates are based on listenership, which is calculated by independent survey companies. The largest of these is the Arbitron Company. Surveys are published throughout the industry and denote the listening audience of particular stations at specific hours of the day, including a breakdown of the audience by age group. The more listeners a radio station has, the higher its rates. Charges are usually quoted for 30 or 60 seconds. The time of day the spot is run affects the price. Prime time (often called drive time in the radio industry) constitutes the most expensive time slot. Rates vary significantly between stations as well as within the time periods the advertiser wishes to run an advertisement. A 30-second drive time spot might be $18 for one station and $60 for another, depending on the survey of listeners. Radio stations, like newspapers, offer discounts to frequent users.

Small business owners should be more concerned with the makeup of the listeners than the number. It does not matter how many listeners a radio station has if they are not your target market. You must choose the station your customers tune in to in order to get the best results. For example, if you are in the business of selling western wear, you might consider using country western stations, but if you sell to teenagers, you would advertise on hard rock or hip hop stations.

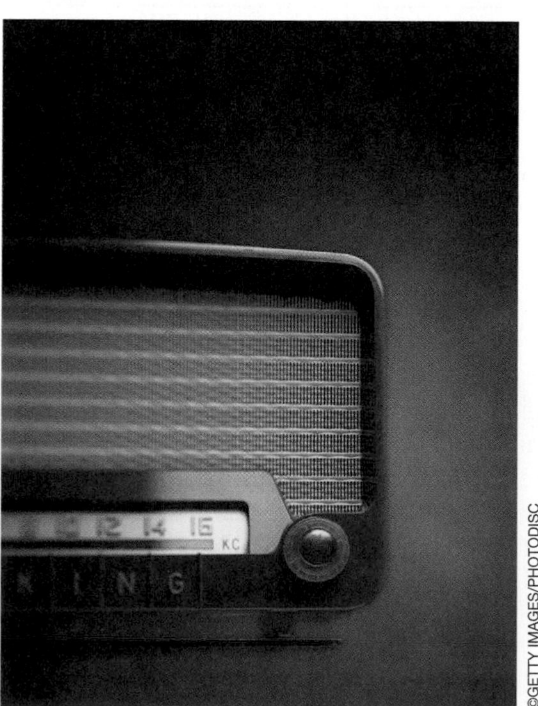

©GETTY IMAGES/PHOTODISC

Radio advertising can offer a degree of personalization. An effectively designed radio commercial often creates a one-on-one connection between the narrator and the listener. This is particularly true with a single car occupant who is free to concentrate on the message. If there are others in the car, such as small children, the "noise factors" surrounding the commercial will reduce the effectiveness and retentiveness of the message.

Television

The expanding number of television stations has opened opportunities for smaller businesses to use television advertising. When the major networks dominated all markets, advertising was too costly and competitive for small enterprises. However, with the growth of local programming through cable and satellite television, TV advertising is now a viable option. With such a large assortment of stations and programs, businesses may choose television stations on the same premise as radio—by the target market served. The advertiser's objective is to choose a program of interest to its specific market. For instance, a sporting goods store may wish to sponsor the televising of a local high school football game.

Rates are based on viewership, which is surveyed by independent companies such as the Nielsen Company. Television rates may be comparable with local radio rates. However, there is a one-time charge for taping the commercial, and, depending on the degree of complexity, this can prove quite costly. The advertiser should be informed and involved with the actual taping as the final product will cast an image of the business that many viewers will see and remember. Television advertising is not as personal as radio advertising, but it adds the visual dimension—"a picture is worth a thousand words"—which is a powerful stimulant and a reinforcement of your basic message.

Billboard Advertising

Many businesses find billboard advertising invaluable. Restaurants, motels, and tourist attractions are examples of businesses that typically make use of this medium. Its appeal is to businesses that target car travelers, particularly those travelers who are visiting an area or are passing through. There are also mobile billboards, which are placed in public transportation vehicles such as buses, subways, and taxicabs. Often less expensive than highway billboards, they also offer better targeting.

Rates for billboards are based on the average number of exposures of a location, measured by the number of people who pass by over a given time period. Exposures are determined by drive-by surveys. This information is available through a state's department of transportation. Rates fluctuate according to the amount of traffic, whether the sign is lighted or unlighted, and its size. Usually advertisers are billed on a monthly basis, as stipulated in a signed contract covering a specific period of time. Design, artwork, and setup charges are billed separately and, like television advertising, demand the entrepreneur's close attention as the image will tell a story to the many potential customers who see the billboard.

©GETTY IMAGES/PHOTODISC

Ethics for ENTREPRENEURS

Some entrepreneurs rely on trickery to achieve a sale. Two common unethical sales methods are bait-and-switch advertising and deceptive closing tactics.

In bait-and-switch advertising, a seller advertises a special price on a product that he or she does not intend to sell. When buyers inquire, they may be told that the product is sold out or that it is of inferior quality, but that there is another product available, at a higher price.

Deceptive closing tactics come into play when a salesperson tells a potential buyer that the product the buyer is interested in will be sold to another waiting buyer if it is not purchased immediately, when in actuality there is no waiting buyer.

Think Critically

1. Have you ever been victimized by either of the above tactics? If so, describe the situation and explain the best way to handle it.
2. The Latin expression *caveat emptor* means "let the buyer beware." Do you believe this warning is necessary when buying products in the U.S.?

Telephone Directories

Telephones are an indispensable convenience tool for consumers. For this reason, small businesses selling consumer products or services should consider advertising in telephone directories. For many businesses, such as restaurants, repair services, and highly specialized products, this kind of advertising is essential. The challenge is to place ads where the target market will be looking. Many product classifications overlap, and there may be a temptation to advertise under multiple headings, which can lead to overreaching and become very expensive. Again, the better you understand your target market, the more effectively you will control your advertising expenditures.

Rates are determined by the number of telephone books in circulation and the size of the advertisement. If you advertise in the local Yellow Pages, the charges are billed monthly as part of your telephone bill. Supplemental telephone directories bill separately.

Direct Mail

For many small businesses the most efficient, cost-effective advertising vehicle is **direct mail**, printed information sent through a delivery service or electronic mail to potential customers. Designed properly, it provides the desired one-to-one connection. Direct mail places a message in front of the potential customer, often with minimum "noise factors" that cause distortion. The challenge lies in designing a format that is inviting as well as informative.

Strategies Since the strength of a small business is its capacity for a more personal connection with its customers, its direct mail pieces should be as personal as possible. You should address your mailing piece to an individual—for instance, "Mrs. Mary Jones"—rather than to "Resident." It is better to address the piece by hand or make it look as if it was personally typewritten rather than to use stick-on labels, which make the piece appear to be part of a mass mailing. In a crowded mailbox of advertisements, the recipient is more likely to open mail pieces that look personally addressed.

The same holds true for the salutation and the message itself. "Dear Ms. Jones"—or, in the case of a regular customer whom you know personally, "Dear Mary"—will be much better received than "Dear Customer." Whenever possible the message should begin with a personal touch, such as "Thank you for..." or perhaps some reference to a past relationship.

Besides being personal, a direct mail message must also look professional. The use of photographs, graphs, or illustrations shows professionalism and breaks the monotony of the written message. When using photographs, include pictures of people, pets, or places of local interest rather than generic copied images. Use high-quality paper to help create the image you desire for your business.

Mailing Lists Direct mail can be used to send information letters, brochures, or catalogs. Mailing lists are available through mailing houses and can be tailored for the intended market. The cost is based on the number of names and addresses required.

The best mailing list consists of customers who have used or visited the business in the past. Designing an effective system for collecting and maintaining a database of past and current customers is a must for every new business. Mailing a letter to regular customers announcing a new product or development in your business is the most cost-effective form of advertising you can use.

The cost of mailing pieces can be significant. If you use direct mail as a regular part of your promotional program, bulk rates are available through the postal service that will mean significant savings in mailing expenditures. Mailing fees are determined by the size and weight of a mailing piece. Check with the postal authorities before designing your mailing piece.

Small Business Technology

In the past, getting the word out about a new product or special event could take several days. Sellers had to design and place newspaper ads two to three days in advance or submit radio spots one or two days in advance. Through the use of the Internet and fax machines, information can be sent out much more quickly today. A special sale can be announced in minutes via a company's database of customer e-mail addresses or fax numbers. Businesses often use e-mail or fax to preannounce a special sale or event to their established customers while using traditional media to attract new customers.

Telecommunications Advertising

Internet advertising is attracting more and more customers. E-mail pop-ups and banners are designed as a quick hit-and-move-on technique. As such they do not hold much appeal for most small businesses. They offer little in the way of personalization and have not been determined as cost-effective for most vendors of small consumer goods as they cannot be effectively targeted.

However, web site merchants do use services that direct customers to their sites. Pay-per-click ads are offered by Internet search services. For a fee for each customer directed to a web site, the server lists an entrepreneur's product as a sponsor under the desired category or name. If a business wishes its web site to be listed when a search is being conducted for a product—baseball pennants, for instance—the business agrees to pay the server a specified amount to make sure its web site is listed as a source for baseball pennants. When the words "baseball pennant" are entered into an Internet search, the names of

©GETTY IMAGES/PHOTODISC

vendors who have subscribed to the service show up on the page. Fees range from a few cents to several dollars per hit, depending on the number of businesses bidding for a listing and in what place or order the subscriber wishes to be listed. Businesses with web sites are very dependent on this type of advertising.

Another form of advertising commonly used in conjunction with the telecommunications industry is fax broadcasting. The seller pays a fax broadcasting service to distribute a specified number of faxes to a particular market. Although it can be targeted in the same way a mailing list is, this form of advertising cannot be personalized and is generally not an effective medium for small businesses.

Create Copy

The best source of information for creating advertising copy is the entrepreneur. It is important to recognize that any promotional piece will carry the image of your business. You are responsible for maintaining a positive image, and it is therefore your job to screen all representations of the business. Certainly you should make use of the art departments of print media and the production design skills of radio and television personnel, but final control should remain in your hands. You know your product and your target customer best.

FIGURE 11-2

Effective Advertising Copy

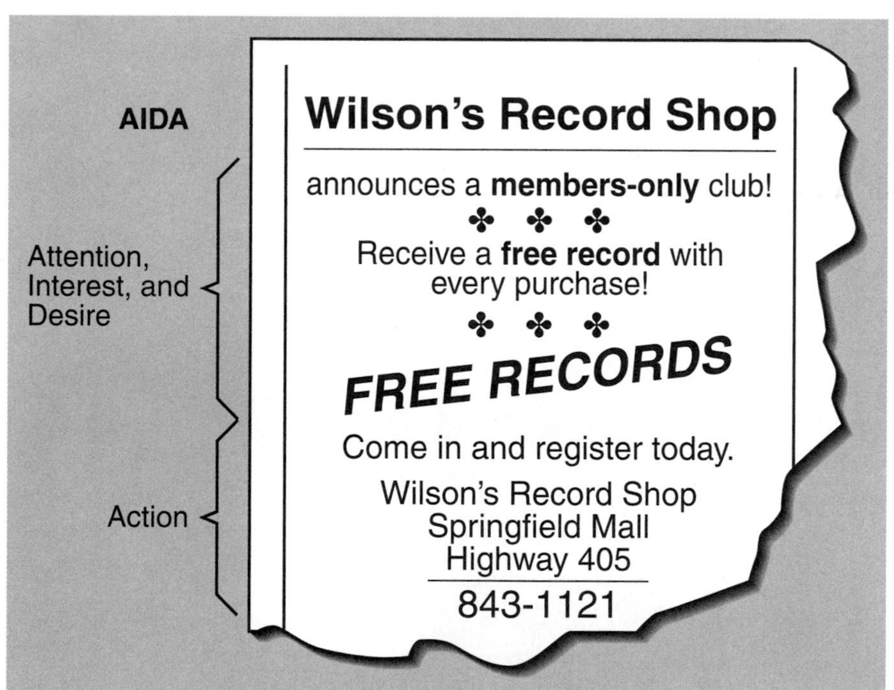

Advertising copywriters often use two acronyms to guide them in creating copy: **AIDA** (attention, interest, desire, action) and **KISS** (keep it simple, stupid). An effective ad, such as the one in Figure 11-2, must, of course, attract the attention of the target market. Usually this is accomplished with a headline, photograph, or illustration. The features of the product or service and the benefits the customer will receive after purchasing it are explained in clear, concise language or illustrations.

The action part of the advertisement asks the customer to do something to gain the satisfaction being offered. "Buy now," "come on down," and "save today" are examples of action statements. All advertisements, whether in print media, radio, television, billboards, Yellow Pages, or direct mail, should contain the four AIDA ingredients. And they should be simple. Keep in mind that the customer is busy and will not take the time to decipher long and complicated messages. The message must be clear, concise, and understandable to everyone: KISS.

Evaluate Advertising Results

Rarely can an entrepreneur effectively measure the results of an individual advertisement. An entrepreneur who spends $1,000 on a one-time advertisement with the objective of selling enough of the product to pay for the ad and make a profit will, in most cases, be disappointed in the results. Evaluating the effectiveness of an advertising program requires looking at the benefits of image enhancement and customer exposure over the long term rather than immediately. A business that spends money on a consistent, well-planned advertising program will show steady growth. Over a period of months or years, it will outperform the growth statistics of its industry.

To get the most out of your advertising dollars, you must make both a long-term approach and consistency a central part of your planning. Consistency assures the regular exposure that will keep the business in the customer's awareness. Large businesses know the importance of consistency, which is why they run advertisements repeatedly on television, radio, and print media. The more times people are exposed to an ad, the more likely those in the target market are to remember it.

STAGE A PROMOTIONAL EVENT

A **promotional event** is a planned program created to build goodwill for a business by offering an added value to the customers. An event can be as simple as distributing pens or calendars to customers or as elaborate as staging contests and awarding prizes. Planning a promotion for a small business can be a very rewarding and surprisingly affordable method of increasing sales and exposure.

Promotions should be fun for the customer and the business. The primary objective is to create goodwill. A simple contest of guessing the number of jelly beans in a jar for a prize creates excitement for customers and leaves them with a good feeling about the business. The cost is nominal and might include a fish bowl, jelly beans, copies of entry forms, and a prize, normally a product or gift certificate from the business. In exchange, customers enjoy participating and often encourage friends and family members to participate as well, giving the business a broader exposure. Once the word is out, potential customers stop in to enter the contest and, of course, are exposed to the products or services of the business.

Another example of a contest that attracts community members is one that offers prizes for the best artwork or science experiment by a child. Such a contest gains the attention of the entire family several times—first as the child is creating the artwork or experiment, next when the work is on display at the business. Then family and friends come by to see the child's entry. When the contest is over and the entries are judged by a source outside the business, such as the local art league or science club, the winner and runner-ups are announced with

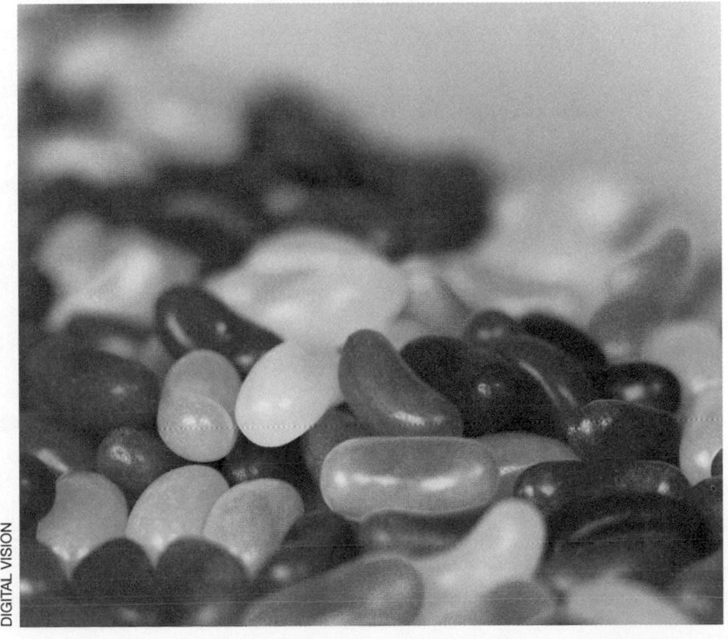
DIGITAL VISION

great fanfare to the local newspaper or television station. A contest generates free publicity and goodwill for all concerned. The cost to the business is minimal and is returned many times over.

The small business should work from an annual calendar, which helps not only with budgeting but also with highlighting certain sales periods. Successful merchandisers use a calendar that features at least one promotional event per month. For example, a January sales event might be a white sale, February might feature a President's Day or Valentine's Day sale, and August might feature a back-to-school sale. If you market on an occasional or irregular basis, the competition may succeed in taking away your customers and changing their buying habits.

Small businesses, particularly retailers, should be socially oriented. People should enjoy visiting the store not only to see what is new on the shelves but also to interact with other customers, friends, and the staff in a welcoming environment. By staging promotions, the business is entertaining its customers, fostering good feelings, and, in the long run, increasing sales.

A grand opening is another kind of promotion that reaps benefits for a new business. A grand opening serves multiple purposes. It is an exciting way to announce that the enterprise is open for business and, done correctly and creatively, also announces that the business is fun, cares for its customers, and is socially oriented. Customers enjoy looking at new things, and they will respond to the invitation. Serving refreshments, having a ribbon-cutting ceremony, and providing entertainment are ways to create goodwill, gain excellent exposure, and ensure that new customers will return. Simple ideas such as giving a carnation to everyone who attends is an inexpensive but extremely effective method of building positive attitudes toward the new business.

As with advertising, a promotion judged strictly in terms of dollars returned for a particular event will be disappointing. Promotions must be evaluated as part of an overall marketing package that allows a business to reach its sales goals.

The Global ENTREPRENEUR

Many entrepreneurs who sell through the Internet are taking a global approach to designing their web sites. It is quite simple to add a translation page to a site. Simply list a click that will direct potential customers to the language of their preference. Once there, they will find the information translated into that language. For example, a German clock manufacturer lists "To view in English" at the top of his web page. With one click, all descriptions and metrics instantly transpose to English. This is an especially wise choice for entrepreneurs who market products that are difficult to find.

Think Critically

1. List three examples of products sold on the Internet that should be described in more than one language.
2. Conduct an Internet search for a product normally manufactured outside the U.S. and report your findings to the class. Note whether or not the delivery charges to your hometown make purchase feasible.

THE DYNAMICS OF PERSONAL SELLING

A sales plan may consist of several methods of selling. You must decide the best means of educating potential customers about the features, advantages, and benefits of your product or service.

Retailing Retail selling is the easiest method because the customer comes to the seller. The mere fact that the customer has chosen a particular store in which to shop or browse announces to the seller a need for that store's particular product or service. The seller must make sure to create an environment that encourages browsing and purchasing. Salespeople must be welcoming and knowledgeable in their presentations.

Cold Calling The most difficult sales method is cold calls, which are calls made without prior notice to the potential customer. The salesperson must be armed with techniques designed to quickly determine the needs of potential customers. Cold calling is often not an efficient method, particularly for business-to-business selling, as it requires waiting for the availability of the intended customer. Qualifying prospects is a particularly important ingredient. A salesperson who waits an hour to visit with a potential client may be disappointed to learn that he has called upon the wrong buyer in the wrong department. Proper homework must be done to prevent wasting time.

Telemarketing When done properly, telemarketing is an effective sales method for many small businesses. **Telemarketing** is selling that involves interacting with customers by telephone. An advantage of telemarketing is the ability to communicate one-on-one with the potential customer, but it has been abused so that it has a negative image. Since the product cannot be seen or touched, telemarketing should only be considered for small service companies. Telemarketing can reach large numbers of prospects relatively inexpensively. The rules of etiquette require that sales personnel be articulate, enthusiastic, and well versed in the features and benefits of the product or service. A good telemarketing script proceeds through the following steps:

1. Address the customer by name, and identify yourself, your company, and the reason you are calling.
2. Pause. Ask if the time is convenient. If it is not, arrange a better time.
3. Make an opening statement describing the features and benefits of the product or service, such as "I'm calling to tell you about a new insurance policy that will better protect your home against catastrophic natural occurrences."
4. Determine if the prospect qualifies by asking fact-finding questions.
5. Overcome any objections.
6. Sell the benefits.
7. Use a trial close.
8. Close.
9. Summarize and confirm.
10. Express your appreciation for the time or order.
11. Determine the follow-up method and date.

©GETTY IMAGES/PHOTODISC

The most effective use for telemarketing is as a follow-up to a direct mail piece, particularly if the piece closes with the announcement that a service representative will contact the recipient at a later date. When used in this manner, the telephone is viewed less as an intrusion and more as a tool that offers additional information. The bottom line of telephone etiquette is not to use any method that the caller might personally find objectionable, and not to violate times normally reserved for family matters or privacy, such as dinner hours. For small businesses, telemarketing is better suited for business-to-business contact during regular business hours than for residential calling.

Trade Shows Trade shows bring industry buyers and sellers together. A **trade show** is a gathering of many producers in the same industry to display products to customers. This promotional tool is normally used to communicate with businesses that purchase a product for the purpose of using it within their own production process or reselling it to consumers or other organizations. Since the potential client is part of the seller's industry, product knowledge is extremely important. Smiles and personality alone will not sell to an informed buyer who is looking out for what is best for his or her business.

Product Demonstrations Often part of the cold caller's repertoire, demonstrations show how a product is used to bring about the desired benefits. Often used in on-site industry presentations or staged promotional events, demonstrations present an excellent format for effectively handling objections.

This sales method is successful only if the full support of the company is behind the sales representative and the product. Sales personnel must be equipped with knowledge, support tools (warranties, dependable shipping schedule, and so on), merchandising aids, and the confidence that the company supports them.

©GETTY IMAGES/PHOTODISC

Sales Training A good sales training course or manual will help motivate and hone the selling skills of representatives. It will not transform a highly technical introvert into a dynamic sales personality, but it will teach proven sales techniques. A training program must match the sales philosophy and approach of the business. The primary requirement for successful sales training is hiring motivated, proactive individuals who want to become professional salespeople. Since training programs also serve as motivators, it is important that they be offered on a regular basis. In order to keep motivation high and skills sharp, salespeople should undergo further training at planned intervals.

PUBLIC RELATIONS AND PUBLICITY

Successful entrepreneurs know the value of public relations, whether paid or free publicity. Public relations is exactly what it says—creating good relationships with the public. Building a good reputation for integrity and fair value will, in the long run, determine how successful a business will be. New businesses must start from scratch to develop good public relations, and, although it might take a long time and a sacrifice of time and money, it should be part of the overall promotional plan. It ties together all the elements of the promotional mix as well as the social responsibilities of the business.

Good public relations is gained by companies that work effectively within their community and industry. They go beyond what is expected to earn goodwill. Whether that means community service or financial support of not-for-profit organizations, public relations demands attention and planning. Just as an advertising calendar helps when planning advertising, a public relations program lays out what is needed for a business to be considered a responsible and trusted member of the community.

©GETTY IMAGES/PHOTODISC

Public relations cannot be evaluated quantitatively. There is no way to measure the financial return on sponsoring a Little League team. The results may show up many years later in the form of favorable word-of-mouth advertising and loyal clients who do not leave a small business to save 5 percent by buying from a large business.

Good public relations also produces more publicity. **Publicity** is free exposure for the business through media channels. It is invaluable because not only is it free, it also carries more credibility than paid advertisements. A newspaper article that describes in glowing terms the activities or products of a business organization is worth far more to the bottom line than any ad.

Entrepreneurs who build good relations with the media receive favorable treatment. They may be able to release information to a media contact about new products or developments within their company and soon thereafter find themselves being interviewed on television or written up in the local newspaper. Imagine the value to a bridal shop of a newspaper feature story that describes new bridal fashions and identifies that shop as the place to find them.

A feature story that identifies the store assigns credibility to the business and identifies it as a leader among bridal stores. Readers will discuss the article with their friends and visit the store to see the new fashions. A favorable article in a newspaper or an interview on television or radio is more advantageous to a business than a paid advertisement.

Ship in a BOTTLE

Implementing the Marketing Plan

Things were really heating up for Ship in a Bottle. Success at the gift shows, good Internet traffic, and positive feedback were leading to a very optimistic forecast. The question now was how to keep the momentum going.

Fred knew the answer to enticing and keeping customers lay in how effective his promotional strategy was. He was pleased with his web site and brochure, but those two pieces were not the total program. He went to work on further developing his advertising program, critically examining his sales program, and developing a public relations plan.

Fred turned his attention to magazine classified advertising to help build a customer mailing list. He decided to run ads under the headline "European Crafted Ships in Bottles" in magazines that were targeted to the boating community. He found over 12 such national magazines but settled on the three that most closely matched his ideal customers—sailors. The average cost of his ads, which ran approximately 20 words and included a toll-free telephone number, a small product sketch, and web site information, was $325. The ads suggested that interested readers call for information and a brochure. Out of curiosity, he also placed a small classified ad in *USA Today* and a home decorating magazine.

By this time Fred had hired two part-time assistants to help with telephone answering and shipping. He knew it was important that these representatives have knowledge of the product and a warm, accommodating telephone personality. He had both of them review a video that Johann had sent showing how a ship in a bottle was built. It was an intricate process that demanded careful study to fully understand the complexities of the craft. He quizzed his assistants to make sure they had a firm grasp of the information and could answer customers' questions.

Fred also spent considerable time going over telephone etiquette with his assistants. He was learning that the way customers were treated when they called for information or to place an order was a very important ingredient in the success ratio of calls to sales. He also discovered that specialty product customers wanted specific information and wanted to feel secure about their credit card transactions. At one point Fred considered a more sophisticated order processing system on his web site that would eliminate personal contact, but he quickly rejected the notion. Speaking to customers via telephone allowed a more personal connection than he had anticipated. He could answer specific questions and build a first-name rapport with each customer.

Part of his question regarding a public relations plan was answered when he received a request for an interview from one of the nautical magazines. Fred realized the craft was a mystery to most people and that regular interviews with different media would keep the business before the public eye. He also decided to explore the possibility of showing Johann's video at trade shows and community craft shows.

The results of all these activities started to pour in. The magazine ads garnered not only many requests for information but also higher direct sales than he had expected. The ads in *USA Today* and the home decorating magazine were a total

continued

bust. The published interview was a great source of telephone inquiries and sales. Throughout this growth period, Fred was more than pleased with how professionally his staff handled telephone inquiries and sales.

Think Critically

1. Explain the pros and cons of three other advertising strategies that Fred might consider.
2. Describe some promotional ideas for Ship in a Bottle.

Summary

Entrepreneurs must develop their promotional mix and strategy after reviewing their competitive advantage. They must determine what is most important to communicate about the business and how it is to be communicated. Because of their limited capital resources, entrepreneurs must be careful to develop promotional strategies that communicate directly with their intended target market.

A common mistake is to overreach a business's market, which causes additional expenditures. An effective advertising program requires consistency. It is important to keep the name of the business in the minds of its customers and keep them informed of new developments, new offerings, special offers, and so on. An advertising program should be designed that takes into consideration the business's stage of development. Good business owners take an active role in designing their ads, as they know their business better than advertising media representatives.

Advertising strategies that allow for a more personal, one-to-one presentation are the best choice for small businesses. Direct mail, telemarketing, and print or broadcast media directed at specific target markets are viable communication vehicles.

Planned promotional events are often effective tools for bringing public attention to particular features of the product and the business. Promotions should be designed to generate goodwill. Whether they consist of giveaways, contests, or entertainment, the entrepreneur's objective with any promotion is to make the customer feel good about the business.

Small enterprises must select selling methods that reflect their image and philosophy. The business owner must ensure that all sales personnel are properly trained in regard to product knowledge and presentation skills. Sales training is only effective if it is reinforced with a consistent, regularly scheduled, follow-up training program.

The final piece of the promotional mix is public relations. A good public relations program is essential to building goodwill in the marketplace and the community. Although it is not possible to quantify the value of public relations in terms of dollars and cents, there is no doubt that an ongoing public relations program contributes to the long-term success of any business enterprise. It often leads to free publicity, which is a very effective means of bringing new customers to the business and reminding current customers that the business is growing and thriving.

A Case in POINT

Do It Yourself

Phil Taylor was disappointed with the results of the television commercials for his car dealership. The commercials were no different from all the rest on TV, and very few customers were being enticed by them. He had always left the advertising copy decisions to Steve Farr, the sales representative at WATZ Television, because he felt that Steve had more experience in this area. Now he was wondering if Steve was missing the mark.

At his next meeting with Steve, Phil addressed the issue. "Steve, if you can't put some excitement into these commercials, I'm going to drop them and do something different. Why can't they be fun? Why do they have to show that boring guy droning on and on about great deals? Spark it up! I want my customers to be happy when they think about my dealership."

"Phil, why don't you design your own ads?" Steve replied. "I'll help with the production techniques and make sure they look good. You know your business the best, and I think you need to get involved."

Think Critically

1. Do you agree with Steve that Phil should design his own commercials? Why?
2. Give Phil some suggestions for writing ad copy.
3. How would you create a fun and exciting commercial for a car dealership?

Vocabulary Builder

Write a brief definition of each word or phrase.

1. AIDA
2. column inch
3. competitive stage
4. direct mail
5. institutional advertising
6. KISS
7. network promoting
8. pioneering stage
9. product advertising
10. promotional event
11. publicity
12. pull strategy
13. push strategy
14. retentive stage
15. telemarketing
16. trade show
17. viral promotional strategy
18. zoned editions

Review the Concepts

19. What is the difference between push and pull strategies?
20. Explain how viral promotions are implemented.
21. What makes network promoting effective?
22. What is the function of advertising?
23. What are the three advertising stages and their objectives?
24. What is the difference between product and institutional advertising?
25. How are rates determined for newspaper ads? For radio ads? For television commercials?
26. Why is direct mail particularly suitable for small businesses?
27. How does a promotional event build goodwill?
28. Name and describe five methods of personal selling.

Critical Thinking

29. How much would a 6-by-4-column-inch newspaper ad cost at $25 per column inch?
30. Describe the various strategies that are employed at different stages of the advertising spiral.
31. Keeping in mind the acronyms AIDA and KISS, design a grand opening announcement for a new shoe store.
32. Explain what makes an effective direct mail campaign.
33. How can you keep a sales force motivated?
34. Describe a recent promotional event that you attended in terms of how successful it was at creating goodwill and encouraging product acceptance.
35. How does a good public relations program generate free publicity?

Project

Build Your Business Plan

1. Describe your intended promotional strategy. Defend your choice of type of media.
2. Allocate a percentage of projected annual revenues for an advertising budget. Check industry sources for the average spent on advertising.
3. On a blank sheet of paper, write the acronyms AIDA and KISS in pencil across the top. Design a newspaper ad that announces the opening of your business.
4. Using the same acronyms, write the copy for a 30-second radio ad telling listeners why they should patronize your business. Read it aloud to make sure it fills exactly 30 seconds. You may use music or other background noise to help get your message across.

Chapter 12

E-Entrepreneurship

Objectives

12-1 Explain the difference between bricks-and-mortar and virtual businesses.

12-2 Discuss the scope of the e-entrepreneurship market and how to address e-entrepreneurship in the business plan.

12-3 Explain the process of creating an e-business web site.

12-4 Discuss e-entrepreneurship and the law.

12-5 Evaluate an e-business web site according to a checklist of important factors.

12-6 Discuss the myths of e-entrepreneurship.

12-7 Analyze common e-entrepreneurship mistakes.

BRICKS AND MORTAR, VIRTUAL, OR BOTH

An entrepreneur is an individual who is willing to take the risk of investing time and money in a business that has the potential to make a profit or incur a loss. An **e-entrepreneur** is defined as an individual willing to take the risk of investing time and money in an electronic business that has the potential to make a profit or incur a loss. **E-entrepreneurship** is the act of managing an electronic enterprise that has the potential to make a profit or incur a loss.

More often than not, an electronic business uses the Internet to conduct financial transactions. The business may be referred to as a virtual business, online business, e-business, or cyber business. These terms will be used interchangeably in this chapter as various aspects of electronic business are discussed.

What is the difference between a bricks-and-mortar business and a virtual business? A **bricks-and-mortar business** is one that has a material presence such as a storefront, storage facility, office space, manufacturing facility, or other tangible location where potential customers can actually walk in and interact with employees. A **virtual business** is one that does not have a material space designed to receive customers and transacts most of its business online.

Virtual businesses, which started to make their presence felt in the business world in the early 1990s, are an interesting adaptation of the basic business model. A virtual business can deal with customers from any location that offers Internet capability. This flexibility eliminates the need for a physical space, a major concern in setting up a bricks-and-mortar business.

The major advantage of a virtual business is that wherever the entrepreneur is, the business can be there also. As long as reliable telephone and Internet services exist, your business can be run from anywhere in the world. It also requires few personnel, especially in the beginning when cash flow is low. Employees can be hired as needed.

Does the emerging entrepreneur have to choose between a bricks-and-mortar and virtual business, or can he or she have both? The reality of doing business in the current Internet age is that you can start a virtual business and never have to worry about a physical space for customers to visit. If you start a bricks-and-mortar business, however, you will probably have to maintain at least a minimal Internet presence. A business that does not offer at least basic descriptive information on the Internet is at a significant competitive disadvantage.

©GETTY IMAGES/PHOTODISC

THE E-ENTREPRENEURSHIP MARKET

According to the most recent statistics from Nielsen//NetRatings, approximately 75 percent of Americans have access to the Internet from home. That's a 9 percent increase over the previous year. That means over 200 million people are potential customers for the entrepreneur with an Internet site.

Nielsen//NetRatings also offers some very interesting demographic data concerning Internet use. Internet home use for females 25 to 34 is 77 percent. For females 35 to 54, penetration is 81.7 percent. For males the same age, it is 80.2 percent. During February 2003, the average user visited the Internet 36 times and spent almost 20 hours viewing over 1,200 pages.

Other interesting Internet use statistics include the following:

1. According to Nielsen//NetRatings, favorite Internet sites for both home and work are Internet search engines and travel sites.
2. According to Arbitron, 74 percent of online radio listening takes place between 5 a.m. and 5 p.m. on weekdays.
3. Informa Media Group estimates that worldwide revenues from e-gambling will climb to $14.5 billion by 2006.
4. In a recently survey, the majority of Internet sites said site traffic was heaviest during work hours.
5. Another recent survey reported that Napster music-swapping software was found on approximately 20 percent of over 15,000 work PCs examined.
6. According to OneStat.com, over 15 percent of worldwide Internet traffic occurs on Monday, which makes it the most popular online day of the week.
7. According to Nielsen//NetRatings, news sites reach 35.5 percent more users at work than at home, and work users spend 68 percent longer online.
8. Nielsen//NetRatings reports that finance sites reach over 30 percent more work users than home users, and work users spend nearly twice as much time online.
9. eBay and Amazon.com currently dominate online shopping.
10. A recent survey found that over 20 percent of consumers shop online from work.

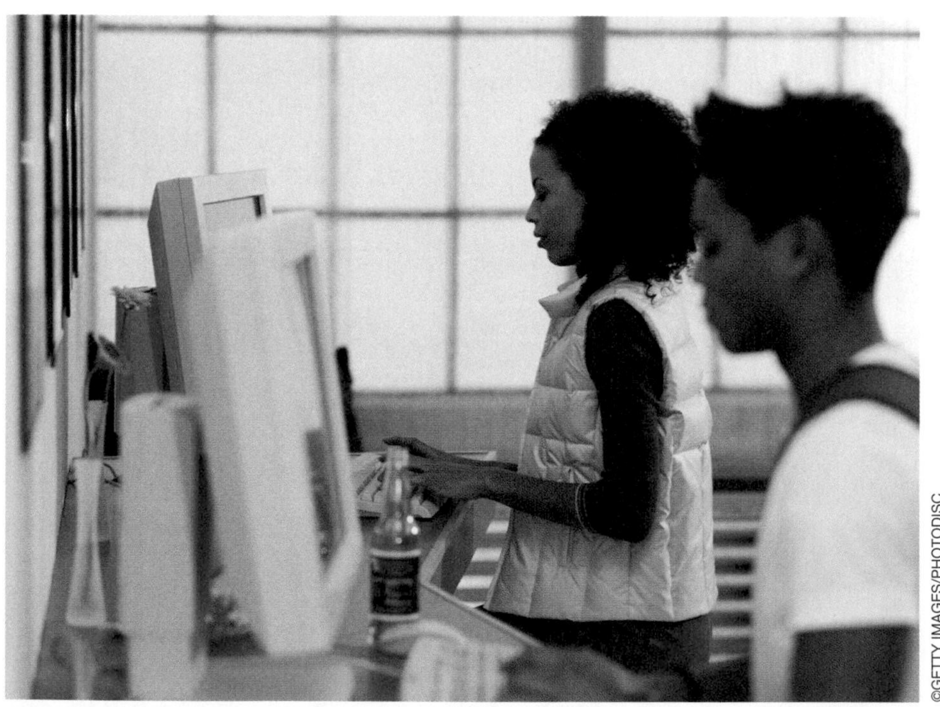

History of E-Entrepreneurship

The e-entrepreneurship market has seen rapid growth. The events that led to the statistics listed above began in the early 1990s, when electronic data interchange was standardized and companies could reliably complete transactions among themselves. In 1992, Compuserve offered online retail products to its customers. This event represented the first time in history that consumers could buy things using their computers.

Netscape arrived on the scene in 1994 and provided users with a simple and colorful browser with which to surf the Internet. It also provided a safe online transaction technology called Secure Sockets Layer. The following year saw the launch of Amazon.com and eBay, now two of the biggest names in e-commerce.

Digital Subscriber Line In 1998, DSL, or Digital Subscriber Line, which provided fast, always-on Internet service, was offered to customers across California. DSL service encouraged people to spend more time and money online. By 1999 retail spending over the Internet reached an estimated $20 billion. Internet sales have continued to rise every year since, attracting the attention of governments looking for more sales tax revenue. In 2004, the U.S. government extended the original 1998 moratorium on Internet taxes until at least 2009. Supporters say the moratorium is an important way to encourage the growth of the Internet in the U.S. With or without the moratorium, the Internet is rapidly becoming an everyday part of American life.

With an estimated 75 percent of Americans having access to the Internet from home, most Americans will soon be a few keystrokes away from any e-entrepreneurship site in the world. Such unprecedented access to businesses everywhere will have a significant impact on business in general. The most positive impact will no doubt be on profitability. In a recent survey of 400 small businesses by ACNielsen, 58 percent of respondents reported that the Internet helped in their growth and expansion. Fifty-one percent said the Internet helped their businesses become more profitable, 49 percent that the Internet helped them reduce costs, and 15 percent that their businesses rely on the Internet to survive.

The e-entrepreneurship market is a reality of contemporary business life. It is not just a technological trend; it is here to stay. To ignore it is to ignore the potential for enormous profitability. Mastery of virtual business is a requisite skill for modern entrepreneurs.

E-Entrepreneurship in the Business Plan

The business planning process around which most of this text is written will ultimately form your basic business model. In other words, it will dictate how you operate your business. It deals primarily with bricks-and-mortar start-ups. If you intend to include a virtual component in your new business, you will need to add e-business considerations to each component of the business plan outline discussed in Chapter 2.

The e-entrepreneurship components of the business planning process integrate your Internet site and your basic business model. They should address web site planning, development, marketing, legal, financial, management, and special considerations. They should be designed to ensure that your Internet content reaches the right customer while leveraging the full value of the Internet as a marketing tool. They must create a process for educating and communicating with your customers.

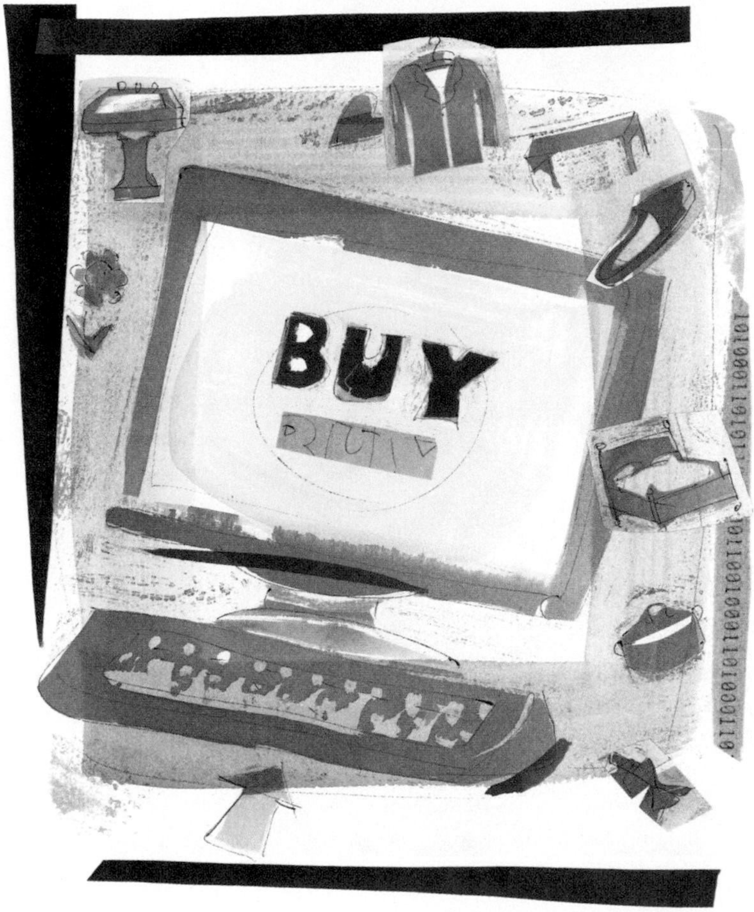

©GETTY IMAGES/PHOTODISC

Every successful entrepreneur has learned the importance of a traditional business plan. That lesson is often forgotten with the addition of a virtual component. Blatant in their absence are usually the various parts of the marketing plan. Are the customers the same? What about the competition? Invariably, the geographic market changes. What about pricing? Promotion of the virtual business will also be different.

The other aspects of traditional business planning are also important. Do you possess the required knowledge and skill to make the new virtual business a success? What about additional financial requirements? Organization, planning, and staffing will certainly be different and will require additional thought. The special considerations involved in a bricks-and-mortar business become considerably more important when applied to a virtual business.

The industry analysis portion of the business plan also ratchets up a few notches. Not only should the analysis cover the basic components discussed in Chapter 6, it must also view each component from the perspective of e-entrepreneurship. Industry trends, laws or legal issues, technological issues, and barriers to entry take on a heightened level of importance.

Careful planning for a virtual business is a must. Do your homework. Look for successful companies to benchmark. Integrate what works and discard those things that do not. When you consider the high failure rate of virtual businesses over the past 10 years, you will agree there is no such thing as overplanning.

CREATE AN E-BUSINESS

The first step toward e-entrepreneurship is usually the selection and registration of a **domain name**, which is the unique name that identifies an Internet site. The selection of a domain name is a chief concern when doing business online. Although a superior domain name does not guarantee success, it will most certainly have an impact on almost every aspect of an online business.

Domain Name Process

A superior domain name is one that is easy to remember and is not easily confused with other names. Before you make the final choice of a domain name, use a search engine to check for other companies using the same name or a derivation of it. An official check will be conducted during the registration process. You cannot just pick any domain name and start to use it, however. The name must first be registered. Through registration it becomes a legitimate part of the **Domain Name System (DNS)**.

Domain Name System The DNS is a directory organized under the familiar domains ".com," ".gov," ".org," and so on. It consists of all domain names and their matching computers registered to particular companies and persons using the Internet. When you register a domain name, it will be associated with the computer you assign to it during the period the registration is in effect. From that computer you can create a web site that will be accessible to Internet users around the world.

©GETTY IMAGES/PHOTODISC

The Domain Name System helps Internet users find their way around the Internet. Every computer linked to the Internet has an exclusive address, called its **Internet Protocol (IP) address**. Like a telephone number, an IP address is a set of numbers that computers can read. The DNS makes using the Internet easier by allowing a recognizable string of letters (the domain name) to be used instead of the numeric IP address. So instead of keying a long number, you can key the **URL** (Uniform Resource Locator), for example *http://domainname.com.*

ICANN Registration of domain names is controlled by a private-public partnership called the **Internet Corporation for Assigned Names and Numbers (ICANN)**. It is responsible for managing and coordinating the Domain Name System to ensure that every address is exclusive and that all users of the Internet can find all legitimate addresses. It does this by managing the distribution of unique IP addresses and domain names and by ensuring that each domain name corresponds to the correct IP address.

Numerous companies have been accredited by ICANN to act as registrars, which means they can identify and set minimum standards for the performance of registration functions, recognize persons or entities meeting those standards, and enter into accreditation agreements that set forth the rules and procedures applicable to the provision of registrar services. Fees are charged for these services and can vary by company.

Domain names can be registered through the many different registrar companies. E-entrepreneurs pick one company to register their name. A current listing of these companies can be accessed on the ICANN Internet site. Upon contact, the registration company you choose will ask you to provide an assortment of contact and technical information. It will keep records of the contact information and submit the technical information to a central directory called the registry. You will be required to enter a registration contract with the registrar that sets forth the terms under which your registration is accepted and will be maintained.

The registry receives data concerning registrations of domain names and name servers from registrars and handles the dissemination of information concerning those registrations. Domain name servers translate the human-readable domain name into the machine-readable IP address. The unique name that identifies your Internet site provides other computers on the Internet the information necessary to find your web site.

Components of an E-Business Site

Once you have chosen and registered a domain name, you can proceed to the rest of the site development process.

Web Site Design The first decision you must make is whether to design your web site in-house or contract the project to a professional Web design company. If you are unsure about your ability to create a top-notch site, by all means hire a professional to do it for you. The money you spend up front will be more than worth it when online orders start to roll in.

If you hire a web site contractor, set realistic budgets and timelines before you begin. Make sure you understand the process, the scope of work and commitment, what you are getting for your money, and how long the whole process will take. Ask the contractor to show you a project plan and timeline. Visit other sites the contractor has developed and check out the quality of work.

Whether you design the site yourself or hire a professional, the most important point to remember is ease of use. If a visitor to the site has difficulty navigating it or cannot find the product for which he is searching, you have just lost a customer.

Content The "face" of your site is its content. Visitors will either like the content or not. Content includes the actual written text, product information, graphics, and any data incorporated into your company's site. Remember, ease of use is the most important aspect of content, followed closely by uniqueness. What makes your site stand out from the thousands of others in your business? Choose a promotional appeal that fits the desired image of your new business venture. It may be informative, authoritarian, humorous, provocative, or any number of other possibilities.

One of the first things visitors should see is a brief site description, possibly in the window's title area. Tell them what the company does. This is especially important to the new e-entrepreneur who is an unknown. If you need to give the site visitor more information about the company than can be associated with the page title, put a link in a visible area, such as high left on the page.

What is it you want the site to accomplish? Highlight the top four to six things and provide links. These may include a product list, product information, how to order, company news releases, published articles about the company, customers' frequently asked questions, and so on. Provide the links in an easy-to-use format.

Be careful with graphics. They should illustrate real content, not just adorn your home page. If you use photos, less is probably better than more. Each photo will appear less cluttered and more pleasing to the eye if it depicts fewer people and objects. Close-up images with simple backgrounds usually work the best. Graphics are great for grabbing attention, but refrain from going over the top with them.

Once you have your page up and running, keep it current. If you feature news releases and news articles, include the dates of release. Information in your site relating to products and uses should be updated on a regular basis. Nothing is more detrimental to the e-entrepreneur's success than an outdated web site.

You can never pay too much attention to your web site's content. Remember, content is the first place consumers start building their image of your business. Better content will result in a better image.

Web Host A service that, for a fee, allows your company's web page to be connected to the Internet is called a **web host**. During the site planning process, you need to make a decision concerning the host for your site. Different web hosts use different computer hardware that dictates which software can be used in site development. The type of web site you are planning will determine the services required, how much storage space you need, e-mail requirements, and the level of technical support you need.

Even though the term web host is often used interchangeably with **Internet Service Provider** (ISP), they are not synonymous. An Internet Service Provider is a company that provides access to the Internet for organizations and/or individuals. Access services provided by ISPs may include web hosting, e-mail, and support for many other applications. Not all ISPs, however, provide web-hosting services. Make sure you choose one that does.

There are other concerns you must address when you select an ISP. An important one is e-mail. How many e-mail accounts do you need? Is one enough? Probably not, since you are running a small business. Will your company have employees other than the owner? If so, you will need numerous e-mail addresses. Not all ISPs offer multiple e-mail accounts.

Customer and owner privacy should also be a high priority. Does the ISP have an acceptable privacy policy? Will it protect the privacy of both your company and your potential customers?

ISP technical support is another important concern. You should consider issues such as software used, download times, technical support via toll-free telephone numbers, and how the ISP responds to online problems.

ISPs are not all the same. They differ in both size and the services they offer. Local ISPs, by virtue of their location, are generally smaller, but they offer competitive rates. National ISPs are bigger and host thousands of users. You must decide which is a better fit for your virtual business.

Security and/or Firewalls Will your web site be secure against hackers and others seeking unauthorized entry? The first line of security for most web sites is a **firewall**, a system designed to prevent unauthorized access to or from a private computer network. Firewalls can be implemented in both hardware and software, or a combination of both. They are frequently used to prevent Internet users from accessing private networks connected to the Internet, especially **intranets**, which are Internet networks inside a company not accessible to the public. All messages entering or leaving the intranet pass through the firewall, which examines each message and blocks those that do not meet the specified security criteria. Web site security is crucial for any online merchant, and firewalls are an essential part of that security. They prevent hackers from gaining access to your customers' personal and financial information or your in-house company files.

©GETTY IMAGES/PHOTODISC

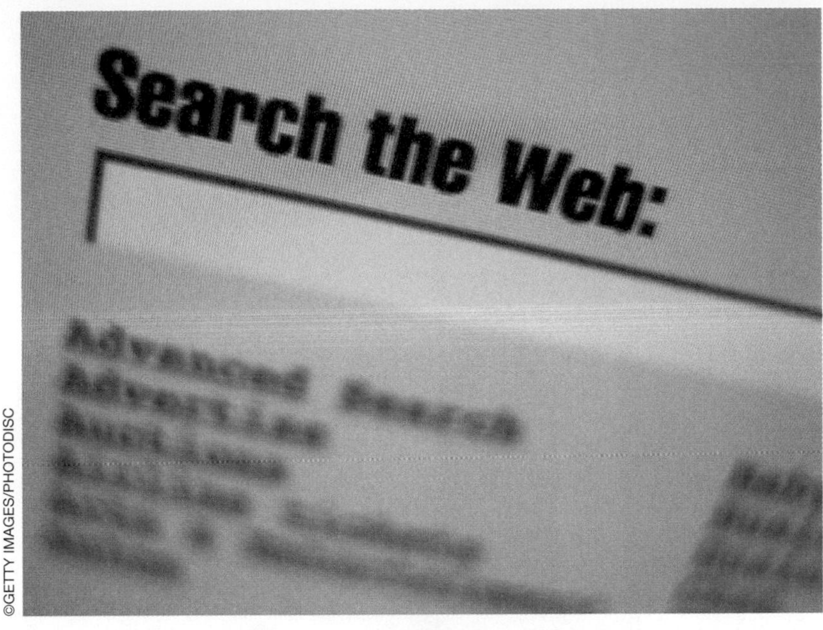

©GETTY IMAGES/PHOTODISC

Search Site Submission You have created your e-business web site and chosen an ISP. Customers will now start visiting your site and the orders will start to roll in, right? Not if popular Internet search engines do not know you exist. An **Internet search engine** is a program that searches documents on the Internet for specified keywords and returns a list of documents in which the keywords are found. Although search engines are really a general class of programs, the term is often used to specifically describe systems like Google, Yahoo, MSN Search, and Ask Jeeves that enable users to search for documents. According to Nielsen//NetRatings, one in three Americans uses a search engine. In a typical month, 114.5 million or 39 percent of Americans used a search engine to find information on the Internet.

Search engines do not automatically reference your site. Specific site reference can be a complex process. You can research the required process and submit the site yourself or use a service to complete the process for you, usually for a fee. The do-it-yourself solution is not as difficult as it may seem. After you become familiar with each search engine's compliance procedure, it is essentially a matter of typing in your URL and other applicable information required by the search engine site. Do not be disappointed if your site does not show up immediately on a specific engine search. After submission, it can take several weeks for the process to complete. Remember to factor the delay into your business planning timeline.

On-site Search Engine Many e-entrepreneurship sites are large and contain massive amounts of content. Some consumers may be overwhelmed by all that information and cannot find the items for which they are searching. If that is a possibility, the web site should provide visitors with an on-site search engine, which is a search engine that only searches the site in question. Take Cabelas.com as an example. As many of you know, Cabela's is one of the biggest sporting goods retailers in the country. Its site is huge and contains thousands of items. An on-site search engine dedicated to searching only Cabela's thousands of items makes online shopping much easier.

If you use an outside contractor to design and develop your site, the on-site search engine can be included in the contract. Also, many companies in the world of virtual business offer free or low-cost search engines for use on your site.

Database Software Your new e-business will need some database software to identify and maintain your customer and product data. Again, if you use a web design contractor, you can include this as part of the total package. Despite what you see on TV and read in print, most web sites still cannot process credit cards online. Many sites that do accept credit cards actually process them offline. They use the online forms to gather required customer information and then input the data manually. Make sure you understand what your software will and will not do.

BRAND X PICTURES

Online Payment If you plan to accept orders online and take credit cards or other forms of online payment as part of your e-business, you will need to plan on the web site features described below. Professional assistance is advisable as you consider these additional features.

- **Product Catalog** Customers should have a listing of all products offered on the site. A well-designed catalog allows you to create categories of products and manage the product list within each category. The catalog should include basic product definitions and any variations available, plus high-quality photos, product features, accessories, and consumer reviews if available.
- **Shopping Cart** A familiar icon on many e-business sites is the **shopping cart**. It is used online to keep track of and record customers' purchasing decisions as they are made without going back and forth to an order form. If you are considering the addition of a shopping cart to your site, make sure it is the best way to process sales (other choices are online order forms, toll-free numbers, and so on). If it is, numerous options are available, including online shopping cart services, off-the-shelf shopping cart software, and inclusion in turnkey web site building packages.

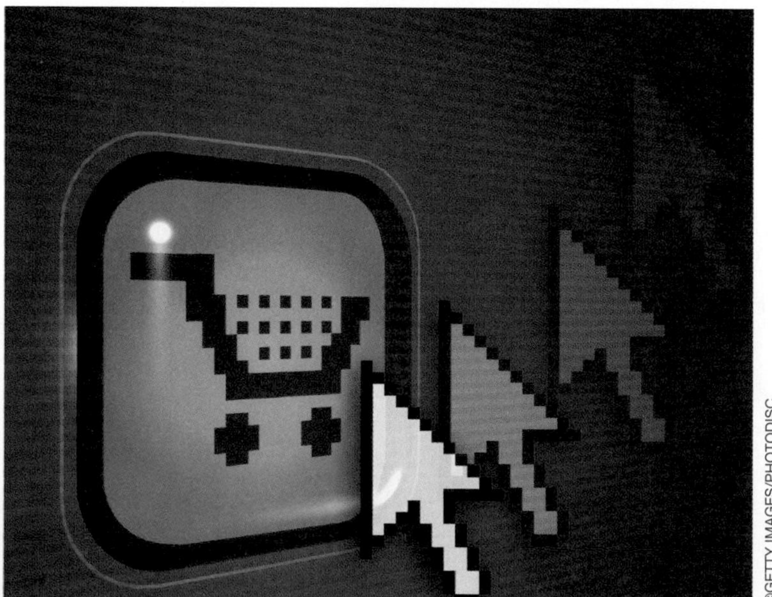
©GETTY IMAGES/PHOTODISC

- **Merchant Account Provider** A bank or financial institution that provides you with a means for accepting and processing credit card transactions over the Internet is a **merchant account provider**. Referred to as a MAP, it may charge you a monthly fee, yearly fee, setup fee, and per-transaction fee. Acquiring a MAP is not easy, and the business requirements can be quite strict. Requirements include clearly displaying your return policy, having a U.S. checking account, having a U.S. postal address, not being in active bankruptcy, never having been convicted of credit card fraud, and others.

- **Alternative Payment Options** For younger customers and others who do not have credit cards, you should provide alternative payment options that allow them to make purchases online. These options would also be helpful for international customers. In many countries, credit cards do not enjoy the popularity they do in the U.S.
- **Order Fulfillment** To guarantee that customers get their orders, you must develop an order fulfillment system. The number of repeat customers visiting your site will be significantly impacted by the system you design. Customers ordering on the Internet may be located anywhere in the world. Remember that as you decide whether to handle orders yourself or contract out the shipping component. You need to ensure that a profit can be made after delivery costs are factored into every sale.
- **Customer Service** An overall customer service plan must be designed for online customers. How will complaints and returns be handled? What mechanism will be in place to facilitate correspondence with customers? These and other customer service issues must be addressed.
- **E-mail Notification** Your e-business will need an automated system of sending e-mail notification messages to your customers to let them know the status of their orders. Order tracking is another service you may need to offer. Techno-savvy consumers will want a way to log on to your site and look up the status of their order.
- **Customer FAQs** It may be advantageous to the new business to establish a list of customers' frequently asked questions, especially those relating to orders, along with their answers.

Small Business Technology

Beware of modem redialing! According to the FTC, you can log on to the Internet and visit an entertainment site, but first you have to download a special viewer program. Your next phone bill is for thousands of dollars. What happened?

When you download the viewer software, it disconnects your computer from your local ISP and reconnects it to a phone number in some other part of the world, without your knowledge. Because the software turns off your modem speaker, you can't hear the disconnect or the dialing of an international number. To compound the problem, the program does not disconnect from the international number until you turn off your computer. It has happened to thousands of consumers who incurred hundreds of thousands of dollars in international long distance charges.

E-ENTREPRENEURSHIP AND THE LAW

As the number of companies and consumers shopping online soars, fraud and deception have become major issues. Virtual business is not above the law, however. Fraud and deception are unlawful no matter what the medium. The Federal Trade Commission has enforced and will continue enforcing its consumer protection laws online to ensure that products and services are described truthfully in online ads and that consumers get what they pay for. According to the FTC, these activities also benefit sellers who expect and deserve a fair marketplace.

Advertising

Online consumers are protected by many of the general principles of advertising law that also apply to Internet ads. However, new issues arise as rapidly as new technology develops. In order to comply with the law, e-entrepreneurs should consider the relevant FTC policies as they develop online ads.

The same consumer protection laws that apply to commercial activities in other media apply online. The FTC

©GETTY IMAGES/PHOTODISC

Act's prohibition of "unfair or deceptive acts or practices" encompasses Internet advertising, marketing, and sales. To avoid being misleading, to ensure that consumers receive material information about the terms of a transaction, or to further public policy goals, ads must display certain clear and conspicuous disclosures.

FTC rules and guidelines that use specific terms such as "written," "writing," "printed," or "direct mail" are adaptable to new technologies. In other words, rules and guidelines that apply to written ads or printed materials also apply to visual text displayed on the Internet.

"Direct mail" solicitations include e-mail. If e-mail invites consumers to call the sender to purchase goods or services, that telephone call and subsequent sale must comply with Telemarketing Sales Rule requirements.

CAN-SPAM Act of 2003 The Controlling the Assault of Non-Solicited Pornography and Marketing Act establishes requirements for those who send commercial e-mail, spells out penalties for spammers and companies whose products are advertised in spam if they violate the law, and gives consumers the right to ask e-mailers to stop spamming them. **Spam** is defined as unsolicited "junk" e-mail sent to large numbers of people to promote products or services.

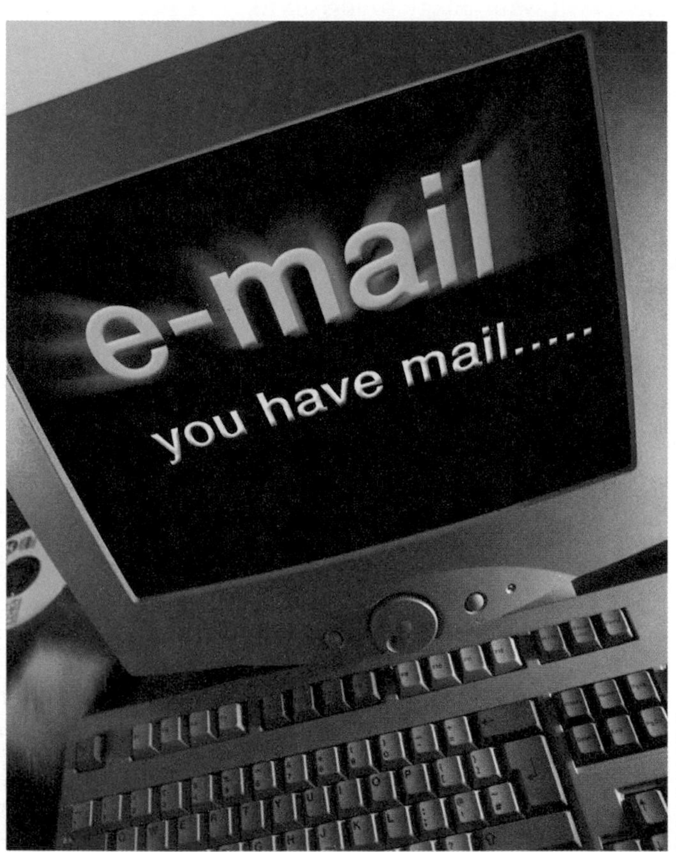

BRAND X PICTURES

The law, which became effective January 1, 2004, covers e-mail whose primary purpose is advertising or promoting a commercial product or service, including content on a web site. Its main provisions are:

- It bans false or misleading header information. A commercial e-mail's "From" and routing information, including the originating domain name and e-mail address, must be accurate and identify the person who initiated the e-mail.
- It prohibits deceptive subject lines. The subject line cannot mislead the recipient about the contents or subject matter of the message.
- It requires that commercial e-mail be identified as an advertisement and include the sender's valid physical postal address.
- It requires that the e-mail give recipients an opt-out method. It must provide a return e-mail address or another Internet-based response mechanism that allows a recipient to ask the sender not to send future e-mail messages to that e-mail address, and the sender must honor the

request. There may be a menu of choices that allow the recipient to opt out of certain types of messages, but it must include the option to end all commercial messages from the sender.

Each violation of the provisions listed above is subject to fines of up to $11,000.

E-Consumer Complaints

The FTC has an online general complaint form that can be used by consumers to register complaints relating to online transactions in the U.S. Another FTC form may be used for e-business complaints involving a foreign company. The information contained in an individual complaint may be entered into the *Consumer Sentinel*, a consumer complaint database maintained by the FTC and made available to certified government law enforcement agencies in participating countries. The information is used to spot new trends, uncover new scams, and target suspect companies and individuals for law enforcement action. The FTC stresses that submitting a complaint will help law enforcement agencies worldwide in their effort to keep the Internet safe for consumers.

Global E-Entrepreneurship Agreement

The growth of online commerce brings with it the need for international cooperation. Newly established international guidelines are helping to answer many business questions for e-entrepreneurs seeking business outside the U.S. The U.S. and 29 other countries, working together as members of the Organization for Economic Cooperation and Development (OECD), have agreed to several guidelines that call for:

- fair business, advertising, and marketing practices
- enough information to allow consumers to make informed choices, including disclosures about online businesses, their goods and services, and the terms and conditions of sale
- clear processes for confirming transactions
- secure payment mechanisms
- timely and affordable dispute resolution and redress processes
- privacy protection
- consumer and business education
- international government cooperation

©GETTY IMAGES/PHOTODISC

The Global ENTREPRENEUR

According to recent Internet alerts and articles, online selling has developed into a perilous venture. As with most criminal activity, ignorance and apathy are the main culprits. Online merchants need to pay careful attention to the dangers and plan accordingly. If they do not, international criminals will identify the site's vulnerability and take advantage of it. Such activity could result in losses that would put most small companies out of business.

One study found that more than 40 percent of all online credit card fraud experienced by U.S. companies was committed by international criminals. Certain countries, such as Yugoslavia, Nigeria, Romania, Pakistan, and Indonesia, seem to be riskier for e-entrepreneurs than others. Of these "bad boys," Yugoslavia was the worst. The study estimated that about 13 percent of purchases initiated from that country were fraudulent, compared to the U.S. fraud rate of about 1.7 percent. Other research shows that overall global fraud rates are four times higher than domestic rates.

To avoid online losses to international crime, many e-entrepreneurs simply steer clear of overseas sales. As many as one-third of medium and large web sites do not sell to global customers.

The news is not all negative, however. Online sales to New Zealand, Switzerland, Japan, France, and Italy actually experienced lower fraud rates than domestic U.S. sales did. The point here is to remember that international e-entrepreneurship is not without risks.

In spite of those risks, many Internet experts say e-entrepreneurs should not retreat from online international selling. You should, however, pay more attention to overseas shipments and carefully review orders beforehand. If you question an order for any reason, honor your instincts and do not send the merchandise. This is especially true if the order is substantial and deviates from what you consider a normal order.

Think Critically

1. What safeguards can you implement to protect your site from international fraud?
2. Do you think e-entrepreneurs should stay away from international e-business altogether? Why or why not?

The overall goal of the guidelines is to build consumer confidence in the global electronic marketplace by ensuring that consumers are just as safe shopping online as offline, no matter where they live or where the company they do business with is based. E-businesses that adhere to OECD guidelines apply them in specific ways.

COMSTOCK IMAGES

1. They follow fair business, advertising, and marketing practices. They provide truthful, accurate, and complete information to consumers and avoid deceptive, misleading, or unfair claims, omissions, or practices.
2. They provide accurate, clear, and easily accessible information about the company and the goods or services it offers. They disclose the information consumers need to understand whom they're dealing with and what they're buying.
3. They disclose full information about the terms, conditions, and costs of the transaction. They provide consumers with a full, itemized list of the costs involved in the transaction, designating the currency involved, the terms of delivery or performance, and the terms, conditions, and methods of payment.
4. They ensure that consumers know they are making a commitment to buy before closing the deal. They take steps to protect consumers who are merely "surfing" the Internet from unknowingly entering into a sales contract. They give the consumer a chance to change the order before committing to purchase or to cancel it altogether.
5. They provide an easy-to-use and secure method for online payments. They adopt security measures appropriate to the transaction to make sure that personal information is less vulnerable to hackers.
6. They protect consumer privacy during electronic transactions. They disclose their privacy policies or information practice statements prominently on their web sites and offer customers choices as to how their personal information is used.
7. They have policies and procedures to address consumer problems quickly, fairly, and without excessive cost or inconvenience to the consumer.
8. They adopt fair, effective, and easy-to-understand self-regulatory policies and procedures. They extend to electronic commerce the same basic level of protections that cover other forms of commerce.
9. They help educate consumers about electronic commerce, thereby contributing to a consumer-friendly electronic marketplace. These businesses work with governments and consumer representatives to ensure that consumers understand their rights and responsibilities when participating in online commerce.

Better Business Bureau/BBB Online

In addition to laws and policies put forth by the FTC, the Better Business Bureau has developed its own "Code of Online Business Practices." It is based on five basic principles:

1. **Truthful and Accurate Communications** Online businesses must not deceive or mislead potential customers.
2. **Disclosure** Information about the business, the goods or services it offers, and any transactions conducted must be fully disclosed to the customer.
3. **Information Practices and Security** Online businesses must post and follow a privacy policy with regard to customers' personal information, use a secure system for all transactions, and honor customers' wishes concerning spam e-mail.
4. **Customer Satisfaction** Merchants must stand behind all claims and promises, answer customers' questions, and resolve complaints in a responsible manner.
5. **Protecting Children** Merchants who direct advertising at children under the age of 13 must follow specific, self-regulatory guidelines for children's advertising.

WEB SITE CHECKLIST

The checklist in Table 12-1 is provided as a quick evaluation tool that you can use to determine if your web site meets the basic requirements for e-entrepreneurship success and is ready to receive e-customers.

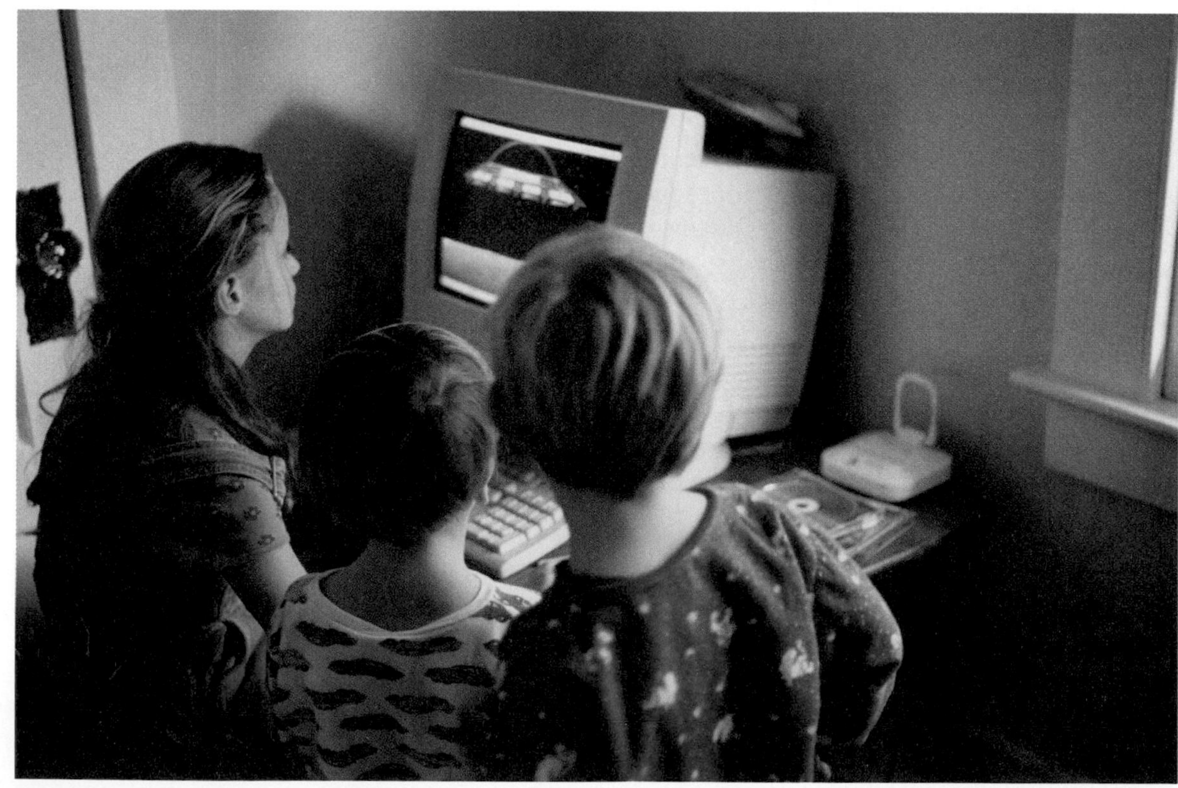

TABLE 12-1 SITE EVALUATION CHECKLIST	YES	NO
Your domain name is easy to remember and not easily confused with other names.		
Your domain name has been registered.		
A web host has been selected.		
The site loads quickly.		
Content is attractive and user friendly.		
Page navigation is simple and easy to understand.		
The site is compatible with most popular web browsers.		
The site has been submitted to pertinent search engines.		
An on-site search engine has been developed, if appropriate.		
The optimum number of company e-mail accounts has been determined, and accounts have been started.		
A consumer privacy policy has been established.		
Security for the site has been developed and implemented.		
Customers are notified of security measures taken.		
Database software has been purchased and installed.		
Online products have been carefully selected for their suitability to the medium.		
A product catalog has been developed.		
A simple and easy-to-use shopping cart program has been added to the site.		
A merchant account provider has been selected and the system is in place.		
Alternative payment options have been developed.		
An efficient order fulfillment system is in place.		
A customer service policy has been developed.		
The company phone number is listed in a prominent location on the site.		
An automated customer e-mail notification system has been developed.		
The e-entrepreneurship site has been fully integrated with your conventional bricks-and-mortar business, if appropriate.		
The site's functionality has been thoroughly tested.		
An e-entrepreneurship marketing plan has been developed.		
Your e-marketing is not based on spam promotion.		
Employees who will be handling e-business orders have been trained.		
Site maintenance and content updating have been scheduled.		
Your site meets all the requirements of the law according to the FTC.		

MYTHS OF E-ENTREPRENEURSHIP

A great deal of misinformation exists relating to e-entrepreneurship. The following are a few of the myths in circulation.

E-entrepreneurship is a no-brainer. There is much more to online selling than setting up a web site and a credit card ordering system. Behind-the-scenes tasks like filling orders, handling vendor issues, managing databases, and endless others make e-entrepreneurship just as complicated as any bricks-and-mortar business.

E-entrepreneurship is cheap. Just because you may not have a building or full-time employees does not mean there are no costs associated with an e-business. The cost of Web design, hosting, software, shipping, and any number of other components can put pressure on the bottom line.

The best price is always online. If you are a smart shopper, you know this is not so. Consumers often use online prices to negotiate better deals in regular stores.

E-commerce will kill traditional retail. Jeff Bezos of Amazon.com has predicted that Web retail sales will end up comprising only about 10 percent of annual retail sales, not the 50 percent or more that some people predicted when interest in e-retailing started to grow.

DIGITAL VISION

E-entrepreneurships make an obscene amount of money. With the growing competition online, most companies try to keep their profit margins as low as possible. Any extravagant amounts of money that have been made were the result of public stock offerings back in e-commerce's early days. Those amounts had more to do with the perceived potential of the Internet than with actual profits. E-entrepreneurship is not a shortcut to extreme wealth; it is merely another tool in successful business operation.

E-entrepreneurship is not safe. The number-one concern among consumers shopping on the Internet is and has been for some time credit card safety. The ability of e-business to encrypt orders transmitted over the Web has all but eliminated that problem.

E-entrepreneurship success depends on the right technology. Although technology is important, it does not eliminate the need for sound business practices.

Getting products to consumers is an e-entrepreneur's biggest cost. Although shipping and handling costs are high, they typically lag behind those for business technology. This is even truer when the business enters a period of rapid growth.

Most Web consumers are "young." This statement was true in the beginning, but no longer. Recent online research has found that the age distribution of online shoppers is almost identical to that of in-store shoppers.

If a product or service can be sold, it can be sold on the Web. Many products are ill-suited for web sales. Luxury products and products requiring a lot of salesperson interaction are not good candidates for online selling. Many personal services cannot be sold online. For products that do not fit the mold for online sales, web sites are typically used for information only.

Everyone else is selling online. According to a recent nationwide survey, only 25 percent of traditional companies employ any form of e-commerce. E-commerce is rapidly growing, but it has not overtaken traditional bricks-and-mortar commerce.

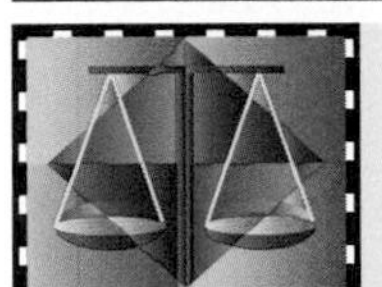

Ethics for ENTREPRENEURS

Jen Mangrum has been a professional writer for over 25 years. She worked for 10 years as an editor at a large publishing company, then freelanced as a technical writer, producing corporate reports and editing technical training manuals for Fortune 50 companies. As a sideline she wrote advertising brochures and articles for travel magazines. For the past five years she has concentrated on fiction, and one of her novels was recently published.

While lunching with a friend recently, Jen shared the many facets of writing she had experienced during her long and very successful career. Phyllis, her friend, suggested that with everything Jen knew about writing, she could probably write a how-to book. Why, she could even take it a step further and franchise a home writing business.

The more Jen thought about Phyllis's idea, the more intrigued she became—so intrigued, in fact, that she spent the next three months writing a how-to guide. Jen titled it *Publishing for $$$*. She was less sure about the franchising idea, but she thought there would be a large market for the guide. After all, who wouldn't want to pick up a few extra dollars in their spare time?

Jen started an online business to sell the guide. She registered the domain name publishingfor$$$.com, built a web page, and began promoting the guide. Since she had made $4,000 to $8,000 a month as a technical writer, she stated that anyone using the guide could potentially earn $4,000 or more per month. The guide sold for $99.99. Sales started slowly but have increased steadily the past few months.

Yesterday Jen received a letter from the Better Business Bureau. Her hands shook as she read it. The BBB had received several complaints from disgruntled customers who had made $0 using the guide. The letter asked Jen to document the methodology behind her advertising claim and case histories of all clients who had earned the promised income. What was she going to do now?

Think Critically

1. Do you think Jen broke the law?
2. Do you think Jen violated any of the five principles of the BBB Code of Online Business Practices? Please explain your answer.

COMMON E-ENTREPRENEURSHIP MISTAKES

Achieving success as an e-entrepreneur is no easier than achieving success in a bricks-and-mortar business. Some would say it is even more difficult. The path to e-business success is fraught with potential mistakes. The following are 15 of the most common.

1. **Trying to sell the wrong product online** Just because a product sells well in your bricks-and-mortar store does not mean it will sell well in your virtual location. Evaluate your products for their suitability to sell online. Try to think as your customers will think.
2. **Misjudging the web site's potential** Many entrepreneurs establish a web site simply because it is fashionable and therefore do no planning for it. Part of e-entrepreneurship planning should be an educated projection of sales. This projection should be compared to actual sales as the site goes online and then updated regularly. One of the most disheartening problems faced by entrepreneurs occurs when sales exceed the ability to procure and deliver the product. When that happens, the success of the business can actually kill the business because of disgruntled customers who cannot get products advertised as available.
3. **Forgetting that a first impression can only be made once** If your site is not immediately impressive, with visually appealing graphics and user-friendly functions, potential customers will leave and never come back. Good first impressions get and keep customers.
4. **Making the site too complicated** A web site can only do so much. Think about your target market and tailor content and functions to the appropriate level.
5. **Using a complicated navigation system** If customers have difficulty getting around your site and cannot determine basic functions like adding to a shopping cart or completing the order, they will simply leave.

©GETTY IMAGES/PHOTODISC

6. **Forgetting to list your phone number** Guess what? Many customers will use your site to gather information and complete comparison-shopping. When they get ready to order, however, they want to talk to a real person. List a phone number in a prominent location.
7. **Supporting only one browser** A **web browser** is a software application used to locate and display web pages. The two most popular browsers are Netscape Navigator and Microsoft Internet Explorer. Both

of these are graphical browsers, which means they can display graphics as well as text. Browser incompatibility occurs when a web site is designed to support only one browser. Customers using a different browser may not be able to access the web site.

8. **Featuring out-of-date content** Internet content should be regularly updated. Outdated product information and price lists will contribute very quickly to the demise of your e-business. Based on the nature of your business, devise and adhere to a timeline of scheduled updates.
9. **Requiring excessive download times** Internet customers by nature tend to be impatient. They are accustomed to having information at their fingertips whenever they desire. Time is important to them. Most web site designers understand this and design sites that will download to the customer's computer very quickly. Failure to do this will drive customers away from your site before they have a chance to see your product.
10. **Ignoring customer service** This is probably one of the most troublesome areas for entrepreneurs starting an e-business. Plan carefully and avoid this costly mistake.
11. **Not validating the functionality of your site** Web sites by design can be technically complex. Once the site is developed, it should be tested extensively before being made available to the public. After the site is up and running for customers, test it on a regularly scheduled basis. Encourage customers to report any problems they encounter when using the site.
12. **Not merging your web site with your conventional business** After setting up your web site, print the address on all your business cards and business correspondence. Any advertisements for the business should prominently display the Internet address. Print it on your receipts and display it by registers. Encourage your bricks-and-mortar customers to use the site. Encourage employees to mention the site to customers.
13. **Not promoting the site** How will potential customers know your web site is up and available for business? Your e-business will need a marketing plan. Run ads on other sites, advertise the web site address, put posters in bricks-and-mortar locations—promote the site in any way you can think of.

©GETTY IMAGES/PHOTODISC

14. **Using spam promotion** Buying an e-mail list and sending information about your site to thousands of potential customers is probably not the best way to promote your business. The use of spam promotional techniques carries a certain disreputable connotation.
15. **Failing to deliver products** Like bricks-and-mortar business, e-business depends on repeat customers. If your e-business does not deliver ordered products to customers in a timely fashion, they will probably become one-time-only customers.

Ship in a BOTTLE

Expanding the Web Site

Fred was discovering that the further he reached into his new business, the more exciting it became. His initial venture into e-entrepreneurship had proven quite successful. His web site, www.shipinabottle.com, had a clear and easy-to-remember domain name, and the site was attractive, simple to navigate, and secure. His business had grown dramatically, particularly since he had listed "ship in a bottle" as a search term with pay-per-hit advertising offered by two host services. Although he had originally achieved a good no-charge reference listing under "ship in a bottle" with most host services, he was finding that the number of reference listings continued to grow for all products and that he needed additional insurance that his domain would stand out from the competition. Since he had such a specialty listing, the pay-per-hit service was available at the minimum charge, 5 cents per hit. This fee assured him that he would hold one of the top three web site reference listings at all times. Many advertisers paid as much as $3 per hit in more competitive product listings.

It was becoming obvious to Fred that he should consider expanding his offerings. Just as in a retail store, once the customer was already visiting the web site, why not try to sell other, related products? Fred started his search by consulting with Johann. Johann had expanded into gift items, nautical apparel, weather instruments and clocks, and flags. He put Fred in contact with his suppliers for each product line.

An apparel line that had been successful for Johann proved to be less so for Fred. The apparel was European designed and nautically styled. Fred was sure at first that it would have an appeal because it was unique to the U.S. market. He featured Johann's most popular clothing but ran into problems with size translations and inventory planning. The investment to carry a full size selection for 40 apparel items was staggering, and the risk outweighed the gain. He abandoned the idea after a three-month trial.

Nautical clocks and weather instruments were more successful. The German manufacturer who supplied Johann was delighted to find an American distributor. His prices were competitive and his quality outstanding. Fred added the items to his site and reinforced them by advertising in two nationally distributed sailing magazines. Within six months, they proved to be a profitable addition.

Of some surprise to Fred was the success of historical European and German flags. Flags did not appear to fit his product focus, but Johann insisted they would do well. Sure enough, Fred found out that, like ships in bottles, historical European flags were almost impossible to find in the U.S. By creating a listing with the pay-per-hit hosting services under "European flags," he attracted enough traffic to his web site that flags became a good investment.

Fred was learning a valuable lesson: if you turn over a stone, new ideas sometimes leap out. While discussing his venture with the manager of a large museum store that sold his ships in bottles, he learned that the museum store did not have a web site for the art and gift pieces it made in-house. The manager agreed to allow Fred to list some of the museum's limited-edition art prints and one-of-a-kind gift items on his site. This connection added a whole new dimension to Fred's business.

continued

Fred reviewed his expanded web site and inventory selection and realized that his business had matured to the point where it would demand his full-time attention. A hobby business was now at the critical juncture of becoming a full-fledged enterprise with unlimited sales potential.

Think Critically

1. Create a list of other products that Fred should consider offering. Defend your reasoning.
2. Did Fred give his apparel experiment a serious enough try?
3. Research hosting companies that offer pay-per-hit listings. Do you believe it is necessary for e-entrepreneurs to use these services, or should they be content with generating interest from information reference listings?

Summary

An e-entrepreneur is defined as an individual who is willing to take the risk of investing time and money in an electronic business that has the potential to make a profit or incur a loss. E-entrepreneurship is the act of managing an electronic enterprise that has the potential to make a profit or incur a loss. Electronic businesses are also called virtual businesses, online businesses, e-businesses, or cyber businesses. A bricks-and-mortar business is one that has a material presence such as a storefront, storage facility, office space, manufacturing facility, or other tangible location where potential customers can walk in and interact with employees. A virtual business does not have a material space for receiving customers and completes most of its business online. The major advantage of a virtual business is that wherever the entrepreneur is, the business can be there also, as long as reliable phone and Internet service exist. Over 200 million people are potential customers for an entrepreneur with an Internet site.

If your new business will have a virtual component, you will need to add e-business considerations to each component of your business plan. These components should address web site planning, development, marketing, legal, financial, management, and special considerations. They should make certain your Internet content reaches the right customer and create a process for educating and communicating with your customers. Your industry analysis should not only analyze the basic components but must also view each from the perspective of e-entrepreneurship. Industry trends, laws or legal issues, technological issues, and barriers to entry become more important.

The first step toward e-entrepreneurship is usually the selection and registration of a domain name, the unique name that identifies an Internet site. The Internet Corporation for Assigned Names and Numbers (ICANN) manages and coordinates the Domain Name System to ensure that every address is exclusive and that all users of the Internet can find all legitimate addresses.

Once the domain name has been chosen and registered, you must decide whether to design the web site in-house or contract the project to a professional web design company. The "face" of the site is its content—the actual text, products, information, graphics, and any data incorporated into the site. Another important decision concerns the web host for your site. A web host is a business that, for a fee, allows a company's web page to be connected to the Internet. Other considerations include the Internet Service Provider, site security, search site submission to Internet search engines, on-site search engine, database software, and other components required for online order acceptance.

As online shopping soars in popularity, fraud and deception are major concerns. The Federal Trade Commission enforces laws to ensure that products and services are described truthfully in online ads and that consumers get what they pay for. These laws benefit both consumers and sellers.

There are many misconceptions about e-entrepreneurship, such as: it is a no-brainer, it is cheap, it is not safe, most consumers are young, and others. Starting an e-business and achieving success are no easier than starting and achieving success in a bricks-and-mortar business.

The growth of online commerce has spurred the need for international cooperation. The Organization for Economic Cooperation and Development (OECD), consisting of the U.S. and 29 other countries, has established new guidelines for international e-commerce. The Better Business Bureau has also developed its own Code of Online Business Practices.

A Case in POINT

Michael Bakchos's family has been in the orchard business for 40 years. His grandfather, Makhaon, emigrated from Greece to America as a small child. Like many immigrants, Makhaon contributed to the family's livelihood as soon as he was old enough to work in the orchards of the high mountain valley where they lived.

Makhaon worked in the peach orchards until he was middle-aged. Then, through a bit of good luck, he was able to buy an orchard of his own. With the help of Michael's father he built the orchard into a thriving business. After Makhaon retired, Michael's father bought several contiguous orchards and greatly expanded the peach crop.

Two years ago, Michael's father retired and turned over management of the family business to him. Unlike his father and grandfather, Michael has a college degree, in business administration. He thinks the time is right to implement some of the things he has learned. He believes that the worldwide accessibility of the Internet offers an almost endless market for the "Bakchos Peach." Michael feels that he can sell "a ton of fresh peaches to the big-city folks back East."

As a first step in the process, Michael has registered the domain name Bakchospeaches.com. He has hired you to help him build his web site.

Think Critically

1. Prepare an evaluation of the domain name for Michael.
2. Evaluate the product Michael intends to sell online and prepare a brief report concerning its suitability for Internet commerce.
3. In the Site Evaluation Checklist (Table 12-1), what do you think Michael's number-one concern for his e-business would be?

Vocabulary Builder

Write a brief definition of each word or phrase.

1. bricks-and-mortar business
2. domain name
3. Domain Name System (DNS)
4. e-entrepreneur
5. e-entrepreneurship
6. firewall

7. Internet Corporation for Assigned Names and Numbers (ICANN)
8. Internet Protocol (IP) address
9. Internet search engine
10. Internet Service Provider
11. intranets
12. merchant account provider
13. shopping cart
14. spam
15. URL
16. virtual business
17. web browser
18. web host

Review the Concepts

19. How is a virtual business different from a bricks-and-mortar business?
20. In a virtual business plan, which component is often absent?
21. What is the first step in the creation of an e-business?
22. What is considered the "face" of the web site?

Critical Thinking

23. When reading Internet usage statistics, what strikes you about work hours?
24. Which aspect of the Internet's history do you find most interesting? Why?
25. Discuss the importance of including e-entrepreneurship in a business plan.
26. Discuss the function of the Domain Name System.
27. What is the difference between a web host and an ISP?
28. Do you think the CAN-SPAM Act of 2003 is fair to advertisers? Explain.
29. Why are global agreements necessary in international e-commerce?
30. What do you think is behind the myth about young Internet consumers?
31. Based on your own experience online, what are the three most serious mistakes an entrepreneur can make?

Project

Build Your Business Plan

Give careful thought to whether or not the Internet is a suitable way to market your product or service.

1. Does your business need a web site? Justify your answer.
2. Using a search engine, check if another business is using your domain name or something similar to it.
3. From the Site Evaluation Checklist, choose the five issues you consider most relevant to your business. Justify your answer.

A Dream Retirement

Ray Heath has lived in California all his life. For 25 years he worked in the aerospace industry in Long Beach. Then, after a successful corporate career, Ray retired with a handsome retirement income.

His company had made it a policy to give employees one share of stock for every two they purchased. Beginning with his second year of employment, Ray invested 10 percent of his annual income in company stock. When he retired, his stock was worth more than $1,600,000.

Alhough Ray had enjoyed his many years with the company, he had resented the times he was affected by upper-management decisions in which he had no input. He knew that at some point in the future he wanted to be in a decision-making position. He often shared with his wife, Jill, his desire to own a business someday.

Ray's retirement meant that "someday" had arrived. Now he could start his own business and run it the way he thought best. There would be no more corporate boardroom politics to affect decisions. He would make all decisions himself, based on what he thought was most appropriate for his business and his goals.

When Ray and Jill had dreamed about and planned for their retirement, they had discussed the idea of buying a small motel. So for the past year, as Ray's retirement date approached, they focused their attention on motels. They read everything that was available about motel management. They tried to determine which parts of the country were experiencing growth or had growth potential in the travel and tourism industry. They concentrated their research on coastal areas, since they both enjoyed the ocean very much.

Ray and Jill knew they needed to identify an area that had clear growth potential but was not yet fully developed. Property there would still be reasonably priced. They could afford to buy a small motel and turn it into a profitable retirement venture.

After much research, they found the perfect spot on a section of the Texas Gulf Coast adjacent to a high-growth zone. Within the next 10 years, Ray and Jill calculated, the area would grow to match or even surpass its high-growth neighbor. They pinpointed the small town of Port Aransas as the location that most closely matched their needs.

Port Aransas is on the northern tip of Mustang Island, about 30 minutes' drive from Corpus Christi, three hours from the Rio Grande Valley, three hours from San Antonio, and four hours from Houston or Austin. In 2000 its population was approximately 3,370. The most recent statistics Ray and Jill found estimated the population in July 2002 at 3,505, an increase of 4 percent. Further research yielded other useful information on the town: the median age of its residents was 45.1 years, median household income was $39,432, and median house value was $110,500.

Port Aransas is a working port and one of the most popular tourist towns in Texas. Numerous tourist attractions in the area include:

- Aransas Wildlife Refuge
- *U.S.S. Lexington*, Museum on the Bay, Corpus Christi
- Texas State Aquarium, Corpus Christi

- Mustang Island State Park, Mustang Island
- Texas Maritime Museum, Rockport
- Padre Island National Seashore
- Goose Island State Park, Rockport

With an annual average temperature of 71.5°, an annual average rainfall of 31.92 inches, and an estimated 600-plus species of saltwater fish in the waters off the island, Port Aransas seemed the ideal location for the Heaths.

After Ray retired, he and Jill sold their home, moved to Port Aransas, and spent the next month talking to real estate agents. Among the 23 motels in the immediate area, only two of the owners were interested in selling. After visiting both properties and talking to the owners, the Heaths decided on a motel overlooking Aransas Pass, a major shipping lane leading into Corpus Christi Bay.

The motel had 35 rooms, an outdoor swimming pool, and a spacious lobby with a view of the Pass. The stucco building was about 40 years old. The only apparent problem was that the rooms were decorated in an outdated olive green, orange, and gold color scheme. The swimming pool was in good shape, although some of the tiles on the deck were loose and crumbling. Overall, though, the Heaths fell in love with the grounds and the view. They decided to make some changes, and Jill's brother, an engineer, said he would inspect the place when he came to visit in a month or so.

After an exchange of offers and counteroffers, the owners of the motel accepted Ray and Jill's contract. A month later the Heaths moved into the motel, which was currently open for business during the quiet off-season. The start of the tourist season was about six months away. By that time, the Heaths had to make sure they had done everything possible to ensure a steady flow of guests.

Ray and Jill understood they could not keep the motel going the way it was and assume it would make money. They needed business and marketing plans to guide them through the experience of motel ownership.

Their first action was to search the local chamber of commerce listing for a marketing company to assist them. They had no luck finding a local company; the closest one was in Dallas. They did, however, discover a visitors' guide that was published locally for tourists. They needed to be listed in the guide, of course, but what should they emphasize about their motel?

The Heaths had their work cut out for them. They had to address a number of issues right away. The accuracy of their responses could mean the difference between business success and business failure.

Case Questions

1. How can the Heaths determine who their potential customers are?
2. How should the Heaths determine what to charge for their rooms and any other services they offer?
3. How do you suggest the Heaths promote their hotel?
4. Do you think the Heaths should consider Internet marketing? Why?
5. If the Heaths decide to create a web site for their motel, what are some of the mistakes they should try to avoid?

Unit 4

Manage and Finance the Small Business

Profile of an Entrepreneur

Soichiro Honda 1906–1991

Soichiro Honda was a well-known businessman in Japan long before he decided to become an international entrepreneur. As he pondered the decision to take his products into the international marketplace, he was advised that America would pose the greatest challenge and thus should be put off. Not one to avoid challenges, Honda decided to meet the biggest one head-on and take his motorcycle to America.

The 1959 advertising slogan "You Meet the Nicest People on a Honda" changed the way Americans felt about motorcycles. Until then, they had associated riding motorcycles with undesirable people, loud noise, and an unsavory way of life. That all changed when the unknown entrepreneur from Japan introduced his Cub motorcycle to American consumers. The Honda Company crafted an advertising campaign that linked the Cub with good clean fun and, after an initial glitch, won over a generation of Americans who likely never would have considered buying a motorcycle.

Soichiro Honda's success began many years earlier. He was born in Japan in 1906 and grew up helping his father repair bicycles in the little town of Komyo. At 16 he went to Tokyo to pursue an apprenticeship at an automobile repair shop, then returned home and opened his own shop.

Honda was a risk-taker by nature. That part of his personality led to a lifelong interest in car racing. But, following a terrible crash, his wife convinced him to retire from the sport.

After the excitement of racing, his repair business was not enough to keep him occupied. He launched a piston ring manufacturing enterprise in 1937 and by 1948 had started producing motorcycles. That same year he started the Honda Corporation. A year later his first motorcycle, the Dream, rolled out of the factory. It was an immediate success.

Honda was successful even though he ignored the Japanese business culture of the time. In post–World War II Japan, whom you knew and the school you graduated from were prime elements of business success. Honda's lack of respect for this tradition, called *gakubatsu,* was unusual and one of the traits that defined his entrepreneurship. It has been said that Honda "was a results-oriented pragmatist who suffered no fools gladly."

An article by the American Honda Motor Company provides an unusual glimpse into the true nature of Soichiro Honda. His knowledge of his fellow countrymen made him an effec-

HARUYOSHI YAMAGUCHI/BLOOMBERG NEWS/LANDOV

GETTY IMAGES

tive leader. He required in others talents he himself did not have. “Honda demanded practical results, and he found a way of working that brought those results. He learned to regard failures as necessary steps toward understanding. He instilled in others the drive to learn without fear of failure. Such was the road to success.”

Honda believed that having a good idea was not enough. Nor were a strong will and a willingness to put in the hours. If your products were no better or no worse than your competitor's, the customer had no reason to prefer yours. Honda believed success would come from continual reinvestment in technology, which would lead to the discovery of new things that people would want.

By the early 1950s Honda's company had developed into an engine manufacturer, and its products included most motorcycle parts. In 1952 Honda introduced the Cub. It was a hit with the transportation-starved Japanese—small, easily operated, and inexpensive to run. Sales took off, and by 1959 Honda was the leading motorcycle manufacturer in Japan.

Honda was a great believer in market research, much of which he conducted himself. One of his preferred market research techniques was to travel to races around the world and study the competition's motorcycles. Once a standard was set by a competitive product, Honda took this information back to the research shop and did his utmost to improve upon it.

Honda's interest in racing was not limited to gathering competitive intelligence. He also entered Honda motorcycles in competitions. His interest in continual product improvement took the company from a disappointing finish in its first international race in 1954 to a manufacturer's team prize in the Isle of Man race in 1959, its first year in that race.

Honda's racing successes were about performance, not ego. Every time a Honda motorcycle won a race, sales successes followed. By 1959, not only had Honda topped the Japanese motorcycle sales chart, it was selling at an unbelievable rate of 100,000 units a month!

In 1959 Soichiro Honda brought his product to America, because he believed his products were the best in the world. Who could argue, given his phenomenal sales success in Japan? As history would soon show, the American consuming public would argue. America's experience with the new Cub was anything but inspiring. Honda motorcycles began blowing head gaskets and losing clutches. The Cub might have been good enough for Japan, but it was not meeting muster in the U.S.

Bewildered, Honda took the motorcycles back to Japan to regroup. He quickly discovered that the problem, though mechanical, was really tied more closely to culture. Americans were accustomed to greater speeds than the Japanese, and that was causing the failures. Once Honda exposed the problem, it was quickly addressed. By 1963 Honda had become the top-selling brand of motorcycles in the United States.

Soichiro Honda was no stranger to these kinds of problems. He had a saying for difficult times: “To me, success can be achieved only through repeated failure and introspection. In fact, success represents 1 percent of your work and results from the 99 percent that is called failure.”

The manufacture of automobiles proved no easier for Honda. In the early 1960s Japan's Ministry of International Trade and Industry (MITI), now called the Ministry of Economy, Trade, and Industry (METI), felt that Japan's automotive industry of 10 manufacturers should be merged into two international majors, Toyota and Nissan. In defiance of MITI's desires, Honda announced his intention to enter automobile production. His exceptional leadership propelled the Honda Motor Company to international acclaim and unparalleled success in the automotive arena.

With its track record of innovation, Honda has become a formidable global force in the motorcycle and automobile industries. Today it is the largest motorcycle manufacturer and one of the top 10 automobile manufacturers in the world.

Chapter 13

Human Resource Management

Objectives

13-1 Define the three management functions.

13-2 Explain the concept and procedures of staffing.

13-3 Discuss theories of management style.

13-4 Explain the concept of controlling.

13-5 List and describe the primary laws that govern employment.

THE THREE MANAGEMENT FUNCTIONS

The successful entrepreneur knows the importance of having the right personnel. Just as capital, equipment, and inventory are essential resources for success, so are people—the human resources. Without the right personnel, even a well-equipped, well-capitalized business will flounder.

Finding and keeping good employees requires the competent performance of three management functions—staffing, directing, and controlling. In addition, a thorough knowledge of labor laws ensures compliance throughout the entire human resource management process.

STAFFING

At this point in the business planning process, the entrepreneur must determine if employees will be necessary in the new business. Sometimes they are; sometimes they are not. **Staffing** is the process that determines the number of employees needed and defines a process for hiring them.

Labor expense can be a significant line item in the overall budget. Many small businesses fail because the owner overstaffs. Be very careful with staffing—try not to hire more employees than you need. But this is much easier said than done. How exactly can you determine the number of employees you need?

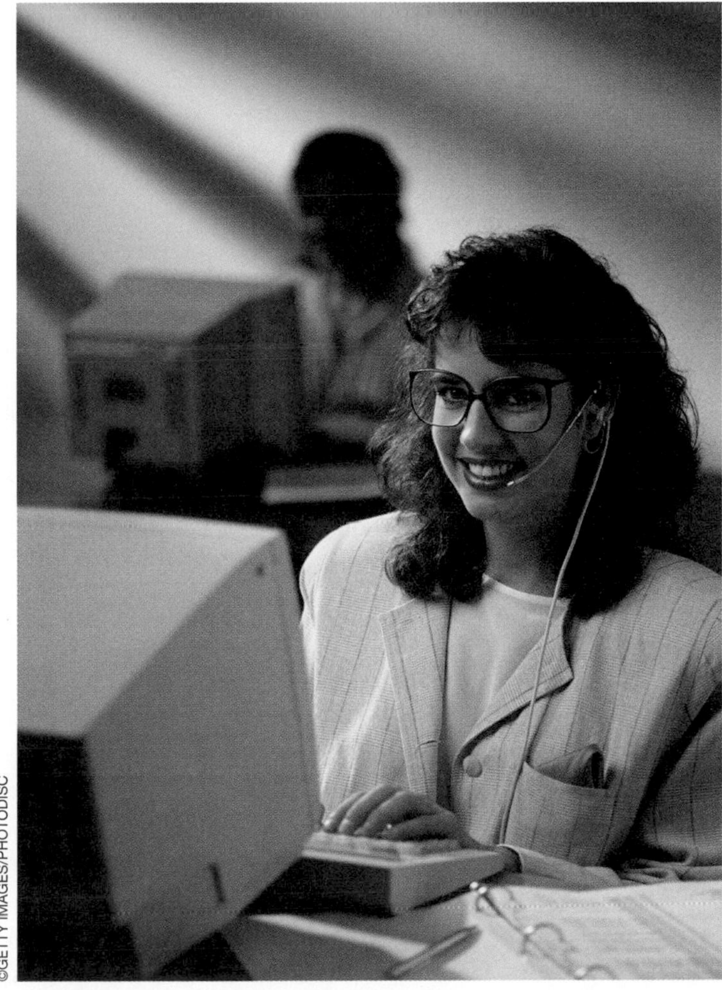
©GETTY IMAGES/PHOTODISC

First, staffing begins with calculating how much money is available for personnel. Entrepreneurs use sales projections as guides not only for purchasing initial inventory and equipment but also for determining how to staff the business and how much money to pay employees. Check with industry sources to see what percent of sales revenues is normally allocated for payroll expenses. This figure is often discovered during the industry analysis portion of business planning. Then multiply your own projected revenues by that percentage. The result will be an approximate amount you can use as a guide.

After you have determined how much money is available for personnel, you must decide how many employees you need. The type of business you are planning will determine this number as well as the skills those employees will need. The size of the physical facility and hours of operation are other factors. If your business is retail, how much coverage will you need on the sales floor? If your business will involve selling to other businesses in a defined geographic region, how big is the territory to be covered?

After establishing employee skills and numbers, you need to develop a job description for each major category of employees, such as assistant manager, sales staff, bookkeeper, and so on. As you will discover later, a good job description is essential during the recruiting and hiring stages of the new business.

The next step is to investigate how much other local businesses are paying for similar employees. Check your local newspaper, call the state employment service, review local online salary survey data, and ask knowledgeable people in your industry about prevailing wage rates. This information will help determine how much your employees should be paid. The approximate payroll cost, including employer-paid taxes and benefits, if offered, should then be calculated for each potential employee. Compute this amount for all projected employees to determine total labor costs.

The Organization Chart

As part of the staffing process, it is helpful to carefully analyze the business's needs by means of an organization chart. An organization chart is a picture of a business's distribution of its human resources. A well-developed organization chart, such as that in Figure 13-1, has both planning and management uses. During the planning phase, it identifies the number and types of employees needed. It lists positions in the organization and the primary responsibilities of each. The names of the individuals who hold the positions are added to the chart as they join the business.

FIGURE 13-1

Organization Chart

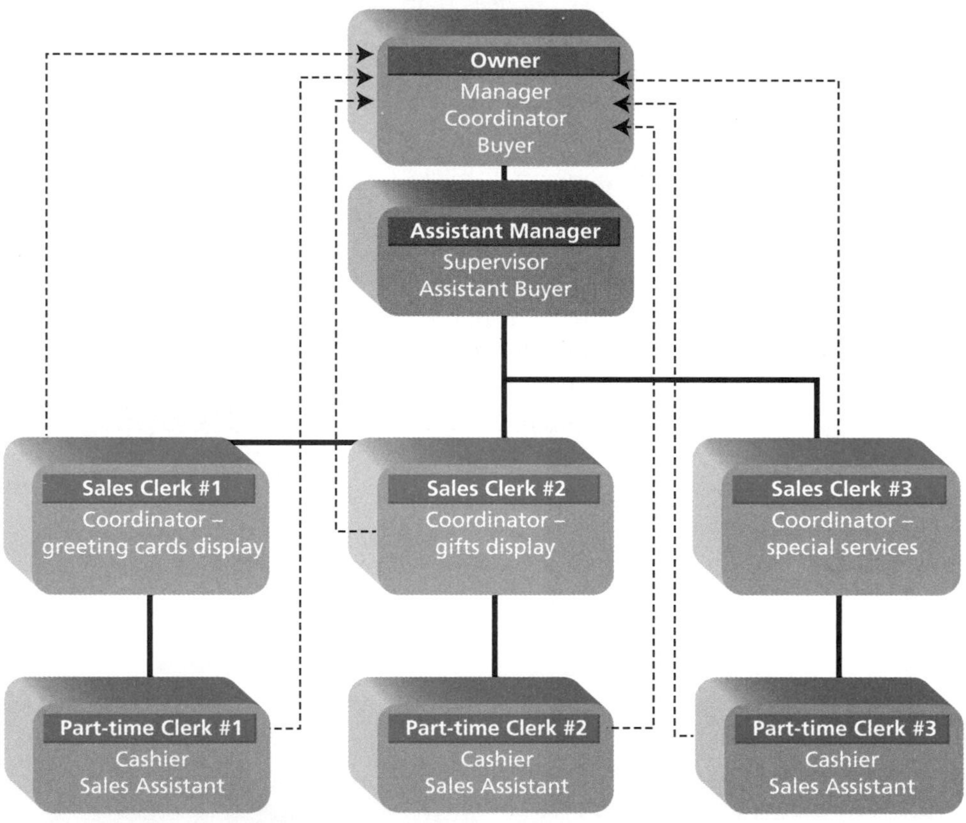

The lines on the chart indicate reporting relationships. It is important to include specific instructions about who oversees whom, or the **chain of command**. Solid lines indicate formal reporting relationships. Broken lines indicate that all employees have direct access to the manager.

Management uses the organization chart to identify the positions that must be filled and the skills needed for each one. It is an important part of the business planning process because it gives owners a clear picture of their personnel needs. To identify the positions to be filled, the owner must first determine what type of organization the business is.

Small businesses are normally characterized as **line organizations**. A line organization's mission is to actually create and sell products or services. Larger organizations, characterized as **line and staff organizations**, may have staff positions such as personnel manager, safety officer, and accountant to assist the line employees who perform the actual work of creating and selling the products or services. One staff position that is often found in a small business is that of bookkeeper.

The organization chart is also a very important tool for employees. All employees have the right to know what their areas of responsibility are, to whom they must report, and what other positions they may pursue within the organization. If this information is not readily available, employees may not be motivated to do their best work, and morale—as well as productivity—may suffer. No matter how large or small the organization, an organization chart should be designed and made available as a reference tool for both management and employees.

Too many small businesses overlook this tool, believing that because their organizations are small their employees automatically know what is expected of them. It is usually not that clear, however, particularly in a small business in which responsibilities may overlap. Illustrating supervisory relationships in chart form helps to eliminate confusion.

Recruiting

Finding and recruiting the right employees for a new business are not easy. Entrepreneurs usually have capital limitations that can make those tasks even more difficult. Small business owners—especially new small business owners—cannot always offer the same wages or salaries to prospective employees as large businesses can. Their benefit packages may not be as lucrative. Large businesses often offer incentives such as well-funded profit sharing plans, comprehensive insurance packages, and paid vacations. For these reasons, small business owners are often forced to hire less experienced individuals. Less experienced does not always mean less skilled, however. With effective training, these employees can perform the same functions as well as or even better than employees who join a company with prior training.

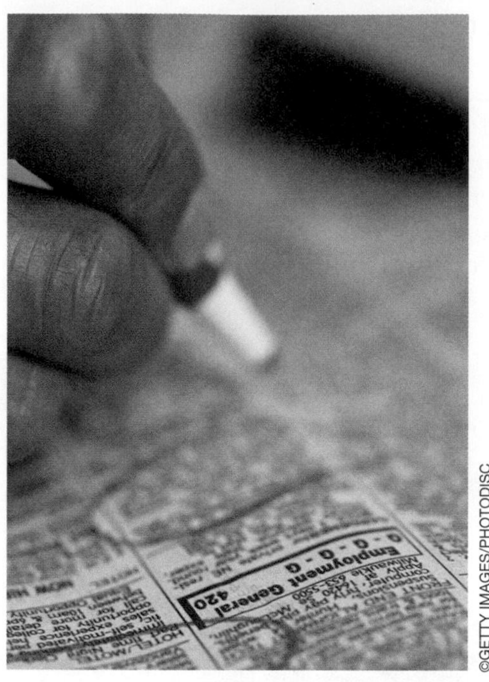
©GETTY IMAGES/PHOTODISC

How do small business owners find and recruit quality personnel? There are several ways to "shop" for applicants.

Classified Advertisements Placing ads in the help wanted sections of local newspapers is usually a good way to attract large numbers of applicants. A descriptive ad should list job requirements, such as education or previous experience, as well as the responsibilities of the open position. Resumes should be requested from applicants in addition to cover letters. It is sometimes helpful to ask that specific information be included in the cover letter, such as salary requirements, date of availability, or other pertinent information. For employers who do not wish to disclose the business's name, many newspapers offer mailbox facilities for use with their classified ads. Resumes can then be screened to determine which applicants are worth interviewing.

Employment Agencies Employment agencies keep records of people who are looking for work and their qualifications. Seeking applicants through an employment agency saves some of the time involved in screening applicants, but the cost is much higher than the cost of classified advertising. Employment agencies charge a fee from either applicants or employers, or sometimes both.

College Placement Services Many colleges keep records and resumes of students and alumni who are looking for work. This placement service is offered at no charge.

In-Store Advertising Posting a sign in the business's window may attract pedestrians or motorists. With this method, you have two options. After applicants complete the application, you can inform them that they may be called for an interview or you can interview them immediately. The first option allows you to do some initial screening of the applicants. The second option requires interviewing all applicants. The latter course often means dedicating several days to interviewing alone, with the result that not much other work will get done during those days.

Referrals Your friends or employees are often good sources of referrals. If you consider the person who is making the recommendation reliable, a referral may require very little screening. However, many business owners are reluctant to hire people related to, or too closely affiliated with, other employees. There is the possibility of alienating one at the expense of the other, creating conflicts within the organization, or losing two employees if one decides to leave or must be let go.

Internet Recruiting With so many people using the Internet, it makes good sense to consider using it to recruit employees. Most online employment options allow you to post jobs, then search the resumes that are sent in response to the posting. One of the largest online job services is Monster, which claims that over 1.6 million job seekers visit its site daily. There is a downside to online recruiting, however: it can cost several hundred dollars to post a job and review resumes. Make sure you carefully consider all aspects of this recruiting option.

Regardless of the methods you use, it is to your advantage to attract a large number of applicants. Having more people to choose from allows you to be more selective and hire the most suitable person.

Job Applications

Tailoring an employment application to your specific business is a good idea. With a tailored application you can gather specific information that might not be included on a resume and use that information to decide what to ask during the interview.

One suggestion is that you do not buy and use a "canned" generic job application. Many commercially available hiring guides and software programs offer generic application forms. The problem with these is that they are designed so that a wide range of businesses can use them. They rarely fit the needs of a specific business.

Using the job description you have written as a guide, tailor the application to fit your own entrepreneurial vision. Ask questions relevant to the specific job and its requirements. Avoid asking questions that are not job related.

In addition to asking potential employees to complete a job application, most savvy businesses also ask for a resume. Small businesses should not overlook this requirement. You should be aware, however, of a growing trend in the employment marketplace, that of job applicants lying on their resumes. In 2003 a major news organization reported that over 50 percent of the people on whom it had conducted background checks had provided bogus information in their resumes. That statistic compared with about 40 percent in 2002.

As an entrepreneur, how can you be sure potential employees are being truthful? Probably the easiest and least expensive method is to check their references. You would be surprised by how many employers fail to take this simple precautionary step and how many job applicants are very much aware of that fact. If the job is a sensitive one, you might want to take the inquiry a step further and pay for a criminal background check.

When it comes to college degrees or special training, verify the applicant's claims. Request that an official transcript of all courses and grades be sent by the alma mater directly to you, rather than through the applicant. This is common practice for colleges.

Another note of caution: There has been a proliferation of "diploma mills" in the past few years. For the right price, a person can get a phony degree in almost any subject from one of hundreds of businesses offering this service. Make sure the purported degree is legitimate. If in doubt, call your local college or university and ask for a list of accredited schools. Caution at this stage of the hiring process will save your business countless hours and possibly dollars in the future.

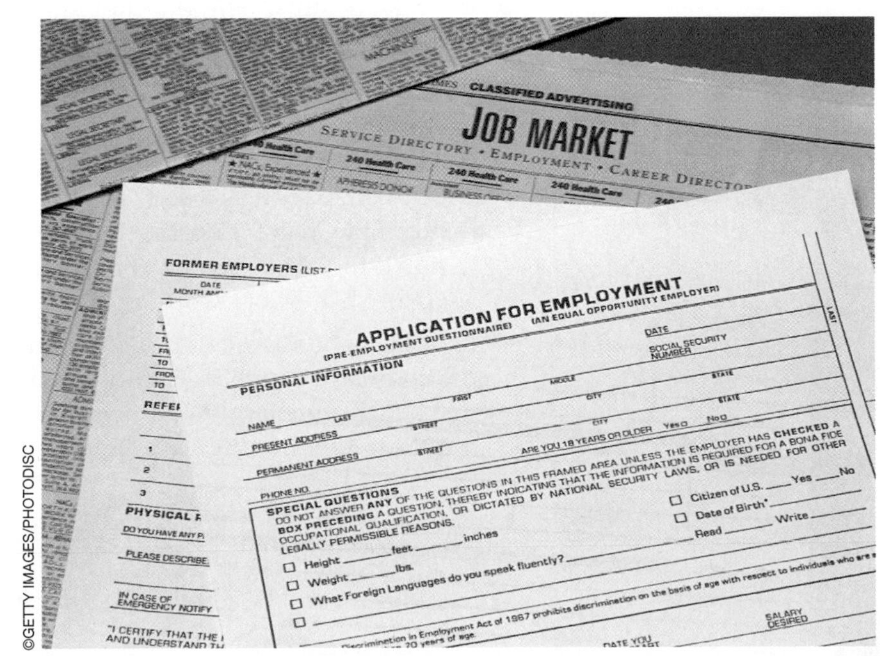

©GETTY IMAGES/PHOTODISC

Interviewing

Once job descriptions are written and candidates have been selected, the interview process can begin. As with any interview, you should plan carefully and write out a list of questions beforehand. A lot of information must be gathered in a relatively short period of time, and it is easy to get caught up in conversation and forget to ask important questions.

DIGITAL VISION

Interviews should be held in a quiet, relaxing environment. Focus on the applicant's personal characteristics with regard to teamwork and cooperation. Two important characteristics to look for are a positive attitude and reliability. Skills are obviously desirable, but if they are inadequate, they can generally be taught. A positive attitude cannot be. The discussion should allow you to determine whether the applicant will do well in the team environment of a small business.

In many cases, more than one interview will be needed before the final decision can be made. If the interview indicates that the applicant is right for the position, you should take time to fully explain the job, show the applicant the operation, and list several good reasons for joining the team. The following are some of the ways you can make your small business appealing to a prospective employee.

- Express the excitement of participating in a new venture. Many people prefer to work in an environment in which they can see the outcome of their work. Employees of small businesses know their contributions are important to the success of the business. They have strong self-actualization needs. For them, working for a small business is worth a possible sacrifice of financial benefits.
- Tell potential employees how much the company needs them. By being direct about this, you can help them visualize the roles they will play in the operation and success of the business.
- Share your values with the applicant. If it is clear the goal is to create an ethical and responsible business, the applicant will feel proud to become part of the organization.
- Create an environment of flexibility and caring, and be sure to describe that environment to potential employees. Small businesses should not need to enforce the kinds of rules necessary in larger businesses. Explain, for example, that you understand that additional time off is sometimes required for family responsibilities. Reinforce the impression that there are many benefits to working in a friendly, informal environment.
- Establish a bonus system whereby employees benefit from the success of the company. Emphasize that if the business does well, the employees will benefit financially. When extra profits are generated, employees should receive bonuses in recognition of their contributions.

New employees should be hired on a probationary basis for a set period of time—four to six weeks is common. Both employer and employee must clearly understand that if either party is dissatisfied at the end of this period, the relationship will be terminated. Specific reasons for termination should be reviewed. Tardiness, dishonesty, unreliability, and poor attitude disrupt the activities of the team and cannot be accommodated in a small business.

Thorough interviewing is important because training new employees is expensive. An employee in training is not usually able to produce at full speed, and neither is the trainer. Two employees are therefore performing at below-normal levels for a certain period of time, which ultimately results in higher payroll expenses. If the interview and selection process is inadequate, there will be excessive turnover of employees and, therefore, a continual need for training.

Ethics for ENTREPRENEURS

Jared graduated from high school six years ago and moved to a larger city 250 miles away. For several years he worked at a series of low-level retail jobs. Then he became an assistant manager at a locally owned clothing store. He enjoyed the work, felt he had learned a tremendous amount about the retail business, and was ready to take on the added responsibilities of managing a store.

Jared spoke with the owner of the store and learned that opportunities for advancement were slim at best. The owner agreed that Jared was competent enough to manage a store on his own. He understood Jared's desire to advance his career and offered to write letters of recommendation and personally visit any potential employers.

Jared felt very good after the conversation. He was aware of several openings for retail store managers in the area. With his experience, he felt it would just be a matter of time before he would find the right job.

Two months later Jared saw a newspaper ad for the perfect job. A national men's-wear chain was looking for experienced managers to support a major expansion. Individuals with at least two years of management experience and a college degree would be considered. Those hired would be trained for six months in an established store and then placed as store managers in one of the new locations.

Jared thought the job was a great fit except for one thing—he didn't have a college degree. In fact, he had no college credits at all. "What a stupid requirement," he thought. He knew he could do the job. As he stewed over the degree requirement, he began to think, "What if I faked the degree? I'd be moving to a part of the country where no one knows me. I'll never get caught."

During the next week, Jared used the Internet to investigate his options. He discovered a site that for $500 would give him a toll-free telephone number to put on his resume. When called, operators would "verify" the academic qualifications listed on the resume. Jared decided to pay the fee and apply for the job.

Thirteen months later, Jared was managing a successful new store in Florida. He was happy he had faked the college degree. After all, the store's success was proof it wasn't necessary. He wasn't worried. Even if his deception were discovered, what could be done?

Think Critically

1. Do you agree with Jared's action? Explain.
2. Do you think Jared broke any laws? What could happen to him?

DIRECTING

FUN FACTS

Only three companies have reached the highly sought number-one spot on the Fortune 500 since 1954: General Motors, ExxonMobil, and Wal-Mart. Sam Walton would be proud of his entrepreneurial venture some 40-plus years after he began it.

Directing is influencing people's behavior through motivation, communication, group dynamics, leadership, and discipline. Once the business is staffed, efficient management and leadership skills are necessary to keep valuable employees. Successful small business owners understand that they lead by example. A small business does not have an "ivory tower" from which the boss looks down on the employees. The boss is right in the middle of things, taking an active part in the running of the business alongside the workers. If the boss is not willing to pick up the trash, employees won't be either.

Motivating

As instructor and organizer, the business owner decides what must be done, which is a planning function, and how it will be done, which is a directing function. Good instructors are patient. They do not expect students to do the impossible, but they do expect students to do their best. Enthusiasm and efficiency in the workplace are dependent on the employer's ability to motivate employees. By allowing plenty of time and creating a proper learning environment, the owner can supply employees with the tools they need for good performance. This requires coordination, attention to detail, and the ability to give directions and assign tasks.

Management Styles

In the 1960s, Douglas MacGregor, a professor of industrial administration at the Massachusetts Institute of Technology, observed two distinct management styles that he termed Theory X and Theory Y. **Theory X managers** are those who direct with little consideration for human relations. They are very task-oriented and are most concerned with making sure that assigned jobs are completed in the most efficient manner. They operate under the assumption that workers prefer to be directed and do not wish to take on responsibility. Theory X managers believe the majority of employees must be forced to work, with the threat of punishment if they do not. They believe security is a primary employee desire and getting paid is the major incentive for their attendance in the workplace.

Theory Y managers are more concerned with human relations. They direct under the assumption that workers like their work and enjoy responsibility. They believe that, given the opportunity, people will use their creativity and intellectual capabilities. Effective managers operate under a Theory Y philosophy. They realize that to build an effective team and accomplish all the work on hand, workers must receive satisfaction from the job itself and not just from the pay they receive.

This theory reinforced the results of a study conducted by Frederick Herzberg in the late 1950s. According to his study, worker enthusiasm is created by the following job satisfaction factors, ranked in order:

1. sense of achievement
2. recognition for achievement
3. interest in the work itself
4. opportunity for growth
5. opportunity for advancement
6. responsibility
7. peer and group relationships
8. compensation
9. supervisor fairness
10. reasonable company policies and rules
11. status
12 job security
13. supervisor friendliness
14. good working conditions

©GETTY IMAGES/PHOTODISC

The study clearly indicates that employees are more concerned with the nature and potential of the job itself than with security or status. They prefer an environment that encourages a sense of achievement and personal growth. They desire recognition for accomplishments and enjoy working with others who have similar goals.

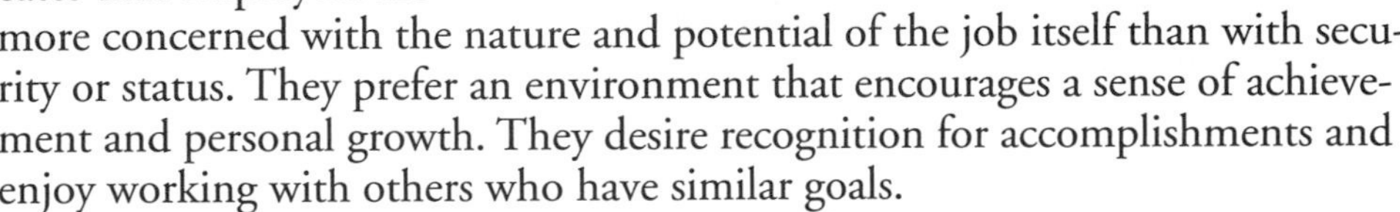

Herzberg went on to separate job-related factors into two categories—motivators and hygiene factors. **Motivators** are personal job factors affecting the individual worker. They include:

- the work itself
- achievement
- recognition
- responsibility
- growth and advancement

Hygiene factors have more to do with the company's management and the workplace environment and include:

- salary
- supervision
- company policies
- interpersonal relationships
- working conditions

Workers will perform their assigned duties in a satisfactory manner when the hygiene factors are acceptable, but if management expects peak performance, the workplace must also offer the motivators.

Small Business Technology

Scheduling personnel has always been a problem for the small business that has to deal with more than one shift seven days a week. A restaurant is a good example. How does the owner keep up with scheduling two shifts, seven days a week? Personnel scheduling software is one solution. It can show when and where each staff member is expected to work, highlight schedule exceptions such as vacations and sick leave, tally the hours scheduled for each employee, and emphasize scheduled overtime. It can even alert management when people are double-booked or when the number of hours, days, shifts, or breaks scheduled are not possible for individual employees.

Many small businesses can offer a combination of Theory Y management and Herzberg's motivators more easily than large organizations can. Because of their size, large organizations must generally rely on rigid company policies and structured supervision to control operations. Small business managers can work with all their employees and instill a sense of involvement, achievement, and challenge.

An Alternative Theory Another theory of management styles that has gained acceptance was developed by William Ouchi in his book, *Theory Z: How American Management Can Meet the Japanese Challenge.* **Theory Z managers** give employees a great deal of freedom and trust. They assume workers feel loyalty to the company and have an interest in team building. Theory Z is more worker oriented than MacGregor's XY theory, which views motivation primarily from the manager's and company's point of view.

Theory Z is a good fit for most small businesses because the entrepreneur must place a great deal of faith in the employees. Whether you choose Theory X, Y, Z, or some combination thereof, remember that your management style will have a large impact on your employees and ultimately on the success of your entrepreneurial venture.

CONTROLLING

Controlling is the process of establishing performance standards based on the firm's objectives, measuring and reporting actual performance, comparing the two, and taking corrective or preventive action as necessary. The controlling function is often the most difficult for human resources managers to master. To excel in this function, business owners must constantly consider employees' roles in the business.

Employee Input

Employees who are in line positions work directly with customers, and often with suppliers as well. A good manager is open to suggestions from employees because they know what customers want and expect.

DIGITAL VISION

Large businesses, of necessity, tend to establish objectives from the top down. Upper management sets sales goals and company policies, often without direct employee input. Making decisions without collecting information from the people most affected—the employees—forces new policies on those employees and ultimately hurts company morale.

For example, when ABC Company, a large organization, sets its sales goals for the upcoming year, it typically does it from the top down. The president of the company reports the results of the past year to the Board of Directors and awaits their response. If the company achieved a 5 percent increase in sales the previous year, the response might be to try for a 6 percent increase in the coming year. The president, not wanting to disappoint the board, accepts the challenge. She meets with the vice president of sales and sets a goal for a 7 percent increase—she wants to look good to the Board of Directors even if the sales team misses the mark. The vice president meets with the regional sales managers and sets an 8 percent increase as their objective, using the same protective strategy the president did. The regional sales managers relay a 9 percent objective to the district managers, who relay a 10 percent objective to sales personnel.

In this case, the original goal has almost doubled by the time it reaches the unfortunate sales representatives. During the coming year, pressure to reach the objective will build, particularly for the sales reps, who are responsible for the most difficult task. This is top-down management; managers neither listen to nor request information from the bottom, as illustrated in Figure 13-2.

FIGURE 13-2

Top-Down Management

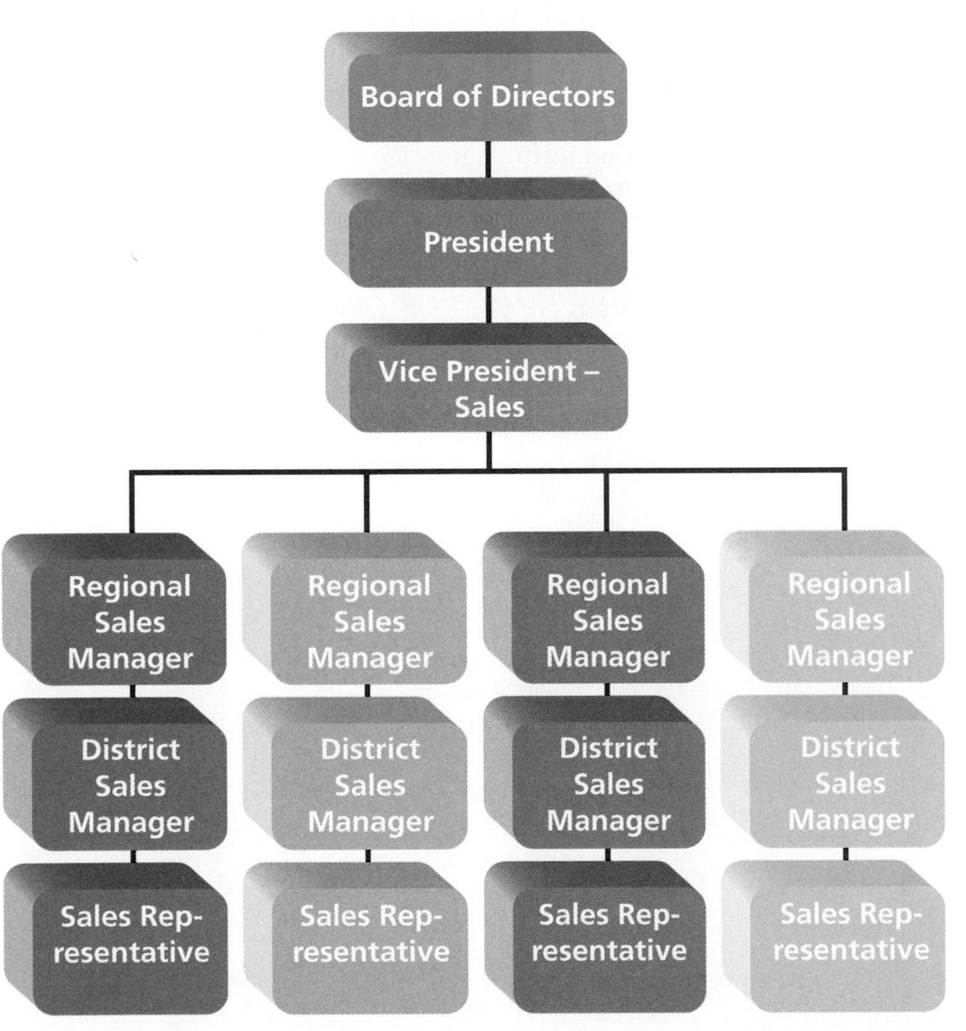

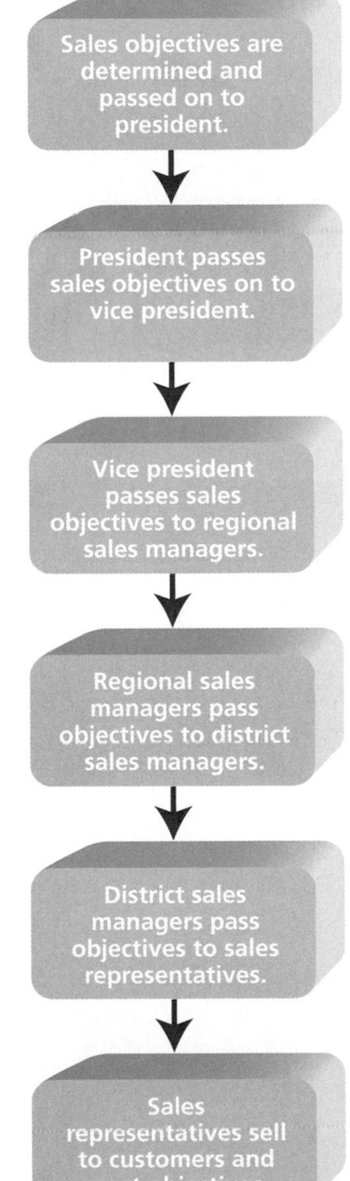

The small business owner, on the other hand, works more closely with employees and should always get direct input from them before making important decisions. For example, a retail store owner who is considering adding a new product line should ask sales personnel for suggestions, since they work with the customers daily. A business owner who wants to make an accurate sales forecast should ask sales personnel what they think is happening in the market. Most small business owners find that they are most successful when they are willing to listen.

Performance Evaluations

FUN FACTS

In 1943, the chairman of IBM was asked his opinion on the future of computers. His answer was, "I think there is a world market for maybe five computers." What do you think he would answer today?

Employees need to know how their employers feel about their performance. Large businesses usually have an elaborate system for appraising employees' work. This system often requires rating performance in selected areas such as dependability, punctuality, attitude toward job and coworkers, and success in achieving predetermined objectives. The ratings are used to let the employees know how their supervisors perceive their performance. They also serve as useful management control tools because they provide a means of determining whether the objectives for a particular job are being met. They should be used in every business, large or small.

Performance evaluations are conducted at regular intervals, usually every 6 or 12 months. They are most productive when conducted away from the business, where employer and employee have an uninterrupted period of time to share their thoughts about the direction of the business. Focusing on positives rather than negatives helps the employee feel more at ease. Productivity can be reviewed and new objectives set in a nonthreatening way that is helpful to everyone involved.

Employee evaluations provide an excellent opportunity for praise and, when necessary, suggestions for improvement. As an employer you need to devise an employee evaluation form. Figure 13-3 is an example of an effective evaluation form for a small business employee.

FIGURE 13-3

Sample Evaluation Form

JAN'S SHOE EMPORIUM
Employee Evaluation

Employee name ______________________ Date ____________

1. Employee's evaluation of his/her work accomplishments

   ____

   Employer's comments ______________________________

   ____

2. Employee's evaluation of the company's overall performance, including areas that could be improved ______________________

   ____

3. Employee's specific comments regarding

   employee morale ______________________________

   customer relations ____________________________

   policies/procedures ___________________________

4. Manager's evaluation of employee's contribution toward company goals ______________________________________

   ____

   Employee's response, including points of agreement/disagreement

   ____

   ____

5. Goals agreed upon for future development of company __________

   ____

Evaluation forms will likely differ considerably from those of a large business. The best system does not use rankings or ratings—it uses comments. There should be a list of the areas to be discussed, prepared ahead of time, with space to record comments made during the discussion. Clearly stated work objectives make it easy to determine what has or has not been achieved. Employer and employee should ultimately agree on the points discussed and the objectives that have been set for future performance.

LABOR LAWS

Entrepreneurs who plan to hire other people must learn the regulations that protect them and their employees from unfair labor practices. Small businesses can be susceptible to personnel trouble because often the person doing the hiring is not a trained personnel specialist. That is why familiarity with these laws is so important. Without this knowledge, employers may infringe upon applicants' or employees' rights without knowing it. There are many labor laws and new ones are constantly being added, so it is in your best interest to keep up with legislative activities affecting employment.

The Equal Employment Opportunity Commission (EEOC), a government agency established by Congress in 1972, regulates the labor laws described below and others. The commission receives charges of discrimination, investigates them, and, if they appear to be true, attempts to remedy the problem through reconciliation. If reconciliation is not achieved, the commission may bring suit in federal court. The commission handles 75,000 to 80,000 charges annually.

©GETTY IMAGES/PHOTODISC

Fair Labor Standards Act of 1938 The FLSA established a minimum wage and required overtime pay for employees working more than 40 hours per week. The act provides minimum standards for both wages and overtime entitlement and spells out administrative procedures by which covered work time must be compensated. Included in the act are provisions related to child labor and equal pay. In addition, it exempts specified employees or groups of employees from the application of certain of its provisions. The main objective of the act is to eliminate labor conditions detrimental to the maintenance of the minimum standards of living necessary for workers' health, efficiency, and well-being.

The law originally contained a large number of special industry exemptions, many of which were designed to protect traditional pay practices in small rural businesses. Most of these exemptions have been repealed. Currently, the most important issues relate to so-called "white-collar" exemptions applicable to professional, administrative, and executive employees.

The most contentious issues in recent years were related to technical employees, such as computer programmers, who have a great deal of specialized knowledge but no formal academic credentials. Such employees often exercise no direct management or even administrative authority, and so are arguably ineligible for any of the FLSA white-collar exemptions. By legislative amendment, some employees of this sort are now exempt from the overtime provisions of the FLSA, but many issues remain unsettled.

Civil Rights Act of 1964 This is "an Act to enforce the constitutional right to vote, to confer jurisdiction upon the district courts of the United States to provide injunctive relief against discrimination in public accommodations, to authorize the Attorney General to institute suits to protect constitutional rights in public facilities and public education, to extend the Commission on Civil Rights, to prevent discrimination in federally assisted programs, to establish a Commission on Equal Employment Opportunity, and for other purposes." Title VII of the act prohibits employment discrimination based on race, color, religion, sex, and national origin.

©GETTY IMAGES/PHOTODISC

Age Discrimination in Employment Act of 1967 The overall purpose of this act is to promote employment of older persons based on their ability rather than age, to prohibit arbitrary age discrimination in employment, and to help employers and workers find ways of meeting problems arising from the impact of age on employment. It specifically prohibits personnel practices that discriminate against people aged 40 and older. An amendment in 1986 extends protections to employees over age 70.

Occupational Safety and Health Act (OSHA) of 1970 The "OSHA Act" was based on the fact that Congress found that personal injuries and illnesses arising out of work situations impose a substantial burden upon, and are a hindrance to, interstate commerce in terms of lost production, wage loss, medical expenses, and disability compensation payments.

The OSHA Act is administered nationally by the Occupational Safety and Health Administration, also called OSHA, which is a division of the U.S. Department of Labor. In general, the act is designed to assure that employers provide "worker protection." It promotes a healthy and safe working environment by regulating exposure to hazardous substances and setting requirements for safety equipment.

Immigration Reform and Control Act of 1986 This act requires that employers check the identification of employees hired after 1986 to ensure that they are legal citizens of the United States.

The Global ENTREPRENEUR

Recruiting and hiring competent employees is a daunting task for many entrepreneurs. What happens if you recruit a promising employee who is not a U.S. citizen? What does the law require you to do?

The Immigration Reform and Control Act was written primarily to control the unlawful employment of aliens (non–U.S. citizens). Employers are responsible for verifying the employment eligibility and identity of all employees hired to work in the U.S. after November 6, 1986. They must complete Employment Eligibility Verification forms (Form I-9) for all employees, including U.S. citizens.

The employer must list the documentation he or she inspected that shows the employee is legal and must attest that the documents "appear to be genuine and relate to the employee named... and that to the best of my knowledge the employee is eligible to work in the United States." The employee must fill out a section attesting to his or her legal status in the U.S. The form is kept on file by the employer and reviewed by government officials only if there is an inquiry into that employee or employer.

Frequently asked questions about employment eligibility include these:

1. *Do citizens and nationals of the U.S. need to prove to their employers that they are eligible to work?* Yes. While U.S. citizens and nationals are automatically eligible for employment, they too must present proof of employment eligibility and identity and complete an Employment Eligibility Verification form (Form I-9).
2. *Do I need to complete a Form I-9 for everyone who applies for a job with my company?* No. You need to complete Form I-9 only for people you actually hire.
3. *Can I fire an employee who fails to produce the required document(s) within three business days?* Yes.
4. *What is my responsibility concerning the authenticity of document(s) presented to me?* You must examine the document(s) and, if they reasonably appear to be genuine and to relate to the person presenting them, you must accept them.
5. *May I accept a photocopy of a document presented by an employee?* No. Employees must present original documents. The only exception is a certified copy of a birth certificate.
6. *What happens if I properly complete a Form I-9 and the government discovers that my employee is not actually authorized to work?* You cannot be charged with a verification violation, but you cannot knowingly continue to employ this individual.

Think Critically

1. Do you think the above law is fair to small business? Please explain.
2. Secure a Form I-9 and bring it to class. Discuss its requirements.

Americans with Disabilities Act The ADA prohibits employment discrimination based on workers' disabilities. The General Rule of the Act is that "no covered entity shall discriminate against a qualified individual with a disability because of the disability of such individual in regard to job application procedures, the hiring, advancement, or discharge of employees, employee compensation, job training, and other terms, conditions, and privileges of employment." Additionally, it prohibits discrimination in employment (Title I), in the provision of state and local government programs, services, and benefits (Title II), and by private businesses and other entities that operate places of "public accommodation" (Title III).

General prohibitions under the law include:

- Discrimination on the basis of a wide range of physical and mental disabilities
- Making inquiries of job applicants regarding past or current medical conditions
- Requiring job applicants to take a medical exam prior to the job offer
- Maintaining work sites with extensive material barriers to the passage of employees with physical disabilities

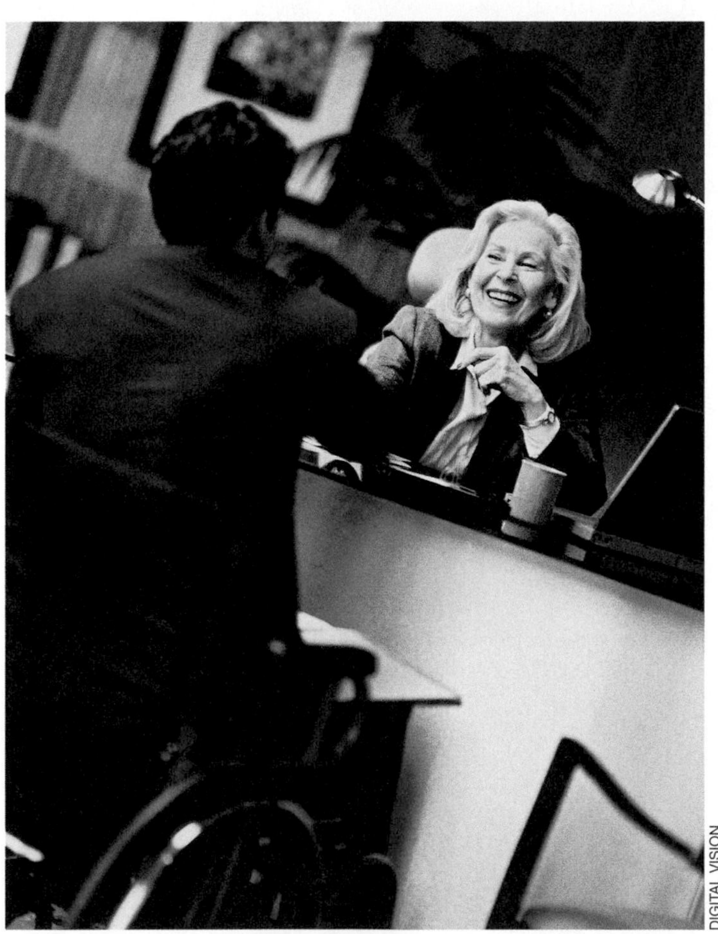
DIGITAL VISION

To be considered legally disabled, an employee must have a physical or mental impairment that substantially limits a major life activity and have a record of that impairment. A worker may have physical impairments, such as a cosmetic disfigurement or a missing limb, or mental and psychological disorders. People who are not themselves disabled but who encounter discrimination on the basis of their association or relationship with a person who has a disability, such as parents of children with disabilities, are also covered.

Disability does not automatically mean eligibility under the requirements of the ADA. A person is not disabled under the law if his or her impairment is corrected and does not substantially limit a major life activity.

The intent of the ADA is to protect job applicants and employees who are legally disabled yet still qualified for a specific job. An employee is qualified if he or she can carry out the necessary functions of the job with some type of reasonable accommodation.

Employees and applicants who are presently involved in the use of illegal drugs are not covered by the ADA. The employer may act on the basis of the drug use. Tests for illegal drugs are not subject to the ADA's limitations on medical examinations. Employers may require illegal drug users and alcoholics to meet the same performance standards as other employees.

Guidelines for Job Interview Questions

The laws regarding employment may seem hopelessly complex. How can you reduce all the information down to a usable format? How can you make sure you don't run afoul of the law? The following information about questions that can be legally asked during a job interview should prove helpful.

- **Name** Employers are not allowed to ask questions about a name that would reveal national origin. Employers may ask if the applicant has ever been employed under a different name.
- **Gender** Exercise extreme caution when structuring questions in this area. A voluntary request may be made of the applicant if the answer is not used to discriminate. Except in the rarest of circumstances, such as hiring a bathroom attendant, gender is not a bona fide occupational qualification. Do not request information from females if it is not also requested of males. Just because a job has always been labeled "men's work" does not make it legal to exclude female applicants.

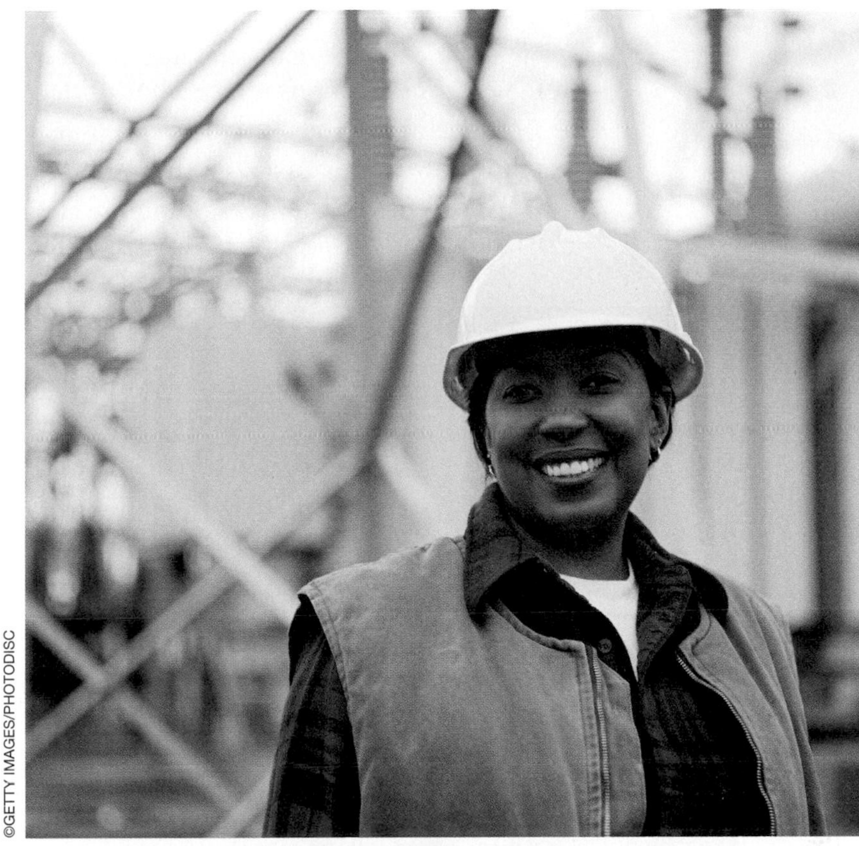
©GETTY IMAGES/PHOTODISC

- **Education** You are legally entitled to inquire about an applicant's academic preparation, degrees and dates conferred, and names of schools attended.
- **Job Attendance** You may inquire about attendance at prior jobs, but the question must be limited to days off or number of days late for any reason. Do not inquire about days off due to illness.
- **Home Address** You may ask for the applicant's address and length of stay at the current address, but you may not inquire about other people staying at the address or whether the applicant owns or rents the residence.
- **Age** If by law an employee, such as a bartender, must be a particular age, you may require proof of age after the applicant is hired. Be careful with job advertisements that imply age-based limitations that are not legally required.
- **Marital Status** You may not ask about marital status. Never ask a female applicant if she has children, and never inquire as to childcare arrangements. If you have a concern in this area, simply ask if the applicant can meet the attendance policy and anticipated work schedule.

- **National Origin** You may inquire about languages the applicant reads, speaks, or writes fluently if another language is required for the job. Inquiries into the applicant's lineage, ancestry, national origin, birthplace, or native language are not allowed.
- **Place of Birth** You may not ask for the birthplace of an applicant or of an applicant's parents or spouse. A birth certificate may not be required prior to employment. A better way to determine U.S. citizenship, if it is a job requirement, is to ask if the applicant can, after employment, submit a birth certificate or other evidence of U.S. citizenship.
- **Race** Employers may not inquire about the applicant's race. After employment, race may be requested for affirmative action purposes. Only in very rare situations is race a bona fide occupational qualification.
- **Convictions/Court Records** You may inquire about conviction for a crime only if the conviction is relevant to employment.
- **Dependents** You may not inquire about dependents. This area is violated regularly, especially in relation to female applicants.

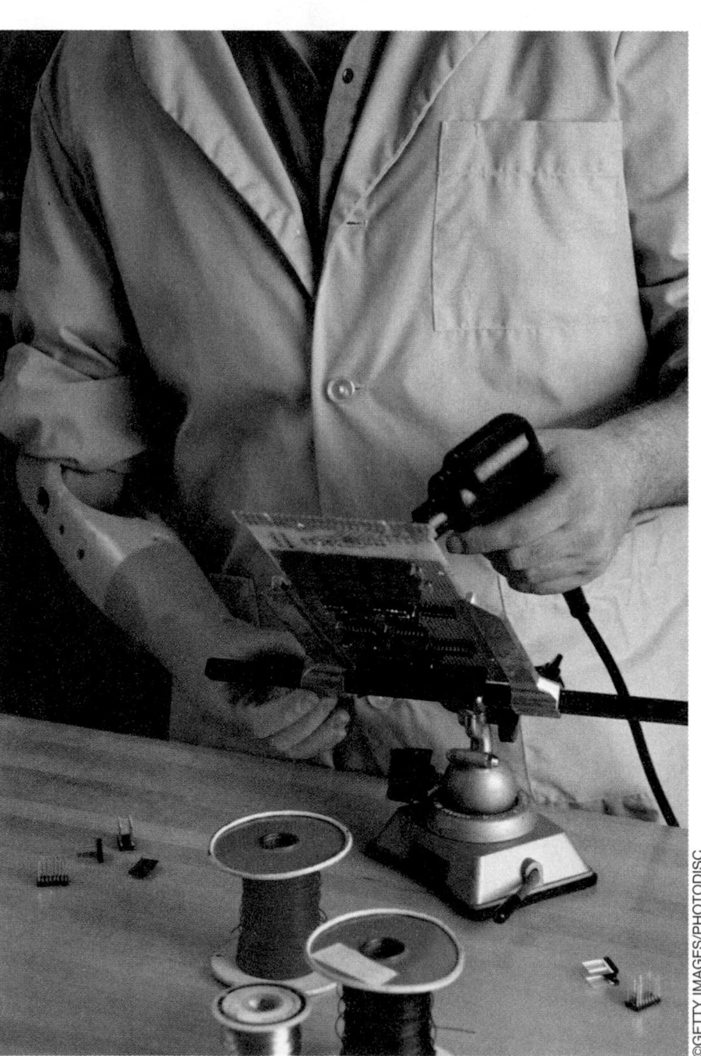
©GETTY IMAGES/PHOTODISC

- **Obvious Disability** Do not ask how the person became disabled or the long-term diagnosis. If you believe the disability may interfere with the performance of essential functions of the job, you may ask the applicant to explain or demonstrate how she or he can perform those essential functions with or without a reasonable accommodation.
- **Unknown Disability** You cannot ask if the applicant has any disabilities. You can, however, give the applicant a comprehensive job description listing all essential functions and ask if all functions can be performed with or without reasonable accommodation.
- **Medical History** Any questions about the applicant's medical history are usually illegal unless they are job related. If the job requires a medical examination, you must inform applicants that any job offer is contingent upon acceptable results from the exam. You may ask about current use of illegal drugs or alcohol. You should explain the company's standards and ask if the applicant can meet them. You should also state the company's polices concerning on-the-job alcohol and drug consumption.

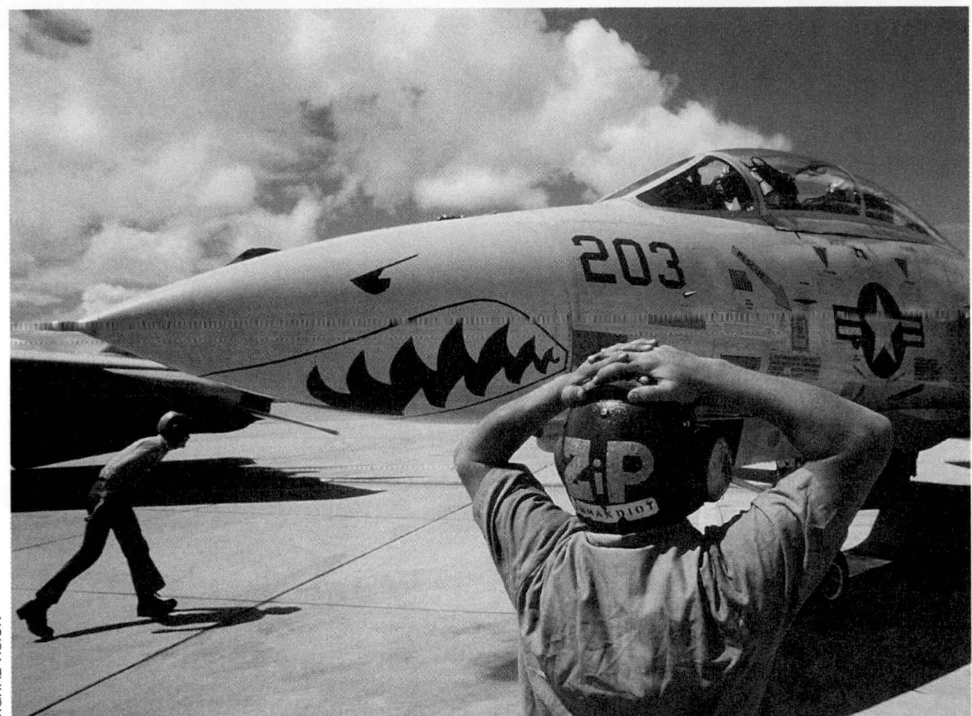

DIGITAL VISION

- **Military Service** You may not ask about type of discharge. You may ask about education and experiences in the service as they relate to a specific job.
- **Photograph** You may not require a photograph with the application or suggest that a photograph is optional. A photograph may be required for identification after the applicant is hired.
- **Physical Characteristics** Measurements such as height and weight may be requested if necessary after the applicant is hired. If asked, you must be prepared to prove that they are bona fide occupational qualifications.
- **References** You may ask if another person referred the applicant. You may also ask about individuals who are willing to provide personal and/or professional references for the applicant.
- **Emergency Contact** It is legal for an employer to require the name of a person or persons to be contacted in case of an emergency, but illegal to specifically require the name of a relative for that purpose.
- **Relatives** You may not inquire about any relative of an adult applicant. Job applicants who are underage may be asked for names and addresses of parents or guardians. It is legal to ask for the names of relatives already employed by the company as long as the information is not determined to be detrimental to the employment of minority groups underrepresented in the workforce.
- **Religion** You are prohibited from asking questions that identify religious denominations or customs. Except in cases of hardship to the company, you are required to make reasonable accommodation for employees' religious practices.
- **Misinformation** Applicants should be given notice that any misinformation or omission of pertinent facts during the application process may be cause for dismissal at any time such deception is discovered.

Ship in a BOTTLE

The original concept had been quite simple: a part-time Internet business that Fred and Jeanie could manage in the evenings and on weekends, with occasional sales trips to visit retail stores. But, with growth, the picture had changed and demands on their time had increased. Fred and Jeanie were having trouble fitting the order taking, shipping, and inventory control into their tight schedules, which included full-time jobs. They reviewed their options: either slow down the rate of growth, which neither wanted to do, or find some help.

Fred wrote job descriptions for two part-time associates: one to work the telephone and help with packing, the other to assist in maintaining business records. For the first position it was important to find someone who could converse sincerely with customers over the telephone and be meticulous when preparing shipments or posting and filing information. The person filling the other position would need a good working knowledge of computer applications. Although the pay would be minimal, Fred hoped he could attract the right people by describing the flexible hours, the benefits of being on the ground floor of a growing business, and the rewards of working with Jeanie and him. His goal was to create a team atmosphere.

After reviewing the job descriptions, Fred decided the job would be a perfect opportunity for a college student or a young mother looking for flexible hours. He posted the job openings with the community college placement office and ran a classified ad in the local newspaper.

Within a matter of days Fred and Jeanie received five inquiries from the college placement office. They called the applicants and asked them to fill out application forms and provide resumes. Interviews were scheduled with three of them. After spending two hours with each applicant, they chose a delightful young man, Lee Harris, for the position of working the telephone and preparing shipments. Lee was enthusiastic and an aspiring entrepreneur—a perfect fit. After a thorough indoctrination and on-the-job training, Lee joined the team.

The second position was more difficult to fill. The applicants from the college placement office lacked the background and experience that Fred and Jeanie were hoping to find. One well-qualified candidate answered the newspaper ad but was not interested because of the low pay and limited hours. Just when it seemed that a less qualified candidate would have to be hired, Jeanie was approached at her job by a trusted colleague whose wife, Susie, was looking for a position that would allow her sufficient time at home with their newborn daughter. Pay was not as important as personal considerations. Susie, a former office manager, was more than qualified. In addition to being a pleasant person, she knew computer applications and had three years' experience in office organization.

The initial team was on board. Fred wondered what the organization might look like in a year or five years down the road. Would he and Jeanie be full-time managers of a team of telephone and computer operators, shipping personnel, and office assistants? He envisioned an exciting workplace with everyone working toward the same goals. He knew that creating that kind of environment would entail offering profit

continued

sharing or bonus plans that would allow employees to benefit from the organization's success. He had already designed a program whereby Lee and Susie would receive bonuses if the business grew and they stayed with the job. The possibilities were endless.

Think Critically

1. Write a classified help wanted ad for the part-time office assistant for Ship in a Bottle.
2. Design an incentive program for Ship in a Bottle employees.

Summary

Entrepreneurs must realize the importance of bringing together a team of employees who are well schooled in creating and/or selling the product or service. Developing a good team involves three management functions: staffing, directing, and controlling.

Staffing begins with writing job descriptions and creating an organization chart that clearly defines all positions, responsibilities, and reporting relationships. Finding and recruiting the right employees for various organizational roles is a difficult task. Sources include classified ads, employment agencies, college placement services, in-store advertising, referrals, and Internet recruiting.

Tailored employment applications allow business owners to gather specific information that might not be included on a resume. This information can be useful in deciding what to ask during the job interview. A written list of questions is essential for effective interviewing.

Once the team is in place, the owner must be a skillful director or manager. Directing is influencing people's behavior through motivation, communication, group dynamics, leadership, and discipline. Business owners usually fall into one of three management styles known as Theory X, Theory Y, and Theory Z.

Controlling is a management function that evaluates and corrects personnel performance. To excel in this function, owners must constantly consider employees' roles in the business. Proper employee evaluation procedures and the ability to listen are essential. Employers can motivate employees by letting them know they are integral parts of the business and allowing them to assume challenging responsibilities.

Entrepreneurs must be familiar with the laws that govern employment and protect both them and their employees from unfair labor practices. The Fair Labor Standards Act of 1938 established a minimum wage and required overtime pay for employees working more than 40 hours per week. The Civil Rights Act of 1964 prohibited discrimination based on sex, race, color, religion, or national origin. The Age Discrimination in Employment Act of 1967 prohibited personnel practices that discriminate against people aged 40 and older. The Occupational Safety and Health Act (OSHA) of 1970 deals with personal injuries and illnesses arising out of work situations. The Immigration Reform and Control Act of 1986 requires employers to check the identification of employees to ensure they are U.S. citizens. The Americans with Disabilities Act (ADA) prohibits employment discrimination on the basis of workers' disabilities.

The laws concerning employment are complex. It is helpful to be familiar with the kinds of questions that may not be asked on a job application or during a job interview.

A Case in POINT

"I think you'll find this store an enjoyable place to work, Susan. What we can't provide in wages we more than make up for with a comfortable environment. I try to be as flexible as possible. Let me introduce you to Sharon and Jim. They'll be showing you the ropes."

Susan was happy to have found a nice store to work in that was not far from her home. Roger, the owner, seemed friendly and sincere.

Sharon and Jim were cordial but somewhat reserved. They taught her the cash register procedures and the inventory control system. After two weeks Susan felt comfortable with her assignments, but she still felt like an outsider with Sharon and Jim. She learned that although they liked their work, they were fearful of Roger's moods. Some days he was easygoing; other days he was temperamental and impulsive.

Susan's first encounter with Roger's mood swings occurred when she was at the cash register writing a ticket for a customer refund. "Who told you to write the ticket that way?" Roger demanded.

"Jim did," Susan answered.

"Well, it's all wrong. Doesn't he know anything? I'll go talk to him. Meanwhile, please pick up that paper on the floor. This place looks like a pigsty." Roger took the refund ticket, went to Jim, and reprimanded him in front of a customer.

After this incident, Jim and Sharon were more open with Susan. They complained about their boss's erratic behavior, and Jim vented his frustrations. "I won't be treated like this. The next time he's in one of his moods, I'm staying out of his way. I'll say I'm sick and leave early."

It wasn't long before Roger lost his temper again and fired Jim. His replacement lasted less than two weeks. Sharon and Susan started looking for new jobs because they never knew when their turn might come. Susan didn't want to leave, but working for such an unpredictable person was causing her great anxiety—both on the job and off.

Think Critically

1. Which management style is Roger exhibiting during his bad moods?
2. What effect is Roger's inconsistency having on the business's productivity and payroll?
3. What can Susan do about her situation?

Vocabulary Builder

Write a brief definition of each word or phrase.

1. chain of command
2. controlling
3. directing
4. hygiene factor
5. line and staff organization
6. line organization
7. motivator
8. staffing
9. Theory X manager
10. Theory Y manager
11. Theory Z manager

Review the Concepts

12. What are the three management functions?
13. How do entrepreneurs determine how much money to allocate to payroll expenses for new businesses?
14. What is the purpose of an organization chart?
15. How do line organizations and line and staff organizations differ?
16. What do the connecting lines on an organization chart represent?
17. What effect might capital limitations have on the recruiting process?
18. What are five methods of finding potential employees?
19. In what ways can a small business owner interest potential employees?
20. Why are inadequate interviewing and employee selection methods expensive for small business owners?
21. How do Theory X, Theory Y, and Theory Z managers differ?
22. What are the two kinds of job satisfaction factors and what are their effects?
23. What are the characteristics of an effective performance evaluation?
24. With which labor laws should small business owners be familiar?

Critical Thinking

25. What can happen in a business that does not have an organization chart?
26. Name some advantages and disadvantages of working for a small business.
27. Have you ever worked for a Theory X manager? A Theory Y manager? Relate your experiences to the class.
28. What aspects of a job do you consider motivators? Hygiene factors? Does your list differ from Herzberg's?
29. Do you think minimum wage laws can raise the cost of living? Why or why not? Could they affect job availability for certain groups, such as teenagers?

Project

Build Your Business Plan

In your business plan notebook, develop a human resources plan for your hypothetical business. Address the following six tasks. Determine how many employees you will hire. Create an organization chart. Write a job description for each position, including areas of responsibility. Decide how much you will pay your employees. Decide how you will find and recruit your employees. Describe your intended management style.

Chapter 14

Build a Financial Plan

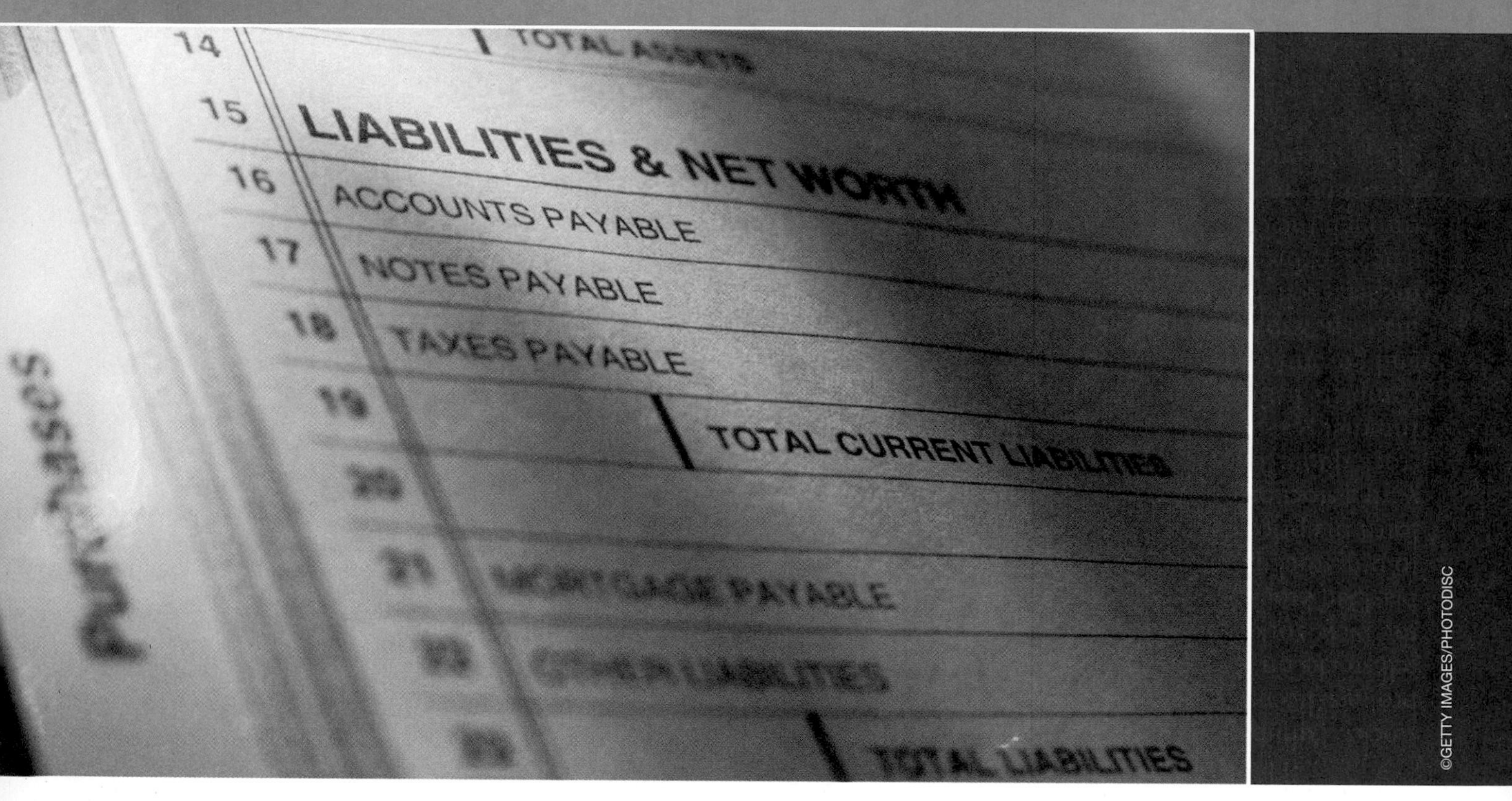

©GETTY IMAGES/PHOTODISC

Objectives

14-1 Explain how entrepreneurs use their personal assets to start a business.

14-2 Discuss the sources of debt capital available to entrepreneurs.

14-3 Discuss the various sources of equity capital.

14-4 Describe the overall process of putting together the initial capitalization for a new business.

PERSONAL CONTRIBUTIONS

When setting out on their own, entrepreneurs must realize that the primary financial contributions will come from their own pockets. Some entrepreneurial pursuits rely heavily on the individual's talents and knowledge, while others require a sizable financial investment. All ventures require that entrepreneurs look first at what they can contribute in terms of abilities and money before looking to others for help. Securing the initial financing for a new business is often the straw that breaks the camel's back. It does not have to be, as long as the entrepreneur is determined and the business plan is well researched.

The Personal Resume

Your new business will be successful only if you have the personal skills to assume the responsibility of owning and managing it. A **personal resume** describing those skills helps to demonstrate that your background is suitable for the business you wish to start and should be part of your business plan.

A well-written resume, such as the one in Figure 14-1, includes the following information:

1. your name, address, telephone number, and e-mail address
2. a statement declaring your business objective and why you are qualified to achieve that objective
3. a chronological list of your work experiences, with a brief description of responsibilities and accomplishments for each position
4. a description of all formal education and training programs you have undertaken
5. a list of personal activities that indicate character and ambition, including community work, significant hobbies (particularly if they relate to the business), and awards and distinctions
6. three references—people who can attest to your achievements

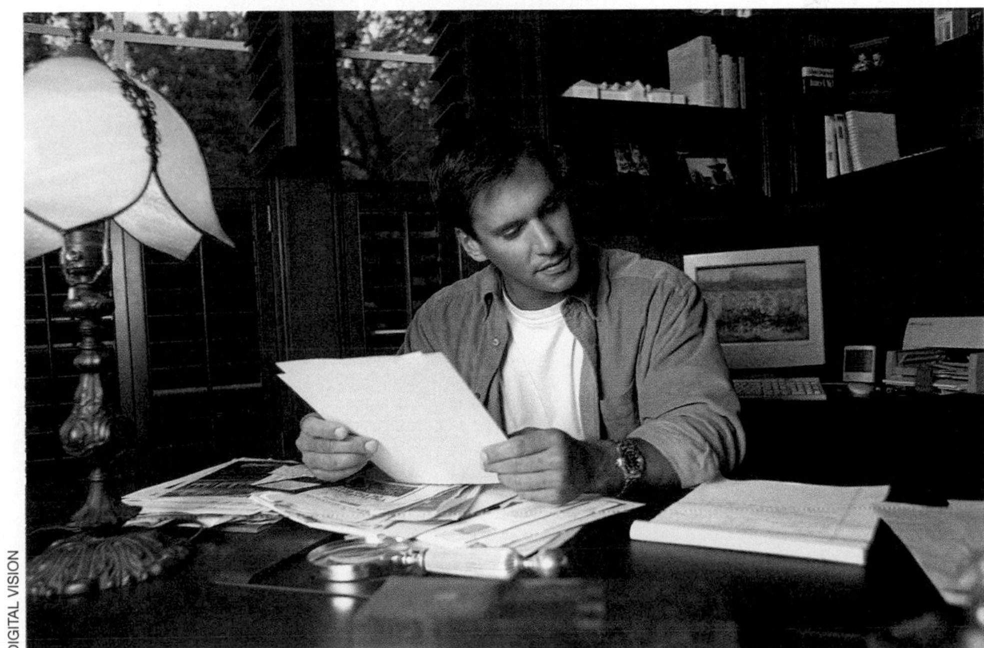
DIGITAL VISION

If partners, investors, or family members will play important roles in the business start-up, their resumes should be included as well. The goal is to present a clear and complete picture of all the skills and expertise available to ensure the success of the new business. If your resume does not show this, you will have to earn the appropriate qualifications. This might mean taking related educational courses or working in the industry in order to gain knowledge and experience.

FIGURE 14-1

Personal Resume

James L. Sullivan
111 Meredith Circle
Fort Walton Beach, FL 32548

Objective	To own and operate Precision Electronics Service Company and make use of management and vocational abilities.
Employment and Business Experience	Executive Airlines 1520 Locust Drive Atlanta, GA 33604 1983 – present Responsibilities: Supervised 10-person maintenance crew for charter aircraft carriers. Named 1990 Employee of the Year.
	Bureau of Land Management 907 Buena Vista Road Boise, ID 68745 1981 – 1983 Responsibilities: Repaired and installed radios. Supervised two employees.
Education	Marietta College Marietta, OH BA in Business Administration, 1981 GPA 3.2/4.0
	Vocational Technical Institute Twin Falls, ID Television Radio Repair Course, 1976
Community Activities	Fulton County Chamber of Commerce, Membership Committee South Metro YMCA Board of Directors Kiwanis Club, Treasurer
Hobbies	Ham radio operator, golf, model train collector
References	Mr. Milton Causey, Vice President Executive Airlines 1520 Locust Drive Atlanta, GA 33604 (404) 555-3440
	Ms. Phyllis Charles, Personnel Manager Executive Airlines 1520 Locust Drive Atlanta, GA 33604 (404) 555-3440
	Dr. William H. Hershey, Dean School of Business Administration Marietta College Marietta, OH 38973 (213) 555-6756

Resume Do's and Don'ts A proper resume demonstrates your:

- self-image
- communication skills
- ability to achieve results
- direction and focus toward goals
- personal character, as evidenced by community activities, personal interests, and hobbies

You should avoid the following:

- excessive length (one page is sufficient in many cases)
- poor organization
- irrelevancies (include only significant information that gives evidence of your abilities)
- poor grammar, misspellings, typographical errors
- photos, fancy paper stock, or borders

References A proper resume offers as references people who can verify that what is represented is accurate. List two or three names with addresses and phone numbers, or state at the end of the resume that references are available upon request. It is customary to ask permission beforehand from people you would like to use as references.

It is important that your references be people who have witnessed the accomplishments listed on your resume. They should not be simply a list of friends or relatives. A potential lendor or investor expects to discuss with the references your career achievements, not whether you are pleasant to be around.

FUN FACTS

It has been reported that almost 25 percent of resumes exaggerate the education of the individual. In an increasingly competitive job market, there is greater pressure to pad credentials in order to get the attention of potential employers. Almost 50 percent of those who review resumes believe there is an increase in padding.

Ethics for ENTREPRENEURS

Bob High was preparing a resume to include with his business plan for a new restaurant. He was going to present the plan to his bank for consideration for a line of credit. Bob was on familiar terms with the bank personnel, who were aware of his successful career as a master chef. His career had been one of steady growth as he moved up the ladder of fine institutions. It was now time to venture out and open his own restaurant.

As he reviewed his resume, Bob was concerned that the bank might consider his lack of business experience a problem. He had entered the restaurant business after college, where he had been an English major. Since then he had enrolled in and successfully completed a number of cooking and restaurant programs, but he had not received any direct business training. Bob wondered if he should list business administration as his college major instead of English. After all, it was highly doubtful that the bank would request his college transcript.

Think Critically

1. What risk is Bob taking by changing his resume?
2. What other action might he take to satisfy the bank regarding his lack of business experience?

The higher the authority, the more credible the reference is. Previous supervisors or colleagues who have worked with you on career or community efforts make good references. Former instructors do too, since they have witnessed your educational achievements.

Net Worth

To determine your financial capabilities, use the method of calculation shown in the example in Table 14-1.

The format used to determine a person's financial worth is the same as that used in a business balance sheet, which will be discussed in Chapter 15. It lists the person's assets (owned property) on one side and liabilities (debts owed) on the other. The difference between the assets and the liabilities is the **personal net worth.**

TABLE 14-1 NET WORTH CALCULATION

ASSETS		LIABILITIES	
Cash on hand and in bank	$18,000	Notes payable to bank (auto)	$2,000
Government securities	6,000	Notes payable to others	0
Stocks and/or bonds	14,000	Accounts and bills due:	
Accounts and notes receivable	0	Credit cards	2,000
Real estate: lot	$10,000	Real estate mortgage (lot)	3,000
Automobile	8,000	Other debts	
Cash surrender value, life insurance	5,000	College loan	3,000
Other assets			
Personal belongings	16,000		
Certificate of deposit	6,000		
Total assets	**$83,000**	**Total liabilities**	**$10,000**

NET WORTH	
Total assets	$83,000
Total liabilities	$10,000
Net worth (total assets less total liabilities)	$73,000

Available Cash

Entrepreneurs must identify which of their assets can be turned into cash for financing the business and which assets can be used as collateral for borrowing purposes. The items listed in the assets column in Table 14-1 can help you identify which of your assets can be used in one of these ways.

Cash on Hand Cash on hand includes all money held in checking and savings accounts that is readily available upon request. One of the advantages of using personal savings to start a business is that the entrepreneur keeps more of the business's profits.

Entrepreneurs frequently seek financial assistance from family members. Any money offered by a family member should be included. If the money is an outright gift, it should be listed as cash on hand. If it is in the form of a loan, after the relative (or friend) reviews the business plan thoroughly and fully understands the risks, a personal note should be drawn up promising repayment after the business is firmly on its feet. The repayment note should appear on the personal net worth statement as notes payable to others. Entrepreneurs must be aware that they are required by the federal government to pay interest on such loans if they are to be considered legally enforceable.

Government Securities Savings bonds and treasury notes are two types of **government securities**. You may invest in the U.S. government by allowing it to use your money in exchange for repayment, including interest, at a later date. **Interest** is the payment made to lenders for the use of their money. Government securities can be redeemed for cash at federally insured financial institutions.

Stocks The certificates representing ownership in a corporation are called stocks. Publicly traded stocks are normally bought and sold through stockbrokers, licensed agents who buy and sell stocks on stock exchanges such as the New York Stock Exchange or the NasDaq Stock Exchange. If you wish to buy stock in a corporation, you can learn the price per share by checking with a stockbroker or clicking on the stock quote icon on most major Internet search sites. There is also a complete listing of stocks, bonds, and government securities in most major newspapers or financial news media, such as the *Wall Street Journal*. The stockbroker places a buy order through the exchange to find a seller. Discount trading brokerage firms offer direct trading through their web sites at reduced trading commission fees. Buyers of publicly listed stocks are always available, although the selling price is never guaranteed until the transaction is actually made. To sell stock, thereby converting it to cash, individuals place a sell order with their stockbroker. The completion of the sale normally takes only a few days, and the seller receives his or her cash at that time.

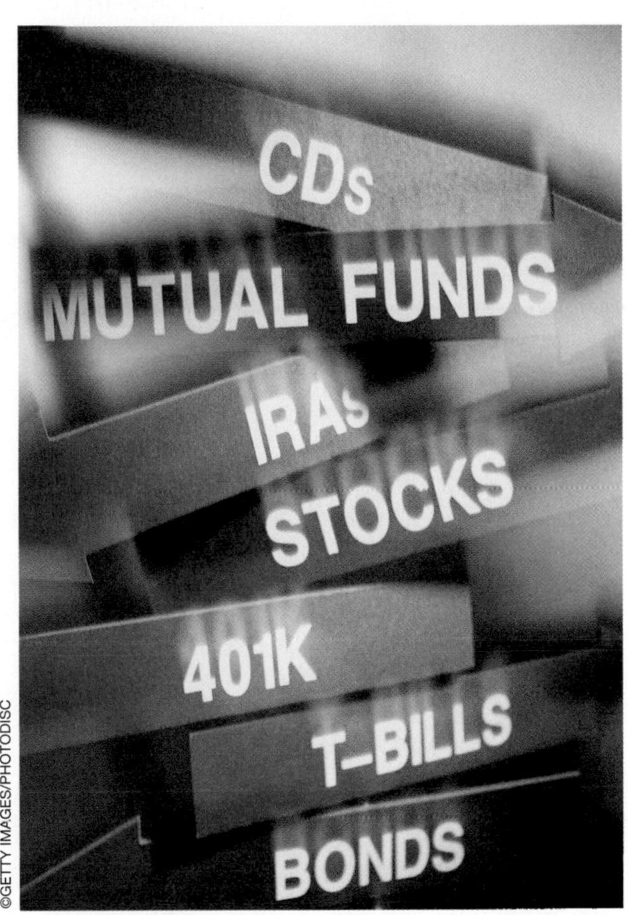

Bonds Like government securities, **bonds** are contracts of indebtedness issued by corporations or governmental units that promise payment of the principal plus interest at a specified date, or **maturity date**. An individual holding a bond can redeem it at any time for cash, although it loses some of its original value if it is exchanged before the maturity date.

Profit Sharing and Pension Plans Many individuals have accumulated investments in profit sharing and pension plans with current or former employers. Often these investment plans are held by the company until the individual leaves the company. Entrepreneurs who have worked for such companies and plan to resign and pursue a business start-up can consider these investment plans as money available to start a business. They should be aware, however, that money withdrawn before a specified date or age may be subject to taxes and/or penalties.

Insurance Policies Another source that can be considered available funds is the cash value of a life insurance policy. **Whole life insurance** policies serve as investments for their owners. Over a period of time, premium payments accumulate and the policy acquires a cash value because the insurance company uses a certain portion of the premium payments to make investments. As these investments grow, the cash value of the policy grows as well. Whole life policies allow the owner either to redeem the cash value at any time or to borrow against the policy at a very attractive interest rate. The policyholder must be aware, however, that any money taken out or borrowed against the policy will decrease the amount of money distributed at the time of death.

Assets Not Considered Available Cash Automobiles are not usually considered sources of available cash because they are needed for transportation. Other assets may include personal belongings, such as furniture and jewelry, but these are also not usually counted as available assets. Homes are not considered readily available cash assets because they are used as residences and cannot be sold on short notice.

©GETTY IMAGES/PHOTODISC

DEBT CAPITAL

The primary financial contribution for a new business comes from the entrepreneur's personal savings and investments. You must take a careful look at your financial resources and how much of those resources you are willing to contribute to the business venture. Although it is important to show confidence in an idea by investing personal resources, it would be foolish to risk *all* your financial assets.

After you have identified all possible sources of personal wealth, it may be clear that your business plan will require more investment capital than you have available. You may find it necessary to turn to outside sources for financial help in the form of loans, also called **debt capital**.

It is imperative that you set aside enough money to provide for personal emergencies. You should also keep in reserve enough to cover several months' living expenses in case the business venture does not work out as planned. Determining the amount of money necessary to open a business will be discussed more thoroughly in Chapter 15.

Friends and Relatives

Establishing trust is usually a requirement for borrowing money. Who trusts the entrepreneur more than friends and relatives? In many cases it is encouragement from these people that prompts the idea to start the business in the first place.

Most people use family money, if it is available, during the start-up phase of a new business. Friends and family may be willing to lend more money than other sources would, and they often allow more time for repayment. In addition, they probably do not scrutinize the business plan as closely as other lenders would, and they are usually more understanding during times of hardship.

If you accept an offer of a loan from friends or family, a formal agreement should be signed by all parties stating the duration and the interest rate to be paid. If there is no signed personal note, the Internal Revenue Service will not recognize it as a debt and you will not be able to deduct interest payments as a business expense. A signed agreement will also assure the lender of repayment as promised. If payment must be delayed in the future, it is fairly easy to draw up a new agreement.

A word of caution regarding borrowing money from friends or family: They may feel that since you used their money, you should also take their advice. A good rule to follow is not to ask for help from family or friends, but if it is offered, do not turn it down.

Borrowing Against Collateral

Some assets that are not easily converted into cash can be used as collateral against which to borrow. This is true if the lender believes that the assets can be converted to cash at a future date in the event the borrower defaults on the loan.

Home Equity The equity in one's home or other real estate is an excellent source of collateral because the real estate market is considered reasonably stable. **Home equity** is the difference between the money owed (mortgage) on a home and its appraised value. For instance, the equity of a home with an appraised value of $150,000 and an outstanding mortgage loan of $100,000 is $50,000. A lending institution might lend money against a certain portion of this equity by holding the house as collateral. In the event the borrower cannot pay back the loan, the lender has the right to force the sale of the house to recapture the money owed. To make sure the loan is well secured, or collateralized, the lender will usually loan only up to 80 percent of the equity in a home to protect itself in case the real estate market experiences a slump. In the example above, the borrower could borrow up to $40,000—or 80 percent of the home equity of $50,000—if he or she were willing to place the home as collateral against a loan that would finance the new business. Since a home is often considered a precious investment, a decision to borrow against it should be made only after very careful deliberation.

©GETTY IMAGES/PHOTODISC

Small Business Technology

More and more businesses are paying their bills via electronic fund transfer. The debtor sends payments to the vendor over the Internet, and these payments are automatically subtracted from the business checking account. Paying this way speeds up transactions and improves the business's cash flow. Payers can also wait until the last possible day to pay and still receive early payment discounts. Many small businesses use automatic deductions to pay bank notes. The bank debits the business account for monthly installment payments. The entrepreneur saves time preparing and mailing the payment and is less likely to miss the due date.

Investments Instead of selling their investments and using the cash to finance the start-up, many entrepreneurs decide to use their investments as collateral. This can be a good idea particularly if the investments are expected to grow at a rate equal to, or higher than, the interest cost of borrowing against them. Just as in the case of home equity, the lender will loan only a certain portion of the market value of the investment to protect against a downward turn of the market. For example, stock you own might have a collateral value of 70 percent of its current market value. You could place $10,000 of that stock with a lender as collateral and receive a $7,000 loan. The stock remains in your name but is in the lender's possession until the loan is paid.

Cash can be used for collateral when it is placed in a **certificate of deposit** with a bank. A certificate of deposit, or CD, is money that is deposited for a specified period of time (six months, one year, or longer) and cannot be withdrawn without penalty. The interest rate is higher than on a standard savings account, and the longer the duration of the CD, the higher the interest rate. When a CD is used as collateral, the bank keeps control over it until the debt is paid. It is important to note that during the time stocks and/or CDs are held by a lender, the interest payments on the CDs and dividends on the stocks continue to be paid to the borrower.

Commercial Banks

Most entrepreneurs think of commercial banks when it comes to borrowing funds. They have a bank they deal with on a regular basis and are inclined to begin their quest for funds there. However, you may find that your bank is not able or willing to meet your business needs. Banks are very aware of the risks of loaning money to a new business start-up—remember, the majority do not survive past five years. Since they have a responsibility to their shareholders, banks normally do not offer start-up loans unless there is suitable cash or stock collateral available from the borrower. You should investigate and shop around for banks to help, but do not be surprised if you are not welcomed with open arms.

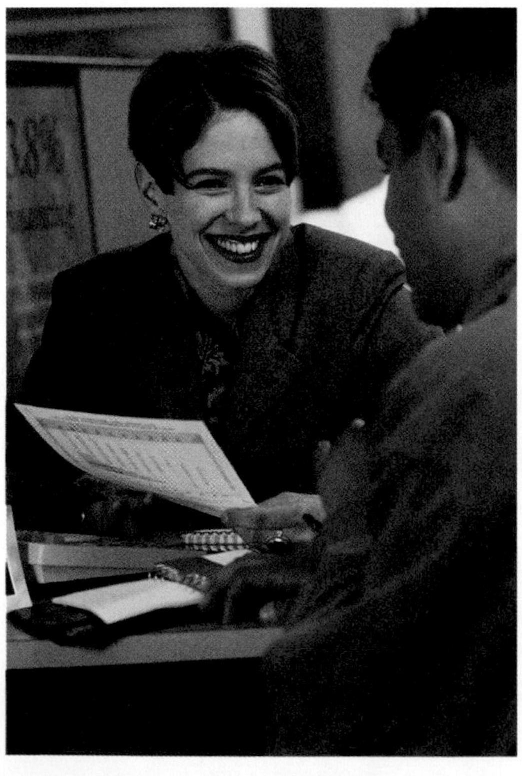

©GETTY IMAGES/PHOTODISC

Before approaching a bank for funds, you should understand the various types of financing available. The following seven types of loans are the most common:

1. **Traditional Loans** This type of loan is normally short-term (less than one year's duration) and often unsecured (no collateral required). Traditional loans may not be available to new business owners.
2. **Line of Credit** There are two types of line-of-credit financing. The **regular line of credit** allows business owners access to a preapproved, prearranged amount of money for a specific period of time, usually one year. The **revolving line of credit** also allows business owners access to a certain amount of money, but it provides an option for renewal at the end of the original term.

The interest rate for a line of credit is usually 1.5 to 3 percent above the **prime rate of interest**. The prime rate is the publicly stated rate that major commercial banks charge their most creditworthy business customers for short-term loans. In most cases interest is charged only on the amount drawn, but the bank may charge a fee (1.5 to 2 percent of the total line) for reserving the funds.

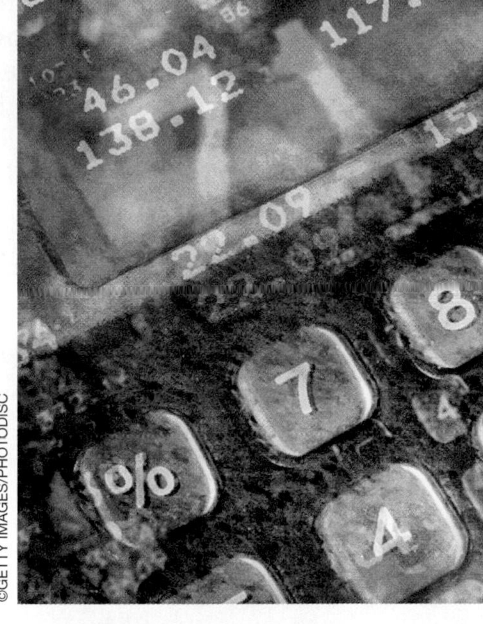

©GETTY IMAGES/PHOTODISC

A business owner who needs extra cash several times during the year may be able to save time and money by obtaining a line of credit. Once a line of credit is approved, loans of this amount are automatic. No additional paperwork or approvals are required up to the preapproved amount. A line of credit helps business owners through the highs and lows that can occur over the course of a year. If a retail business has a dip in sales in October, it may not have the money to stock up on inventory for the busier Christmas season. A line of credit can provide the funds to increase inventory when sales are slow.

3. **Installment Loans** Entrepreneurs often use installment loans to finance equipment. The term of the loan is based on the expected life of the asset purchased. If you purchase an expensive piece of equipment, such as a computer system, it is likely that your business will not generate enough profit to pay for it in one year. If the loan is spread out over several years, however, the computer will add enough value to the business to justify its expense.

   The interest rate on installment loans is based on the bank's cost of funds and is usually 2 to 4 percent higher than the prime rate of interest. Installment loans for business equipment are handled in the same manner as installment loans for personal assets. They are often obtained through the private lending division of the bank rather than the commercial lending division. It is common for the bank to request that the equipment serve as collateral for the loan.

4. **Mortgage Loans** Mortgage loans are given to businesses that have property to serve as collateral for the loan. Two types of mortgage loans are usually available to entrepreneurs. The first is a loan on new property, such as a building that houses the business. For this type of loan, the building becomes collateral. The maximum amount of the loan is determined by the value of the property. Many commercial banks will approve a loan of up to 90 percent of the appraised value of the building.

   The second type of mortgage uses property that is already owned and listed on the personal financial statement, such as the owner's residence, as collateral. This is known as an **equity loan**. The maximum amount for this type of loan is determined by the amount of equity the owner has in the secured property—that is, the appraised value of the property less the existing debt. As with home equity loans, many banks will approve a loan up to 80 percent of the equity amount.

   Acquiring a mortgage loan may require payment of closing costs, including loan origination fees, appraisal fees, and other fees. Interest rates for these loans vary. Some are based on the prime lending rate, others on the treasury bond interest rate.

5. **Accounts Receivable Financing** This type of loan is available to accounts receivable businesses, which permit their customers to charge merchandise or services. If an entrepreneur has accounts receivables worth $10,000—in other words, customers owe the business $10,000—then the loan is based on that amount. Banks will loan a business up to 85 percent of the total face value of its accounts receivable if the business's debtors are deemed good credit customers. As the receivables come in, payments are forwarded to the bank. The interest rate for this type of financing is often higher than that for other types of loans.
6. **Inventory Financing** If you choose this type of financing, the inventory that is held by your business is used as collateral for the loan. Banks will probably require that the value of the inventory be at least double the amount of the loan. This type of loan is available only when you have paid for the inventory. Banks are sometimes reluctant to use inventory as collateral because if the entrepreneur defaults and they end up in possession of the inventory, they often do not have a way of reselling it.
7. **Sales Contracts** Some entrepreneurs own businesses that sell products or services on a contractual basis. For example, Michael Jacob owns a small furniture manufacturing plant in North Carolina. He recently obtained a contract with a large chain of retail furniture stores. He will supply them with 8,000 entertainment centers over a period of three years. Michael's company has never had such a large order, and he does not have enough equipment or employees to produce the merchandise. To meet his contractual obligation, he must buy four new machines and add six new employees. He does not have enough money on hand to cover these costs. The contract is with a well-known business, so he can take the contract to the bank and request a loan based on the value of the contracted sales. Most banks are receptive to this type of request as long as the purchaser has a sound business reputation.

Trade Credit

A company that supplies merchandise to a business can provide a source of working capital known as **trade credit** to that business. Vendors provide trade credit as a way of enticing sales and meeting competition. Typically trade credit gives the business 30 to 90 days to pay for merchandise. Effective use of trade credit can be a valuable cash flow tool. Purchasing goals and plans will be discussed in Chapter 16.

Another form of trade credit is **factoring.** In many industries there are companies that, in effect, buy an entrepreneur's accounts receivable at a discounted amount, then collect the amount due from the purchaser. For example, if ABC Company is owed $5,000 by Smith Brothers, the factor will pay ABC $4,500 for that receivable and assume the liability for the $5,000 balance due.

Equipment Vendor Loans

Equipment vendors often allow entrepreneurs to lease equipment or buy it on credit. The vendor usually requires a down payment of 25 to 50 percent of the cost of the equipment. The balance is paid in installments over a specified period, thereby making it possible for businesses to use profits from the use of the equipment to cover their costs. The equipment that is being financed is the collateral for the loan. In the event of default the equipment vendor takes back the equipment. Usually equipment vendors offer a larger line of credit on the equipment they sell than banks do because they can resell the equipment if they are forced to take back ownership because of a loan default.

A large part of the cost of starting a new business is often the purchase of equipment. When vendors allow entrepreneurs to lease or buy on credit, they provide a reduction in immediate expenditures and, therefore, an increase in working capital.

FUN FACTS

Did you know that such well-known companies as Nike, Apple, FedEx, AOL, Ben & Jerry's Ice Cream, Intel, and Compaq received initial financing support from a federal agency such as the SBA?

Credit Cards

Almost everyone is bombarded with invitations to apply for credit cards. Many credit card companies charge excessive interest charges and should be avoided. However, there are companies that offer more competitive rates—although usually higher than direct bank-loan rates—and these cards may be considered for short-term credit for business purposes. Some companies offer cash advances to card holders, although generally at higher rates than for direct purchases.

If a new business is in need of short-term credit, there is nothing wrong with using a credit card as long as the finance charge is fair and the amount charged is not part of the long-term capitalization plan of the business. Often these cards can be used to purchase inventory before credit is arranged between the entrepreneur and the vendor. The entrepreneur can use a personal credit card or, better yet, apply for a bank credit card in the name of the business.

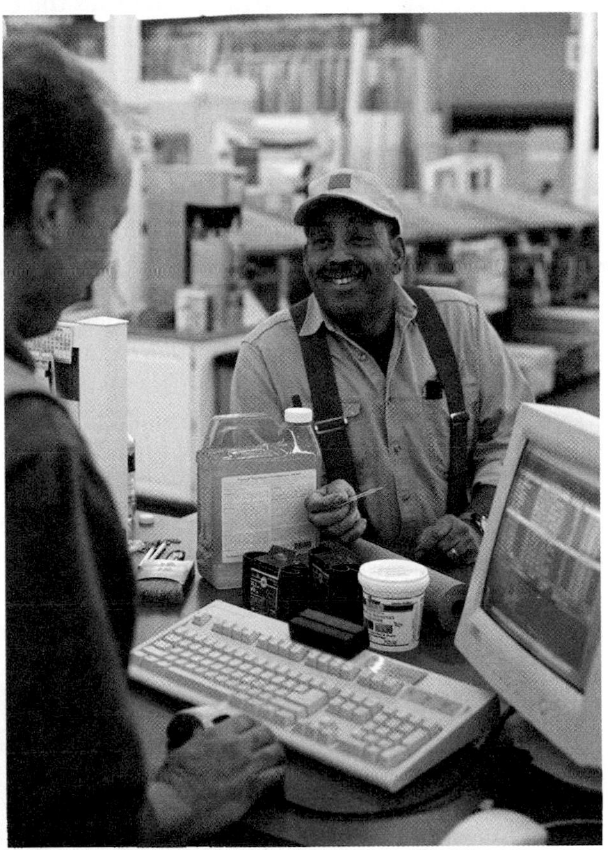

State and Local Business Development Funds

Most states and many communities have funds available for business start-ups. An example of this type of funding at the state level is the Colorado First Customized Training Program. This program, which began with the passage of a law in 1984, provides money to new businesses for employee training. An example at the local level is the Allentown Economic Development Commission in Allentown, PA, which provides loan assistance to qualified small businesses.

The purpose of these assistance programs is to help create businesses that will bring jobs to an area and thus increase the community and state tax base. They are not handouts, but they do offer very appealing low-interest loans with attractive payback terms. Not all businesses qualify for these programs—manufacturing and technology-based companies are most favored.

Small Business Administration

As you have learned, the Small Business Administration is a federal agency established in 1953 to aid the development of small businesses. One of its primary purposes is to provide financial assistance to small business owners.

The SBA's loan guarantee program is for small business owners who are unable to obtain financing through a bank or other private lending source. The maximum amount of the loan guarantee is 90 percent, and the maximum amount that can be borrowed is $750,000. If a loan request is approved, the SBA guarantees the lender that in the event the borrower cannot repay the obligation, the SBA will use funds appropriated by Congress to pay the guaranteed portion of the loan. SBA "contact banks" include most commercial banks. The same bank that denies the entrepreneur a loan may be quite helpful in assisting the same entrepreneur to apply for an SBA guarantee, as it relieves the bank of much of the loan risk.

The SBA also has a smaller program designed to assist small businesses in their operations. The 7(m) Micro Loan program provides short-term loans of up to $35,000. These loans are designed to provide existing small businesses with working capital for purposes such as inventory, supplies, or other operational expenses.

Very few groups of business owners qualify for direct loans from the SBA. They include businesses that employ the handicapped, promote energy conservation, or are being started in communities of great need.

It should be noted that the government is not in the business of giving handouts to small businesses. SBA programs are designed to assist in financing, not to provide free money. There is a very limited budget set aside in the Small Business Innovation Research (SBIR) program to provide grants to small businesses for innovative research and development in the areas of public assistance and government contracts. Applications and information about the program are available at local SBA offices or through the SBA Internet website.

Information regarding SBA loans is easily obtained at participating banks, Small Business Development Centers at local colleges or chambers of commerce, or by visiting a regional Small Business Administration office.

EQUITY CAPITAL

Equity capital is the money invested in a business by the owner or owners. This might include the owner's personal savings or investment by others, such as private investors, venture capitalists, stockholders, investment bankers, or partners.

Entrepreneurs who need additional funds and wish to finance their business entirely through equity capital need investors. If they want people to invest in their business, they may be required to provide a substantial portion of the needed capital themselves. Many potential investors consider the amount of money you are willing to invest an indicator of how dedicated you are to the new venture. However, if the business is one that involves a truly innovative idea, someone may be willing to invest the entire amount needed.

Private Investors

Entrepreneurs may be able to obtain financial assistance from people who are willing to take a gamble and invest in a sound business plan. These **private investors** often have a personal association with the entrepreneur or learn of the opportunity through contacts in the local community. Since they are generally not professional investors, most have a conservative investment philosophy and may not be willing to finance businesses that involve high risk. A personal banker, lawyer, or accountant may be able to provide a referral to such a source.

Taking private investors can be accomplished through the sale of stock. As discussed in Chapter 4, selling stock in your company means giving up a portion of the ownership in exchange for needed funds. It can be done when you start the business or after it is established, perhaps to expand the business operation. Selling stock this way is not the same as public offerings through a major stock exchange, which is how large businesses trade and sell stock.

Figure 14-2 is an example of a cover sheet for a private stock offering to investors. The cover sheet is usually supported by a formal business plan that further explains the intent and goals of the business attempting to raise capital.

FIGURE 14-2

Cover Sheet of a Private Stock Offering

Number ____________ Offeree ____________

PRIVATE PLACEMENT MEMORANDUM

Unique Expectations, Inc.
2196 Cheshire Bridge Road
Atlanta, GA 30303

THESE ARE SPECULATIVE SECURITIES. SEE "RISK FACTORS." THE SECURITIES ARE SUBJECT TO CERTAIN RESTRICTIONS ON TRANSFER. THERE IS NO MARKET FOR THEM AND NO MARKET LIKELY TO DEVELOP. CONSEQUENTLY, THEY WILL NOT BE READILY TRANSFERABLE.

	Price to Purchaser 1	Proceeds to Corporation 2
Per share	$50	$50
Total	$2,000,000	$2,000,000

THE OFFERING

The Company hereby offers to sell **40,000** of its authorized Common Stock having a par value of $1 per share. Upon completion of this offering, there will be **75,000** of such shares outstanding.

The offering price is **$50.00** per share, with minimum investment of **$50,000.00** per investor. If any investor desires to purchase more than **1,000** shares, he/she may do so, provided the additional investment is in increments of **$5,000.00.**

The full amount of each subscription shall be due and payable upon the Company's acceptance of a stock subscription agreement signed by the investor.

The Company believes that it should not attempt to conduct the business described herein until such time as it shall have received a minimum of **$500,000.00** in payment for shares of Common Stock offered hereby. Therefore, until **$500,000.00** has been received, all monies paid to the Company for the offered shares will be deposited in a special escrow account at Capital City National Bank for the benefit of the subscribers and will be held in that account until the required minimum amount has been raised, and if less than **$500,000.00** is raised, the escrowed funds will be refunded to the subscribers without interest.

The Global ENTREPRENEUR

In Europe, businesses receive financial support from the European Investment Bank (EIB), which serves as a financing institution for the member countries of the European Union. Its goal is to foster business development and create closer ties among EU nations through economic growth. In 2003, the EIB was instrumental in providing over 35 billion euros in financing to European businesses.

Think Critically

1. Find out more about the European Investment Bank and compare it to what you have learned about the Small Business Administration.
2. Do you believe that trade agreements reducing trade barriers among members of the European Union have added to the need for the EIB? Why?

Venture Capitalists

Financial assistance from **venture capitalists** should generally be considered only as a last resort. Venture capitalists are professional investors who seek larger, high-risk business investment opportunities. They rarely invest in small start-ups, preferring established businesses and/or businesses that have the potential for an extremely high return on investment.

Venture capitalists often insist on being involved in the management of the business. They usually require agreements that allow them to take full control of the business if it is not meeting their expectations. Profit becomes the highest priority, often overriding the entrepreneur's ideas about product quality or how the business should be run. Accepting venture capital is often a matter of accepting that it is better to own a significantly reduced portion of the business than no business at all.

Investment Banks

Investment banks specialize in bringing together entrepreneurs who need funds and individuals or groups that have money to invest. The latter include, for example, insurance companies and pension fund administrators. Most major metropolitan areas have investment banks. Entrepreneurs in other areas may not have access to this funding source.

Partnerships

Entrepreneurs may seek a partner or partners for one of two reasons: to increase the business's capital or to acquire expertise in areas unfamiliar to them. The percentage of ownership is usually based on the percentage of the total capital each partner invests. A partnership agreement should be drawn up that clearly shows the amount invested by each partner. Many entrepreneurs prefer to form a corporation and share the stock in the same proportions as in the intended partnership.

CREATE A FINANCIAL PACKAGE

It is not uncommon for the finished business plan to require more money to implement it than is available. Sometimes this is—or should be—the inhibitor that stops or delays a business start-up. It can also be a challenge to the entrepreneur's determination, creativity, and confidence.

In most cases, initial capitalization of a start-up business comes from a number of sources discussed in this chapter, starting with the entrepreneur's personal savings. An example is an entrepreneur who, after reviewing all sources of personal wealth, comes up with half the funds required. She may visit the bank for start-up capital but will likely be turned down unless she can offer ample collateral that can be easily converted to cash. She turns next to family and friends. If she is reluctant to make a direct request, her enthusiasm for the idea may generate an offer of a loan or investment money. Next, she explores the industry for assistance in the form of equipment loans and trade credit. She may consider using a personal or business credit card for a small portion of the money. Once most of the funds are in place, another trip to the bank, with a business plan that includes a strong personal resume and a complete market and financial analysis, might be in order. The same bank that would not give her a start-up loan may be willing to grant a short-term line of credit once it ascertains that she has put together her initial capitalization and will soon be making deposits on a regular basis.

As you consider sources of additional funds, keep in mind that the best source is the one that fulfills your business's particular needs at the lowest cost. Cost can mean either monetary loss or ownership reduction, which forces you to give up a portion of your interest in the business.

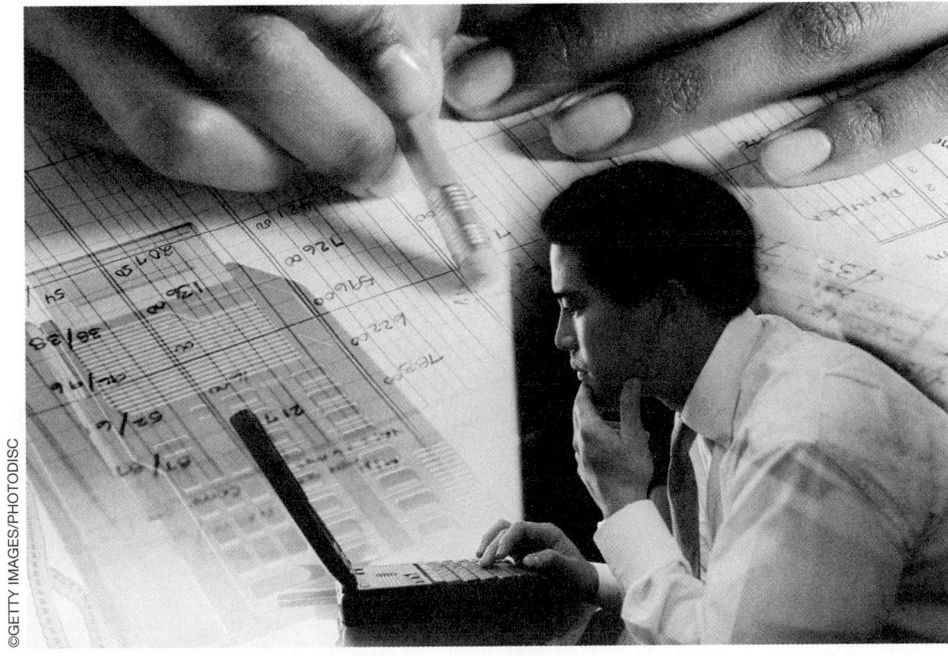

You must be knowledgeable about the various financial sources and how each could serve your business. Take the time to determine the true cost—in both money and ownership—of capital obtained from each source. Choose alternatives as well, since your first choice may not be available. For example, if you don't have enough capital to purchase inventory, you should probably try to make use of trade credit or seek a short-term loan from a bank. If you need equipment, you might consider equipment vendors or banks.

Financing a business start-up carries undeniable risks. You must be willing to show confidence in your idea by taking the largest risks and hoping others will follow your lead.

Ship in a BOTTLE

Financial Considerations

The initial cost of researching his business idea had not been a problem for Fred. He had paid for the initial samples, about $500, out of his savings. He had covered the cost of the first trade show and basic supplies the same way. However, when the idea had grown to the point of designing brochures, creating a web site, and stocking inventory, Fred realized he would need to create a financial plan.

His initial estimates of his expenses were:

inventory	$4,500
brochure	2,000
web site design and setup	1,800
computer upgrade	1,100
immediate trade show expense	2,300
supplies	450
miscellaneous	500
Total	$12,650

These figures were only a start-up projection. Fred knew he would have to do a full 12-month projection as well, but that could wait until after he had a better feel for the new enterprise. His initial plan was to finance the first three months' activity himself and then look further down the road and decide if 12-month and long-term capitalization plans were needed, based on the initial trial.

Fred went to work on phase one. He had already spent over $2,000 of his personal savings at this point, which left only $3,000 in his savings account. He completed a personal net worth statement that showed some clear deficits. In addition to the $3,000 he had a stock and bond portfolio of $5,000. He had a whole life insurance policy, but it was only two years old and had no loan value yet. Outside of these tangible listings there was nothing else he could use in the business. He needed his car, and his personal belongings were not items he could sell. The small amount of equity in his home was out of bounds, as he did not believe in putting up everything he owned to pursue his dream. He and Jeanie had two personal credit cards, each with $5,000 credit available. He decided to take his business plan to Bill Barron at First National Bank for advice.

Fred and Bill had known each other for a number of years, and Fred was confident that Bill would give him solid direction. After reviewing the business plan, Bill suggested a two-tier financing plan.

"This idea has great potential, Fred, but as you admitted, it's too early to go full speed. I'd advise you to stay the course and see where you stand in another three months. You have the $3,000 in savings and $5,000 in stock. You can sell the stock, or the bank can loan you $4,000 against it as collateral. I think you can find the rest of the $12,650 in trade credit with Johann on inventory purchases, or, if necessary, use one of your credit cards for a short-term loan. If the business keeps developing over the next three months, you might have enough history to qualify for at least a line of credit with our bank. Once we see that the business can support short-term

continued

credit, the door will be open to discuss a longer-term financing plan to build this business into a full-function import business with unlimited potential."

Leaving the bank, Fred felt good. He called Johann and requested 90-day payment terms on the $1,600 merchandise order. Johann agreed on the condition that Fred pay $1,000 in advance. Having reduced his $12,650, three-month need to $9,150, Fred could now move ahead with his plan.

Think Critically

1. Are there other ways that Fred could have solved his financial dilemma?
2. Why is the banker willing to work with Fred in three months, but not now?
3. If you were Fred, would you sell your stock and bonds, or borrow against their value?

Summary

When putting together a business plan, entrepreneurs must look first at what they can personally contribute to the endeavor. Calculating personal net worth is part of this process. Sources of personal contributions include cash on hand, government securities, stocks and bonds, profit sharing and pension plans, and insurance policies.

If it is necessary to seek other financial sources, a personal resume should be included with the business plan. A personal resume gives an overview of the skills and leadership capabilities of the person who will manage and operate the business. A resume should be prepared for each person actively involved in the proposed new business.

Entrepreneurs must also provide evidence of financial capability. A personal net worth calculation shows what financial resources can be used for the business. It indicates the amount of readily available cash and any assets the entrepreneur owns that can be used as loan collateral.

If the entrepreneur does not have the needed financial resources, he or she must turn to borrowing money, called debt capital, or attracting investors, who supply equity capital. In either case a sound financial plan must be prepared that demonstrates the business's ability to pay back the debt or achieve sufficient profits to share with investors.

The entrepreneur has many financial sources to choose from. Debt capital is available from friends and relatives, commercial banks, supply vendors, equipment vendors, personal credit cards, state and/or local business development funds, and the SBA. Equity capital is available from personal savings, private investors, venture capitalists, partners, investment bankers, and sale of stocks, bonds, or government securities.

Matching financial sources to business needs is very important. The entrepreneur should remember that the best source of financing is the one that fulfills the business's needs at the lowest cost. It is not uncommon for the entrepreneur to use many different sources to arrive at the total capitalization needed for a new business start-up.

A Case in POINT

Too Soon to Expand

Eleanor War was so pleased with the success of her ladies' fashion boutique after one year that she began looking for a second location. She quickly found an opportunity in a neighboring community.

She thought it would be much easier to open and operate the second store than the first. She had learned a great deal in a year and had established good credit with all her suppliers. She saw no reason to go through all the financial planning she had done for the first store. She could order all the inventory on credit and would not have to pay for it for 30 to 60 days. By then she would have sold enough to pay for the first orders. She also knew that the fixture and equipment manufacturers would give her a note for most of her purchases since she had been paying on time for the first store's fixture and equipment note. She was so confident that she opened without a cash reserve for operating expenses.

It didn't work. Business started at a very slow pace. After the first month, Eleanor had sold barely enough to cover her operating expenses, let alone the initial inventory bills and monthly fixture note. At the end of 60 days she was in serious trouble. She was forced to stock the new store with inventory from her other store because she could not order from her suppliers until she paid for the initial inventory shipments. This, of course, hurt business at the original store. Eleanor had overestimated the success of the second store. She wondered what she should do.

Think Critically

1. What did Eleanor fail to do before opening her second store?
2. What should she do at this point?
3. What will happen if Eleanor fails to correct the situation immediately?

Vocabulary Builder

Write a brief definition of each word or phrase.

1. bonds
2. certificate of deposit
3. debt capital
4. equity capital
5. equity loan
6. factoring
7. government securities
8. home equity
9. interest
10. investment banks
11. maturity date
12. personal net worth
13. personal resume
14. prime rate of interest
15. private investor
16. regular line of credit
17. revolving line of credit
18. trade credit
19. venture capitalist
20. whole life insurance

Review the Concepts

21. Why is a personal resume important to a business plan?
22. What information should a personal resume include?
23. How is a person's net worth calculated?
24. What is the difference between stocks and bonds?
25. What types of financing options are available from commercial banks?

Critical Thinking

26. Approximately how much money would a bank be willing to lend as a home equity loan on a house with an appraised value of $150,000 and an outstanding mortgage of $90,000?
27. Why would an individual use stocks as collateral to borrow against, rather than selling them?
28. What is the net worth of an individual with the following assets and liabilities? How much money do you believe this person could raise for business purposes?

ASSETS	LIABILITIES
Cash, savings $3,500	Home mortgage $80,000
Stocks, bonds $8,400	Automobile loan $8,200
Automobile $12,400	Accounts payable $2,400
House $165,000	Student loan $2,800
Personal belongings $26,000	

29. Make a list of all potential sources of capital, both debt and equity, describing the advantages and disadvantages of each.

Project

Build Your Business Plan

Your hypothetical business plan has now progressed to the point where you need to start thinking about acquiring capital. Begin this process by doing the following:

1. Prepare a net worth calculation (hypothetical or real), indicating which funds could be invested in a business operation.
2. Develop a list of all possible funding sources in your community. Include both debt capital and equity capital sources.
3. Rank the funding sources based on the type of business you are planning. The first source on the list should be the one you consider your best choice for financing.

Chapter 15

Capitalization and Financial Projections

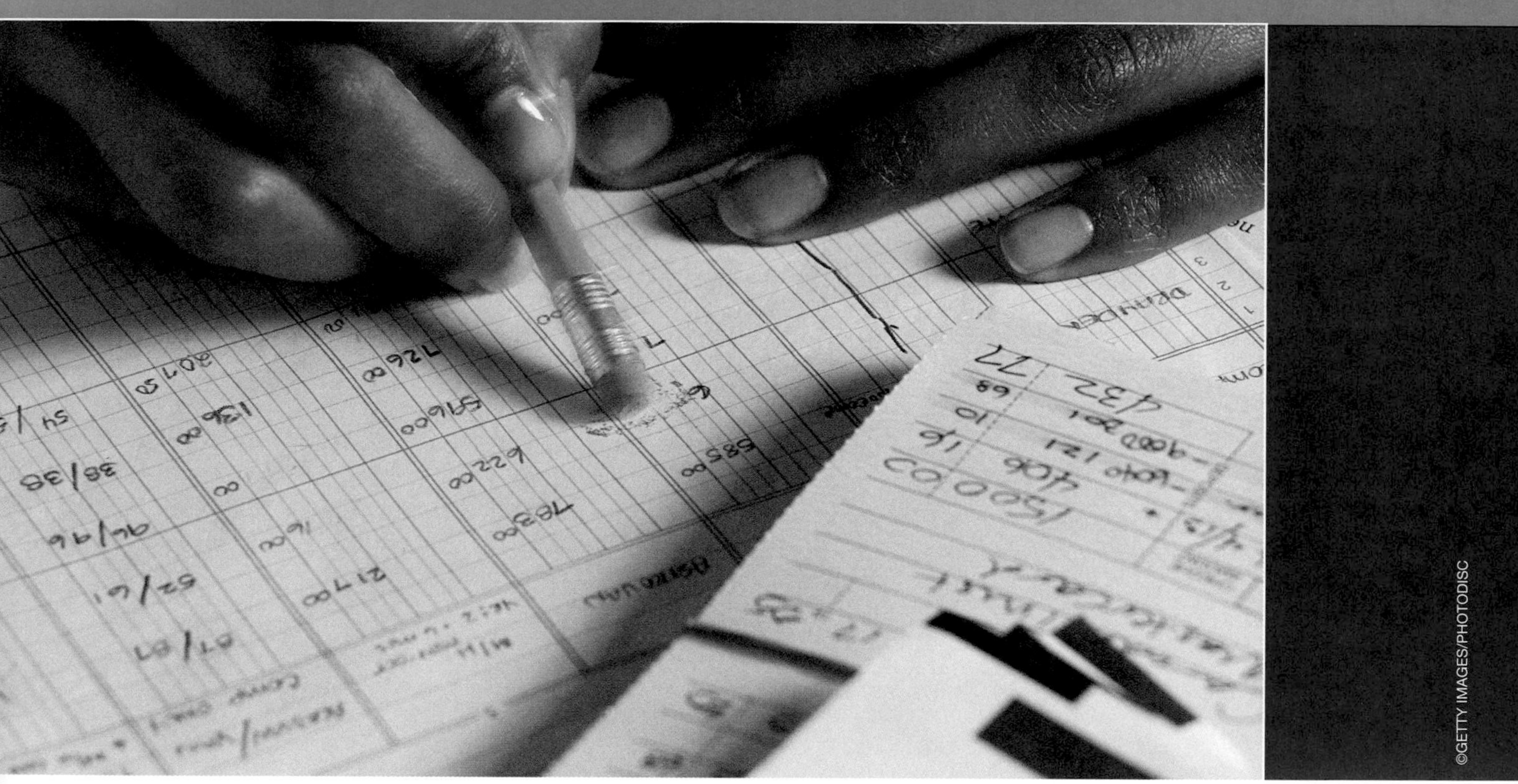

©GETTY IMAGES/PHOTODISC

Objectives

15-1 Explain the process of determining the capitalization needs of a new business.

15-2 Describe how to put together the various financial statements that comprise a financial plan.

15-3 Discuss the financial records every entrepreneur should maintain.

WHAT IS CAPITALIZATION?

The biggest obstacle for many entrepreneurs is initial capitalization. **Capitalization** is the activity of obtaining all the capital assets necessary to operate a business. **Capital assets** include all the equipment, inventory, and operating resources (including cash) that the business owns and uses in its operations. The challenge for the new business owner is determining where to obtain the money to purchase and/or lease the items needed to start a business—the initial capitalization. As noted in Chapter 14, more often than not there is a deficit between the financial resources that are needed and the financial resources that are on hand. In this chapter we will examine more closely putting the initial capitalization plan together and projecting the future financial needs of a business operation.

The Total Financial Package

Before you can complete your business plan, you need to ask yourself how much money you need for the type of business you are considering. The path to the answer starts with your personal financial objective. How much income will you need for personal living expenses? What is the minimum profit you consider adequate? Personal rent or mortgage expenses, car payments, utility bills, groceries, and so on must be covered whether you are employed or self-employed.

Write an objective statement outlining your expenses and the minimum profit you require. Whether the objective is $5,000 per year for a part-time business or $100,000 for a heavily invested enterprise, you will use this financial objective statement to direct your business plan.

Your minimum profit figure will dictate the amount of capital you will need to achieve your objective. For example, if your objective is to make $25,000 per year, you must design the financial or capitalization plan to ensure that enough capital assets are purchased or leased to achieve the sales volume that will ensure a $25,000 net profit. **Net profit** is the income left over after all expenses, including taxes, are paid. If you need to make sales worth $150,000 to net $25,000, you must purchase whatever inventory, equipment, and other capital assets are required to ensure sales revenues of $150,000. Many entrepreneurs do not develop a realistic plan of investment to earn the needed profits. When they cannot obtain the resources to meet the business's objective, the business is considered **undercapitalized**.

Ethics for ENTREPRENEURS

There is a tendency among many entrepreneurs to overstate their profits when they apply for a small business loan. By making the business look more profitable than it is, they are hoping that bankers will be more willing to make a loan. Most bankers, however, have ways of validating the accuracy of an income statement. They can check industry sources regarding expected profits from businesses of a particular size, request copies of the borrower's income tax and sales tax forms, or request audited financial statements from a certified public accounting firm.

Think Critically

1. What would be the future ramifications for an entrepreneur who uses deceitful financial statements to apply for a business loan?
2. Can you think of other ways a lending institution can validate financial statements?

Initial Capital Needs

Calculating initial capital needs begins with a sales projection. As an example, take an entrepreneurial couple, Dorothy and Bill, and their new store, The Emporium—Decorative Gifts for the Home. Their first-year objective is to make a $25,000 profit selling retail products with an average markup of 50 percent. They hope to make more than that eventually, but $25,000 is what they will need to meet all their personal obligations during the first year of operation. They need a plan to help them achieve their objective.

©GETTY IMAGES/PHOTODISC

While researching the industry, Dorothy and Bill learned that successful stores selling similar products can expect to make a profit of 12 to 18 percent of gross, or total, sales. This translates into a sales goal in excess of $150,000 per year to achieve a profit of $25,000. After proper market research to validate that the market need is at least $150,000, they must purchase whatever inventory, fixtures, and equipment will ensure that they reach their minimum sales objective.

Initial Inventory To determine the amount of inventory you should purchase, you need to estimate how often the inventory will turn over. **Inventory turnover** is the number of times a business sells the amount of its base inventory in a year. If the average inventory turnover rate for a product is 5, divide projected sales by 5 to determine the minimum amount of inventory that should be available at all times. Average inventory turnover rates can usually be found by consulting an industry trade association or asking other entrepreneurs active in the industry. To achieve $150,000 in sales, Dorothy and Bill will need to sell $30,000 worth of retail inventory five times per year. Since the markup is 50 percent of the retail price, Dorothy and Bill must have a minimum of $15,000 of initial inventory to open their business.

FUN FACTS

The number of post-secondary schools, colleges, and universities that offer entrepreneurship courses has grown tenfold in the past 15 years. Many programs offer majors and even graduate study programs in entrepreneurship. Nearly all community colleges and technical schools offer training in financial and spreadsheet software programs.

One-Time-Only Start-up Costs Many costs are incurred only once by the business during its start-up phase. When you have calculated the minimum amount of inventory, you should determine what kinds of equipment, fixtures, and leasehold improvements you will need. Equipment includes machinery, computers, cash registers, and other capital items used in the production and sale of products or services provided by your business. Some equipment can be leased. Fixtures include what is needed to house and display inventory, such as shelving units, gondolas, tables, and display cases. **Leasehold improvements** consist of improvements to the property such as carpeting, wallpaper, lighting, and so on. Money should also be available for signs, grand opening advertising and promotional events, utility deposits, and other one-time miscellaneous expenses related to opening the business.

Table 15-1 is a statement of one-time-only capital needed for a new business such as The Emporium. It represents the amount of money that will get the doors open. However, money will also be needed to cover operating expenses while the business gets established.

TABLE 15-1 THE EMPORIUM: ONE-TIME-ONLY CAPITAL NEEDS

Fixtures and equipment	$25,000
Decorating and remodeling	18,000
Installation cost	5,000
Starting inventory	15,000
Utility deposits	1,000
Legal and other fees	1,000
Grand opening promotion	4,000
Cash on hand	1,000
Other	5,000
Total one-time-only expenses	$75,000

Monthly Operating Expenses In addition to start-up costs, entrepreneurs must also estimate the average monthly cost of keeping the business running smoothly. It will take time to generate sufficient sales to cover all expenses, so the business owner should set aside enough money to cover initial expenses without depending on sales revenues. It is generally recommended that you keep three months of operating expense capital in an operating reserves account so that you can concentrate on building sales without worrying about how you're going to pay the bills. One method of calculating the optimum operating reserve is to add up the monthly rent, employees' salaries, average cost of utility services, insurance premiums, and all other expenses. Then multiply the total projected monthly operating expenses by three (representing three months) to arrive at the amount that should be available in the initial capitalization plan for operating expenses. An example of these calculations is shown in Table 15-2 for Dorothy and Bill's business, The Emporium.

TABLE 15-2 THE EMPORIUM: INITIAL OPERATING EXPENSES

Item	Expenses (One Month)	Expenses (Three Months)
Owner's salary	$2,000	$6,000
Other salary	900	2,700
Rent	1,600	4,800
Operating supplies	270	810
Taxes and licenses	125	375
Utilities	300	900
Advertising	250	750
Insurance	200	600
Accounting and legal	165	495
Loan principal and interest	225	675
Miscellaneous	150	450
Total monthly expenses	$6,185	$18,555

Adding the total amount of one-time-only capital needs to your initial operating expenses will give you the total amount you will need to fund your business idea—your initial capitalization. For instance, to determine total capitalization for The Emporium, you would add its one-time-only capital needs (Table 15-1) to its three-month operating expenses (Table 15-2).

$$\$75{,}000 + \$18{,}555 = \$93{,}555$$

Once you have determined this figure for your business, your next step is to devise a plan to make sure the money is available to you.

FINANCIAL STATEMENTS

Financial statements are important control tools for the entrepreneur. They help the entrepreneur stay on target by making adjustments when results do not match projections. The business plan for a new business should include a **pro forma financial statement**, which is a projected statistical report that describes the expected financial status of a business at a future date. To demonstrate the validity of a business idea, entrepreneurs must project success in its pro forma income statements, balance sheets, and cash flow spreadsheets.

Income Statements

An **income statement** shows the revenues, or monies collected, and the expenses, or monies paid out, of a business over a specified period of time. It also shows the business's profits. New business owners should make pro forma income statements for the first year of operation as well as for future years (usually the first three). If they are properly done and show a realistic profit, these income statements will serve to support the reasons for starting the business.

A simplified pro forma statement for the first year of operation of The Emporium, after one-time capital expenditures have been paid, might look like Table 15-3.

TABLE 15-3 THE EMPORIUM: SIMPLIFIED PRO FORMA INCOME STATEMENT

Sales	$150,000	
Cost of goods sold (incl. freight charges)	78,000	
Gross profit		72,000
Operating expenses		
Payroll	10,800	
Rent	19,200	
Maintenance and repairs	600	
Operating supplies	3,200	
Taxes and licenses	1,500	
Utilities	3,600	
Advertising	3,000	
Insurance	2,400	
Accounting and legal	1,980	
Miscellaneous	1,800	
Total operating expenses		48,080
Net operating profit		$23,920

This statement makes use of the itemized expenses in the initial operating expenses statement in Table 15-2. It shows the expected sales and operating expenses for one year. In this case, it is evident that if the business is properly managed and the location is suitable, it can expect to realize the goal of a $24,000 profit the first year.

Future projections indicate the planned growth of the business. Growth projections are based on factors such as industry growth, market population growth, and growth that can be expected as the business becomes better known. In the case of The Emporium, Dorothy and Bill have determined that they can expect revenue growth of 15 percent in the second year ($150,000 to $172,500 = 15 percent increase), and 10 percent in the third year ($172,500 to $189,750 = 10 percent increase). The pro forma income statement for the second and third years of this business is shown in Table 15-4 on the next page.

TABLE 15-4 THE EMPORIUM: SIMPLIFIED PRO FORMA INCOME STATEMENT, SECOND AND THIRD YEARS		
	Second Year	**Third Year**
Sales	$172,500	$189,750
Cost of goods sold	88,000	90,200
Gross profit	84,500	99,550
Operating expenses		
Payroll	12,000	13,000
Rent	19,000	19,000
Maintenance and repairs	1,100	1,200
Operating supplies	3,300	3,400
Taxes and licenses	1,600	1,700
Utilities	3,600	3,600
Advertising	3,400	3,800
Insurance	2,500	2,600
Accounting and legal	2,100	2,200
Miscellaneous	2,000	2,200
Total operating expenses	50,600	52,700
Net profit	$33,900	$46,850

Balance Sheets

A **balance sheet** is a financial statement that shows the worth, or value, of a business. A pro forma balance sheet projects the growth of a business in terms of how much capital value the business will have at a particular date in the future. The business plan should include a pro forma balance sheet for its opening date as well as one indicating what the business should be worth one year from opening and possibly later. Table 15-5 shows a simplified pro forma balance sheet for the Novelties Gift Shop.

TABLE 15-5 NOVELTIES GIFT SHOP: SIMPLIFIED PRO FORMA BALANCE SHEET			
Assets		**Liabilities and Owner's Equity**	
Current assets		Current liabilities	
Cash	$ 6,400	Accounts payable	$ 5,200
Inventory	15,000	Current portion of long-term debt	3,300
Total current assets	21,400	Long-term liabilities	6,700
Fixed assets	17,900	Total liabilities	15,200
		Owner's equity	24,100
Total assets	$39,300	Total liabilities and owner's equity	$39,300

The balance sheet has two sides: assets and liabilities. The **assets** side shows all property and capital to which the business claims ownership. The **liabilities** side shows all the debts of the business. The **net worth** of a business, also called value or owner's equity, is determined by adding all the value of what is owned (the assets) and subtracting from this the total debt of the business (the liabilities). Table 15-5 is called a balance sheet because the net worth is added to the liabilities to achieve the "balanced" totals on each side of the ledger.

Assets are listed as current and fixed. **Current assets** include cash and assets that are easily converted into cash, such as inventory and accounts receivable. **Fixed assets** are those capital purchases that generally take a longer time to convert or liquidate into cash, such as property, equipment, and fixtures that require a special buyer.

©GETTY IMAGES/PHOTODISC

Liabilities are listed as current or long term. **Current liabilities** are debts that are to be paid within 12 months of the date of the balance sheet. **Long-term liabilities** are usually debts that come due more than 12 months after the date of the balance sheet. Long-term liabilities are generally associated with the purchase of fixed assets such as mortgage notes on property and equipment. By breaking liabilities down into short and long term, it is easy to calculate how much money the business could raise on short notice for emergency purchases or expansion. The goal of the business owner is to always keep current assets greater than current liabilities. Otherwise the business will be considered "technically bankrupt."

Liquidity A balance sheet allows entrepreneurs, bankers, and investors to quickly determine the liquidity of a business operation. **Liquidity** is defined as a business's ability to meet its debt obligations as they become due. Two common methods of determining a business's liquidity are current ratio tests and acid-test ratios.

The **current ratio** test compares cash, as well as any assets that can be converted into cash within a year, with the debt (liabilities) that will become due and payable within the year. The assets are the current assets listed on the balance sheet, and the liabilities are the current liabilities. The ratio is expressed as:

current ratio = current assets ÷ current liabilities

The current ratio of the business described in Figure 15-5 is:

2.52 = \$21,400 ÷ \$8,500

A favorable current ratio would be 2:1. A minimum acceptable ratio would be 1:1, which indicates that there are sufficient current assets on hand so that, if sold, the business would be able to meet all its obligations.

The **acid-test ratio** is more restrictive as it eliminates inventory, the least liquid of current assets, from the numerator.

acid-test ratio = (current assets – inventory) ÷ current liabilities

The acid-test ratio for the Novelties Gift Shop is:

0.753 = (\$21,400 – \$15,000) ÷ \$8,500

The acid-test ratio will, of course, be lower than the current ratio and will give a better indication of a business's liquidity in an emergency situation.

FUN FACTS

It is estimated that 95 percent of all entrepreneurs depend primarily on their own investment money to start a new business. Fewer than 1 percent of start-ups are capitalized by venture capital sources. The SBA assisted over 76,000 small businesses with loan guarantees in 2003.

The Novelties Gift Shop has a reasonably good current ratio but a somewhat questionable acid-test ratio.

Cash Flow

To get a better idea of how well your business will operate during the first year, you must break the year down into a month-by-month projection of financial activities, or a **cash flow statement**. This analysis allows you to prepare for potential cash flow problems, which are caused by changing sales and payment patterns often created by seasonal and industry fluctuations. A cash flow statement tells you what your business's cash position really is. For example, since many of your customers will purchase goods on credit, you may not receive payment (cash) for those purchases for a month or more. Although on paper the purchases may show up as sales, they do not involve cash payment. Also, goods are sometimes purchased and paid for by the

TABLE 15-6 12-MONTH CASH FLOW CYCLE PLANNING FORM

NAME OF BUSINESS	TYPE OF BUSINESS								DATE		
	Pre-start-up position		Month 1		Month 2		Month 3		TOTAL		
YEAR MONTH									Months 1-12		
	Estimate	Actual	Estimate	Actual	Estimate	Actual	Estimate	Actual	Estimate	Actual	
1. CASH ON HAND (Beginning of month)											**1.**
2. CASH RECEIPTS											**2.**
(a) Cash sales											(a)
(b) Collections from credit accounts											(b)
(c) Loan or other cash injection (specify)											(c)
3. TOTAL CASH RECEIPTS (2a + 2b + 2c = 3)											**3.**
4. TOTAL CASH AVAILABLE (Before cash out) (1 + 3)											**4.**
5. CASH PAID OUT											**5.**
(a) Purchases (merchandise)											(a)
(b) Gross wages (excludes withdrawals)											(b)
(c) Payroll expenses (taxes, etc.)											(c)
(d) Outside services											(d)
(e) Supplies (office and operating)											(e)
(f) Repairs and maintenance											(f)
(g) Advertising											(g)
(h) Car, delivery, and travel											(h)
(i) Accounting and legal											(i)
(j) Rent											(j)
(k) Telephone											(k)
(l) Utilities											(l)
(m) Insurance											(m)
(n) Taxes (real estate, etc.)											(n)
(o) Interest											(o)
(p) Other expenses (specify each)											(p)
(q) Subtotal											(q)
(r) Loan principal payment											(r)
(s) Capital purchases (specify)											(s)
(t) Other start-up costs											(t)
(u) Reserve and/or escrow (specify)											(u)
(v) Owner's withdrawal											(v)
6. TOTAL CASH PAID OUT (Total 5a thru 5v)											**6.**
7. CASH POSITION End of month, 4 minus 6											**7.**

business even when the goods are still in inventory. For these reasons the business may appear more cash-rich than it really is.

Many seasonal businesses make the great majority of their annual profits in a relatively short period of time. An income statement shows how much profit the business makes but not when the profit is realized. It is the cash flow analysis that reveals this and makes it clear that the business must spread out its profits to compensate for slower sales periods during the year.

The owner of a business such as the Novelties Gift Shop needs to understand how the projected $150,000 in sales will occur. Particularly in a retail business, in which a great portion of sales might be made at the end of the year during the holiday season, the new owner must plan for the impact that different seasons have on the cash flow cycle. Consulting industry sources to find the percentage of total sales normally received each month of the year allows the owner to budget expenses to accommodate these fluctuations. Table 15-6 is an example of a form available from the Small Business Administration for calculating and recording cash flow.

A cash flow spreadsheet is simply a cash budget similar to one you might use to keep track of your personal cash inflow and outflow. In your personal budget, you schedule your payouts according to when you get paid. A business declares its cash on hand at the beginning of each month and adds to it all projected revenues for the coming month. Table 15-7 is the 12-month cash flow spreadsheet of the Novelties Gift Shop.

TABLE 15-7 NOVELTIES GIFT SHOP 12-MONTH CASH FLOW

	Jan.	Feb.	March	April	May	June	July	Aug.	Sept.	Oct.	Nov.	Dec.
Beg. cash	10,000	825	4,500	6,875	9,600	10,975	10,700	9,775	9,950	8,975	15,550	20,925
REVENUES												
Retail	8,000	12,000	13,000	15,000	14,000	11,000	8,000	8,000	7,000	14,000	18,000	26,000
TOTAL REV.	8,000	12,000	13,000	15,000	14,000	11,000	8,000	8,000	7,000	14,000	18,000	26,000
Avail. cash	18,000	12,825	17,500	21,875	23,600	21,975	18,700	17,775	16,950	22,975	33,550	46,925
EXPENSES												
Goods	13,000	4,000	6,000	7,000	8,000	7,000	5,000	4,000	4,000	3,000	7,000	9,000
Freight	200	200	200	200	250	200	100	100	100	100	100	300
Rent	1,500	1,500	1,500	1,500	1,500	1,500	1,500	1,500	1,500	1,500	1,500	1,500
Payroll	1,000	1,200	1,200	1,400	1,300	1,000	1,000	1,000	1,000	1,200	1,500	2,000
Advertising	200	300	500	500	400	300	200	200	200	200	1,000	1,000
Supplies	100	150	150	150	100	100	150	50	50	250	350	350
Travel	100	0	100	0	100	100	0	0	0	0	0	0
Phone	125	125	125	125	125	125	125	125	175	125	125	125
Utilities	100	100	100	100	100	100	100	100	100	200	200	200
Maintenance	100	100	100	150	100	150	100	100	100	150	150	150
Accountant	100	100	100	600	100	100	100	100	100	100	100	100
Interest	100	100	100	100	100	100	100	100	200	100	100	200
Bank fees	150	50	50	50	50	100	50	50	50	100	100	150
Insurance	150	150	150	150	150	150	150	150	150	150	150	150
Misc.	250	250	250	250	250	250	250	250	250	250	250	250
EXPENSES PAID OUT	17,175	8,325	10,625	12,275	12,625	11,275	8,925	7,825	7,975	7,425	12,625	15,475
End cash	825	4,500	6,875	9,600	10,975	10,700	9,775	9,950	8,975	15,550	20,925	31,450

Total revenues for the year = $154,000

Total cost of goods for the year = $79,050 (includes freight charges)

Total operating expenses for the year = $53,500

Keep in mind that not all sales count as revenues in businesses that allow credit. Also, revenues can come from sources other than sales, such as loan proceeds and accounts receivable. Therefore the cash inflow is only the actual cash that is received and deposited in a particular month.

The same is true of projected payments. You project the bills that are to be paid that month, which do not necessarily include all your bills. Some invoices may have extended billing terms, and others may be disputed. "Expenses paid out" lists only that portion of debts that will actually be paid in that particular month. When you have totaled the projected expenses paid out, subtract it from the total of the beginning cash balance plus projected cash inflow to arrive at an estimated cash position at the end of the month. Then carry this figure over to the next month as the beginning-of-the-month cash on hand.

$$\text{Beginning cash} + \text{revenues collected} = \text{total cash available} - \text{expenses paid out} = \text{ending cash balance} = \text{next month's beginning cash balance}$$

You should keep a cash flow spreadsheet on your computer at all times. A software spreadsheet program such as Excel or Lotus allows you to post daily cash flow changes that can be incorporated immediately into a projected 12-month cash flow plan. If your cash flow falls short or exceeds expectations in a given month, you can enter the change on the spreadsheet and it will automatically calculate the impact on the remainder of the year. If sales are not as expected on a particular day, the results are reflected immediately in the cash flow projection for the rest of the month, and you can make the necessary corrections immediately. This is particularly useful for any new business owner who is not experienced at making projections.

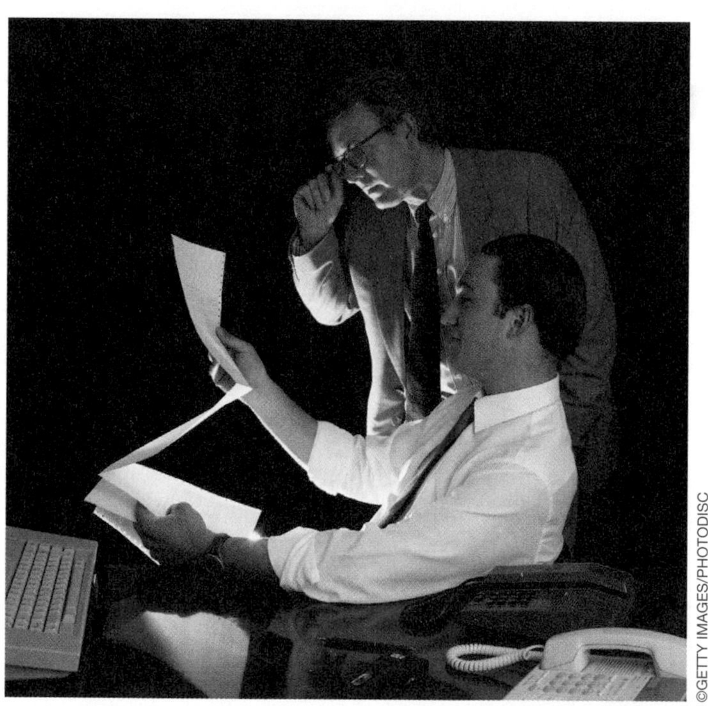
©GETTY IMAGES/PHOTODISC

It is very common for a business to show some months with excess cash coming in while other months may show too little to meet obligations. You must keep this possibility in mind and properly allocate money in different cycles. If there are cash deficits during slow seasons, you can use a line of credit at the bank. Bankers will want to review your cash flow projections before issuing a line of credit.

It is not difficult for entrepreneurs to go bankrupt if cash is flowing out of the business much faster than it is flowing in. They may be making a profit on the items they sell, but if cash is coming in too slowly, the business may have to close. An example of a cash flow problem that could destroy a successful business is illustrated by the following example.

Edith Brown's linen supply business had a very promising start. She had lined up a number of impressive contracts with hotels and hospitals, from whom she expected sales of $100,000 per month. The gross margin of the business was slim—approximately 20 percent—so she would have to make up for it with volume. Since she was new to the industry, she agreed to pay her cleaning service and linen suppliers cash on delivery and planned to bill her clients on a net 30 payment basis. Therefore, although her business showed sales of $100,000 for the first month, it had no income, only the cost-of-goods expense of $80,000 and the expected operating expense payments of $20,000. The $100,000 was scheduled to be collected during the second month. To cover this initial imbalance she arranged a $100,000 bank loan and created a first-month cash flow projection:

Beginning cash on hand	$ 0
Sales collected	0
Bank loan proceeds	100,000
Total cash available	$100,000
Cash paid out	
Cost of goods	80,000
Operating expenses	20,000
Total cash paid out	$100,000
Ending cash position	0

Although Edith recognized that the ending cash balance was zero, she knew that she would be collecting $100,000 in receipts in month two. Besides, she was adding more contracts and business was good. In fact, business continued to be excellent, increasing at a rate of 5 percent each month. Despite the brisk pace, however, Edith found herself in a very deep cash flow hole five months down the road. Her anticipated 30-day collections were not on schedule—instead, she received 50 percent in 30 days and the other 50 percent in 60 days. Edith was still paying cash on delivery for her goods.

©GETTY IMAGES/PHOTODISC

	Month 2	Month 3	Month 4	Month 5
Beg. cash on hand	0	($55,000)	($61,500)	($68,000)
Sales	[105,000]	[110,000]	[116,000]	[122,000]
Sales collected	50,000	102,500	107,500	113,000
Total cash available	50,000	47,500	46,000	46,000
Cash paid out				
Cost of goods (80% sales)	84,000	88,000	93,000	98,000
Operating expenses*	21,000	21,000	21,000	21,000
Total cash paid out	105,000	109,000	114,000	119,000
Ending cash position	(55,000)	(61,500)	(68,000)	(73,000)

**Increased $1,000 due to interest on $100,000 loan.*

Edith was scrambling from one month to the next trying to make it all work. She went back to the bank and asked for help. The banker explained that the problem was not with the business, which was operating at a profitable pace, but with the cash flow. He showed Edith how her cash flow would work for the next month if she were paying on 30-day credit terms for her goods and collecting in 30 days as she had originally projected.

Sales	[$130,000]
Sales collected (from month 5)	122,000
Total cash available	122,000
Cash paid out	
Cost of goods (due on month 5 purchases)	$98,000
Operating expenses	21,000
Total cash paid out	119,000
Ending cash position	$3,000

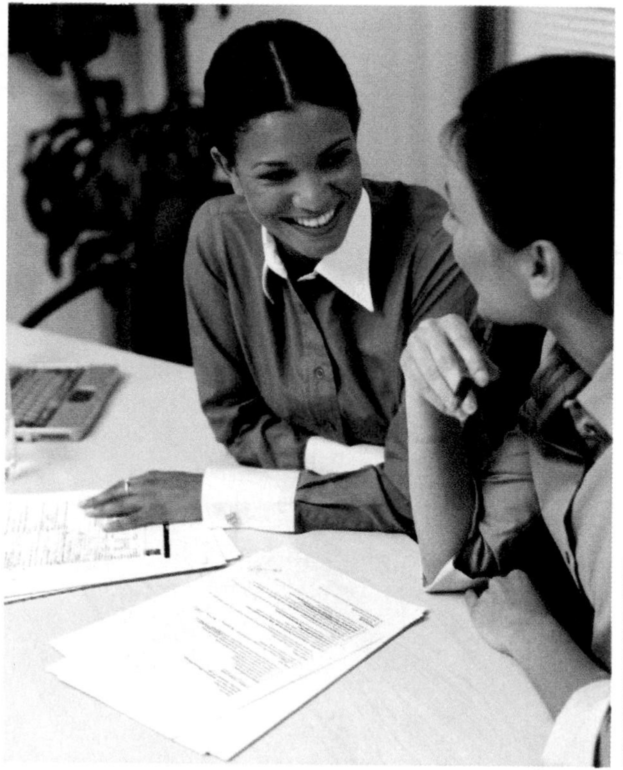

©GETTY IMAGES/PHOTODISC

The banker explained that because Edith was paying before collecting, the faster her business grew, the more money she had to pay in advance. It was a catch 22 situation. Unless she gained control of her cash flow, the bank would not be able to help her and the situation would only worsen. Once she had resolved the issues with her suppliers and clients, however, the bank could work with her as her enterprise appeared to be very profitable.

Edith met with her suppliers, explained the situation, and managed to arrange credit with them. She then imposed on her clients stiff penalties for late payments. Eventually she pulled all the pieces together, received a sufficient line of credit from the bank to help her through the cash flow problem, and was on her way to a successful entrepreneurial career.

Cash Flow Projections and Initial Capital Needs

A cash flow projection can be used to help determine the initial capital reserve for a start-up operation. Instead of multiplying the operating expenses estimate by three months, as illustrated earlier, enter zero in the opening cash-on-hand column of the cash flow spreadsheet. By listing projected monthly revenues and operating expenses in the cash flow spreadsheet, you will see the deficit that will be incurred in the first few months of operation. Carry the deficits forward until you reach the month in which a surplus

The Global ENTREPRENEUR

The Securities and Exchange Commission, a federal agency, has assisted in the creation of an International Accounting Standards Committee. The purpose of the committee is to develop a global financial reporting framework that ensures access to high-quality financial information by investors and businesses in all markets. This measure is meant in part is to encourage participation by small business owners in the growing global market.

Think Critically

1. Why is this standardization important to a small business owner who wishes to enter a contractual agreement with a foreign company?
2. What other financial information, in addition to formal accounting statements, would you require before doing business with a foreign company?

occurs. The total deficit incurred before reaching that month is the amount of operating reserve you should include in your business plan. When you enter that figure in the opening cash-on-hand column, the cash flow statement will not show any deficits in the opening months.

	Month 1	Month 2	Month 3	Month 4	Month 5
Beg. cash	$ 0	($5,000)	($7,000)	($7,000)	($6,000)
Cash collected	5,000	10,000	12,000	14,000	15,000
Cash paid out	10,000	12,000	12,000	13,000	13,000
Ending cash bal.	(5,000)	(7,000)	(7,000)	(6,000)	(4,000)

In the scenario above, you could find the point of greatest deficit ($7,000) and insert that figure as cash collected in month 1 as a personal contribution or as loan proceeds, thus eliminating any cash flow deficits in the cash flow plan.

A word of caution to optimistic entrepreneurs: When you project the cash flow for your new business, use a conservative approach. It is very easy to change a figure to ease the need. If there is a $5,000 deficit, for instance, it may be tempting to simply hit a button that increases the sales projection by $5,000, thereby eliminating the need for $5,000 to cover the deficit. It would be wiser in the long run to use a worst-case scenario as you prepare your cash flow projection.

When you have put together a capital needs statement, pro forma income statements, balance sheets, and a monthly cash flow projection, you will have your financial plan in place. The information you have gathered will indicate how much money you will need to open and operate the business during its start-up phase; the income that the business should generate in its first, second, and third years of operation; and the expected value of the business upon opening and at the end of the first year or later. These are essential ingredients of the business plan. They will determine whether or not you will need to borrow money for your business idea or attract investors to share the risks and profits.

Small Business Technology

The original accounting software programs of the 1980s were few and very basic. Most programs had to be tailored by local computer experts to fit specific businesses. Now hundreds of software programs are available for almost any kind of business. Well-known programs for small businesses include Oracle Small Business, Microsoft CRM, QuickBooks Pro, and Business Works.

FINANCIAL RECORDS

With the variety of software programs now available, maintaining business records has never been easier. Popular accounting programs such as QuickBooks have eliminated the need for many accounting services. Entrepreneurs should maintain their own daily and monthly accounting records and use accountants for preparing tax returns and formal financial statements. Business owners who do not stay on top of their accounting records run the risk of having an incomplete and therefore inaccurate picture of their financial position, which will then hamper their decision-making.

Small business owners should have easy access to the financial records described below.

Income and Expense Register All accounting software programs keep an up-to-date transaction accounting of income and expenses. When you enter sales receipts, they will be broken down into gross amount received, sales tax collected, and any extra charges received, minus credit card fees, refunds, returns, and so on. The check disbursement register (Table 15-8) will show the date, check number, name of payee, and amount paid. It will also enter the payment in its proper expense classification, such as rent, utilities, and supplies. If you post daily, you can count on always having an up-to-date record of all your financial transactions, which will help you make important business decisions. You can also create reports that show daily, weekly, monthly, quarterly, or year-to-date receipts and expenses.

TABLE 15-8 CHECK REGISTER SPREADSHEET

	DATE	CHECK No.	TO WHOM PAID	AMOUNT	PAYROLL	RENT	MAINT.	SUPPLIES	TAXES	UTILITIES	ADVERTISING	INSURANCE	ACCTG./ LEGAL	MISC.
1														
2														
3														
4														
5														
6														
7														
8														
9														

Accounts Payable Ledger It is crucial that you keep up with all the debts you owe. An accounts payable ledger will list by account name all the bills your business needs to pay. It will show the amount owed, the due date, and the vendor's name and address. When you have paid the bill, the ledger will show the amount and date paid, any discounts taken, and year-to-date purchases from that particular vendor.

Accounts Receivable Ledger As illustrated by the story of Edith Brown and her linen supply business, keeping track of monies owed to the business is vitally important. An accounts receivable ledger keeps track of who owes the business money, invoice due dates, and the payment history of each customer. When a payment is received, it is entered into the accounts receivable ledger, which automatically reduces the balance due the business by the amount paid.

Furniture, Fixture, and Equipment Ledger All purchases of fixed assets should be recorded in a separate ledger. This will maintain an up-to-date record of business assets and the dates they were purchased. This is important because these assets are eligible for depreciation deductions, which are allowed on any equipment that will wear out or have to be replaced in the future. The Internal Revenue Service allows businesses to deduct a percentage of the cost of the equipment each year as a way to retain earnings to replace the equipment at a later date. Various depreciation schedules are used, depending on the industry and the type of equipment. The most common is a straight-line seven-year schedule, which allows the business to deduct a depreciation expense 1/7th of the cost of the equipment each year for seven years. With a furniture, fixture, and equipment ledger, the accounting software can quickly calculate the depreciation expense of each capital equipment purchase.

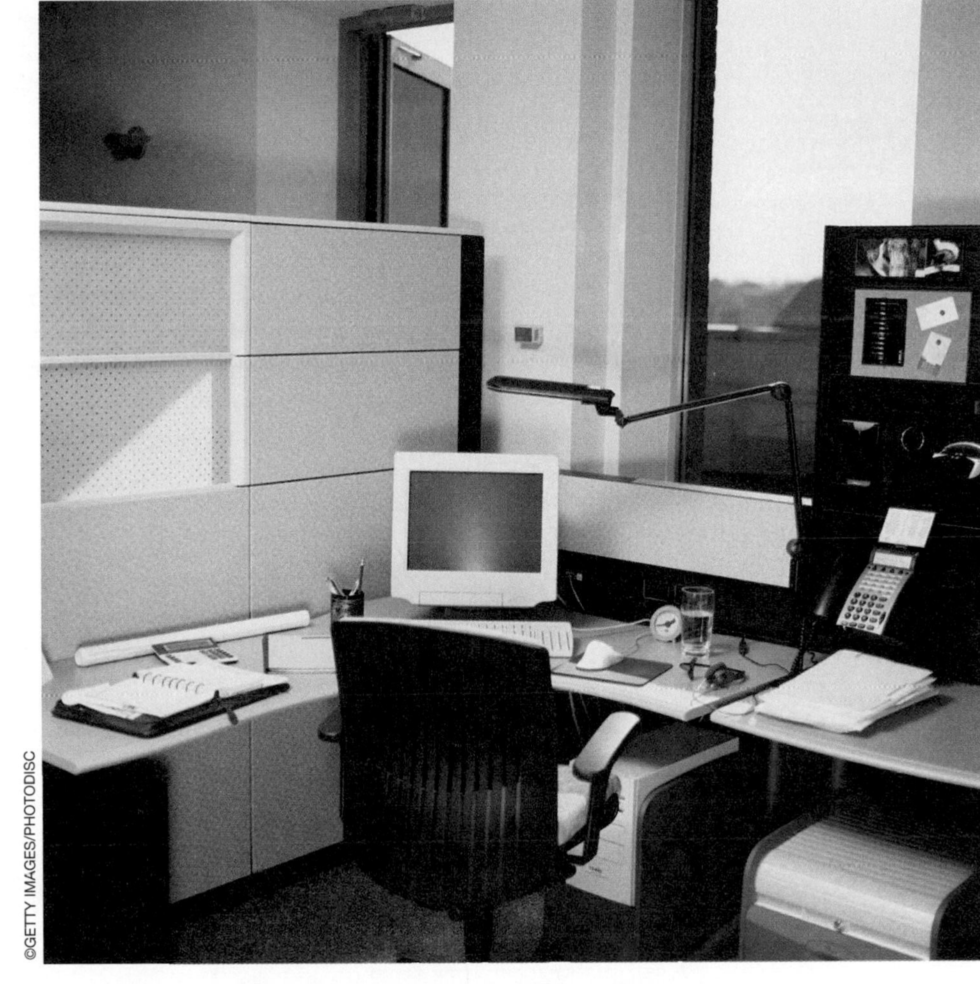

Notes Payable Ledger Any money borrowed for the business should be recorded, showing the lender, the date the note becomes due, the interest rate to be paid, and any special payment arrangements. If the ledger is kept current, it will automatically record all payments and show an up-to-date accounting of outstanding principal.

Payroll Records Keeping payroll records on your computer greatly eases the burden of payday. Accounting software will keep a record of all employees, the wages paid, taxes withheld, benefits expenses deducted, and so on. Some programs even write the checks. At the end of a pay period, all payroll expenses are totaled and classified. At the end of the calendar year, the business issues W-4 statements to employees or 1099 forms to independent contractors using the information recorded each payday.

Successful entrepreneurs understand the importance of staying on top financially. They are not intimidated by accounting and financial management. Electronic bookkeeping software is not difficult to use and is an important asset for any entrepreneur trying to grow a business.

Ship in a BOTTLE

The Financial Plan

It was time for Fred to tackle the future financial plan for Ship in a Bottle. He had a starting point from which to project and was ready to complete three-year pro forma income statements, pro forma balance sheets, and a 12-month cash flow spreadsheet. He started by stating his objectives.

Year one Launch the business on a part-time basis, gain experience, and prepare for a full-time venture.

Year two Become a full-time entrepreneur by developing the business to the point that a major expansion could be considered that would allow Jeanie to join him and open opportunities for other family members and friends to become part of the team.

Year three Own and manage a growing, dynamic imported-nautical-gift business with a full staff, including outside sales personnel.

"I might as well think big," Fred thought. "I can always change my plans, depending on how quickly it grows, but for now, I'm going for it!"

Year one was reasonably easy to project, based on his initial assessments of trade show and web site sales and his current investment. Sales would be equally split between wholesale and retail. His conservative estimate of first-year revenues was $40,000.

Sales	
Retail	$20,000
Wholesale	20,000
Total sales	40,000
Cost of goods (including freight charges)	18,000
Gross profit	$22,000
Operating expenses	
Advertising (brochures, Internet services)	2,900
Payroll (2 part-time independent contractors)	1,200
Mailing	600
Travel (4 trade shows, visits to wholesalers)	1,500
Van lease	3,000
Telephone	1,200
Web site maintenance	600
Accounting	400
Supplies (packaging materials, etc.)	600
Interest (credit card)	300
Trade show exhibit fee	4,500
Miscellaneous (bank fees, petty cash, etc.)	2,400
Total operating expenses	$19,200
Net operating profit	$2,800

Fred realized this was not a get-rich-quick business, but he was being conservative in his estimates and felt confident he could build from this base. Projecting the second year was exciting, although he did not feel quite as confident as with the first year. He predicted a dramatic growth in wholesale sales based on four trade-show exhibits and reorder sales from existing accounts.

continued

He was also excited about the idea of featuring more products on his web site, including high-priced nautical weather instruments, art, and home décor. Since he would be able to work full-time on the venture, he felt he could easily double the first-year revenues, for a total of $80,000.

But what about the third year? Just how big could his business become? Could he fully develop an import business in such a short time? Why not plan it? He could slow down the pace if necessary and make adjustments if it turned out that growth would take longer than expected. Fred created a third-year pro forma income statement showing $400,000 in revenues for an operation that included Jeanie, an office staff, and commission sales representatives.

	Year 1	Year 2	Year 3
Sales			
Wholesale	$20,000	$40,000	$200,000
Retail	20,000	40,000	200,000
Total revenues	40,000	80,000	400,000
Cost of goods	18,000	36,000	180,000
Gross profit	22,000	44,000	220,000
Operating expenses			
Advertising	2,900	4,000	12,000
Payroll/commissions	1,200	4,800	80,000
Trade shows	4,500	4,500	13,500
Travel	1,500	3,000	6,000
Van lease	3,000	3,000	4,800
Telephone	1,200	1,400	2,500
Supplies	600	1,200	4,800
Interest	300	300	1,000
Miscellaneous	2,400	3,000	5,000
Total operating expenses	17,600	25,200	129,600
Net operating profit	$4,400	$18,800	$ 91,000

Fred was a little concerned that he would have to survive on an income of less than $20,000 during year two. But they would still have Jeanie's salary that year, and the thought of getting to year three made it seem worthwhile. Although he was currently a proprietor, he decided to change to a subchapter S corporation before year three. His payroll arrangement would not change, as he and Jeanie would declare the net profits as their income.

Making a cash flow spreadsheet for his first year of operation was not as difficult as he had feared. Since more than 50 percent of his business was retail and paid on sale and his outstanding accounts receivables came from carefully screened and qualified accounts, he did not anticipate collection problems. He felt sure that almost all accounts would be paid in the 30-day credit time. Therefore, once he was established, he could count on the 50 percent of his monthly sales that came from the web site being paid for immediately, and the remainder of the cash would be collected from the previous month's wholesale sales. If a month of $4,000 in sales was followed by a month of $3,000 in sales, the cash received would be $1,500 from the second month's web site sales and $2,000 (50 percent of $4,000) from the previous month's wholesale sales, to equal total receipts of $3,500. He would also have to show his arrangement with Johann and other vendors, which was to pay within 30 days of receiving the goods. Fred was also aware that he had to incorporate the Christmas holiday selling season into his wholesale and retail volume projections. For goods sent out to stores in October, he would show a wholesale revenue

continued

increase in November and a large retail increase in December. He laid out a 12-month cash flow spreadsheet (Table 15-9).

Fred turned his attention next to creating a pro forma balance sheet to prove that the venture would make a good investment. He already had the opening balance sheet in place from his current start-up expenses.

Assets		Liabilities	
Cash	$1,500	Credit card loan	$3,000
Inventory	4,500	Accounts payable	3,500
Supplies	450	Total liabilities	6,500
Brochures	2,000	Equity	4,350
Computer	2,400		
Total assets	$10,850	Total liabilities/equity	$10,850

Reviewing his second-year projections, Fred realized he would have to increase his inventory to realize the goal of doubling sales. He was willing to reinvest the $2,800 projected net profit from year one and felt sure that Bill Barron at the bank would grant him a $5,000 line of credit. The beginning of year two would look like this:

Assets		Liabilities	
Cash	$ 1,500	Credit card loan	$2,700
Inventory	11,500	Accounts payable	2,950
Supplies	450	Note payable	5,000
Brochures	2,000	Total liabilities	10,650
Computer	2,400	Equity	7,200
Total assets	$17,850	Total liabilities/equity	$17,850

Although this progress was not overwhelming, reinvesting the $2,800 and reducing the credit card and accounts payable debts helped improve his equity. Bill Barron was impressed, particularly since the projections seemed conservative, and reassured Fred that the bank would assist him if the pro formas turned out to be reasonably accurate.

Bill also encouraged Fred to draw out his plan for the leap to the $400,000 sales level. Fred knew a jump this large would require additional capitalization, but it was not impossible. To reach a sales level of this magnitude and set up a sales force, office staff, and proper technology, Fred estimated he would need an inventory worth $50,000, additional equipment worth $5,000, and a professional-looking catalog for $20,000—approximately $75,000 of additional capitalization. Counting on higher profits along the way, he calculated that he would have to borrow $50,000 on a five-year note to make his dream come true. When the time was right, he was certain he would find the money either by taking out a bank loan or taking in an investor.

With his limited financial training, this was by far the hardest part of the business plan for Fred. But when he was done he felt good about what he had accomplished. He felt he was in control of his business.

Critical Thinking

1. Is Fred getting ahead of himself by making a $400,000 sales projection for year three?
2. What problems might he encounter that he has not considered?
3. Can you suggest ideas that will help Fred further develop his business?

TABLE 15-9 SHIP IN A BOTTLE 12-MONTH CASH FLOW												
	Jan.	**Feb.**	**March**	**April**	**May**	**June**	**July**	**Aug.**	**Sept.**	**Oct.**	**Nov.**	**Dec.**
Beg. cash	600	140	80	620	260	-600	2,790	-170	320	1,695	3,770	6,745
REVENUES												
Retail	1,500	1,000	1,500	1,500	1,500	1,200	1,000	1,400	800	2,300	4,300	7,400
Wholesale	1,300	1,300	1,300	1,400	1,400	1,200	1,500	1,300	2,100	1,700	1,700	1,800
Loan						3,000						
TOTAL REV.	2,800	2,300	2,800	2,900	2,900	5,400	2,500	2,700	2,900	4,000	6,000	9,200
Avail. Cash	3,400	2,440	2,880	3,520	3,160	4,800	5,290	2,530	3,220	5,695	9,770	15,945
EXPENSES												
Goods	500	1,000	1,200	500	1,500	400	1,700	500	200	1,000	1,200	2,000
Freight	0	200	0	0	800	0	0	600	0	0	500	500
Credit card	150	150	150	250	150	150	600	150	150	150	150	150
Web site		100	0	100	0	100	100	100	100	100	100	100
Advertising	100	100	50	100	400	400	300	100	100	100	100	400
Office	100	100	50	100	100	100	50	50	50	50	50	50
Travel	100	0	100	0	100	100	0	0	0	0	0	0
Phone	125	125	125	125	125	125	125	125	175	125	125	125
Misc.	100	100	100	100	100	100	100	100	100	200	200	200
Auto loan	335	335	335	335	335	335	335	335	400	0	400	0
Trade show	1,500	0	0	1,500	0	0	2,000	0	0	0	0	0
Interest	100	100	100	100	100	100	100	100	200	100	100	200
Bank fees	150	50	50	50	50	100	50	50	50	100	100	150
Loan pay												3,000
EXPENSES PAID OUT	3,260	2,360	2,260	3,260	3,760	2,010	5,460	2,210	1,525	1,925	3,025	6,875
End cash	140	80	620	260	-600	2,790	-170	320	1,695	3,770	6,745	9,070

Summary

When starting a business operation, the entrepreneur must have a financial plan to arrange for the purchase of all necessary components. The plan starts with a realistic objective of desired profits and a calculation of what must be purchased to achieve that objective. Determining how much inventory is needed, what kind of equipment is required, and how much money will meet initial operating expenses is done by researching industry sources and talking to suppliers.

Once a total capitalization figure is determined, pro forma income statements and balance sheets are created to validate whether or not the business is a good investment and potentially profitable. These financial statements also show whether or not it will be necessary to borrow money or raise money from investors to open the business.

Successful entrepreneurs know the importance of maintaining a healthy cash flow into and out of the business operation. A cash flow spreadsheet shows how the money circulates in a business. It reflects changes in monthly revenues due to seasonal fluctuations and incorporates the business's sales collections and accounts payable arrangements. A poor cash flow plan can harm even the most profitable of businesses.

Many business owners use an accountant to assist in important financial and tax decisions because accountants are educated in these matters. But successful entrepreneurs maintain basic bookkeeping systems themselves and rely on accountants for advisory consultation, special reports, and tax matters. Today's accounting software has facilitated bookkeeping responsibilities considerably.

A Case in POINT

A Capital Idea

Paula Zelski was excited about the prospect of mass-producing her own line of designer T-shirts. She had produced a limited number, 200, which sold quickly in three local boutiques.

Paula expanded her line and hired Walt Crosby, a manufacturer's rep, to sell her shirts at a 15 percent commission. She planned to produce 10,000 units for a net profit of $1.12 per unit. If she could increase her production run to 20,000, economies of scale would raise her per-unit profit to more than $3 per shirt. She calculated her one-time-only capital needs at $14,500 and monthly operating expenses at $3,200. She had $3,000 in the bank and borrowed $15,000 on a home equity loan. After buying new equipment and purchasing the initial inventory, she had only one month's operating funds in her checking account. Everything else looked good. Walt had sold the 10,000 shirts to retailers at the Chicago spring fashion show.

Unfortunately, Paula had done a poor job of planning for accounts receivable. She encountered cash flow problems and ran out of money for payroll and rent. She was forced to borrow funds with her credit card at a much higher interest rate than on her home equity loan.

Eventually she collected all the money that was due and paid her bills, including the credit card debt, although the additional interest charges reduced her net profit. But her product continued to do well. Walt returned from the next show with orders for 18,000 more shirts. Paula's elation turned to panic when she realized she could not pay for the materials she would need to produce that many shirts.

Think Critically

What did Paula neglect to do in her initial capitalization plan? What can she do now to keep the business going?

Vocabulary Builder

Write a brief definition of each word or phrase.

1. acid-test ratio
2. assets
3. balance sheet
4. capital assets
5. capitalization
6. cash flow statement
7. current assets
8. current liabilities
9. current ratio
10. fixed assets
11. income statement
12. inventory turnover
13. leasehold improvements
14. liabilities
15. liquidity
16. long-term liabilities
17. net profit
18. net worth
19. pro forma financial statement
20. undercapitalized

Review the Concepts

21. How are capital assets used in the operation of a business?
22. What is the starting point for determining a business's financial needs?
23. How are operating expenses calculated for a new business?
24. What is the difference between an income statement and a balance sheet?
25. Why should a business conduct a cash flow analysis?
26. What is the difference between current and fixed assets?
27. What are the financial records every entrepreneur should keep?
28. What financial transactions should be included in the daily bookkeeping system?

Critical Thinking

29. Why is a financial plan such an important part of the overall business plan?
30. How does knowing the inventory turnover of a business help determine its capital needs?
31. What problems might an entrepreneur encounter if she does not conduct a cash flow analysis for her new business?
32. If the asset value of a business increases by $2,000 and the liabilities decrease by $1,000, by how much would the owner's equity change?
33. What would be the net profit of a business with total sales of $350,000, a 50 percent retail markup, and operating expenses of 35 percent of total sales?
34. An entrepreneur has calculated one-time-only capital needs at $10,000 and monthly operating expenses at $3,000. He decides to open with only $12,000. The first year's profits are expected to be $30,000. What problems would you warn him about as a result of undercapitalization?

Project

Build Your Business Plan

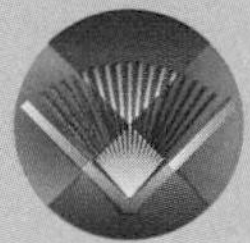

In your business plan, make a one-time-only needs statement for your chosen business. Create a balance sheet showing assets and any liabilities that may be incurred. You may need to consult someone with experience in your chosen industry for this information.

Based on your sales projection, make a pro forma income statement to determine the feasibility of your idea. In addition, research the revenue fluctuations of the industry and create a monthly cash flow spreadsheet on your computer. A local SBA office or Small Business Development Center would be glad to assist you.

Chapter 16

Management Control Tools

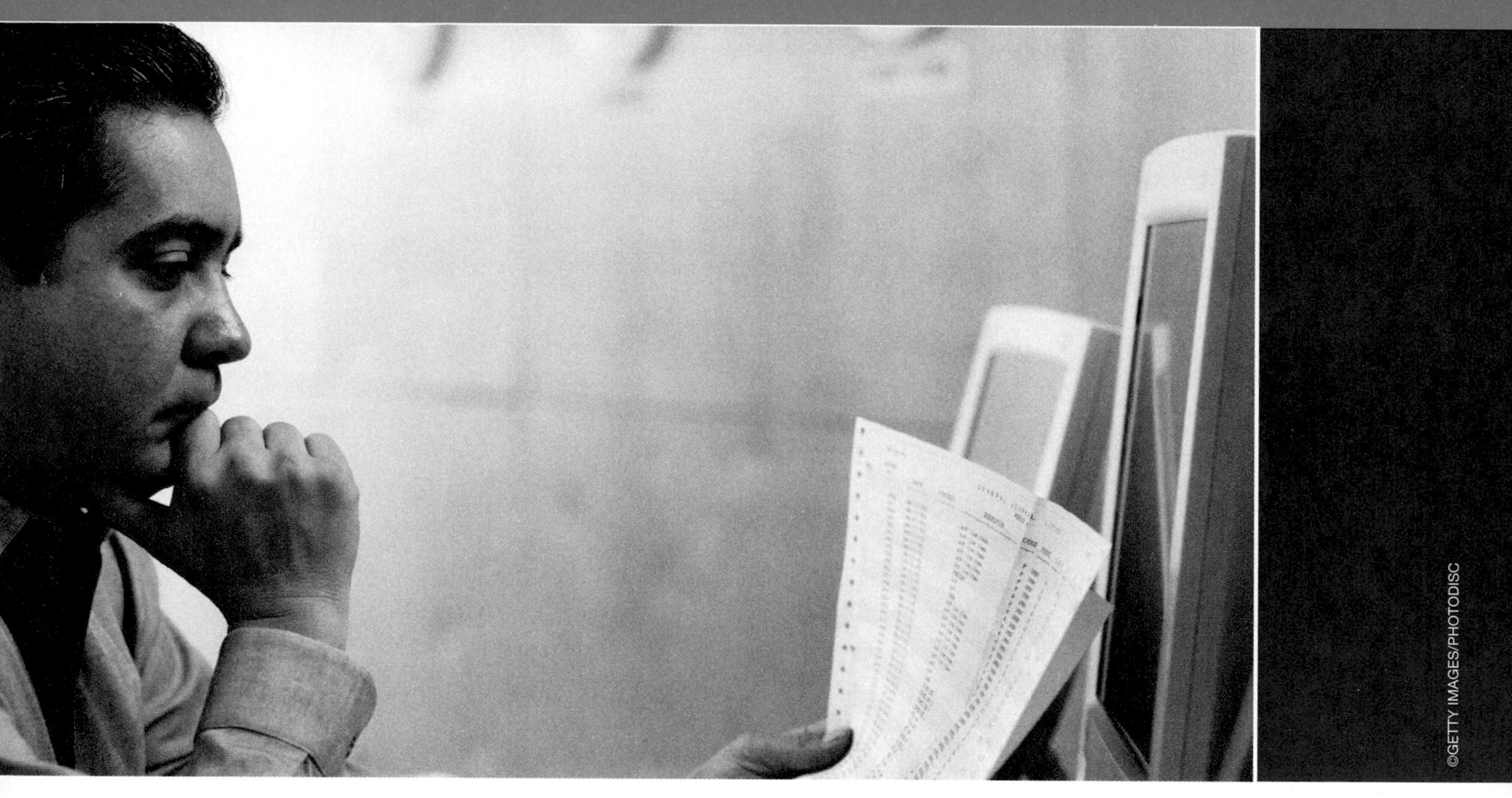
©GETTY IMAGES/PHOTODISC

Objectives

16-1 Describe management techniques used by small businesses.

16-2 Explain the importance of monitoring and controlling revenues.

16-3 Discuss the most effective ways to control inventory.

16-4 Analyze how inventory fluctuations affect business operations.

16-5 Describe technology tools that assist entrepreneurs.

16-6 Discuss methods of preventing employee and customer theft.

THE CONTROL FUNCTION

Along with planning, organizing, and directing, controlling is one of the four management functions. Controlling requires developing programs to monitor the activities of a business and make corrections when necessary. Again, the small business owner has the advantage of faster and more flexible responses. When things get out of line, you can make quick decisions to correct the imbalance without calling numerous meetings and waiting for the go-ahead from top management.

In her book *When Giants Learn to Dance*, Dr. Rosabeth Ross Kanter points out that large businesses have become so bureaucratic that they can no longer keep up ("dance") with the times. She goes on to say that they must become more flexible, like small businesses, to be successful in today's marketplace. At the same time she warns that without well-established policies, procedures, and discipline, small businesses run the risk of losing their focus and going off track. It is a balancing act—small businesses need policies and procedures, but not to the extent that those become handicaps in reaching the business's goals.

The importance of monitoring cash flow, performing effective appraisals of employee performance, and operating with a suitable accounting system has been discussed in earlier chapters. These are all essential control tools for managing small businesses. But if management does not have a clear vision of how the business is to be controlled, the business will flounder. Two management theories that guide many small businesses are management by objectives and total quality management.

Management by Objectives

By clearly stating the goals of the business and meshing them with the goals of the employees, entrepreneurs make use of a management technique called **management by objectives**, or MBO. MBO serves as a planning tool when the objectives are being set and as a control tool when the results are monitored and measured. Objectives should be set in all areas of the business's operations to ensure that resources are used efficiently. The planning function—setting the objectives—should follow the steps shown in Figure 16-1.

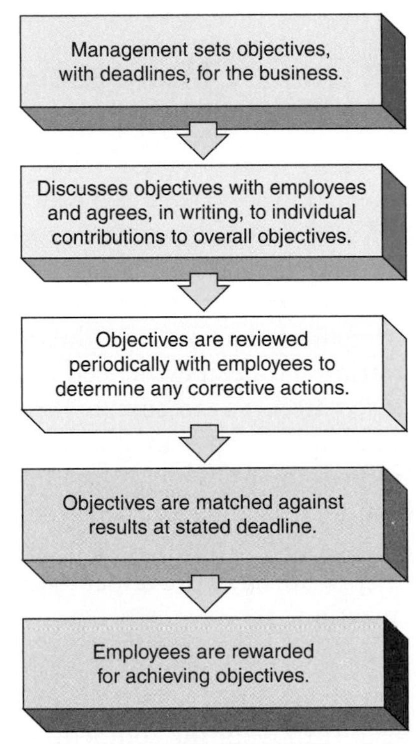

Management sets objectives, with deadlines, for the business.
Discusses objectives with employees and agrees, in writing, to individual contributions to overall objectives.
Objectives are reviewed periodically with employees to determine any corrective actions.
Objectives are matched against results at stated deadline.
Employees are rewarded for achieving objectives.

FIGURE 16-1
MBO Planning Steps

The control function—monitoring results—can be effective only if the standards against which results are measured are fairly and uniformly established. Proper standards

MBO Control Cycle

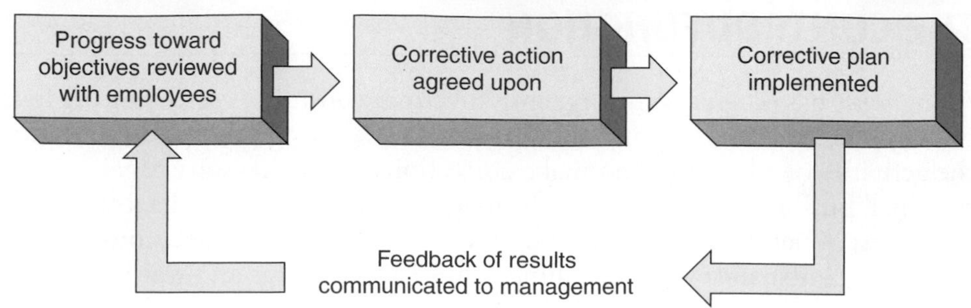

allow an effective feedback system that is consistent and clearly understood by everyone concerned. Figure 16-2 illustrates the steps involved in the controlling function of the MBO technique.

Although both large and small businesses can benefit from the MBO technique, it is better suited for small businesses. In large businesses the bureaucratic process of setting, monitoring, and changing objectives can be too slow and often results in missed opportunities. Small business owners can tailor a system to their particular business that establishes and monitors their objectives in a fair, efficient, and responsive manner. It is not enough simply to announce what you expect to achieve in a particular area of your business operation. Detailed objectives must be defined, discussed, and agreed to by all employees concerned, and the results should be closely monitored.

Small business owners use a variety of reports that serve as checklists for achieving objectives. Sales objectives are the first to be set. Nearly every aspect of a business is dependent on achieving sales objectives, so entrepreneurs must accurately estimate what sales totals will be for different time periods. Sales affect inventory levels, cash flow, personnel scheduling, and all other operating conditions.

Total Quality Management

The total quality management theory (TQM) has become a buzzword representing quality and efficiency throughout the business world. In Chapter 10, it was discussed how the idea was adapted from the Japanese after World War II in an effort to increase quality and at the same time decentralize (spread out) decision-making in businesses. Dr. Edward Deming was one of the first to cite the Japanese as operating with a superior system of control in production and customer service techniques. Its adaptation has been evidenced by improved quality of U.S. products and increased attention to customer service and product warranties.

The underlying principle of TQM is a relentless push toward continuous improvement, which is accomplished through better relationships with customers and suppliers, reduced production or replacement time, and more open input from employees. It requires implementing a large number of small improvement steps to reach goals in all areas of the organization.

TQM strategies include:

- **Benchmarking** The company continually measures its products against those of the competition and, when necessary, not only copies what the competition does but improves on it.

- **Outsourcing** The company relies on outside sources to perform certain functions that the company does not do well, such as creating graphics or managing payroll.
- **Quality circles** Teams of employee volunteers meet regularly to freely discuss how products and customer services can be improved.

The TQM way of thinking was new to many large businesses in the beginning, but in some ways it has always been practiced by successful smaller companies. Small businesses have traditionally placed great emphasis on constantly improving customer service and doing whatever it takes to produce products superior to those of their larger competitors. The most effective way to do this is to set high standards and make sure those standards are understood and achieved by all employees.

CONTROL REVENUES

If you set your business's sales objective at $200,000 at the beginning of the year, the business will be in sad shape if you do not discover until July that sales are running 30 percent behind the objective. It would be too late at that point to take corrective action. By monitoring your sales income daily, weekly, and monthly, you are better equipped to detect any problems early and then design and implement a plan to correct them. The plan that calls for sales to total $200,000 per year might require that 7 percent of sales be received in January. Therefore the January sales objectives would be $14,000—approximately $3,500 per week or $500 per day. The comparison of actual sales results with sales objectives can be shown on a daily and weekly sales report and summarized in a monthly report. For future reference, it is a good idea to add written notes explaining any change or discrepancy. Examples of such reports are shown in Tables 16-1 and 16-2.

If the numbers in your daily or weekly report are higher or lower than the sales objective, you may need to adjust those objectives. For example, if the sales income for the first two weeks of the month is $7,800 instead

TABLE 16-1 DAILY AND WEEKLY SALES REPORT

Week of: June 14

Daily Sales	Objective	+/(-)
Monday	$1,400	$150
Tuesday	$1,200	$75
Wednesday	$1,400	($200)
Thursday	$1,500	$125
Friday	$2,100	($350)
Saturday	$2,600	$400
Sunday	$1,000	$100
Weekly Total	$11,200	+ $300 [$11,500]

Comments: Antique car show in mall added to Saturday traffic. Poor weather on Friday.

TABLE 16-2 MONTHLY SALES TO OBJECTIVES REPORT

Month	Sales	Objective	+(–)	Comments
January	$21,200	$20,500	+700	Increase open-to-buy $500
February	18,400	18,550	(-150)	No action necessary
March	23,000	24,500	(-1,500)	Decrease open-to-buy $1,000
April	26,700	24,300	+2,400	Increase open-to-buy $2,000
May	23,100	22,900	+200	No action necessary
June	19,650	19,900	(-250)	No action necessary

of the $7,000 projected, you might reset the monthly sales objective at $15,600 instead of the $14,000 originally set. If this new objective is achieved, your annual sales objective might be reset for an additional $1,600. The same logic would apply if sales are not meeting your daily or weekly objectives.

Cash Flow Budgeting

If you have a firm grasp on how to handle a cash flow budget, you will learn how to best utilize extra available cash or react to a negative cash flow situation. Extra cash might be used to make an early note payment, which would save on interest, or it might be put in an interest-generating account to increase revenues. Extra cash may also allow early payment of an invoice, thereby increasing the vendor discount. Payroll hours might be increased to spur production or sales. Often extra income is used to pay for more advertisements or promotional activities. Used correctly, it can generate a snowball effect on the entire operation.

On the other hand, not meeting cash flow expectations can be devastating. As discussed in Chapter 15, entrepreneurs must be prepared to handle difficult cash flow situations with contingency plans such as a revolving line of credit arranged in advance to overcome short-term cash shortages.

Collecting Accounts Receivable

Small business owners who operate with an accounts receivable system must stay on top of collections at all times. It may be tempting to allow a favorite or important customer to take extra time to pay off invoices. But giving an extension one time sets a precedent that customers will often take advantage of. Allowing someone to pay you late might cause you to pay someone else late, which is not fair to you and not fair to the party you owe.

The credit record of a business is so important that it should not be placed in jeopardy by a poor collection system. Good businesses can quickly go bad when they cannot collect the money owed to them in a timely and efficient manner. Strict enforcement of company policies on bill collecting is essential to avoiding future revenue problems.

CONTROL INVENTORY

There is a direct correlation between sales and **inventory**. Inventory is the number of units, and the value of those units, that are available for sale or manufacture. Theoretically, the more units a business has on hand to sell or manufacture, the more it should sell. In this way, inventory affects sales, and consequently inventory levels are controlled by sales. If a business does not have sufficient inventory, there will be a drop-off in expected sales revenues. If it sells more units than expected, its inventory will fall below the desired level. If a business does not sell the expected number of units, the inventory will be higher than the desired level. Closely monitoring sales revenues allows the entrepreneur to adjust inventory levels to the demands of the market.

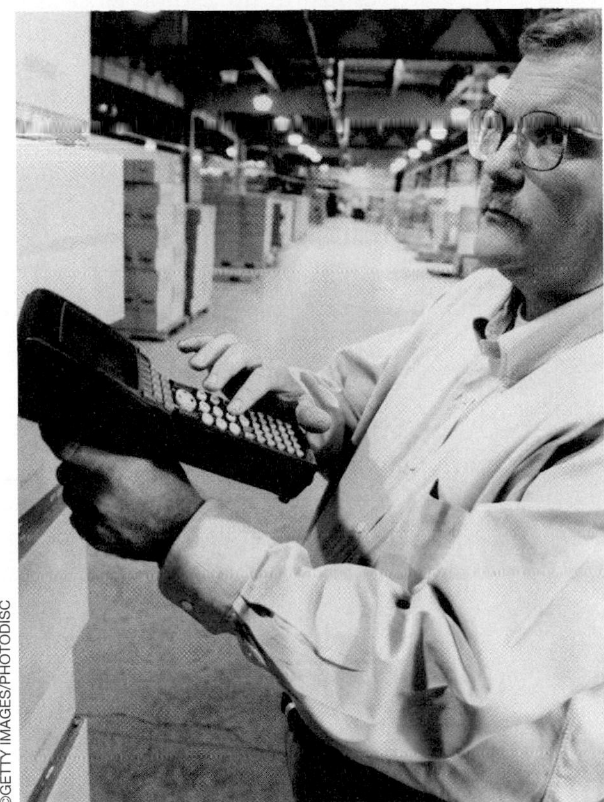
©GETTY IMAGES/PHOTODISC

As a business owner, your goal is to have the quantity of goods available that will give you the highest level of sales without over-investing in inventory. It is impossible to always have the exact amount of inventory on hand that will yield the greatest profit, but with the proper controls in place, you can maintain a level that will produce a healthy sales income and a profitable return on investment. For example, if you invest $10,000 in inventory and the net profit received from the sale of that inventory is $2,000, you have received a return on investment of 20 percent.

Business owners must make a profit from the purchase of inventory. If they have leftover or excess inventory, they are forced to sell it at a price that yields less profit or possibly a loss. If the inventory does not sell, it decreases the return on investment. Having too little inventory, on the other hand, can be even more dangerous. A deficit will lead to lost sales, lost profits, and dissatisfied customers. Manufacturers who run out of parts or materials may be forced to shut down production until replacement parts or materials arrive. Retailers who run out of merchandise before a major holiday lose business at a time when they should be making high profits. In addition, they are sending customers to their competitors with no assurance that those customers will return when inventory levels are brought back in line.

The Purchasing Process

Inventory suppliers, called **vendors**, must be carefully chosen. They must be dependable, stand behind their products, ship efficiently, and care about their customers. Good vendors are not out to make a quick profit but instead appreciate the long-term value of every customer. They understand that if

FUN FACTS

Atlanta's AmericasMart claims that it is the largest wholesale marketplace of its kind in the world. It hosts 23 different wholesale markets that attract 548,000 trade show attendees from every state in the U.S. and 80 foreign countries. Its gift show market alone has 2,000 permanent exhibitor showrooms and 4,000 temporary exhibitor display booths.

their customers do well with the goods or materials they supply, they will do well also. Vendors work closely with each customer to build a partnership. Everyone profits from this partnership as long as there is open communication and dependable and consistent service.

The ideal inventory plan is the **just-in-time inventory plan**. The inventory arrives just in time, or as close as possible to the time needed, to make the sale. The advantage to receiving inventory as close as possible to the point of selling it is that less money is tied up in inventory. With today's efficient production and transportation capabilities, it has become the norm not to accumulate inventory in warehouses six months in advance of selling the goods. Retailers and manufacturers have come to expect quick delivery from most of their vendors and will quickly change suppliers if orders are not delivered on time.

Entrepreneurs begin to purchase inventory after they have established their purchase plan objective. Depending on the industry, goods might come from one or more of a number of sources: trade shows, sales calls, print or online catalogs, and telemarketers.

Trade Shows Industry representatives frequently gather at central points in the marketplace and invite potential buyers to visit their exhibits. Trade shows can be as small as a few companies renting space at a local motel or as large as thousands of vendors exhibiting their goods, entertaining customers, and making new contacts at a permanent commercial arena in a major city. A trade show is an opportunity for buying, selling, and networking. **Networking** is the process of making business contacts by meeting people who can assist in business development. Trade shows can be exciting ventures whether entrepreneurs are shopping for goods or selling their own. For potential buyers, trade shows are an opportunity to discover what is new in their industry that can help increase profits and gain competitive advantages over the competition. They can buy unique goods, compare the prices of different vendors, or learn about new opportunities and industry developments.

Ethics for ENTREPRENEURS

Some vendors violate the rules at trade shows. They may "pad" orders by adding small increments to the number of units purchased in the hope that a small change will not be noticed. The buyer orders 15 dozen units, but the vendor records 16 dozen. This 6 percent add-on can make a significant difference to a seller who writes dozens or even hundreds of orders in a day. If the buyer happens to notice the discrepancy, the vendor apologizes for an "unintentional" error. However, the buyer with a sound purchase plan will notice and may sense what is happening. The vendor is risking a long-term relationship in an effort to sell a dozen more units—not a sound decision.

Think Critically

1. This type of violation correlates to cheating. Many students cheat. Discuss the ethical issues involved.
2. Can you think of any ways that buyers might violate vendors at trade shows?

Many trade shows offer educational seminars as well as buying and selling opportunities.

Sales Calls When not selling at trade shows, sales representatives are usually traveling through their assigned sales territories demonstrating their goods or services to customers—business owners, purchasing agents, and store managers, among others—at their places of business. Often, sales representatives make presentations and contacts at trade shows and then close the sales deal with the entrepreneur later, at the business itself. Buyers may also purchase a certain amount of inventory at a trade show and hold back a portion of their "open-to-buy" to have available when the sales representative visits their business. **Open-to-buy** is the term used to express the purchasing budget of a business.

Catalogs/Internet Just as people use catalogs and the Internet at home for convenient buying, entrepreneurs can use them to purchase inventory. Vendors often spend considerable amounts of money on designing web sites and creating catalog presentations of their products or services. Catalogs and web sites offer a method of ordering inventory that allows entrepreneurs to order whenever they find it convenient, without having to travel.

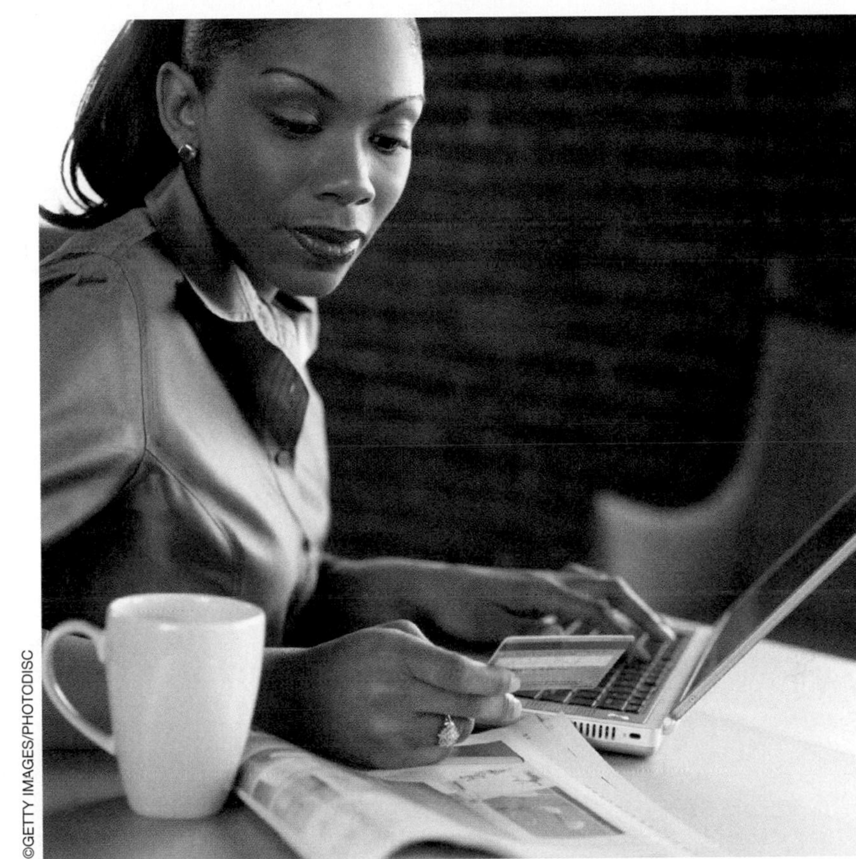
©GETTY IMAGES/PHOTODISC

Telemarketers Some vendors contact potential clients over the telephone. Obviously, when acquiring new inventory, business owners cannot rely on telemarketing. However, the telephone is an excellent means for sales follow-up and sometimes for sales closing. It is less effective as a cold-call tool since it does not allow the customer—in this case, the business owner—to see or touch the product.

The Inventory Purchase Plan

The amount of inventory a business should purchase can be calculated from the sales forecast. You must ask the question "How many units do I need to add to what is presently available to reach my sales objective for a particular period of time?" You need to know how much inventory is on hand at the beginning of the sales period and how much inventory you desire at the end of the sales period. For instance, if you wish to increase the amount of inventory on hand at the end of the period, you must add the amount of the desired increase to your purchase plan. If you want less inventory on hand, you subtract the amount.

The formula for calculating inventory purchases is:

beginning inventory + purchases – sales – markdowns = ending inventory

Suppose that a merchant has a beginning inventory worth $45,000 and projected sales of $100,000 over a period of six months. She wishes to increase the inventory on hand to $50,000 at the end of the six months and plans to mark down $10,000 of the inventory and sell it at cost. Since markdowns represent inventory that is sold without profit, that amount must be subtracted from the plan. To calculate the needed purchase (represented as *x*), the merchant inserts these figures into the formula.

$$\begin{aligned} \text{beginning inventory} + \text{purchases} - \text{sales} - \text{markdowns} &= \text{ending inventory} \\ \$45{,}000 + x - \$100{,}000 - \$10{,}000 &= \$50{,}000 \\ x - \$65{,}000 &= \$50{,}000 \\ x &= \$115{,}000 \end{aligned}$$

Once the inventory purchase amount has been determined, the entrepreneur must make sure the inventory arrives at the proper time. If all the inventory arrives at the same time, such as at the beginning of the sales period, it would all have to be paid for at one time. This could cause serious cash flow problems, and there would be no control tools available to raise or lower the inventory level in the event that sales were higher or lower than planned. A better strategy is to break the plan into smaller periods of time and stagger inventory purchases. With a detailed purchase plan it is easier to maintain the desired inventory levels. A six-month purchase plan for the example described above could be broken down into a month-by-month plan such as that in Table 16-3.

TABLE 16-3 6-MONTH RETAIL SALES AND INVENTORY PURCHASE PLAN

	July	August	September	October	November	December	TOTAL
Beginning Inventory	$45,000	$45,800	$47,600	$48,200	$50,600	$55,600	
+ Purchases	14,000	15,000	16,000	20,000	27,000	23,000	115,000
(–) Sales	12,000	12,000	14,000	16,000	20,000	26,000	100,000
(–) Markdowns	1,200	1,200	1,400	1,600	2,000	2,600	10,000
= Ending Inventory	45,800	47,600	48,200	50,600	55,600	50,000	

Note that in the table, the merchant plans to gradually increase the inventory level as the Christmas selling season approaches. It is imperative that the inventory level at the beginning of each month be sufficient to accommodate projected sales for that particular month. The key to proper inventory levels is being flexible and changing course in midstream when necessary to adjust to sales that are higher or lower than projected. Table 16-3 can apply to a retail store. A manufacturing company would have a new-materials inventory (unfinished raw materials), a work-in-process inventory (goods in the manufacturing process), and a finished goods inventory (goods ready for delivery).

For example, if September sales are $5,000 lower than the objective, there will be a $5,000 inventory surplus (in terms of sales dollars) on hand at the beginning of October. As soon as it is clear that the sales slippage is a trend, the entrepreneur should alter the purchase plan to reflect the situation. Otherwise there is a risk of ending up with an increasing disparity at the end of each month. Conversely, if sales are higher than projected, it may be wise to order additional inventory. Smart entrepreneurs keep an open-to-buy reserve to handle such situations. An **open-to-buy reserve** is money available for additional purchases outside the detailed purchase plan. When sales are poor it is not used, but when sales are on the upswing it is money that is immediately available to help cover additional purchases.

Small business owners should keep a running written record of inventory levels, called a **perpetual inventory**, at all times. By recording the amount of inventory a business receives and how much it sells on a daily, weekly, and monthly basis, you will have a record that shows approximate inventory levels at any given time. This informal record will not be exact because it does not take into account defective or stolen inventory. Nor does it include an accurate account of markdowns taken. It must be corrected for accuracy at least once a year with a **physical inventory**, an actual physical count of all the inventory the business owns. The items are counted manually and recorded on a list with a detailed description that may include size, color, and, if used, a stock number. Table 16-4 shows a sample physical inventory sheet.

TABLE 16-4 PHYSICAL INVENTORY REPORT

Description	Qty.	Sizes	Colors	Wholesale Each	Retail Each	Wholesale Total	Retail Total
Bags, duffle, equipment, nylon	9	n/a	black, navy, gray	3.50	7.00	31.50	63.00
Bags, duffle, equipment, canvas	9	n/a	same	4.50	9.00	40.50	81.00
Belts, stretch, cinch, women's	45	S, M, L	yellow, white, pink, gray, blue	2.50	5.00	112.50	225.00
Gloves, Triangle, leather	24	n/a	gray, white	10.00	20.00	240.00	480.00
Jump rope, heavy rope, rubber	3	3-1/2 lb	black	12.50	25.00	37.50	75.00
Jump rope, heavy rope, rubber	3	5 lb	black	15.00	30.00	45.00	90.00
Jump rope, aerobic	6	n/a	white	5.00	10.00	30.00	60.00
Leg warmers, Softouch	72	n/a	yellow, white, pink, gray, navy, orchid, black, blue	7.00	14.00	504.00	1,008.00

Inventory Delivery

Because sales projections never exactly match actual sales, you must build flexibility into your purchase plan. Most businesses make planned purchases well in advance of the targeted sales period. For example, a retail store might place orders for the Christmas selling season six to nine months beforehand to ensure receiving the best selection of merchandise from vendors. When doing this, the entrepreneur must recognize that numerous conditions might change that would require altering sales projections made so far in advance. Poor economic cycles, natural catastrophes, and terrorist threats are examples of events in the external environment that can cause a major disruption of a business's plans. For this reason, dependable suppliers and a flexible open-to-buy program are essential.

Astute business owners place orders in advance for the sales they feel most confident about. Many industries need lead time to produce or possibly import their products, so a high percentage of purchasing may have to be done well in advance. It is extremely important to have a well-thought-out backup plan, an open-to-buy reserve, and dependable suppliers in order to accommodate any unexpected changes. It is also important to recognize that customer tastes can change quickly, particularly in the retail sector. New fashions, fad products, and overnight technology changes are some of the reasons product demand might change between the time the original purchase plan is created and the selling season arrives. Good entrepreneurs have the flexibility and cash flow to adjust their plans as dictated by changes in the marketplace. As an example, a business owner operating with the plan in Table 16-3 might place orders totaling $70,000 at a trade show at the beginning of the sales period and keep $45,000 available as an open-to-buy. If sales are higher than expected, more than the planned $45,000 in inventory should be purchased. If sales are lower, some amount less than $45,000 should be spent.

The Global ENTREPRENEUR

The greatest concern about selling to overseas buyers is getting paid. Suing in a foreign court for unpaid goods is extremely difficult and expensive. Most international transactions are performed on a CIA, COD, or credit card basis, at least initially. If credit has been established, collection techniques must be given close attention. One alternative is to use the services of an international factor that performs the collection process for the exporter. Factors research the credit record of buyers and offer to pay, in this case, the exporter at the time the shipment is delivered and accepted by the buyer. The exporter must accept a discount on the invoice total for this service, but using a factor alleviates a major concern of international entrepreneurs.

Think Critically

1. What do you believe would be a reasonable fee for a factoring service?
2. Is it ethical to build the cost of the factoring service into the invoice total?

Terms of Sale

It is very important to buy from sources that offer fair terms of payment. Payment terms, also known as trade credit, on goods and services vary from industry to industry. However, in most industries it is common for vendors to give discounts to buyers who order large quantities and pay promptly. Vendors must be paid in order to maintain a positive cash flow and have the money available to reinvest in inventory as soon as possible.

The terms of sale are shown on the **invoice**, a statement the seller delivers to the buyer that lists the contents of a shipment or delivery, the number of units or items delivered, the unit price, the total cost, and the payment terms of the sale.

Some examples of the more common terms of sale are as follows:

- **CIA (cash in advance)** The invoice is paid in full to the vendor before being released for shipment.
- **COD (cash on delivery)** The amount of the invoice is collected by the deliverer upon delivery of the goods.
- **2/10/n30 ROG** The buyer receives a 2 percent discount if the invoice amount is paid within 10 days of the date the buyer receives the goods. The net amount (n) is due by the 30th day after receipt. ROG stands for "receipt of goods."
- **2/10/n30 EOM** The buyer receives a 2 percent discount if the invoice amount is paid by the 10th day of the month following delivery. The net amount is due by the 30th day of that month. EOM stands for "end of month."
- **3/10, 1/15, n60** The buyer receives a 3 percent discount if the invoice is paid within 10 days of delivery, or 1 percent if it is paid within 15 days. The net amount is due in 60 days.
- **EOM** The amount billed is due at the end of the month. No discounts apply.

©GETTY IMAGES/PHOTODISC

Terms of sale can have a significant impact on cash flow projections. Business owners wish to have as much time as possible to pay for inventory purchases. Ideally, they would prefer not to pay the vendor until ample time has passed to sell the inventory. For cash in advance (CIA) or COD purchases, the money for the inventory is invested immediately and taken out of the cash flow. If generous terms, such as n/60 or n/90, are granted to the buyer, the total sales price, including the profit, might be collected before money is taken out of the cash flow. This can make quite a difference to a business that makes a high percentage of its annual sales during the Christmas holiday selling season. Paying in January for merchandise sold in November and December, instead of paying in September when the merchandise is delivered, has a very positive cash flow impact. If merchandise must be paid for before it has had a chance to sell, business owners often find it necessary to borrow money from the bank until the merchandise sells. Paying interest on the borrowed money decreases the potential net profit. Taking advantage of discounts for early invoice payment, on the other hand, means additional profit.

Since it is in your best interest to tie up money in inventory for the shortest time possible, you must devise an inventory system that allows for the most efficient use of money. A just-in-time inventory system avoids having inventory that sits in a stockroom. Again, the key to this system is knowing the capability and reliability of vendors and closely monitoring inventory levels.

Most businesses assign a reorder point for inventory used on an everyday basis. When the stock of an item falls to this level—the reorder point—the item is automatically reordered. The reorder point is determined by the delivery time of the replacement inventory. Some businesses use a computerized inventory system that alerts management when it is time to reorder. This type of system is often used in cashiering systems that record each sale by a stock number. You can also create your own manual system to check inventory levels on a daily or weekly basis.

INVENTORY AND SALES FLUCTUATIONS

What happens when sales objectives are either exceeded or not met? Using the sales and inventory purchase plan in Table 16-3, assume that August's total sales are a disappointing $10,000 rather than the $12,000 projected. The immediate result is that the cash flow projection is $2,000 less than planned and the inventory level is $2,000 higher. Unless there is reason to believe that the lower sales are a long-term trend, simple short-term corrections should be made.

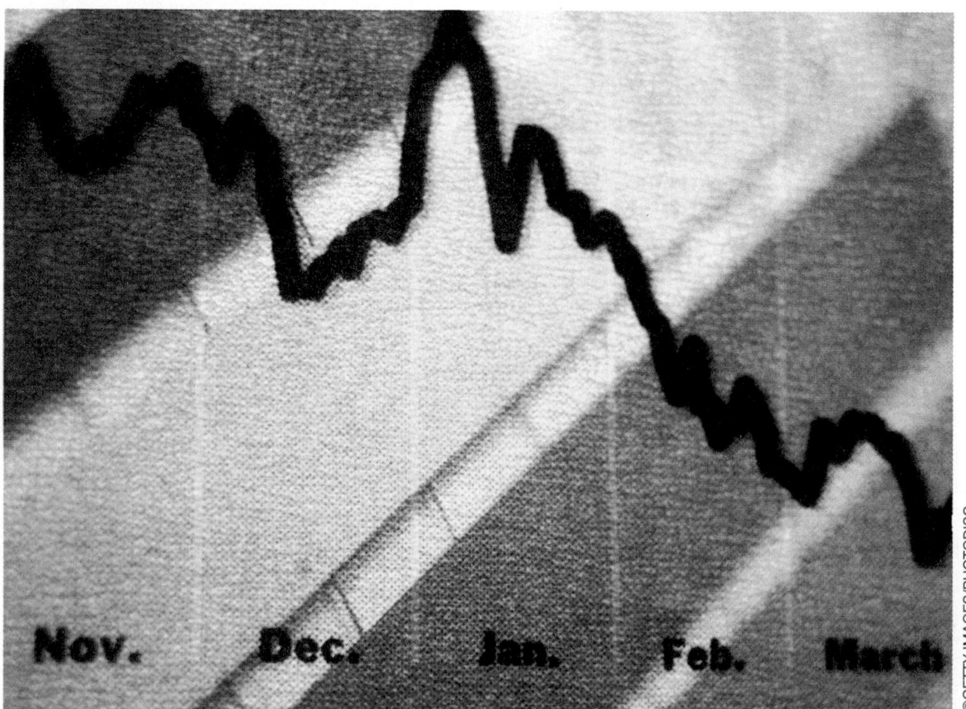

Postponing planned inventory arrivals by $2,000 in the next 30 days will correct the inventory level by October 1. At the same time, the planned future inventory purchases could be reduced by $2,000. In this way, the cash flow deficit will also be brought back in line.

If sales had exceeded the projection by $2,000, the business owner should attempt to speed up the planned inventory arrivals and at the same time order additional inventory using the open-to-buy reserve. If she fails to do this, the $2,000 inventory shortage will cause a decrease in anticipated sales sometime in the near future. As you can see, fluctuations in sales can easily get out of hand when they are not closely monitored. If corrections are not made immediately, a string of three or four months of sales revenue not being met or exceeding expectations will seriously disrupt the entire operation. This is why control reports must be kept up to date.

Poorly planned and controlled sales and inventory purchase objectives can have a domino effect throughout the entire business operation. In addition to cash flow problems, the business will experience disruptions in personnel scheduling, insurance expenditures, and promotional efforts.

Personnel Scheduling

The organization chart and personnel needs are designed to accommodate projected sales objectives. In the event these projections get out of line, the entrepreneur has to adjust personnel schedules. If sales are too low, there will be employees with not enough work to do. Some may have to be laid off, or their hours may need to be decreased. Some companies reduce their employees' pay rate. All these measures have a negative impact on employee morale. Poor morale can cause excessive personnel turnover, which could result in the expensive task of employee recruiting and training.

If sales exceed objectives, the owner may have to hire extra personnel or pay overtime to handle the added business. If the business is understaffed, customers may not receive the quick, efficient assistance to which they are accustomed, and they might go to the competition instead.

Personnel schedules, like inventory purchase plans, should be designed with flexibility. Successful business owners have a contingency plan of action to handle both slow and busy sales periods. They cross-train employees, who are then qualified to handle additional responsibilities. They also keep the names of people who can work on a part-time or temporary basis always on hand.

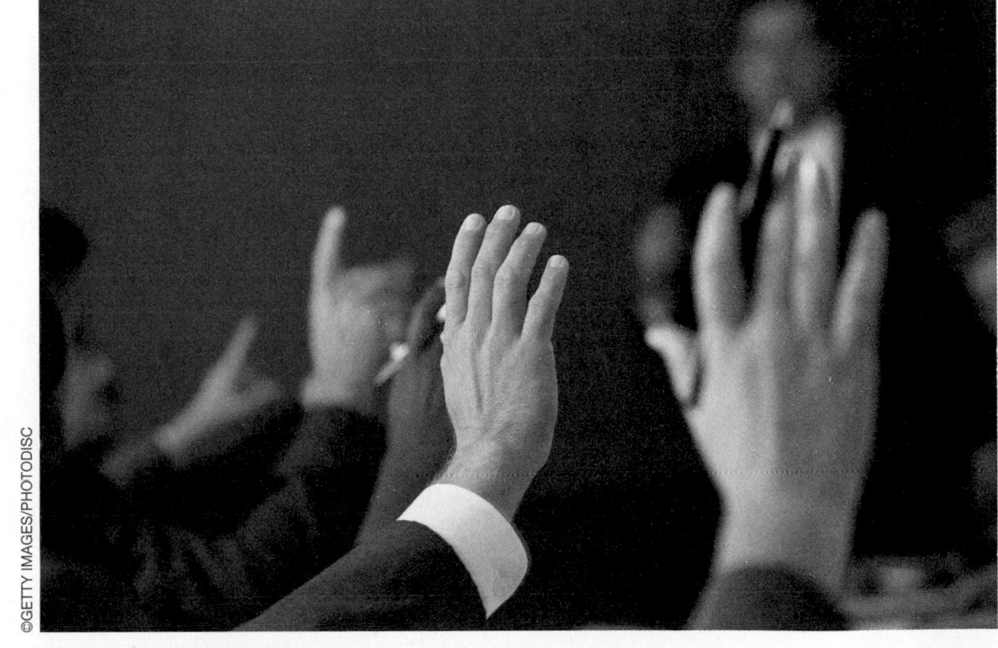
©GETTY IMAGES/PHOTODISC

Business owners should warn employees in advance of possible courses of action the company will take to handle periods of high or low sales. For example, there may be times when employees are asked to work overtime or their working hours are cut back. Entrepreneurs and their families should be prepared to work extra hours themselves when needed. If it is necessary to lay off employees because of poor sales, owners should provide as much notice as possible to give the affected personnel time to search for other jobs.

Insurance

Unexpected changes in sales and inventory plans also have an impact on the insurance requirements of the business. Entrepreneurs must carry insurance to protect against losing their investments as a result of fire, accidents, or other unexpected events. Insurance premiums are based on the value of the business. The more property that is insured, the higher the premiums. Additional inventory increases the value of the business, which in turn means that additional insurance coverage should be purchased. If the value of inventory increases by $25,000, the insurance should increase by the same amount. The insurance company should be informed of changes in the value of the business, or coverage will not be sufficient. Many businesses carry "peak season" coverage that automatically expands during times of the year when inventory increases are anticipated. In case of fire or other emergency, the owner will not receive reimbursement for lost property that has not been reported to the insurance company.

Promotions

Since promotional events and sales activities are often scheduled months in advance, a change of inventory levels can be devastating to a planned promotion. If the business is planning an event to showcase its newest products, but poor sales have forced the business to cut back or postpone delivery of inventory, plans will have to be changed as soon as possible. Seasonal advertising will be misspent if the proper amount of inventory is not on hand to satisfy the demand created by the advertising.

©GETTY IMAGES/PHOTODISC

Likewise, if a manufacturer does not have the completed goods ready for shipment, the business's sales force will have nothing to sell. In this situation poorly planned inventory production will demoralize the sales force and cause resignations as sales personnel who receive commissions will suffer financially.

Future Implications

When a business fails to meet its sales objectives, the ramifications can be felt for a long time. Coming out of a fall selling season with too much inventory reduces the amount of money available to buy spring goods, which then adversely affects purchases for the following fall season. Unless contingency plans and control tools are planned and implemented, this domino effect can gain momentum until it crushes the operation. Conversely, dramatic upswings can change not only the immediate but the long-term opportunities of a business. Good business cycles open up *strategic windows* of opportunity—times when opportunities and expansion should be sought and will only be available for a certain amount of time. You must take the time to formulate strategic, long-term plans that take into consideration all possible outcomes to your decisions.

COMPUTERS AS CONTROL TOOLS

Personal computers have become great tools for business owners. There is a wide range of hardware to choose from. Among the many software packages available for business use, some are designed for manufacturers and others for service, retail, or wholesale businesses.

Entrepreneurs must shop carefully for the software system that best fits their particular business, then find the computer hardware that accommodates the chosen system. Computer hardware consists of the computer, monitor, keyboard, printer, and speaker system. For many start-up businesses, systems that cost less than $2,000 are sufficient. As the business matures, so should the system. It might start as an individual PC and end up a network of computers, all tied into one central system. If you are not up to date in the use of PCs, look into taking courses at a local college or private computer learning center. In today's world it is becoming almost impossible to operate a business without at least a rudimentary knowledge of computer technology.

With proper training, you can keep records and monitor activities as efficiently as large businesses do. Business operations that can be handled efficiently through the use of computers include:

- **Financial Statements** Updated income statements, balance sheets, and cash flow statements can be easily maintained and reproduced as needed.
- **Inventory Control Records** Perpetual inventory totals can be tracked by product line as well as accumulated totals. Many businesses have computerized sales terminals that automatically subtract each item sold from its product category.

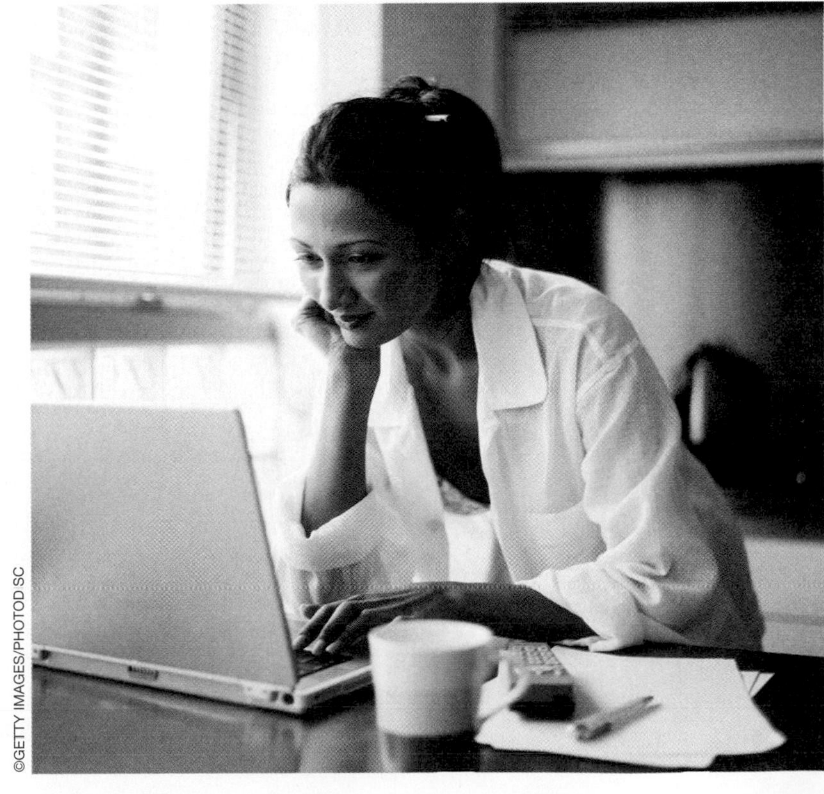
©GETTY IMAGES/PHOTODISC

Small Business Technology

Entrepreneurs carry their control tools with them—laptops on airplanes and PDAs at trade shows. Cell phones have become part of their wardrobe, clipped to their belts each morning. When they travel, business owners check in with the office, pull up daily cash flow information on their computers, and keep track of their schedules. At trade shows they calculate changes in their open-to-buy budget with each order placed. In today's marketplace it is essential to stay in touch with what's going on around you.

- **Personnel Payroll Records** Payroll software makes it possible to maintain year-to-date payroll records showing all tax and other payroll deductions per employee. A payroll program automatically calculates all tax and other deductions for each pay period and prints the paychecks. This saves considerable time for the person in charge of payroll.
- **Accounts Payable and Receivable Records** By recording all incoming and outgoing invoices, the business keeps current and convenient records of all monies owed by vendors and customers.
- **Correspondence** Word processing software programs make writing and keeping records of all business correspondence simple. Numerous graphic art and publishing programs assist in developing brochures, advertising layouts, and announcements.

Database Applications

Most entrepreneurs routinely develop lists of various kinds of information. The names of customers, potential customers, vendors, and competitors are examples of information that should be collected and organized. A **database** is a collection, depository, and list of information used by businesses to stay informed about their customers. Database software is a set of instructions used with a computer to set up and provide access to this listing of data.

A database stored in a computer makes it easy to organize information, keep the information up to date, and produce printed copies of the information. A database is organized so that many people can retrieve information from it, use it for different reasons, and format it in different ways. Table 16-5 is an example of how information about customers can be stored in a database.

TABLE 16-5 CUSTOMER DATABASE

Name	Address	Phone	Purchases Year to Date
Dinges Works	341 Colfax Rd.	303-243-5436	$ 10,365.89
Johnson Sales	802 South St.	303-245-9898	30,143.09
Reed Manufacturing	104 Constitution Ave.	303-248-1010	18,296.54
Stein Manufacturing	143 S. Hampton Rd.	303-245-7777	76,243.65
Sultan Manufacturing	2101 Industrial Rd.	303-243-1999	25,389.89
Wong Energy	567 Wales Ave.	303-248-0753	100,945.10
Zu Welding	557 Colorado St.	303-245-9183	7,512.76

When creating a database, you must first decide what information about your customers is important to keep on file. The entrepreneur who developed the database in Table 16-5 wanted a list of all customers, including the address, phone number, and year-to-date purchases of each. If the entrepreneur later decides that other information would be useful as well, that information can be added to the database. For instance, the year that each customer began purchasing from the business could be added as a fifth category.

Information can be retrieved from the database and sorted on the basis of a particular characteristic that you choose. For example, if you want to know which customers are located in the area of town that has phone numbers with the prefix 243, you could search the database for all phone numbers that begin with 243. The search would yield two customers: Dinges Works and Sultan Manufacturing. You can use this information to arrange to call on both customers when you are in that part of town. Or perhaps you decide to reward all customers who have ordered at least $25,000 worth of merchandise in the year to date. Your search brings up Johnson Sales, Stein Manufacturing, Sultan Manufacturing, and Wong Energy.

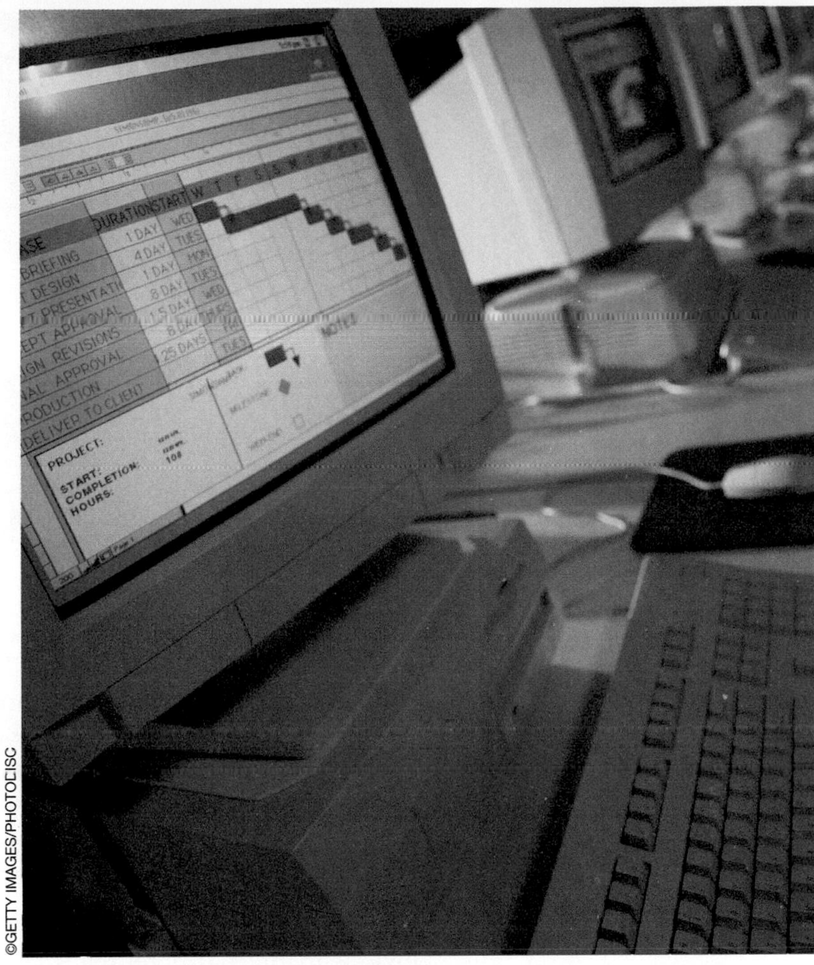

©GETTY IMAGES/PHOTODISC

Searches based on many other characteristics can also be made. A restaurateur in need of additional revenues can keep a list of customers and their birthdays. Sending an invitation for a free dessert on their special day is bound to bring in extra business.

A database can be used to create mailing labels, generate reports, and track accounts payable and receivable. The ability to store and organize information in different ways can be a valuable asset for the busy entrepreneur.

Spreadsheet Applications

As discussed in Chapter 15, one of the major responsibilities of an entrepreneur is to maintain accurate accounting records. The most efficient way to keep these records is with spreadsheet software. A **spreadsheet** is an electronic replacement for an accountant's columnar ledger, pencil, and calculator. You can use spreadsheets to calculate budgets, prepare financial statements, and analyze financial problems—in fact, you can apply them to almost any math problem that can be solved with a calculator. As numbers are changed on the spreadsheet, totals are automatically recalculated. This feature facilitates planning different financial scenarios. For example, when you are completing the initial capitalization portion of your business plan, you will find it very useful to experiment with different figures to determine actual operating costs and cash flow. If you wanted to see what your total operating costs would be with a building rent of $650 per month instead of the $800 per month you had originally estimated, you could substitute the $800 figure with $650. The spreadsheet would then automatically recalculate your initial operating cost estimates, as shown in Table 16-6. To recalculate all the figures with pencil and paper would be time consuming, but the computer can perform the same function for you instantly.

TABLE 16-6 SAMPLE SPREADSHEET OF BUSINESS START-UP COSTS: FIRST AND SECOND ESTIMATES

	Expense Item	First Estimate	Second Estimate
1	Telephone	$ 100	$ 100
2	Equipment	10,000	10,000
3	Wages	4,000	4,000
4	Rent	800	650
5	Utilities	350	350
6	Advertising	400	400
7	Merchandise	20,000	20,000
8	TOTAL	$35,650	$35,500

CONTROL THEFT

It is an unfortunate fact of life that some people steal. Businesses are often victims of theft by customers and employees. If business owners do not take proper security measures, inventory theft can have a serious impact on their inventory control system and their profits.

The best method of controlling inventory theft is through prevention. Measures for preventing customer theft include the following.

- Train the staff to watch all customers closely, but not in an annoying or obvious manner. If potential thieves know they are being watched, they generally will not steal. In a retail environment, all customers should be acknowledged as they enter. It is not only polite, but it also gives notice to shoplifters that the employees are aware of their presence.

©GETTY IMAGES/PHOTODISC

- Teach employees the procedures to follow in the event they witness a theft. Call your local police department and ask about procedures or training available to business owners. If a shoplifter is apprehended and arrested, it serves as notice to others that the business does not tolerate shoplifting.
- Invest in security devices. Alarm systems, hidden cameras, and security tags on merchandise are commonly used devices. The cost of some security systems may be partially offset by reduced insurance premiums. As a prevention tool, it is usually a good idea to publicly post the security measures being used.

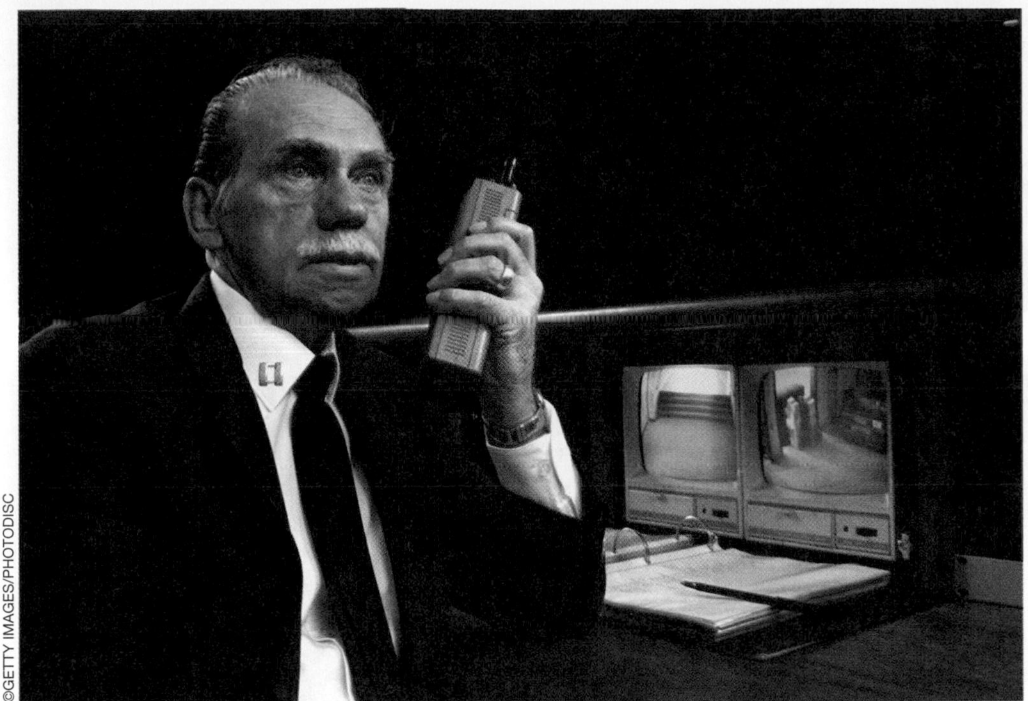
©GETTY IMAGES/PHOTODISC

Businesses must also establish prevention measures against employee theft, which is actually far more common in many industries than customer theft. Common methods include the following.

- Set a policy that allows checking all articles taken out of the business at closing time or at employee work shift changes. Articles that may be checked include purses, tote bags, briefcases, and lunch bags.
- Devise a system of checking inventory levels against sales results. If an item is not accounted for, compare sales receipts with physical inventory to determine whether it may have been stolen.

The best way to ensure employee honesty is to cultivate an open relationship between employees and management. Employees who work as a team and take pride in their work are less likely to be tempted to steal from the business. In the event there is theft, loyal employees will find a way to report infractions by their fellow employees.

The amount of stolen inventory can be calculated when a physical inventory is taken. Business owners can assume that merchandise, products, or parts not accounted for by sales, use, or damage have been stolen. A significant incidence of theft reduces inventory levels and causes problems in achieving sales objectives.

Successful entrepreneurs are very attuned to properly monitoring operations in all areas of their business. Whenever things go astray—whether it be cash flow, inventory fluctuations, or stolen goods—a business will suffer in its profitability. There is no perfect business plan that is able to predict and project its operations exactly. There are times that circumstances arise that are a total surprise and are impossible to predict. Good managers develop guidelines to rely on when plans change and are able to move quickly and decisively to correct imbalances. This contingency planning ability is developed through experience and instilling a strong monitoring program throughout the business operation.

FUN FACTS

According to the U.S. Department of Commerce, employee theft is responsible for nearly one-third of business bankruptcies. The 2002 National Retail Survey estimates the cost of shoplifting at $10 billion per year. There are a reported 800,000 shoplifting incidents every day.

Ship in a BOTTLE

Taking Control

With five product lines, three employees, and an operating budget of over $2,000 per month, Ship in a Bottle was on its way to becoming a full-fledged business. Fred was ready to take the plunge into full-time ownership/management and build the business into a $1,000,000-per-year operation. But if he was going to reach that objective, he would have to install some management controls that he had neglected.

He started by reviewing his objectives. No longer could he get by with "guesstimating" sales. He would have to set annual sales objectives and strategies to achieve them. He consulted with his employees, with Johann, with the nautical weather instrument and clock manufacturer, and met with his flag, nautical print, and home decor vendors at trade shows. He reviewed each vendor's production and delivery capabilities. Fred then reviewed his retail accounts and decided to visit the stores on a regular basis. He considered hiring a sales representative to do this.

Fred developed a purchase plan for each product line based on three-month periods. The difficult part was coordinating various production and delivery schedules. Flags were available almost immediately, ship in a bottle took three months, clocks and weather instruments one month, and nautical prints and decor four to six weeks. He had decided months earlier that he would rather be too long on inventory than too short. Losing orders because of shortages would be unacceptable because he knew customers would find a substitute product.

Fred had also learned that the seasons varied greatly in terms of promotional possibilities. December was the best month for the retail web site, October was good for the wholesale trade, June offered Father's Day and graduations, Valentine's Day was a bright spot, but January stank. He would need to arrange his inventory arrivals to coordinate with the various seasons. He hoped to persuade his vendors to loosen up in their selling terms as they got to know him better. Of course, he knew his retail store accounts would request the same treatment—they would want special terms, too. One of the first policies he put into effect was that all customers would be treated equally no matter their size or status.

Fred had learned the value of a computer in a small business. It made his job much easier and allowed him to keep an eye on important financial information. He would soon need to add some computers to the network for the telephone answering crew to forward orders.

It was exciting, exhilarating—and frightening. A year earlier he had been looking for a ship in a bottle, and now he was setting up a business that would support his family. He was living the American dream of business ownership. Fred Johnson, Entrepreneur: it sounded pretty good.

Think Critically

1. Do you think Fred is ready to operate his business on a full-time basis?
2. Make a list of policies Fred can use to stay on top of his enterprise.
3. What areas should Fred investigate for future expansion?

Summary

Entrepreneurs must control all aspects of their business operations. Management by objectives clearly states the goals of the business and meshes them with the goals of the employees to ensure that everyone is involved. Objectives are stated for all operational aspects of the business, and results are measured against fair and uniform standards. Another management technique is total quality management, or TQM, which involves implementing a program of continuous improvement through stronger relationships with customers and suppliers, reduced production or replacement time, and greater employee involvement.

Once sales objectives are set, sales results are monitored on a daily, weekly, and monthly basis to make sure the business is operating as planned. If objectives are off the mark, there will be a ripple effect throughout the operation. Missed sales objectives force changes in inventory levels, personnel scheduling, insurance requirements, and promotional plans. Cash flow budgeting and the timely collection of accounts receivable are two ways to control revenues.

Entrepreneurs should monitor inventory and design purchase plans. The purchase plan must be flexible to accommodate changes in sales revenue forecasts. The just-in-time inventory plan is ideal. Building a strong relationship with dependable and cooperative vendors allows the entrepreneur to negotiate for the best payment terms, manage inventory levels, and maintain a positive cash flow.

Personal computers are invaluable control tools. Database and spreadsheet software programs are used to create financial statements, budgets, inventory control records, payroll records, accounts payable and receivable records, and customer databases.

Employee and customer theft are an unavoidable aspect of running a business. Security measures must be built into the business plan, and an open relationship must be cultivated between management and employees.

A Case in POINT

Unrealistic Expectations

Benny's desk was piled high with invoices. He was discussing his problem with Suzanne, a consultant from the local Small Business Development Center. "I can't keep up with all these bills, Suzanne. I'm totally confused about which to pay now and which to hold off on."

Suzanne was not surprised. Benny's business *was* a mess—a gift shop stuffed with random goods and no theme or direction. "How many vendors do you have, Benny?"

"Fifty or 60, maybe more. When I go to trade shows I buy whatever looks like it'll sell."

Suzanne handed him a blank pad. "A shop this size doesn't need so many suppliers. List all of your suppliers by category so you can see what percentage of your total sales comes from each category."

A week later Benny presented a list to Suzanne.

Classification	# of Suppliers	% of Sales
Greeting cards/stationery	11	21
All occasion gifts	15	23
Special occasion gifts	12	20
Novelty gifts	18	26
Fine gifts	7	10

continued

Chapter Review

"Benny, you have 63 suppliers. That's less than 2 percent of sales per supplier. If you consolidate your buying, you'll get better service and have a better grip on your business. If you cut the list to 20 or 25—so 4 or 5 percent comes from each supplier—you'll save on shipping costs, and possibly get discounts for your higher-volume purchases."

Working together, Benny and Suzanne made a new list.

Classification	# of Suppliers	% of Sales
Greeting cards/stationery	5	25
All-occasion gifts	6	25
Special-occasion gifts	4	20
Novelty gifts	5	20
Fine gifts	3	10

"Well, that's a start," Suzanne said. "Choose your vendors carefully. Buy only from those you can depend on, who will offer help when you need it. Choosing the best vendors will make your inventory selection better. Also, the more established the vendor, the more flexible the payment terms. Design a detailed purchase plan and a strict budget before you go to the next trade show—and stick to it. Hold some money back as an open-to-buy after the show so that you can adjust to any changes in your projected sales during the selling season."

Think Critically

1. What caused Benny's inventory problem in the first place?
2. What control tools should he implement now for the future?

Vocabulary Builder

Write a brief definition of each word or phrase.

1. database
2. inventory
3. invoice
4. just-in-time inventory plan
5. management by objectives
6. networking
7. open-to-buy
8. open-to-buy reserve
9. perpetual inventory
10. physical inventory
11. spreadsheet
12. vendors

Review the Concepts

13. Why is management by objectives both a planning and control tool?
14. What are the primary components of total quality management?
15. Why is it necessary to monitor sales results daily, weekly, and monthly?
16. Explain two important ways to control revenues.
17. What is the advantage of a just-in-time inventory control system?
18. What are four ways that a business owner can shop for inventory?
19. What does the notation 2/10/n30 mean?

20. How do inventory and sales fluctuations affect personnel scheduling, insurance, and promotion?
21. Name five ways that a small business owner can use a computer.
22. Name three uses for a database and three uses for a spreadsheet.

Critical Thinking

23. What is the starting point of a purchase plan, and how are planned purchases determined?
24. What can happen to a business owner who fails to maintain an open-to-buy budget after planned purchases have been ordered?
25. Discuss the importance of establishing trust and dependability with vendors.
26. What do you believe is management's responsibility to employees when poor sales force a reduction in payroll?
27. How much should a business purchase if it has a beginning inventory of $75,000, a planned ending inventory of $80,000, projected sales of $200,000, and projected markdowns at cost of $10,000?
28. Why is building a database on a computer essential for a small business owner?

Project

Build Your Business Plan

Prepare a six-month purchase plan for your hypothetical business. Start by stating what you believe will be your beginning inventory and your ending inventory. (Note: Since it is a new business, the inventory should be in a growth stage.) By inserting your six-month sales forecast and calculating a percentage for markdowns, you will be able to determine your initial open-to-buy. Refer to Table 16-3 to create your plan.

Now determine from which vendors you will purchase inventory. Visit would-be competitors in your community. Find out if any trade shows are scheduled for your industry in or close to your locale. If possible, find out if you can attend as a guest.

Determine the type of database your new business should maintain. Consider a separate database for customers, vendors, and competitors.

It is now time to conclude your business plan by writing the executive summary, which is placed at the beginning of the report. Review your total plan and summarize its most attractive features. Remember the executive summary should act as a catalyst for the reader to continue. Tell your reader what lies ahead in the report.

Best wishes for an exciting entrepreneurial career!

The Banker

Mary Yost was reviewing Gavin Ross's loan application for his proposed candy manufacturing and distribution company. Mary is a commercial loan officer at First National Bank. Her primary responsibility is to review business loan applications, interview applicants, and make recommendations to the loan committee for approval or disapproval.

Her first task was to determine whether Gavin had the expertise and experience to run a business. She was pleased to note from his resume that he had worked for a large confectionery for over five years, honing his managerial skills. He also had an outstanding personal credit rating.

Mary had to determine whether Gavin's financial proposition was a good risk. The bank directors were cautious about granting new business loans because so many new businesses fail. The bank usually required that a new business loan be 100 percent collateralized by easily liquidated personal assets. Exceptions were sometimes made if the applicant had a strong business plan. Gavin's loan would have to be an exception—he did not have enough collateral to fully support his $50,000 loan request. Mary reviewed Gavin's personal financial statement.

Assets		Liabilities	
Cash on hand	$ 1,500	Notes payable (automobile)	$ 4,500
Stocks and bonds	25,000	Credit card debt	1,300
Real estate (home)	110,000	Mortgage loan	70,000
Automobile	8,000	Misc. accounts payable	900
Personal assets	11,000		
Total assets	$155,500	Total liabilities	$76,700

Total assets ($155,500) – Total liabilities (76,700) = Net worth ($78,800)

The financial plan to start the business called for a total of $75,000. Gavin, willing to contribute $25,000 from the sale of stocks and bonds, was $50,000 short. Mary reread the statement for other possible sources of collateral. Gavin's car was too old, and his personal belongings could not be easily liquidated if the bank had to call in the loan. But the home equity—the $40,000 difference between the mortgage loan and the value of the home—could be used to help secure the loan. The bank could lend Gavin up to 80 percent of his home equity, or $32,000.

There was still an $18,000 deficit in available start-up funds. Mary turned her attention to the pro forma balance sheet for the new business.

Assets		Liabilities and Owner's Equity	
Current assets		Current liabilities	
Cash	$15,500	Accounts payable	$ 300
Inventory	19,300	Current portion of long-term	
Supplies	2,200	debt (3 yr. $50,000)	16,700
Total current assets	37,000	Total current liabilities	17,000
Fixed assets	37,500	Long-term debt	33,300
		Owner's equity	24,200
Total Assets	$74,500	Total liabilities/owner's equity	$74,500

Although Gavin had hoped to use the inventory and equipment as collateral, Mary knew they would be difficult for the bank to liquidate if necessary. After contacting a buyer of used candy-making equipment she penciled in $5,000 as its true collateral value. She still needed to find $13,000 in collateral for a $50,000 loan.

She reviewed Gavin's pro forma income statement. He had prepared both best- and worst-case scenarios. Mary studied the worst-case scenario to determine the level of risk.

Based on Gavin's conservative projections, the business could afford a $1,400 monthly payment, the approximate amount required for a three-year payout of $50,000 at 6.5 percent interest. This would pinch Gavin's cash flow a little during the first year, but the second- and third-year projections indicated that by then he could easily meet the payment.

Mary reviewed the capital-needed statement again. She noted approvingly that Gavin had put in a reserve fund of $10,000 for unexpected expenses. The cash flow projection did not indicate any months of excessive deficits.

Pro Forma Income Statement, Year Ending June 30, 2006		
Sales	$250,000	
Cost of goods sold	97,000	
Gross profit		$153,000
Operating expenses		
Payroll (including owner)	75,000	
Rent	18,700	
Operating supplies	9,900	
Maintenance	6,000	
Utilities	8,600	
Interest	3,600	
Advertising	2,500	
Insurance	3,700	
Depreciation	4,000	
Other	4,000	
Total operating expenses		$136,000
Net Profit (before taxes)		$17,000

Mary decided to propose that the bank lend Gavin $40,000 on a three-year note, collateralized by his $32,000 home equity and liquid business assets of $5,000. She would also recommend approval of a short-term $10,000 line of credit in case of a cash flow shortage. The loan committee would have misgivings about issuing a loan to a new business that was less than 100 percent collateralized, but the bank would benefit from the use of Gavin's deposits of $250,000. Mary recognized the risks but also felt it was a solid recommendation. If the business failed, she would be held responsible for recommending the loan. If it succeeded, her recommendations would be treated with greater respect. Mary wrote "Recommend Approval" across the top of the application.

CASE QUESTIONS

1. Do you believe the loan committee should accept Mary's recommendation? Why or why not?
2. Do you think Gavin should accept the loan as recommended, or should he hold out for his original request of a $50,000 three-year loan?
3. Do you believe commercial lending institutions are too cautious about making new business loans? Can you think of anything they could do to lower the risks associated with new business loans?

APPENDIX

Small Business Assistance

Federal Agencies

Federal/State Cooperatives

State Agencies

Community Resources

Professional Sources

Sample Listing of Small-Business Incubators by State

Because entrepreneurs are often the sole creators and/or directors of their enterprises, they sometimes work in isolated environments. As you have learned, entrepreneurs must become knowledgeable in many areas to successfully operate their businesses and compete in today's sophisticated marketplace. This appendix provides a partial listing of resources you can turn to for information on establishing and maintaining a business. For additional information, visit the agencies' Internet sites or contact them directly.

FEDERAL AGENCIES

Many types of support and assistance are available through government agencies. Entrepreneurs can generally obtain most of the information, education, and direction they need from these sources.

Small Business Administration

The U.S. government recognizes the important role that small businesses play in our society. Congress authorized the formation of the Small Business Administration (SBA) in 1953 to encourage the development of small businesses and the important inventions and innovations they provide. The SBA helps small businesses secure government contracts and acts as a special advocate with other federal agencies as well as state and private agencies. It helps small businesses increase their revenues and profits, which increases tax revenues for the government and helps to maintain Americans' standard of living. More than 100 SBA offices are located throughout the country. Assistance includes loans, counseling, and publications.

SBA Loan Assistance The SBA provides assistance in financing thousands of businesses that would not qualify for conventional financing. It offers two basic types of business loans, guaranteed and direct, as discussed in Chapter 14.

Counseling One of the sources of SBA counseling services is the **Service Corps of Retired Executives (SCORE)**. There is no cost for these services, as SCORE is a volunteer organization. Volunteers come from all areas of business, including commercial and industrial, and use their business experience to advise and guide small business owners. SCORE also offers comprehensive workshops for prospective and new business owners. Keep in mind that counselors can provide information about business basics but may not be able to answer questions specific to a particular business.

Another source of free counseling is the **Small Business Institute (SBI)**. Student teams at many colleges provide SBI counseling services. Contact your local SBA office for information about these services, which are available only during certain periods of the school term.

SBA District Offices Most major cities in the U.S. have an SBA district office. These offices offer a full range of services, usually including counseling and publications.

Women's Business Centers (WBCs) The number of women entrepreneurs is growing daily. In response to their specific needs, the SBA developed Women's Business Centers. There are currently more than 80 such centers across the U.S.

Online Training Courses With the growing popularity of the Internet, the SBA has made various online classes available to entrepreneurs. They are accessible on the SBA Internet site, www.sba.gov.

National Ombudsman This service provides assistance to entrepreneurs who have encountered business-operating problems created by the government.

Law Library The Law Library is a valuable resource for entrepreneurs seeking legal and business information. The site also contains a vast amount of small business research and statistical information.

Publications The SBA offers numerous publications and videotapes addressing a variety of topics of interest to small business owners. Most are available at nominal cost and can be ordered through any SBA office.

Other Federal Agencies

Small business owners can also obtain assistance from other government agencies. Their offices are widely distributed throughout the U.S., and their services cover the full range of business needs.

U.S. Department of Commerce The Department of Commerce encourages, serves, and promotes international trade, economic growth, and technological advancement. Its wide variety of programs provide assistance and information, including social and economic statistics for business, as well as research and support for scientific, engineering, and technological development. It also grants patents, trademarks, and service marks, helps promote economic development, and assists in the growth of minority businesses. These functions are served through 12 different bureaus within the Department, the most prominent of which are the Bureau of the Census and the Bureau of Economic Analysis.

The **Bureau of the Census** collects, tabulates, and publishes a wide range of statistical data about the people and the economy of the U.S. The principal means by which the Bureau assists small businesses is through its printed reports, computer tapes, and special tabulations.

The **Bureau of Economic Analysis (BEA)** strives to provide a clear picture of the U.S. economy through analysis of national economic statistics, including personal income, business activity, and investment activity. Results of BEA analyses are published monthly in the *Survey of Current Business and Business Conditions Digest*.

Other bureaus of the Department of Commerce provide technical information; assistance for international trade (both import and export) and minority business development; extensive research for scientific and technological businesses; environmental monitoring; telecommunications development; incentives for invention, research and development, and commercialization; and information about travel and tourism.

Federal Trade Commission The primary purpose of the FTC is to ensure fair business practices in the U.S. The FTC has the authority to make and enforce rules to regulate trade and protect consumers.

Government Printing Office The GPO prints and binds documents for all divisions of the federal government. Although it does not produce government publications, it does produce and distribute catalogs of all government publications and processes orders for these publications.

Internal Revenue Service A division of the Department of the Treasury, the IRS is responsible for collecting taxes and ensuring compliance with tax laws. The IRS also provides services to taxpayers. It issues federal taxpayer identification numbers for businesses, distributes (upon request) publications that explain tax rules, and assists with tax-related questions, both by telephone and through representatives at local IRS offices.

FEDERAL/STATE COOPERATIVES

Some sources of assistance are funded by both the federal government (through the SBA) and state governments. One such agency is the Small Business Development Center (SBDC). The SBDC program is a cooperative venture between the SBA and each state's business development department, with active participation by local chambers of commerce and colleges and universities.

STATE AGENCIES

Assistance is also available to small businesses at the state level.

State Departments of Development

Each of the 50 states has a **Department of Development (DOD)**. This department administers federal community development programs and is usually made up of several divisions.

Division of Business Development This division coordinates the various business programs, including tax incentive and financial assistance programs, that are designed to enhance the state's business climate. Subdivisions of the DBD promote the state to out-of- state industries and businesses and encourage existing companies to maintain and/or expand their facilities. They also provide information about locations, markets, labor, taxes, and finances, and often sponsor customized job training programs.

Economic Development Financing Division This division administers various state economic-development financing programs.

Minority Business Development Division Aiding the growth of the state's minority-owned businesses and monitoring state-administered loan and funding programs for these businesses is the mission of this division.

Small Business Division This division assists small businesses in the areas of licensing, business structure, taxes, and financing. It also serves as a liaison between the small business community and state government agencies.

Other DOD Divisions In addition to the divisions described above, each state's DOD comprises several others, including an International Trade Division, a Community Development Division, a Division of Energy, a Marketing and Research Division, a Policy and Intergovernmental Relations Division, and an Administration Division. Many state DODs also have one department that supplies new business owners with all the information, and sometimes the applications, they need to meet licensing and permit requirements.

Other State Agencies

Other state agencies also provide assistance to small business owners. The following operate in most states in the U.S.

Office of the Secretary of State General business information, information and forms for incorporation, and forms for registering state trademarks and business names are provided by this office.

State Department of Agriculture and Consumer Protection Division These departments issue permits for businesses involved with the processing, handling, storage, or distribution of food products. They also issue permits for businesses of public interest, such as day-care centers, schools, financial institutions, and employment agencies.

State Department of Labor This department provides information regarding employer responsibilities in relation to unemployment insurance. All employers must contribute a specified percentage of wages to the state's fund for compensation for displaced workers.

State Sales and Use Tax Division This agency issues identification numbers to retail businesses, which must collect and remit sales taxes. It also provides instructions for collecting, reporting, and remitting sales taxes to the state.

Worker's Compensation Board All business owners who have employees must provide insurance that gives employees or their survivors benefits in the event of work-related injuries or death. The Board works with employers to provide this protection at a reasonable cost.

An Example of State Resources

The state of Colorado has an official web site with links to various departments, agencies, counties, cities, and schools. Other resources include the following.

The Colorado Business Assistance Center provides a one-stop shop for information regarding federal, state, and local licensing requirements for starting a business. It offers two important publications. The *Colorado Business Resource Guide*, developed by the Colorado Office of Economic Development, provides most of the regulatory information necessary to establish a business in Colorado as well as useful tools and references for successful business operation. *Doing Business in Colorado* provides links to relevant state agencies.

The Colorado Department of Revenue answers state tax questions.

The Colorado Secretary of State offers a searchable database for Colorado businesses registered with the Secretary of State. Its Business Center provides information regarding the functions, services, and activities pertaining to business organizations such as partnerships, corporations, LLCs, and so on. Other information addresses business names and trademarks.

COMMUNITY RESOURCES

Many communities offer their own assistance centers for small business owners. The principal community assistance center is often the chamber of commerce.

Chambers of Commerce

The purpose of chambers of commerce, which are operated and funded by local municipalities and businesses, is to stimulate local economic growth. Economic growth is important to all communities, as it ensures that there will be enough jobs and income to attract and keep residents. The chamber of commerce is usually staffed by people who are well versed in the commercial activities of the community. They are an excellent source of information for owners of both new and established businesses.

Local business owners and managers are eligible for membership in the chamber of commerce. Serving in this capacity is an excellent way to meet and network with other business owners.

Small-Business Incubators

A small-business incubator is an excellent place for an entrepreneur to receive the business services necessary for the initial survival of a small, usually nonretail business. Robert E. Bernier of the University of Nebraska at Omaha, in a research paper titled "Small-Business Incubators and the Entrepreneurial Environment," defines a small-business incubator as "an attempt to influence the entrepreneurial environment by providing an entrepreneurial subculture, access to capital, flexible and low-cost space, sharing of overhead expenses, and management and technical assistance." Hundreds of small-business incubators around the country currently provide services to entrepreneurs.

A good example is the Western Colorado Business Development Corporation (WCBDC) in Grand Junction, CO. According to its Internet site, the WCBDC "is a place for tenants to operate businesses. It is a source for small business loans. It provides consultation, training and classes for incubator tenants and other small businesses. It offers access to financial, legal, marketing and management expertise. This wide range of business support services under one roof is a unique feature of WCBDC, and the organization has received national recognition for its excellence. WCBDC is a public or not-for-profit center, sponsored by government and nonprofit organizations primarily for economic development, job creation, economic diversification and/or expansion of the tax base."

You will find a sample listing of small-business incubators at the end of this appendix. It is a good starting point for entrepreneurs needing start-up assistance.

Other Community Resources

Colleges, universities, and technical schools often offer community outreach services through educational training and research support. If these resources are available in your community, you should take advantage of them.

A trip to City Hall or the county courthouse will help you determine what municipal and county government agencies exist in your community. Other offices that may be of assistance to you are the Licensing and Permit Office, for business licenses; the County Health Department, for local health and safety regulations; and the County Extension Services, for resources for agricultural businesses.

PROFESSIONAL SERVICES

Small business owners can also obtain assistance from various professionals. Their services seldom come without a cost. Be sure to plan ahead and include such services in your budget.

Attorneys

Many business owners seek legal help to make sure they follow the proper procedures in all the legal aspects of their business operation, such as drafting and/or signing lease agreements. Attorneys provide valuable information about business owners' rights, the best legal structure for a business, protecting assets, preventing legal action, obtaining patents and trademarks, and tax and business legislation. Business owners should establish a relationship with an attorney even if legal services are not needed on a regular basis.

Accountants

In addition to designing and maintaining bookkeeping systems, accountants can often provide planning and management advice. In particular, they may be able to make valuable recommendations for minimizing tax liability.

Insurance Agents

Certified insurance agents have extensive training related to insurance requirements and regulations. Good agents help small business owners determine how to obtain the coverage they need at the lowest possible cost. They can also suggest ways to reduce existing insurance costs—for example, by implementing certain safety and security measures.

SAMPLE LISTING OF SMALL-BUSINESS INCUBATORS BY STATE

Please note that this is a partial listing; not all incubators are listed for each state. You may find more complete, up-to-date information for your state by visiting the web sites of the National Business Incubator Association (listed below) and the Small Business Development Center National Information Clearing House.

National Business Incubator Association
20 East Circle Drive, #37198
Athens, OH 45701-3571
Tel.: (740) 593-4331
Fax: (740) 593-1996

ALABAMA
Alabama Business Incubation Network (ABIN)
Chairman: Jerry W. Davis
c/o Shoals Entrepreneurial Center
3115 Northington Court
Florence, AL 35630
Tel.: (205) 760-9014
Fax: (205) 740-5530
E-mail: jdavis@floweb.com

ARKANSAS
Arkansas Business Incubator Manager Association
c/o GENESIS Technology Incubator
Engineering Research Center
University of Arkansas
Fayetteville, AR 72701-1201
Tel.: (501) 575-7227
Fax: (501) 575-7446
E-mail: spruett@comp.uark.edu

Arkansas Small Business Development Center
100 South Main Street, Suite 401
Little Rock, AR 72201
Tel.: (501) 324-9043
Fax: (501) 324-9049

ARIZONA

Arizona Small Business Development Center Network
2411 West 14th Street
Tempe, AZ 85281
Tel.: (602) 731-8720

Border Region Business Incubator
Drawer 104
One Main Street
Bisbee, AZ 85603
Tel.: (520) 432-7823
Fax: (520) 432-7826
E-mail: brbi@theriver.com

CALIFORNIA

California Business Incubation Network (CBIN)
225 Broadway, Suite 2250
San Diego, CA 92101
Tel.: (619) 237-0559
Fax: (619) 237-0521
E-mail: sheilawash@aol.com

Central California Small Business Development Center
Fresno/Madera County Office
3419 West Shaw, Suite102
Fresno, CA 93711
Tel.: (209) 275-1223
Fax: (209) 275-1499
Kings/Tulare County Office
430 West Caldwell, Suite D
Visalia, CA 93277
Tel.: (209) 625-3051
Fax: (209) 625-3053

Greater Sacramento Small Business Development Center
1410 Ethan Way
Sacramento, CA 95825
Tel.: (916) 563-3210

Inland Empire Business Incubator
155 South Memorial Drive
Building 409, Suite B
San Bernardino, CA 92408
Tel.: (909) 382-0065
Fax: (909) 382-8543

Pacific Incubation Network (PIN)
111 North Market Street, Suite 604
San Jose, CA 95113
Tel.: (408) 367-6134
Fax: (408) 351-3334
E-mail: info@pacificincubation.org

Renaissance Entrepreneurship Center
275 5th Street (near Folsom)
San Francisco, CA 94103
Voicemail: (415) 541-8580
Fax: (415) 541-8589

Silicon Valley Small Business Development Center
298 South Sunnyvale Avenue, Suite 204
Sunnyvale, CA 94086
Tel.: (408) 736-0680
Fax: (408) 736-0679

COLORADO

Western Colorado Business Development Corporation
Business Incubator Center
2591 B-3/4 Road
Grand Junction, CO 81503
Tel.: (970) 243-5242
Fax: (970) 241-0771

FLORIDA

Florida/NASA Business Incubation Center
1311 North U.S. 1, Suite 129
Titusville, FL 32796
Tel.: (321) 383-5200

University of Central Florida Small Business Development Center
College of Business Administration
315 East Robinson Street, Suite 100
Orlando, FL 32801
Tel.: (407) 420-4850

University of North Florida Small Business Development Center
12000 Alumni Drive
Jacksonville, FL 32224
Tel.: (904) 620-2477

GEORGIA

Kennesaw State University Small Business Development Center
1000 Chastain Road #0409
Kennesaw, GA 30144-5591
Tel: (770) 423-6450

HAWAII

Hawaii Small Business Development Center
University of Hawaii at Hilo
200 West Kawili Street
Hilo, HI 96720-4091
Tel.: (808) 974-7515
Fax: (808) 974-7683
E-mail: darrylm@interpac.net

IDAHO
Idaho Small Business Development Center
Boise State University
1910 University Drive
Boise, ID 83725
Tel.: (208) 385-1640
Fax: (208) 385-3877
E-mail: jhogge@bsu.idbsu.edu

ILLINOIS
Illinois Small Business Development Association
Small Business Development Center
Rock Valley College
Technology Center
3301 North Mulford Road, Room 277
Rockford, IL 61114-5640
Tel.: (815) 636-6353
Fax: (815) 636-4074

Western Illinois University Small Business Development Center
Seal Hall 214
Macomb, IL 61455
Tel.: (309) 298-2211
Fax: (309) 298-2520
E-mail: SB-Center@wiu.edu

INDIANA
Entrepreneur Business Center (EBC)
55 South State Avenue
Indianapolis, IN 46201
Tel.: (317) 236-0143

Indiana Business Incubator Association (IBIA)
c/o 5th Avenue Executive Office Mall
487 Broadway, Suite 202
Gary, IN 46402
Tel.: (219) 881-4400
Fax: (219) 881-4402

Indiana Small Business Development Corporation
One North Capitol Avenue, Suite 900
Indianapolis, IN 46204
Tel.: (317) 234-2082
Fax: (317) 232-8872

KENTUCKY
Greater Louisville Small Business Development Center
600 West Main Street, 4th Floor
Louisville, KY 40202
Tel.: (502) 574-4770

Kentucky Small Business Development Centers
University of Kentucky
225 Gatton College of Business and Economics
Lexington, KY 40506-0034
Tel.: (888) 475-SBDC

LOUISIANA
Louisiana Business Incubation Association
South Stadium Drive/LSU
Baton Rouge, LA 70803
Tel.: (225) 578-7555
Fax: (225) 578-3975
E-mail: lbtc@lsu.edu

MASSACHUSETTS
The Enterprise Center at Salem State College
121 Loring Avenue
Salem, MA 01970
Tel.: (978) 542-7528
Fax: (978) 542-8387

MICHIGAN
Michigan Business Incubator Association
c/o Hastings Industrial Incubator
1035 E. State Street
Hastings, MI 49058
Tel.: (616) 948-2305
Fax: (616) 948-2947
E-mail: edohost@im4u.net

MISSISSIPPI
Mississippi Business Incubator Network
Executive Director:
c/o Gulf Coast Business Technology Center
1636 Popps Ferry Road
Biloxi, MS 39532
Tel.: (601) 392-9741
Fax: (601) 392-9743
E-mail: btc@datasync.com

NEVADA
Nevada Small Business Development Center
Las Vegas NSBDC Office
851 East Tropicana, Bldg. 700 (physical location)
UNLV, 4505 Maryland Parkway, Box 456011 (mail)
Las Vegas, NV 89154
Tel.: (702) 895-4270

NEW HAMPSHIRE
New Hampshire Small Business Development Center
120 Main Street
Littleton, NH 03561
Tel.: (603) 444-1053

NEW JERSEY
New Jersey Small Business Development Center
Rutgers Business School
Graduate Programs, Newark and New Brunswick
49 Bleeker Street
Newark, NJ 07102
Tel.: (973) 353-1927

NEW YORK
New York State Small Business Development Center
University at Albany
1 Pinnacle Place, Suite 218
Albany, NY 12203-3439
Tel.: (518) 453-9567

NORTH CAROLINA
North Carolina Business Incubator Association
c/o Smoky Mountain Small Business & Industry Center
100 Industrial Park Drive
Waynesville, NC 28734
Tel.: (704) 452-1967
Fax: (704) 456-1352

OKLAHOMA
Oklahoma Business Incubator Association
1500 West 7th
Stillwater, OK 74074-4364
Tel.: (580) 743-5574
Fax: (580) 743-6821
E-mail: jim_comer@okvotech.org

PENNSYLVANIA
Pennsylvania Incubator Association (PIA)
c/o Corry Incubator
154 Enterprise Road
Corry, PA 16407
Tel.: (814) 664-3884
Fax: (814) 664-3885
E-mail: rnovo@gremlan.org

Uniflow Center
1525 East Lake Road
Erie, PA 16510
Tel.: (814) 899-6022
Fax: (814) 899-0250

University of Scranton Small Business Development Center
Estate Building, 2nd floor
200 Monroe Avenue
Scranton, PA 18510
Tel.: (570) 941-7588

SOUTH CAROLINA
The Frank L. Roddey SBDC of South Carolina
University of South Carolina
Moore School of Business
1705 College Street
Columbia, SC 29208
Tel.: (803) 777-4907
Fax: (803) 777-4403

TEXAS
Texas Business Incubator Association
c/o E.D.C.
8845 Long Pt. Road
Houston, TX 77055-3019
Tel.: (713) 932-7495, x13
Fax: (713) 932-7498
E-mail: cdkring@aol.com

STARTech Foundation
1302 East Collins Boulevard
Richardson, TX 75081
Tel.: (214) 576-9800
Fax: (214) 576-9849

VIRGINIA
New Century Venture Center
1354 Eighth Street SW
Roanoke, VA 24015
Tel.: (540) 344-6402
Fax: (540) 345-0262

WISCONSIN
Webster Business Incubator
7421 Main Street West
PO Box 147
Webster, WI 54893
Tel.: (715) 866-4211

Wisconsin Business Incubator Association
Coulee Region Business Center
1100 Kane Streets
LaCrosse, WI 54603
Tel.: (608) 782-8022
Fax: (608) 784-5505
E-mail: dloomis@execpc.com

Glossary

A

absentee management the owner oversees the business but is not present on a regular basis (p. 14)

acid-test ratio a test that takes the current assets minus the inventory divided by the current liabilities to find the business's liquidity (p. 329)

advertising paid-for, nonpersonal presentation of a sales-enticing message (p. 104)

AIDA advertising copywriters often use this acronym to describe what their copy needs to accomplish; the acronym stands for attention, interest, desire, and action (p. 238)

anchor store larger store that advertises nationally and attracts customers from an entire community (p. 166)

assets all property and capital to which the business claims ownership (p. 329)

attitude how a person feels about something (p. 11)

autonomy anchor career anchor describing free thinkers, who like to do things their own way and are seldom concerned with security (p. 10)

B

bait and switch advertising the practice of advertising a lower-priced item to lure customers into the store for the real purpose of selling them a different, higher-priced item (p. 78)

balance sheet a financial statement that shows the worth, or value, of a business (p. 328)

big box store center shopping center comprised of very large shopping goods stores that sell in great quantities, usually at discounted prices (p. 167)

black box approach this model has been used to describe the mystery of what goes on in a buyer's mind. Entrepreneurs can apply a stimulus (an advertisement or sales presentation) and observe the reaction, but cannot be positive of the customer's actual decision-making process (p. 196)

bonds contracts of indebtedness issued by corporations or governmental units that promise payment of the principal plus interest at a specified date, or maturity date (p. 307)

breakeven point when the cost of producing and/or selling a product or service is covered (p. 209)

bricks-and-mortar business a business that has a material presence such as a storefront, storage facility, office space, manufacturing facility, or other tangible location where potential customers can actually walk in and interact with employees (p. 249)

business brokers brokers who represent sellers and bring them together with potential buyers (p. 43)

Business.com the resource for entrepreneurial planning that covers over 28 industries and provides a directory of industry web sites (p. 118)

business plan plan that serves as a manual to help the entrepreneur during the design and start-up phases of the business (p. 26)

C

capital assets all the equipment, inventory, and operating resources (including cash) that the business owns and uses in its operations (p. 323)

capitalization activity of obtaining all the capital assets necessary to operate a business (p. 323)

career anchors five factors identified by Dr. Edgar Schein that influence one's career choice; the five anchors are technical, managerial, security, creativity and autonomy (p. 9)

cash flow statement a month-to-month projection of financial activities (p. 330)

cash in advance term of sale in which the invoice is paid in full to the vendor before being released for shipment (p. 355)

cash on delivery term of sale in which the amount of the invoice is collected by the deliverer upon delivery of the goods (p. 355)

Census Bureau States Initiative ongoing effort to make economic data and statistics more widely available at the state and local levels (p. 119)

certificate of deposit money that is deposited for a specified period of time (six months, one year, or longer) that pays a higher interest, but cannot be withdrawn without penalty (p. 310)

chain of command reporting relationships in the workplace; who oversees whom (p. 280)

channels of distribution the available distribution networks to get the product to the consumer (p. 103)

Clayton Act a follow-up to the Sherman Antitrust Act which provides additional powers for dealing with companies involved in illegal deals (p. 141)

cocooning the tendency of people to create a home retreat and then to stay there (p. 127)

cognitive dissonance the uncertainty consumers feel after they have purchased an item (p. 107)

collateral something of value pledged as security for a loan (p. 34)

column inch newspaper advertising space one column wide and 14 newsprint lines deep (p. 233)

community shopping center shopping center designed to serve residents of many neighborhoods (p. 166)

competition the rivalry between companies that sell similar products or services (p. 139)

competitive analysis the examination of the characteristics of a specific competing firm (p. 150)

competitive impact the ability to effectively compete with other businesses (p. 139)

competitive intelligence a systematic and ethical program for gathering, analyzing, and managing external information that can affect a company's plans, decisions, and operations (p. 155)

competitive stage advertising stage in which business emphasizes distinctive or exceptional features of the product not shared by the competition (p. 231)

conscious needs needs that a buyer is totally aware of at the time of purchase (p. 189)

consideration the legal term for the value received by each of the parties involved in a contract (p. 84)

contract a legally enforceable agreement negotiated between two or more persons (p. 82)

contributing margin the gross profit derived from the sale of the product (p. 210)

controlling the process of establishing performance standards based on the firm's objectives, measuring and reporting actual performance, comparing the two, and taking corrective or preventive action as necessary (p. 288)

convenience goods products that people expect to find in many places (p. 164)

corporation a legal entity created by law (p. 72)

creativity anchor career anchor describing individuals who enjoy coming up with unique ideas and do not like routine tasks (p. 10)

creativity process according to Graham Wallas, six-step process that individuals pass through in developing new ideas; the process begins with discovery and interests, proceeds through research, and ends with the entrepreneur (p. 18)

current assets include cash and assets that are easily converted into cash, such as inventory and accounts receivable (p. 329)

Current Industrial Reports Census Bureau program that provides monthly, quarterly, and annual measures of industrial activity (p. 117)

current liabilities debts that are to be paid within 12 months of the date of the balance sheet (p. 329)

current ratio test that compares cash, as well as any assets that can be converted into cash within a year, with the debt (liabilities) that will become due and payable within the year (p. 329)

customer profile detailed description of the customer that tells the entrepreneur to whom the marketing plan should be directed (p. 101)

customers individuals or organizations with unsatisfied needs that possess the resources needed to fulfill those needs (p. 187)

D

database a collection, depository, and list of information used by businesses to stay informed about their customers (p. 360)

debt capital loans for a business (p. 308)

deceptive advertising any advertising containing information that would mislead the average consumer about a particular product or service (p. 77)

demographics the characteristics of a population as classified by age, sex, income, and other factors for market and other forms of research (p. 122)

direct competition the businesses that derive the majority of their profits from the sale of products or services that are the same as or similar to those sold by another business (p. 148)

directing influencing people's behavior through motivation, communication, group dynamics, leadership, and discipline (p. 286)

direct mail printed information sent through a delivery service or electronic mail to potential customers (p. 236)

discount outlet center shopping center usually owned by the manufacturer of the products it sells; becoming more widespread, but not an option for a new entrepreneur (p. 167)

domain name the unique name that identifies an Internet site (p. 253)

Domain Name System (DNS) a directory of domain names organized under the familiar domains ".com," ".gov," ".org" (p. 253)

E

early adopters the consumers who use a new product after the innovators have already tried it (p. 194)

early majority consumers who wish to emulate opinion leaders (p. 194)

earnings approach method of determining whether a business will be able to pay a buyer for his or her time (p. 50)

economies of scale manufacturing in greater quantities to lower the unit cost (p. 103)

e-entrepreneur an individual willing to take the risk of investing time and money in an electronic business that has the potential to make a profit or incur a loss (p. 249)

e-entrepreneurship the act of managing an electronic enterprise that has the potential to make a profit or incur a loss (p. 249)

entrepreneur a person who possesses vision and ambition to reach goals in business and industry in the hope of achieving profits, but also with the understanding of the risks involved (p. 5)

EOM term of sale in which the amount billed is due at the end of the month; no discounts apply (p. 355)

equity capital the money invested in a business by the owner or owners (p. 314)

equity loan this loan is based on the property that is already owned and listed on the borrower's personal financial statement. The maximum amount for this type of loan is determined by the amount of equity the owner has in the secured property (p. 311)

executive summary provides a two- to three-page summary that describes the business plan (p. 28)

expectations the minimum goals that you attempt to achieve (p. 11)

express warranty a clearly stated fact, either written or verbal, about the quality or performance of a product (p. 80)

extensive decisions the most difficult purchasing decisions because they are characterized by the belief that the decision is extremely important and has a long-term impact on personal budgets or lifestyles. An example would be buying a home (p. 195)

external factors elements surrounding a business that indirectly affect its operations (p. 217)

F

factoring a form of trade credit where industries buy an entrepreneur's accounts receivable at a discounted amount, and then collect the amount due from the purchaser (p. 312)

false advertising any advertising containing information that is not true or would cause the average consumer to reach a false conclusion about the product or service concerned (p. 77)

Federal Trade Commission federal administrative agency charged with the responsibility of ensuring fair, free, and open business (p. 77)

Federal Trade Commission Franchise Rule according to the Federal Trade Commission, "The Rule is designed to enable potential franchisees to protect themselves before investing by providing them with information essential to an assessment of the potential risks and benefits, to meaningful comparisons with other investments, and to further investigation of the franchise opportunity." (p. 56)

financial plan contains the entrepreneur's estimates for the following categories: cost of starting the business and maintaining it, projected income, projected operating expenses, projected cash flow, and initial balance sheet (p. 33)

firewall a system designed to prevent unauthorized access to or from a private computer network (p. 256)

fixed assets the capital purchases that generally take a longer time to convert or liquidate into cash, such as property, equipment, and fixtures that require a special buyer (p. 329)

fixed costs costs that do not vary even when there are changes in production and/or sales volume (p. 209)

FOB type of pricing in which the buyer must pay transportation charges to deliver the products, and the title or ownership of the products is passed to the customer when the items are loaded on the shipping vehicle (p. 220)

franchise the contractual right to market a product or service (p. 52)

franchisee the party that pays a royalty (percentage of sales or outright fee) and often an initial fee for the right to do business under the franchisor's name and system (p. 53)

franchising a method of doing business in which a franchisee is granted the right to engage in offering, selling, or distributing goods or services under a marketing format that is designed by the franchisor (p. 53)

franchisor the party that lends his or her trademark or trade name and a business system (p. 53)

G

general partner a partner who actively engages in the day-to-day management of the business and is fully liable for any actions for, by, and against the business (p. 70)

goodwill an intangible, but salable, asset, such as the reputation or location of a business (p. 50)

government securities money invested in the government, such as savings bonds and treasury notes, in exchange for repayment, including interest, at a later date (p. 307)

H

hiving urban trend involving people without children who seek an in-city environment (p. 127)

home equity the difference between the money owed (mortgage) on a home and its appraised value (p. 309)

Hoover's Online a database that lists 12 million companies and delivers comprehensive company, industry, and market intelligence that drives business growth (p. 118)

hygiene factors job satisfaction factors related to the company's management and the workplace environment (p. 287)

I

ideal self the self that you would like to be (p. 192)

implied warranty an unwritten warranty ensuring that a product will perform under normal use and circumstances (p. 80)

income statement a document that shows the revenues, or monies collected, and the expenses, or monies paid out, of a business over a specified period of time (p. 327)

incubator subsidized business rental facility in which compatible businesses share space and common operating expenses (p. 169)

indirect competition competition from businesses that derive only a small percentage of their profits from the sale of products or services that are the same as or similar to those sold by another business (p. 149)

industry analysis a form of exploratory business research that examines the overall condition of a particular industry (p. 117)

innovators consumers who are the first to buy a new product (p. 194)

institutional advertising used in the retentive stage of a business, it is designed to broadcast a good image of the business itself by emphasizing the benefits and advantages of doing business with it (p. 232)

interest the payment made to lenders for the use of their money (p. 307)

internal factors elements within a business that directly affect prices (p. 219)

Internet Corporation for Assigned Names and Numbers (ICANN) a private-public partnership that is responsible for managing and coordinating the Domain Name System to ensure that every address is exclusive and that all users of the Internet can find all legitimate addresses (p. 253)

Internet Protocol (IP) address exclusive address that every computer linked to the Internet has (p. 253)

Internet search engine a program that searches documents on the Internet for specified keywords and returns a list of documents in which the keywords are found (p. 257)

Internet Service Provider (ISP) a company that provides access to the Internet for organizations and/or individuals (p. 256)

intranets Internet networks inside a company not accessible to the public (p. 256)

inventory number of units, and the value of those units, that are available for sale or manufacture (p. 349)

inventory turnover the number of times a business sells the amount of its base inventory in a year (p. 325)

investment banks banks that specialize in bringing together entrepreneurs who need funds and individuals or groups that have money to invest (p. 316)

invoice a statement the seller delivers to the buyer that lists the contents of a shipment or delivery, the number of units or items delivered, the unit price, the total cost, and the payment terms of the sale (p. 355)

J

just-in-time inventory plan inventory plan in which the inventory arrives just in time, or as close as possible to the time needed, to make the sale (p. 350)

K

KISS advertising copywriters use this acronym to remind them what they need to do in an ad, which is "Keep it simple, stupid." (p. 238)

L

laggards consumers who are the last to try new products (p. 194)

late majority the consumers who adopt a product or style after it has been out for a while and the innovators and early adopters have been using it for a while (p. 194)

leasehold improvements improvements to the property such as carpeting, wallpaper, lighting, and so on (p. 325)

lessee the tenant of a leased space (p. 172)

lessor the landlord who owns the building and rents it to the lessee (p. 172)

liabilities all the debts of a business (p. 329)

limited liability company an alternative form of ownership that has been in existence since the late 1980s that offers the limited liability protection of a corporation, but is taxed like a partnership (p. 76)

limited partner a partner who does not actively engage in the day-to-day management of the business and whose liability is limited to the extent of his or her investment in the business (p. 70)

line and staff organization larger organization which has staff positions—such as personnel manager, safety officer, and accountant—and line employees who perform the actual work of creating and selling the products or services (p. 281)

line organization business whose mission is to create and sell products or services (p. 281)

liquidation value the immediate cash value of all the assets of a business (including the present value of future income) (p. 51)

liquidity a business's ability to meet its debt obligations as they become due (p. 329)

list price the standard price charged to customers (p. 220)

long-term liabilities debts that come due more than 12 months after the date of the balance sheet (p. 329)

looking-glass self the way people want others to perceive them (p. 192)

loss leader pricing a strategy of pricing some products at a level that eliminates profit to increase customer traffic and the likelihood of selling related products at a normal or higher markup (p. 214)

M

management by objectives (MBO) planning tool that sets objectives in all areas of operation to ensure efficient use of resources; clearly stating the goals of the business and meshing them with the goals of the employees (p. 345)

managerial anchor career anchor describing generalists, as opposed to specialists, who enjoy working with people and are able to handle many responsibilities (p. 10)

markdown the difference between the original selling price and the price at which an item is actually sold (p. 210)

marketing concept the belief that consumer wants and needs are the driving force behind any product development or marketing effort (p. 97)

marketing mix product, place, price, and promotion—the heart of a marketing plan for any business (p. 102)

marketing plan defines and quantifies consumers, demand, competition, geographic market, and pricing policy for a specific small business (p. 30)

marketing research the gathering, recording, and analyzing of data about problems relating to the marketing of goods and services (p. 97)

market penetration pricing selling at the lowest possible price to entice people to try a new product in hopes of gaining market share; this method often is used to introduce a new product or business (p. 213)

market segmentation process of breaking down the total market for goods and services on the basis of who benefits from the product or service, age, geographic location, or other demographic or psychographic factors (p. 101)

market value price at which buyers and sellers trade similar items in the open marketplace (p. 43)

markup the amount added to the cost of an item to arrive at a selling price (p. 210)

maturity date the specified date that a bond contract promises to pay back principle plus interest (p. 307)

merchant account provider a bank or financial institution that provides a means for accepting and processing credit card transactions over the Internet (p. 258)

merchant association association of commercial tenants that collects dues from tenants and uses these funds for advertising and for paying for entertainment events designed to attract customers (p. 168)

micropolitan term used to designate areas with at least one urban cluster of 10,000 to 50,000 people (p. 119)

monopoly a business environment in which a single company, by controlling a specific supply of products or services, sets prices, prevents other businesses from entering the market, and controls the available supply of the product or service (p. 141)

motivations internal tensions that direct an individual to satisfy unsatisfied needs (p. 190)

motivator personal job factor affecting the individual worker (p. 287)

N

needs the tangibles (the things you see) and the intangibles (the things you feel) that you must have to maintain an acceptable lifestyle (p. 11)

need satisfaction theory Dr. Abraham Maslow's theory which states that once you fulfill your lower-level physiological and safety needs, you begin to feel the upper-level needs for love and belonging, self-esteem, and self-actualization (p. 188)

neighborhood shopping center shopping center whose customers are primarily nearby residents who shop there for convenience; generally consists of a supermarket and small service and convenience good stores (p. 166)

net price the balance remaining after all discounts are subtracted (p. 220)

net profit the income left over after all expenses, including taxes, are paid (p. 323)

networking the process of making business contacts by meeting people who can assist in business development (p. 350)

network promoting using personal references to spread the word and sell products (p. 230)

net worth the value of the owner's equity, determined by subtracting the total debt, or liabilities, of a business from the value of what is owned (assets) (p. 329)

niche small, manageable market segment that can be effectively reached and influenced (p. 101)

nonroutine decisions infrequent or first-time purchase decisions that may require a greater utility exchange, like buying new tires for a car (p. 194)

O

open-to-buy the term used to express the purchasing budget of a business (p. 351)

open-to-buy reserve money available for additional purchases outside the detailed purchase plan (p. 353)

organization chart part of the business plan that deals with the actual management and defines who will be responsible for tasks such as purchasing, advertising, accounting, and hiring personnel (p. 33)

P

partnership an association of two or more persons to carry on as co-owners of a business for profit (p. 68)

partnership agreement the understanding between two or more entrepreneurs who are considering a partnership arrangement; the agreement can be either written or verbal (p. 68)

percentage rent clause lease clause that requires the tenant to pay additional rent if and when revenues exceed a certain dollar amount (p. 172)

perceptions the way you view and understand things as determined by your background and mental framework (p. 189)

perpetual inventory a running written record of inventory levels (p. 353)

personal financial statement a document that describes the borrower's financial situation (p. 34)

personal net worth the difference between a person's assets and liabilities (p. 306)

personal resume a document that describes a person's skills, education, and background (p. 303)

physical inventory an actual physical count of the entire inventory the business owns (p. 353)

pioneering stage the stage when a new business introduces itself to the marketplace (p. 231)

preconscious need need that is not fully developed or conscious (p. 189)

price bundling selling a product in multiple units (such as two for the price of one) (p. 215)

price discrimination the practice of charging different prices to different customers for the same goods (p. 141)

price fixing the agreement between competitors to establish and maintain prices for their goods and services, which is illegal (p. 141)

price lining grouping products at certain price points (p. 214)

price points the price levels with which consumers feel psychologically comfortable (p. 215)

pricing policy the last part of the marketing plan which determines how the business will set prices for the product or service provided (p. 31)

primary data original research data often collected through surveys and questionnaires (p. 98)

prime rate of interest the publicly stated rate that major commercial banks charge their most creditworthy business customers for short-term loans (p. 311)

private investors people who are willing to take a gamble and invest in a business (p. 315)

product advertising advertising that focuses on the benefits and advantages of buying the particular products or services of a business (p. 232)

product mix mixture or portfolio of products a business offers for sale (p. 102)

profit margin the markup on a good, which is the difference between the cost of a good or service and its selling price (p. 167)

pro forma financial statement a projected statistical report that describes the expected financial status of a business at a future date (p. 326)

promotion the way a business communicates with its market (p. 104)

promotional event a planned program to build goodwill for a business by offering an added value to the customers (p. 239)

promotional mix the activities used by a business to communicate with its market, which are advertising, sales promotion, personal selling, visual merchandising, and public relations (p. 104)

psychographics data regarding the lifestyle of the population in a particular market (p. 97)

publicity free exposure for the business through media channels (p. 243)

public relations planned events that demonstrate goodwill of a business (p. 107)

pull strategy a strategy to create interest in the product, but not to make it available at first so that the customers are literally demanding the product (p. 229)

push strategy a strategy to attract customers that depends on the seller making the product immediately available (p. 229)

R

real self the way a person really is (p. 192)

reference groups buyers with similar needs (p. 194)

regional shopping center shopping center designed to attract customers from a region, or more than one community; usually has three or more anchor stores and more than 50 other stores (p. 167)

regular line of credit preapproved, prearranged amount of money made available as a loan for a specific period of time, usually one year (p. 310)

replacement value current replacement value of assets; usually higher than asset value (p. 51)

retained earnings profits that remain in the business for either future use for business expansion or for distribution to the owner(s) as investment payback (p. 13)

retentive stage once a business is firmly established, it enters this advertising stage, in which the intention is to maintain market share (p. 232)

return on investment portion of business earnings available to pay back the owner, or investors, money that has been previously paid into the business (p. 13)

Reuters Investor a source of information that describes key, up-to-date developments in the industry including statistics, price performance, company rankings, news, market capitalization, research reports, and risk alerts (p. 118)

revolving line of credit prearranged amount of money made available as a loan, with an option for renewal at the end of the original term (p. 310)

Robinson-Patman Act extended the Clayton Act in 1936 by outlawing price discrimination (p. 141)

routine decisions simple, almost reflex buying decisions that do not require scrutiny or research; an example would be someone buying toothpaste—people do not give it a lot of consideration (p. 194)

royalty a percentage of sales or an outright fee (p. 53)

S

sales promotion directing customer attention to a product or service with planned activities or public relations campaigns; the entrepreneur is a message sender hoping for a positive response from the message receiver, such as confirmation of a sale (p. 105)

secondary data public information about the number of people living in a community, the average education of the population, the per capita income, and the gender ratios (p. 98)

security anchor career anchor describing individuals who perform best in large organizations that offer regular paychecks, benefits, and the assurance of long-term employment (p. 10)

selective distortion hearing what you want to hear and seeing what you want to see; perceptions of a product that are based on past experiences (p. 189)

selective retention remembering and retaining only information that aligns with personal beliefs and values and discarding or ignoring information that does not (p. 190)

self-image the way people think other people see them (p. 192)

shareholder/stockholder person who buys stocks or shares in a company and holds partial ownership in the corporation according to the amount of stock he or she owns (p. 72)

Sherman Antitrust Act passed in 1890, this act makes any business deal illegal that unreasonably restricts trade or commerce among states (p. 141)

shopping cart online feature that keeps track of and records customers' purchases as they are made without requiring the customer to go back and forth to an order form (p. 258)

shopping goods goods normally found in all communities, for which consumers often comparison-shop as they look for the best values (p. 164)

skimming setting prices very high in anticipation of a short selling period (p. 213)

Small Business Administration a federal government agency created to assist the development of the country's small businesses (p. 7)

sole proprietorship a business established, owned, and controlled by a single person (p. 66)

spam unsolicited "junk" e-mail sent to large numbers of people to promote products or services (p. 260)

specialty goods products that people are willing to go out of their way to buy (p. 165)

spreadsheet an electronic replacement for an accountant's columnar ledger, pencil, and calculator; used to create budgets, prepare financial statements, and analyze financial problems (p. 361)

staffing the process that determines the number of employees needed and defines a process for hiring them (p. 279)

stand-alone store store that depends on drive-by traffic (p. 169)

Statistical Abstract of the United States basic statistics on industries compiled by the Census Bureau since 1878 (p. 118)

status quo pricing strategy in which price levels are firmly established and remain relatively fixed until something happens in the marketplace that requires a change or adjustment (p. 215)

Statute of Frauds collective term describing assorted statutory provisions that render certain types of contracts unenforceable unless they are executed in writing (p. 87)

stock share of ownership in a corporation (p. 72)

subchapter S corporation form of ownership that has all the advantages of a corporation but that eliminates double taxation (p. 73)

super regional shopping center shopping center found in major metropolitan areas, may contain more than a hundred of the most contemporary stores (p. 167)

supply and demand relationship of the supply of a product or service and demand for the product or service; in the role of pricing a product, if consumers perceive the price to be too high for an item, the demand will be low so the supply will be high; if the consumers perceive that the price of the product is below its value, the demand will be great (pp. 208–209)

T

target market specific description of most likely customer group for a business, which then develops a marketing plan to attract this segment of the market (p. 101)

technical anchor career anchor describing individuals who gain satisfaction from being able to do a specific job correctly (p. 10)

telemarketing selling that involves interacting with customers by telephone (p. 241)

Theory X managers managers who direct with little consideration for human relations, are very task-oriented, and are most concerned with making sure jobs are completed in the most efficient manner (p. 286)

Theory Y managers managers who direct with concern for human relations, and assume workers like their work and enjoy responsibility (p. 286)

Theory Z managers managers who give employees a great deal of freedom and trust (p. 288)

Thomas Register of American Manufacturers one of the most comprehensive online resources for finding companies and products manufactured in North America (p. 119)

tie-in sales requiring the purchase of one product line in order to purchase another one (p. 220)

total customer concept business practice of making every effort to ensure the customer's return (p. 198)

total pricing concept setting prices that allow a business to cover the cost of goods and operations, generate retained earnings, reward the owner(s), and offer customers fair value (p. 207)

total quality management (TQM) a management style taken from the Japanese method of manufacturing that encourages continuous improvement in quality and customer service (p. 222)

trade credit short-term debt arrangement provided by vendor to entice sales and meet competition (p. 312)

trade name any name other than the full first and last name(s) of the owner(s) of a business entity, including a general partnership (p. 65)

trade show a gathering of many producers in the same industry to display products to customers (p. 242)

tying agreements when a customer must buy one type of product before he or she can buy another type from the same seller; this was made illegal by the Clayton Act (p. 141)

U

unconscious need an unsatisfied need exposed years before and suppressed until the purchase opportunity is presented (p. 189)

undercapitalized term used to describe when an entrepreneur cannot meet the business's objective (p. 323)

URL global address of documents and other resources on the World Wide Web (p. 253)

utility satisfaction choosing products that will give the greatest satisfaction in exchange for money or barter (p. 194)

V

values beliefs and inner convictions that a person holds dear (p. 11)

VANE an acronym that stands for values, attitude, needs, expectations—intangible feelings an entrepreneur should match to a business opportunity (p. 11)

variable costs costs that fluctuate with changes in production and/or sales volume (p. 209)

vendors inventory suppliers (p. 349)

venture capitalists professional investors who seek larger, high-risk business investment opportunities (p. 316)

viral promotional strategy just as a virus spreads from one person to another, some marketers set in motion a plan to capture the attention of a particular segment of the market with the expectation that the opinion leaders of that segment will spread the word (p. 229)

virtual business a business that does not have a material space designed to receive customers and transacts most of its business online (p. 249)

visual merchandising visual displays of merchandise designed to attract customers' attention (p. 107)

W

web browser software application used to locate and display web pages (p. 268)

web host a service that, for a fee, allows your company's web page to be connected to the Internet (p. 256)

whole life insurance life insurance policy that acquires a cash value over time due to the insurance company's investments (p. 307)

Z

zoned editions newspaper editions that are distributed only in specific areas to serve the needs of marketers in that area (p. 232)

zone price the price set for a particular geographic area (p. 220)

Index

B

C

D

E

F

G

H

I

J

N

O

P

Q

R

S

T

U

V